ECONOGUIDE® SERIES

ECONOGUIDE® WALT DISNEY WORLD® RESORT, UNIVERSAL ORLANDO®

Also Includes SeaWorld®
and Central Florida

Fifth Edition

COREY SANDLER

INSIDERS' GUIDE®

GUILFORD, CONNECTICUT
AN IMPRINT OF THE GLOBE PEQUOT PRESS

To Willie and Tessa,
May their lives always be a magic theme park

The prices and rates listed in this guidebook were confirmed at
press time. We recommend, however, that you call establishments
to obtain current information before traveling.

To buy books in quantity for corporate use
or incentives, call **(800) 962–0973**
or e-mail **premiums@GlobePequot.com.**

INSIDERS' GUIDE®

Copyright © 2003, 2004, 2005, 2006, 2007 by Word Association, Inc.

Insiders' Guide is a registered trademark of Morris Book Publishing, LLC.
Econoguide is a registered trademark of Word Association, Inc.

Text design by Lesley Weissman-Cook
Maps by XNR Productions, Inc. © Morris Book Publishing, LLC
Interior photographs by the author unless otherwise indicated.

ISSN: 1541-7158
ISBN: 978-0-7627-4169-4

Manufactured in the United States of America
Fifth Globe Pequot Press Edition/First Printing

CONTENTS

PART VIII: TAMPA

ACKNOWLEDGMENTS

As always, dozens of hardworking and creative people helped move my words from the keyboard to the book you hold in your hands.

Thanks to the editorial and production staff at Globe Pequot, including Mary Luders Norris, Elizabeth Taylor, and Justine Rathbun.

Thanks to original champion Gene Brissie and current torchbearer Ed Claflin.

My appreciation extends to the theme parks and public-relations staffs who helped me assemble the massive stack of specifications, itineraries, and prices and wrangle them into manageable shape.

As always, thanks to Janice Keefe for running the office and putting up with me, a pair of major assignments.

And thanks to you for buying this book. We all hope you find it of value.

ABOUT THE AUTHOR

Corey Sandler is a former newsman and editor for the Associated Press, Gannett Newspapers, Ziff-Davis Publishing, and IDG. He has written more than 160 books on history, travel, video games, and computers; his titles have been translated into French, Spanish, German, Italian, Portuguese, Polish, Russian, Bulgarian, Hebrew, and Chinese. When he's not traveling, he hides out with his wife and two children on Nantucket, 30 miles off the coast of Massachusetts.

INTRODUCTION TO THE FIFTH EDITION

NOT ALL THAT LONG AGO, Orlando was home to thousands of alligators, cows, and steers, and not a single cartoon mouse. In the mid-1960s Walt Disney and his aides secretly bought up thousands of acres of swamp and forest and planned the world of wonders we now are gathered to celebrate and explore.

In 1971 Walt Disney World opened with just a single theme park: the Magic Kingdom. Today there are four theme parks within Walt Disney World, two water parks, a permanent circus, a baseball stadium, a racetrack, ninety-nine holes of golf, and much more.

About fifteen minutes away is Universal Orlando, which opened in 1990 with one park and added a second in 1999. In between is SeaWorld, with two more.

And all around, a world of other enticements has grown: dinner theaters, museums, golf courses, thrill rides, restaurants fancy and fast, and just about anything else that might lure a visitor into spending some time and money.

That's not to say that a bit of real Florida can't still be found. In one ten-day period, I petted a giraffe on the Serengeti Safari at Busch Gardens Tampa Bay, stroked a penguin on a behind-the-scenes tour at SeaWorld Orlando, swam with a dolphin at Discovery Cove, and entered a crocodile pen with the aid of a keeper at Gatorland.

This is the fifteenth year we have published an Econoguide to Walt Disney World (and the fifth edition brought to your hands by The Globe Pequot Press), and there are changes in every section of the book. Some are big, some are small; all are important to travelers who want to know how to get the very most for their time and money on a vacation trip.

WAY BEYOND INFINITY

Walt Disney World is a wonderful mélange of things real and fantastic, amusing and terrifying. Perhaps best of all is the opportunity to jump from one place to another. In just one place you can hang glide over California, blast off to Mars, take a boat ride in Mexico, and enter the Twilight Zone.

The Econoguide Best of Orlando and Central Florida

▶ **WALT DISNEY WORLD ATTRACTIONS**
Magic Kingdom
Disney's Animal Kingdom
Disney–MGM Studios
Epcot Center
Downtown Disney
Cirque du Soleil
Blizzard Beach
Typhoon Lagoon

▶ **UNIVERSAL ORLANDO**
Universal Studios Florida
Universal Studios Islands of Adventure
Universal CityWalk

▶ **OTHER ATTRACTIONS**
SeaWorld Orlando
Discovery Cove
Kennedy Space Center Visitor Center
Wet 'n Wild
Gatorland
Busch Gardens Tampa Bay

Theme-Park Attendance Champs

The Walt Disney Company continued to own the top five spots in theme-park attendance in 2005, and six of the top seven parks, according to the trade magazine *Amusement Business*. In California, Disney's California Adventure moved up a notch to seventh place in 2005.

In Orlando, Walt Disney World was the big guy in town, followed by Universal's two parks and SeaWorld Orlando.

Overall attendance at North American amusement parks increased by about 4.2 percent in 2005, continuing a two-year recovery from a slight slump. The magazine estimates that 176 million guests passed through the turnstiles at the top fifty parks.

Here are the magazine's estimates:

1. The Magic Kingdom, Walt Disney World, Orlando: 16.1 million visitors, up 6.5 percent from 2004.
2. Disneyland, Anaheim: 14.5 million, up 8.5 percent.
3. Epcot, Walt Disney World: 9.9 million, up 5.5 percent.
4. Disney–MGM Studios, Walt Disney World: 8.6 million, up 5 percent.
5. Disney's Animal Kingdom, Walt Disney World: 8.2 million, up 5 percent.
6. Universal Studios Florida, Orlando: 6.1 million, down 8.5 percent.
7. Disney's California Adventure, Anaheim: 5.8 million, up 3.6 percent.
8. Universal's Islands of Adventure, Orlando: 5.76 million, down 8.5 percent.
9. SeaWorld Orlando: 5.6 million, unchanged.
10. Universal Studios Hollywood: 4.7 million, down 6 percent.
11. Adventuredome at Circus Circus, Las Vegas: 4.5 million, up 2.3 percent.
12. Busch Gardens, Tampa Bay: 4.3 million, up 5.1 percent.
13. SeaWorld California, San Diego: 4.1 million, up 2.5 percent.
14. Paramount Canada's Wonderland, Maple, Ontario: 3.6 million, up 7 percent.
15. Knott's Berry Farm, Buena Park, California: 3.47 million, down 3 percent.

Around the world in 2005, Disney paid tribute to the fiftieth anniversary of the opening of Disneyland in California, and in doing so they kept true to one of Walt Disney's promises: The Magic Kingdom (and all that has grown from that original idea) will never be completed.

In the fall of 2006, that party came to an end and a new one began: the "Year of a Million Dreams." The celebration (at both Walt Disney World and the Disneyland Resort in California) intends to bestow a million dream gifts—some small and some monumental—to randomly selected guests.

The most spectacular prize at Walt Disney World will be a free overnight in Cinderella's royal bedchamber within Cinderella Castle, with a view previously enjoyed only by Tinker Bell. The lavishly decorated bedroom is in a space originally planned as an in-park apartment for the use of the Disney family.

At Disneyland, one guest will be given the key for the night to the new Mickey Mouse Penthouse at the Disneyland Hotel, with extraordinary views of both Disneyland and Disney's California Adventure parks. The penthouse is decorated in all things Mickey.

Other Disney dreams that will be handed out by cast members will include:
- An expedition to each Disney resort around the world to serve as grand marshal in a Disney parade
- A variety of unique Disney vacation experiences
- Admission to special parties and other experiences in the Disneyland and Walt Disney World parks
- Private meetings with favorite Disney characters
- A Golden FastPass ticket with unique access rights to some of Disney's most popular attractions

The celebration is scheduled to continue through September 2007.

Meanwhile, the company debuted four new attractions in Florida, including the latest—and perhaps the greatest—peak in the Disney mountain range. **Expedition Everest** at Disney's Animal Kingdom is a modern triumph of Disney Imagineering, a smooth and fast roller coaster with some truly impressive (and fun) details of the high Himalayas.

The Seas with Nemo & Friends at Epcot picks up where the film *Finding Nemo* left off. Advanced technology gives the stars of the film the appearance of swimming amid the live marine life of the 5.7-million-gallon saltwater aquarium in The Living Seas pavilion. Guests aboard "clam-mobiles" float into a coral reef where they meet Mr. Ray and his class on a field trip. Along the way, familiar characters such as Dory, Bruce, Crush, and Marlin join in the search.

At Disney's Animal Kingdom, ***Finding Nemo—The Musical*** is a live-action musical stage show also based on the *Nemo* movie. The show features original songs by Tony Award–winning *Avenue Q* composer Robert Lopez and a cappella musical *Along the Way* composer Kristen Anderson-Lopez. The musical immerses us in the story of Nemo and his overprotective clownfish father, Marlin, in a dazzling production that combines puppets, dancers, acrobats, and animated backdrops. The Theater in the Wild was enclosed and air-conditioned for the show.

The Laugh Floor Comedy Club at the Magic Kingdom invites guests to laugh, joke, sing songs, and match wits with animated stars of *Monsters, Inc.* The attraction features the one-eyed hero of the film, Mike Wazowski, who has opened a comedy club to collect laughs that will generate electricity for the monster world of Monstropolis.

And by popular demand, Epcot guests will have two options when it comes to riding **Mission: SPACE.** There's still the wild and original thrill attraction, but there's also a milder ride experience for those with more delicate constitutions. The new version, which is created by turning off the spinning centrifuge, may be more suited for some guests, such as those who are prone to motion sickness or have other conditions.

In 2005 Epcot opened **Soarin'**, a unique and truly impressive simulation of a hang-glider tour of California; the attraction, at the Land pavilion, was imported from Disney's California Adventure park. Nearby, that most excellent turtle Crush from Pixar's *Finding Nemo* opened an outpost at The Living Seas. *Turtle Talk with Crush* is a highly advanced real-time computer graphics interactive short; that means what we've got here is an animated character that can speak with the audience.

At the Magic Kingdom the classic **It's a Small World** has received an extreme makeover with new costumes, fresh colors, and an enhanced audio system.

Disney's Typhoon Lagoon gained a white-knuckle "water coaster," **Crush 'n' Gusher,** that sends riders down flumes through the Disneyfied remains of the Tropical Amity fruit-packing plant.

And at Disney–MGM Studios, the screech of tires now has a bit of a French accent with the opening of *Lights, Motors, Action! Extreme Stunt Show,* an import from Disney Studios Paris.

Other recent additions include a major concert stage at the Magic Kingdom for the mouse who started it all. *Mickey's PhilharMagic* delivers music, magic, and maestro Mickey Mouse in a state-of-the-art 3-D film, live-action, and puppet extravaganza.

Over at Universal Studios Florida, the winds of change swept out a trio of older favorites and replaced them with what's new. **Universal 360** is a spectacular nighttime cinema, music, laser, and fireworks show presented during summertime.

In 2005, the park unwrapped **Revenge of the Mummy,** an indoor roller coaster that is definitely out there. And the park also invited guests to test their own limits—as viewers or participants—at a *Fear Factor* show.

Also at Universal, *Shrek 4-D* moved into the former location of *Alfred Hitchcock: The Art of Making Movies*. Nearby, *Jimmy Neutron's Nicktoon Blast* displaced *The Funtastic World of Hanna-Barbera.*

Universal Orlando has gotten the bugs out of its high-tech Universal Studios Islands of Adventure park, while it gets the bugs in at **Men in Black** at the Universal Studios Florida park. The technological and storytelling marvel known as Islands of Adventure includes **Spider-Man,** the most technologically advanced theme-park ride in town, as well as **The Hulk** and **Dueling Dragons,** two roller coasters that seem several steps beyond the laws of physics. Nearby, Universal CityWalk is an entertainment and dining magnet by night.

Back at Walt Disney World, other big draws include the wild **GM Test Track** at Epcot, the fabulous *Fantasmic!* show and the thrilling **Rock 'n' Roller Coaster** or the perennially failing elevator of the **Tower of Terror** at Disney–MGM Studios, and a state-of-the-art old-fashioned dark ride, **The Many Adventures of Winnie the Pooh,** at the Magic Kingdom. At Downtown Disney the weird and wonderful Cirque du Soleil is in residence in a permanent circus tent. Across the way, DisneyQuest is an indoor virtual-reality theme park.

SeaWorld, renowned for its devotion to things natural, is now the home of an impressive thrill ride: **Kraken,** a truly unnatural roller coaster. The new hangout is the **Waterfront at SeaWorld,** an entertainment and dining venue along the central lake at the park. Across the road is Discovery Cove, an ultra-exclusive marine park with some of the best facilities (and absolutely the highest prices) anywhere.

The Kennedy Space Center Visitor Complex continues to expand its peek into the world of space exploration.

In Tampa Bay, Busch Gardens debuted in 2005 another animalistic coaster: **SheiKra,** the nation's first dive coaster. A few years before, the park made a bit of a splash with **Rhino Rally,** an unusual safari ride into the midst of its animals, which begins as a truck ride and ends as a river raft adventure.

And while 2004 saw the departure of one small but intriguing attraction, Splendid China, 2005 brought the revival of one of Florida's original tourist attractions, **Cypress Gardens.**

How in the world can you keep track of everything worth knowing about in central Florida? You can start here.

AN INSIDER'S GUIDE

I've been to Orlando enough times that I'm on a first-name basis with flight attendants, car-rental clerks, and hotel check-in staff. I swear that the ghoul in charge of the Tower of Terror saves me the front row in the soon-to-be-out-of-control elevator, and I know exactly which seat to choose for the best Soarin' over California or the most out-of-control trip Back to the Future.

I am a huge fan of Orlando as a theme park of theme parks, and much more. I don't know of many other places with so much to do, so many interesting places to visit . . . and so many ways to spend hard-earned dollars. *Not that there's anything wrong with that . . . if you're careful.*

My goal in the Econoguide series is to help you get the most for your money and make the best use of your time. This is not a guide for cheapskates; you will, though, learn how to travel well—considerably better than the folks in front of and behind you in line. (Oh, and I'll offer some tips on how to reduce the chances of finding long lines.)

Once again I've gone back and walked every mile of every major park and attraction and looked everywhere for changes and new features. There are thousands of changes, minor and major, from last year's edition of the book.

ABOUT WALT DISNEY WORLD AND ORLANDO

Walt Disney World is a magical kingdom of fantastic delights for children of all ages; I recommend it highly.

Disney's greatest accomplishment in Orlando was the creation of an entire world of entertainment: four theme parks, two water parks, half a dozen golf courses, a baseball stadium, a world-class automobile racetrack, dozens of hotels, hundreds of restaurants, and thousands of major and minor diversions from tennis, horseback riding, boating, and bicycling to cartooning lessons. There's a whole island of restaurants and nightclubs, a gigantic movie theater complex, and a permanent circus. For many guests a week's visit to Orlando can be spent entirely within the boundaries of the Walt Disney World resort.

Now Disney has serious competition for multiday visits. Universal Orlando has two parks on its property: Universal Studios Florida and Universal Studios Islands of Adventure, plus the Wet 'n Wild water park nearby, a huge rock 'n' roll club, its own island of restaurants and clubs, and its own hotel complex. And SeaWorld has expanded within its own boundaries and across the road in an exclusive upscale park. There are also dozens of other excellent attractions and recreational opportunities in the Orlando and central Florida region, from fine arts to Major League Baseball spring training and a National Basketball Association home team.

But let's get something straight here: As wonderful an entertainment opportunity as they are, Walt Disney World, Universal Orlando, SeaWorld, and all the rest are basically gigantic vacuum cleaners aimed at your wallet. *Be careful out there.*

NOT TOO CUTE

After visits that have totaled months at Walt Disney World, the Disneyland Resort, Disneyland Paris, and Tokyo Disneyland, I've come up with my All-Purpose Disney Attraction Classification Guide. I've decided that Disney attractions can be divided into "Disney Cute," "Disney Smart," and "Disney Wow."

■ **Disney Cute** is Mickey Mouse; *Turtle Talk with Crush;* Winnie the Pooh; Aladdin; It's a Small World; *Mickey's PhilharMagic;* the Tiki Birds; Snow White; Cinderella; and Dumbo. That's where the hook is set with young children and their parents.

■ **Disney Smart** is Disney's Animal Kingdom; Epcot's Future World; Epcot's World Showcase; and Epcot's Innoventions. At the Magic Kingdom it's the Hall of Presidents. At Disney–MGM Studios it's the Special Effects and Production Tour. This is where Disney magic helps us learn.

■ **Disney Wow** is Soarin'; Expedition Everest; the *Lights, Motors, Action! Extreme Stunt Show;* Mission: SPACE; GM Test Track; Rock 'n' Roller Coaster; Dinosaur; Space Mountain; Tower of Terror; Star Tours; The Great Movie Ride; Thunder Mountain Railroad; and Splash Mountain. These are the things that make us say, "Ooh."

One reason for Disney's success is that they have learned to mix Cute, Smart, and Wow. It's the reason children come back as adolescents and then as parents; it's the reason adults can enjoy accompanying their youngsters. Add to this Disney's impressive devotion to expanding its attraction to adults with things such as water parks, golf courses, tennis courts, nightclubs, and spectacularly sybaritic hotels, and it's only just begun: Disney's Wide World of Sports, the spring training baseball facilities for the Atlanta Braves, the national headquarters of the Amateur Athletic Union, and much more. Call those "Disney for Adults," and they will be the reason this place will continue to be a lure for us all once we are too jaded for Cute, too educated for Smart, and (alas) too old for Wow.

WHY THIS BOOK?

Now, don't get me wrong: Walt Disney World and Universal Orlando may be the best-designed, best-run, and most overall satisfying tourist attractions on this planet, but you also have the right to spend your time and money as carefully as possible. That's what this book is all about—helping you get the very most from your time and money as you travel to Orlando and visit the parks and attractions there.

ABOUT INDEPENDENCE

The author and publisher of this book have no connection with Walt Disney World, Universal Orlando, SeaWorld, Busch Gardens, or any of the other attractions written about here. Our profit comes from you, the readers of this book, and it is you we hope to serve as best we can.

We'd be happy to hear your comments and suggestions, too. Please send e-mails to us at: info@econoguide.com.

You can receive a free subscription to the Econoguide newsletter for updates, announcements, and special offers. To subscribe, go to our Web page at www .econoguide.com and click on the "Subscribe to Newsletter" link. You can also subscribe by sending an e-mail with your name and e-mail address to: newsletter@ econoguide.com.

I hope you'll also consider the other books in the Econoguide series. You can find them at bookstores, or ask your bookseller to order them. All are written by Corey Sandler.

Econoguide Disneyland® Resort, Universal Studios Hollywood®
Econoguide Las Vegas
Econoguide Cruises
Econoguide Buying or Leasing a Car
Econoguide Buying and Selling a Home

PART I

ON THE ROAD TO ORLANDO

CHAPTER ONE

WHEN: THE SEASONS OF CENTRAL FLORIDA

HERE ARE TWO HYPOTHETICAL DAYS from a vacation trip to Orlando:

July 4. It wasn't exactly the flight you wanted. However, you're grateful for the privilege of forking over $705 for a coach seat in the jammed cabin of the jet. All of the rooms inside the park—at $289 per night—are sold out, but you were lucky enough to pay just $150 for a very ordinary hotel room that is a twenty-minute bumper-to-bumper drive from the parking lots.

According to the driver of the tram, you are parked near the Magic Kingdom, although you're not sure you're in the same county. When you get to the ticket booths, there's a thirty-minute wait just to get on the monorail to the entrance. Once inside you sprint to Tomorrowland to find that the line for Space Mountain includes what seems to be the occupants of every car you passed on the long, long ride through the gigantic parking lot.

Or perhaps you are determined to start your day with an African safari—the lions are more active in the cooler morning—and then give yourself a chill with a face-to-face fly-by with a yeti at the latest addition to the Disney Mountain Range, Expedition Everest. But when you arrive at Disney's Animal Kingdom, the wild things are in a line that looks like it stretches from the ticket booths back to Nairobi.

Then again, you might prefer to gracefully hang glide over California at Epcot's Soarin' ride, or blast off for Mars on the stomach-churning Mission: SPACE, or take a thrilling spin around the GM Test Track at Epcot. In your mind's eye you imagine zipping around the fifty-degree curves at 65 miles per hour; when you get there, you find a traffic jam with people in line all the way back to the airport. At Disney–MGM Studios you want to be a millionaire, but all the money in your pockets is not enough to get you into *Who Wants to Be a Millionaire—Play It!*

CENTRAL FLORIDA WEATHER AVERAGES

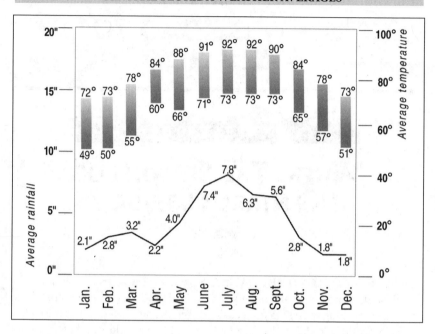

At Universal's Islands of Adventure, the lines for the Incredible Hulk Coaster are incredible, for Dr. Doom's Fearfall they're fearsome, and the only way you're going to get into Back to the Future is to go back to the past.

And you'd better plan on showing up for lunch at 10:45 A.M. and dinner at 4:30 P.M. if you hope to find a table at the lowliest overpriced burger stop. But there are always the cooling thrills at Blizzard Beach, right? True, but the line for Florida's only ski resort stretches back to Philadelphia.

March 20. It seems like it's just your family and a crew of flight attendants, stretched out at 30,000 feet. Even nicer, you were able to grab a deep-discount ticket on a major airline for just $150. Your hotel room outside the parks costs $29.95, and the road to the kingdom is empty. The sleek monorail stands empty and waiting for you at the transportation center. Your leisurely walk to Space Mountain puts you into a ten-minute queue; later in the day you can drop into a rocket car without breaking stride. At Epcot your private vehicle awaits your arrival at the GM Test Track. Over at Universal's Islands of Adventure, Spider-Man senses your arrival personally, and The Cat in the Hat is looking for company.

Take your pick of restaurants, and feel free to take a break in the afternoon and run over to Typhoon Lagoon; temperatures often reach eighty degrees, and the lagoon is like a beach on a semiprivate tropical island.

Do I have to point out which trip is likely to be more enjoyable?

OUR GUIDING RULE

The basic Econoguide strategy to getting the most out of your trip is this: Go when most people don't; stay home when everyone else is standing in line. Specifically, I suggest you try to make your visit to Florida when school is in session and in the weeks between holidays: between Labor Day and Thanksgiving, between Thanksgiving and Christmas, between New Year's Day and Presidents' Week, between Presidents' Week and spring break or Easter, between Easter and Memorial Day.

I'm not just talking about crowds at Walt Disney World, Universal Studios Orlando, SeaWorld, and elsewhere in central Florida. There's also the availability of discount airline tickets, off-season motel rates, and restaurant specials to consider. You'll find lower prices when businesses are anxious for your patronage. The best deals can be found in low season or what travel agents call the "shoulder season," midway between the slowest and busiest times. But this doesn't mean you can't have a good time if your schedule (or your children's) requires you to visit at high season. I'll show you ways to save money and time, any time of the year.

A WALT DISNEY WORLD VACATION CALENDAR

Walt Disney World is, and probably always will be, the number one attraction in Orlando; the crowd estimates in this calendar are based on the history of that four-theme-park resort. However, the same relative crowd levels can be expected at Universal Studios Orlando's theme parks and at other attractions in Florida.

■ JANUARY

🚹 🚹 🚹 New Year's Eve and New Year's Day

🚹 Second week of January through end of the month

🚹 🚹 Walt Disney World Marathon, early January
Warm and semiprivate. Room rates at low-season level, except during special events.

New Year's Day and a few days afterward are the crowded aftermath of the Christmas rush. But when the kids go back to school and most of the adults return to work after the

Key to Calendar

🚹 = Semiprivate

🚹 🚹 = Moderate crowds

🚹 🚹 🚹 = Heavy crowds

🚹 🚹 🚹 🚹 = Elbow-to-elbow

Christmas–New Year's holiday, the population at the parks drops off very sharply. The second week of January through the first week of February is usually the second least crowded period of the year, with daily attendance averaging about 25,000 visitors at the Magic Kingdom. There's a spike in early January when the Walt Disney World Marathon is held at the resort, attracting as many as 24,000 runners plus families and spectators. During this time the parks close early and do not offer nighttime parades or fireworks, but you'll be able to walk right onto most major rides and attractions; room rates are at their lowest level.

■ FEBRUARY

👤 👤 First ten days of February

Moderate crowds. Warm but not hot. Room rates lower than at peak-season levels.

Early February is a period of average attendance, reaching 30,000 to 35,000 visitors daily. The parks generally close early except for weekends, and there are no nighttime parades or fireworks.

👤 👤 👤 Presidents' Week holiday period

Heavy crowds for holiday week. Room rates at high-season level.

Presidents' Week (celebrated in many school districts in and around the period from February 12 to February 22) is a time of fairly heavy attendance, up to about 45,000 visitors daily. Watch out for Race Week in Daytona, too. The parks are open late, with nightly parades and fireworks.

👤 👤 Late February

A quiet time. Rooms drop to shoulder-season levels.

■ MARCH

👤 👤 Entire month

March comes in like a lamb. Back to moderate attendance. Thermometer nudges into the eighties. Room rates at shoulder-season level.

Attendance falls off to moderate levels from the end of February through the first week of April, averaging about 35,000 visitors. There are days in early March when you will have the parks to yourself, but at other times you will join thousands of college kids on early spring break or fans drawn south for baseball spring training. Weatherwise, though, this is not a bad time to come to Florida—with luck you will run into eighty-degree water-park days. The parks generally close early, and there are no nighttime parades or fireworks in the first half of the month; during spring break the parks are open later.

■ APRIL

👤 👤 First and fourth weeks of April

Usually a lovely time, with moderate attendance and room rates below peak-season levels.

Sneak in before or after the spring-break rush. The parks generally close early, and there are no nighttime parades or fireworks.

🚶 🚶 🚶 **Second and third weeks of April**
The Easter Parade can attract a lot of bunnies and college breakers. Consistent eighty-degree weather. Room rates at high-season levels.

The second and third weeks of April are among the most crowded times, as Easter visitors and spring-break students clog the turnstiles at rates of up to 60,000 per day. The parks are open late, with parades and fireworks.

MAY

🚶 🚶 **Entire month**
Moderate attendance, swimming weather, and shoulder-season rates.

Another relatively quiet period is from the end of April through the first week of June. Expect average attendance of about 30,000 per day. The parks generally close early, and there are no nighttime parades or fireworks.

JUNE TO AUGUST

🚶 🚶 🚶 **The crazy days of summer**
Hot sun, lots and lots of company, and high-season rates.

Just after Memorial Day the throngs of people come—and stay. Crowds of about 60,000 per day can be expected from the first week of June through the third week of August. Room rates are at high season. Temperatures average in the nineties, and you can expect a few heavy downpours or steady rains. Parks are open late, with nighttime parades and fireworks.

SEPTEMBER TO MID-NOVEMBER

🚶 **The post-summer doldrums**
Theme-park heaven: no lines, no crowds, and low, low rates. Watch out for Golf Classic weekend, though. Temperatures still high.

Where have all the tourists gone? On the day after Labor Day, the turnstiles slow to a crawl, averaging about 20,000 visitors per day. Room rates reach bottom, too. The weather is quite good, although the occasional tropical storm or hurricane can dampen a few days here and there. The parks generally close at 6:00 or 7:00 P.M., but the lack of lines should allow you to see everything you want. There are some late hours on weekends, with parades or fireworks.

In recent years the Golf Classic has occupied a weekend in late October, bringing thousands of PGA fans to hotels and the parks.

NOVEMBER

🚶 🚶 🚶 **Thanksgiving for what?**
Airlines, hotels, and restaurants give thanks for the huge crowds at Thanksgiving. Rates at high-season level.

Thanksgiving week brings the brief return of NO VACANCY signs at motels and in attraction lines. Average attendance is about 55,000 visitors. The parks generally close early, except for the holiday week and weekends surrounding it.

■ DECEMBER

♠ First through third weeks

This is it: the secret season. Mickey can get lonely at times like these, and hotels will almost pay you to come and stay.

From after Thanksgiving until the day Christmas vacation starts is the quietest time of the year for a visit. Attendance levels average 15,000 to 20,000 per day, and lines are rare. Room rates are rock-bottom, too. The parks generally close early, and there are no nighttime parades or fireworks, except on weekends.

♠ ♠ ♠ ♠ Christmas holiday

The not-at-all-secret season. Your sisters and cousins and aunts will all be in line, in front of you. You may need a loan for the super-high-season room rates.

The Christmas–New Year's holiday is the most crowded, least time-efficient time to visit central Florida. You'll be shoulder to shoulder with an average of 75,000 to 80,000 other visitors each day at Walt Disney World, with large crowds and long lines at Universal Studios, SeaWorld, and other area attractions. Parks are open late with a full schedule of parades by day and night, capped off by fireworks.

The crowds can become so large that some of the parks actually close the gates by midmorning. Don't feel too bad if you're shut out. It could be worse: You could be inside . . . in line. You cannot count on air temperatures warm enough for swimming, either. Room rates are at their highest levels, too.

It's a festive, happy time, but frankly, we'd rather be alone or close to it. If you must go, be sure to arrive at the park early and follow the Power Trip plan you'll find in each theme-park chapter for your best chance.

THE BEST DAY TO GO TO THE PARK

ATTRACTION	GO	DON'T GO
Magic Kingdom	Sunday Tuesday Wednesday Friday	Monday Thursday Saturday
Disney's Animal Kingdom	Sunday Thursday Friday Saturday	Monday Tuesday Wednesday
Epcot	Sunday Monday Wednesday Thursday Saturday	Tuesday Friday

ATTRACTION	GO	DON'T GO
Disney–MGM Studios	Monday Tuesday Thursday Friday Saturday	Sunday Wednesday
Universal Studios Florida, Universal Studios Islands of Adventure, and other area attractions	Sunday Monday Tuesday Friday	Wednesday Thursday Saturday
SeaWorld	Weekdays	Weekends

When Mom, Dad, William, and Tessa arrive in Orlando on Sunday (the most common arrival date) for a week's visit (the most common length of vacation), the first place they will go is the Magic Kingdom on Monday. Epcot comes next, then the Disney–MGM Studios. The remainder of the week is usually given over to other area parks and attractions. But we believe the best plan for your visit is to adopt what we call a "contrarian view." In other words, go against the common logic of others that says, "We came here for the Magic Kingdom, and that's where we'll go first." Most visitors come to Orlando for Walt Disney World and will head there first; a contrarian approach says head to Universal Studios Orlando early in the week instead of later.

By the way, it should be obvious that seven days is not enough time to experience all that Orlando and central Florida have to offer; if time and money are no object, I'd suggest a ten-day to two-week visit with about half of the time devoted to Disney World and the other days for Universal Studios Florida, SeaWorld, Busch Gardens, and all the other attractions in the area.

Here is one schedule you might want to consider if you are visiting central Florida during one of the busy times of the year. It starts with arrival on Saturday, which is a bit against the tide; if you get to Orlando early enough, you may be able to visit a water park or other attraction (other than the Magic Kingdom) that night.

THE ECONOGUIDE CONTRARIAN SCHEDULE

Saturday	Arrive in Orlando. Visit Disney–MGM Studios, water parks, smaller attractions, dinner theaters, or Pleasure Island
Sunday	Magic Kingdom, Animal Kingdom, Epcot, Universal Studios Florida, or Universal's Islands of Adventure
Monday	Universal's Islands of Adventure, Epcot, or Disney–MGM Studio

Tuesday	Magic Kingdom, SeaWorld, beach, golf, water parks, or other attractions
Wednesday	Busch Gardens, Space Center, Magic Kingdom, or Epcot
Thursday	Epcot Center, Animal Kingdom, or smaller attractions
Friday	Magic Kingdom, Animal Kingdom
Saturday	A second chance at the park of your choice (avoid Magic Kingdom, Universal Studios Florida, Universal Studios Islands of Adventure, and SeaWorld)

SPECIAL EVENTS AT WALT DISNEY WORLD

The Walt Disney World Happy Easter Parade marches down Main Street in the Magic Kingdom and is broadcast nationally; check with Disney reservations before you visit to find out if the parade will be taped a few days to a week ahead of Easter itself—it usually is.

The lovely **Epcot International Flower & Garden Festival** takes place within the gates of Epcot from mid-April through June 1.

At the end of October, the park celebrates **Mickey's Not-So-Scary Halloween Party,** which is just what it sounds like. Guests are invited to dress in costumes and trick-or-treat throughout the park from 7:00 P.M. to midnight over a three-day weekend. The party also includes parades, live music, and storytelling, culminating in a special fireworks display. In recent years special tickets for the Halloween party were priced separately from general park admission and at a lower price. For information contact any Walt Disney World ticket location or Ticketmaster.

The Magic Kingdom promises a 100 percent chance of snow flurries in balmy central Florida for **Mickey's Very Merry Christmas Party** each year. Of course, this is Disney, and it's not really snow. But then again, that's not really a mouse wearing those size 48 shoes, either. (Sorry to disillusion you.) Instead, there's a phalanx of artificial snow machines set up behind Main Street, U.S.A., to blanket the crowds at the end of the nightly Mickey's Very Merry Christmas Parade. There are also special stage shows and fireworks shows with a holiday theme. The Christmas party requires a separate admission ticket; in recent years the park was cleared at the end of each

Winter Wonderland

Each Christmas season Walt Disney World Resort is "decked" with more than 11 miles of garland, 3,000 wreaths, and 1,500 Christmas trees. Traditionally the tallest is a 70-foot tree in Disney's Contemporary Resort. Other large trees are placed in prominent positions in the theme parks.

Special Events and Celebrations at Walt Disney World

▶ **Walt Disney World Marathon,** early January. A 26.2-mile race through all four Disney theme parks. On the same weekend is a half-marathon, two-day health expo, and 5K race.

▶ **Chinese New Year,** late January to February. Epcot.

▶ **Mardi Gras,** mid-February. Pleasure Island.

▶ **Atlanta Braves Spring Training,** February–March. Preseason workouts and baseball games at Disney's Wide World of Sports.

▶ **St. Patrick's Day Celebration,** Mid-March. Pleasure Island.

▶ **Walt Disney World Easter Parade,** Easter. Magic Kingdom.

▶ **Epcot International Flower & Garden Festival,** April–June. Epcot blooms with more than thirty million colorful blossoms, workshops with national gardening experts, and interactive garden activities for kids.

▶ **Night of Joy,** September. Top contemporary Christian music performers throughout Disney's Magic Kingdom.

▶ **Walt Disney World Golf Classic,** October. Annual PGA tournament held at Disney's Magnolia and Palm golf courses.

▶ **Epcot International Food and Wine Festival,** October–November. A monthlong festival of live entertainment, guest chefs, culinary demonstrations, seminars, and winemaker dinners.

▶ **ABC Super Soap Weekend,** November. Favorite soap stars from shows including *All My Children, One Life to Live,* and *General Hospital* meet with fans at Disney–MGM Studios.

▶ **Holiday Splendor,** Thanksgiving to New Year's Day. Dazzling lights, spirited song, and even snow flurries. Highlights include Spectacle of Lights, a display of five million twinkling lights at Disney–MGM Studios; Mickey's Very Merry Christmas Party at Magic Kingdom; Candlelight Processional at Epcot; plus caroling, tree-lighting ceremonies, and visits by Santa.

day and then reopened at 8:00 P.M., remaining open until 1:00 A.M. Certain length-of-stay ticket packages included the extra night's admission.

At Disney–MGM Studios the park looks like a hardware store gone crazy with the **Osborne Family Light Extravaganza.** Epcot celebrates **Holidays Around the World** at World Showcase pavilions.

At Universal Studios Florida big annual events include a monstrous Halloween party and an extended Mardi Gras celebration in late winter.

CHAPTER TWO

HOW: PLANES, TRAINS, AND AUTOMOBILES

I LOVE TO TRAVEL, but I hate to waste time and money. It all but kills me to know that I spent $200 more than I should have for an airline ticket, or that the next guy over has a nicer hotel room at a better price. Put another way, my goal is to take more vacations and spend more time in wondrous places than most people, and to have a better time while I'm at it.

Let's get something straight here, though: This book is not a guide for the cheapskate who wants a $10-a-night tour of dreadful dives and uninspiring-but-free sights. I'm perfectly willing to spend a reasonable amount of money for good value. In this book I'll help you make the same sort of good use of your own money and time.

AIR TRAVEL

The way I figure it, one major airline is pretty much like another. Sure, one company may offer a larger bag of peanuts while the other promises its flight attendants have more accommodating smiles. Me, I'm much more interested in other things: safety, the most convenient schedule, and the lowest price. Though I'm sometimes willing to trade price for convenience, I'll never risk my neck for a few dollars. But that doesn't mean I don't try my hardest to get the very best price on airline tickets. I watch the newspapers for seasonal sales and price wars, clip coupons from the usual and not-so-usual sources, consult the burgeoning world of Internet travel agencies, and happily play one airline against the other.

Here are some things to look for:

■ **A new airline.** In recent years, we have seen the arrival of carriers like JetBlue and the growth of no-frills discount carriers like Southwest. Almost all of the new carriers make a big splash with low fares and extra amenities.

■ **New service.** When airlines come into a market, they often offer "introductory" prices. I've seen prices as low as $19 in fare wars; in recent years there have been several periods during which you could buy cross-country tickets for $79 to $99 each way.

■ **The right airport.** When one airline dominates a particular airport, chances are that prices are not as competitive as they should be. You'll get the best prices at an airport where two or more airlines fly between the same pairs of cities; even better, when one of the low-cost carriers (including Southwest and JetBlue) offers tickets, the major airlines generally match their prices on some or all flights, at huge cost to their own bottom line.

■ **The best time.** The busiest travel days of the year are usually the days before Thanksgiving, Christmas, and school holidays. You can bet that deep-discount tickets will be rare at those times of the year, and seats themselves will be in short supply. On the other hand, you can expect the best prices and availability during slack periods that include the time between Thanksgiving and Christmas, and in the dead of winter. In this book, we're exploring vacation trips, and in theory, you can make some adjustments to your plans to get the best possible rate.

> ### Receive Econoguide Updates
>
> You can receive a free subscription to the Econoguide newsletter for updates, announcements, and special offers. To subscribe, go to our Web page at www.econoguide.com and click on the "Subscribe to Newsletter" link. You can also subscribe by sending an e-mail with your name and e-mail address to: newsletter@econoguide.com.

Let's start with a real-life scenario. I want to get away from New England to the Walt Disney World Resort and Universal Studios Orlando. I know to stay away from the busiest and most expensive times of the year: the Christmas–New Year's holiday, the Presidents' Week vacation, and the heart of the summer (yes, I know it can be unbearably hot, but the desert vacationland still draws millions). The availability of online reservation systems from the hotels and from travel portals makes it easy to see when rates are high or low.

It is also usually less expensive to fly during the middle of the week—Tuesday through Thursday instead of on Monday or Friday; Saturday is sometimes a good day to travel, too. And most importantly, in this example, I am willing to consider saving some money by driving a bit farther to the airport.

Here are some real prices I found for round-trip flights to one of the Orlando-area airports in the summer: I could fly early in the morning, arriving at Orlando International Airport in Florida in time for dinner and a fireworks show for as little as $241 from Manchester, New Hampshire; $258 from Boston; or $261 from Providence.

Orlando International is about twenty to thirty minutes from Walt Disney World, but it is such a huge airport that sometimes it can take as much as an hour to collect your bags and get to your rental car or bus transportation. So, I sometimes use an alternate airport such as Tampa (just over an hour away by car). I usually can make up some of the extra driving time by zipping through the terminal to baggage claim and my rental car.

In my quick check of prices for this chapter, I found flights from Boston to Tampa for $213 and from Providence for $216. For a family of four, that's a potential savings of about $120; even with high gasoline prices, it's worth considering alternate airports. (Besides Tampa, there's also Daytona Beach and Sanford.) And I know that if I went on searching, and kept an eye out for airline sales, I could probably drop the price a bit more.

■ ALICE IN AIRLINELAND

In today's strange world of air travel, there is a lot of room for the dollarwise and clever traveler to wiggle. You can pay an inflated full price, you can take advantage of the lowest fares, or you can play the ultimate game and parlay tickets into free travel.

Should you use a travel agent? If an agent can save you money or offer you some service you cannot obtain by doing it yourself, go ahead; the fact is, though, that very few traditional travel agencies are still in the business of selling airline tickets and hotel reservations. Most airlines have severely cut or eliminated commissions on tickets, and there's not much money to be made on hotels, either. The surviving traditional travel agencies instead concentrate on big-ticket items such as cruises or all-in-one airline, hotel, car rental, and entertainment packages. If you were to ask a travel agency to sell you an airline ticket, they might slap a service charge on the price.

And there is a built-in major conflict of interest here, because under the traditional arrangement, the agent was paid by the seller, not the buyer; and an agent would usually make more commission on a $500 ticket than a $250 ticket.

The modern replacement for agencies is the online travel portal, where you can compare prices, departure times, and other considerations. Here you'll find computerized travel agencies that offer airline, hotel, car, cruise, and package reservations. You won't receive personalized assistance, but you will be able to make as many price checks and itinerary routings as you like without apology. Several of the services feature special deals, including companion fares and rebates you won't find offered elsewhere.

At an online travel Web site, your purchase is charged to your credit card (which adds a layer of protection for you), and in most cases you will receive an electronic confirmation code instead of a paper ticket, which speeds up the whole process and cuts costs. There are three golden rules when it comes to saving hundreds of dollars on travel: Be flexible, be flexible, and be flexible. Here's how to translate that flexibility into extra dollars in your pocket:

■ Shop around. Consult several online travel Web sites for the best availabile fares and connections, and then check the Web site for the airline itself to see if an even better fare is available there. You can also call the airline; although prices online are usually less than those quoted by a reservations agent, you can ask questions for free. And in some cases, the reservations agent will match the online price quote if you make that specific request. It doesn't hurt to ask.

■ Be flexible about when you choose to travel. Go during the off-season or low season when airfares, hotel rooms, cruises, and attractions are offered at substantial discounts. Try to avoid school vacations, spring break, and the prime summer travel months of July and August, unless you enjoy a lot of company.

- Be flexible about the day of the week you travel. In many cases you can save hundreds of dollars by bumping your departure date one or two days in either direction. Ask the airline reservations agent (or read the fine print on the Web site) about current fare rules and restrictions.

Double Indemnity

Your homeowner's or renter's insurance policy may include coverage for theft of your possessions while you travel, making it unnecessary to purchase a special policy. Check with your insurance agent.

The days of lightest air travel are generally midweek, Saturday afternoon, and Sunday morning. The busiest days are Sunday evening, Monday morning, and Friday afternoon and evening. In many cases, you will receive the lowest possible fare if your stay includes all day Saturday; this class of ticket is sold as an excursion fare. It used to be standard practice by airlines to use this as a way to exclude business travelers from the cheapest fares, assuming that businesspeople will want to be home by Friday night. Most airlines have been forced by economic conditions to end this discrimination against business travelers, but you may still run into price differentials.

- The day of the week on which you *buy* your tickets may also make a price difference. Airlines often test out higher fares over the relatively quiet weekends. They're looking to see if their competitors will match their higher rates. If the other carriers don't bite, the fares often float back down by Monday morning. Know the prevailing rates and look for up-and-down fluctuations.
- In general, you will receive the lowest fare if you buy a round-trip ticket, and if the flights on the itinerary are all on the same airline or on codeshare partners. However, in certain circumstances, you may find it less expensive to buy one-way tickets in each direction. Some of the low-fare airlines, including JetBlue and Southwest, usually allow you to buy an outbound and return ticket separately without additional cost. There is no reason I can think of not to choose different carriers for different directions if you can save cash in the process.
- Take advantage of frequent-flier programs only when they make economic sense. If you need to accumulate 50,000 miles to earn a ticket worth between $350 and $500—a fairly typical equation—that means that your miles are worth somewhere between a penny and a penny and a half each. So, if you are buying a 6,000-mile round-trip transcontinental ticket, the miles could be worth between $60 and $90—if you end up using them. But if you could find a fare on a different airline priced $200 less, it doesn't make sense to pay more for a ticket with frequent-flier mileage. (One possible exception: if you need just a few hundred or a thousand miles to reach a free-ticket plateau. But before you buy a more-expensive ticket just for that reason, check to see if you can purchase miles directly from the airline or earn them in other ways, such as through affinity credit-card programs.)

The Best Policy

Consider buying trip-cancellation insurance from a travel agency or tour operator or directly from an insurance company (ask your insurance agent for advice). The policies are intended to reimburse you for any lost deposits or prepayments if you must cancel a trip because you or certain specified members of your family become ill. Read the policy carefully to understand the circumstances under which the company will pay.

Take care not to purchase more coverage than you need; if your tour package costs $5,000 but you would lose only $1,000 in the event of a cancellation, then the amount of insurance required is just $1,000. Some policies will cover you for health and accident benefits while on vacation, excluding any preexisting conditions.

And be sure you understand your contract with your airline. You may be able to reschedule a flight or even receive a refund after payment of a service charge; some airlines will give full refunds or free rescheduling if you can prove a medical reason for the change.

■ Be flexible about the hour of your departure. There is generally lower demand—and therefore lower prices—for flights that leave in the middle of the day or very late at night. The highest rates are usually assigned to breakfast-time (7:00 to 11:00 A.M.) and cocktail-hour (4:00 to 7:00 P.M.) departures.

■ Be flexible on the route you will take and be willing to put up with a change of plane or stopover. Once again, you are putting the law of supply and demand in your favor. For example, a nonstop flight from Boston to Orlando for a family of four may cost hundreds more than a flight from Boston that includes a change of planes in Atlanta (a Delta hub) before proceeding on to Florida. (Sometimes, though, it works the other way: On a popular route, the nonstop may be less expensive than a connecting flight.)

(You should also understand that in airline terminology, a "direct" flight does not mean a "nonstop" flight. *Nonstop* means the plane goes from Point A to Point B without stopping anywhere else. A *direct* flight may go from Point A to Point B, but it may include a stopover at Point C or at more than one airport along the way. A connecting flight means you must get off the plane at an airport en route and change to another plane. And just to add one more level of confusion, some airlines have "direct" flights that involve a change of plane along the way—the flight number stays the same, but passengers have to get off at an intermediate stop, dragging all their carry-on luggage to another gate and aircraft. Go figure.)

Consider flying on one of the newer, deep-discount airlines, but don't let economy cloud your judgment. Some carriers are simply better run than others. Read the newspapers, check with a trusted fellow traveler, and use common sense. As far as I'm concerned, the best thing about the cheapo airlines is the pressure they put on the established carriers to lower prices or even to match fares on certain flights. Look for the cheapest fare you can find, and then call your favorite big airline and see if it will sell you a ticket at the same price—it just might work.

■ Don't overlook the possibility of flying out of a different airport either. For example, metropolitan New Yorkers can find domestic flights from LaGuardia, Newark, White Plains, and a developing discount mecca at Islip. Suburbanites of Boston might want to consider flights from Providence or Manchester as possibly cheaper alternatives to Logan Airport. Chicago has O'Hare and Midway. From southern California, there are major airports at Los Angeles, Orange County, Long Beach, Burbank, and San Diego.

■ Plan way ahead of time and purchase the most deeply discounted advance tickets, which usually are nonrefundable. Most carriers limit the number of discount tickets on any particular flight. Although there may be plenty of seats left on the day you want to travel, they may be offered at higher rates.

■ Understand the difference between nonrefundable and noncancelable. Most airlines interpret *nonrefundable* to mean that they can keep all of your money if you cancel a reservation or fail to show up for a flight. You can, though, apply the value of the ticket (minus a fee of as much as $150) toward the purchase of another ticket. A *noncancelable* fare means that you have bought a specific seat on a specific flight. If your plans change or you are forced to cancel your trip, you lose the value of the ticket. (Think of it as missing a concert performance. You can't use the ticket another day.) Of course, if the airline cancels your flight or makes a schedule or routing change you find does not meet your needs, you are entitled to a refund of your fare.

■ If you're feeling adventurous, you can take a big chance and wait for the last possible moment, keeping in contact with charter tour operators and accepting a bargain price on a leftover seat and hotel reservation. You may also find that some airlines will reduce the prices on leftover seats within a few weeks of your departure date; don't be afraid to check with the airline regularly or ask your travel agent to do it for you. In fact, some travel agencies have automated computer programs that keep a constant electronic eagle eye on available seats and fares.

■ Take advantage of special discount programs such as senior citizens' clubs, military discounts, or offerings from other organizations to which you may belong. If you are in the broadly defined "senior" category, you may not even have to belong to a group such as AARP; simply ask the airline ticket agent if there is a discount available. You may have to prove your age or show a membership card when you pick up your ticket or boarding pass.

■ Consider doing business with discounters or ticket brokers, known in the industry as consolidators or, less flatteringly, as bucket shops. These companies buy the airlines' slow-to-sell tickets in volume and resell them to consumers at rock-bottom prices. Search the Internet for listings; you may also find ads in the classified listings of many Sunday newspaper travel sections. Be sure to weigh the savings on the ticket price against any restrictions attached to the tickets. For example, they may not be changeable, which could be a big problem, and they usually don't accrue frequent-flier mileage, which is a less-important issue.

■ Shop online through one of the Internet travel sites or the Web sites of individual airlines. You can expect to receive the lowest possible airfares—usually a few percent below the best prices offered if you call the airline directly—but little assistance in choosing among the offerings. Be sure to pay close attention to details such as the number of connections required between origin and destination. Note, too, that tickets sold in this way may have severe restrictions on changes and cancellations.

Some of the best Internet agencies include:

Microsoft Expedia, www.expedia.com

Orbitz, www.orbitz.com

Travelocity, www.travelocity.com

Among the airlines that offer online booking are:

American Airlines, www.aa.com

Continental Airlines, www.continental.com

Delta Airlines, www.delta.com

JetBlue, www.jetblue.com

Northwest Airlines, www.nwa.com

Southwest, www.southwest.com

United Airlines, www.united.com

US Airways (now combined with America West), www.usairways.com

Consider, very carefully, buying tickets from an online travel auction site such as www.priceline.com or www.hotwire.com. These sites promise to match your travel plans with available seats on major airlines at deep-discount prices; you will not be able to choose departure or arrival times or a particular airline. The way to use these sites is to do your research beforehand on one of the regular Web sites to find the best price you can; compare that to the "blind" offerings from the auction sites.

Although the auction sites can often deliver the best prices, the tickets come with some detractions: You cannot time your arrival for a particular time of the day; it may be impossible to make changes or obtain a refund if your plans change; and you may not be permitted to stand by for another flight with your limited ticket. And read the fine print carefully: Prices may not include taxes and fees, and the sites may tack on a service charge. Be sure to compare the true bottom line to the price quoted on other Web sites or from a travel agent.

These auction sites have also begun offering a more traditional form of ticket booking, where the airline and flight times are displayed before you make your purchase. Be sure to check the prices against another travel Web site to make sure you are receiving a real discount from the regular fare.

Use an electronic ticket when it is to your advantage. Most major airlines have dispensed with their former practice of producing an individualized ticket for your travel and mailing it to you; instead, you'll be given a confirmation number (sometimes called a record locator) and asked to show up at the airport with proper identification and receive your ticket and boarding pass there. If you absolutely insist on receiving an actual ticket in advance of your flight, some airlines charge as much as $50 per ticket for their trouble.

In general, electronic ticketing works well. At many major airports, airlines have begun installing automated check-in machines, similar in operation to a bank's ATM. You'll be asked to insert a credit card or a frequent-flier ID card just for the purposes of identification, and the device will print out your ticket and boarding pass there. A nearby attendant will take your bags and attach luggage tags.

■ OTHER MONEY-SAVING STRATEGIES

Airlines are forever weeping and gnashing their teeth about huge losses due to cutthroat competition. And then they regularly turn around and drop their prices radically with major sales. I don't waste time worrying about the bottom line of the airlines; it's my own wallet I want to keep full. Therefore, the savvy traveler keeps an eye out for airline fare wars all the time. Read the ads in newspapers and keep an ear open for news broadcasts that often cover the outbreak of price drops. If you have a good relationship with a travel agent, you can ask to be notified of any fare sales.

The most common times for airfare wars are in the weeks leading up to the quietest seasons for carriers, including the period from mid-May to mid-June (except Memorial Day weekend), between Labor Day and Thanksgiving, and again in the winter, with the exception of Christmas, New Year's, and Presidents' Day holiday periods.

Study the fine print on discount coupons distributed by the airlines or third parties such as supermarkets, catalog companies, and direct marketers. In my experience, these coupons are often less valuable than they seem. Read the fine print carefully and be sure to ask the reservationist if the price quoted with the coupon is higher than another fare for which you qualify.

Don't be afraid to ask for a refund on previously purchased tickets if fares go down for the period of your travel. The airline may refund the difference, or you may be able to reticket your itinerary at the new fare, paying a penalty of about $100 for cashing in the old tickets. Be persistent: If the difference in fare is significant, it may be worth making a visit to the airport to meet with a supervisor at the ticket counter.

■ YOUR RIGHTS AS A CONSUMER

Whether you are buying your ticket through a travel Web site, a travel agent, or directly with the airline, here are some important questions to ask:

■ Is the price guaranteed, or can it change from the time of the reservation until you actually purchase the ticket?

■ Can the price change between the time you buy the ticket and the date of departure?

■ Is there a penalty for cancellation of the ticket?

■ Can the reservation be changed without penalty or for a reasonable fee? Be sure you understand the sort of service you are buying.

■ Is this a nonstop flight, a direct flight (an itinerary where your plane will make one or more stops en route to its destination), or a flight that requires you to change planes one or more times?

■ What seat has been issued? Do you really want the center seat in a three-seat row, between two strangers?

A savvy traveler also pays attention to the newspapers and consults others to consider:

■ Is there anything I should know about the short-term financial health of this airline that might affect my flight?

■ Are there any threats of work stoppages or legal actions that could ruin my trip? Your best protection against bankruptcies, strikes, and fraud is to use a major credit card to purchase your tickets and enlist the aid of that company in disputing charges for services not delivered.

■ BEATING THE AIRLINES AT THEIR OWN GAME

In my opinion, the airlines deserve all the headaches we travelers can give them because of the costly pricing schemes they throw at us—deals such as take-it-or-leave-it fares of $350 to fly 90 miles between two cities where they hold a monopoly and $198 bargain fares to travel 3,000 miles across the nation. Or round-trip fares of $300 if you leave on a Thursday and return on a Monday, but $1,200 if you leave on Monday and return the next Thursday.

But a creative traveler can find ways to work around most of these roadblocks. Nothing I'm going to suggest here is against the law; some of the tips, though, are against the rules of some airlines. Here are a couple of strategies:

Round-trip ticket for a one-way flight. Some airlines offer their very best fares for round-trip bookings, with prices often considerably less than the cost of a one-way ticket. For example, a promotional round-trip from New York to Orlando may cost $198, while a one-way ticket is priced at $279.

If you find yourself in a situation where you need only a one-way ticket—for example, a complex multileg trip, or if you plan to drive or take a train in one direction—consider buying a round-trip ticket and throwing away the return coupon. In theory this violates airline policies, but that doesn't mean savvy travelers don't use this technique. The airline is not likely to object unless it detects a large number of such no-shows in a short period of time.

Nested tickets. This scheme generally works in either of two situations: where regular fares are more than twice as high as excursion or special fares, or in situations where you plan to fly between two locations twice in less than a year.

Let's say you want to fly from Boston to Orlando. Buy two sets of tickets in your name. The first is from Boston to Orlando and back. This set has the return date for when you want to come back from your second trip. The other set of tickets is from Orlando to Boston and back to Orlando, this time making the first leg of the ticket for the date you want to come back from the first trip, and the second leg of the trip the date you want to depart for the second trip.

If this sounds complicated, that's because it is. It will be up to you to keep your tickets straight when you travel. Some airlines have threatened to crack down on such practices by searching their computer databases for multiple reservations. I have seen no evidence of this, though.

One solution: Buy one set of tickets on one airline and the other set on another carrier. Or, buy one set of round-trip tickets from Boston to Orlando and back, and the other from Tampa to Boston and back.

Split tickets. Fare wars sometimes result in supercheap fares through a connecting city. For example, an airline seeking to boost traffic through a hub in Cincinnati creates a situation in which it is less expensive to get from New York to Orlando by buying a round-trip ticket from New York to Cincinnati and then a separate round-trip ticket from Cincinnati to Orlando.

Be sure to book a schedule that allows enough time between flights; if you miss your connection, you could end up losing time and money.

Standing Up for Standing By

One of the little-known secrets of air travel on most airlines and most types of tickets is the fact that travelers with valid tickets may be allowed to stand by for flights other than the ones for which they have reservations. If there are empty seats on the flight, standby ticket holders are permitted to board.

Some airlines are very liberal in their acceptance of standbys within a few days of the reserved flight, while others will charge a fee for changes in itinerary. And some airline personnel are stricter about regulations than others.

Here's what I do know: If I can't get the exact flight I want for a trip, I make the closest acceptable reservations available after that flight and then show up early at the airport and head for the check-in counter for the flight I really want to take. Unless you are seeking to travel during an impossibly overbooked holiday period or arrive on a bad-weather day when flights have been canceled, your chances of successfully standing by for a flight are usually pretty good.

One trick is to call the airline the day before the flight and check on the availability of seats for the flight for which you want to try. Some reservation clerks are very forthcoming with information; many times I have been told something like, "There are seventy seats open on that flight."

Be careful with standby maneuvers if your itinerary requires a change of plane en route; you'll need to check the availability of seats on all of the legs of your journey. Some deep-discount fares may include prohibitions against standing by for other flights; read the fine print, especially if you are booking your own flight over the Internet.

The fly in the ointment in today's strict security environment is this: Airlines are required to match bags to passengers before a flight takes off. It is difficult, if not impossible, to stand by for a flight other than the one for which you hold a ticket if you have checked a bag. Your chances are much better if you limit yourself to carry-on bags (if allowed). And security screeners may not let you into the concourse for flights more than two hours before scheduled departure. Consult with the ticket agents at check-in counters outside of the security barriers for advice.

A final note: Be especially careful about standing by for the very last flight of the night. If you somehow are unable to get on that flight, you're stuck for the night.

Overbooking

Overbooking is a polite industry term for the legal business practice of selling more than an airline can deliver. It all stems, alas, from the rudeness of many travelers who neglect to cancel flight reservations that will not be used. Airlines study the patterns on various flights and city pairs and apply a formula that allows them to sell more tickets than there are seats on the plane in the expectation that a certain percentage of ticket holders will not show up.

But what happens if all passengers holding a reservation do show up? Obviously, the result will be more passengers than seats, and some will have to be left behind.

The involuntary bump list will begin with passengers who check in late. Airlines must ask for volunteers before bumping any passengers who have followed the rules on check-in.

Now, assuming that no one is willing to give up his or her seat just for the fun of it, the airline will offer some sort of compensation—either a free ticket or cash, or both. It is up to the passenger and the airline to negotiate a deal.

Some air travelers, including this author, look forward to an overbooked flight when their schedules are flexible. My most profitable score: $4,000 in vouchers on a set of four $450 international tickets. The airline was desperate to clear a large block of seats, and it didn't matter to us if we arrived home a few hours late. We received the equivalent of three tickets for the price of one, and we went on to earn some more free travel on future tickets purchased with those vouchers.

The U.S. Department of Transportation's consumer protection regulations set some minimum levels of compensation for passengers who are bumped from a flight due to overbooking:

■ If you are bumped involuntarily, the airline must provide a ticket on its next available flight. Unfortunately, there is no guarantee there will be a seat on that plane or that it will arrive at your destination at a convenient time.

■ If the airline can get you on another flight that will get you to your destination within one hour of the original arrival time, no compensation need be paid. If you are scheduled to get to your destination more than one hour but less than two hours late, you're entitled to receive an amount equal to the one-way fare of the oversold flight, up to $200. If the delay is more than two hours, the bumpee will receive an amount equal to twice the one-way fare of the original flight, up to $400.

■ It is not considered bumping if a flight is canceled because of weather, equipment problems, or the lack of a flight crew. You are also not eligible for compensation if the airline substitutes a smaller aircraft for operational or safety reasons, or if the flight involves an aircraft with sixty seats or fewer.

How to Get Bumped

Why in the world would you want to be bumped? Well, perhaps you'd like to look at missing your plane as an opportunity to earn a little money for your time instead of an annoyance. Is a two-hour delay worth $100 an hour to you? For the inconvenience of waiting a few hours on the way home, a family of four might receive a voucher for $800—that could pay for a week's hotel plus a heck of a meal at the airport.

If you're not in a rush to get to your destination—or to get back home—you might want to volunteer to be bumped. We wouldn't recommend doing this on the busiest travel days of the year or if you are booked on the last flight of the day, unless you are also looking forward to a free night in an airport motel.

■ BAD WEATHER, BAD PLANES, STRIKES, AND OTHER HEADACHES

You don't want pilots to fly into weather they consider unsafe, of course. You also don't want them to take up a plane with a mechanical problem. No matter how you feel about unions, you probably don't want to cross a picket line to board a plane piloted by strikebreakers. And so, you should accept an airline's cancellation of a flight for any of these legitimate reasons.

Here's the bad news, though: If a flight is canceled for an "act of God" such as bad weather, an earthquake, or a plague of locusts, or because of a strike or labor dispute, the airline isn't required to do anything for you except refund your money. In practice, carriers will usually make a good effort to find another way to get you to your destination more or less on time, which could mean rebooking on another flight on the same airline or on a different carrier. But you could be facing a delay of a day or more in the worst situations, such as a major snowstorm.

Here is a summary of your rather limited rights as an air passenger:

■ An airline is required to compensate you above the cost of your ticket only if you're bumped from an oversold flight against your will.

■ If you volunteer to be bumped, you can negotiate for the best deal with the ticket agent or a supervisor; for your inconvenience, you can generally expect to be offered a free round-trip ticket on the airline.

■ If your scheduled flight is unable to deliver you directly to the destination on your ticket, and alternate transportation such as a bus or limousine is provided, the airline is required to pay you twice the amount of your one-way fare if your arrival on the alternate transportation will be more than two hours later than the original airline ticket promised.

■ If you purchased your ticket with a credit card, the airline must credit your account within seven days of receiving an application for a refund.

All that said, in many cases you will be able to convince an agent or a supervisor to go beyond the letter of the law. I've found that the best strategy is to politely but firmly stand your ground. Ask the ticket clerk for another flight, for a free night in a hotel and a flight in the morning, or for any other reasonable accommodation. Don't take no for an answer but remain polite and ask for a supervisor if necessary. Sooner or later, they'll do something to get you out of the way.

And then there are labor problems, including those that have faced airlines such as American Airlines and US Airways in recent years. Your best defense against a strike is to anticipate it before it happens: Keep your ears open for labor problems when you make a reservation. Then keep in touch with your travel agent or the airline itself in the days leading up to any strike deadline. It is often easier to make alternate plans or seek a refund in the days immediately before a strike; wait until the last minute, and you're going to be joining a very long line of upset people.

In the face of a strike, a major airline will attempt to reroute you on another airline if possible. If you buy your own ticket on another carrier, you're unlikely to be reimbursed. If your flight is canceled, you'll certainly be able to claim a full refund of your fare or obtain a voucher in its value without paying any penalties.

AIRLINE SAFETY

There are no guarantees in life, but in general, flying on an airplane is considerably safer than the drive to the airport. All the major air carriers have very good safety records; some are better than others. I pay attention to news reports about Federal Aviation Administration (FAA) inspections and rulings and then make adjustments. And although I love to squeeze George Washington until he yelps, I avoid start-up and super-cut-rate airlines because I have my doubts about how much money they can afford to devote to maintenance.

Among major airlines, the fatal-accident rate during the last twenty-five years stands somewhere between 0.3 and 0.74 incidents per million flights. Not included in these listings are small commuter airlines (except those that are affiliated with major carriers). Put another way, if you were to take one flight per day—randomly selected—chances are it would be about 22,000 years before you would end up as a statistic on a fatal crash.

The very low numbers over such a long period of time, experts say, make them poor predictors of future incidents. Instead, you should pay more attention to reports of FAA or National Transportation Safety Board (NTSB) rulings on maintenance and training problems.

THE NEW WORLD OF AIRPORT SECURITY

Travel has become more complicated and less convenient in the wake of the terrorist attacks of 2001. The bottom line for well-meaning, nonviolent business and pleasure travelers is this: You'll need to add an hour or more to the check-in process, and your options to stand by for a different flight or make other changes to your itinerary are severely limited.

Here are some things you can do to lessen the pain:

- Consult with the airline or your travel agent about current policies regarding check-in times.
- Consider your departure time; lines for check-in and security clearance are longest during peak travel times—early morning and late afternoon.
- An alternate airport may have shorter lines. Some major hubs may, by necessity, be more efficient at processing huge crowds; at the same time, smaller airports with fewer crowds may be easier to navigate.
- Try to avoid carrying unnecessary metallic items on your person. Choose a belt with a small buckle rather than the one with the three-pound world-championship steer-wrestling medallion. Put your cell phone, keys, coins, and wristwatch in a plastic bag and place it in your carry-on bag as you approach the magnetometer; this will speed your passage and reduce the chances of losing items.
- Travel in a pair of shoes that are easy to remove and put on again.
- Be cooperative and remember that the screening is intended to keep you safe, and hope that the guards do their job well.

TOUR PACKAGES AND CHARTER FLIGHTS

Tour packages and flights sold by tour operators or travel agents may look similar, but the consumer may end up with significantly different rights.

What you end up with is greatly dependent on whether the flight is a scheduled or nonscheduled flight. A scheduled flight is one that is published in the Official Airline Guide and available to the general public through a travel agent or from the airline. This doesn't mean that a scheduled flight will necessarily be on a major carrier or that you'll be flying on a 747 jumbo jet; it could just as easily be the propeller-driven pride of Hayseed Airlines. In any case, though, a scheduled flight does have to meet stringent federal government certification requirements.

A nonscheduled flight is also known as a "charter flight." The term is sometimes also applied to a complete package that includes a nonscheduled flight, hotel accommodations, ground transportation, and other elements. Charter flights are generally a creation of a tour operator who will purchase all the seats on a specific flight to a specific destination or who will rent an airplane and crew from an air carrier.

Charter flights and charter tours are regulated by the federal government, but your rights as a consumer are much more limited than those afforded to scheduled flight customers. You wouldn't buy a hamburger without knowing the price and specifications (two all-beef patties on a sesame seed bun, etc.). Why, then, would you spend hundreds or even thousands of dollars on a tour and not understand the contract that underlies the transaction?

When you purchase a charter flight or a tour package, you should review and sign a contract that spells out your rights. This contract is sometimes referred to as the "Operator Participant Contract" or the "Terms and Conditions." Look for this contract in the booklet or brochure that describes the packages; ask for it if one is not offered.

Remember that the contract is designed mostly to benefit the tour operator, and each contract may be different from others you have agreed to in the past. The basic rule here is this: If you don't understand it, don't sign it.

How to Book a Package or Charter Flight

For charter flights and packages, consider using a travel agent, preferably one you know and trust. The tour operator usually pays the agent's commission. Some tour packages, however, are available only from the operator who organized the tour; in certain cases, you may be able to negotiate a better price by dealing directly with the operator, although you are giving up one layer of protection for your rights.

Pay for your ticket with a credit card. I consider this a cardinal rule for almost any situation in which you're paying in advance for a service or product. If you end up in a dispute with the travel provider or a

Don't Wait to Drop a Card

If you have booked a trip through a travel agent or tour operator, keep in touch. In many cases they can anticipate major changes before departure time and will let you know. And many operators will try hard to keep you from demanding a refund if you find a major change unacceptable. They may offer a discount or upgrade on a substitute trip or adjust the price of the changed tour.

If you have booked a flight directly through an airline, make sure they have your phone number in case of a change in the schedule. Call the airline a few days before your first flight to confirm your reservation and check for any changes.

Second Chance

Most tour operators, if forced to cancel, will offer another package or other incentives as a goodwill gesture. If a charter flight or charter tour is canceled, the tour operator must refund your money within fourteen days.

travel agency, you should be able to enlist the assistance of the credit-card issuer on your behalf.

Keep in mind that charter airlines don't have fleets of planes available as substitutes in the event of a mechanical problem or an extensive weather delay. They may not be able to arrange for a substitute plane from another carrier.

If you're still willing to try a charter after all of these warnings, make one more check of the bottom line before you sign the contract:

■ First of all, is the air travel significantly less expensive than the lowest nonrefundable fare available from a scheduled carrier? (Remember that you are, in effect, buying a nonrefundable fare with most charter flight contracts.)

■ Have you included taxes, service charges, baggage transfer fees, or other charges the tour operator may put into the contract?

■ Are the savings significantly more than the 10 percent the charter operator may (typically) boost the price without your permission? Do any savings come at a cost of time? Put a value on your time.

■ Finally, don't buy a complete package until you have compared it to the a la carte cost of such a trip. Call the hotels offered by the tour operator, or similar ones in the same area, and ask them a simple question: "What is your best price for a room?" Be sure to mention any discount programs that are applicable, including the American Automobile Association (AAA) or other organizations. Do the same for car rental agencies, and place a call to any attractions you plan to visit to get current prices.

If you miss a flight because of a problem with an unrelated carrier, you could forfeit nonrefundable tickets. Try to avoid such combinations; if you can't, allow extra hours between connections.

Some tour operators offer travel insurance that pays for accommodations or alternate travel costs made necessary by certain types of delays

■ ORLANDO INTERNATIONAL AIRPORT

Orlando's airport has grown from a backwater strip to one of the busiest—and most efficiently operated—terminals in the country. Located about thirty minutes west of Walt Disney World, it is served by several major highways as well as bus and limousine service. For information consult www.orlandoairports.net.

This large airport can seem very confusing to a new visitor, but its design is actually unusually logical. Think of the place as a giant X with central facilities at the intersection of the axes. There are four main clusters of gates at the airport, and each cluster is connected to the single ticketing and baggage claim area by an automated monorail. You won't be the first to observe that the first semi-thrill ride of your vacation is at the airport.

Here are the gate assignments as they existed in 2006 (be sure to check with your airline on arrival for any changes):

ORLANDO INTERNATIONAL AIRPORT

Hyatt Hotel

Terminal Top
Parking
Levels 4–10

Gates
100–129

A

Gates
1–29

P

3

2

1

Gates
60–99

P

Gates
30–59

B

Courtesy Greater Orlando Aviation Authority

■ **Airside Terminal 1** (Gates 1–29). Air Jamaica, Air Transat, Alaska, American Airlines, Bahamasair, Canjet, Cathay Pacific, Champion Air, Continental Airlines, Copa Airlines, Iberia, Japan, Lan, Lot, LTU, Martinair, Mexicana, Skyservice, SN Brussels, TAM, WestJet.

■ **Airside Terminal 2** (Gates 100–129). AirTran, ATA, JetBlue, Midway, Southwest, Spirit, Sun Country Airlines.

■ **Airside Terminal 3** (Gates 30–59). Air Canada, America West, ANA, Austrian, bmi, Independence, KLM, Lufthansa, Northwest Airlines, Scandinavian, Spirit, Swiss, United, US Airways.

■ **Airside Terminal 4** (Gates 60–99). AeroMexico, Air France, British Airways, China, Condor, Delta, Delta Connection, El Al, Frontier, Korean, MiamiAir, Midwest, Royal Air Maroc, Ryan International, South African, Sun Country Airlines, TSA, Virgin Atlantic.

■ ORLANDO SANFORD AIRPORT

Sanford's airport is located about 25 miles northeast of Orlando, off Interstate 4. The airport is served by many domestic and international charter airlines as well as a few smaller scheduled airlines such as

Lug It Yourself

If you are connecting between a charter and a scheduled airline, your bags will likely not be transferred "interline"—you will have to pick them up and deliver them between counters.

Allegiant and Icelandair. For information call (407) 585–4000 or consult www
.orlandosanfordairport.com.

■ AREA TRANSPORTATION INFORMATION

■ **Orlando International Airport Visitor Information.** (407) 825–2352; www
.orlandoairports.net.

■ **I-Ride.** (407) 248–9590; www.iridetrolley.com. A bus service along International Drive, connecting hotels, attractions, and restaurants. The Main line of the trolleylike bus runs daily from 8:00 A.M. to 10:30 P.M., about fifteen minutes apart, making more than fifty scheduled stops between SeaWorld Orlando and the Belz Factory Outlet World. The Green line begins and ends on International Drive but primarily travels along Universal Boulevard. The service carries more than a million passengers a year. A single adult fare is $1.00; children age twelve and younger ride free when accompanied by a paying adult. One-day passes are $3.00, three-day passes are $5.00, and seven-day passes are $9.00. The Mercado also has its own shuttle that serves hotels on International Drive.

■ **LYNX/Tri-County Regional Transportation Authority.** (407) 841–8240; www.golynx.com. Public transportation in Orlando and nearby. Several buses serve Walt Disney World, although the trip may involve several transfers. The standard fare is $1.50. A single-day pass costs $3.50, and multiday passes are also available. Transfers between buses are free. Senior discounts are available for riders age sixty-five or older.

■ **Amtrak.** (800) 872–7245 or (407) 843–7611; www.amtrak.com. Daily train service to Orlando from New York, Tampa, and Miami. Stops include downtown Orlando, Winter Park, and Sanford. Service from New York to Orlando is scheduled to consume between seventeen and twenty-seven hours, depending on time of departure. The Auto Train transports passengers and their cars from Lorton, Virginia, each day, departing in the afternoon and arriving about 8:30 A.M. the next day in Sanford, 25 miles northeast of downtown Orlando.

■ **Greyhound Bus Lines.** (407) 292–3424; www.greyhound.com. The Orlando terminal is located at 555 North John Young Parkway; for information call (407) 292–3440. The Kissimmee terminal is at 103 East Dakin Avenue; for information call (407) 847–3911. Service from New York to Orlando is scheduled to consume between twenty-two and twenty-six hours, depending on time of departure.

■ **Mears Transportation.** (407) 423–5566; www.mearstransportation.com. Shuttle van, town car, limousine service, and taxi from Orlando International Airport to hotels and attractions.

DRIVE?, HE SAID

Everyone's conception of the perfect vacation is different, but for me, I draw a distinction between getting there and being there. I want the getting there part to be as quick and simple as possible, and the being there part to be as long as I can manage and afford. Therefore, I fly to most any destination more than a few hundred miles from my home. The cost of driving, hotels, meals en route, and

FLORIDA HIGHWAYS

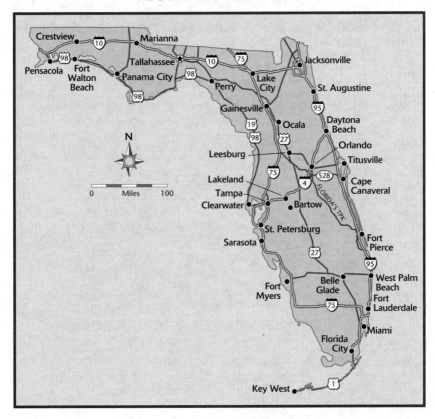

general physical and mental wear and tear rarely equals a deeply discounted excursion fare.

If you do drive, though, you can save a few dollars by using the services of AAA or another automobile club. And before you head out, make certain your vehicle is in traveling shape: A tune-up and fully inflated, inspected tires will save gas, money, and headaches.

If you plan to travel by bus or train, be aware that the national carriers generally have the same sort of peak and off-peak pricing as the airlines. The cheapest time to buy tickets is when the fewest people want them.

■ RENTING A CAR FOR A FLORIDA TRIP

If you are planning to stay at a hotel within Walt Disney World, you may be able to get by without renting a car, although you will not be able to get to attractions and restaurants outside the Disney boundaries without calling a cab or car service.

If you are staying outside Walt Disney World, you may be able to use a hotel shuttle bus to the parks, but you will find your options limited by the bus schedule. You should consider renting a car. The good news is that Orlando is one of

Interstate 4 Exits in Kissimmee/Orlando Area

New	Old*	
64A	(25A)	US 192 east. Motel strip toward downtown Kissimmee. Water Mania, Old Town, Medieval Times.
64B	(25B)	US 192 west. Magic Kingdom, Disney–MGM. Motel strip, Splendid China (now closed).
65	(26C/D)	Osceola Parkway, Animal Kingdom, Wide World of Sports.
67	(26A/B)	Epcot Center, Downtown Disney.
68	(27)	Highway 535 to Kissimmee and Lake Buena Vista. Hotel Plaza Resorts, Disney Village Resorts, Fort Wilderness.
71	(27A)	SeaWorld. Central Florida Parkway eastbound (toward Orlando) only.
72	(28)	Highway 528 east (Beeline Expressway) to SeaWorld, Orlando International Airport, and Kennedy Space Center (toll road).
74B	(29B)	Universal Studios.
75A	(30A)	Highway 435 (Kirkman Road). Universal Studios.
75B	(30B)	Kirkman Road (Universal Studios).
77	(31)	Florida Turnpike south to Miami or north to Wildwood.
80	(33)	Highway 441, 17-92 (South Orange Blossom Trail).
82C	(38)	Anderson Street, Orlando. Church Street area.

* Florida renumbered exits on I–4 in 2003; signs will indicate both old and new exit numbers for a number of years to come.

the most competitive markets anywhere in the country. Except during peak periods, rental rates for a small car are as low as $150 to $250 per week; a larger or more luxurious car rents for about twice that amount.

Rental rates generally follow the same low-shoulder–high-season structure as airlines and hotels. I have paid as little as $59 a week for a tiny subcompact (a convertible, no less) in low season.

Every major car rental agency, and many not-so-major ones, has operations in Orlando. Consider the value of your time in choosing among rental companies with locations at the Orlando airport—including Alamo, Avis, Budget, Dollar, and National—and those who conduct their business a few miles away.

The lowest rates are generally offered by companies that put you on a bus and take you to their lot; you'll have to wait for a bus in both directions, adding as much as thirty minutes to each end of your transaction. Among companies located off the airport property are Enterprise, Hertz, Payless, and Thrifty.

One advantage to bringing a car to the park is the chance to save a bit of money and get a more relaxed, better meal by ducking out of the park at lunch and visiting a decent buffet or menu restaurant. You can then return to the park for some evening rides and the fireworks. (Get your hand stamped when you leave the park and hold on to your ticket stub—both are needed for readmission on the same day. Your parking receipt is also valid for reentry to any of the parking lots.)

Check with your insurance agent to determine how well your personal automobile policy covers a rental car and its contents. I strongly recommend you use a credit card that offers rental-car insurance; such insurance usually covers the deductible below your personal policy. The extra auto insurance by itself is usually worth an upgrade to a "gold card" or other extra-service credit card. The only sticky area comes for those visitors who have a driver's license but no car, and therefore no insurance. Again, consult your credit-card company and your insurance agent to see what kind of coverage you have or need.

> ## Caveat Driver
>
> Before you give your airline frequent-flier number to a rental car company to earn "free" miles while you drive, ask if there is a service charge for giving the miles. In other words, free is not necessarily free. Airlines miles—if you end up using them on a ticket—are usually worth about a penny or two each. I have seen situations where a car rental agency charges $2.00 to award 50 cents' worth of miles.

Although it is theoretically possible to rent a car without a credit card, you will find it to be a rather inconvenient process. If they cannot hold your credit-card account hostage, most agencies will require a large cash deposit—perhaps as much as several thousand dollars—before they will give you the keys.

Pay attention, too, when the rental agent explains the gas-tank policy. The most common plan says you must return the car with a full tank; if the agency must refill the tank, you will be billed a service charge plus what is usually a very high per-gallon rate. Other optional plans include one where the rental agency sells you a full tank when you first drive away and takes no note of how much gas remains when you return the car. Unless you somehow manage to return the car with the engine running on fumes, you are in effect making a gift to the agency with every gallon you bring back. I prefer the first option, refilling the tank on the way to the airport on getaway day.

Super Rental Deals

If you can figure out a way to get to Florida inexpensively in the spring, you can take advantage of the glut of rental vehicles of all description that agencies wish were elsewhere—mostly up north. Companies including Avis, Budget, Hertz, and National offer cars for as little as $6.00 a day, provided you drop off the car in one of a few dozen northeast cities. Under most plans you can hold on to the

MAJOR ROADS NEAR WALT DISNEY WORLD

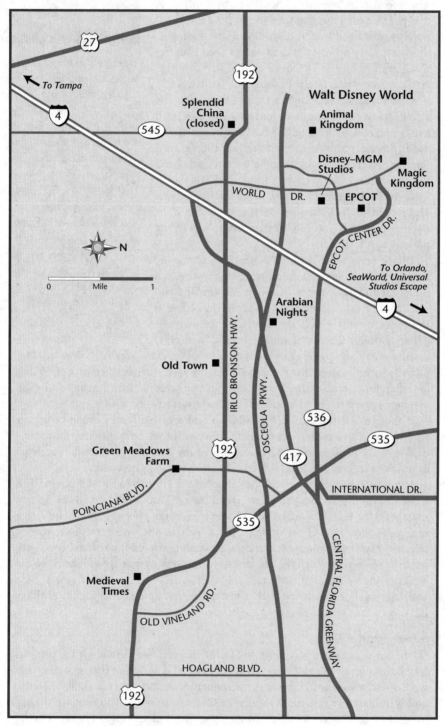

WALT DISNEY WORLD EXITS ON I–4

Exit 65 (Old 26C/D)
- Animal Kingdom, Wide World of Sports

Exit 67 (Old 26A/B)
- Epcot
- Downtown Disney
- Magic Kingdom Resorts: Disney's Grand Floridian Resort & Spa, Disney's Contemporary Resort, Disney's Polynesian Resort, Disney's Wilderness Lodge, Disney's Fort Wilderness Resort and Campground
- Epcot Resorts: Disney's Yacht and Beach Club, Disney's BoardWalk Inn and Villas, Disney's Caribbean Beach Resort
- Downtown Disney Resorts: Disney's Old Key West Resort, Disney's Dixie Landings, Disney's Port Orleans

Exit 64B (Old 25B)
- Disney's Animal Kingdom, Magic Kingdom, Disney–MGM Studios, Wide World of Sports
- Disney–MGM Resorts: Disney's All-Star Movies, Disney's All-Star Music, Disney's All-Star Sports, Disney's Coronado Springs Resort
- Magic Kingdom Resorts: Disney's Grand Floridian Resort & Spa, Disney's Contemporary Resort, Disney's Polynesian Resort, Disney's Wilderness Lodge, Disney's Fort Wilderness Resort and Campground
- Animal Kingdom Lodge

car for as long as two weeks. The situation is reversed in the fall, when car agencies want to send vehicles down south for the snowbirds.

■ A GUIDE TO HIGHWAY 192

A road-sign system helps demark a 12-mile stretch of the confusing U.S. Highway 192, also known as Irlo Bronson Highway. In the initial project, markers are numbered from 4 at the western end near the now-closed Splendid China attraction and the entrance to Walt Disney World to 15 at the eastern end of the Kissimmee tourist area just short of Hoagland Boulevard.

Here are a few landmarks:
- **4.** Splendid China (closed)
- **5–6.** A World of Orchids
- **6–7.** Walt Disney World main gate
- **7–8.** Disney's Wide World of Sports. I–4 to Disney's Celebration, SeaWorld, Universal Studios Florida, downtown Orlando, Orlando International Airport
- **8–9.** Arabian Nights, Water Mania
- **9–10.** Old Town, Pirate's Cove
- **10–11.** Poinciana Boulevard intersection with US 192, Green Meadows Farm
- **11–12.** Capone's, Vineland Road intersection
- **12–13.** Congo River Golf
- **13–14.** Manufacturer's Outlet Mall
- **14–15.** Medieval Times, Jungleland, River Adventure Golf, Hoagland Boulevard intersection

CHAPTER THREE

WHERE: YOU'VE GOT TO SLEEP AND EAT

EVERYBODY'S GOT TO SLEEP AND EAT. The trick is to sleep and eat well . . . and no two people seem to place the same value on a bed and a meal. When I travel, I usually spend as little time as possible in my room—I collapse into bed much too late to visit the pool or stroll the lobby, and I'm off on my next adventure at sunrise. So I'm looking for something quiet, clean, safe, and convenient to my next day's plans. Others, though, focus more on glass elevators, room service, retail shops, and the number of channels on the television set in the room. And, when I travel to a theme park, my main gustatory goal is to find a place to eat where there are cloth napkins and the butter does not come in the shape of mouse ears. For others, that's exactly the goal.

In this chapter we'll take an Econoguide tour through some of the best options for sleeping and eating in and around Walt Disney World and Universal Studios Orlando. I'll begin with the hotels and restaurants within the boundaries of the park.

In 2006, there were more than 500 hotels with an excess of 113,000 rooms in the greater Orlando area; about 34,000 of those rooms are at the 20 resorts within Walt Disney World or very nearby. That represents an increase over the year before, taking into account the closing of a major hotel and the addition of several new sites within the park. Orlando has the second-largest collection of hotel rooms in the nation, second only to Las Vegas, where there were about 152,000 rooms in 2006.

There are also more than 26,000 vacation-home rentals available and more than 16,000 vacation ownership units.

According to industry reports, average room occupancy in Orlando in recent years has approached 75 percent; during peak holiday and summer periods occupancy is nearly 100 percent within 5 to 10 miles of the parks. Average room rates close to Walt Disney World were about $110; in greater Orlando the aver-

Disney's Pop Century Resort

age rate was about $85. Again, rates rise to their highest levels at times of peak demand.

At Walt Disney World the most exciting upscale hotel for animal lovers is Disney's Animal Kingdom Lodge. This lovely hotel is like a theme park of its own, with many of the rooms overlooking a savanna stocked with herds of giraffe, zebras, kudu, and more. The hotel itself is a stunning re-creation of an African lodge, and it features two of the best restaurants in town.

The newest resort within the park is Disney's Pop Century Resort, a massive 5,760-room "value" complex located between Disney's Wide World of Sports and Disney's Caribbean Beach Resort.

At Universal Orlando there are three impressive, upscale places to stay: the lovely Portofino resort, the Hard Rock Hotel, and the Royal Pacific Resort at Universal Orlando.

NEGOTIATING FOR A ROOM

Notice the title of this section: It's not called "buying" a room. The price of hotel rooms, like almost everything else, can be negotiated by the savvy traveler at most locations; you're a lot more likely to have success whittling down the price outside of the Walt Disney World resort itself, where list prices are pretty firmly set for a particular time period.

Anywhere else, here is how to pay the highest possible price for a hotel room: Walk up to the front desk without a reservation and say, "I'd like a room." If there are any rooms available, you may be charged the "rack rate," which is the published maximum nightly charge.

Here are a few ways to pay the lowest possible price:

■ Research hotel rates on the Internet. Start with one of the general travel Web sites that can display rates at many different chains and independent locations. Once you have narrowed down the available choices, check some of the company chains to see if their rates are lower. For example, if Expedia.com shows you an acceptable rate at a Quality Inn in Kissimmee, check with www.choicehotels .com or www.qualityinn.com to see if you can find a better price, or one that comes with a more acceptable cancellation policy.

Here are some worthy Internet sites for booking hotel rooms:

General travel sites

Expedia, www.expedia.com

Hotels.com, www.hotels.com

Orbitz, www.orbitz.com

Travelocity, www.travelocity.com

Hotel companies

Choice Hotels (Clarion, Comfort, Econolodge, Quality, Rodeway, Sleep), www.choicehotels.com

Days Inn, www.daysinn.com

Doubletree, www.doubletreehotels.com

Holiday Inn, www.holiday-inn.com

Hyatt, www.hyatt.com

Marriott, www.marriott.com

Ramada Inns, www.ramada.com

Residence Inn, www.residenceinn.com

Super 8, www.super8.com

Travelodge, www.travelodge.com

■ Spend an hour on the phone and call a half dozen hotels directly that seem to be in the price range you'd like to spend. You'll find many listings for hotels in Orlando and Kissimmee in this book; you can also find listings in the AAA tour book available to members.

Start by asking for the "room rate." Then ask them for their "best rate." Does that sound unnecessary? Trust me, it's not: I can't begin to count the number of times the rates have dropped substantially when I have asked again.

True story: I once called the reservation desk of a major hotel chain and asked for the rates for a night at a Chicago location. "That will be $149 per night," I was told. "Ouch," I said. "Oh, would you like to spend less?" the reservationist answered. I admitted that I would, and she punched a few keys on her keyboard. "They have a special promotion going on. How about $109 per night?" she asked.

Not bad for a city hotel, I reasoned, but still I hadn't asked the big question. "What is your best rate?" I asked. "Oh, our best rate? That would be $79," said the agent.

"OK, I'll take it. I'm a AAA member, by the way." Another pause. "That's fine, Mr. Sandler. The nightly room rate will be $71.10. Have a nice day."

When you feel you've negotiated the best deal you can obtain over the phone, make a reservation at the hotel of your choice. Be sure to go over the dates and prices one more time, and obtain the name of the person you spoke with and get a confirmation number if available.

■ But wait: When you show up at your hotel on the first night, stop and look at the marquee outside and see if the hotel is advertising a discount rate. Most of the hotels that surround the Walt Disney World area adjust their prices based on attendance levels at the park. It is not uncommon to see prices change by $10 or more over the course of a day. Here's where you need to be bold. Walk up to the desk as if you did not have a reservation, and ask the clerk what the best room rate is for the night. If the rate quoted is less than the rate in your reservation, you are now properly armed to ask for a reduction in your room rate.

Similarly, if the room rate advertised out front on the marquee drops during your stay, don't be shy about asking that your charges be reduced. Just be sure to ask for the reduction before you spend another night at the old rate, and obtain the name of the clerk who promises a change. If the hotel tries a lame excuse, such as "That's only for new check-ins," you can offer to check out and then check back in again. That will usually work; you can always check out and go to the hotel across the road that will usually match the rates of its competitor.

■ The way to make the most flexible choice, in the low season only, is to come down without a reservation, and then cruise one of the motel strips such as U.S. Highway 192 (Irlo Bronson Memorial Highway) or International Drive. Check the outdoor marquees for discount prices and make notes. Find a phone, and make a few calls to the attractive ones. Once again, be sure to ask for the best price. The later in the day you search for a room, the more likely you are to find a hotel ready to make a deal.

■ DIALING FOR DOLLARS

As I cited in my "true story," you must be aggressive in guarding your checkbook in dealing with a reservation agent. Sometimes you will also need to be persistent. The fact is that a single room may be offered at four different prices by four different agents. You may find the lowest price by calling directly to the hotel; in some cases a chain's toll-free central reservations service may have some special deals. Occasionally travel agents are offered special promotional rates.

If you're doing your own booking, call the central reservations number for a chain and follow up with a direct call to the hotel. If you use a travel agent, request that the agent verify the lowest rate indicated on the agency's computer with a direct call to the hotel. Think of it this way: If you can save $20 a night on a week's stay, your first few meals are free.

Here's My Card

Membership in AAA brings some important benefits for the traveler, although you may not be able to apply the club's usual 10 percent discount on top of whatever hotel rate you negotiate. (It doesn't hurt to ask, though.) Be sure to request a tour book as well as Florida and Orlando maps from AAA, even if you plan to fly to Florida; they are much better than the maps given by car rental agencies.

Wrong Numbers

Be sure you understand the telephone billing policy at the motel. Some establishments allow free local calls, while others charge as much as $1.00 for such calls. (I'm especially unhappy with service charges for 800 numbers.) Be sure to examine your bill carefully at checkout and make sure it is correct.

Nearly all motels tack ridiculously high service charges on long-distance calls, and there is no reason to pay it. You'll almost always be better off using your cell phone or a telephone credit card for long-distance calls.

WHERE SHOULD YOU STAY?

Except during the most busy holiday travel times of the year—Christmas through New Year's, spring break, and the Fourth of July through mid-August among them—you're not going to have any trouble locating a decent place to stay in the Orlando and Kissimmee area. In fact, the biggest problem is choosing among the various options.

How should you choose a place to stay? I'd suggest you start by deciding on a price range you'd be willing to pay. Then decide what sort of accommodations fit your needs—in the Kissimmee-Orlando area you can find single rooms and spacious suites in nearly every price range. At the extremes—the least expensive and the most expensive—the difference in quality can be substantial. In the middle price ranges, the difference among rooms is often mostly related to location.

If you're traveling with a family, do you want a luxury multibedroom suite or a set of connecting single rooms? Do you need a refrigerator or kitchen? (You can easily save $20 per day for a family of four by eating breakfast in your room; but if a room with a refrigerator costs $25 more per day, it's no deal at all.) Are you willing to drive fifteen minutes in the morning and at the end of the day to save money or obtain a better room for the same price?

Families or groups may also want to consider renting a condo or home in the area, buying several bedrooms and a kitchen for not much more than the price of two or three tiny hotel rooms.

Few would argue with the statement that some of the most exciting and most convenient hotels are to be found within the Walt Disney World park boundaries, but they come at a not insignificant premium. Following are ranges for low-season rooms (high-season rates can be as much as double):

$25 to $60 per night. East and west of Interstate 4 on US 192 (also known as Irlo Bronson Highway). The farther east or west you go on Bronson, up to about 8 miles from I–4, the lower the prices in general. You'll also find some very basic budget motels in the South Orange Blossom Trail area and in some downtown Orlando districts, about twenty to thirty minutes from Walt Disney World. Some of the budget hotels are *very* basic, well below the standards you may be used to; watch out, too, for "service" charges for more than one person in the room, for housekeeping, for soap....

$50 to $124 per night. Walt Disney World budget hotels, including the very basic All-Star Sports, Music, Movies, and Pop Century Resorts. Other moderately priced places are on International Drive; resort motels can be found on US 192 and in the Apopka–Vineland Road area. Half-an-hour-away rooms in this range can be found in downtown Orlando and near Orlando International Airport.

$125 to $300 per night. Walt Disney World premium hotels, first-class hotels in Lake Buena Vista, and better establishments along International Drive and within Universal Studios Orlando.

HOTELS WITHIN WALT DISNEY WORLD

Within Walt Disney World are five clusters of hotels and resorts. Reservations can be made through travel agencies or through the Disney central travel desk at (407) 934–7639, or consult www.disneyworld.com/vacation.html. Hotels accept American Express, MasterCard, Visa, and the Disney Credit Card. In most cases reservations must be canceled more than seventy-two hours prior to the arrival date; check-in time is 3:00 P.M. and checkout 11:00 A.M.

Disney classifies their hotels in "value," "moderate," and "deluxe" groups. All of the Disney properties are well maintained and connected to the parks and other attractions by bus, monorail, or boat service. If you do not intend to leave the resort, you can get by without a rental car—but that will also mean you will be totally reliant on Disney restaurants and eateries.

■ MAGIC KINGDOM RESORT AREA

★★★ Disney's Wilderness Lodge $$$$
901 Timberline Drive, Lake Buena Vista; (407) 824–3200. A rustic, 728-room lodge patterned after the famed Old Faithful Inn at Yellowstone National Park. The lodge includes massive log columns, totem poles, and stone fireplaces—just the sort of thing you'd expect in central Florida, right? But wait: There's also a twelve-story geyser, a waterfall, and a rocky swimming pool that begins in the lobby as a hot spring and works its way outside.

Located between the Contemporary Resort and Fort Wilderness, the Wilderness Lodge is one of Disney's "deluxe" category resorts. The lodge is hidden away on the shores of Bay Lake and surrounded by towering pine, cypress, and oak forests. The 728-room hideaway is accessible by boat across Seven Seas Lagoon to the Magic Kingdom and by bus to the rest of Walt Disney World. Most rooms include a balcony with views of waterfalls, "geysers," courtyards, Bay Lake, or the surrounding woods.

The resort features a volcanic meadow with bubbling color pools, babbling brooks, and geysers spewing misty streams up to 100 feet into the air beside the swimming pool and white-sand beaches. A bubbling hot spring in the main lobby expands into a geo-

Disney Hotels

★★ Better hotels
★★★ Superior hotels
★★★★ Econoguide Best
$$ Value: $79–$137
$$$ Moderate: $139–$215
$$$$ Deluxe: about $205 and up

Econoguide to the Best Hotels in Kissimmee and Orlando

★★★★ Animal Kingdom Lodge, Walt Disney World
★★★★ Disney's BoardWalk Inn, Walt Disney World
★★★★ Disney's Grand Floridian Resort, Walt Disney World
★★★★ Gaylord Palms Resort, Kissimmee
★★★★ Hard Rock Hotel, Universal Orlando
★★★★ The Peabody Orlando, Orlando
★★★★ Portofino Bay Hotel, Universal Orlando
★★★★ Royal Pacific Resort, Universal Orlando
★★★★ Renaissance Orlando Resort at SeaWorld, Orlando

thermal area outside the building, flowing under a picturesque window wall to become Silver Creek in the upper courtyard. The creek widens and is transformed into a roaring waterfall that plummets 15 feet past Overlook Point, another traditional National Park icon, and widens again in the swimming area.

The Cub's Den offers a supervised dining and Western-theme entertainment club for children ages four to twelve, including movies and video games. The club is open from 5:00 P.M. to midnight, at a charge of about $6.00 per hour.

Transportation to the Magic Kingdom includes boat service from the hotel dock and buses to the other theme parks and elsewhere in Walt Disney World.

★★ Disney's Contemporary Resort $$$$

4600 North World Drive, Lake Buena Vista; (407) 824–1000. Is it a hotel with a monorail running through the middle, or a monorail station with a hotel surrounding it?

Either way, it's a most unusual setting and just a mouse trot from the main gate of Walt Disney World. The hotel, one of just two that opened with the Magic Kingdom in 1971, was ahead of its time in construction methods. While the hotel's steel skeleton was being constructed at the site, individual rooms were being built and finished at Walt Disney World on an "assembly line," with workers completing fifteen units per day. As each room passed through the specially constructed building, the electrical, mechanical, and plumbing facilities were added piece by piece. Once furnished, the nine-ton guest rooms were trucked to the site, lifted by crane, and slid into the steel structure, like an oversize set of dresser drawers. The entire structure was then covered by specially designed sun-resistant glass.

The Contemporary is a great place to view the nightly Electrical Water Pageant in season, especially

Artistic License

The mosaic mural in the fourth-floor lobby of Disney's Contemporary Resort was created in 1971 with 1,800 1-square-foot tiles and took eighteen months to construct. Look closely: There's a five-legged goat facing the monorail track.

Disney Resort Prices at a Glance

$$ Value (about $79–$137)
Disney's All-Star Movies Resort
Disney's All-Star Music Resort
Disney's All-Star Sports Resort
Disney's Pop Century Resort

$$$ Moderate (about $139–$215)
Disney's Caribbean Beach Resort
Disney's Coronado Springs Resort
Disney's Port Orleans—French Quarter
Disney's Port Orleans—Riverside Resort

$$$$ Deluxe (about $205 and up)
Disney's Animal Kingdom Lodge ($205–$625)
Disney's Beach Club Resort ($305–$695)
Disney's BoardWalk Inn ($305–$710)
Disney's Contemporary Resort ($249–$725)
Disney's Grand Floridian Resort & Spa ($359–$890)
Disney's Polynesian Resort ($315–$780)
Disney's Wilderness Lodge ($205–$500)
Disney's Yacht Club Resort ($305–$695)
Dolphin and Swan Resorts ($295–$490; suites $610–$2,850)

Camping
Disney's Fort Wilderness Resort Cabins ($239–$349)
Disney's Fort Wilderness Resort Campsites ($39–$92)

Disney's Vacation Club
Disney's Beach Club Villas ($305–$1,070)
Disney's BoardWalk Villas ($305–$2,020)
Disney's Old Key West Resort ($269–$1,545)
Disney's Saratoga Springs Resort & Spa ($269–$1,545)
The Villas at Disney's Wilderness Lodge ($295–$1,040)

Rates are per night, vary by season, and are subject to change. Hotels within the resort start at the value level; lower-priced accommodations are available outside the Disney border. All Disney hotels offer free roll-away beds, up to the room's limit on occupancy. Children age eighteen and younger stay at no additional charge in rooms with parents; there is an additional charge of $10 per adult for more than two adults in value hotels, $15 per adult in moderate hotels, and $25 per adult in deluxe hotels.

Vacation Club rooms are rented on a nightly basis when time-share owners make them available and include studios, one- and two-bedroom villas, and Grand Villas.

(continued)

Disney hotels have as many as four "seasons" for room prices. Supervalue rates are generally in effect in January and September. Value rates are offered in early February, post-Easter to early June, the end of August, and from October 1 through mid-December. Regular rates are generally in effect from mid-February through mid-April, and from mid-June through mid-August. Top holiday rates are charged from mid-December through New Year's Eve.

if your room faces the lagoon. The resort includes 1,052 rooms, a health club, and a marina.

Note that not all of the rooms are in the fifteen-story, A-shaped main building with the monorail station but may be located in the more ordinary annex buildings along the lake. There are suites on the hotel's fourteenth floor that include private concierge and special services.

Sports facilities include a white-sand beach, six clay tennis courts, two heated outdoor swimming pools with a water slide, and a tony fitness center. Guests can rent Water Sprites from the marina, or a waterskiing boat with driver and skis.

The Mouseketeer Clubhouse is open from 4:30 P.M. to midnight for children ages four to twelve; rates are about $8.00 per hour per child. For reservations call (407) 824–3038. Two movies (Disney titles, of course) are shown each night in the theater at the Fiesta Fun Center, which is also the home of a large collection of video arcade machines.

Transportation to the parks is by monorail, water taxi, and bus. You can also catch a water taxi to Discovery Island.

Disney's Contemporary Resort

Flying through the Airport

Some ideas are good, some are mere marketing flash, and some truly magical: We award Econoguide pixie dust to the inventor of Disney's Magical Express, which offers complimentary airport shuttle, luggage delivery, and airline check-in for guests staying at Disney's own on-property hotels.

Under the program, which began in the summer of 2005, guests who sign up for the plan can check their bags at their hometown airport, bypass baggage claim at Orlando International Airport, and board motor coaches to the Walt Disney World Resort. The idea is that bags will "magically" appear in their room upon check-in or soon thereafter.

Disney announced in 2006 it would continue the program indefinitely. Guests flying any airline in or out of the Orlando airport can take advantage of the motor coach transportation between the airport and their Walt Disney World hotel; guests departing on participating airlines (in 2006, including American, Continental, Delta, JetBlue, Northwest, and United) can also avoid airport check-in lines by checking their luggage and receiving a boarding pass for domestic flights before departing their select Walt Disney World hotel at the end of their stay.

As an added benefit, guests with flight departures later in the day no longer have to worry about their luggage after they check out of their hotel. They can simply check their luggage at the Resort Airline Check-in Desk and then enjoy the last day of their stay.

With Disney's Magical Express service, a family of four can save more than $80 (based on round-trip shuttle or taxi transportation, plus tip, for two adults and two children). The service must be booked at least ten days prior to arrival through www.disneyworld.com, through the Disney Reservation Center by calling (407) 934–7639, or through a travel agent. The Magical Express service is not available to guests of the Walt Disney World Swan and Dolphin hotels, the Shades of Green, the seven hotels near Hotel Plaza Boulevard, or hotels not on Walt Disney World property.

★★★★ Disney's Grand Floridian Resort & Spa $$$$

4401 Grand Floridian Way, Lake Buena Vista; (407) 824–3000. This opulent resort along the shores of Seven Seas Lagoon with its own monorail station is a mixture of Victorian elegance and modernity in white and coral trim. In typical Disney fashion, it is probably much prettier than the real thing ever was. The hotel drew its design from some of the grand old hotels of Palm Beach at the turn of the twentieth century, including the Royal Poinciana.

The spectacular five-story Grand Lobby is topped by stained-glass skylights and lit in the evening by grand chandeliers. A big band entertains nightly. Some of the rooms include quirky dormers and turrets, as well as balconies that offer close-up views of the Magic Kingdom. There are fifteen honeymoon suites and

Disney's Grand Floridian Resort & Spa

other suites with as many as three bedrooms. The resort includes 901 rooms, a health club, tennis courts, a marina with Water Sprites and sailboats, and a white-sand beach fronting Seven Seas Lagoon.

The resort accommodations are among the most luxurious at Walt Disney World. The concierge and suite rooms with private elevator access in the Sugar Loaf Key building include in-room facilities such as a wet bar and lavish decor. One of the resort's five lodge buildings also features personal concierge service.

An open-cage elevator, aviary, palms, and ferns set the mood in the sitting area of the Grand Lobby, which reaches five stories to a Victorian ceiling adorned with three illuminated stained-glass domes, ornate chandeliers, and metal scrolls.

Luxury accommodations at the resort include the Walt E. Disney Suite, with two bedrooms, a living room, and entry hall. Much of the decor salutes Disney's love of trains, including vintage photographs and a replica of the founder's Carolwood Pacific Railway locomotive in the entry hall.

Weekly, Not Weakly

Are you staying a full week? Ask for the weekly rate. If the room clerk says there is no such rate, ask to speak to the manager; he or she should be willing to shave the price for a long-term stay.

The Mouseketeer Club, for children ages four to twelve, is open 4:30 P.M. to midnight. Rates are $8.00 per hour, with dinner included. Call (407) 824–2985 for reservations.

Guests looking for an intimate setting for dinner can arrange through the front desk for a private dinner for two, served against the elegant backdrop of the Grand Floridian beach or with a personal butler aboard the *Grand 1,* the most luxurious watercraft at Walt Disney World Resort.

There are two clay tennis courts and a heated swimming pool; the marina at the white-sand beach offers watercraft for rent. Other amenities at the Grand Floridian Resort & Spa include deluxe concierge services and a 44-foot yacht available for private parties on the lake right outside its doors.

Transportation to the parks is by monorail, water taxi, and bus. The parking lot is across the road; at the end of a long day, it can feel like the next county.

★★★ Disney's Polynesian Resort $$$$

1600 Seven Seas Drive, Lake Buena Vista; (407) 824–2000. A Disneyfied version of Hawaiian island architecture and landscaping, including palm-lined, torch-lit walkways; tropical gardens; two exotic swimming pools (one with a slide built into a volcano); and a station on the monorail. Oh, and did I mention the indoor waterfall in the lobby? This place is especially magical at night.

The resort includes 855 rooms in two- and three-story island-style longhouses, plus a marina and a kid's club. You can rent Water Sprites, sailboats, and other watercraft at the marina.

Every room has a patio, with most offering a view of the lagoon or one of the swimming pools. Special suites that include King Kamehameha concierge serv-

Rent a Tree

If you visit Walt Disney World during the Christmas holidays, you can order up a holiday tree for your room, fully decorated, for a fee. For a bit more the tree can be shipped back home after your vacation. Contact Guest Services for information.

Disney's Polynesian Resort

Vegetarian and Health-Conscious Dining

Not everything at Walt Disney World has been through a deep-fryer or is based on meat. Many restaurants, especially those in the better resorts, offer some inventive vegetarian, low-fat, or low-carbohydrate meals.

Among places to grab some greens: **Cosmic Ray's Starlight Café** at the Magic Kingdom, where you can find Caesar salad and vegetable soup; **Restaurant Marrakesh** at the Morocco pavilion of Epcot, which serves vegetable couscous; and, also at Epcot, the **Sunshine Season Food Fair at the Land,** which offers salads and vegetable pita.

At Disney–MGM Studios you can enjoy a bowl of vegetarian minestrone at **Mama Melrose's Ristorante Italiano.** Nearby, at the **ABC Commissary,** you'll find tabbouleh wraps.

Jiko–The Cooking Place offers some unusual low-fat chicken and fish dishes, and the chef promises to whip up special vegetarian platters on request.

ices are on the lagoon side of several of the longhouses.

Kids have their own club at Neverland, for guests ages four to twelve. It's open from 5:00 P.M. to midnight, with a three-hour minimum, at $8.00 per hour; there's even a special buffet for the kids served from 6:00 to 8:00 P.M. Call for reservations at (407) 824–2170.

The resort includes two heated outdoor swimming pools, a sand volleyball court, and a white-sand beach. Transportation to the parks is by monorail, water taxi, and bus. You can also see the nightly Electrical Water Pageant from the resort.

★ Fort Wilderness Resort and Campground $$–$$$$

4510 North Fort Wilderness Trail, Lake Buena Vista; (407) 824–2900. Park your camper, pitch a tent, or rent one of Disney's Fleetwood Trailer Homes, complete with air-conditioning, television, telephone, kitchen, and daily housekeeping service. All of the 784 campsites at the secluded 780-acre site include electrical hookups, water, and a charcoal grill; most have sanitary hookups. The sites are intended for tent or trailer campers up to 65 feet. Comfort stations, a trading post, and shower and laundry facilities are nearby. Pay attention to the campsite number you are assigned; a savvy visitor may be able to improve on the location. Numbers from 100 to 599 are near the beach and Pioneer Hall. The high numbers, from 1,500, are quiet and remote.

Inside one of the 408 wilderness homes you'll probably have a hard time remembering you are in the woods; the one-bedroom units include a double or bunk bed, and a double Murphy bed in the sitting area. There's a full kitchen, daily maid service, and air-conditioning, too. Disney's Fort Wilderness Resort and Campground also offers wilderness cabins. Yes, they're cabins, but they also feature daily maid service, cable television, and air-conditioning, with sleeping space for six and a full kitchen and outdoor grill. Nightly rental rates range from $229 to $329.

The resort opened with the Magic Kingdom in 1971. Recreation options include horseback riding, nature trails, white-sand beaches, canoeing through streams, swimming in two pools, boat and bike rentals, fishing excursions, and a petting farm and pony rides for children.

Guests can also participate in a nightly campfire sing-along and marshmallow roast with Disney characters, followed by Disney movies in a theater under the stars.

The Tri-Circle D Petting Farm is located between Pioneer Hall and Horse Barn, open to children of all ages, for free. Kids ages two to eight and weighing less than eighty pounds can also ride a pony at the farm for $3.00; the ponies are available daily from 10:00 A.M. to 5:00 P.M.

There are two heated swimming pools and a large beach on Bay Lake. Nearby are the Osprey Ridge and Eagle Pines golf courses, and the mothballed River Country water park. There's a nightly campfire gathering near the Meadow Trading Post, including free Disney movies and sing-alongs with Chip 'n Dale. Fort Wilderness is also a good place to watch the nightly Electrical Water Pageant.

In the center of the resort is Pioneer Hall, which includes the Hoop-Dee-Doo Musical Revue.

You can purchase groceries at the Crossroads of Lake Buena Vista shopping center just outside of the Walt Disney World park or bring them in your own vehicle. Transportation to the parks is by bus, tram, and water taxi. A limited number of tents are available for rent if you don't want to bring your own equipment.

> ## Safety First
>
> The small safes available in some hotels can be valuable to the traveler; be sure to inquire whether there is a service charge for their use. We've been in hotels that apply the charge regardless of whether we used the safe or not; look over your bill at checkout and object to any charges that are not proper. In any case, we'd suggest that any objects that are so valuable you feel it necessary to lock them up should probably be left at home.

★★ Shades of Green on Walt Disney Resort—U.S. Armed Forces Recreation Center

(407) 824–3600. The former Disney Inn, situated between two PGA-tour golf courses (probably the only ones in the world with sand traps shaped like Mickey Mouse), this rustic resort is offered to vacationing servicemen and -women from all branches of the armed forces, as well as civilian employees of the Department of Defense and certain other present and former employees and spouses of military branches.

■ EPCOT AND DISNEY–MGM RESORT AREA

★★★ Disney's Yacht and Beach Club Resorts $$$$

1800 Epcot Resorts Boulevard, Lake Buena Vista; (407) 934–8000. A pair of attractive resorts near Epcot Center and Disney–MGM Studios and set around their own lake. The luxury club hotels on the shores of twenty-five-acre Crescent Lake were designed by noted architect Robert A. M. Stern, best known for his East Coast seaside homes. The 1890s theme features fancy-cut shingles, French doors, and other postmodern embellishments.

The Yacht Club is the more formal of the two, made to appear like a New England grand hotel with its own small lighthouse. Both hotels share Storm-

Econoguide to the Best Food at Walt Disney World

▶ Best food with a view: **California Grill**, Disney's Contemporary Resort.

▶ Best new dining experience: **Boma**, Disney's Animal Kingdom Lodge.

▶ Best steak dinner: **Yachtsman Steakhouse**, Disney's Yacht Club Resort, or **Concourse Steakhouse**, Disney's Contemporary Resort. Second place: **Le Cellier**, Canada pavilion, Epcot.

▶ Best seafood: **Fulton's Crab House**, Downtown Disney, and **Coral Reef**, The Living Seas at Epcot. Close seconds: **California Grill**, Disney's Contemporary Resort, and **Flying Fish Cafe**, Disney's BoardWalk.

▶ Best theme eatery: **Rainforest Cafe**, Disney's Animal Kingdom. Close second: **House of Blues**, Downtown Disney.

▶ Best sushi: **California Grill**, Disney's Contemporary Resort. Close seconds: **Kimono's**, Walt Disney World Swan, and **Matsu No Ma Lounge**, in Japan at the Epcot World Showcase.

▶ Best vegetarian fare: **Spoodles**, Disney's BoardWalk Resort. Second place: **California Grill**, Disney's Contemporary Resort.

▶ Best hot dogs: **Sunset Ranch Market** at Disney–MGM Studios.

▶ Best milk shakes: Mom's specials at the **'50s Prime Time Cafe**, Disney–MGM Studios, and **Beaches and Cream Soda Shop**, Disney's Beach Club Resort.

▶ Best high tea: **Rose & Crown Pub & Dining Room**, in the United Kingdom in Epcot World Showcase, and **Garden View Lounge**, Disney's Grand Floridian Resort & Spa.

▶ Best wine cellar: **Victoria and Albert's**, Disney's Grand Floridian Resort & Spa. Close seconds: **California Grill**, Disney's Contemporary Resort; **Spoodles**, Disney's BoardWalk Resort; and **Jiko–The Cooking Place**, Disney's Animal Kingdom Lodge.

▶ Best beer selection: **Big River Grille and Brewing Works**, Disney's BoardWalk Resort. Close second: **ESPN Club**, Disney's BoardWalk.

▶ Most exclusive table: The Chef's Table in the kitchen at **Victoria and Albert's**, Disney's Grand Floridian (booked six months in advance).

along Bay, a fantasy lagoon reminiscent of a Nantucket beach with a life-size shipwreck with water slides, snorkeling in a sandy lagoon, and a meandering swimming area. A fleet of boats is available for rent, too.

The Yacht Club includes 635 rooms and the Beach Club an additional 580; it also has a health club, tennis courts, a marina, a beach, and a pool. The Sand-castle Club is for kids ages four to twelve, open from 5:00 P.M. to midnight, with a charge of about $4.00 per hour for the first child and $2.00 per hour for additional kids. Dinner is available for an additional charge. Call (407) 934–6290 for information.

The resorts are within walking or quick tram distance of the International Gateway entrance to Epcot Center; you can also catch a water taxi to Disney–MGM Studios or a bus to the Magic Kingdom.

★★★ Walt Disney World Dolphin $$$$
1500 Epcot Resorts Boulevard, Lake Buena Vista; (407) 934–4000.

★★★ Walt Disney World Swan $$$$
1200 Epcot Resorts Boulevard, Lake Buena Vista; (407) 934–3000; www.swan dolphin.com. Why not a triangular hotel with a huge dolphin's head on top, or a rounded building graced by a pair of tremendous swans? This is Walt Disney World, after all. Two of the most distinctive hotels of the park face off across a grotto pool that has a waterfall and whirlpools. ·

The Dolphin, operated by Sheraton, offers 1,509 rooms and includes several interesting eateries.

The Swan and Dolphin hotels underwent a major redecorating project in 2003, with an aim to make rooms more luxurious. The two hotels are aimed mostly at business travelers, catering to corporate meetings, industry conventions, and trade shows. Among changes is a step away from theme-park bright colors in favor of all-white linens and down bedcovers and pillows.

The resorts include a health club, tennis courts, a marina, a beach, and Camp Dolphin and Camp Swan for kids ages four to twelve. The camps are generally open evenings from about 4:00 P.M. to midnight; call to check hours and make reservations.

Disney's Fantasia Gardens and Fantasia Fairways Miniature Golf are located across the road from the Swan and Dolphin. Both hotels are within walking distance of, or a short tram ride to, the International Gateway entrance of Epcot near the France pavilion. Water taxis run to Disney–MGM Studios. Buses head to the Magic Kingdom and other parts of Walt Disney World.

★★ Disney's Caribbean Beach Resort $$$
900 Cayman Way, Lake Buena Vista; (407) 934–3400. One of the best bargains within the park, the sprawling 2,112-room resort spreads across five "villages" named after Caribbean islands (Aruba, Barbados, Jamaica, Martinique, and Trinidad). Each colorful village has its own pool and beach, with rooms in two-story buildings. In addition, the five communities are linked to the Old Port Royale food court along Barefoot Bay.

Footbridges over the lake connect the "mainland" with the one-acre Parrot Cay island play area for children and a 1.4-mile promenade with scenic views of the lake for walking or bike riding. The Barefoot Bay Boat Yard marina rents

---

Beach Front

Stormalong Bay, Disney's Beach Club Resort swimming area, holds 750,000 gallons of water. Disney claims it is the largest sand-bottom pool in the world.

small sailboats, Mercury WaterMouse, pontoon boats, canoes, and other watercraft. Guests can rent a bike or boat at the marina. Transportation to the parks is by bus.

★★ Disney's All-Star Sports Resort $$

1701 West Buena Vista Drive, Lake Buena Vista; (407) 939–5000. Together with the All-Star Music and All-Star Movies Resorts, this is Disney's "economy" zone; the hotels are spiffed-up motels with comparatively small rooms. The 246-acre site is just southwest of Disney–MGM Studios and near the Blizzard Beach water park. Transportation to the theme parks is by bus.

The 1,920-room All-Star Sports Resort focuses on five sports themes: football, baseball, basketball, tennis, and surfing. All around are unusual sports scenes, including palm trees arranged to look like a basketball team at tip-off, an interior courtyard that resembles a football field, a quiet pool in the shape of a baseball infield, and wild sports icons.

At the Surf's Up building, bold colors glisten on 38-foot-tall surfboards, and nearly a thousand colorful fish appear to be swimming along a wavy balcony; two giant shark fins encircle a free-form pool surrounded by swaying palms. At the Hoops Hotel huge pennants from favorite college teams cover the roofline, and 5-foot basketballs hang from the railings. The baseball-theme Home Run Hotel features stadium lights, scoreboards, and an outfield fence. Footballs and helmets big enough for Godzilla welcome guests to the Touchdown Hotel, and stairwells shaped like cans of tennis balls decorate the Center Court Hotel.

The central check-in is at Stadium Hall, which features red, white, and blue seats; caged basketball court lighting; and red lockers. At the End Zone food court, open from 6:00 A.M. to 11:00 P.M., giant sports figures perch atop brightly colored dining booths. Guest rooms feature sports bedspreads, megaphone light fixtures, and bold artwork.

★★ Disney's All-Star Music Resort $$

1801 West Buena Vista Drive, Lake Buena Vista; (407) 939–6000. The 1,920-room All-Star Music Resort features country, rock, Broadway, calypso, and jazz themes. Top hats, musical notes, and an oversized Broadway-show marquee add to the facade at Broadway. Giant amplifiers, speakers, microphones, and a neon-lit, oversized jukebox rock on at the Rock Inn. Check-in for the music-theme hotel is in Melody Hall, where you'll also find the Intermission food court, open from 6:00 A.M. to 11:00 P.M. Guests can cool off at one of two themed pools, one in the shape of a guitar, the other a grand piano.

In 2006, nearly 400 guest rooms at the resort were converted into family suites. Featuring two bathrooms and sleeping up to six people, each suite also includes a kitchenette with sink, microwave, coffeemaker, and refrigerator. The private "master" bedroom has its own flat-screen television, desk, and lounge chair.

★★ Disney's All-Star Movies Resort $$

1901 West Buena Vista Drive, Lake Buena Vista; (407) 939–7333. The third installment in the All-Star group features giant icons from favorite Disney movies, including *101 Dalmatians, Toy Story, Fantasia, The Mighty Ducks, Fantasia 2000,* and *The Love Bug.* There are 1,920 more rooms, plus a hockey-rink swimming pool and a Fantasia pool where Sorcerer Mickey directs a liquid symphony.

Pongo and Perdita from *101 Dalmatians* and Buzz Lightyear from *Toy Story* tower more than 35 feet tall. Giant sorcerer's hats, spell books, brooms, and buckets decorate the Fantasia area, and the Mighty Ducks section scores points with giant hockey sticks, goalie nets, and duck-shaped hockey masks.

Also at the resort is an area that salutes a segment from *Fantasia 2000* named "The Steadfast Tin Soldier," with larger-than-life icons that include a ballerina, a jack-in-the-box, and tin soldiers.

★★ Disney's Pop Century Resort $$

1050 Century Drive, Lake Buena Vista; (407) 934–7639. The newest hotel project at Walt Disney World, the first half of this massive 5,760-room resort spread across twenty buildings opened at the end of 2003; the remainder stands ready to open when tourism levels warrant.

The hotel sends guests on a trip through American popular culture, highlighting the toys, fads, technological breakthroughs, dance crazes, and catchphrases that defined each decade of the twentieth century. One building is festooned with signs reading DUH! YO! GET REAL! Y2K WAZZUP? Each pair of buildings is themed to a different decade.

The first phase of the resort salutes the "Classic Years" of the 1950s and 1960s. The 1950s area features giant sock-hoppers dancing on the sides of the lodge buildings; a 40-foot-tall tabletop jukebox anchors the courtyard. A bowling pin–shaped pool offers a cool dip. The canine character stars from Disney's 1955 *Lady and the Tramp* gaze at each other across the courtyard.

Decked out in tie-dyed hues and psychedelic colors, the 1960s buildings celebrate the era of Flower Power. Play-Doh Pete, the artful child of Play-Doh labels, is featured on a giant can. Peeking out the top of the can are several animal creations, including a blue elephant and a yellow giraffe. Baloo and Mowgli from Disney's 1967 *The Jungle Book* are hand-in-hand across the courtyard. Giant Duncan Imperial yo-yos, with "strings" that measure more than 1 foot in diameter, bookend each building. The centerpiece of the area is the Hippy Dippy Pool, a flower-shaped pool complete with squirting petals on the periphery.

In the 1970s courtyard a colorful Big Wheel riding toy gets ready to roll, while a classic Mickey Mouse rotary-dial telephone calls from across the courtyard. Between the two towering icons, table-soccer players stand at the ready for guests to wander amid their imaginary game. Eight-track tapes, the popular musical medium of the decade, corner each building.

In the 1980s area a giant Rubik's Cube puzzle towers more than 40 feet tall on each building. Across the courtyard one of the original Sony Walkman models, and accompanying headphones, anchors the building.

Closing out the century, the 1990s area pays tribute to personal technology marvels: the cellular telephone and the computer. A giant laptop computer is the centerpiece, while early-model cellular telephones stand at each corner. In the middle of the courtyard is a computer-shaped pool, complete with a spongy keyboard that offers guests an alphabet-filled pool deck area.

The second half of the resort covers the "Legendary Years," from 1900 to the 1940s.

Priced in the same budget range as the All-Star resorts, Pop Century is located in the northeast quadrant of Osceola Parkway and Victory Way, between Disney's Wide World of Sports and Disney's Caribbean Beach Resort.

★★★★ Disney's BoardWalk Inn $$$$
(407) 939–5100.

★★★★ Disney's BoardWalk Villas $$$$
2101 Epcot Resorts Boulevard, Lake Buena Vista; (407) 939–6200. Way back before there was such a thing as a Disney theme park (yes, kids, there was such a time), our forebears ventured to the beach to grand "boardwalk" resorts, including famed Coney Island in New York and others along the Jersey Shore. It's a place of striped awnings and balconies like those of oceanfront inns of the 1930s.

Flash forward to Disney's BoardWalk resort, which re-creates some of the old-time fun with 378 hotel rooms and 532 Vacation Club time-share units in a forty-five-acre area along Crescent Lake near Epcot, across the water from Disney's Yacht and Beach Club Resorts with views of Crescent Lake or gardens. Guests can walk around the lake on the boardwalk to Epcot, take a boat to Epcot or Disney–MGM Studios, or take a bus to the Magic Kingdom and other destinations within Walt Disney World.

This is one of the loveliest spots at Walt Disney World, with hardly a mouse in sight. Take the time to explore some of the eateries and stores around the lake; there is a fascinating collection of old photos and pageant tickets from beach towns like Atlantic City. In the lobby of the hotel, treasures include metal Nanny Chairs from a nineteenth-century European carousel, hand painted and gold leafed. Nearby is a photo and beautifully detailed wooden model of Flip Flap, a 1910 coaster at Coney Island; the ride went into a complete inverted loop, not much different from today's metal coasters.

Outside the BoardWalk Inn, one of the vacation resorts, is a fully operational miniature carousel dating from the 1920s from famed carousel maker Marcus Illions.

The original concept for this resort seemed to imply that Disney would add a rock-'em, roll-'em wooden coaster; as built, the coaster is a water slide that enters into the Luna Park swimming pool, including a 200-foot roller-coaster water slide and water-spouting elephants.

Among the guest rooms are fourteen two-story Garden Suites, luxury accommodations made to look like New England homes that have white picket fences and gardens. The foremost place to stay is the 2,000-square-foot Steeplechase Suite at the Innkeeper's Club.

The Little Toots child care facility is open from 4:00 P.M. to midnight for youngsters ages four to twelve, at a rate of $4.00 per hour.

Admission and parking are free for the boardwalk, shops, and restaurants; valet parking is also available.

★★★ Disney's Coronado Springs Resort $$$

1000 West Buena Vista Drive, Lake Buena Vista; (407) 939–1000. A moderately priced convention hotel, this attractive 1,967-room spread pays homage to Francisco de Coronado's explorations from Mexico to the American Southwest. It is also the only place in the world where Mexico and Santa Fe face Polynesia across a lake.

Located on 136 acres on the west side of World Drive, near Blizzard Beach and Disney–MGM Studios, the resort's haciendas lie in the shade of palm trees, near a white-sand beach on fifteen-acre Lago Dorado and four themed pools, including one large water hole with a slide. The resort appears as a series of three- and four-story *palacios* (Spanish for palaces) tinted in shades of desert sand, sunset pink, and tropical green. There are also two-story cabanas on the northern shore of the lake. At the edge of the lagoon, the five-story Mayan pyramid is the splashy centerpiece of a family fun pool, complete with twisting water slide.

Guests stay in one of three major areas: the Casitas, representing urban centers such as Santa Fe; the Ranchos, villas landscaped with sagebrush and cactus; and the Cabanas, inspired by beachside resorts along the Gulf Coast.

The lobby and reception area is built around La Fuente de las Palomas, a fountain that bubbles up from a Spanish urn under a domed ceiling painted with images of white clouds and doves against a perfect blue sky.

The resort features a 95,000-square-foot convention center and the largest hotel ballroom in the Southeast. Oh yes, there are also colorful plazas, palm trees, and a rocky shoreline along a lake.

Recreational facilities include a sand volleyball court at the "Dig Site" pool area. Bicycles and watercraft are available for rent at La Marina.

■ DISNEY'S ANIMAL KINGDOM AREA

★★★★ Disney's Animal Kingdom Lodge $$$

2901 Osceola Parkway; (407) 938–3000. Inspired by the splendor of a South African game reserve, the 1,307-room, five-story deluxe resort features hand-carved furnishings and views of a thirty-three-acre tropical savanna stocked with free-roaming animals. The lodge, located near Disney's Animal Kingdom but not directly on the theme-park property, is based on a traditional semicircular kraal or corral, a design used in African villages to keep homes and livestock safe from harm.

The six-story resort features towering thatched roofs complemented by rich woods and golden tones. The grand lobby includes a large mud fireplace, natu-

The Animal Kingdom Lodge at Walt Disney World

ral lighting, and giant dormer windows that provide spectacular views of sunrises and sunsets over the savanna. The hotel shares the same architect, and much of the same impressive atmosphere within the grand lobby, as Disney's Grand Californian Hotel at the Disneyland Resort.

At night, twinkling lights resemble fireflies and soft-glowing campfires. Just outside the lobby, Arusha Rock, an elevated kopje, or rock outcropping, puts guests within 15 feet of the animals and gives an extraordinary, near-panoramic view of the animal reserve. Many of the resort's guest rooms feature balconies overlooking savannas that are home to more than 200 mammals and birds, including giraffe, zebra, Thomson's gazelle, ostrich, and sacred ibis. And the Uzima Pool includes a 67-foot-long water slide.

Disney's Animal Kingdom Lodge also offers guests a chance to get up close with some of the hotel's local wildlife. Guests staying in concierge-level rooms and suites can book a place on the Wanyama Safari, a three-hour sunset photo safari that includes dinner at Jiko—The Cooking Place. Tickets for the safari, limited to no more than eight people age sixteen and older, are $150.

■ DISNEY VILLAGE RESORT AREA

★★ Disney's Port Orleans—Riverside Resort $$$

★★ Disney's Port Orleans—French Quarter $$$

2201 Orleans Drive, Lake Buena Vista; (407) 934–5000. This re-creation of the French Quarter of New Orleans is packed with G-rated Disney detail. The resort's swimming pool is located at Doubloon Lagoon and includes a sea-serpent water slide, on which you slide down the tongue and into the water.

The popular French Quarter section of Port Orleans hotel was reopened in spring 2004 after renovation. The Riverside section underwent reconstruction phase by phase. Improvements included new furnishings and fixtures.

The French Quarter opened in 1991. Riverside, originally a separate operation called Dixie Landings, accepted its first guests a year later.

The resort includes 1,008 rooms in seven three-story buildings, a marina, and a pool. Transportation to the parks is by water taxi or bus.

The former Dixie Landings Resort is now merged with Port Orleans as Port Orleans–Riverside. A bit of the old South, this is another of Disney's moderately priced resorts. The huge 2,048-room resort, divided into "parishes," includes a marina and five pools. The buildings are styled after plantation mansions and low bayou homes. The mansion rooms are a bit more formal, evoking memories of grand staircases and columns; the bayou rooms in tin-roofed structures look as if they would fit in well with the swamp. There's a stocked fishing hole and a country-style water slide at Old Man Island at the center of the resort. Boats and bicycles are available for rent at Dixie Levee.

Transportation to the parks is by water taxi and bus.

Music to Your Eyes

The musical staff notes across the registration desk at Disney's Port Orleans Resort–French Quarter spell out the first verse of "When the Saints Go Marching In."

★★ Disney's Village Resort $$$$

Magnolia Way, Lake Buena Vista; (407) 827–1100. This is a collection of light and open town houses, "tree houses," and multilevel villas in the woods near Disney–MGM Studios and Epcot Center. For some families, renting one of these villa rooms may be less expensive or more convenient than taking two small hotel rooms. Most of the smaller one-bedroom Club Suites include refrigerators, and one- and two-bedroom Vacation Villas include fully equipped kitchens.

Nearby are the Lake Buena Vista Golf Course, five lighted pools, tennis courts, and a marina. The resort includes 585 units and a health club. Villas range from one- and two-bedroom units to the fancier Fairway and Treehouse Villas. You can also rent one of four Grand Vista Suites, fully furnished homes originally intended as model homes for a residential or time-sharing resort.

Some of the best bass fishing in Walt Disney World is in the canals right outside the door of many of the villas. The resort is across the lagoon from Pleasure Island and next to the Disney Village Marketplace shops and restaurants. Groceries for the villas are available at the Gourmet Pantry within the resort, or you can take a short drive outside the park to the Crossroads of Lake Buena Vista shopping center (outside the park, it is nevertheless on Disney property . . . don't want to let any of those dollars leak out of the company's hands, do we?).

Transportation to the parks is by bus.

★★ Disney's Old Key West Resort $$$$

1510 North Cove Road, Lake Buena Vista; (407) 827–7700. These deluxe studios and one- to three-bedroom vacation homes with whirlpool tubs have shared facilities that include a video library, four pools, tennis courts, and a marina.

■ DISNEY VILLAGE HOTEL PLAZA

Seven hotels built and operated by major (non-Disney) hotel companies are clustered near the Disney Village Marketplace and Pleasure Island. Guests can drive to the theme parks (and pay for parking) or use Disney buses. These are high-quality hotels with the sort of amenities you would expect elsewhere, but mostly without Disney touches.

★★ Buena Vista Palace Resort & Spa

1900 Hotel Plaza Boulevard; (800) 327–2990 or (407) 827–2727; www.buenavistapalace.com. Formerly the Wyndham Palace, and before then (and now once again) the Buena Vista Palace, this twenty-seven-story lakeside tower has views of much of Walt Disney World, nine restaurants, and a Recreation Island with three pools.

The new owner of the place has a collection of luxury hotels around the world as well as the LaQuinta Inns and Wellesley Inns chains.

The resort includes 1,013 rooms and suites, a health club, tennis courts, and pools. Restaurants include the top-of-the-tower haute cuisine Arthur's 27 and the Top of the Palace Lounge. There's also the less-formal Outback restaurant with seafood and steaks.

★★ Holiday Inn Walt Disney World

1805 Hotel Plaza Boulevard; (866) 655–4669 or (407) 828–8888; www.holiday-inn.com. A family-oriented hotel with a fourteen-story central atrium and 323 rooms, this was originally the Howard Johnson Resort Hotel until it was converted lock, stock, and towels to a Courtyard by Marriott, and in 2005 to a Holiday Inn.

★★ Doubletree Guest Suites in the Walt Disney World Resort

2305 Hotel Plaza Boulevard; (800) 222–8733 or (407) 934–1000; www.doubletreehotels.com. Each one- or two-bedroom suite includes a microwave, refrigerator, and small wet bar, and the 229-room hotel offers a pool and tennis courts. The showplace eatery is the Streamers Restaurant.

★★★ Grosvenor Resort in Walt Disney World Resort

1850 Hotel Plaza Boulevard; (800) 624–4109 or (407) 828–4444; www.grosvenorresort.com. This lakeside tower has 625 rooms and includes a large recreation facility featuring tennis and handball courts, a children's playground, and heated swimming pools. Baskerville's, a British-theme restaurant, is modeled after Sherlock Holmes's 221B Baker Street home in London. Next door is Moriarty's, a pub named after the great detective's archenemy.

★★★ Hilton in the Walt Disney World Resort

1751 Hotel Plaza Boulevard; (800) 782–4414 or (407) 827–4000; www.hilton.com. A large resort and conference center, the Hilton is directly across from the Disney Village Marketplace. The hotel recently underwent a top-to-bottom renovation with a Main Street Disney theme. It includes nine restaurants and lounges, among them Covington Mill and a Benihana Japanese steak house. Also featured is an outdoor spa. The Vacation Station Kid's Hotel caters to kids ages four to twelve; guests at the hotel can park their kids for two hours for as little as $2.25, with additional charges for more hours.

★★ Hotel Royal Plaza in Walt Disney World Resort

1905 Hotel Plaza Boulevard; (800) 248–7890 or (407) 828–2828; www.royal plaza.com. This 396-room hotel includes two restaurants and lounges with nightly entertainment, a pool, and tennis courts.

★★ Best Western Lake Buena Vista Resort Hotel

2000 Hotel Plaza Boulevard; (800) 348–3765 or (407) 828–2424; www.bestwestern .com. This lakeside hotel has a Caribbean flavor and a rooftop nightclub known as Toppers that offers a spectacular view of Walt Disney World. Traders restaurant offers breakfast and dinner, and Parakeet Cafe has pizza and snacks.

■ WHY STAY AT A HOTEL WITHIN WALT DISNEY WORLD?

The hotels within Walt Disney World are among the most attractive, imaginative places to stay at any major tourist area we know of. They offer all sorts of extras not available outside the park and quite a few conveniences. However, all of this comes at a price. The lowest rates at hotels owned or operated by Disney—or those operated by major chains on the park property—generally start at around $79 per night in low season, which is the middle to high end of most standard off-site hotels.

It is up to you to decide what value to place on the extras that come with your higher room rates; you should also consider the possibility of obtaining similar special treatment outside the park. (I heard of one family who booked perfectly nice rooms a few miles outside the park and used just some of the money they saved to engage limousine service to and from the park.)

Insider advantages to guests who stay at Walt Disney World resorts include: free parking within Walt Disney World for the length of the stay; complimentary use of the Walt Disney World transportation system, including monorail, bus, ferryboat, and launch transportation to the parks, avoiding crowded parking lots; advance reservations for dining, Disney Dinner Shows, and Disney Character Breakfasts (guests can make reservations as soon as they receive confirmation of hotel reservations); and preferred access to tee times on all five

Babysitter Club

Guests at hotels at Walt Disney World can hire an in-room babysitter by consulting with Guest Services or the In-Room KinderCare Learning Center.

championship golf courses. Also available are horseback riding, swimming, tennis, health clubs, and other facilities (golf, horses, tennis, and other activities, though, are not free).

DINING OPTIONS AT WALT DISNEY WORLD RESORTS

You can find just about any kind of food, served at the most casual or (almost) most formal level, within the boundaries of Walt Disney World. Some of the eateries are aimed at children and the families who brought them to Orlando, and others are intended for adults who do not require crayons to color the place mats.

In this section I'll give a tour of many of the dining places at the Disney hotels. You'll also find coverage of restaurants within the theme parks in the chapters about each later in the book.

■ DISNEY'S ALL-STAR MOVIES RESORT
World Premiere Food Court
Food court
American **(B, L, D, S)** $
DDP

■ DISNEY'S ALL-STAR MUSIC RESORT
Intermission Food Court
Food court
American **(B, L, D, S)** $
DDP

Key
B = Breakfast
L = Lunch
D = Dinner
S = Snacks
DDP = Disney Dining Plan
SDE = Signature Dining Experience
$ Budget
$$ Moderate
$$$ Expensive

■ DISNEY'S ALL-STAR SPORTS RESORT
End Zone Food Court
Food court
American **(B, L, D, S)** $
DDP

■ DISNEY'S ANIMAL KINGDOM LODGE
Boma—Flavors of Africa
Buffet restaurant
(B, D) $$
DDP
Reservations recommended
Boma—Flavors of Africa features curries, chutneys, and other Indian and Asian influences for grilled fish, meats, and vegetables served in an attrac-

Room and Board

If living and sleeping entirely within the bounds of Walt Disney World is not enough for you, the resort also offers the **Disney Dining Plan (DDP),** a meal plan that assures that you'll do all of your dining at one or another location of Chez Mickey. The DDP is available as an add-on to guests staying at Disney Resorts.

In 2006, the plan worked like this: For each night of the package, you were entitled to one table-service meal (appetizer, entree, dessert, and a nonalcoholic beverage) or one full buffet meal. You were also allowed one counter-service meal, including entree, dessert, and nonalcoholic beverage. And finally, the package included one snack, such as ice cream, fruit, chips, or an additional drink. All gratuities were included.

If you wanted to upgrade your dining experience, you could exchange two table-service meals for one **Signature Dining Experience (SDE)** at a selection of some of the resort's better restaurants, such as Citrico's at Disney's Grand Floridian Resort, or for one Disney Dinner Show, such as the Hoop-Dee-Doo Musical Revue.

In the listings in this chapter, we have indicated participating Disney Dining Plan establishments with a DDP notation, and Signature Dining Experience restaurants with an SDE notation.

tive buffet setting. Highlights of the menu include soups from hearty seafood gumbo to curry-infused mulligatawny. A most unusual entree on one of my visits was nut-crusted baked salmon. Many of the servers and hosts are from African nations. The restaurant serves breakfast and dinner; guests can watch the preparation of their meals in an exhibition kitchen.

Jiko—The Cooking Place
Restaurant
(B, D) $$$ (dinner)
DDP, SDE
Reservations recommended

Jiko—The Cooking Place has an African and Mediterranean menu that is among the best at any Walt Disney World restaurant. Entrees, which range in price from about $18 to $29, include golden bass steamed in parchment paper with spicy "chaka-laka" sauce; chermoula (Moroccan marinade) roasted

Reservations

To make a reservation at any Disney restaurant that accepts them, call (407) WDW–DINE (939–3463).

chicken with preserved lemons, olives, herbs, and harissa (Tunisian pepper sauce); and pomegranate-glazed quails. The restaurant also features one of the most extensive collections of South African wines in North America; most of the sixty-five vintages are available by the glass as well as the bottle.

The Mara
Food court
American (B, L, D, S) $; fast casual dining (B, S) $
DDP

■ DISNEY'S BEACH CLUB RESORT

Beaches & Cream Soda Shop
Restaurant
American (L, D, S) $$
DDP

Cape May Café
Restaurant
American (D) $$ (buffet)
Character breakfast (buffet): $$
DDP
Reservations recommended
A nightly indoor New England–style clambake with clams, mussels, chicken, chowders, and more, served buffet style from 5:30 to 9:30 P.M.

■ DISNEY'S BOARDWALK INN

Big River Grille & Brewing Works
Restaurant
American (L, D) $$
DDP
The brewmaster crafts five specialty beers, served along with pub pies, sausages, gourmet burgers, and more substantial entrees, including yellowfin tuna marinated in teriyaki sauce, breast of chicken with shiitake mushrooms in Rocket Red Ale sauce, and "tilted" veal loaf, from 10:00 A.M. to 2:00 A.M. Flagship beers brewed on the premises are the aggressive Rocket Red Ale, Title Pale Ale, and Wowzer's Wheat, the lightest in body and flavor, featuring orange peel added during the brewing.

BoardWalk Bakery
Bakery
American (B, L, D, S) $

■ DISNEY'S CARIBBEAN BEACH RESORT

Old Port Royale Food Court
Food court
American (B, L, D, S) $

DDP

You'll find a wide range of fast-food choices, including Wok Shop (for basic Chinese fare), Cinnamon Bay Bakery, Montego's Deli, Port Royale Hamburger Shop, Bridgetown Broiler (grilled chicken and fajitas), and Royale Pizza & Pasta Shop.

Shutter's at Old Port Royale

Restaurant
American **(D)** $$
DDP
Reservations recommended

■ DISNEY'S CONTEMPORARY RESORT

California Grill

Restaurant
Californian **(D)** $$$
SDE
Reservations recommended

High above it all, on the fifteenth floor, is by most accounts one of Disney's best (and among the priciest) gourmet eateries. The California Grill has offerings ranging from sushi and lemongrass soup to spicy braised lamb shank with Thai red curried lentils, Atlantic salmon baked under a black-olive crust with grilled vegetable ratatouille, and pan-seared yellowfin tuna with black beans. Dinner is served from 5:30 to 10:00 P.M. You can watch specialties being prepared within the exhibition kitchen or catch a view of the fireworks or water parade from the windows.

Chef Mickey's

Restaurant
Character buffet **(B, D)** $$
DDP
Reservations recommended

Chef Mickey's Restaurant offers breakfast or dinner with the majordomo mouse himself. Dinner selections include shrimp, prime rib, carved meats, and a salad bar. Breakfast is served from 7:30 to 11:30 A.M. Dinner is available from 5:00 to 9:30 P.M.

Concourse Steakhouse

Restaurant
Steak house **(B, L, D)** $$
DDP

The Concourse Steakhouse has trellised ceilings that allow peeks through to the 90-foot-high atrium lobby and the monorail trains passing through. Breakfast, lunch, and dinner are offered from 7:00 A.M. through 10:00 P.M., with dinner entrees starting at about $15. Specialties include charbroiled steak, oven-roasted chicken, pasta dishes, and seafood.

Food and Fun Center
Counter
American (B, L, D, S) $
DDP

■ DISNEY'S CORONADO SPRINGS RESORT
Maya Grill
Restaurant
American (B, D) $$$
DDP
Reservations recommended
Located along the lake, Maya Grill is open for breakfast from 7:00 to 11:30 A.M. and for dinner from 5:00 to 10:00 P.M. The restaurant is operated by one of the premier restaurateur families of Mexico—operators of the famed San Angel Inn in Mexico and its sister eatery of the same name at Epcot—and features a wood-fired grill where cooks braise meats and fish over an open fire. The relatively small restaurant is a hidden gem at Walt Disney World.

Pepper Market
Food court
American (B, L, D) $$
DDP
Southwest, Mexican, and American dishes for all meals. You'll pick up your food from various serving stations and have your dinner card punched; a cashier translates the punch into a bill when you are ready to leave.

■ DISNEY'S FORT WILDERNESS RESORT & CAMPGROUND
Crockett's Tavern
Restaurant
American (D, S) $
Fast food and snacks.

Hoop-Dee-Doo Musical Revue
Dinner show: $$$
DDP
Reservations recommended
All-you-can-eat hoedown dinner show presented three times a night in peak season and featuring fried chicken, spare ribs, corn on the cob, and strawberry shortcake.

Mickey's Backyard BBQ
Dinner show buffet: $$$
DDP
Reservations recommended
A character dining experience with live music and line dancing, offered seasonally.

Trail's End Restaurant
Restaurant
American **(B, L, D) $$**
DDP
Basic American fare and pizza, all day long, served beneath a dramatic high-beamed ceiling.

■ DISNEY'S GRAND FLORIDIAN RESORT & SPA
1900 Park Fare
Restaurant
Character dining **(B, D) $$**
DDP
1900 Park Fare offers buffet breakfasts and dinners in an attractive room that features carousel horses, a one-hundred-year-old band organ named Big Bertha, and Disney characters. There's a breakfast buffet with Mary Poppins and friends featuring pancakes and waffles, and dinner with Mickey and Minnie from 5:30 to 9:00 P.M.

Citricos
Restaurant
(D) $$$
DDP, SDE
Citricos, a posh eatery featuring Mediterranean, Caribbean, Italian, and south Florida cuisine, is a mix of new- and old-world design and menu with an "on-stage" kitchen. Specialties include Florida lobster ratatouille with lamb loin, and a citrus soufflé. Most dishes are prepared without butter or cream sauces, emphasizing oils infused with herbs and spices. Decadent desserts include chocolate ravioli with licorice ice cream.

Garden View Lounge
Lounge
American **(L)**, British **(S)**, character dining **(L)**
(L) $$$$, (S) $$
Reservations recommended
Afternoon tea and light fare.

Gasparilla Grill & Games
Counter
American **(B, L, D, S) $**
DDP
Pizza, burgers, and sandwiches.

Grand Floridian Café
Restaurant
American **(B, L, D) $$**
DDP
The Grand Floridian Café offers a coffee-shop menu all day, including Pasta

Havana with garlic, cilantro, white wine, lemon juice, and cream sauce served with your choice of vegetables, chicken, or shrimp; mango chicken; and filet mignon.

Narcoossee's

Restaurant
Seafood **(D) $$$**
DDP

A showplace seafood and steak eatery, Narcoossee's seats diners in front of an open kitchen in a building that is built out into Seven Seas Lagoon. Open for lunch from 11:30 A.M. to 3:00 P.M. and dinner from 5:00 to 10:00 P.M.; entrees start at about $15 and climb sharply. The chef calls the menu "Floribbean," with specialties such as oven-roasted Caicos baby conch and roasted grouper with crabmeat crust. *Narcoossee,* by the way, is a Native American word that means "little bear."

Victoria & Albert's

Restaurant
American prix-fixe menu **(D) $$$$**
SDE
Reservations required

One of Disney's prime restaurants is Victoria & Albert's, with just sixty-five seats and a most refined atmosphere, where you'll be attended by a butler and maid in Victorian dress. The prix-fixe menu, which usually includes meat, fish, and poultry offerings, is priced at about $80 per person before orders from the extensive and expensive wine list.

Some samples: salmon sautéed in olive oil with olives, capers, and tomato; roasted rack of lamb with Madeira almond sauce; and Bailey's Irish Cream soufflé. The restaurant is one of the few in Walt Disney World that requires men to wear jackets. Depending on the season, there may be just one or two seatings per evening; reservations are a must. And for the ultimate in up-close dining, you can attempt to reserve the Chef's Table, located right in the kitchen; you and your guests can watch and interact with the chef and his team as they prepare a dinner based on your preferences. The Chef's Table seats up to six and is often booked up to six months in advance.

■ DISNEY'S OLD KEY WEST RESORT

Good's Food To Go

Counter
American **(B, L, D, S) $**
DDP

Olivia's Café

Restaurant
American **(B, L, D) $$**
DDP

Open all day with outdoor and indoor seating. Key West specialties are served, including conch egg rolls; conch chowder; Mangrove Snapper, wrapped in a banana leaf and steamed with herb butter; Florida Paella; and Mojo Chicken, drizzled with fresh lime vinaigrette. A character breakfast with Winnie the Pooh and Tigger is offered Sunday and Wednesday.

■ DISNEY'S POLYNESIAN RESORT

Captain Cook's Snacks Company
Counter
American (B, L, D, S) $
DDP

Disney's Spirit of Aloha Show
Polynesian dinner show: $$$
DDP
Hula and fire dancers perform nightly.

Kona Cafe
Restaurant
American (B, L, D) $$
DDP
Reservations recommended
An energetic casual restaurant that mixes Pacific Rim spices and American classics for breakfast, lunch, and dinner. Pots of Kona coffee are ground to order all day.

'Ohana
Restaurant
American (D) $$
DDP
The 'Ohana Feast, served nightly from 5:00 to 10:00 P.M., includes fire-grilled meats, fowl, and shrimp and stir-fried vegetables and noodles.

'Ohana's Best Friends Breakfast with Lilo & Stitch
Restaurant
American (B) $$
DDP
Reservations recommended

■ DISNEY'S POP CENTURY RESORT

Everything Pop Shopping and Dining
Food court
American (B, L, D, S) $
DDP
Features updated versions of comfort foods: peanut butter–Fluff sandwiches; buttermilk-soaked, deep-fried chicken; warm cinnamon buns; oversize sloppy joes; slow-cooked pot roast; and beef stew with buttered noodles. You'll even

find TV-tray dinners with molded tin compartments. But the sloppy joes are made with a cabernet-sauvignon sauce and topped with aged Wisconsin cheddar, and the veggies are slow roasted and include creamed spinach with Gruyère and fresh microgreens with infused oils.

■ DISNEY'S PORT ORLEANS–FRENCH QUARTER

Sassagoula Floatworks and Food Factory Food Court
Counter
American **(B, L, D, S) $**
DDP
Decorated with Mardi Gras props, the food court features the King Creole Broiler, with Creole specialties; Basin Street Burgers and Chicken; Preservation Pizza Company; and Jacques Beignet's Bakery, featuring New Orleans beignets (fried dough fritters).

Boatwright's Dining Hall
Restaurant
Southern and American **(B, D) $$**
DDP
A Cajun and American menu in a reproduction of a shipbuilding shed overlooking the Sassagoula River. Specialties include gumbo, grilled catfish Bayou Teche, roasted chicken, and prime rib, with dinner entrees from about $5.00 to $20.00, served from 5:00 to 10:00 P.M. Breakfast is also served, from 7:00 to 11:30 A.M.

Riverside Mill Food Court
Food court
American **(B, L, D, S) $**
DDP

The Artist's Palette
Counter
American **(B, L, D, S) $**
DDP

■ DISNEY'S WILDERNESS LODGE

Artist Point
Restaurant
American **(B, D) $$$**
SDE
Artist Point celebrates the flavors of the Pacific Northwest with items such as maple-glazed king salmon, elk sausage, and pan-seared rainbow trout at dinner, served from 5:30 to 10:00 P.M. The gourmet eatery is transformed in the early morning from 7:30 to 11:15 A.M. as the site of a character breakfast with Pocahontas, John Smith, Meeko, and more.

Roaring Fork Snacks
Counter
American (B, L, D, S) $
DDP
Roaring Forks offers counter-service burgers, sandwiches, salads, and other basic fare.

Whispering Canyon Café
Restaurant
American (B, L, D) $$
DDP
Reservations recommended
The Whispering Canyon Café features all-you-can-eat buffets for breakfast and dinner and a family-style cookout each evening. At lunchtime an a la carte menu includes sandwiches, burgers, and chili.

■ DISNEY'S YACHT CLUB RESORT
Yacht Club Galley
Restaurant
American (B, L, D) $$
DDP
Reservations recommended
Dinner includes pot roast, barbecue pork ribs, pasta primavera, and Seafood Sunrise, which is a dish of shrimp, scallops, crab cake, and rice pilaf with saffron Dijon and spicy tomato sauce.

Yachtsman Steakhouse
Restaurant
Steak house (D) $$$
SDE
Reservations recommended
Serving dinner from 5:30 to 10:00 P.M., featuring Chateaubriand, steak, fish, or poultry.

■ WALT DISNEY WORLD SWAN
Garden Grove Café
Restaurant
American (B, L) $$
Character breakfast: $$
A dining room in a greenhouse.

Gulliver's Grill
Restaurant
American (dinner buffet) $$
At night the Garden Grove becomes Gulliver's, which serves beef and seafood specialties in a fanciful setting.

Kimonos
Restaurant
Japanese **(D)** $$
An Asian lounge and sushi bar.

Palio
Restaurant
Italian **(D)** $$$
Reservations recommended

Splash Grill & Deli
Counter
American **(L, S)** $

■ WALT DISNEY WORLD DOLPHIN

Cabana Bar & Grill
Restaurant
American **(L, S)** $

Dolphin Fountain
Restaurant
American **(L, D)** $

Fresh Mediterranean Market
Restaurant
Mediterranean **(B, L)** $$

Picabu's
Counter
American **(B, L, D, S)** $

Shula's Steak House
Restaurant
Steak house **(D)** $$$
SDE
Reservations recommended
The restaurant, partly owned by former Miami Dolphins coach Don Shula, is one of the best beeferies in town.

Todd English's bluezoo
Restaurant
Seafood **(D)** $$$
SDE
Reservations recommended
Acclaimed Boston chef Todd English brings his high-tone (mostly) seafood offerings to a sophisticated, handsome restaurant. Specialties include a selection

of fresh fish simply grilled with a choice of sauces, or more fancy offerings such as miso-glazed Chilean sea bass or seared nori-wrapped tuna. You can also get a slow-roasted pork chop or pan-roasted chicken breast. Entrees range from about $24 to $52.

■ DISNEY'S BOARDWALK

ESPN Club

Sports bar
Casual dining **(L, D, S) $$**
DDP

A sports fan's heaven, with more television monitors and big screens than your average appliance store; they display a wide range of sporting events. The menu offers a selection of bar food and drink, including Bloody Mary Chili. Specialties include Tailgate BBQ Pork, Mighty Duck "Chick Trick," penne pasta, and the Slider Burger.

Flying Fish Café

Restaurant
Seafood **(D) $$$**
SDE

Seafood and steaks each evening from 5:00 to 10:00 P.M. and later on weekends. Subtle decorations include a floor-to-ceiling backlit glass Ferris wheel, a roller coaster studded with light bulbs, and a high-energy color pattern of rich reds and blues. Guests can dine at the chef's counter by the show kitchen to watch the chefs in action.

Specialties include a fritto misto of rock shrimp, squid, and the catch of the day served with lemon pepper aioli and braised cranberry beans; oak-wood-grilled center-cut pork chop; spicy barbecue-glazed salmon fillet with corn pudding and sugar snap peas; and potato-wrapped striped bass with leek fondue and cabernet sauvignon reduction.

Spoodles

Restaurant
American, Mediterranean **(B, L, D) $$**
DDP

Mediterranean cuisine from France, Spain, Italy, Greece, and North Africa for breakfast, lunch, and dinner, from 7:00 A.M. to 10:00 P.M. A breakfast buffet offers traditional and unusual baked and stir-fried offerings. The dinner menu features bite-size tapas, and entrees include pasta with chicken, spinach, and roasted peppers; mushroom risotto; tuna with Moroccan spices and sun-dried tomato couscous; or a grilled rib eye with garlic mashed potatoes, fennel, and tomatoes.

■ DISNEY'S WIDE WORLD OF SPORTS COMPLEX

Official All Star Café
Restaurant
American (L, D) $$
DDP

■ DOWNTOWN DISNEY

Bongos Cuban Café
Restaurant
Cuban (L, D) $$

Cap'n Jack's Restaurant
Restaurant
American (L, D) $$
DDP

Rainforest Café–Downtown Disney
Restaurant
American (L, D) $$

Earl of Sandwich
Counter–full meals
American (B, L, D, S) $
DDP

FoodQuest at DisneyQuest
Counter–full meals
American (L, D, S) $
DDP

Fulton's Crab House
Restaurant
Seafood (L, D) $$$
SDE
Reservations recommended

Ghirardelli Soda Fountain & Chocolate Shop
Ice cream shop
American (S) $

House of Blues
Restaurant
Southern and American (L, D) $$
Reservations recommended

McDonald's
Counter
Fast food (B, L, D, S) $

Planet Hollywood
Restaurant
Themed dining (L, D) $$
DDP

Portobello Yacht Club
Restaurant
Italian (L, D) $$$
SDE
Reservations recommended

Raglan Road Irish Pub and Restaurant
Restaurant
Irish (D) $$
Reservations recommended

Wolfgang Puck Café
Restaurant
Californian (L, D) $$
DDP

Wolfgang Puck Express—Marketplace
Wolfgang Puck Express—West Side
Counter
Californian (B, L, D, S) $

HOTELS AT UNIVERSAL ORLANDO

Universal Orlando offers 2,400 luxury rooms within its boundaries, at three handsome hotels. All three hotels are connected to each other and to Universal Studios, Universal Studios Islands of Adventure, and Universal Studios CityWalk by walkways and scenic waterways plied by water taxis. One of the best perks for guests at the on-site hotels is Universal Express: A quick flash of their room key allows guests to bypass the regular lines at most Universal Orlando rides and attractions. Guests are also offered priority reservations at restaurants in the hotels and the parks. All three hotels are managed by Loews.

★★★★ Royal Pacific Resort $$$$
6300 Hollywood Way, Orlando; (407) 503–3000; www.universalorlando.com. The newest and largest hotel at Universal Orlando, the Royal Pacific Resort

The Royal Pacific Resort at Universal Studios Orlando. © *2003 Universal Studios Orlando. All rights reserved.*

opened in 2002, adding 1,000 rooms in a campus of buildings that suggests the tropically lush region of Asia Pacific and the South Pacific. The fifty-three-acre property includes swaying palm trees, exotic plants, a bamboo forest, and a tropical lotus lagoon.

There are five restaurants and lounges, including Emeril Lagasse's Tchoup Chop ($$$), a Polynesian eatery with waterfalls, sculpted gardens, and giant woks. A lagoon-style swimming pool—said to be the largest in Orlando—includes a beach area. Rooms are decorated in Dutch colonial style, including hand-carved wooden accent panels carved in Bali, Indonesia. Standard room rates range from about $159 to $299, with suites priced to $1,499.

★★★★ Portofino Bay Hotel $$$$

5601 Universal Boulevard, Orlando; (407) 503–1000; www.universalorlando .com. An especially attractive resort set alongside a lagoon, Portofino re-creates a bit of the charm and romantic harbor setting of the Mediterranean seaside village of Portofino in Italy.

Guest rooms occupy buildings patterned after Portofino's waterfront homes and restaurants. As visitors would find in Italy, the hotel features elaborate trompe l'oeil paintings on the building exteriors. Hundreds of years ago the residents of the poor fishing village of Portofino could not afford the detailed marble columns, window surrounds, and moldings found in Rome and Venice and instead employed local artisans to paint in the look of more elaborate construction.

The hotel includes eight restaurants and lounges, two swimming pools, a pair of bocce-ball courts, and a large convention and meeting space. Standard room rates range from about $249 to $359, with suites priced to $2,100.

The signature restaurant at the hotel is Bice, an outpost of the international chain of old-world Italian restaurants. Bice draws its lineage back to 1926 as a neighborhood trattoria in Milan run by Beatrice "Bice" Ruggerri. Today there are sixteen eateries in locations including Milan, Paris, Tokyo, New York, and São Paulo. The restaurant, which opened in early 2005, overlooks the re-created Portofino Bay. Trattoria del Porto ($$$) is a family-style

Hotel Restaurant Price Ranges

$ Budget
$$ Moderate
$$$ Expensive
$$$$ Very expensive

Portofino Bay Hotel

restaurant offering diverse regional offerings. At Mama Della's Ristorante ($$–$$$), Mama herself greets and entertains guests and supervises preparation of pasta, pizzas, cannolis, and more.

★★★★ Hard Rock Hotel $$$$

5800 Universal Boulevard, Orlando; (407) 503–7625; www.universalorlando .com. The rock is hard, but the accommodations are soft and luxurious at this mission-style hotel. The public areas are decorated with pieces from Hard Rock's huge collection of rock 'n' roll memorabilia. Some of the gems of the hotel include a military-style vest, peach floral drawstring shirt, and black silk pants worn by Jimi Hendrix in the summer of 1968; one of Elton John's most outlandish stage costumes from his 1984 world tour, a reproduction of the outfit worn in painter Thomas Gainsborough's *Blue Boy*, complete with blue satin breeches, gold filigree accents, and ostrich-plume hat; and a rhinestone-encrusted bell-bottom jumpsuit and cape worn by Elvis during one of his Las Vegas engagements.

Approaching from the gatehouse, guests can hear the hotel before they see it, as rock music rumbles from hidden speakers. Out front of the entry is a fountain made up of forty-two bronze guitars swirling upward in a double helix—

Hard Rock Hotel

Econoguide to the Best Food at Universal Orlando

▶ Best menu: **Emeril's Restaurant Orlando**, CityWalk. Bam! Quirky New Orleans and American fare.

▶ Best scene: **Latin Quarter**, CityWalk. Serves spicy food and hot dancers.

▶ Best house party: **Pat O'Brien's**, CityWalk. Offers Cajun fare and exotic drinks. Second place: **Bob Marley—A Tribute to Freedom**, CityWalk. A tribute to Jamaican country cooking and great music.

▶ Best theme-park eatery: **Mythos**, Universal Studios Islands of Adventure. Mysteriously well prepared.

the DNA that binds musicians to their art. The Lobby Lounge overlooks the cabanas, pool deck, and sand of the Hard Rock Beach Club; underwater speakers play music into the pool. Rooms and suites have rock themes, up to and including the Graceland Suite. Standard room rates range from about $199 to $359, with suites priced to $1,575.

HOTELS OUTSIDE OF THE THEME PARKS

■ U.S. HIGHWAY 192/IRLO BRONSON MEMORIAL HIGHWAY/ VINE STREET KISSIMMEE

Katella Avenue, which fronts the main entrance to Disneyland in California, turned out to be one of Walt Disney's worst nightmares. When Disneyland was first built, it was surrounded by lush green orange groves, but with the success of the park, the environs became an unending stretch of unattractive strip motels, gift shops, and fast-food restaurants. When Disney began secretly buying up tens of thousands of acres of swamp and cypress groves in central Florida in the 1960s, it was with the intention of shielding his new park deep within a green barrier. There was to be no Katella Avenue at Walt Disney World.

In the end, Disney was successful. The Magic Kingdom, Epcot Center, Disney–MGM Studios, Disney's Animal Kingdom, and all of the other attractions within the park seem to exist in a world unto themselves. There are more than 27,000 hotel rooms within the bounds of Walt Disney World, and tens of thousands more in the neighborhood. Even so, the sheer size of the park swallows them up and hides them from sight of each other. But, of course, the Walt Disney Company cannot own every square mile of Florida, even though it probably would if it could. There are two principal places where Disney meets the real world: at Apopka–Vineland Road (Highway 535) and at US 192. And then there is the rest of the Orlando-Kissimmee area.

Prices for Non-Disney Hotels

★ Ordinary Hotels
★★ Better Hotels
★★★ Superior Hotels
★★★★ Econoguide Best
$ Economy: $25–$45 low season; $45–$65 high season
$$ Budget: $45–$75 low season; $65–$90 high season
$$$ Moderate: $75–$125 low season; $100–$200 high season
$$$$ Deluxe: $125–$200 low season; $200–$400 high season

Note that properties without a star rating are acceptable but not recommended.

(Bronson = Irlo Bronson Highway, also known as US 192)

US 192 bears several different names in its traverse from U.S. Highway 27 west of the park to and through downtown Kissimmee. For much of its length near the park, it is known as Irlo Bronson Memorial Highway. (Bronson was a prominent local politician and developer.) Near Kissimmee it is called Vine Street; past Kissimmee toward St. Cloud, it is named Thirteenth Street. Some segments are also known as Space Coast Highway. You can call it 192 anywhere and people will know what you mean.

Most of the hotels and attractions on US 192 can be found between Interstate 4 and Highway 441 (Main Street/South Orange Blossom Trail) in Kissimmee. The section where I–4 meets US 192 actually lies within the southern end of the huge Walt Disney World property. West of I–4, toward US 27, is the less popular side of US 192, although a number of new hotels have been built in the area. Room rates at low season range from as low as $29 at US 27 to about $75 per night closer to the park; high-season rates are about double. Hotels in this area often include "Main Gate" or "West Gate" in their names.

The busier side of US 192 runs about 10 miles from I–4 east to Main Street in Kissimmee. The area closest to I–4 is often called "Main Gate East." Near I–4 you will find attractions including Arabian Nights, Old Town, and Water Mania. Between the intersection of Highway 535 and Kissimmee are Medieval Times and Fun 'n Wheels. A few miles past South Orange Blossom Trail and just short of the intersection with the Florida Turnpike is Osceola County Stadium, the spring-training home of the Houston Astros.

The far distant reaches of US 192 and the back roads outside the obvious tourist areas are the homes of the lowest rung on the ladder—I have seen rates as low as $19.99 for the night. Be sure to read the fine print; some prices are for single guests only, with an additional $5.00 or $10.00 for a second person. Several hotels advertise a low price and then add a "service charge" to the nightly bill.

■ LAKE BUENA VISTA, APOPKA–VINELAND ROAD, CROSSROADS, WORLD CENTER

The "back door" to Walt Disney World can be found off Highway 535: Apopka–Vineland Road. Here Hotel Plaza Boulevard leads into the Disney Village Hotel Plaza area, Disney Village, and Pleasure Island. Farther along the road are the gates to the Magic Kingdom, Epcot, Disney–MGM Studios, and the other attractions within the park. Some of the property in this area is actually owned and controlled by the Walt Disney Company, although it is not technically within the park.

Many of the area hotels offer free transportation to Walt Disney World, and some may be on the route for transportation companies that pick up passengers at Orlando International Airport. Inquire when you call for information.

★★ Courtyard by Marriott Lake Buena Vista at Vista Centre $$–$$$

8501 Palm Parkway; (800) 635–8684 or (407) 239–6900; www.marriott.com. A family-oriented resort with 308 rooms; suites include a refrigerator and microwave. The Courtyard Cafe ($$) offers a breakfast buffet and dinner from a menu.

★★ Embassy Suites Resort Lake Buena Vista $$$–$$$$

8100 Lake Avenue; (800) 257–8483 or (407) 239–1144; www.embassysuites.com. An all-suite hotel in Lake Buena Vista, with bedroom; living room, dining, and kitchen areas; refrigerator; and microwave.

★★★★ Gaylord Palms Resort $$$–$$$$

6000 West Osceola Parkway, Kissimmee; (407) 586–0315; www.gaylordpalms .com. If you're not going to a convention at this fabulous resort about five min-

> ## From Cows to Mice
>
> For many decades, way before the arrival of the Hollywood mice, Kissimmee was among Florida's premier cattle-raising areas, best known for its Brahma cattle.

Under the atrium of the spectacular Gaylord Palms Resort

The Real Old Town

Orlando was established as a campground for soldiers during the Seminole Indian War of 1835 to 1842, and it then continued as a trading post. The war resulted in removal of most Native Americans in Florida to reservations in Oklahoma.

utes away from Walt Disney World at the intersection of International Drive and Osceola Parkway, see if you can get invited as a guest speaker. This hotel, which opened in 2002, is a theme park all by itself.

Modeled after classic old Floridian architecture, with salutes to Saint Augustine, Key West, and Everglades architecture, the design includes four acres of gardens under glass. The exterior looks like a turn-of-the-twentieth-century Florida grand hotel, modeled after the former Ponce de Leon Hotel in St. Augustine, now Flagler College.

There are 1,406 guest rooms, including 115 suites and nine presidential suites, restaurants, lounges, shops, a world-class Canyon Ranch spa, fitness center, two swimming pools, and a wedding gazebo.

Meetings and conventions—the heart of the hotel's business, although unaffiliated guests can reserve rooms through most of the year—are accommodated with 400,000 square feet of convention, meeting, exhibition, and prefunction space, including a 178,000-square-foot exhibition hall. All this takes place beneath a spectacular four-acre glass atrium.

At the heart of the atrium is Emerald Bay, a separate 362-room area with its own suites, boardrooms, and meeting facilities, which was designed to be a hotel within a hotel. The upscale guest rooms, additional services, and meeting facilities convey the look and feel of a boutique hotel within the destination resort. Every room includes free high-speed T-1 Internet connection, and the room safe is large enough to hold a laptop computer and has a plug inside to recharge your equipment.

Tucked in the resort's Everglades locale, along a rustic walkway that winds past the "river of grass" and cypress trees draped in Spanish moss, Old Hickory Steakhouse ($$) appears as a weatherworn, tin-roofed respite in the backwoods of south Florida. The menu, though, is not backwoods, including an extensive wine list. Specialties include aged beef, lobster, tuna, and an artisanal cheese course.

A meandering wooden boardwalk leads across a pond to the *Gaylord*, a 60-foot docked sailboat that serves as the bar for Sunset Sam's Fish Camp ($$–$$$). The restaurant re-creates a bit of Mallory Square in Key West, serving fresh oysters, clams, and spicy conch fritters. Seafood offerings include yellowtail, Chilean sea bass, pompano, and Gulf Coast grouper, each served sautéed, blackened, broiled, or grilled and finished with sauces such as champagne-dill or citrus-tomato vinaigrette. The signature dessert is a "mile-high" Key lime margarita pie served in a margarita glass. (I'm still working it off.)

During its early planning and construction, the hotel was originally envisioned as the Opryland Hotel. Its owner, Gaylord Entertainment, decided that the hotel and convention center were going to be much more upscale and sophisticated than the Opryland name might have suggested. This assessment turned out to be correct.

★★ Holiday Inn Sunspree—Lake Buena Vista $$–$$$

13351 Highway 535; (800) 366–6299 or (407) 239–4500; www.holiday-inn.com. This family resort is just outside the Disney Village Marketplace area on Highway 535. All 507 rooms include a refrigerator and microwave; some offer Kidsuites, a miniroom for the youngsters within the parents' suite. There is also Camp Holiday, offering activities for children ages four to twelve from 4:00 to 10:00 P.M. for a nominal fee.

Restaurants include Maxine's ($$), with breakfast and dinner buffets. Max's Funtime Parlor ($–$$) has breakfast and dinner buffets with character shows, featuring the Kidsuite Gang: Max, Maxine, Paully Wog, Grahammie Bear, Mollee Mouse, and Mattie Mole. Kids eat free with an adult.

> ## A Growing City
>
> The Orlando metropolitan area was the sixteenth-fastest growing area in the country, according to the 2000 Census. Its population grew 34 percent between 1990 and 2000, to 1,644,561.

★★ Hyatt Regency Grand Cypress $$$$

1 Grand Cypress Boulevard, near the Disney Village Hotel Plaza; (800) 233–1234 or (407) 239–1234. Villas of Grand Cypress $$$$. (800) 835–7377 or (407) 239–4700; www.hyatt.com. A 750-room tower plus 146 villas in and around forty-five holes of golf, twelve tennis courts, and a huge pool with waterfalls and a 45-foot water slide.

★★★ Orlando World Center Marriott Resort and Convention Center $$–$$$$

Highway 536 and I–4; (800) 228–9290 or (407) 239–4200; www.marriottworld center.com. The complex sprawls across 200 landscaped acres and includes 1,501 rooms and suites, an eighteen-hole golf course, several large pools, and tennis courts. There are five restaurants, including Mikado's ($$–$$$), a Japanese steak house. Child care can be arranged through the conceirge. The Orlando World Center is often used for large conventions, offering Disney and other entertainment for spouses and children while business goes on within its meeting rooms.

■ INTERNATIONAL DRIVE (SEAWORLD TO UNIVERSAL STUDIOS ORLANDO)

The next major stop on our tour is the International Drive area, a 5-mile uninterrupted stretch of every national hotel and restaurant chain you've ever heard of, and some you probably haven't. This road serves no purpose other than for the tourist; it's a convenient midway location for the visitor looking to explore in all directions. Room rates run from about $50 to $100 during low season at motels; a few fancy hotels have rooms at about double those prices.

One end of International Drive begins south of the Beeline Expressway at the entrance to SeaWorld. From there it wanders more or less northerly to pass by the Orange County Convention and Civic Center, the Mercado shopping area, across Sand Lake Road (Highway 482), in front of Wet 'n Wild, and then heads east across Kirkman Road near the main entrance to Universal Studios.

International Drive is, then, just minutes from SeaWorld, Universal Studios, Wet 'n Wild, and half a dozen other smaller attractions. There are restaurants of all descriptions on the road, as well. The road is about a fifteen-minute drive south to Walt Disney World or north to Orlando. North of the Beeline, International Drive branches into exotically named circles: Hawaiian Court, Samoan Court, Austrian Court, and Jamaican Court. North of Sand Lake Road, you will be across the road from Wet 'n Wild. Just before Kirkman Road, look for American Way on the left side. Nearby to Universal Studios are Kirkman Road, Turkey Lake Road, and Universal Boulevard (renamed from Republic Drive in 1998).

★★★★ Peabody Orlando $$$–$$$$

9801 International Drive; (407) 352–4000; www.peabodyorlando.com. The queen of International Drive, this elegant and somewhat unusual hotel has rooms that range in price from about $300 to $390 and suites that climb to $1,450. (There are special rates for seniors and promotions throughout the year.) Facilities include an Olympic-size swimming pool, a health club, and extensive meeting and convention facilities.

Restaurants include the gourmet eatery Dux ($$$), a Northern Italian trattoria known as Capriccio ($$$), and the B-Line Diner ($$), which is reminiscent of a 1954 burger-and-milk-shake diner.

The Peabody has ambitious plans for expansion, including a tower with 750 additional guest rooms and 125,000 square feet of flexible meeting space.

While Disney has a mouse, SeaWorld has a whale, and Universal Studios has a shark, the Peabody has a squad of trained ducks. Every day at 11:00 A.M., five somewhat-trained mallards march down a red carpet to the lobby fountain, accompanied by the official duck master, to the tune of John Philip Sousa's "King Cotton" march. At 5:00 P.M. the procession goes the other way, and the ducks return to their Royal Duck Palace. The show is free and open to visitors as well as guests. The hotel's shuttle to the theme parks, by the way, is known as the Double Ducker.

★★ Nickelodeon Family Suites by Holiday Inn $$–$$$$

14500 Continental Gateway; (407) 387–5437; www.ichotelsgroup.com. New in 2005 is the first Nickelodeon-themed hotel, appropriately located off International Drive between Walt Disney World and Universal Studios Orlando. You can rent a one-, two-, or three-bedroom Kidsuite themed around popular Nickelodeon characters; some include whirlpool tubs and kitchens. Outside is a water park with slides, flumes, and play areas. The hotel was formerly the Holiday Inn Family Suites Resort.

■ ORLANDO INTERNATIONAL AIRPORT AREA

The Orlando airport is located about thirty minutes away from Walt Disney World. If your plane arrives late or if you are preparing for an early-morning departure, you might want to consider staying near the airport. Room rates for "name" hotels are higher than those in the tourist areas of Kissimmee; expect to pay $60 to $125 per night in low season for a standard room and from $70 to $150 per night in high season.

The closest hotel to your airline's arrival gate doesn't even require you to leave the airport. The Hyatt Regency Airport Hotel is within the main airport building; you might want to consider one night's stay there if your plane arrives very late or leaves very early. Rates at the Hyatt range from about $99 to $245, depending on the season. For information consult www.orlandoairport.hyatt.com.

Other hotels close to the airport can be found along Semoran Boulevard (Highway 436), which leads into Frontage Road and McCoy Road, two service roads that run parallel to the Beeline Expressway (Highway 528). Also in the neighborhood are T. G. Lee Boulevard and Augusta National Drive. Moving west from the airport, you are heading for the South Orange Blossom Trail area.

■ SOUTH ORANGE BLOSSOM TRAIL/SAND LAKE ROAD/ FLORIDA MALL AREA

Near the intersection where the Beeline Expressway comes to the combined Highway 17–92 and 441—which is better known as the South Orange Blossom Trail—you will find a collection of more than a dozen brand-name motels. The farther north you travel, toward Orlando, the more likely you are to find lower-priced locally owned motels. (You'll also find some adult bookstores, strip joints, and other sites and people not on the tourist bureau's recommended list.) Nightly rates in this area range from about $40 to $100 in off-season and $50 to $150 per night in high season.

Rumor has it that there once was grass in the neighborhood; it's almost all asphalt now. This is strictly a place to sleep, with the exception of the intersection of South Orange Blossom Trail with Sand Lake Road (Highway 482). Here you will find the Florida Mall, with shopping, movie theaters, and chain restaurants. Sand Lake connects to the east with McCoy Road and runs directly into the airport.

EATING FOR LESS OUTSIDE OF DISNEY

As a tourist magnet, the Orlando area offers just about every type of restaurant from fancy to ordinary, from American to European to Asian. (One of the most eclectic gatherings of foreign restaurants can be found within the World Showcase pavilions of Epcot Center.) But the emphasis seems to be on "family" restaurants. If there is a single major franchise fast-food restaurant in America that is not represented in the Orlando area, I don't know about it.

The biggest collections of fast-food restaurants can be found on US 192 and International Drive. If you're really into deep-fried grease, you can probably find seven different McDonald's, Burger Kings, or Pizza Huts, one for every night of a week's stay.

Somewhat unique to the South are the all-you-can-eat buffets, which usually offer breakfasts in the range of $2.00 to $5.00, lunches from $4.00 to $8.00, and dinners from $6.00 to $12.00. Chains include Ponderosa Steak House, Sizzler, and Shoney's. Be aware that quality can vary from one buffet to the next. A great buffet deal is at Sweet Tomatoes on International Drive near Universal Orlando. By the way, don't hesitate to ask to inspect the buffet before buying your way into the buffet line.

CHAPTER FOUR

WALT DISNEY WORLD:
YOU'VE GOT TO HAVE A TICKET

AS IF YOU DON'T ALREADY face enough tough decisions—dates, airlines, hotels, and more—there is also the matter of those little pieces of cardboard called "admission tickets." Actually, they are not all that little: A family of four, including two children under ten years of age, visiting Walt Disney World for five days could easily spend—are you ready for this?—$930 plus tax for a set of Park Hopper tickets, or $1,130 if you also want to visit the water parks, DisneyQuest, and Wide World of Sports.

The very best thing you can do is to sit down with a piece of paper and make a plan before you leave for Florida. Don't wait until you are standing at the ticket counter with a hundred people eyeing your back, your children tugging at your sleeves, and tears in your eyes to decide on your ticket strategy. Instead, fit your plans to one of the available ticket packages. And don't overlook the money-saving strategies we discuss here.

FIRST, THE BAD NEWS

Remember what I said about Walt Disney World being a giant vacuum aimed at your wallet? Well, the great sucking sound begins at the ticket counter. If one of the Disney ticket plans matches your schedule exactly, you're in luck and you will save some money. But if the plans are not exactly what you need, you could end up wasting money instead of saving.

AN ECONOGUIDE TO DISNEY TICKETS

Disney generally raises prices once a year. The most recent version of pricing is a scheme called "Magic Your Way," which offers visitors "a la carte" tickets that begin with the one-park-per-day **Base Ticket** and then add options: **Park Hopping** (the ability to go to more than one park on one day) and **Water Park Fun & More** (a specified number of visits to water parks and other extra-price attractions at Walt Disney World).

Perhaps the most significant a la carte option for some visitors is the ability to pay a bit more to add a **No Expiration** option to multiday tickets. This comes at a price, but it might allow visitors to reduce the average daily cost for Disney World visits over time.

So, which ticket do you buy? That's simple: It depends.

You'll have to do some advance thinking and planning. How many days do you plan to spend at Walt Disney World? Which of the four theme parks, two water parks, one indoor interactive gaming palace, one nighttime entertainment district, and one sports complex do you want to visit?

Do you want the freedom to begin your day at the Magic Kingdom and end it at Epcot? Do you want to spend the morning at Animal Kingdom, the hot afternoon at Blizzard Beach, and then duck into Disney–MGM Studios for the late show of *Fantasmic* or a quick drop on the perpetually failing elevator at Twilight Zone Tower of Terror? How about holding an ace in the hole for a rainy afternoon admission to DisneyQuest?

And then ask yourself: Is this going to be your one and only visit to Walt Disney World, or do you plan to return? And if you expect to come back, will it be within a year? Within two or three years?

The question of future plans is an important one if you want to strategize on ways to save money over time. Among your options: paying extra to make multiday tickets (up to ten-day passes) usable without an expiration date, or buying an annual pass and making two trips within a twelve-month period.

The Base Ticket, the Park Hopper, the Water Park Fun & More option all come with a relatively short shelf life—the ticket completely expires fourteen days after the first day it is used. You can get around this by buying the No Expiration feature—for a charge that boosts the per-day cost between $5.00 and $16.00 for most tickets.

And Disney not only taketh away: Under the current scheme it also giveth a discount between $2.00 and $17.00 for tickets that are purchased in advance outside of Florida at a Disney-authorized location or over the Internet.

Did I say it was simple to make a buying decision? Well, here's the way I analyze it: If you plan to come back to Walt Disney World one or two times over the course of a few years, it probably makes sense to buy a ten-day Park Hopper with Water Park & More and No Expiration ($466 for an adult and $427 for a child

Walt Disney World Ticket Prices

Prices were in effect in the fall of 2006 after Disney raised prices for the second time in the same year; they do not include 6.5 percent Florida sales tax.

BASE TICKET

(One park per day. Tickets expire fourteen days after first use.)

	1-DAY	2-DAY	3-DAY	4-DAY	5-DAY	6-DAY	7-DAY	8-DAY	9-DAY	10-DAY
ADULT	$67	$132	$192	$202	$206	$208	$210	$212	$214	$216
(Approx. cost/day)	$67	$66	$64	$50	$41	$35	$30	$27	$24	$22
CHILD (AGES 3–9)	$56	$110	$160	$168	$169	$171	$173	$175	$176	$177
(Approx. cost/day)	$56	$55	$53	$42	$34	$29	$25	$22	$20	$18

ADD PARK HOPPER

(Multiple parks per day)

	1-DAY	2-DAY	3-DAY	4-DAY	5-DAY	6-DAY	7-DAY	8-DAY	9-DAY	10-DAY
ANY TICKET	$45	$45	$45	$45	$45	$45	$45	$45	$45	$45
(Addl. cost/day)	$45	$23	$15	$11	$9	$8	$6	$6	$5	$5

ADD WATER PARK FUN & MORE

(Adds a specified number of visits, from three to six, to Blizzard Beach, Typhoon Lagoon, DisneyQuest, Pleasure Island, or Wide World of Sports Complex)

	1-DAY	2-DAY	3-DAY	4-DAY	5-DAY	6-DAY	7-DAY	8-DAY	9-DAY	10-DAY
ANY TICKET	$50	$50	$50	$50	$50	$50	$50	$50	$50	$50
(Addl. cost/day)	$50	$25	$17	$13	$10	$8	$7	$6	$6	$5
(Number visits)	3	3	3	4	4	5	6	6	6	6

ADD NO EXPIRATION

(Unused days never expire)

	1-DAY	2-DAY	3-DAY	4-DAY	5-DAY	6-DAY	7-DAY	8-DAY	9-DAY	10-DAY
ANY TICKET	N/A	$10	$15	$40	$55	$60	$90	$125	$150	$155
(Addl. cost/day)	n/a	$5	$5	$10	$11	$10	$13	$16	$17	$16

TOTAL COST OF PARK HOPPER, WATER PARK FUN & MORE, NO EXPIRATION TICKET

	1-DAY	2-DAY	3-DAY	4-DAY	5-DAY	6-DAY	7-DAY	8-DAY	9-DAY	10-DAY
ADULT	$162*	$237	$302	$337	$356	$363	$395	$432	$459	$466
(Cost/day)	$162*	$119	$109	$84	$71	$61	$56	$54	$51	$47
CHILD (AGES 3–9)	$151*	$215	$270	$303	$319	$326	$358	$395	$421	$427
(Cost/day)	$151*	$108	$90	$76	$64	$54	$51	$49	$47	$43

* No Expiration option not available.

ADVANCE PURCHASE SAVINGS

Park Hopper and Park Hopper Plus Water Park Fun & More tickets purchased outside of Florida prior to arrival at Walt Disney World include a small discount. Prices indicate Park Hopper/Park Hopper Plus Water Park Fun & More.

	1-DAY	2-DAY	3-DAY	4-DAY	5-DAY	6-DAY	7-DAY	8-DAY	9-DAY	10-DAY
ADULT	*	*	*	$2/$12	$5/$15	$6/$16	$7/$17	$7/$17	$7/$17	$7/$17
CHILD (AGES 3–9)	*	*	*	$2/$10	$2/$10	$2/$10	$2/$10	$3/$11	$3/$11	$3/$11

* No Advance Purchase Savings offered.

(continued)

ANNUAL PASS	
(Unlimited admission for 365 days to theme parks, plus free parking)	
ADULT	$434
CHILD (AGES 3–9)	$382
PREMIUM ANNUAL PASS	
(Unlimited admission for 365 days to theme parks, water parks, Pleasure Island, DisneyQuest, and Wide World of Sports, plus free parking)	
ADULT	$559
CHILD (AGES 3–9)	$493

in 2006); you can save a bit more by ordering the ticket ahead of time. There is very little chance that the cost of admission to Walt Disney World is going to go down in price over time, and you'll have the tickets in the bank. (And Disney will have your money, but that's the deal.)

Spreading out your use of such a ten-day ticket over two or three visits to Orlando also allows you to plan time to visit some of the other attractions in the area, including the two theme parks of Universal Studios Florida and SeaWorld Orlando, and even venture farther to places like the Kennedy Space Center or Busch Gardens Tampa.

The new pricing scheme may make some visitors less likely to use what I used to call the "Annual Pass Eleven-Month Year." The idea is to purchase an annual pass—which includes unlimited park-hopping—and then make two visits within 365 days. For example, visit Orlando in March of one year and February of the next. The new pricing scheme makes that less attractive unless you plan to spend more than ten days at Walt Disney World on those two trips; the cost of a ten-day Base Ticket plus Park Hopper privileges and No Expiration is still less than an annual pass. Go figure.

■ I GROW OLD, I GROW OLD

What do you do if your child graduates to adult ticket status while you still have days left on your nonexpiring multiday ticket? Go to Guest Services, where you can apply the value of the ticket against a new adult ticket. Or, tell your eleven-year-old to look like a nine-year-old at the ticket turnstile.

■ TRANSFERABILITY

In recent years Disney has made it difficult to use one nifty money-saving trick. The tickets have always been "nontransferable," but Disney had no way to enforce that rule. It used to be that you could give your unused tickets to a friend or other family member, or sell your unused passes to one of the many "gray market" ticket booths in the vicinity of the park. The gray marketeers would buy and sell extra tickets at a discount.

Disney has tried various methods to make it hard to transfer ownership of a ticket. One recent experiment uses a "biometrics" device that measures the length

Other Disney Ticket Prices

Prices were in effect in early 2007 and do not include 6.5 percent Florida sales tax. They are subject to change.

	ADULT	CHILD (AGES 3 TO 9)
DISNEYQUEST	$36.00	$30.00
DISNEYQUEST ANNUAL PASS	$89.00	$71.00
BLIZZARD BEACH	$36.00	$30.00
TYPHOON LAGOON	$36.00	$30.00
WATER PARKS ANNUAL PASS	$99.95	$80.50
WATER PARKS/DISNEYQUEST ANNUAL PASS	$129.00	$99.00
PLEASURE ISLAND		
1-night Multi-club	$21.95	$21.95
Annual pass	$55.95	$55.95*
WIDE WORLD OF SPORTS	$10.28	$7.71
CIRQUE DU SOLEIL	$61.00–$95.00	$49.00–$76.00

Parking $10.00
Stroller rental $10.00 per day or $8.00 per day for length-of-stay rental
Double stroller rental $18.00 per day or $16.00 per day for length-of-stay rental
Wheelchair $10.00 per day or $8.00 per day for length-of-stay rental
Electric Convenience Vehicle $35.00 per day plus $5.00 deposit

*At Pleasure Island, admission to clubs is restricted to guests eighteen or older unless accompanied by a guest twenty-one or older with the following exceptions. All guests must be twenty-one or older to enter Mannequins Dance Palace and BET Soundstage Club on select nights. Single-club ticket can be used anywhere on the island except Adventurers Club and The Comedy Warehouse.

and width of your fingers in a special reader at the turnstiles and compares it to information on file. And the tickets themselves do not indicate the remaining value on a ticket.

I cannot suggest you trade or sell passes to friends, relatives, or strangers; not that I think it is necessarily wrong to do so—you paid for that ticket, after all— but because they may not hold the value you think they have.

And for the same reasons, I cannot recommend buying tickets from gray marketeers outside the park. If it were my money, I would stay away from any of the credit-card media and would consider buying only a standard cardboard ticket, and only after I examined the ticket very carefully for signs of alteration or fraud. Then I would pay for the tickets with a credit card so that I could challenge payment if necessary.

BUYING DISCOUNT TICKETS

Yes, you can get Disney tickets for less, but it takes a bit of doing. Officially, you buy tickets from Disney either at the gate, online, or from a Disney store. Unofficially, you may be offered tickets from tourist bureaus, time-share come-ons, and from unidentified stands off the Disney property. These unofficial tickets may well be legitimate, or they may not; I would recommend exercising extreme caution when making a purchase that could amount to hundreds or thousands of dollars. Insist on using a credit card, and be prepared to enlist the assistance of the credit-card company if you end up the victim of fraud.

The following include official ways to purchase tickets:

■ Visit the Disney Web site for advance purchase of multiday tickets. In 2006 Disney offered discounts of about 4 to 5 percent through its Internet portal at www.disney.com. Typical savings for a family of four were about $50. Tickets can be mailed to your home for a small fee or held at the park for pickup.

Disney's Advance Purchase and Savings plan is also moving into Disney Stores around the nation, where visitors can purchase tickets from an electronic kiosk.

(You can also buy tickets, not necessarily at a discount, by calling 407–824–4321.)

■ Book an all-inclusive hotel and park admission package from the Walt Disney Company. Packages include rooms and tickets; some other deals add in use of recreational facilities, and breakfast, lunch, and dinner every day at the hotel or within the parks. Be sure to figure the true value of the package. Ask for the regular room rate, and then add in the value—to you—of recreation and meals to determine if there is a real discount. If the package includes airfare, compare its value against the best ticket prices you could obtain on your own.

■ Book a hotel and admission package from one of the hotels outside the park. Again, find out the regular hotel charge to determine if your admission tickets are being offered at a discount.

■ Be on the lookout for occasional promotions by the Walt Disney Company through some of the official tourist agencies in the Orlando area. One good place to check is the Orlando/Orange County Convention & Visitors Bureau, which is located at 8445 International Drive. Write to the bureau at P.O. Box 690355, Orlando, FL 32869. Call (877) 460–6849, or log onto www.orlandoticket sales.com or www.orlandoinfo.com/tickets.

Disney regularly offers special deals to Florida residents, sometimes extending the discounts to neighboring states. Some of the programs allow buyers to bring guests. Do you have any friends or relatives down south?

■ Buy tickets through AAA or other travel associations or through credit-card issuers that may offer slightly discounted tickets.

FREE TICKETS!

Two Disney tickets for $5.00! Free Universal Studios passes! Impossible? Not at all. Completely free? Well . . . you can't help but notice the come-ons as you travel in the prime tourist areas of Irlo Bronson Highway (US Highway 192) in Kissimmee and International Drive in Orlando. And in many hotels you'll be assaulted in the lobby.

The pitch works something like this: "All you've got to do is go to this wonderful resort, eat a free breakfast, and listen to our two-hour presentation about our time-sharing/interval ownership/vacation club. Even if you don't buy, we'll give you two free tickets to Walt Disney World. There's no pressure." It's all true, except for the "no pressure" part.

You'll start by filling out a simple form. There are usually a few qualifying questions to see if you have sufficient income to make a time-sharing purchase—the threshold is usually pretty low, around $30,000 per year in annual income—and you'll likely be asked to make a "deposit" of about $20 to hold your place at the presentation. The deposit will be returned along with your "free" tickets. (There are two reasons for the deposit: The deposit is the commission earned by the ticket broker for delivering you to the sales group, as well as an inducement to make sure you show up for your appointment.)

I've sat through a few of the presentations and have earned my free tickets and the return of my deposit, just as promised. I've also had to fight off some pretty insistent sales pitches. Sometimes the two or nearly three hours of my time have been worth the value of a pair of tickets; sometimes I've felt like it would be worth paying $100 to the salespeople to let me escape before my promised time was up.

Should you consider buying a time-share? Most hard-nosed financial experts consider them to be less-than-wonderful investments. They talk about the fact that you may be locked into a location or time period that may not always work with your changing lifestyle, and they worry about unexpected expenses—if the elevator fails or the swimming pool leaks or other major expenses occur, the bill will come to the homeowners. Finally, there is not a very good history of increasing monetary value for time-share purchases.

Several agencies in and around Orlando specialize in unloading time-shares from private parties. If there is a big disparity between buying from the developer and buying from a reseller, or if the reseller has an unexpectedly large inventory of shares for sale, you should be very suspicious. In any case, consult an accountant or attorney before signing anything.

TICKETS FOR OTHER ATTRACTIONS

Non-Disney attractions in the Orlando area are much more willing to strike a deal. You can usually purchase discounted tickets for Universal Orlando, SeaWorld, many dinner theaters, and other entertainment from brokers in hotels and on tourist strips. Shop around before you buy and examine the tickets carefully.

Check the Web sites for the attractions for advance-purchase discount tickets; some destinations such as SeaWorld and Busch Gardens allow you to buy tickets over the Internet and print them out to take to the park.

AAA and other membership groups may offer discount tickets on their Web sites or through their offices.

CHAPTER FIVE

WALT DISNEY WORLD (AND UNIVERSAL ORLANDO) WITH CHILDREN

CHILDREN AND WALT DISNEY WORLD? Could there possibly be a better fit? Well, yes and no. For many kids a visit to Walt Disney World or Universal Orlando is the biggest thing that has ever happened to them—and although it almost always will be a most wonderful vacation, there are also special concerns for youngsters and their parents. Here are ten suggestions to make a trip with young children go well:

1. Involve the children in the planning. Obtain maps and brochures and study them at the dinner table; read sections of this book together. Work together on a schedule for the places you want to visit on each day.

2. Draw up the "rules" for the visit and make sure each child understands them and agrees with them. The basic rule in our family was that our young children always had to be within an arm's length of Mom or Dad.

3. Study and understand the height and age minimums for some of the more active rides at the parks. Don't build up expectations of your 41-inch-tall child for an attraction that requires riders to be 42 inches in height. (Did we hear someone say something about lift pads in shoes? Just remember that the rules are there to protect children from injury.)

4. Come to a family agreement on financial matters. Few parents can afford to buy everything a child demands; even if you could, you probably wouldn't want to. Consider giving your children a special allowance they can spend at the park, and encourage them to wait a day or two into the trip before they hit the gift shops so they don't hit bottom before they find the souvenir they really want.

5. Choose a place to meet if you become separated. Landmarks at Walt Disney World include Cinderella's Castle or the carousel in the Magic Kingdom, Spaceship Earth in Epcot, a particular spot near the *Tree of Life* at Disney's Animal Kingdom, and the Sorceror's Hat in Disney–MGM Studios.

At Universal Studios Florida, a prominent landmark is the *Back to the Future* steam locomotive. At Universal Studios Islands of Adventure, a good place to meet is One Fish, Two Fish, Red Fish, Blue Fish in Seuss Landing or the Dueling Dragons coaster at the back of the park.

Beyond that, instruct your children to find a uniformed park attendant if they are lost, and plan on checking with attendants yourself if you misplace a child.

Attach a name tag to youngsters (available at Guest Services if you don't have your own) or put a paper in your child's pocket with your name, cell phone number, and hotel on it. Some parents even give their kids walkie-talkie radios or cell phones.

6. For much of the year, the sun in central Florida is quite strong. Keep your kids (and yourself) under hats, and be sure to use a sunscreen, especially at midday; I'd suggest a waterproof lotion with an SPF of 30 or 45. You may want to bring bottles of water for the entire family—it's a lot cheaper than soda at the snack bars, and better for you, too.

7. You are not supposed to bring food into the park. In this book, I used to say that I'd never seen a paying guest searched for hidden sandwiches; unfortunately, that has changed in the current security environment. Guards are not supposed to permit you to bring cans or glass bottles into the parks, but peanut butter sandwiches—in clear plastic wrapping—will probably be waved through. You may choose to leave lunch in a cooler in your car and come out for a break. This is easy at Epcot, Disney–MGM Studios, or Animal Kingdom because of the relative proximity of the parking lot to the park but more of a problem at the Magic Kingdom or Universal Studios, where the car can be thirty minutes away.

8. A good strategy with youngsters, especially if you are staying inside Walt Disney World or Universal Studios Florida or nearby, is to arrive early and then leave at lunchtime for a quick nap or a swim; return at dusk to enjoy the evening at the park. You'll miss the hottest and most crowded part of the day and probably enjoy yourself much more. Be sure to have your hands stamped when you leave the park and hold onto your tickets (including your parking pass) if you intend to return.

Mom and Dad, I Promise . . .

One of the best things about going to Walt Disney World or Universal Studios with kids is that a resourceful parent should be able to milk a few weeks of "If you don't behave right now, I'm not taking you to Florida" threats. My resourceful son Willie came up with his own contract:

The Ten Theme-Park Commandments

I. Thou shalt not leave thy parents' sight.

II. Thou shalt not go on twister rides after a meal.

III. Thou shalt not complain about the lines.

IV. Thou shalt not fight with thy sister or brother.

V. Thou shalt not ask to buy something at the shops that costs more than the admission ticket.

VI. Thou shalt enjoy any of the boring things that Mom and Dad want to see.

VII. Thou shalt stand still so Dad can take at least one picture.

VIII. Thou shalt not pester the characters to talk.

IX. Thou shalt not sing "It's a Small World After All" more than sixteen times in a row.

X. Thou shalt go on at least one educational ride, even if it has a long line.

9. Although you can bring your own stroller, it is also easy to rent one for the day at the parks. Park the stroller near the exit to the attraction so it is waiting when you come out. Don't leave any valuables with the stroller. If you move from one Disney park to another during a single day, show your receipt at the new park to obtain a stroller when you arrive.

10. There are changing tables in most restrooms and private places for nursing mothers. You can also purchase diapers and formula; ask at Guest Services. Disney's Baby Center, at each park, is designed to assist in nursing or changing infants; most other restrooms throughout the parks have some accommodation for these needs. The Baby Center also offers for sale emergency rations of formula, replacement pacifiers, bottles, and diapers. Strollers are available for rent beneath the railroad overpass at the park entrance.

A KID'S-EYE VIEW

What are the best attractions for youngsters (three to ten years old)? Well, you know your particular child's interests and fears better than anyone else, but here are some favorites and a few warnings. (Key appears on next page.)

MAGIC KINGDOM

Mickey's PhilharMagic
Dumbo, The Flying Elephant ❷
Cinderella's Golden Carrousel
It's a Small World
Jungle Cruise
Pirates of the Caribbean ❶
Peter Pan's Flight
Mad Tea Party ❷
The Magic Carpets of Aladdin ❷
Splash Mountain ❸❹

The Many Adventures of Winnie
   the Pooh
Mickey's Toontown Fair
The Barnstormer
Ariel's Grotto
Country Bear Jamboree
Tom Sawyer's Island
Tomorrowland Speedway ❸
Enchanted Tiki Room

EPCOT

Body Wars ❹
Imagination!
Honey, I Shrunk the Audience
Turtle Talk with Crush
Universe of Energy ❶
GM Test Track ❶❹

Soarin' ❷
Cranium Command ❹
Wonders of Life ❷
The Living Seas
River of Time (Mexico)

DISNEY'S ANIMAL KINGDOM

Kilimanjaro Safaris
Kali River Rapids ❹
Festival of the Lion King
Tarzan Rocks! ❶
It's Tough to Be a Bug!

TriceraTop Spin ❷
Primeval Whirl ❷❹
Dinosaurs ❹
Affection Section
Pangani Forest Exploration Trail

DISNEY–MGM STUDIOS

Fantasmic! ❶
Jim Henson's Muppet*Vision 3D ❶
The Great Movie Ride ❶
Honey, I Shrunk the Kids Movie Set
   Adventure

Playhouse Disney—Live on Stage
Voyage of the Little Mermaid ❶
Beauty and the Beast—Live on Stage
Sounds Dangerous ❶
Star Tours ❹

UNIVERSAL STUDIOS FLORIDA

Woody Woodpecker's KidZone
Shrek 4-D ❶
Jimmy Neutron's Nicktoon Blast ❷
Fievel's Playground
E.T. Adventure
Twister ❶

Back to the Future ❹
Animal Actors Stage
Earthquake–The Big One ❶❸
Jaws ❶❹
Men in Black ❹

UNIVERSAL'S ISLANDS OF ADVENTURE

The Cat in the Hat
If I Ran the Zoo
Dudley Do-Right's Ripsaw Falls ❷
The Eighth Voyage of Sindbad ❶
Pteranodon Flyers ❷
One Fish, Two Fish, Red Fish,
   Blue Fish

Caro-Seuss-el
Storm Force Accelatron ❷
Me Ship *The Olive*
Jurassic Park River Adventure ❶❷
Camp Jurassic

Key:
❶ Loud noises and special effects (pirates, skeletons, beasts) may startle unprepared children.
❷ Can make some children dizzy.
❸ Adult must accompany small children.
❹ **Disney–MGM Studios:** Star Tours may be too rough of a ride for the youngest visitors.
Epcot: Body Wars, Cranium Command, and GM Test Track may be too intense for the very young. Parental guidance advised for *The Making of Me* film at the Wonders of Life.
Universal Studios Florida: Back to the Future and Men in Black may be too intense for some children; use your judgment based on your knowledge of your own child. Jaws, Twister, and Earthquake have some wild effects, but most children find them fun. **Magic Kingdom:** Splash Mountain is charming, but it does include one drop over a waterfall; it's not as scary as it looks, but some children may not be ready. **Disney's Animal Kingdom:** Dinosaurs is a wild ride through animatronic dinosaurs and exploding meteors. Some youngsters may be scared, but most will beg for a second, third, and fourth trip. Kali River Rapids is a relatively wild river-raft ride that may frighten some youngsters. Primeval Whirl is wilder than it appears and is not appropriate for children unprepared for roller coasters. And I haven't even listed the thrilling Expedition Everest here; if your child is 44 inches or taller and loves roller coasters, this is a great one; otherwise, you're going to have to pretend that the huge mountain in Asia is not there.

Disney Character Spotting

For some kids—and more than a few adults—one of the highlights of a visit to Walt Disney World is exchanging a high-five with a Disney character or collecting his or her autograph. (Yes, most of us know that it's just a cast member in a rubber head or a fanciful costume, but that doesn't prevent long lines for a meet-and-greet.)

Check the park maps for a white Mickey's glove that indicates the location for character greetings and the time schedule for their appearance; you can also ask a cast member for assistance. At the Magic Kingdom there's a large gathering of characters at Mickey's Toontown Fair—so many that you'd swear there was more than one Mickey and Minnie, but that can't possibly be true, right? The Fantasyland Character Festival also has a regular gathering.

At Epcot characters sometimes ride a double-decker bus through World Showcase Plaza and make regular appearances at most of the pavilions—look for Belle and friends from *Beauty and the Beast* at France and Aladdin and buddies at Morocco. Disney's Animal Kingdom has Camp Minnie-Mickey, where Mickey and friends hang out in the shade.

BABYSITTING

What? You've come all the way to Walt Disney World with the kids, and now you want an adult's night out? Trust us, we understand.

Depending on your comfort level, you might want to hire a professional babysitter to come to your room and watch the kids. In doing so, remember that not only are you leaving your kids in the hands of a stranger, you're also walking away from all of your stuff in the room. Or, if you are traveling with friends, you could consider swapping nights off.

Check with the concierge about available services offered by the hotel or endorsed by them. Walt Disney World does endorse one company for in-room babysitting for guests at its own resort: **Kid's Nite Out,** which can provide child care in the room or serve as a mother's helper during your stay. Reservations can be made in advance by calling (800) 696–8105 or (407) 828–0920 or by consulting www.kidsniteout.com.

ORGANIZED PROGRAMS AT DISNEY RESORT HOTELS

Check with the concierge for available programs offered to guests at Walt Disney Resort hotels. Some are limited to the hotel where you are staying, while others will accept guests from other company-owned hotels.

Walt Disney World Dolphin. Camp Dolphin. (407) 934–4000, ext. 4241.

Supervised evening activities for children ages three to twelve including sports, games, arts and crafts, as well as special events. Dinner Club available.

Walt Disney World Swan. Camp Swan. (407) 934–3000, ext. 1006. Supervised evening activities.

Disney's BoardWalk. The Harbor Club. (407) 939–6301. Nightly supervised activities; dinner available.

Contemporary Resort. Mouseketeer Clubhouse. (407) 824–1000, ext. 3038. Nightly supervised activities and movies; dinner available.

Grand Floridian Resort. Mouseketeer Clubhouse. (407) 824–2985. Nightly supervised activities; dinner available.

Polynesian Resort. Neverland Club. (407) 939–3463. Nightly supervised activities and movies; buffet dinner available.

Disney's Yacht and Beach Clubs. Sandcastle Club. (407) 939–3463, ext. 3750. Nightly supervised activities; dinner available.

Disney's Wilderness Lodge. Disney's Grand Adventures for Kids. (407) 939–3463. Nightly supervised activities; dinner available.

CHILDREN'S ACTIVITIES

Guests at one of the resorts within Walt Disney World can enroll their children in one of several special activities offered at Disney's Grand Floridian Resort. Reservations (which are recommended) can be made by calling (407) 939–3463.

Grand Adventures in Cooking. Children hand-paint their own aprons and chef hats, read a story, and make a snack. Tuesday and Friday mornings.

Pirate Cruise. Kids will follow clues to search Bay Lake and the Seven Seas Lagoon for buried treasure and lunch. Offered daily from 10:30 A.M. to noon.

Wonderland Tea Party. Tea party for children, hosted by characters from *Alice in Wonderland.* Call for days and hours.

Coloring in the Garden. Arts and crafts in the Grand Floridian's garden, among Disney characters. Daily at 9:00 A.M. outside 1900 Park Fare.

BABY STROLLERS AND BABY SERVICES

Baby strollers are available for $10.00 per day (or $8.00 per day for the length of stay) at the entrance to the Magic Kingdom, at the base of Spaceship Earth and at the International Gateway at Epcot, at Oscar's Super Service just inside the gates of Disney–MGM Studios, and at the entrance to Disney's Animal Kingdom. Changing, feeding, and nursing facilities are available adjacent to the Crystal Palace on Main Street, U.S.A, in the Magic Kingdom; at Odyssey Center in Future World in Epcot; at the Guest Services building at the main entrance of Disney–MGM Studios; and at Discovery Island in Disney's Animal Kingdom. Disposable diapers, baby bottles, formula, and other baby supplies are available for purchase. Additional changing areas are available in most ladies' restrooms and some men's restrooms.

PART II

WALT DISNEY WORLD

CHAPTER SIX

THE KEYS TO THE KINGDOM . . . AND THE REST OF WALT DISNEY WORLD

SO, YOU WANT TO GO TO WALT DISNEY WORLD. Great! Which Walt Disney World?

■ The world of Mickey and Minnie and Dumbo and 1,000 live elephants, okapi, giraffes, two-toed sloths, gorillas, and black rhinos? (The Magic Kingdom and Disney's Animal Kingdom)

■ The place where you find Nemo . . . or the abominable snowman? (Epcot and Disney's Animal Kingdom)

■ The location of the vacation home away from home for Jack Sparrow and his nemesis, Barbossa, as well as Donald Duck's rehearsal hall and Minnie's kitchen? (The Magic Kingdom)

■ A place where you can gently soar over California, strap yourself into a centrifuge and simulate the first manned mission to Mars, or volunteer as a crash-test dummy? (Soarin', Mission: SPACE, and GM Test Track, all three at Epcot)

■ A hotel where the guy next door may be a giraffe and room service delivers munchies to the okapi? (Disney's Animal Kingdom Lodge)

■ The only place on the planet where China touches Norway, or where Santa Fe overlooks Polynesia? (Epcot Center and Disney's Coronado Springs)

■ The home of R2D2, Humphrey Bogart, the Alien, Kermit the Frog, and an elevator guaranteed to fail hundreds of times a day? (Disney–MGM Studios)

■ The stately adult pleasure dome of Merriweather A. Pleasure, where you can boogie all night (almost)? (Pleasure Island)

■ Florida's only ski resort and the summer golf course for Santa's elves? (Blizzard Beach and Winter Summerland)

■ The place where you can take a terrifying plunge down Humunga Kowabunga or a chairlift to the top of Florida's only ski resort? (Typhoon Lagoon and Blizzard Beach)

Cinderella Castle at the Magic Kingdom

WALT DISNEY WORLD ROADWAYS

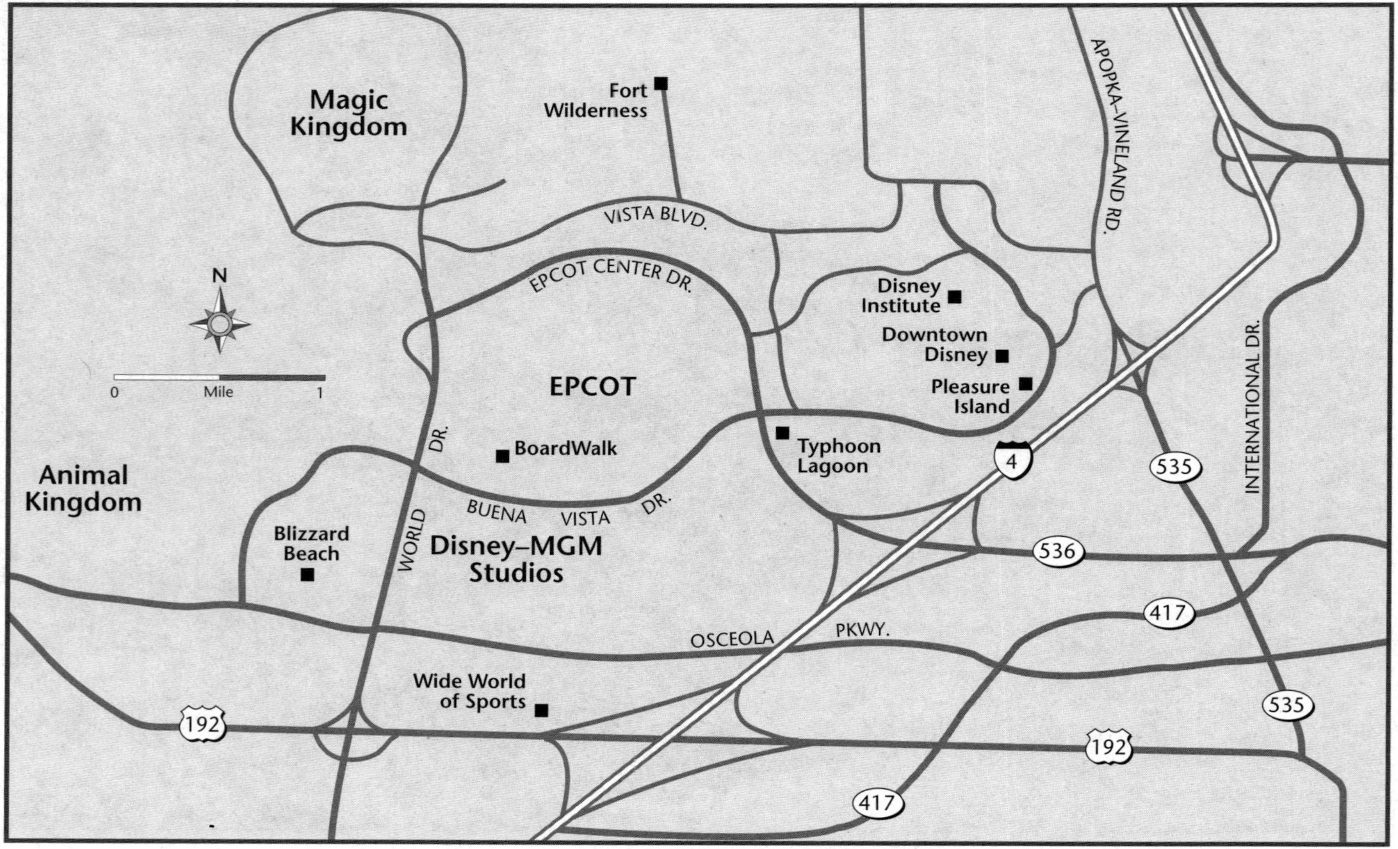

Magic Kingdom

Fort Wilderness

VISTA BLVD.

EPCOT CENTER DR.

EPCOT

BoardWalk

BUENA VISTA DR.

Disney–MGM Studios

WORLD DR.

Animal Kingdom

Blizzard Beach

Wide World of Sports

Disney Institute

Downtown Disney

Pleasure Island

Typhoon Lagoon

APOPKA–VINELAND RD.

INTERNATIONAL DR.

4

535

536

535

417

192

417

OSCEOLA PKWY.

192

N

Mile

0   1

- The place where you can hitch a ride in rock group Aerosmith's speedy luxury limo or drive among the dinosaurs? (Rock 'n' Roller Coaster at Disney–MGM Studios and Dinosaur at Animal Kingdom)
- A place with five championship-level golf courses? (The Magic Linkdom)
- The home port of the largest private flotilla in the world, bigger than many navies? (The Walt Disney World Marinas)
- A dinner table in a rain forest or parked at a drive-in movie? (Rainforest Cafe or Sci-Fi Dine-In Theater)
- A spectacular old-style baseball park, home to the spring-training camp of a major-league team? (Disney's Wide World of Sports)
- The place where you can take a steam train to fantasy, adventure, and tomorrow? (The Magic Kingdom)

Oh, *that* Disney World.

Let's start with an important definition: Walt Disney World is the entertainment complex that includes the **Magic Kingdom, Epcot, Disney's Animal Kingdom,** and **Disney–MGM Studios** as well as **Blizzard Beach, Typhoon Lagoon,** the six Disney golf courses, **Downtown Disney** (including **Pleasure Island, Disney Village,** and **Disney West Side,** encompassing **DisneyQuest** and **Cirque du Soleil**), **Disney's Wide World of Sports,** and hundreds of Disney-operated and Disney-licensed restaurants and hotels within the property lines of the World.

Covering 47 square miles, Walt Disney World is about the size of San Francisco, or twice the size of Manhattan. Of more than 30,000 acres, only about one-fourth has been developed, with another quarter set aside as a wilderness preserve.

My goal in this, the largest section of the book, is twofold: first, to break down the huge World into smaller and more understandable pieces and, second, to put them back together in a way that shows how to get the most out of it. There are nine chapters in this section: The Keys to the Kingdom . . . and the Rest of Walt Disney World, The Magic Kingdom, Epcot, Disney's Animal Kingdom, Disney–MGM Studios, Disney Water Parks, Downtown Disney, Educational Opportunities and Tours at Walt Disney World, and Inside the World of Disney.

Each of the theme-park chapters begins with a list of Econoguide "Must-See" attractions and the exclusive "Power Trip" tour. I hope you'll take the time to read the chapters before you go and once again when you're in Florida. Later on in the book, we'll return to Walt Disney World to discuss dinner theaters, sports, recreation, and educational opportunities.

A FEW WAYS AROUND THE WAITING LINES

The good news about Walt Disney World is that things are getting better and better all the time. Just consider these spectacular recent additions: **Expedition Everest,** a wild and woolly coaster at Disney's Animal Kingdom; the technologically advanced and wondrously uplifting **Soarin'** at Epcot; and the white-knuckle blastoff of **Mission: SPACE,** also at Epcot. Over at the Magic Kingdom,

Relativity

All of Disneyland in California could fit within the lagoon at Epcot, or within the boundaries of the parking lot at the Magic Kingdom. Disney's Animal Kingdom, at 500 acres, is the largest Disney theme park in the world.

the most famous mouse in the world took up a baton in *Mickey's PhilharMagic*.

Also recently arrived are a pair of fish tales based on the film *Finding Nemo*: **The Seas with Nemo & Friends** at Epcot and **Finding Nemo—The Musical** at Disney's Animal Kingdom. And the longtime favorite Pirates of the Caribbean at the Magic Kingdom gained a few new residents, including some of the stars of the recent movie series based on the attraction: welcome Jack Sparrow and Davy Jones.

And if it's been a while since you've visited, you may have yet to ride the hard-rockin' coaster at Disney–MGM Studios, enjoy amazing animal encounters at Disney's Animal Kingdom, or take a wild automobile ride at Epcot.

The not-so-good news: There are thousands of people in line ahead of you, especially during the busy summer season and holiday periods.

■ THE FASTPASS SYSTEM

Disney's Fastpass offers some welcome relief to waiting lines; the advanced ride-reservation system is available at many of the most popular attractions in all four theme parks. To use the system, insert your admission ticket into a card reader to receive a Fastpass with a scheduled return time. At the appointed hour you can walk right into the preshow area without waiting in line. Here's the fine print: You'll have to wait until after your current Fastpass appointment or two hours—whichever is sooner—before you can obtain another reservation.

And one more wrinkle: Disney has shown signs it may be pulling back from

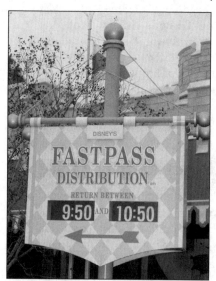

A Fastpass distribution site in Fantasyland

the concept. It seems that the Fastpass has disrupted the carefully engineered traffic flows at the parks; although some people are able to happily cruise right onto a ride at their appointed time, the waiting lines for those without passes at some attractions have grown unacceptably long. It is unclear if Fastpass will be a permanent element of Disney parks, if it will be reconfigured, or if it will be ended.

Among attractions with Fastpass distribution in late 2006:

Magic Kingdom: The Haunted Mansion, The Many Adventures of Winnie the Pooh, Jungle Cruise, Space Mountain, Buzz Lightyear's Space Ranger Spin, Splash Mountain, Peter Pan's Flight, Stitch's Great Escape!, and Big Thunder Mountain Railroad.

Epcot: Soarin'; Mission: SPACE; GM Test

Track; *Honey, I Shrunk the Audience;* Living with the Land; and Maelstrom.

Disney–MGM Studios: *Lights, Motors, Action! Extreme Stunt Show,* Rock 'n' Roller Coaster Starring Aerosmith, Tower of Terror, Star Tours, *Indiana Jones Epic Stunt Spectacular,* and the *Voyage of the Little Mermaid.*

Disney's Animal Kingdom: Expedition Everest, Kilimanjaro Safaris, Dinosaur, Primeval Whirl, *It's Tough to Be a Bug,* and Kali River Rapids.

Guests staying at select Walt Disney World hotels can take advantage of "Extra Magic Hour" openings. Each day one of the four parks opens a few attractions an hour early at no extra charge. During certain busy times of the year, guests at park resorts can also purchase a special Magic Kingdom E-Ride Night pass. Some of the most popular attractions at the park are held open after hours for guests with these special tickets, usually between 10:00 P.M. and 1:00 A.M.

GETTING TO THE MAGIC KINGDOM BY CAR

The idea behind the transportation system at Walt Disney World probably sounded good at the time: Getting to the Magic Kingdom should be a magical experience. When you leave your car, you should be in an entirely different world.

"We'll have visitors park way on the other side of a large lagoon and then let them take an exciting monorail ride or a soothing ferryboat to the main gate," the planners said. "By the time they're inside the park, they'll completely forget about the outside world."

So far, so good, but let's consider how it works out nearly forty or so years after the planners made their drawings. First you park way out in East Overshoe, practically the next county. Then you must walk to the central aisle of the parking lot and wait for a gigantic snakelike tram to take you to the Transportation and Ticket Center (TTC). At the TTC you'll choose between a monorail around Seven Seas Lagoon or a ferryboat ride. Either way you'll be taken to the main gates.

Total time from parking the car to your first step onto Main Street is about thirty minutes at the start of the day and as much as an hour at peak periods

Hot Dogs

Never leave your cat, dog, mouse, or other pet in your car; heat can build up tremendously in a parked vehicle, and animals can die. If you must bring a pet with you, bring proof of vaccination and use one of the Pet Care Kennels at the Magic Kingdom's Transportation and Ticket Center or at the entrance to Epcot, Disney's Animal Kingdom, Disney–MGM Studios, and Disney's Fort Wilderness Resort and Campground. Animal lovers there will also care for birds, ferrets, small rodents, and nonvenomous snakes in carriers.

Traffic Reports

If you're driving within the Walt Disney World Resort, four low-power radio signals on three AM frequencies keep visitors abreast of current information. Tune to 1030 (driving toward the Magic Kingdom), 900 (exiting the Magic Kingdom), 810 (entering Epcot), and 900 (exiting Epcot).

from about 10:00 A.M. to noon, when there are long lines at the monorail or fer-ryboat. At the end of the day, you'll have to reverse the process. And you did re-member where you parked your car, right?

For most visitors to the Magic Kingdom staying outside the park, there's no easy way around the process except to follow one of our general rules: Arrive early. If you're staying within Walt Disney World, consider taking the monorail, water taxi, or bus right from your hotel. These modes of transportation go directly to the front gate of the Magic Kingdom, skipping the intermediate stop at the TTC.

GETTING TO EPCOT, DISNEY–MGM, OR ANIMAL KINGDOM BY CAR

The situation is different at Disney–MGM Studios, Epcot, and Disney's Animal Kingdom, where you can park and walk or take a single tram ride to the gates. On busy days, or if I know that I will be ending my day at a different park from the one I started at, I leave my car where I want it to be at the end of the day and use Disney transportation to travel to my first park of the day.

For example, if your plan for the day calls for a start at the Magic Kingdom and ends with a special dinner at Epcot, you might try this strategy: Arrive early at Epcot and park there. Ride the monorail to the transfer point at the TTC and pick up the monorail to the Magic Kingdom. Then reverse that route in the af-ternoon and you will be able to stay as late as you want at Epcot and pick up your car there. The alternate plan works, too, on nights when the Magic Kingdom is open later than Epcot; park at the Magic Kingdom and ride the monorail to Epcot to begin your day.

You can also park your car at one of the hotels served by boat service to the International Gateway entrance to Epcot for a graceful exit at the end of the day. Here's one plan: Park at the Swan or Dolphin, take a bus to the TTC for the Magic Kingdom in the morning, and then take the monorail to Epcot.

TRANSPORTATION WITHIN WALT DISNEY WORLD

One of the advantages of a hotel within Walt Disney World is the availability of Disney's own bus, monorail, and boat fleet.

The buses go directly to the Magic Kingdom, Disney's Animal Kingdom, Epcot, and Disney–MGM Studios. Similarly, boat services from some Disney ho-tels go directly to the Magic Kingdom or to Epcot's back-door International Gateway entrance. Visitors staying at a Disney hotel with a monorail stop have di-rect service only to the Magic Kingdom; you'll have to make a transfer at the TTC to an Epcot train or a Disney–MGM Studios bus if either is your destination.

The principal transportation system at the Magic Kingdom is the Mark IV Monorail system, which links the Magic Kingdom and the TTC, and a second route that runs from there to Epcot. A local version of the Magic Kingdom loop stops at several of the major hotels within the park.

Getting around in Walt Disney World

DESTINATION	FROM	RIDE
Magic Kingdom	Disney's Polynesian Resort Disney's Contemporary Resort Disney's Grand Floridian Resort	Monorail
	Disney's Wilderness Lodge Disney's Fort Wilderness Lodge	Boat
	All other Disney resorts	Bus
	Disney–MGM Studios Disney's Animal Kingdom	Bus to TTC*, then monorail or ferryboat
	Epcot	Monorail to TTC, then monorail or ferryboat
Disney–MGM Studios	Disney's BoardWalk Disney's Yacht Club Resort Disney's Beach Club Resort Walt Disney World Swan Walt Disney World Dolphin	Boat
	All other Disney resorts Epcot Disney's Animal Kingdom	Bus
	Magic Kingdom	Monorail or ferryboat to TTC, then bus
Epcot	Disney's Polynesian Resort Disney's Contemporary Resort Disney's Grand Floridian Resort	Monorail to TTC, then transfer to Epcot monorail
	Disney's BoardWalk Disney's Yacht Club Resort Disney's Beach Club Resort Walt Disney World Swan Walt Disney World Dolphin	Boat or walk
	All other Disney resorts Disney–MGM Studios Disney's Animal Kingdom	Bus
	Magic Kingdom	Monorail or ferryboat to TTC, then Epcot monorail
Disney's Animal Kingdom	All Disney resorts Disney–MGM Studios Epcot	Bus
	Magic Kingdom	Monorail or ferryboat to TTC, then bus
Downtown Disney Disney's Typhoon Lagoon	All Disney resorts	Bus

(continued)

DESTINATION	FROM	RIDE
Disney's Blizzard Beach Disney's Winter Summerland	All Disney resorts	Bus (until 9:00 P.M.)
Disney's Fantasia Gardens	All Disney resorts	Bus to TTC, transfer to Swan/Dolphin bus, walk from Swan resort
Disney's Wide World of Sports	All Disney resorts	Bus to Disney–MGM Studios, transfer to Disney's Wide World of Sports bus (during Disney–MGM Studios hours)
Any Disney Resort	Any Disney resorts	Bus to downtown Disney, transfer to resort bus

*TTC is the Transportation and Ticket Center, a hub near the Magic Kingdom that brings together the monorail, many buses, and the ferryboat to the Magic Kingdom.

■ EVERYTHING YOU ALWAYS WANTED TO KNOW ABOUT THE MONORAIL

Well, almost everything.

The trains have eight 113-horsepower motors in various cars; the train can't be split up into smaller units. The monorails run on 600-volt DC power drawn from Disney's own power plant north of the Contemporary Resort, across the road from the monorail maintenance shop.

The Disney tracks stretch nearly 14 miles, including spur lines and maintenance areas. Just more than half of that is the Epcot "beam"; the Lagoon beam to hotels and the Exterior beam to the Magic Kingdom are each about 2.5 miles long. The monorail trains travel on rubber tires on a 26-inch-wide precast concrete beamway supported by tapered concrete columns. The height of the beam ranges from 18 feet off the ground to more than 60 feet at its highest elevation.

The Walt Disney World monorail system has been in operation since 1971. In 1982 the system was expanded with the extension to Epcot, and in 1990 and 1991 new trains were delivered. On a typical day more than 150,000 guests will ride the monorail system.

By the way, there is one row of seats in the front cab with the driver of the monorail. Ask one of the attendants to place you there for an interesting and different perspective. You may have to let a train pass by if there are many people waiting in line.

■ FIVE IF BY MONORAIL, SEVEN IF BY FERRY

Another component of the transportation system to the Magic Kingdom is decidedly low-tech: Disney's fleet of ferryboats that cross the lagoon from the TTC to the gates of the park. At most times there are two boats in constant operation, with a third available for peak periods.

The scaled-down versions of the famous Staten Island Ferries in New York are double-ended vessels, meaning they don't need to turn around at either end of their trip. You walk on at one end and walk off at the other. By the way, the ferries are free-floating; unlike the riverboat at the Magic Kingdom, there is no rail beneath the water.

Although the monorail may look speedy, in truth it is only about a minute or two faster than the ferryboat in getting from the TTC to the Magic Kingdom. And the two ferryboats can carry about three times as many passengers as one monorail train. So, if the line for the monorail is lengthy, go by sea. The ferries are a very pleasant way to travel, especially on a pretty evening at the end of a long day.

THE MAGIC KINGDOM'S UNDERGROUND

Among the most amazing wonders of the Magic Kingdom is one that most visitors never see. Below you are nine acres of underground "Utilidor" corridors hiding the sewers, water pipes, air-conditioning, electrical cables, communications links, and garbage-collection facilities. There is also an extensive system of tunnels that allows employees to come and go within the park virtually unseen. (Have you ever wondered why you have never seen Mickey walking to work, or seen a Mike Fink keelboat captain strolling through Tomorrowland?)

Actually, the tunnels are the first level of the Magic Kingdom. Because of the high water table of much of Florida, the tunnels were put in place first and then covered over with dirt, much of it from the excavation of the lagoon.

About that trash: As you might expect in a Magic Kingdom, Disney does not use an ordinary garbage truck. Refuse is sucked to a central collection point through a vast network of pneumatic tubes.

The Utilidor is not open to ordinary guests at the Magic Kingdom; you can, though, book a "Keys to the Kingdom" tour that includes a brief visit to the ground floor of the park along with other backstage areas. For more details see the Educational Opportunities and Tours at Walt Disney World chapter.

All the People on the Bus

Can you park at a Disney hotel lot and ride a monorail, boat, or bus directly to one of the parks? The answer is yes . . . and no. In theory, you must have a guest ID card to ride one of the internal modes of transport. However, I have never seen a driver ask for a card. And, Disney encourages guests at Walt Disney World to sample the restaurants and shops at its hotels. If you absolutely insist, Disney also quietly sells a daily transportation ticket for about $3.00, although you may have to try hard to find someone to take your money since these tickets aren't advertised.

Helpful Phone Numbers

▶ Walt Disney World dining reservations: (407) 939–3463

▶ Disney resort hotel reservations: (407) 934–7639

▶ Golf tee times: (407) 824–2270

▶ Pleasure Island: (407) 934–7781

CHAPTER SEVEN

THE MAGIC KINGDOM

ONCE UPON A MOUSE, back in 1928, Walter Elias Disney created a short cartoon he called *Steamboat Willie*. Its star was a guy named Willie who soon thereafter underwent a name change and achieved stardom as Mickey Mouse. Everything else since then has been built upon the slender shoulders of the cute little rodent, along with his gal, Minnie, and buddies Donald, Daisy, Snow White, as well as a cast of thousands of other cartoon and movie favorites.

Disney's film studio began to grow rapidly, and he set up a little park alongside his first movie studios to entertain visitors, exhibiting his collection of scale model trains, among other things. When he moved into television in the early 1950s, Disney struck a deal with ABC Television to help fund the construction of the Disneyland park in California, which opened in a former orange grove in 1955. Although much has changed in the nearly fifty years since Disneyland was first planned, the basic structure of that park, and all that have followed, is the same. Walt Disney World's Magic Kingdom opened in 1971. In 1995 Disney bought the entire ABC network. From mid-2005 deep into 2006, Disney threw itself into the eighteen-month Happiest Celebration on Earth, a salute to Disneyland's fiftieth birthday at all of today's Disney parks.

Today, breathes there a man, woman, girl, boy, duck, or mouse who has not dreamed of visiting the Magic Kingdom? Walt Disney's entertainment vision—along with the incredible marketing skills of the company he left behind—has made Disney's parks and symbols probably the world's best-known popular icons. You can see Mickey Mouse T-shirts worn on the streets of Moscow, Epcot towels on the beaches of the Caribbean, Minnie dresses on the boulevards of Paris, and Roger Rabbit hats in the alleys of Tokyo.

In 1992 Disneyland Paris joined the three other parks—Disneyland, Walt Disney World, and Tokyo Disneyland—on the global map. Disneyland became a two-park resort in 2001 with the opening of Disney's California Adventure, and Disneyland Paris doubled in 2002 with the arrival of Walt Disney Studios. Hong Kong Disneyland opened at Penny's Bay on Lantau Island in September 2005.

In Florida, by far the largest of all the Disney parks, the empire sprawls across miles of land and includes four major theme parks and dozens of other attractions. However, it is still the Magic Kingdom—home of Fantasyland, Adventureland, Frontierland, Tomorrowland, and Main Street, U.S.A.—that visitors think of when they first set out for Orlando.

In this section you'll find the details of the Ultimate Unauthorized Tour of the Magic Kingdom, area by area. I'll tell you which rides are "must-sees" and which ones might not be worth crossing the road for.

THE OPENING DASH

The Magic Kingdom usually opens at 9:00 A.M., although it may open at 8:00 A.M. during extremely busy times of the year, when guests at Walt Disney resorts are allowed a head start to certain areas of the park on some days.

The first part of the park that officially opens is Main Street; you can visit some of the shops or grab a bite to eat at the bakery or restaurants before the attractions open. Visitors are stopped at rope lines at the top of Main Street—one to the left near the Crystal Palace, one in the center heading toward Cinderella Castle, and one to the right just short of Tomorrowland.

The first rule of the Power Trip calls for you to get to the park early; the second is to get yourself a good position at one of the three gates. Bear to the left if your first goal is Splash Mountain, Big Thunder Mountain, or elsewhere in Adventureland or Frontierland. Line up at the rightmost gate if your goal is Space Mountain, Stitch's Great Escape!, Tomorrowland Indy Speedway, or another Tomorrowland ride. Head up the center if you intend to visit Fantasyland, home of Dumbo the Flying Elephant and *Mickey's Philhar-Magic.* Just before the gates open for the masses, you'll hear a bit of music and an announcement that quotes Walt Disney's dedication of the park; the speech ends with a polite request that visitors walk slowly and carefully into the park. Of course, the crowds will stampede wildly instead.

Whether you walk or run, if you are anywhere near the front of the waiting line when the gates

MUST-SEES

Space Mountain
(Tomorrowland)

Buzz Lightyear's Space Ranger Spin
(Tomorrowland)

The Laugh Floor Comedy Club
(Tomorrowland)

Tomorrowland Indy Speedway
(Tomorrowland)

It's a Small World
(Fantasyland)

The Many Adventures of Winnie the Pooh
(Fantasyland)

Mickey's PhilharMagic
(Fantasyland)

Mickey's and Minnie's Country Houses
(Mickey's Toontown Fair)

The Haunted Mansion
(Liberty Square)

Pirates of the Caribbean
(Adventureland)

Jungle Cruise
(Adventureland)

Big Thunder Mountain Railroad
(Frontierland)

Splash Mountain
(Frontierland)

Tom Sawyer Island
(Frontierland)

Power Trip: A Fastpass Plan

For years a big crowd at the Magic Kingdom guaranteed big lines and long waits at the most popular attractions. There are few things less appealing to a four-year-old than waiting an hour for a ride on Winnie the Pooh, a teenager chilling out in a slow-moving queue for Space Mountain, or an adult stuck in the very slow lane at the corral on the dock at the Jungle Cruise.

In years past we have offered detailed battle plans to visitors to help them beat the crowds. We're happy to report that, for the most part, Disney has come to the rescue of its guests with the creation of the Fastpass, a system that lets visitors reserve a time for a popular ride. Fastpass is not perfect, but it's a whole lot better than life without it.

Here's how it works: You insert your admission ticket into a reader at special booths near attractions and receive a Fastpass ticket imprinted with an assigned time period. When you return, you'll enter a special gateway to the attraction with a promise of no more than a fifteen-minute wait. You can't get another Fastpass for two hours or until after your appointed time, whichever comes first. (For attractions that offer the Fastpass ticket, look for the ≡*FAST* icon in this book.)

Disney sometimes adjusts the availability of Fastpass tickets depending on the crowd levels at the park. Waiting times for the major rides are listed on a board near the Plaza Restaurant, just outside the entrance to Frontierland and Adventureland at the top of Main Street, U.S.A. Cast a quick eye on the waiting times when you first arrive to help adjust your Power Trip, and check it out anytime you're in the neighborhood. Your goal: Go where the crowds are not. So the Power Trip for Walt Disney World works like this:

1. Start by coming up with a list of the attractions you most want to see.
2. Divide the list into Fastpass attractions and waiting-line attractions.
3. Get to the park as early as you can.
4. Begin your day by making a beeline to the first Fastpass attraction on your list and grab a ticket.

On busy days the gates will open about thirty minutes before the park itself; you will be able to stroll to a rope barrier at the top of Main Street. On extremely busy days attractions may be open earlier than officially announced.

At busy times of the year, your first Fastpass reservation will tell you to come back in an hour or two; later in the day, the gap may extend to several hours. Now put your Fastpass in your pocket and head for the first attraction on your non-Fastpass list. With a bit of luck, you can ping-pong back and forth between ride reservations and waiting lines.

We've already suggested you arrive early. You should also plan to eat lunch and dinner early in order to avoid lines and to take advantage of a break in the crowds when the rest of the world is chowing down. Another reduction in crowds at attractions comes during the daily parades, shows, and fireworks.

(continued)

Depending on how crowded the park is, you may want to go back after dark for a repeat on a few of the rides. I especially like after-dark rides on Big Thunder Mountain and the Jungle Cruise. You can also catch some of the story rides at Fantasyland and (for the hopelessly romantic or the hopelessly child-directed) It's a Small World. During peak season and holidays you will still be able to catch the late performance of the fireworks show to end your day with a bang.

open, you should be able to get onto any ride in the park with no more than a fifteen-minute wait, which is about as good as it gets. Or try this: Enter the park before the opening, and go up to the Disney World Railroad platform; you'll find a train that will depart the moment the park officially opens. Ride to the Splash Mountain station and get off and into line; you should be able to beat most of the thundering horde racing across the park on foot.

A general rule for any part of Walt Disney World is to head immediately for the ride or rides you expect will have the longest lines and get them out of the way early. Even better, grab a Fastpass for your number-one target on your way to the second attraction on your list; with a bit of luck you should be able to ride both attractions within the first hour you're at the park. Then go on as many other major attractions as you can before the lines become too long. Spend the afternoon visiting lesser attractions, and then go back to major draws at the end of the day as the crowds lessen and the parades and fireworks pull people out of line.

ATTRACTIONS AT THE MAGIC KINGDOM

■ MAIN STREET, U.S.A.

Somewhere, someplace, at some time, there was an America like this. It's a place of small stores with friendly proprietors, where the streets are clean and the landscape neat, and where a paper scrap never lingers on the ground. At the start of your visit to the Magic Kingdom, you'll think of Main Street, U.S.A., as an interesting place to walk through on the way to somewhere else. But be sure to leave time to come back later to browse, shop, or eat. If you are following our advice, you will have arrived early at the park with a specific destination in mind.

Main Street is a fanciful version of Disney's birthplace of Marcelline, Missouri, at about the turn of the twentieth century—about the time of the arrival of electricity. If you look around carefully, you'll note a mixture of old gas lighting and some newfangled electrical lamps and devices.

Disney conceived of his theme park as an extension of his movies and cartoons. As you approach the entrance to Walt Disney World, the train station blocks the view of Main Street, U.S.A., like a curtain at a movie theater. After guests pass through the turnstiles, they walk through the tunnel beneath the rail-

MAGIC KINGDOM

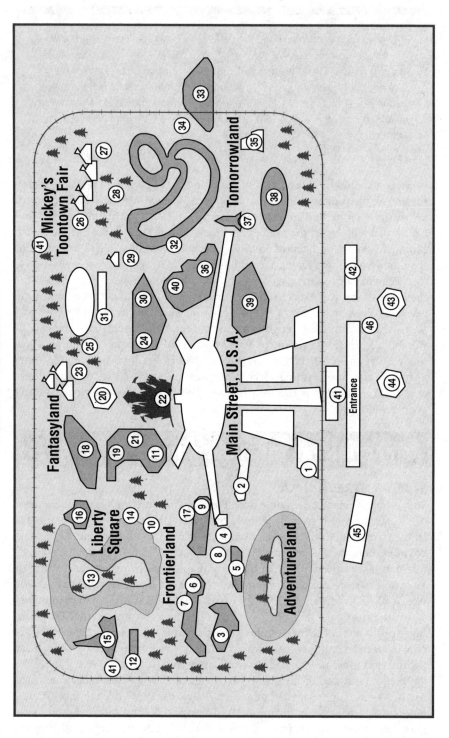

MAGIC KINGDOM

① City Hall	㉖ Toontown Hall of Fame
② First Aid	㉗ Mickey's and Minnie's Country
③ Pirates of the Caribbean	Houses
④ Swiss Family Treehouse	㉘ The Barnstormer at Goofy's Wiseacre
⑤ Jungle Cruise	Farm
⑥ Enchanted Tiki Room	㉙ Mad Tea Party
⑦ Country Bear Jamboree	㉚ The Many Adventures of Winnie the
⑧ The Magic Carpets of Aladdin	Pooh
⑨ Diamond Horseshoe Saloon Revue	㉛ Fantasyland Character Festival
⑩ Liberty Square Riverboat	㉜ Tomorrowland Indy Speedway
⑪ The Hall of Presidents	㉝ Space Mountain
⑫ Splash Mountain	㉞ Tomorrowland Transit Authority
⑬ Tom Sawyer Island	㉟ Tomorrowland Stage
⑭ Mike Fink Keelboats	㊱ Stitch's Great Escape!
⑮ Big Thunder Mountain Railroad	㊲ Astro Orbiter
⑯ The Haunted Mansion	㊳ Carousel of Progress
⑰ Frontierland Shootin' Arcade	㊴ The Laugh Floor Comedy Club
⑱ It's a Small World	㊵ Buzz Lightyear's Space Ranger Spin
⑲ Peter Pan's Flight	㊶ Walt Disney World Railroad stations
⑳ Cinderella's Golden Carrousel	㊷ Magic Kingdom bus transportation
㉑ *Mickey's PhilharMagic*	㊸ Ferryboat to parking
㉒ Cinderella Castle	㊹ Boats to Discovery Island and Fort
㉓ Dumbo the Flying Elephant	Wilderness
㉔ Snow White's Scary Adventures	㊺ Monorail station
㉕ Ariel's Grotto	㊻ Stroller rental

road and then emerge into a new world very different from the one they left on the other side of the curtain.

And then as you walk up Main Street, look up at the windows on the left and right side to see the "credits" for some of the artists, producers, directors, and executives responsible for the creation and growth of Walt Disney World and the Disney Company.

One of the most prominent credits is for Roy O. Disney, who came out of retirement to complete the construction of Walt Disney World after his older brother, Walt, died in 1966. His window is on the right side of Main Street as you face the castle, above the Confectionery.

Also on the right side, above the Main Street Market House, is a salute to the team that secretly purchased thousands of acres of Florida land in the 1960s in preparation for the creation of Walt Disney World. By using shell companies, Disney was able to buy land at a much lower cost than would have been possible if sellers had known of the major plans for a resort. Under the humorous sign M. T. LOTT REAL ESTATE INVESTMENTS are some of the shell companies set up by Disney: Bay Lake Properties, Reedy Creek Ranch Lands, Ayefour Corporation, and Tomahawk Properties.

A barbershop quartet catches a lift on a horse-drawn trolley heading up Main Street, U.S.A.

Above the bakery is a window saluting early Disney animator Ub Iwerks and his son Don Iwerks. On a side alley near the Uptown Jewelers is a window for Elias Disney, Contractor; Elias was Walt and Roy's father. The credit for the man behind the mouse himself is at the end of Main Street, above the Ice Cream Parlor and facing the castle. It reads: WALTER E. DISNEY GRADUATE SCHOOL OF DESIGN & MASTER PLANNING.

Baseball fans should make a pilgrimage to Casey's Corner at the top end of Main Street on the left side as you face the castle. In and around the fast-food restaurant and merchandise for sale there, you'll find an impressive collection of baseball memorabilia from the early 1900s; many of the items come from western Massachusetts in the Springfield, Chicopee, and Athol areas.

Main Street Vehicles

Old-fashioned cars, a horse-drawn trolley, and fire engines move slowly down Main Street to Cinderella Castle. (Following not far behind the horses are uniformed sanitation engineers with shovels.)

You'll find a set of leather and cloth catcher's gear, old bats and balls, and period baseball cards. Check out the unusual photograph of Babe Ruth in midswing, taken from high above in the stands. Advertising material includes a rare commercial endorsement from an umpire, Frank (Silk) O'Loughlin, who tells of his support for a particular brand of old soda: "After a hard game, I feel there is nothing that will relieve fatigue and quench thirst like Coca-Cola."

Photography fans may also want to visit the Main Street Exposition near the railroad station. A Kodak-sponsored exhibit includes a large collection of old cameras dating from the 1890s, including early Brownies. You'll also learn about a Kodak promotion in 1930 where the company gave away 500,000 No. 2 Hawk-Eye cameras to children whose twelfth birthday took place that year.

You'll also find some settings that allow kids of all ages to pose with Disney icons, including alongside Mickey at the wheel of his steamboat; nearby are some interactive computer screens that quiz visitors about Disney history.

One place worth stopping before you begin your exploration is City Hall in Town Square. Step up to the counter to obtain schedules of entertainment and appearances by Disney characters; maps in English, French, German, Spanish, or braille; written show descriptions for visitors with special needs; and other information. City Hall opens when the ticket gates open (up to half an hour or so before the rope is dropped at the top of Main Street), allowing you to make a quick stop there before you join the dash to Space Mountain, Splash Mountain, or Dumbo—or whatever's your immediate pleasure.

Main Street is also the place to be if you are a parade fan; the entertainment moves toward the railroad station just inside the gates, which may be the best seat in the house from which to watch the parade. You can also see the parades at the circle near Cinderella Castle and on the streets of Frontierland, both of which are nearer the major attractions of the park. A secret and slightly less crowded spot from which to watch parades is near the exit from Pirates of the Caribbean and the entrance to Splash Mountain near the Pecos Bill Cafe. A pathway under the railroad is the start or end of most parades. The famous Disney parades change every few years, and in high season there may be as many as three parades a day—an afternoon Disney character parade and two evening electrical events.

Parades and Fireworks

Think Disney theme park, and think magical parades of music and light and favorite characters in fanciful carriages.

The parades, which involve massive floats, choreography, and advanced technology along with a cast of hundreds, usually

The Firehouse on Main Street

Closing Time

Closing time varies according to the season and is sometimes adjusted from day to day based on attendance patterns; it can be as early as 6:00 P.M. or as late as midnight. Check at the park for details. The announced closing time is actually a relative thing, usually meaning the time when the last person is allowed to join a ride line. The parks themselves are cleared out about an hour or so after then, and the final bus or other transportation to parking lots or hotels leaves about ninety minutes after closing time.

are changed every few years and sometimes make triumphal return engagements, which is the case with the classic **SpectroMagic,** which returned in 2005 and ran through all of 2006 as the nighttime parade.

Designed as a moving gallery for audiences along a darkened parade route, the high-tech show creates a moving tableau of pixies and peacocks, sea horses and flying horses, flower gardens and fountains. The show is led by Mickey Mouse, of course, dressed in an amber and purple grand magician's cape and surrounded by a confetti of lights.

The twenty-minute parade, presented on selected nights, uses about 100 miles of fiber-optic cables and 600,000 lights to create its magic. Some thirty computers control the show, and a sequence of electronic triggers along the route activates the audio and visual effects.

In recent years, the Magic Kingdom's daily afternoon moveable spectacle was the **Share a Dream Come True Parade,** featuring one hundred Disney characters, beginning with Mickey Mouse and ending with a fairy-tale finish. Each of the parade's eight major floats features a high acrylic snow globe that encases a Disney star and friends. Among the globes is "It Was All Started by a Mouse," featuring Mickey Mouse and his friends Minnie Mouse and Goofy, along with eleven sculpted figures of Mickey from some of his greatest hits over the years, including *Steamboat Willie, The Brave Little Tailor, Plane Crazy, Mickey's Christmas Carol,* and Sorceror Mickey from *Fantasia.*

"Face the Darkest Fears" brings to Main Street many of the most evil of Disney villains. The Evil Queen from *Snow White and the Seven Dwarfs* rides within a globe, while an 18-foot-tall inflatable Chernabog from the "Night on Bald Mountain" sequence of *Fantasia* hovers overhead. Other nasties surrounding the float include Jafar from *Aladdin,* Malificent from *Sleeping Beauty,* Cruella de Vil from *101 Dalmatians,* and Ursula from *The Little Mermaid.*

"A Dream Is a Wish Your Heart Makes" is a float that features three globes, each holding a famous Disney prince and princess: Cinderella and Prince Charming, Belle and the Beast, and Ariel and Prince Eric. The fairy godmother from *Cinderella* and Flounder and Sebastian from *The Little Mermaid* hover around the globes.

Jiminy Cricket, with a bit of help from the Blue Fairy, narrates the fabulous nightly fireworks show, **Wishes,** a favorite that has been playing at the park for several years. The dazzling twelve-minute display weaves a thrilling story in the sky with hundreds of brilliant pyrotechnic effects exploding above and around Cinderella Castle. Presented most nights, the show includes 683 individual pyrotechnic effects.

Wishes features several new locations for launching fireworks that create brilliant bursts of light around Cinderella Castle, plus pyrotechnic effects never seen before in a Disney theme park, including several developed especially for the show. The show's "wishing star" crests approximately 100 feet above the castle's bright spires. The Blue Fairy is represented by a spectacular star-shaped shell that "paints" each wish high in the sky.

Wishes tells the story of making a wish come true, using classic Disney songs and character voices accompanied by meticulously choreographed fireworks. Among the audio stars are Jiminy Cricket, the Blue Fairy, and Pinocchio; Snow White and the Evil Queen; Cinderella; Ariel from *The Little Mermaid*; Aladdin and Genie; and Tinker Bell and Peter Pan, who flies from atop Cinderella Castle in one of the highlights of the show.

Schedules for parades and fireworks are adjusted based on season and how late the park is open. A typical prime-season calendar would call for an afternoon parade at 3:00 P.M. and a nighttime parade at 9:00 P.M., capped off by fireworks at 10:00 P.M. At the busiest times of the year, when there are special evening hours for guests at Disney resorts, there may be a third nighttime parade, after the fireworks.

Walt Disney World Railroad

A pleasant way to tour the park (our favorite way to end a day), these real steam engines take passengers on a 1.5-mile, thirty-minute circuit of the park. The four engines that are part of the Magic Kingdom's rolling stock were built by the Baldwin Locomotive Works of Philadelphia in the early decades of the twentieth

The Walt Disney World Railroad at Main Street, U.S.A.

century, but they spent much of their working lives in Mexico's Yucatan peninsula hauling sugar cane. The wheels, side rods, and other major parts of the engines are original, although the boilers and cabs have been rebuilt. Originally constructed to burn coal or wood and later converted to oil, the steam engines are now powered by diesel fuel.

Walt Disney was a railroad nut, even running a small-scale system in his own backyard. The *Lilly Belle,* named for Disney's wife, was built in 1928, coincidentally the same year Mickey Mouse made his screen debut. Also on the tracks is the *Roy O. Disney,* named for the boss's brother; the *Walter E. Disney,* named for the man himself; and the less-often-seen *Roger Broggie,* christened after a long-time Disney employee and friend.

The recorded spiel of the conductor has become politically correct in recent years, removing references to marauding Indians and instead extolling the friendly Native Americans waiting to greet visitors. Disney engineers and conductors use traditional railroad whistle signals for communication:

1 short blast: attention;

2 short blasts: ready to leave the station;

2 long, 1 short, 1 long: train approaching a station;

1 long, 1 short, 2 long: train leaving a station; and

4 long blasts: train in distress.

Cinderella Castle

The hallmark of the Magic Kingdom, Cinderella Castle matches every child's mind's-eye image of a fairy-tale castle. It sits at the focal center of the park, marking the top of Main Street, U.S.A., and the entranceway to Fantasyland. It is especially handsome at night, bathed in colored light.

Meeting Places

Try not to select the front of Cinderella Castle as a meeting place for family members who go their own way within the park; it's just way too obvious and not very effective. This location can become quite crowded during the daily parades and other events. Instead, choose the back side of the castle near the carousel or a landmark off the parade route.

The castle is loosely based on Sleeping Beauty's castle from the fairy tale and the Disney movie that brought it to life. It is built of fiberglass and steel beams; not a single brick or stone was used in its construction. Cinderella Castle is 189 feet tall—9 feet higher than Spaceship Earth in Epcot. At Disneyland in Anaheim, California, the original bastion is Sleeping Beauty Castle. It is much smaller; it towers a mere 71 feet tall.

Cinderella Castle was designed as a fanciful composite of French courts such as Fontainebleau, Versailles, and several chateaux of the Loire Valley. Its base evokes the Romanesque architecture of medieval fortresses from the eleventh through thirteenth centuries, while its upper portion is reminiscent of the Gothic styles of Renaissance-era castles.

As part of the commemoration of the fiftieth anniversary of Disneyland, Cinderella Castle was dressed up in party clothes, a transformation inspired by the works of Renaissance artisans of the fifteenth and sixteenth centuries along with a nod to the rich legacy of Disney animated films. The castle was draped with touches of golden trim, rose swags, bunting, and swirling bands of "pixie dust" encircling its blue spires.

Way up top in one of the towers is a small apartment originally intended for Walt Disney and his family, but it was never used. We're told plans were drawn for a place for guests to stay within the castle as part of the park's twenty-fifth anniversary gala; among the problems was how to deal with the fact that guests would have to be inside the park after hours. One solution called for the assignment of a personal escort for all guests, which wouldn't have been too big of a deal because room rates were expected to be several thousand dollars per night. In any case, it never happened, and the rooms within remain unfinished.

You can, though, go halfway up the tower to **Cinderella's Royal Table** for a theme-park theme

Cinderella Castle

breakfast or lunch; reservations are usually required. And be sure to check out the elaborate mosaics in the entranceway; they tell the familiar story of the girl with the glass slipper in Italian glass, real silver, and gold. The coat of arms above the castle on the north wall (facing Fantasyland) is that of the Disney family. Outside the entrance to King Stefan's Banquet Hall are plaques for other Disney executives.

■ TOMORROWLAND

When Tomorrowland was originally conceived, it was as a showcase of the future. Ironically, the world of tomorrow at the Magic Kingdom eventually became the most dated and tired part of the park. In 1995 Tomorrowland underwent the most complete remake of an original area at any Disney park. Today's Tomorrowland looks forward and backward at the same time: The setting is somewhat like a Buck Rogers's science fiction movie of the 1920s and 1930s.

Only in the world of Disney could a place begin way out in the future, fall way behind the times, and then be remade at a cost of millions so that it appears to be a 1930s view of the twenty-first century. The concept was first tried out at Disneyland Paris; a similar remake was undertaken at Disneyland in California. Tomorrowland has been recast as an Interplanetary Convention Center. Space Mountain is now the headquarters for the Intergalactic Tracking Network, and Stitch's Great Escape! is the home away from home for the playfully difficult alien Stitch. Gliding overhead are the trains of the Tomorrowland Transit Authority.

MUST-SEE Space Mountain ≡FAST

Every Disney visitor with a bit of spunk—and his or her mom and dad—has to visit Tomorrowland at least once to catch a rocket ship to Ryca 1. Space Mountain is the big enchilada, the highmost high, the place where hundreds of Magic Kingdom visitors have dropped their eyeglasses, cameras, and hairpieces. It is also one of the most popular of all of the attractions at Walt Disney World (as is the similar—but not identical—ride at Disneyland; another version with an upside-down loop, named Discovery Mountain and based on Jules Verne's book From the Earth to the Moon, is at Disneyland Paris).

Space Mountain is a masterpiece of Disney Imagineering, merging a relatively small and slow (top speed of about 28 miles per hour) roller coaster with an outer-space theme. The small cars zoom around indoors in near-total darkness, the only light coming from the projected images of stars and planets on the ceiling. The ride is a triumph of scene setting, the amusement park equivalent of a big-budget movie's special effects. The cars feel like they are moving much faster than they are because you have no point of reference in the dark. The cars do not turn upside down. This is a ride where the rules of physics apply; the heavier the riders on the train, the faster it will travel—but only up to the limits set by controls on the track.

Lockers

Store extra clothing and other items at one of the coin-operated lockers beneath the Main Street Railroad Station and at the Transportation and Ticket Center. Lockers rent for about $7.00 per day, plus a $2.00 key deposit. Your one-day rental can be transferred to Epcot or Disney–MGM Studios; consult the attendant.

As you enter, you'll see a chart of the FX-1 Intergalactic Tracking Network, representing some of the launches and satellites of a future civilization. When you finally reach the loading area for the ride—the final queue that can give you twenty more minutes of exquisite teasing torture before you are loaded into your spaceship—check out the video monitors hanging from the ceiling. The televisions bring you reports from PNN—the Planetary News Network. You'll hear from the Hubble Traffic scanner on traffic congestion on Route 4066 in the outer galaxy. Wendy Beryllium's weather report calls for a toasty 620 degrees on Mercury and a chilly negative 360 degrees on Neptune. The extended forecast for planet Earth calls for partly cloudy skies, rising oceans, and a giant comet smashing into the planet sometime in the next hundred million years. There's a report on the construction of the Mall of Mars. And if you hang on long enough, you will get to see an episode in the lifestyles of the rich and alien. Be sure to catch the wild ads from Crazy Larry, the used spaceship dealer. What a deal: free floor mats with any intergalactic cruiser!

Overhead, a projector paints the pictures of huge rolling asteroids; you will not be the first to observe that they look like close-ups of chocolate-chip cookies. Disney has never revealed its recipe, although Imagineers insist that the rocks are based on scientific research and are totally nonfattening. Finally, you'll reach the busy launching pad packed with technicians and engineers loading spacecraft.

There are two tracks within the building, and the ride is slightly different on each; the left side has more sharp turns, while the right side has more sharp dips. The waiting line splits into left and right queues as you enter the loading area. Each train seats six persons, one behind the other.

Professional Space Mountain riders—and they are legion—will argue over which seat affords the best ride. The last seat seems to benefit from a "whip" effect as the cars make sharp turns; we prefer the very front chair, where you don't have the back of someone else's head to mar the illusion of space travel and there is a terrific blast of onrushing air as you move on the track. At busy times you probably will not be able to cajole an attendant into allowing you to select the seat of your choice; late at night or on the occasional slow day you might be in luck. It doesn't hurt to ask, politely.

Do keep a hand on your personal belongings; wrap camera and purse straps around your feet and make sure children are properly beneath the restraining bar. (Disney launch technicians will double-check the safety arrangements, too.) And then it's over. The ride is about two minutes and forty seconds in length, and it's nowhere near as fast or as wild as a major roller coaster such as the Rock 'n' Roller Coaster at Disney–MGM Studios, or the even bigger The Hulk or Dueling Dragons at Universal Studios Islands of Adventure in Orlando. But Space Mountain has that certain Disney touch that keeps visitors coming back again and again to wait in line for their next space voyage.

Now, speaking of lines: They can easily extend to ninety minutes or more on a busy afternoon. The general rule to avoid long lines at the Magic Kingdom especially applies here. Get to the ride when the gates first open and you may be able to stroll right on board, or come back to the ride at the end of the day. Another somewhat quiet time is during the dinner hour, from about 6:00 to 7:00 P.M. Another option is to take advantage of Disney's Fastpass system and reserve your spaceflight ahead of time.

Transit Tips

Check out the world of transportation at the right corner of the Space Mountain building near the Carousel of Progress. In one spot you can see the Disney steam train, the modern monorail, and the electric Tomorrowland Transit Authority cars; to your left is the earthbound Tomorrowland Speedway; and above it all are the Astro Orbiters. And don't forget the ride itself—the rocket ships on rails within Space Mountain. Past visitors may look up and miss something: The Skyway no longer crosses the park. It was retired in 1999.

Lost and Found

A family of four touring Walt Disney World for four days and not losing at least one backpack, two sets of sunglasses, and three hats is unlike any we know. On the day of a loss, check at City Hall in the Magic Kingdom or Guest Services at Epcot, Animal Kingdom, or Disney–MGM Studios. After a day, items are taken to a central office at the Transportation and Ticket Center.

If both tracks are operating, a crowd backed up to the front door means a wait of about an hour; sometimes, though, attendants will build up the line outside while the inside queues clear out. This is often done at the end of the day to discourage huge crowds as closing hour approaches.

Children younger than three cannot ride Space Mountain, and kids under seven must be accompanied by an adult. All riders must be at least 44 inches tall, and pregnant women and those with back or health problems are advised against riding. Space Mountain, along with other major rides at Walt Disney World such as Big Thunder Mountain Railroad and Splash Mountain, offers a "switch off" arrangement if not all of the people in your party want to ride the coaster, or if you are traveling with a child too young or too small to ride. Inform the attendant at the turnstile near the launching area that you want to switch off; one parent or adult can ride Space Mountain and change places with another at the exit so everyone can take a turn.

▌MUST-SEE▐ Buzz Lightyear's Space Ranger Spin ≡FAST

It's *Toy Story* live, in a ride that combines a zippy dark ride with a shooting gallery. You'll be teamed with astro-superhero Buzz Lightyear on a daring mission to rescue the universe's crystollic fusion cell supply (better known as batteries) from the clutches of the evil Emperor Zurg.

You'll be assigned to your personal two-seater XP-37 Space Cruiser, spinning through ten scenes of toys, asteroids and meteors, and strange and wondrous aliens in the Gamma Quadrant. Each car includes a joystick to spin the car and a pair of infrared laser guns to knock down all manner of threats by Zurg—basically, shoot any and all of the orange Emperor Zurg insignias scattered throughout the ride. When your laser hits a target, it triggers animation, sound, and light effects, and your score—which varies according to the complexity of the shot—is tallied on an LED screen on the cruiser's dashboard. The final scene takes you through a tunnel of energy, a fun holdover from the Take Flight attraction, which was the former occupant of the building. Each space ranger's score is tallied electronically and displayed on an LED screen on the cruiser's dashboard. As cruisers complete the mission, guests compare their score with the mission profile chart to determine their space-ranger rank.

At a Disney press event, I rode through the Gamma Quadrant with Buzz Aldrin, the famed NASA astronaut (does the name Buzz Lightyear ring a bell?). Aldrin scored pretty well on the ride, by the way, reaching the Planetary Explorer level, which seemed right.

Stitch's Great Escape! ≡*FAST*

Experiment 626, of unknown origin and species, is on the loose after escaping the interstellar custody of Prison Transport Durgon. You may know him better as Stitch, and he is considered four-armed and mischievous . . . and somehow on the loose in the Magic Kingdom.

Once you're in the doors, you learn you have been recruited by the Galactic Federation Grand Council to help guard Stitch. You are a Prisoner Teleportation Officer, guard number 90210 (a little Rodeo Drive joke there, in case you miss the zip code.)

"Welcome, recruits," you're told. "We commend you on your decision to join us as guards." Your assignment is simple: Differentiate between the nice and the naughty.

You've been given a simple little task as a rookie: escorting a Level 2 common criminal of the cosmos, a jaywalker between the moons of Jupiter. All of the "volunteers" are locked into a slightly confining chair. A "scanner" checks you over head to toe to assure that your personal DNA does not get mixed up with that of the prisoner.

But don't you just know it: Something goes wrong. Stitch escapes. In the darkness he steals a chili dog from the hands of a guest in the room . . . and belches a fragrant announcement of his presence. After a wild chase in the dark, Stitch is cornered and the guards are released from protective custody.

Stitch's Great Escape! replaced the darker and scarier ExtraTERRORestrial Alien Encounter with a lighter and more family-friendly show that is loosely based on Disney's Academy Award–nominated film *Lilo & Stitch*. This marks the first time a film made at Walt Disney World provides the story line for an attraction, and one of the fastest turnarounds from movie to ride. Alien Encounter itself replaced the hopelessly outdated Mission to Mars show (so old, it was originally called Voyage to the Moon). There are two theaters, each seating 134 persons; visitors must be at least 48 inches tall.

▓▓▓▓ *MUST-SEE* The Laugh Floor Comedy Club

A high-tech, high-laughter interactive adventure based on Disney-Pixar's *Monsters, Inc.* When the attraction (which replaces *The Timekeeper*) opens in 2007, guests will match wits with the one-eyed hero, Mike Wazowski, and his friends.

Tomorrowland Transit Authority

Trains of twenty-passenger cars of the Tomorrowland Transit Authority Metroliner circle slowly above Tomorrowland, offering a brief peek into Space Mountain (a good way for the faint of heart to get some idea of what the excitement is about) and an even briefer glimpse of Buzz Lightyear's Space Ranger Spin.

World's Fair Fare

Disney was involved in four major pavilions at the 1964–1965 New York World's Fair, including Pepsi's "It's a Small World—A Salute to UNICEF" ride, General Electric's "Carousel of Progress," the Illinois pavilion's "Great Moments with Mr. Lincoln," and Ford's "Magic Skyway" ride. The first three were later recycled for use at Disney parks: "It's a Small World" was moved to Disneyland and became the model for very similar and popular rides at Walt Disney World, Tokyo Disneyland, and Disneyland Paris. The GE "Carousel" was moved to Walt Disney World; it was updated a bit in 1994 but remains essentially unchanged. "Great Moments with Mr. Lincoln" was Disney's first big success with audio-animatronics and was moved to Disneyland's Main Street, where it played for many years.

The former WEDway PeopleMover, reworked a bit as part of the remake of Tomorrowland, loads at **Rockettower Plaza.** The PeopleMover is a pet project of the Magic Kingdom, demonstrating an unusual means of propulsion—the linear induction motor. The track and the car form a motor together, as magnetic pulses pull the car down a flat coil.

There is rarely a significant line for this ten-minute ride, which we find to be about seven minutes too long. Still, it's a seat and a bit of a view.

Astro Orbiter

This basic amusement-park ride has rotating rockets and an up/down lever, but in typical Disney fashion it seems like much more. Nowhere near as threatening (to some) as Space Mountain, it nevertheless is not for people with a fear of heights.

As part of the overall remake of Tomorrowland, the ride was rebuilt and is now one of the most recognizable features of that section of the park, with the Jules Verne theme of rotating planets and moons. It is especially impressive at night. If you think about it, Astro Orbiter is a slightly faster and somewhat higher version of Dumbo, the Flying Elephant.

Carousel of Progress

The future ain't what it used to be, which was very evident as the Carousel of Progress grew further and further out of date in the 1980s. Its concept of the future had moved into the past.

This ride, originally presented at the 1964–1965 World's Fair in New York, tells of the march of technology in American homes. It was interesting in 1964 and quaint in 1984 but hopelessly outdated in the 1990s. In 1994 a slightly updated version of the show debuted, featuring the voice of the late, lamented raconteur Jean Shepherd. The basic Carousel is unchanged; theater seats revolve around a stationary central core populated by audio-animatronic robots. The first few scenes of the show are from the earlier version, with added narration by Shepherd and the original theme song.

The show starts in the early twentieth century as electricity makes its appearance in the home; the second scene takes place at the time of Charles Lindbergh in the 1920s, and then we move on to the promising 1940s. (Many adults will be amused to see a working vibrating-belt exercise machine like those that were popular into the early 1950s.) The fourth stage setting takes us a few years beyond the current day. A young boy loans his grandmother his virtual-reality game, which she takes over; the latest minor tweak to the show gives her an electronic glove. When Grandma calls out her score of 975, the voice-actuated oven burns the turkey.

Even with the small amount of updating, it is still worth noting that the Carousel is an all-white, middle-class world and not all that thrilling, and also one in which Dad is still pretty much the indisputable king of the castle. Note the eyes on the various robot dogs in each scene—the dog is the best actor in the troupe.

The best seat is down front in the center of the auditorium. Note that the Carousel operates during busy times of the year only and may have limited hours any day.

Robo-Stars

Disney claims that the Carousel of Progress has had more performances than any other stage show in the history of America. Of course, it's not really a stage show because all the actors have electric motors.

MUST-SEE Tomorrowland Indy Speedway

Every kid we know dreams of getting behind the wheel of Mommy's or Daddy's car; most adults we know dream of taking a spin around a racecourse. Perhaps that is why this attraction, which doesn't have all that much to do with Tomorrowland that we can think of, is such a popular destination. In 2000 the course received a bit of a face-lift, adding an Indy theme including a brickyard starting line and a position pole.

There are four parallel tracks of about half a mile each, and the little race cars have real gasoline engines that will propel them forward at up to a zippy 7 miles per hour. The steering gear works, too, allowing the driver to move the car left

Tomorrowland Indy Speedway

and right down the course, although there is a center rail that will keep the car from completely leaving the track.

Children must be at least 52 inches tall to ride in one of the cars alone; otherwise their feet won't reach the gas pedal. Mom or Dad, though, can sit alongside and press the pedal while junior happily steers. Waiting lines can reach to nearly an hour on the most crowded days; visit the track early or late to make the best use of your time. A circuit takes about four minutes.

Other Attractions in Tomorrowland
Galaxy Palace Theater. An outdoor theater located between the Transportarium and the Carousel of Progress, used for live shows.

Tomorrowland Arcade. The fanciful power station for the world of the future, located at the exit from Space Mountain, also contains a good-size video arcade, minus any first-person shooting games. Disney designers again looked backward to the rounded, streamlined architecture of the Art Deco 1930s for their presentation of the future.

■ FANTASYLAND
This is the stuff of young dreams: Dumbo, Peter Pan, Alice in Wonderland, Snow White, and the toy riot of It's a Small World. Fantasyland is a bright and cheerful place, decorated in splashes of color and sprinkled with snippets of song. Visible above it all is Cinderella Castle (described already in the section about Main Street, U.S.A.).

Dumbo the Flying Elephant
Disney began with an ordinary amusement-park ride, making it into something very special for the littlest guests. Riders sit in fiberglass elephants, which can be

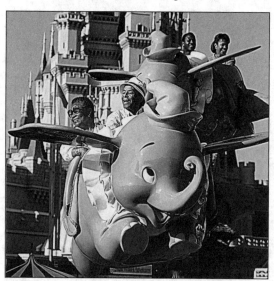

Dumbo the Flying Elephant. © *Disney Enterprises, Inc.*

moved up and down as they circle a mirrored ball and the statue of Timothy Mouse, the very clever rodent who is Dumbo's manager in the classic Disney animated movie. Sixteen Dumbos go around a golden crown with a set of gears and pinwheels, like a kid's drawing of a fantastic machine.

This ride has always been a huge lure for young children, with lines of up to an hour for the ninety-second ride. If your kids insist on an elephant-back ride, head for Dumbo early or late in the day.

One rite of passage, we suspect, is the day the kids tell you they're willing to skip the lines for Dumbo and would rather make a second pass at Space Mountain.

In recent years Disney has added two similar rides elsewhere at Walt Disney World: The Magic Carpets of Aladdin in the Magic Kingdom's Adventureland, and TriceraTop Spin at Disney's Animal Kingdom.

Cinderella's Golden Carrousel

One of the few mostly "real" things in this world of fantasy, Cinderella's Golden Carrousel was built in 1917 for the Detroit Palace Garden Park and later ridden by generations of kids at Maplewood Olympic Park in New Jersey. Many of the horses are hand-carved originals, although the herd has been augmented with some fiberglass replicas, and the overhead canopy has been Disneyfied with images from Disney films. None of the horses are identical. The musical organ, which plays selections from hit movies, is an Italian original. The lines for the two-minute ride ebb and flow; I'd suggest you wait for the times when you can walk right on board.

▐MUST-SEE▐ It's a Small World

It's every little girl's wildest dream: a world of beautiful dancing dolls from all over the world. There is nothing to get your heart beating here, but even the most cynical—including little boys and adults—will probably find something to smile about in this upbeat boat ride. We especially enjoy the animatronic cancan dancers.

The ride underwent a major refurbishment from May 2004 into the spring of 2005, reopening with state-of-the-art animatronics, sound, and music.

This eleven-minute ride was originally designed for the 1964–1965 World's Fair in New York, but unlike the Carousel of Progress, the Small World ride has maintained its timeless appeal. The sound system was updated and improved in recent years. The boats are large and the lines move pretty quickly (if two queues are being formed, the line to the left moves a bit faster), but we'd advise coming to this attraction early or late in the day. Children who like this ride will probably also enjoy the shorter Rivers of Time ride at the Mexican pavilion of Epcot.

Peter Pan's Flight ≡FAST

This is a mellow excursion into some of the scenes from Disney's version of the story of the little boy who doesn't want to grow up. Riders sit in a small pirate ship that suspends them a foot or so off the floor. Everyone's favorite scene is the overhead view of London by night, which does a pretty good job of simulating Peter's flight.

While this ride is strictly for kids, at Disneyland Paris a jazzed-up version is one of the more popular attractions; not so at the Magic Kingdom, although lines still reach to forty-five minutes or more on busy days.

Mad Tea Party

This is a Disney version of a common amusement-park ride in which circular cars move around a track and also spin on platforms. If it sounds dizzying, that's because it is: The very young and others with sensitive stomachs might prefer the carousel across the way.

However, the riders have some control over how fast the cups spin; grab hold of the wheel in the center of the cup and don't let go of it for the least movement.

The ride is covered with a tentlike structure, taking the cups and most of the waiting line out of the elements. The ride has been designed like a scene from Disney's classic 1951 film *Alice in Wonderland*. Our favorite part is the drunken mouse who pops out of the teapot in the center. The ride itself is only about ninety seconds long; the wait can be much more than that. I'd recommend hopping on board only if lines are short.

MUST-SEE The Many Adventures of Winnie the Pooh ≡*FAST*

Oh, bother! It's a blustery day, and the pages of one of our favorite books are blowing out of the building and into Fantasyland. Welcome to a lovingly detailed step into the pages of one of the best-known children's books. Giant honey-pot vehicles carry up to six people into the pages of the book, and we begin in chapter 1, in which Pooh begins his search for honey in a very enchanted place.

"Happy Winds-day," says Gopher. "Maybe for you," replies Piglet. Pooh announces, "I'm in the mood for food," but Eeyore doubts the bear will reach the tree.

We move on to Rabbit's Garden, where Kanga holds onto Roo, flying like a kite in the wind, and into Owl's House. Then we enter the dramatic darkness of the Blustery Night, where we meet Tigger for the first time. "Come bounce with me," he invites, and so we do. Ever sat in a bouncing giant honey pot before?

One of the more dramatic scenes is Pooh's Dream, a view into his nightmare. What could he possibly fear? Why, Heffalump and Woozle honey thieves, of course. Watch for the jack-in-the-boxes. Pooh wakes up in the Floody Place, and here Disney Imagineers pull out all the stops. There's water all about, and we seem to float through the room. The only one who isn't upset about the flooding is Pooh, happy to find that the rising water allows him to float to a honey bonanza high up in a tree.

All in all, this is one honey of a ride, and a great step forward in the venerable history of Disney dark rides. Pooh takes about three and a half minutes, and sixteen to eighteen cars are on the track at any one time. I'd suggest coming early or late to avoid the crowds.

Pooh replaced an old favorite in the park, Mr. Toad's Wild Ride, based on one of Disney's more obscure films, *The Adventures of Ichabod and Mr. Toad,* which was in turn loosely based on the book *The Wind in the Willows.* As good as that ride was, this one is much better. By the way, the catchy music for the Pooh ride is by the composer of the score for *Mary Poppins* and the It's a Small World attraction.

Snow White's Scary Adventures

The word *scary* has returned to the doorway of this attraction, a tip-off to the fact that in some small ways this ride emphasizes the grimmer parts of the Brothers Grimm fairy tale, as presented in Disney's 1938 animated movie. The ride can't hold a fading candle to the spooks in the Haunted Mansion across the way in

Liberty Square, but there are a few more skeletons and witches than very young children might expect.

A remake a few years ago created a kinder, gentler Snow White, removing some of the darker elements of the ride and making the Florida version more like its California, Paris, and Tokyo cousins. Parents be warned: It's still a bit scary at the start with some ghoulish ghouls and wicked witches, but it's happier at the end. The new version uses about half of the old "sets," but now Snow White herself appears for the first time in Florida. In fact, she's there in five scenes: at the wishing well in the courtyard of the castle, in the scary forest, at the dwarf's cottage, with the Prince when he kisses her to break the witch's spell, and (of course) riding off with the Prince to live happily ever after. The revision of the show was accompanied by a 50 percent increase in capacity for the vehicles; cars now carry six passengers instead of four.

MUST-SEE *Mickey's PhilharMagic*

Mickey Mouse makes a triumphant return to the Magic Kingdom with a marvelous show of his own: Think of it as a 3-D *Fantasia* for the twenty-first century.

Well, okay, Mickey does suffer a bit of interference from his good buddy Donald, a distraction by diva Ariel from *The Little Mermaid,* a jaunty cameo by Jasmine from *Aladdin,* a twinkle from Tinker Bell, and a royal encounter with Simba of *The Lion King.*

The show is presented in the Fantasyland Concert Hall in the shadow of Cinderella Castle, the place where Mickey and all his friends visit for a bit of after-hours entertainment when the park is closed to mere mortals.

Mickey, the conductor of the orchestra, leaves the stage for a moment and for some reason leaves Donald Duck in charge. "Don't touch the hat," Mickey warns. And, of course, just like Mickey did half a century ago when he played the Sorceror's Apprentice in *Fantasia,* Donald immediately reaches for the chapeau.

The eye-popping film—Disney's first ever 3-D film created entirely in computer graphics—takes place on the largest seamless screen ever created for a 3-D screen, a 150-foot-wide canvas. When Simba tells us how he can't wait to be king in an adaptation of a scene from *The Lion King,* the image expands from the central screen to a pair of wraparound screens presenting nearly a 180-degree view. The details are vivid (you can see Donald's feathers, Ariel's scales, and Simba's fur), the sound is extreme, and special effects provide windy and watery fun that end with a duck-size blast over your shoulders.

The show uses six projectors, with the main 3-D effects on the center screen. The same film is presented at the new Hong Kong Disneyland.

Donald's voice as heard in the show was created from a classic performance from the past by Clarence "Ducky" Nash, the original voice of Donald Duck. Tony Anselmo, the current voice of Donald, added a few lines that were not recorded by Ducky, such as humming the melody to "Be Our Guest."

Animator Nik Ranieri, who brought Lumière to life for Disney's classic *Beauty and the Beast,* returned to render him in 3-D for *Mickey's PhilharMagic.* Animator Glen Keane, creator of Ariel in *The Little Mermaid,* also made a comeback for the new film.

Songs performed in the show include "The Mickey Mouse Club March," which debuted in 1955; "Be Our Guest" from *Beauty and the Beast;* an orchestral version of "The Sorceror's Apprentice" by Paul Dukas, as presented in the original *Fantasia* movie; "Part of Your World" from *The Little Mermaid;* "I Just Can't Wait to Be King" from *The Lion King;* "You Can Fly! You Can Fly! You Can Fly!" from *Peter Pan;* and "A Whole New World" from *Aladdin.*

The *Mickey* show makes the Magic Kingdom the fourth park at Walt Disney World with a major 3-D film. (The others are *Honey, I Shrunk the Audience* at Epcot; *It's Tough to Be a Bug!* at Disney's Animal Kingdom; and *Jim Henson's Muppet*Vision 3D* at Disney–MGM Studios.)

The Walt Disney Company experimented with animating the Disney characters in 3-D before, most notably in *Working for Peanuts,* a 1953 Donald Duck/Chip 'n Dale cartoon short, but never on a scale as grand as in *Mickey's PhilharMagic.* The attraction was produced jointly by Walt Disney Imagineering and Walt Disney Feature Animation and was rarely seen in 3-D prior to its engagement from December 1987 to December 1993 in Fantasyland Theater in Magic Kingdom as Act 1 of the experience featuring *Magic Journeys.*

The show is in the same theater once used for the Mickey Mouse Musical Revue, in which Mickey made his Magic Kingdom debut as an orchestra conductor in 1971. In 1980 the show moved to Tokyo Disneyland, where it became an opening-day attraction in 1983 and continues to play today. The 3-D film *Magic Journeys* and the live puppet show *Legend of the Lion King* occupied the theater until the installation of *Mickey's PhilharMagic.* The Lion King will continue to be celebrated at Disney's Animal Kingdom in a live show, *Festival of the Lion King.*

The long mural that spans the lobby is a composite of imagery from animated classic Disney movies with musical themes: *Toot, Whistle, Plunk & Boom, Melody Time,* and *Fantasia.*

The best seats are in the middle of the auditorium; each row loads all the way through, so the best strategy is to find a way to hang back a bit so that half the row is filled before you enter.

Other Attractions in Fantasyland

Ariel's Grotto. A watery world in the shadow of Dumbo where fans of *The Little Mermaid* can meet Ariel herself. On hot days visitors young and old may want to dance in the fountains.

Fantasyland Character Festival. Here's your chance to press the fantasy flesh of many favorite Disney characters in front of the former home of 20,000 Leagues under the Sea. That venerable ride has been closed since 1995. In 2005 rumors of a *Finding Nemo* ride that would use the pond began to look like a real plan for sometime in the next few years.

■ MICKEY'S TOONTOWN FAIR

Mickey gets his due, and so do you, in the Mouse's very own little town. There are no outer-space roller coasters or multimillion-dollar water slides here;

instead we have the sort of giddy happiness that has sustained Mickey's popularity for years.

Mickey Mouse, the presiding judge—dare we call him the Big Cheese—of Toontown, greets guests in the Toontown Fair Judge's Office, surrounded by prizewinning fruits and vegetables. Nearby, Mickey's sweetheart, Minnie Mouse, is happy to pose for photographs in the heart-paneled gazebo in her flower garden.

Walt Disney World, Disneyland, and the entire Disney empire were built around the ears of the most famous rodent of all, but until 1989 Mickey didn't have a place of his own. That year Disney honored the mouse's sixtieth birthday with Mickey's Birthdayland, the first new area at Walt Disney World since its opening. After the party was over, the place was kept open as Mickey's Starland, becoming one of the most popular areas of the park for the youngest visitors. Starland was given a major makeover, reopening as Mickey's Toontown Fair as part of the twenty-fifth anniversary celebration party throughout Walt Disney World.

Lines to meet and greet Mickey, Minnie, and the other local stars can become quite lengthy in the middle of the day; come early or late if you can.

⊞ MUST-SEE ⊞ Mickey's Country House

If you have kids, or ever were one, then there's not a whole lot of doubt about this: You've got to visit Mickey Mouse's house. It's a walk-through tour of the Mickster's private digs. In the living room an old-fashioned radio is "tuned" to

Mickey's Country House in Mickey's Toontown

scores from Mickey's favorite football team, Duckburg University. Mickey's clothes are carefully arranged in his bedroom, decorated with baby pictures and a photograph of Minnie. Not quite so neat is the kitchen, the benefit of Donald and Goofy's attempt to win the Toontown Home Remodeling Contest; buckets of paint are stacked in the sink, and paint is splattered on the floor and walls.

In the garden, just outside the kitchen, Mickey's Mousekosh overalls dry on the clothesline above oversize tomato plants, pumpkins (complete with ears), and cactus plants. Out back, in the Judge's Tent, the man—er, the mouse—himself appears to sign autographs.

⫶MUST-SEE⫶ Minnie's Country House

Ms. Minnie is even more sociable than her friend across the street. Minnie waits in the gazebo in her garden from time to time. In addition to her duties as editor of *Minnie's Cartoon Country Living Magazine,* Minnie also quilts and paints and is an avid gardener. You're welcome to tour her office, craft room, and kitchen. Be sure to punch a few buttons on her answering machine to listen to Minnie's latest messages, bake a "quick-rising" cake in the oven, and poke around in her refrigerator.

The Barnstormer at Goofy's Wiseacre Farm

Kid size and with kid-size thrills, this roller coaster has cars that look like old biplanes. The tracks include a wide turn that flies through a barn where kids are waiting their turn to ride. Similar to Gadget's Go-Coaster at Mickey's Toontown at Disneyland, it is about twice as long. In the distance over the top of the coaster is the real thing at Magic Kingdom: Space Mountain.

Other Attractions in Mickey's Toontown Fair

Donald's Boat. The *Miss Daisy,* which has seen better days and sprouts leaks from all over, is a great place to cool off on a hot day. Disney Imagineers have created a dry lake to surround the boat—here's your chance to walk on pseudo-water. And pint-size sailors can clamber aboard to blow the ship's whistle or clang the loud bell.

Toontown Hall of Fame Tent. This shrine to the greatest Disney cartoon characters of all time displays many of the Toontown Fair's blue ribbon–winning entries and also features regular appearances by local celebrities. Parents be warned: There is also a large gift shop within.

Toon Park. Only a toon could have a park like this: a spongy green meadow filled with foam topiary animals including goats, cows, pigs, and horses. Kids can jump and hop on the lily pads to hear the animals moo, bleat, and whinny.

Walt Disney World Railroad. The vintage railroad that circles the Magic Kingdom has a station at the back of Mickey's Toontown Fair. The next stop is Main Street, and the third stop is in Frontierland.

■ LIBERTY SQUARE

This peaceful laid-back corner of America is home of the presidents (robotically assisted), a festive riverboat (which runs on underwater tracks), and a haunted mansion (which is too creepy to pass by without a tour). The square is also home to a massive live oak tree festooned with thirteen lanterns—one for each of the thirteen original colonies—like the Liberty Trees used as political statements in pre-Revolutionary times.

▌MUST-SEE▐ The Haunted Mansion ≡FAST

Scare yourself silly in this masterpiece of an attraction with some of the most sophisticated special effects at Walt Disney World. During the years there have been hundreds of creepy and decrepit little improvements. If it's been a while since you last visited, you should be sure to go back; be sure to bring your death certificate. The ride is something of a rite of passage for kids, moving from Mickey and Minnie to the (humorous) dark side of Disney.

The experience begins in the graveyard waiting line; before you let the tombstones make you feel too creepy, stop and read some of the inscriptions. They're a howl! The attendants, dressed as morticians, are among the best actors in the park, almost always staying in character. They will tell you to "fill in the dead space" in the line. When the elevator at the start of the ride fills up they may announce, "No more bodies." They play their roles well—we've tried our best over the years to make them crack a smile, without any success.

The Haunted Mansion

Tomb with a View

Our favorite Haunted Mansion tombstones include: DEAR DEPARTED BROTHER DAVE. HE CHASED A BEAR INTO A CAVE; HERE RESTS WATHEL R. BENDER. HE RODE TO GLORY ON A FENDER; and HERE LIES GOOD OLD FRED. A GREAT BIG ROCK FELL ON HIS HEAD. And there is REST IN PEACE COUSIN HUET. WE ALL KNOW YOU DIDN'T DO IT.

More favorites, from the cemetery at the exit of the ride: Bluebeard's tomb reads, HERE LYETH HIS LOVING WIVES. SEVEN WINSOME WIVES, SOME FAT SOME THIN. SIX OF THEM WERE FAITHFUL, BUT THE SEVENTH DID HIM IN. Other pun-full names on the wall include Paul Tergyst, Clare Voince, Metta Fisiks, and Manny Festation. Many of the names are drawn from the Imagineers who designed the original ride.

One of the newest tombstones honors the late Walt Disney Imagineer Leota Thomas (whose maiden name, appropriately, was Toombs). If you spend a few moments in contemplation, you'll see that the sculpted head on Leota's tombstone slowly opens and closes its eyes.

Among the gravestones in the pet cemetery is a clever joke: The buried cat has nine dates of death, one for each life.

Stop and take a look at the roofline of the mansion; the decorative parapets of the home are made up of chess pieces. You'll see kings and queens, bishops, rooks, and pawns—everything but knights. Although Imagineers deny they were that clever, Disney tour guides sometimes tell guests: "It's always (k)night inside."

The weather vane atop the building, a bat in shape, is also one of the key lightning rods for the structure. If you look closely, you'll see rods on top of every building at Walt Disney World, which exists within one of the most active lightning regions in the world.

Once you are admitted to the mansion itself, you will be ushered into a strange room that has an interesting visual trick—is the ceiling going up, or the floor going down? Either way, the portraits on the wall are a real scream. (Don't read this if you don't want to know. Okay, you have been warned: At Walt Disney World the ceiling moves up and the floor stays where it is; at Disneyland the floor moves down and the walls are stationary. The stretching room was put into place in California as a way to get visitors to the loading level, which is on the other side of the railroad tracks. When the Florida house was built, there was no need to go down a level, but Imagineers wanted to keep the same illusion even if it was accomplished in a different way.)

The experience is accompanied throughout by a decidedly strange soundtrack that is also among the more literate found at Walt Disney World. Here's part of the introduction from the stretching room:

> When hinges creak in doorless chambers and strange and frightening sounds echo through the halls, whenever candlelights flicker

where the air is deathly still, that is the time when ghosts are present, practicing their terror with ghoulish delight.

Your cadaverous pallor betrays an aura of foreboding, almost as though you sense a disquieting metamorphosis. Is this haunted room actually stretching? Or is it your imagination? And consider this dismaying observation: This chamber has no windows, and no doors.

Which offers you this chilling challenge: to find a way out! Of course, there's always my way.

You'll arrive at a loading station for a moving set of chairs and settle in for a tour through a house that is in the control of the largest collection of spooks this side of the CIA. Says your Ghost Host: "We find it delightfully unlivable here in this ghostly retreat. Every room has wall-to-wall creeps and hot and cold running chills." We've ridden the ride many times and see something different each time. Among the best effects are the dancing ghouls at the dinner party, the moving door knockers, and the face within the crystal ball.

This ride is probably the single best combination of Disney design, filmmaking, and audio-animatronics anywhere at the Magic Kingdom. There are all sorts of delightful details on the ride, enough to make it worth several rides if you have the time. Here are a few you might want to look for: the needlepoint that reads "Tomb Sweet Tomb," the legs sticking out from under the banquet table in the ghostly wedding reception, and the skull-shaped notes rising out of the top of the organ at the reception. You'll meet Madam Leota, a disembodied guide who will help you attempt to make contact with the spirits within the mansion:

> Rap on a table, it's time to respond, send us a message from somewhere beyond. Goblins and ghoulies from last Halloween, awaken the spirits with your tambourine. Wizards and witches wherever you dwell, give us a hint by ringing a bell.

Disney Imagineer Leota Thomas provided the face for the crystal ball and the name for the character; actress Eleanor Audley provided the voice. Audley is also famous as the voice of the evil Maleficent in Disney's classic animated feature *Sleeping Beauty.*

The narrator, the Ghost Host, of the Haunted Mansion is actor Paul Frees, who also gave voice to many of the Pirates of the Caribbean; fans of the *Rocky and Bullwinkle* show may recognize him as the voice of Boris Badenov.

The best special effect of the ride is the wedding-party scene, where guests move from mortal coil to diaphanous spirit and back. The technology that adds transparent ghosts is an old theatrical trick dating from the 1860s. John Henry Pepper, a professor of chemistry in London, introduced the effect on stage and it became known as "Pepper's Ghost." A slanted pane of glass allows viewers to look through it to a screen as well as to see the reflection of lit objects and characters hidden out of sight in front of the glass. At the Haunted Mansion the ghosts reside in a room below the moving doom buggies.

Before They Were Stars

Wayne Brady was a character performer and moved on to be an Anacomical Actor at Epcot before joining Drew Carey on the ABC television show *Whose Line Is it Anyway?* Britney Spears, Christina Aguilera, Justin Timberlake (*NSYNC), and JC Chasez (*NSYNC) each started on *The Mickey Mouse Club* television show before making it big as pop stars. Actor Taye Diggs, whose credits include TV's *Ally McBeal,* started at Tokyo Disneyland in "Festivale Tropical."

After the party, you'll meet the famous Grim Grinning Ghosts, captured within luminous globes. Despite surviving dozens of rides at the Magic Kingdom, Disneyland, and Disneyland Paris, it took us years before we were able to figure out what they were saying. Here's part of their song:

> When the crypt doors creak and the tombstones quake, spooks come out for a swinging wake. Happy haunts materialize and begin to vocalize; grim grinning ghosts come out to socialize.
>
> Now don't close your eyes and don't try to hide, or a silly spook may sit by your side. Shrouded in a daft disguise, they pretend to terrorize; grim grinning ghosts come out to socialize.

In recent years Disney has been subtly increasing the realism of the ride, perhaps in reaction to the overall explicitness of our society. The skeletons are just a bit more real, the ghosts are just a bit more ghoulish. Most noticeable is a new ending, sending your moving chair on a detour through a graveyard full of creepy tombs and ghostly trees. As the ride ends, Madam Leota will urge you to hurry back. Make final arrangements now.

Some very young children may become a bit scared, although most kids of all ages can see the humor among the horrors. And speaking of jokes, stop to read the inscriptions on the tombs at the exit. Lines for this show vary greatly; the best times to visit are early or late in the day. Try not to join the crowds streaming toward the mansion's door each time the Hall of Presidents lets out or the riverboat arrives. The ride lasts about nine minutes, including a two-minute preshow.

The original Haunted Mansion was at Disneyland in California. Because it was to be built near the New Orleans area of Frontierland, the idea was to make it look like an early-1800s Southern mansion; however, it actually ended up looking more like an old home in Baltimore. Walt Disney himself vetoed one design that made the house appear to be derelict (Disney's first falling-down house would come some thirty years later at Disney–MGM Studios with the construction of the Twilight Zone Tower of Terror.)

The original plans called for a walk-through tour, with visitors escorted by a butler or maid who would tell the story. The first story line was quite different, too, and not at all sugarcoated: It told of a wealthy sea merchant who built a fabulous mansion for his new bride but then killed her in a rage when she learned he was really a bloody pirate. Her ghost came back to haunt him and tormented him so much that he finally hanged himself from the rafters, giving the mansion two unhappy spirits. About all that is left of the gruesome story is a brief glimpse of a hanging body above the stretching room, the weather vane in the shape of a sailing ship on the top of the cupola of the mansion, and some nautical-theme paintings.

And here's a bit of trivia you can ask your Disney-expert friends: What major attraction exists at all four parks, but is located in four different lands? The answer, as you might have guessed, is The Haunted Mansion—at Walt Disney World, Liberty Square; at Disneyland, New Orleans Square; at Tokyo Disneyland, in Fantasyland; and at Disneyland Paris, Phantom Manor is in Frontierland.

The Hall of Presidents
Within an ornate theater is a living-history lesson featuring some of Disney's more impressive audio-animatronics. The show is derived from the Illinois pavilion at the 1964–1965 New York World's Fair, designed by Disney. Fairgoers were startled when a seated Abe Lincoln wearily came to life to address the audience. In the Magic Kingdom version of the show, all forty-two American presidents are represented on stage. (Before you send me a correction: There have been forty-three changes of administration, but Grover Cleveland served two nonconsecutive terms.)

> ## The Liberty Tree
>
> Across from the Hall of Presidents is one of the most carefully tended trees in Walt Disney World, a Southern live oak (*Quercus virginiana*) more than a century old. The plaque there reads: UNDER THE BOUGHS OF THE ORIGINAL LIBERTY TREE IN BOSTON IN 1765, PATRIOTS CALLING THEMSELVES THE "SONS OF LIBERTY" GATHERED TO PROTEST THE IMPOSITION OF THE STAMP ACT. IN THE YEARS THAT FOLLOWED, ALMOST EVERY AMERICAN TOWN HAD A LIBERTY TREE, A LIVING SYMBOL OF THE AMERICAN FREEDOM OF SPEECH AND ASSEMBLY.

George W. Bush, in a speech recorded in the Oval Office for Disney, shares the largest speaking role with Abraham Lincoln. Bill Clinton was the first sitting president to have a speaking role in the pageant, with a speech recorded in the Oval Office. In the new version Clinton steps back into the chorus with all the other former presidents.

Shows start on the hour and on the half hour. The first part of the show involves a series of detailed paintings projected on the large center screen; then the curtains pull back to reveal the assembled presidents. President Bush promises that in the "first generation of the twenty-first century, no child, no race, no creed, no ethnic minority will be left out of the American dream."

Lincoln rises wearily from his seat to discuss the Declaration of Independence: "Most governments have been based, practically, on the denial of the equal rights of men, as I have, in part stated them; ours began by affirming those rights," Lincoln says, in a quote from his writings. "True democracy makes no inquiry of color or skin or place of birth."

Shows take about twenty-two minutes. The 700-seat auditorium quickly eats up waiting lines, and the maximum wait should be no more than two shows, or about forty minutes. By the way, the show at the American pavilion at Epcot, the

The *Liberty Belle* loads passengers at Liberty Square.

American Experience, has similar themes but is much flashier, focusing on other great figures from the history of our nation.

Liberty Square Riverboat

A new golden oldie took to the waters in 1997 with the arrival of the *Liberty Belle,* a steam-powered stern-wheeler. The riverboat replaced a pair of older Disney replicas, the *Admiral Joe Fowler* and the *Richard F. Irvine;* they were taken out of service after carrying some ninety million people during their careers.

The boat circles the 0.5-mile Rivers of America connected to an underwater rail. This is by no means a thrill ride, but it is a very pleasant reprieve on a hot day. The narrator is Sam Clemens, best known as author Mark Twain. The cruise takes about twenty minutes.

Mike Fink Keelboats

These small riverboats follow the same circuit as the riverboat but are a bit faster and a bit more personal with your own guide. Mike Fink was a legendary river-boat captain who had an adventure with Davy Crockett. The small boats, the *Bertha Mae* and the *Gullywhumper,* take about ten minutes for a circuit. Because of the small capacity of the boats, we'd advise against joining a long line if there is one; we'd also suggest against duplicating a trip on the keelboats and one on the riverboat. The keelboats run only during the day and may not run during the off-season.

ADVENTURELAND

Ahoy, mateys! Welcome to a most unusual corner of central Florida, where you will find a Caribbean island, an African veldt, a South Pacific bird tree, and more. Adventureland includes some of the most dramatic landscaping touches in the Magic Kingdom and the most popular band of pirates since Penzance.

MUST-SEE Pirates of the Caribbean ≡*FAST*

Yo, ho, ho . . . this ride is one of Disney's very best. After an approach through a dank dungeon waiting area (and past a parrot wearing an eye patch!), you'll settle into a broad-beamed boat for a cruise into the middle of a pirate raid on a Caribbean island town. You'll love the moonlit battle scene as your boat passes beneath the guns of two warring ships; cannonballs will land all around you in the cool water. Pay attention, too, to the jail scene in which a group of pirates tries to entice a mangy dog to bring them the key. The ride includes a wondrous collection of 125 audio-animatronic characters: 65 pirates and villagers and 60 animals and birds, including robotic chickens and pigs.

One of the biggest recent successes of the moviemaking side of the Walt Disney Company was *Pirates of the Caribbean,* which took the title and a few characters from the venerable theme-park ride and spun an entire film around them. In the summer of 2006, the circle was made full when some of the elements of the first two movies in the series were added into the ride.

New members of the buccaneer crew are Captain Jack Sparrow (played by a robot look-alike for Johnny Depp) and his nemesis Barbossa from *Pirates of the Caribbean: The Black Pearl* and Davy Jones from the second movie, *Pirates of the Caribbean: Dead Man's Chest.* In addition to the new characters, the ride also gained some new state-of-the-art special effects. Similar additions were made at the ride of the same name at Disneyland in California. (The Anaheim version of the ride, the original, is almost twice as long at about fifteen minutes and is more detailed than the Orlando attraction.)

The impressive new special effects include a wall of mist used as a projection screen (a similar technology is employed at the *Fantasia* show). The original ship, the *Wicked Wench,* is still in the show—apparently the *Black Pearl* is still out roaming the seven seas—but there's a new master at the wheel, Captain Barbossa.

Jack Sparrow actually makes several appearances in the attraction, including a prominent role in the auction scene.

Some young children may be scared by the simulated cannon fire and the skulls and bones that are fairly liberally strewn about in some of the caves of Pirates of the Caribbean. And some adults may find bones of their own to pick—things such as the depiction of women as objects for sale at auction.

However, the ride might offer an opportunity to discuss such unhappy elements of history with youngsters. The ride begins with a little bit of a watery drop; your boat is dropping below the Disney World Railroad tracks overhead to the ride area, which (like Splash Mountain and Space Mountain) actually lies mostly outside the boundaries of the park. In any case, Pirates of the Caribbean is a masterpiece of Disney artistry. You don't want to miss this one!

Disney has tinkered with the ride for nearly all of its existence, improving the audio system several years ago; I was thrilled to finally be able to understand the background warning at the entrance to the lagoon: "Dead men tell no lies." A bit further into the ride you'll also be able to hear some of the boasts and taunts of the pirates as they go about their good-natured dastardly deeds. Finally, listen for the parrot in the treasure trove at the end of the ride: He sings, "Yo ho, yo ho, a pirate's life for me. We pillage, plunder, we rifle and loot."

Lines can become quite long at midday; head for this popular trip when the park first opens or in late afternoon. As you enter the queue, keep to your left to save a few minutes in line. The waiting area is mostly under cover, which makes it a good place to be when it's raining or on a very hot day. The ride itself takes about seven minutes.

While in the queue, look through a gap in the wall to see two prisoners playing chess; close observers will see that they have reached a stalemate. One of the Disney Imagineers responsible for this ride, and the Haunted Mansion, was a chess fanatic; his interests are evident in a number of places in Walt Disney World.

If you concentrate on the impressive mechanics behind the audio-animatronics of the characters, you just might miss the fact that there are just ten basic faces for more than sixty characters. Everything else is just makeup and costuming.

Swiss Family Treehouse

This is one of those "no accounting for taste" attractions—you'll either love it or hate it, probably depending upon how deeply the story of the Swiss Family Robinson is engraved upon your memory. Actually, this attraction is a remembrance of the 1960 Disney movie version of the classic novel *Swiss Family Robinson,* written by Johann David Wyss and completed by his son Johann Rudolf Wyss in 1813.

The tree house winds up and across a simulated banyan tree (constructed of sculpted concrete and steel). There are a lot of stairs to climb and a few ropewalk bridges; on a busy day your view may be mostly the backside of the tourist in front of you. It takes five to ten minutes to walk up, through, and down the tree. Incredibly, there can sometimes be lengthy lines for the privilege; if there's a line and you're determined to climb this tree, come back late in the day. The "tree" received a remake at the end of 1997, with new and improved details added.

The Magic Carpets of Aladdin

Kids can pilot their own flying carpet at this Disney version of a carnival. Sixteen four-passenger vehicles circle a giant animated genie's lamp, across from the Swiss Family Treehouse. Riders can control their own carpet, moving up or

The Magic Carpets of Aladdin in Adventureland

down or pitching forward or backward. All the while, animatronic camels "spit" at the riders going by. Music from Disney's 1992 animated feature *Aladdin* plays throughout the ride. Alongside the ride the Agrabah Bazaar features a Disney version of a Middle Eastern open-air marketplace, selling vases, brass, spices, clothing, and souvenirs.

MUST-SEE Jungle Cruise ≡*FAST*

Another Disney classic, this is an escorted boat tour through a simulated wild kingdom that somehow stretches from the African veldt to the Amazon rain forest to the Nile valley and the jungles of Southeast Asia.

You'll see some of Disney's most famous special effects, like the automated hippos who lurk just below the water's surface and the cavorting elephants who will spray water from their trunks. The shores are lined with robotic zebras, lions, and giraffes. The best part of the ride is the hokey but still entertaining patter of the tour guides in pith helmets. "Be sure to tell all your friends about Jungle Cruise," our guide told us. "It cuts down the lines." As we were readying to board our boats, we were advised to guard against confusion in loading. "Note that there is one dock to the left, and one to the right: It's a paradox." Ouch. As we passed into a section of Egypt's famous river, we were told, "If you don't believe me, you're in da Nile." Another guide told us, "Don't worry about looking stupid—I'm doing that for you." But my favorite bad joke involved horticultural commentary: "I'd like to point out my favorite plants in the jungle. I like that one, and that one, and that one."

Amateur gardeners may be thrilled by the amazing collection of plants, flowers, and trees—most of them real—that Disney groundskeepers manage to keep alive. One of the tricks is a network of gas heaters that warms the occasionally chilly air of Florida in the winter.

Trees are kept short; most live in planters, and many tropical species are protected by hidden heaters. The water in the "river" is about 4 feet deep; it is colored with a natural dye to hide the depth.

Each of the boats has its own motor, powered by clean-burning compressed natural gas. Although the expedition leader will make a great show of spinning the wheel, the boats actually have a long pylon beneath their keel; rubber wheels on the pylon fit into a channel.

The ride is about ten minutes; the line to get on board, alas, can sometimes wind around and around the corral for more than an hour. Go early or late on busy days. It is actually most dramatic by night, and especially silly. Disney insiders have been predicting a major update for Jungle Cruise for many years.

Enchanted Tiki Room—Under New Management

The Tropical Serenade is among the strangest of all of the attractions at the Magic Kingdom, and you're not likely to enjoy it unless you are in exactly the right frame of mind. In 1998 the birds debuted a new version of the venerable, corny show.

The Tiki Room is the home of the Enchanted Tiki Birds, a collection of more than 200 wisecracking, wing-flapping, automated winged creatures, along with a collection of singing flowers, totem poles, and statues. The interior of the theater is as tacky as ever, and the exceedingly annoying theme song "In the Tiki, Tiki, Tiki, Tiki, Tiki Room" is preserved for the ages.

Hollywood featherweights Iago, from Disney's animated feature *Aladdin*, and Zazu, from *The Lion King*, have become the new landlords of the popular Adventureland attraction that opened with the park October 1, 1971. The original group of animatronic characters continues to star in the show, including José, Michael, Fritz, and Pierre. Walt Disney Imagineers had three of the four original actors re-record audio segments for the new show. But the story line is a bit more interesting, made all the better because of a greatly improved audio system. Now you can hear all of the corny jokes, including Iago's taunting insult to the Polynesian gods. They warn: "When you mess with Polynesia, the Tiki gods will squeeze ya."

The Enchanted Tiki Room—Under New Management blends the original cast into a new version of the corny, strange show. Among the musical highlights is a rendition of "In the Still of the Night," when all of the Tiki icons around the room come to life, complete with a disco mirror ball. One song guests will likely recognize is a stirring rendition of "Friend Like Me," sung by Iago. Midway through the song, Iago, voiced by the professional annoyance Gilbert Gottfried (who provided the voice of Iago for *Aladdin*), interrupts: "Stop the music!" Iago announces the Tiki Room will house a brand-new show. Zazu warns Iago that any changes will anger the Tiki gods. No problem, says Iago. And so, when the new show begins, Uh Oa, the Tiki goddess of disaster, rises up from the center of the room in a horrible blast of green vapor. She raises her staff and sends a bolt hurling toward Iago. When it connects, Iago disappears in a cloud of smoke. After the Tiki gods perform a hip-hop rap number, Iago reappears wrapped in bandages and on crutches, declaring the Tiki gods the greatest act he has ever heard. He joins Zazu and the rest of the animatronic cast for a musical grand finale.

The show also features a funny preshow starring a couple of wisecracking bird-agents, William and Morris, voiced by comedians Don Rickles and the late Phil Hartman. The birds are late for the show. "Maybe they hit traffic," says Morris. "Don't say that!" says William. The waiting area for the show includes a stop in front of a waterfall that features volcano flames.

The Tiki birds were among Disney's first attempts at audio-animatronics, representing the state of the art as it existed around 1963 when a very similar show was introduced at Disneyland. We know some young children who have been absolutely enchanted by the birds; the very young and the very cynical may want to pass. In any case, the show is blissfully short, and it's nice and cool inside on a hot Florida day.

Other Attractions in Adventureland
Shrunken Ned's Junior Jungle Boats. This set of coin-operated remote-control boats stands near the Jungle Cruise. If you say the name quickly, you'll get the minor joke.

■ FRONTIERLAND
Almost anything goes in this wild western corner of the Magic Kingdom, home of Davy Crockett, Tom Sawyer, a bunch of vacationing bears, a runaway mining train, and the park's newest, wettest, and wildest big splash.

▮ MUST-SEE ▮ Big Thunder Mountain Railroad ≡*FAST*
One of the best rides at the park, it is at the same time much more than and much less than it appears. Big Thunder is a Disneyfied roller coaster, one of only three "thrill" rides in the Magic Kingdom (along with Space Mountain and Splash Mountain). As roller coasters go, it is fairly tame, with about a half mile of track and a three-and-a-half-minute ride with a few short drops and some interesting twists and turns. But in the Disney tradition, it is the setting and the attention to detail that make this one of the most popular places to be. The ride is set in the Gold Rush era in the ramshackle mining town of Tumbleweed.

You will ride in a runaway mining train up through a quaking tunnel, across a flooding village, and back down around and through a 197-foot-high artificial mountain, bedecked with real mining antiques from former mines out West. As you enter the

One-Upsmanship

Big Thunder Mountain Railroad at Disneyland Paris has a much sharper drop than its older American cousin.

Early in the morning, Frontierland's storefronts await the crowds.

waiting line, you'll see part of a "stamping mill" made by the Joshua Hendy Works in San Francisco, possibly made for one of the mines of the Comstock in Nevada. Stamping mills were used to crush large pieces of rock into smaller pieces to allow the removal of ore. Look, too, at the audio-animatronic animals and birds, and watch for the old coot of a miner in a bathtub as you zoom by. The telegraph office lists the manager's name as Morris Code—get it? Along the tracks are about twenty audio-animatronic characters, including donkeys, goats, chickens, possums, and the "rainmaker," Professor Cumulus Isobar.

Picking the right time to visit the railroad can make a real difference at this very popular attraction; waits of more than an hour are common at midday in peak season. The shortest lines are early in the day or just before dinnertime. Coaster fans say the best ride (meaning the wildest) can be had by sitting in the last row of seats; we also like the very front of any coaster ride because it gives you a view of the perils ahead, over the top of the engine in front. The line outside, near the rafts to Tom Sawyer Island, is only a small portion of the queue. There is a large upper corral and a winding path down through the mining station to the railroad. The ride takes on a very different feeling at night, and the fun is increased because the darkness hides the track ahead of you. True fans should experience it then as well as during the day.

Children younger than age seven must be accompanied by an adult; no one under 42 inches tall is allowed to ride. Warn young children about the loud noises they will hear as their railway car is pulled up the first lift on the ride.

Construction of the ride, completed in 1981, cost $17 million, which equals the entire price tag for Disneyland when it opened in California in 1955. The Orlando version of the ride is a bit longer than the Disneyland original. In 2003 the Disneyland ride had a fatal accident in one of its tunnels and was shut down for a lengthy renovation. At Walt Disney World the ride was also closed for safety review before reopening.

MUST-SEE Splash Mountain ≡FAST

The Magic Kingdom's "highest, scariest, wildest, and wettest" attraction is a wild ride to contemplate; you may have a long time to contemplate it as you wait your turn on a busy day. Splash Mountain includes three lifts and four drops, with the biggest plunging about 50 feet at a forty-five-degree angle and a top speed of about 40 miles per hour—Disney claims it's the steepest flume ride in the world. The big drop, visible to the crowds along the Rivers of America in Frontierland,

Riders plunge down the face of Splash Mountain in Frontierland.

Charge It

Splash Mountain, because it is one of the high places in the park and because of the watery path, is occasionally forced to close when a lightning storm is in the area.

makes it appear as if the log car has fallen into a pond. Some of the best special effects take place within the mountain, with a story based on Disney's 1946 classic *Song of the South* cartoon. The ride follows Brer Rabbit as he tries to outwit Brer Fox and Brer Bear on a wild journey to the Laughin' Place.

The entrance to Splash Mountain is beneath the reconstructed Frontierland railroad station. (As you approach on the train, you will be able to see a small portion of the interior of Splash Mountain: the *Zip-a-dee Lady* paddle wheeler that is at the end of the ride, after the big drop.) Disney has hidden the waiting lines within an open inner courtyard not visible from the entrance, and then a long and winding queue within the building itself; be sure to ask the cast member at the measuring pole (44 inches minimum for youngsters) about the length of the line. I'd suggest you come back another time—very early or late—if the line is too long. As usual at many of the attractions, you often will save a few minutes by choosing the left-side line over the right. The capacity for the ride is about 2,400 passengers per hour, with fifty log boats in use at a time.

Once you enter the Splash Mountain building, there are a few interesting exhibits, including a series of Brer Fox story needlepoints ("Some critters ain't never gonna learn" and "You can't run away from trouble. Ain't no place that far" among them). Check out the animated shadows on the wall in some of the dark areas. The interior waiting line for Splash Mountain is not a place for claustrophobics. It is dark in places and tight—closer than the waiting queue for Pirates of the Caribbean.

You'll start by loading into your "log"; you may find the seats slightly wet. The logs will climb up into the mountain—you'll see the bottom of the big drop, and first-time riders will certainly be expecting a sudden sharp drop over the precipice they've seen from the ground. And, just to build up the tension a bit, there are several small teasing drops. But instead of the great fall, your log will move gently through a beautiful, tuneful, and peaceful water world filled with some sixty-eight animatronic characters and lots of delightful details. At the end of the first room there's a drop—but again, it's not the big one.

Midway through the ride you'll pass through an opening to the outside and be treated to one of the better views of the park—Thunder Mountain to your left, Cinderella Castle straight ahead, and Space Mountain and the distant Contemporary Resort behind it. (This peek is reminiscent of another Disney classic, the Matterhorn at Disneyland in California.)

How Wet Do You Like It?

Splash Mountain is a watery place, and the log cars make a huge wave as they land at the bottom of the big drop, but the fact is that you won't get very wet on the ride. The two wettest places seem to be the very first row of seats and the last—the wave flies over the car. The front row has the best view of the drop; the last row has the most suspense.

You'll also likely see a crowd of people staring up at you from below—actually, they're looking beyond you to the big drop over your shoulder.

All of a sudden you're back in the mountain, and it's dark. Is this the big drop? Actually, no; you enter into another large room, this time one illuminated with black light. Check out the bees circling around the beehive. There's lots of water now, with splashing fountains and little squirts of water overhead. And there are now some signs of warning: ENTER AT YOUR OWN RISK, DANGER, GO BACK, BEWARE, WATCH OUT.

But instead of going down, you'll go up one more sharp climb. Why do you suppose there are a pair of vultures hanging over the top of the hill? Listen to what they say: "Everybody's got a laughing place, maybe this is yours." This is it, folks. The big one, the spectacular waterfall you've seen from the walkway below. You're over . . . and down in about four seconds. There is one final surprise at the very end, yet another sparkling interior room, home to a "Welcome Home Brer Rabbit" party.

Splash Mountain is actually one of the longer rides at the Magic Kingdom at nearly eleven minutes, and despite the brevity of the final drop, it does give you a lot more for your waiting time than Thunder Mountain or Space Mountain. If you can convince the kids (or the adults) to look past the short drop, they are sure to love the rest of the ride, which is pure Disney. And try the ride again at night; the view of the park from near the top is worth the wait.

There are Splash Mountains at Disneyland and at Tokyo Disneyland; in California guests sit one behind another, while the Japanese and Florida versions load side by side. Disney engineers carefully control the amount of water in the flumes. Too much water will cause too much turbulence and splashing; too little can cause a loaded boat to bottom out. On the big drop about one-quarter of the water is diverted around the boat to control the speed of the drop.

In any case, there's an emergency braking system at the bottom of the big drop; the brake is turned on if an infrared beam determines that two boats are too close together for safety. Pressurized air inflates a set of air bags that lift the underside of the moving boat and push it against rubber strips in a safety channel on the side of the boat, bringing it to a halt.

By the way, the big splash at the bottom of the drop is not caused by the boat—it's an artificial splash produced by water cannons.

MUST-SEE Tom Sawyer Island

Another essential, at least for the youngsters, is the raft ride over to this little island in the middle of the Rivers of America. It's based upon Mark Twain's classic book, and you'll find dark caves, waterwheels, a barrel bridge, and a rope bridge to bounce on. At the far end of the island is a little bridge to Fort Sam Clemens, where kids can scramble around the parapets and fire air guns at passing side-wheelers.

The little snack bar at the fort sells, along with beverages, a most unusual fast

Department of Redundancy Department

If you look carefully, you can spot a fire sprinkler system in the ceiling of the water tunnels within Splash Mountain.

food: whole sour pickles. There's also an interesting little gazebo out on the water known as Aunt Polly's Landing, selling picnic-basket fare: things such as peanut butter and jelly sandwiches, cold fried chicken, and apple pie. Nearby is a half-whitewashed fence with notable graffiti, including a scrawl that declares: Tom ♥ Becky.

Parents will appreciate the space to let their children burn off a bit of energy after standing in lines all day; be advised, though, that it is fairly easy to misplace a youngster in one of the simulated caves or on a trail. Discuss with your children a meeting place in case you become separated. Lines for the raft rarely require more than ten minutes of waiting. The island closes at dusk.

Country Bear Jamboree

This doggedly cute show stars some twenty robotic bears of various sizes, shapes, and personalities, full of corny jokes and strained puns. Where else could you possibly expect to see a trio of bears named Bubbles, Bunny, and Beulah singing a bowdlerized Beach Boys hit, "Wish They All Could Be California Bears"? (The soundtrack is changed annually for a Christmas hoedown.)

The original concept for the Jamboree was as an attraction at Mineral King, a ski resort in northern California that Walt Disney had hoped to develop in the mid-1960s. Mineral King was eventually blocked by environmental and business interests. Instead, Country Bear Jamboree opened at Walt Disney World in 1971.

A stroller parking lot outside Country Bear Jamboree

The similar Jamboree at Disneyland in California was closed in late 2001.

We find this fifteen-minute attraction just barely (sorry) easier to take than the Enchanted Tiki Birds; youngsters and fans of Disney audio-animatronics will probably want to argue strongly in its favor. Despite our opinion, the Jamboree is a very popular show. The best time to visit is early, late, or during one of the parades, and the best seats are at the very front or back of the hall.

Diamond Horseshoe Saloon Revue

Disney's version of a Western dance-hall revue is a lot of fun for young and old; in recent years the cowboys and barmaids stepped aside in favor of a changing series of dance jamborees featuring such Disney and Pixar stars as Woody, Goofy, Chip 'n Dale, Jessie, and Bullseye. One show teaches kids to kick up their heels in classic country dances including "Boot Scootin' Boogie," "Electric Slide," and "Cotton-Eyed Joe," plus the special "Goofy Two-Step." Check the daily schedule for shows.

While you're there, take the time to peruse some of the placards along the walls, old promotions for actors and actresses. Among my favorites, along the right side opposite the bar, are ones for Marie Burroughs as "Ophelia" in Boston from 1893 to 1894, and Emma Juch, born in Vienna in 1865 of American parents. Juch became renowned for Wagner operas and was later head of her own opera company.

Other Attractions in Frontierland

Frontierland Shootin' Arcade. A durn-fancy shooting gallery, sort of a live video game and not like any other shooting gallery you have seen at a county fair. Players aim huge buffalo rifles at a Disney replica of an 1850s frontier town. The rifles fire infrared beams at targets on tombstones, clouds, banks, jails, and other objects; direct hits make the targets spin, explode, or otherwise surprise. Some of the signs on the objects tell a story: OLD TOM HUBBARD DIED WITH A FROWN, BUT A GRAVE CAN'T KEEP A GOOD MAN DOWN. If you hit the skeleton of a steer, his horns will spin around. To use the rifles you must pay an additional charge for a specific number of "bullets."

EATS AND TREATS

There are three types of restaurants at the Magic Kingdom: overpriced and bad, overpriced and barely acceptable, and overpriced and almost good. Well, okay, there are a few meals that are overpriced and good. In any case, we recommend that you not consider meals to be an important part of your experience at the Magic Kingdom; save your time and money for one of the somewhat better Epcot Center or Disney–MGM Studios restaurants or for an evening outside of the Disney borders.

You do, though, have to eat. Disney has a rule against bringing your own sandwiches or other food into the park. In years past I used to say that I had never seen an attendant search a backpack or shoulder bag for tuna fish on rye; alas, in today's heightened security environment, your small backpacks, shoulder bags, and purses will be searched for more dangerous items. I'd still expect that the guards are not likely to confiscate sandwiches, and you certainly can bring a baby's formula and a few candy bars for the kids. If you've got a car in the parking lot, though, one way to save big bucks on meals is to take a midday break and leave the parks for a few hours to eat at a restaurant in Kissimmee or nearby. Your parking pass allows multiple entrances each day.

If you don't pack your own food, it is possible to pick and choose among the offerings at the park. Disney does offer a few nonstandard and more healthful dishes, like pasta salads, turkey burgers, and smoked turkey legs, at some of its stands. Nevertheless, each year guests at Walt Disney World eat more than seven million hamburgers, five million hot dogs, five million pounds of french fries, and 265,000 pounds of popcorn, as well as drink forty-six million Cokes.

We include general price ranges in our listings and mention specific prices for some items. Pricing on food and menus is subject to change. All food establishments within Disney World offer soft drinks at prices of almost $3.00. (I used to recommend that guests throw a few cans of soda in a backpack to save $10 or more on a visit; in today's heightened security conditions, that is no longer a good option.)

■ MAIN STREET, U.S.A.

🍴 **Main Street Wagons.** Located throughout the Main Street area. Espresso, cappuccino, soft drinks. Hot dogs and baked goods. Fresh fruit and vegetables and fruit drinks priced from about $1.00 to $3.00. A few umbrella-shaded tables are available on East Center Street beside the Main Street Market house.

🍴 **Main Street Bakery.** On Main Street near the Plaza Ice Cream Parlor. Unusual baked goods and beverages, $2.00 to $4.00. Watch cookies being made from scratch through the large window fronting on Main Street. There is a small seating area inside the pleasant, floral-decorated shop, but most customers take their goodies to go, either to sit at one of the nearby umbrella tables or to carry with them as they move deeper into the park. The bake shop is very crowded at opening time as guests grab breakfast sweets and coffee. A separate cookies and pastries line is available to the right of the entrance if that is all you want.

🍴 **Plaza Ice Cream Parlor.** On Main Street, near the Main Street Bakery. A pleasant, old-fashioned ice-cream shop; it gets very crowded at times. Most items about $3.00.

🍴 **Casey's Corner.** At the top end of Main Street. Hot dogs, soft drinks, and coffee. Serving staff wearing vintage baseball outfits offer hot dogs (about $2.50 and $3.95) with a toppings bar, plus other snacks.

🍴 **The Crystal Palace.** At the top of Main Street, toward Ad-

The Plaza Ice Cream Parlor at the top of Main Street, U.S.A.

The gardens at the Crystal Palace

ventureland. Breakfast, lunch, and dinner buffets. See chapter 20 for details on the character meals.

The building is a replica of the Crystal Palace, built for the International Exhibition in New York in 1851. The atmosphere is bright and airy with floral designs in a Victorian gazebo setting, and a Dixieland jazz group often entertains diners.

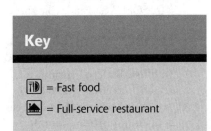 **Tony's Town Square Restaurant.** Just inside the entrance to the right. Italian food, steaks, seafood, hamburgers, and salads, $15.00 to $21.00; appetizers, $3.00 to $8.00. Breakfast, lunch, and dinner from 8:30 A.M.; closing time depends on park hours. Reservations recommended; check in at the restaurant lobby.

The restaurant is modeled after the cafe in Disney's classic *Lady and the Tramp* movie. Seating for about 200. Entrees include steak Fiorentino, a T-bone steak rubbed with garlic and peppercorns; chicken Florentine, a grilled breast served with spinach cream sauce and polenta; and veal marsala with wild mushrooms and marsala wine. Breakfast specialties include Italian frittatas, Lady and the Tramp waffles, and traditional favorites.

The Plaza Restaurant. At the top of Main Street toward Tomorrowland. Gourmet ham-

Key

= Fast food

= Full-service restaurant

burgers, soups, sandwiches, and salads. Lunch and dinner. Open from 11:00 A.M. Entrees, $7.00 to $9.00.

This pleasant nineteenth-century-style dining room offers table service inside and bright yellow and white umbrella tables outside. Specialties include Reubens and other sandwiches, basic burgers and grilled mushroom-and-onion burgers with provolone cheese, and supercalifragilisticexpialidocious sundaes.

ADVENTURELAND

Sunshine Tree Terrace. At the north end of Adventureland, behind the Enchanted Tiki Birds's Tropical Serenade, this is worth a quick stop for a drink or light snack. Offerings include citrus drinks, frozen yogurt, shakes, and desserts, $2.00 to $3.00.

Aloha Isle. Pineapple and fruit drinks, about $2.00. Try fresh pineapple spears for about $1.00 or raspberry/vanilla swirl.

El Pirata y el Perico Restaurante. Mexican fast food for lunch and dinner. Specialties include tacos and nachos.

FRONTIERLAND

Pecos Bill Cafe. Just past the Country Bear Vacation Hoedown. Burgers, chicken barbecue, salads, and hot dogs, $5.00 to $7.00. Western saloon atmosphere in the side-by-side restaurants that share a common menu. Look carefully at the animals mounted on the wall; they're talking and singing robots.

The chicken and bean salad or a barbecue chicken sandwich is a good alternative, but if a hamburger fits your fancy, try the Pecos Bill Trail Bacon Cheeseburger Basket. A fixings bar offers your basic toppings.

Aunt Polly's Dockside Inn. Just what you'd imagine Aunt Polly would pack for Tom and Huck: ham and cheese picnic lunches, apple pie, and ice cream. Located on Tom Sawyer Island.

Turkey Leg Wagon. One of the strangest sights you are likely to see in Frontierland is visitors walking along the pathway absently chewing on what looks like the leg of a large dog. Actually, they're smoked turkey legs sold at a stand directly across from the Country Bear Vacation Hoedown for about $4.00. Just follow the smell to the end of the line. As you carry along one of these interesting treats, watch out for seagulls; they'll sometimes fly right at the turkey leg and try to take a bite out of it!

Diamond Horseshoe Saloon Revue. Sandwiches, ice cream, and snacks with a free Old West vaudeville show. Check daily schedule.

LIBERTY SQUARE

Columbia Harbour House. On Liberty Square across from Ichabod's Landing. Battered shrimp and chicken, cold sandwiches, pasta salads, salads. Lunch and dinner, $3.00 to $7.00. Children's menu includes a chicken sandwich or hot dog for about $4.00. Seafood dining in seafaring atmosphere. The dark, cool decor provides a comfortable respite from the sun. Larger tables seat six to eight. A few small, semiprivate dining rooms accommodate groups.

For an unusual snack or meal, try the clam chowder served inside a round loaf of dark bread. When the chowder is gone, you can eat the bowl. A fruit plate is about $5.25. Sandwiches include smoked ham and cheese, tuna salad, and smoked turkey. Apple cobbler or chocolate and banana cream pies for dessert are about $3.00.

[🍽] Liberty Square Wagon. On the walkway between Columbia Harbour House and the Hall of Presidents. Baked potatoes with toppings and beverages, $2.00 to $3.00. There's also a fresh-fruit and pickle stand nearby. In an area where sandwiches and fast foods average about $5.00, the potato wagon is a popular alternative for a filling, low-cost lunch or snack. Fresh-baked white and sweet potatoes with a variety of toppings, about $2.50.

[🍽] Fruit and Vegetable Wagon. On the square behind the Columbia Harbour House and the Liberty Square Wagon. Various fruits and vegetables from a "farmers' market" wagon. Attractively presented offerings include apples, peaches, grapes, star fruit, and even pickles, squash, and potatoes.

[🏛] Liberty Tree Tavern. Next to Diamond Horseshoe Revue and open for lunch (11:30 A.M. to 4:00 P.M.) and dinner (from 4:30 P.M.). Sandwiches, beef, chicken, seafood, salads, $7.00 to $16.00. Reservations recommended; request a seating time at the door.

Sit-down dining in a colonial atmosphere with a lot of interesting details, including maple bench seats, fireplaces, and simulated peg flooring. A variety of sandwiches is available from about $7.00 to $10.00. Seafood and other entrees range from about $10 to $14. Luncheon specialties include New England pot roast, Pilgrim's Feast turkey dinner, and Cape Cod pasta with shrimp and vegetables.

At dinnertime the Liberty Tree features a Disney characters family-style dinner for about $20 for adults and $10 for children age nine and younger. The meal includes salad, roast turkey, glazed ham, and marinated flank steak.

■ MICKEY'S TOONTOWN FAIR

[🍽] Toontown Farmers Market. An outdoor stand where you can make your own strawberry shortcake for about $3.00.

■ FANTASYLAND

[🍽] Pinocchio Village Haus. Next to It's a Small World. Turkey hamburgers, turkey hot dogs, chicken, salads, pasta. Lunch and dinner.

A large dining hall in a Disneyfied Tudor style. You'll find several small rooms, including a favored location overlooking the It's a Small World ride. Meals from about $5.00 to $6.00 with french fries or grapes and a regular beverage include choice of cheeseburgers (beef or turkey), a quarter-pound turkey hot dog, or a grilled bratwurst. Also available is a smoked turkey sub with provolone cheese, lettuce, and tomatoes for about $4.50. The eatery includes a relish bar with pickles, tomatoes, onions, mushrooms, sauerkraut, barbecue sauce, cheese sauce, and more.

As at many Disney fast-food restaurants, the service lines move slowly at peak time. Come early or late to avoid wasting time.

🍴 **Cinderella's Royal Table.** Upstairs in Cinderella Castle. Character breakfasts, lunches, and dinners. If you enter the castle from the Fantasyland side, the restaurant is on the outside left. Lines for lunch begin early because seating is limited. Among the more expensive restaurants in the Magic Kingdom, Cinderella's Royal Table is a special draw for some children, especially little girls who dream of meeting Cinderella herself. Reservations are accepted at the door on the day you wish to dine; guests at Disney hotels can make telephone reservations up to two days ahead of time.

You enter the restaurant through a "great hall" entrance on the ground floor. This interesting room is complete with torch lanterns and swords on the wall. The slate floor and high, exposed-beam ceiling enhance the "castle" feeling of the restaurant. You'll move upstairs via an interesting, winding stairway or in an elevator.

■ TOMORROWLAND

🍴 **Cosmic Ray's Starlight Cafe.** Cosmic Ray's (get it?) is the largest fast-food eatery in the Magic Kingdom, the former Tomorrowland Terrace. It's decorated in brushed aluminum, purples, and blacks, and there's a little stage at the back of the room for shows. Offerings include hamburgers, vegetarian burgers, chicken, soups, and salads at several food court–like stands within. Specialties include the Chick Encounter family meal for three to four, featuring a whole rotisserie chicken, and the Coop Canaveral chicken drummettes.

🍴 **Plaza Pavilion.** In the walkway between Main Street and Tomorrowland. Pizza, sandwiches, salads, $3.00 to $5.00. Covered outdoor dining in a pleasant setting for about 650 people. There are three dining areas, including one that overlooks a portion of the central lagoon and Cinderella Castle. The area offers cool shade and ample seating away from the main service area and transient crowds.

Try the Italian hoagie at about $4.25 or the chicken Parmesan sandwich for a dollar more. Deep-dish pizza is available by the slice for about $3.25 to $4.75. Get your ice cream with the brownie sundae for about $2.75 or an ice-cream float for about $2.30.

🍴 **Auntie Gravity's Galactic Goodies.** Across the broad plaza from Space Mountain at the base of the Astro Orbiter tower. Juice, snacks, and frozen yogurt, $2.00 to $3.00.

CHAPTER EIGHT

EPCOT

EPCOT IS DISNEY'S PERMANENT WORLD'S FAIR, a place where the nations and the global multinational corporations of the world meet their tourists and customers. Oh, and it's a heck of a lot of fun, too.

Future World, the front half of the park, celebrates things that make us go ZOOM. You enter past **Spaceship Earth,** fly by the **Universe of Energy,** put the pedal to the metal at the **GM Test Track,** and come in for a splashdown at **The Living Seas.**

In a world full of great new things, there are two state-of-the-art flying experiences at Epcot: the gentle and sublimely thrilling **Soarin',** an import from Disney's California Adventure that simulates a hang-glider tour of the Golden States, and the one-of-a-kind **Mission: SPACE,** which blasts off—with a gut-wrenching launch—from Florida to Mars every few minutes. In fact, Mission: SPACE proved to be so stomach-churning for some guests that Disney ended up modifying the ride to allow for two versions. The original ride continues, but there is now also a milder version that turns off the spinning centrifuge that provides most of the G-force thrills (and upset).

Younger visitors gained a new interactive show at The Living Seas, *The Seas with Nemo & Friends.* And nearby at the same pavilion, the turtle-dude Crush has his own high-tech gig. And Figment still charms visitors to **Imagination!**

World Showcase, on the other side of the central lagoon, rejoices in the thrill of international cultures, from Canada to China, Germany to Mexico, and Japan to France.

THE EPCOT STORY

Walt Disney envisioned a modern city built from scratch to include factories, homes, offices, and farms as a showcase for new ideas and technologies from industry and education. Disney gave his dream the name Experimental Prototype

Community of Tomorrow, which is the almost-forgotten name behind the Epcot acronym.

Disney lived long enough to set the broad outlines for Epcot, but the park as built was quite different from the prototype community he first planned. Roughly half the park is given over to imaginative pavilions that explore the frontiers of science: communication, energy, human life, transportation, technology, creativity, agriculture, and the seas. Spread around the World Showcase Lagoon are exhibits, films, and a handful of rides that share some of the cultures of the globe: Canada, France, Morocco, Japan, Italy, America, Germany, China, Norway, Mexico, and the United Kingdom.

Epcot, at 260 acres, is more than twice the size of the Magic Kingdom. The World Showcase Lagoon is about forty acres in size; the promenade that circles it and leads to the pavilions of nations is 1.2 miles long. Construction costs were about $1.3 billion in 1982; at the time it was one of the largest private construction jobs ever undertaken. Hundreds of millions more has been spent since to expand the park.

Although for most visitors it is the Magic Kingdom of Mickey and Minnie that brings them to Walt Disney World, many adults and quite a few children will tell you that the memory they bring home comes from Epcot: blasting off at Mission: SPACE, the wild ride at Test Track, the dinosaurs at the Universe of Energy, the troll at Norway, or the film view of the Great Wall at China. And now millions can come to Florida to hang glide over California.

Epcot has its own parking lot. It is also connected by monorail to the Ticket and Transportation Center (TTC); from there visitors can transfer to another train to continue on to the Magic Kingdom. A ferry connects Epcot's International Gateway to Disney–MGM Studios and to nearby hotels.

EPCOT OPERATING HOURS

Epcot operates on a split schedule, with Future World open for much of the season from 9:00 A.M. to 9:00 P.M. and the World Showcase at the back of the park open from 11:00 A.M. to 9:00 P.M. On most days the gates open at 8:30 A.M., and Spaceship Earth is open for early arrivals.

Remember that operating hours are subject to change; call the park or check at the front desk of one of the hotels within the park for current information.

Epcot is unique among the four parks at Walt Disney World in that it has two entrances—the main gate, which leads directly to the Spaceship Earth, and a second, less-used International Gateway at the World Showcase, between the United Kingdom and France pavilions. Trams or ferries run between the International Gateway and the BoardWalk, Swan, Dolphin, Beach Club, and Yacht Club Resorts. You can also take a ferry between the International Gateway and Disney–MGM Studios, about a thirty-minute trip.

SPECTACLES

IllumiNations: Reflections of Earth is a dazzling finale on and above World Showcase Lagoon; the night is filled with the fiery glow of torches, lasers, high-energy music, and booming fireworks. The sky transforms into a kaleidoscope of colorful pyrotechnic bursts. Comets streak across the sky as video images are displayed on the giant Earth Globe, the floating centerpiece. Then, the sphere blossoms like a flower, revealing a brilliant ball of fire. The music builds, lasers shoot skyward, fireworks light the night, and flames leap across the surface of the lagoon.

ATTRACTIONS AT FUTURE WORLD

MUST-SEE SPACESHIP EARTH

The huge geodesic sphere that is the symbol of Epcot—referred to by most visitors as the "golf ball"—is 180 feet (eighteen stories) high and 165 feet in diameter with 2.2 million cubic feet of space within. The outside of the sphere is made up of some 11,000 triangular tiles, made of a composite of ethylene plastic bonded between two aluminum panels. It weighs almost sixteen million pounds, including 1,750 tons of steel.

As impressive as the shell is, the real excitement of Spaceship Earth can be found on the ride within.

The original ride was designed by a collaboration that included science-fiction author Ray Bradbury, the Smithsonian Institution, and news-

Spaceship Earth. © *Disney Enterprises, Inc.*

EPCOT CENTER

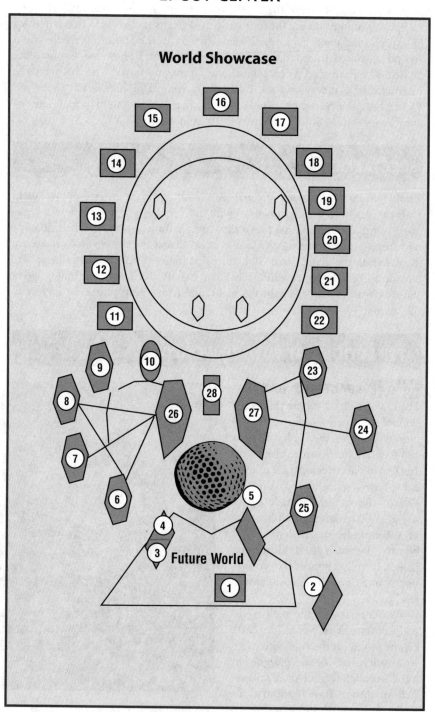

World Showcase

Future World

EPCOT CENTER

① Monorail station
② Bus terminal
③ Banking
④ Strollers
⑤ Spaceship Earth
⑥ Universe of Energy
⑦ Wonders of Life
⑧ Mission: SPACE
⑨ GM Test Track
⑩ Special events
⑪ Mexico
⑫ Norway
⑬ China
⑭ Germany
⑮ Italy

⑯ United States
⑰ Japan
⑱ Morocco
⑲ France
⑳ International Gateway ferry terminal to Epcot resorts
㉑ United Kingdom
㉒ Canada
㉓ Imagination!
㉔ The Land
㉕ The Living Seas
㉖ Innoventions East
㉗ Innoventions West
㉘ Fountain of Nations

man Walter Cronkite. The ride was updated in 1995 with some new areas, a new narration by actor Jeremy Irons, and a new musical score. (The cloying "Tomorrow's Child" song is gone.) There's nothing here that will set your heart to pounding, but the lighting, video, and computerized special effects are among the best at Walt Disney World.

You'll board "time machine" chairs for a trip into the sphere that will take you back through history from the age of the Cro-Magnon some 30,000 years ago to the present, passing through the great ancient civilizations of Egypt, Phoenicia, and Rome along the way. The narration may be a bit beyond the comprehension of young children, but they'll still enjoy and learn from the sights.

You'll note some of the important developments of our time, including the creation of an alphabet and written language, the first books, the development of the printing press, and on to modern communications. You'll also see great cultural figures from Michelangelo at work in the Sistine Chapel to Howdy Doody and Ed Sullivan. At the very top of the ball is the most spectacular sight of all, a huge sky of stars and planets.

Not all of the special effects of this ride are visual ones; Disney engineers created smell cannons that fill the air with appropriate odors, including the ashes of burning Rome. The page from the Bible that Johannes Gutenberg is examining is an exact replica of a page from one of his early bibles. In an ancient Egypt setting, the hieroglyphics on the wall are

Tubular, Dude

The Spaceship Earth sphere is built from four structural parts. The outer shell is strictly for decorative purposes and is connected to an inner waterproof sphere by hundreds of small support columns. A column that runs up the center of the ball supports the internal ride, which circles around the column like a spiral staircase. Finally, a platform at the bottom of the sphere supports the inner structure and the ride itself.

This plan is based on the split schedule that opens Future World two hours before the World Showcase and takes advantage of the Fastpass system. The key to getting the most out of a visit to Epcot, as with every other theme park, is to adopt a contrarian view. Most visitors saunter into the park in midmorning and join the crowds at the pavilions of Future World before beginning a slow—and crowded—circle of the World Showcase section in a clockwise direction.

Our plan begins with an early arrival and quick visits to the most popular pavilions in Future World before moving on to the World Showcase for late morning and the first part of the afternoon. Return to Future World as the sun sinks lower in the sky and miss the crowds who are now moving deeper into the park.

At Epcot, Soarin'; Mission: SPACE; GM Test Track; *Honey, I Shrunk the Audience;* Living with the Land; and Maelstrom at Norway have Fastpass booths. Before you go to the park, make up a list of your personal must-sees. Get to the park early. Soarin' is on the right side of the entrance; if that's your goal, head there first and go for a soar, or pick up a Fastpass reservation for later in the morning and then head for one of the other hot rides at the park.

If you're up for some speed, head directly to Mission: SPACE, and then make tracks to the GM Test Track. Bear to the left from the entrance and follow the signs. Once again, if the lines are short, go ahead and take a spin; otherwise, grab a Fastpass reservation and come back at the appointed hour.

While you're in the neighborhood, retrace your steps a bit to the Universe of Energy pavilion and see the show there. Then sprint across Future World to the **Imagination!** pavilion for the *Honey, I Shrunk the Audience* show. Grab a seat or a Fastpass reservation. By this time it should be near 11:00 A.M. and time to jump out ahead of the crowds. Move into the World Showcase.

The biggest crowds at the World Showcase can usually be found at the **Norway, Mexico,** and **American** pavilions. If you are at the head of the throng, go immediately to Mexico, then next door to Norway, and then continue in a clockwise circle around the lagoon. If you find yourself behind the crowd, you might want to travel in the opposite direction, going counterclockwise and starting at Canada.

After you leave the World Showcase, tour the remaining pavilions of Future World, this time moving in a clockwise direction—starting at the Imagination! pavilion and heading toward the front of the park and **Spaceship Earth.** Double back at the golf ball and visit **Innoventions** and **Wonders of Life** to complete your tour.

With luck, you will complete the tour of Epcot at nightfall and can enjoy a leisurely dinner before coming out to the lagoon for a view of the spectacular *IllumiNations* show.

(continued)

Here's a by-the-numbers Power Trip, pavilion by pavilion. **1:** Soarin';
2: Mission: SPACE; **3:** GM Test Track; **4:** Universe of Energy; **5:** Journey into
Imagination with Figment; **6:** Mexico; **7:** Norway; **8:** China; **9:** Germany;
10: Italy; **11:** The American Adventure; **12:** Japan; **13:** Morocco; **14:** France;
15: United Kingdom; **16:** Canada; **17:** Imagination!; **18:** The Land; **19:** The
Living Seas; **20:** Spaceship Earth; **21:** Innoventions; **22:** Wonders of Life.

reproductions of actual graphics; the words being dictated by the pharaoh were
taken from an actual letter sent by a pharaoh to one of his agents. (If you look
very carefully at the male animatronic figures, you may find that some of them
look familiar. According to Disney insiders, many of the robotic stars of
Spaceship Earth use faces based on the same molds used in the Hall of Presidents
at the Magic Kingdom. The clothing and hair were changed, of course. Look
closely at the lute player in the Renaissance scene: President Dwight D.
Eisenhower makes a cameo appearance.)

Next we move into the near future, where we see a young boy communicating in his room over the information superhighway. At the very top of the golf
ball we move into a startlingly beautiful planetarium-like dome with Spaceship
Earth and the stars all around it. Our chairs move into a view of a futuristic
classroom embarking on a virtual field trip. The dazzling finale puts the audience in the heart of interactive global networks that tie the peoples of Earth together. Fantastic special effects, animatronic robots, and laser beams surround
and encase the visitors on a simulated trip into a microchip. At the exit is the
Global Neighborhood for hands-on demonstrations of new technologies in
voice recognition, video telephony, and the information superhighway. In one
scene an American boy and a Japanese teenage girl exchange experiences via
video telephone. He shows today's karate class; she shows video of her home run
in last night's baseball game.

As befits the unusual building, the time machines in this ride take an unusual
route. You'll slowly spiral up, up, and up around the sides of the ball until you
reach the starfield at top; then your chair will turn around for a steep, backward
descent to the base. Some riders might find the trip down a bit uncomfortable.

Because of its position at the front of the park, lines for this ride are usually
longest at the start of the day, although early arrivals can still expect to be able
to walk right on. If the line builds up, though, we'd suggest coming back in the
afternoon or on your way out of the park at the end of the day.

MUST-SEE MISSION: SPACE ≡FAST

Mission: SPACE is about as real an interplanetary trip as you'll find this side of
the Kennedy Space Center, an attraction that boldly goes where no thrill ride has
gone before: deep space.

The ride is a thrilling combination of Disney storytelling and one-of-a-kind
technology, launching flight trainees into a space adventure, from pulse-racing

A Message from Space

liftoff to weightlessness in outer space. Of course, there is no rocket ship within the fanciful building at Epcot dominated by a huge red planet. Instead, it's a state-of-the-art simulation based on an adaptation of a flight-training centrifuge.

According to some real astronauts who tried the ride, this is about as real an experience as you're going to get without actually strapping into a rocket and blasting off. In fact, it is so real that more than a few nonastronauts became airsick on their short simulated voyage. And so in 2006, Disney began offering two versions of the ride: the original and a much tamer experience that relies on visual special effects without the centrifuge.

Welcome to the International Space Training Center (ISTC), Disney's version of NASA. It is thirty years in the future, and space is accessible to any traveler, although a bit of training is necessary. This is not science fiction; it's a plausible simulation of a down-to-earth training facility for a trip into space: the first crew to Mars.

There will be, of course, hundreds or thousands of other flight trainees preparing to make the same trip. Once you make your way into the building, you'll enter into a jaw-dropping room with a gigantic rotating gravity wheel along one wall. (Anyone who first dreamt of making their own flight to space when they saw astronauts jogging around a gravity wheel in Stanley Kubrick's film *2001: A Space Odyssey* will be ready for immediate blastoff.)

The room includes an original Lunar Rover prototype, on loan from the Smithsonian Institution National Air and Space Museum.

Leaving the gravity wheel, you'll enter into Training Operations, where you'll look over the shoulders of Mission Control. (The workers and the equipment double as the actual ride control.) A lenticular display of the solar system shows various missions in progress.

A time line near the entrance to your ride capsule shows the history of spaceflight, beginning with Soviet cosmonaut Yuri Gagarin's orbital flight in 1961. At the other end—today in the year 2036—is a plaque commemorating the first family in space (the Wilsons, along with Sunspot the Dalmatian), who blasted off on September 1, 2030.

And now you're routed to the Ready Room, where the incoming corps of flight trainees are split into teams: blue, red, gold, or green. There's no difference between the teams—it's just a way to break up the line into groups of forty for their flight.

Entrance to the International Space Training Center at Mission: SPACE

Actor Gary Sinise, who played astronaut Ken Mattingly in the film *Apollo 13,* introduces us to our upcoming ISTC mission in a training video in the Ready Room. He asks us if we're nervous about our upcoming launch, which will take us from 0 to 6,000 mph in six seconds. (Anyone preparing to go to the moon has always felt that way, he assures us.) There are several opportunities to bail out ("opt out") and sign up for Mission Control training.

Then the doors open to the pods, which can hold 160 guests at a time. There are four sets of centrifuges, each with ten pods holding four seats, one for each of the assigned roles: commander, pilot, navigator, and engineer. Each seat has control buttons and a joystick, and each member of the crew a different set of tasks to execute when the Capcom issues an instruction. (The mission cannot fail; if you don't respond properly to instructions, the onboard computer will take over.) The commander is in charge of separation from the booster rocket; the pilot triggers the second stage; the navigator is expected to fire the thrusters; and the engineer monitors the hyperspeed system.

Two teams enter through each door, and you'll see only two of the ten pods. The secrets behind the trip are well hidden outside of the closed capsules; they

The Planetary Plaza near the entrance to Mission: SPACE

spin and rotate in the dark, and visitors' only view is of the interior and the video screens that give representation of space travel.

The view of Earth and Mars are computer generated from data provided by satellites and spacecraft orbiting the planets, including Mars Odyssey and Global Surveyor. Details on Mars include real landforms created from scientific height data and photographic imagery.

Effects on the original version of the ride include a pulse-racing liftoff that provides the sensation of heading straight up in flight, then a brief sensation of weightlessness in the darkness of space, a positive-G "slingshot" maneuver around the moon, an asteroid-dodging dash toward Mars, and a wild landing on the Red Planet.

The ride (with the centrifuge spinning) delivers a very intense simulation of takeoff and all sorts of unusual weightlessness and positive-G feelings. For me, the most unusual moment came when I was called on to press the button to fire the second-stage rocket; when I lifted my hand, it felt like it weighed a few hundred pounds. One of the open secrets of spaceflight is the fact that many astronauts and cosmonauts suffer bouts of "space sickness," which differs from seasickness only in the altitude at which it occurs. Visitors to Mission: SPACE need also consider the possibility of dizziness and stomach upset on the simulation.

As you enter the ride, there are multiple warnings to passengers with fears of enclosed spaces and motion sickness. Most visitors will enjoy the ride without problems, but if you are prone to motion sickness,

Epcot Insider Tip

Here's an insider tip for a classy way to spend the day at Epcot: Take the launch from World Gateway to the BoardWalk Resort for lunch or dinner to escape the madding crowds.

you may want to take some special care. You might want to take a Dramamine or similar motion-sickness preventive half an hour before taking the ride, assuming you do not have a medical condition that precludes its use (check with your doctor).

Once you're in the capsule, here's what not to do: lean forward, close your eyes, or look left or right. Instead, sit back and keep your eyes open and looking forward. Or choose the version without the centrifuge if you'd rather not go for a spin.

The ride was developed by Disney in collaboration with Entertainment Technology Corporation (ETC), a Pennsylvania company that has built aircrew simulation products and related entertainment rides, including the Cyberspace Mountain simulator at DisneyQuest. The company's centrifuges are capable of zooming from 1 to 15 Gs in one second and can reach a maximum of 25 Gs; the ride at Epcot is much less severe, reaching a sustained level of 2.5 Gs. The ride pods can rotate 360 degrees even while spinning.

The technological complexity of the ride system required an enormous amount of equipment, computers, and technology to be carried onboard. Imagineers combined ultra-lightweight carbon fiber materials with airplane wing construction techniques and integration of components into the capsule itself.

Design specifications included the requirement that all the electronics had to be able to withstand multiple "launches" every day, and multiple endurance tests were conducted before the units were released for production. Multiple computers onboard the ride ensure synchronization of the video, audio, and motion of the capsule to create a realistic and powerful experience.

After your four-minute mission is complete, you'll exit your simulator and enter the Advanced Training Lab, where there are the following activities:

■ Expedition Mars, where trainees can learn to use a joystick and jet pack to control an astronaut on the surface of the Red Planet.

■ Mission: SPACE Race, which pits teams of thirty trainees at a time in a challenge to pilot a craft from Mars back to Earth, seeking and replenishing supplies for the mission. You can take a peek at some of the events by going online at www.disneyspacerace.com.

■ Postcards from Space, a set of consoles where you can send one of eight different action videos to an e-mail address of your choice. You'll pose for a video camera and insert your moving image into mini-adventures entitled Space Cadet, Greetings from Space, We Have a Problem, One Small Step, Life on Mars?, Take Me to Your Leader, Alien Abduction, or Saucer Invasion.

The Gardens of Epcot

Epcot is the most meticulously gardened of any of the theme parks at Walt Disney World. Guests age sixteen and older interested in learning more about Epcot landscaping can take the Gardens of the World tour, a three-hour guided walk through World Showcase that explores the styles of landscaping represented in each pavilion. The tour cost is $49 per person. For reservations call (407) 939–8687.

■ Space Base Kids Crawl, which also doubles as the location of a baby-swap area for youngsters too small to blast off for Mars. An intricate set of clear-plastic climbing tubes extends two stories above the lab.

And there is, of course, a gift shop. (Guests can enter directly into the gift shop, and into the Advanced Training Lab, from a doorway at the right side of the building. You can't get on the ride from the lab, though, without waiting in line.)

Speaking of lines, though, there are three ways to get a seat in Mission: SPACE:

1. Waiting in a long queue;

2. Grabbing a Fastpass to make an appointment for a dramatically shortened line; or

3. Joining the singles line to fill in an open pod whenever one is available.

Flight trainees have to be at least 44 inches tall to participate in the mission.

In the outdoor Planetary Plaza near the entrance, take a moment to examine the model of the moon that includes the landing sites for all twenty-nine explorations by U.S. and Russian spacecraft; manned expeditions are in blue, and unmanned explorations have clear markers. Arrayed around the curving wall of the courtyard are quotes from great thinkers and dreamers who paved the way to space travel. Among them:

■ "We set sail on this new sea, because there is knowledge to be gained."—President John F. Kennedy

■ "Exploration is really the essence of the human spirit." —Astronaut Frank Borman

Six-time NASA shuttle astronaut Story Musgrove was one of the consultants on the project. NASA has no formal relationship with Disney for the attraction, although it did allow depiction of its training methods. Corporate sponsor is Hewlett Packard.

The pavilion occupies the former site of the Horizons attraction, one of the sentimental favorites of Epcot. Horizons was an extension of the theme from the Magic Kingdom's Carousel of Progress, presenting a vision of the future that included the Omega Centauri space colony, the Sea Castle underwater city, and the robotic farm station Mesa Verde.

The Lights Fantastic

Disney designers snuck a little extra bit of magic into the construction of the Innoventions building: Fiber optics embedded in the tiles of the walkways outside are computer controlled to dance along with the nightly *IllumiNations* show on the lagoon.

⚏ MUST-SEE INNOVENTIONS

Innoventions is the most commercial part of Walt Disney World, which is saying quite a bit. This is the World's Fair core of Epcot. What Disney has done is truly an amazing thing: It has found a way to charge visitors nearly $50 each to enter a somewhat ordinary convention hall–like building and look at exhibits of commercial products. Even more amazing is the fact that Disney is able to charge major corporations millions of dollars for the right to build their own exhibits.

Although products are not sold in exhibit areas, representatives are on hand to explain and demonstrate. Guests can use computer terminals to request information by mail. Most of the exhibits are changed every few years. Youngsters and fans of electronic gadgets will likely want to bear to the right of Spaceship Earth to **Innoventions West,** home of exhibits by companies that in recent years included Monsanto, Lutron, Xerox, and IBM. On the left side of Spaceship Earth in **Innoventions East** are exhibits aimed mostly at adults, including displays in recent years from Compaq and Motorola.

Fast-food eateries within the Innoventions area include the Electric Umbrella Restaurant and the Fountain View Espresso and Bakery. Parental guidance: Be sure to have a plan to keep track of your children as they roam the sprawling Innoventions buildings.

▮▮▮▮ MUST-SEE ▮▮▮▮ UNIVERSE OF ENERGY

Forward to the past, and back to the future: One of the favorite pavilions at Epcot has been given a fresh jolt of . . . energy. The pavilion is based around an entertaining film known as *Ellen's Energy Adventure,* starring comedian Ellen DeGeneres and featuring some exciting special effects. In the movie Ellen dreams she is a contestant on the *Jeopardy!* television game show. She's up against the reigning champion, Dr. Judy Peterson, played by Jamie Lee Curtis. The third contestant: Albert Einstein. And the categories? They're all about energy, a subject that is clearly not Ellen's specialty. Ellen has a secret weapon, though: her neighbor Bill Nye the Science Guy. She summons him for some hints, and he responds by taking Ellen—and all of the guests seated in the pavilion's famous moving grandstands—on a tour that travels back in time to the birth of the planet, and then on to a world tour of today's energy needs and research.

The show begins with a standing-room-only preshow where we are introduced to Ellen, her cats, her neighbor Bill, and her nemesis, the brainy Dr. Peterson—Ellen insists her nickname was "Stupid Judy." Also making cameo appearances are game-show host Alex Trebek, Willard Scott with the 1 million B.C. weather, and Len Berman with the back, back, back sports report. From the preshow guests move into the old moving theater cars for an expedition 220 million years back to the Big Bang and from there to the dawn of the dinosaurs, with Ellen wisecracking all the way along.

There are six sections; the seats all the way forward to the left lead the parade, while the back right section moves out last. We prefer to be in front. The show still draws healthy crowds and contributes to a lopsided draw to the west side of the park along with the GM Test Track. Head there early, or come back late in the day to avoid lines that may stretch for eons.

▮ WONDERS OF LIFE

A world of its own. Under one geodesic-domed roof you will find two of Epcot's best attractions, plus a healthful Fitness Fairground for children of all ages and entertaining and informative films and presentations on subjects from exercise to reproduction. The geodesic dome for the Wonders of Life pavilion is 250 feet in diameter and 60 feet tall at the center; to construct it, engineers built a temporary tower crane in the center. Rings of triangles were then hoisted by cables attached to the tower and anchored to columns around the circumference. When the dome was up, the crane was dismantled and removed. This is not Epcot's most popular pavilion; perhaps it is just too darned educational. You could easily spend a few hours here; it's an excellent place to escape bad weather. In 2004 Disney began closing the pavilion during the slowest seasons; check ahead of time if this place is one of your goals.

MUST-SEE Body Wars

Strap on your seat belts and prepare for blastoff on a journey to inner space. Body Wars is a fantastic simulator ride that takes you on a repair expedition inside a human body—a training mission to remove a splinter from *within.* (Check out the pilot's cockpit for the Body Wars vehicle; we especially like the pink baby shoes hanging over the windshield.)

As usual in a sci-fi story like this, something goes wrong within the body, and the medical craft begins to lose all power from its fuel cell. Our pilot decides he must go to the brain and cross the blood-brain barrier and park next to a synapse in hopes that it will fire and recharge the cell. Our cabin bounces and twists through the veins and arteries of the human body, ending up with an electrical bang.

Amazingly for a vehicle that doesn't really go anywhere, this ride carries as many health warnings as a roller coaster. Pregnant women and visitors with back or heart ailments are advised not to come aboard, and an adult must accompany any child younger than seven; those younger than three years of age cannot ride. If you're the type who gets queasy on an elevator—and you know who you are— you might want to pass this one by.

Any serious movie fan will recognize the Body Wars story as a spin-off of the classic science-fiction flick *Fantastic Voyage,* which featured Raquel Welch in a bodysuit. At Epcot the Body Wars probe is captained by former fighter pilot Jack Braddock, accompanied by a crew of Walt Disney World guests. The objective is to rendezvous with Dr. Cynthia Lair, an immunologist who also has been miniaturized and beamed inside a patient to study the body's response to a splinter lodged beneath the skin. Soon, however, the voyage evolves into a high-speed race against time when Dr. Lair is swept from the splinter site into the rush of the bloodstream. Going through the pounding chambers of the subject's heart and on through the lungs' gale-force winds, the ship rides the body's current in an effort to rescue Dr. Lair. Once she's safely onboard, though, something goes wrong—you knew that, didn't you?—when the ship loses power and heads toward the brain in search of emergency power and escape.

Super Helix

The huge sculpture at the entrance to the Wonders of Life pavilion is a 75-foot-tall representation of a DNA molecule, the basic building block of life. A human built to the same scale would be about 6 million miles tall.

The monorail passes over Epcot.

The ride was created by Walt Disney Imagineering together with George Lucas's Industrial Light and Magic. The film was directed by Leonard Nimoy, *Star Trek*'s Mr. Spock. "Even though Body Wars is the shortest film I've ever directed, it presented a new set of challenges," Nimoy explained. "We had to take into account that the film will be shown inside a moving theater—the simulator. So, in order to intensify the sense of motion, we built a set that actually moved, and rocked it during filming to match the pitching and rolling of the simulator."

Forty passengers can ride in each of the four twenty-six-ton moving theaters.

MUST-SEE Cranium Command

A wild and offbeat show, unlike almost anything else at Walt Disney World, this is a combination audio-animatronics and film journey into one of the most unstable places on Earth. Your screaming leader, General Knowledge, will inform you that you have been assigned to pilot the most erratic craft in the fleet—the mind of a twelve-year-old boy.

This is a presentation that has something for everyone, from corny jokes and a food fight for the kids to smart one-liners and comic performances from well-known comedians, including George Wendt (Norm from *Cheers*) as superintendent of the stomach, Bobcat Goldthwait as a hysterical adrenaline gland, and Charles Grodin as the smug, all-knowing Right Brain. All this is to teach about the benefits of stress management! It's a very clever show and rarely more than a fifteen- to thirty-minute wait; don't miss it.

Fitness Fairgrounds

The various exhibits in the center of the dome can occupy visitors for hours and are a great place to get out of the sun or rain. Our only warning about this place is that it is quite easy to misplace young children in the busy aisles. Attractions within Fitness Fairgrounds include:

- **Goofy About Health.** You wouldn't ordinarily include our old friend Goofy on a list of contenders for the Olympic team, but this very entertaining film presentation teaches about the value of exercise and health habits as it entertains.
- **AnaComical Players.** A lively and pun-filled tour of the human body, presented by a clever improvisational theater group. Are you really ready for "Flossed in Space"?
- **The Making of Me.** Okay, parents: Here's an opportunity to teach your children some of the facts of life in an entertaining fourteen-minute film starring comedian Martin Short. He begins with a visit to the birth of his mom and dad and follows them right through his own conception (lovemaking is described as a private moment between lovers, with just enough detail to guarantee your kids will come up with their own questions). There is spectacular footage of the beginnings of life and childbirth. Lines for this show, presented in a tiny theater, can begin to stretch to as much as an hour at the most crowded parts of the day; go early or late. Highly recommended.
- **Coach's Corner.** Step up to the batting tee, the tennis net, or the fairway for a quick sports lesson. Your swing will be videotaped, and you'll receive a quick taped comment from one of sports' greatest players. It's all in good fun, although some adults seem to take their moment of stardom very seriously.
- **Wondercycles.** A high-tech set of exercise bicycles that present videodisc images keyed to your pedaling speed. You can "visit" Disneyland, scoot in and among the floats in the Rose Bowl Parade in California, or enjoy a hilarious low-level pedal through Big Town, U.S.A., in which your cycle passes humans, dogs, cars, and furniture at rug-rat level.
- **Sensory Funhouse.** A set of interesting demonstrations of human senses, including sight, sound, and touch. You'll discover some unusual demonstrations, such as an area where you stick your hands through a black curtain so you can't see what you are touching. Like the old story of the blind men and the elephant, it's amusing to hear the descriptions visitors make of items that include a pair of ski goggles, a chess piece, a gyroscope, a toy train, and a toy dinosaur.
- **Met Lifestyle Revue.** A computer will ask you all sorts of personal questions and then offer a personalized set of lifestyle suggestions.

The best way to tour Wonders of Life is to keep an eye on waiting lines for Body Wars and Cranium Command and dive in when they seem reasonable. There is plenty to occupy visitors between trips to those attractions.

🅼🆄🆂🆃-🆂🅴🅴 GM TEST TRACK ≡*FAST*

Fasten your seat belts for the longest, fastest, and most technologically complex ride at Walt Disney World, a wild salute to GM's proving grounds for automobiles. You'll climb hills, careen through hairpin turns, jounce down bumpy roadways, zip along straightaways, and enter into a fifty-degree banked turn at 65 miles per hour, zooming across the front of the pavilion. Trust me, it feels like twice that speed.

The Test Track climbs, spirals, and snakes through the 150,000-square-foot pavilion; the former home of the World of Motion was completely gutted and rebuilt for this attraction at Epcot. About half of the 5,246-foot-long track loops outside the pavilion, where maximum speeds are obtained; a full ride takes about five and a half minutes. (By comparison, Space Mountain lasts about three minutes, reaching a top speed of just 32 miles per hour, half that of the test vehicles here.)

Test Track and Mission: SPACE are the two top draws at Epcot, at least for those with the need for speed. If you have any doubt, consider the fact that Test Track is set up with the largest waiting area in Walt Disney World. If the outside queue is filled, the last person in line can expect as much as a ninety-minute wait. Once you set foot inside the building, the wait should be about forty-five minutes.

One way to get around the waiting lines is to volunteer for the "singles" crew. You'll be ushered right to the training theater, to wait in a much shorter line for the odd open space in the cars. If you choose to take the singles line, you stand a good chance of getting an outside seat as the cars have three chairs in each row. Even better: Make a ride reservation using Disney's Fastpass system.

On the plus side, the inside queue is actually one of the more interesting places I know of to stand around and wait. You'll pass through a simulation of a GM test facility with all sorts of torture devices for vehicles—from door slammers and seat-belt twisters to crash-test dummies in all sorts of extreme distress. The much-abused star here is Chester, who allows himself to be repeatedly thumped in the chest by a swinging weight. By the way, real crash-test dummies cost as much as $100,000 each, wired with as many as 120 data channels for instruments. You'll also learn about emissions, braking, and safety engineering at GM.

At the end of the waiting area, the line is split into groups of twenty-four and ushered into small theaters for a briefing by the test-track coordinator. You'll learn about acceleration, braking, and rollover tests . . . oops, no rollovers today. Note the pictures on the walls of actual GM test tracks around the world. Your guide will select a menu of tests for you and your vehicle:

- **Hill-climb test.** An accelerating climb up a three-story, eighteen-degree hill, demonstrating the measurement of the generation of heat and stress on engines and transmissions.
- **Road-surface test.** Your vehicle will clamber across stretches of rough German and Belgian blocks in a trial for the suspension system.
- **Brake test.** The car makes a high-speed run at a set of traffic cones, with and without computer-controlled ABS braking. Without ABS, of course, the cones become orange roadkill. Monitors give you an instant replay.
- **Environmental chamber.** The vehicles move into a 120-degree heat-lamp oven and then a 20-degree indoor arctic in a test of the effects of temperature and corrosion on the body and system. From there the cars (and passengers) endure a corrosive mist sprayed by industrial robots.

■ **Ride and handling test.** A pass through a hairpin turn and loops set the stage for high-speed trials to come.

■ **Barrier test.** Off to the left side of the car you can watch another test vehicle—with test dummies instead of vacationers—crash into a barrier. And then your vehicle will accelerate rapidly and slam at full speed into a solid wall—not! But it will come very, very close.

■ **High-speed test.** On the other side of the wall is the outdoor high-speed test track, a wild ride into the backyard of the pavilion, and then a great swoop around the front on a fifty-degree bank where the vehicle reaches its top speed of just under 65 miles per hour. Passengers experience about 2 Gs of force on the banked turns.

The ride draws its inspiration from GM's famed Milford proving ground northwest of Detroit; the facility dates from 1924 and includes 132 miles of test roads of nearly every construction. The vehicles are not derived from an actual GM car but instead are adaptations of a HYGE sled. HYGE, which stands for "hydraulic-controlled gas-energized," is a test sled that allows engineers to simplify and standardize the proving-grounds process.

Guests enter into a six-passenger Test Track vehicle; vehicles pull up four at a time. When they leave, cars are spaced about ten seconds apart; the ride should be able to accommodate about 1,800 persons per hour. There are three seats in front and three in back, and each passenger has a shoulder harness and seat belt. (There is no steering wheel, accelerator, or brake pedal—the vehicle is entirely under the control of the computer.) A video screen in front of each row of seats helps explain the testing process.

Passengers will feel the wind; I'd recommend angling for a front seat, where there's a bit more protection from the wind and the view of the track is clearer. The ride will likely continue to operate in light rain but shut down in heavier conditions. Trust me, you wouldn't enjoy the ride in a Florida thunder-boomer. The ride is fun any time of the day, but I particularly recommend the experience by night, when darkness accentuates the outdoor experience.

The gas caps on the body of the car are strictly for show. The vehicles use electric motors in the rear that draw 480 volts of power through a slot in the bottom of the track, like a super-size slot-car racer. The motors generate about 250 horsepower and can accelerate from 0 to 65 miles per hour in about 8.8 seconds; the electric motors are also part of the braking system. A trio of computers manages acceleration, deceleration, and braking; together the onboard computers perform more calculations per second than the brains of the Space Shuttle. A central computer in the ride's control room manages distance between the cars on the track.

The vehicles are constructed entirely out of composite material, with no steel between the front and rear wheels. Cars run about 145 miles per day on a "Tailhook" track surface, based on the coating material used on aircraft carriers. The abuse is tough on the tires, which must be replaced several times a year. During the course of a year, each vehicle will travel the equivalent of twenty-one round-trips from Orlando to Detroit.

Around the curve at the GM Test Track. © *Disney Enterprises, Inc.*

A two-year delay in opening the ride was directly related to the complexity of the technology, one of the most advanced at Walt Disney World. At Test Track, Disney had to invent everything; there were no off-the-shelf mechanisms to be customized. (By comparison, the Rock 'n' Roller Coaster at Disney–MGM Studios uses a track-and-car system already proven at other parks, albeit within a building fitted out with Disney theming.)

The show is not over when you exit your vehicle; you'll walk into an impressive simulation of a robotic assembly line with a stamping mill shaking the floor and parts of vehicles moving by overhead.

In the Driving Technologies Lab, you'll have a chance to sit at one of ten high-tech driving simulators to test out new automotive technologies, including night-vision sensors. Your chair will rumble and bounce in sequence with your driving, and you'll feel the thud of any collisions. (Two of the ten stations are set up with hand controls for drivers who have disabilities.)

Finally, there is a display of some of the latest production cars from General Motors, backed by a flashy set of video walls.

You can enter the GM play area and car showroom without going on the ride; it's also a good place to meet people who have gone ahead of you to try the test track. To enter, head all the way to the right of the entrance to the ride.

■ IMAGINATION!

The heart and soul of the Disney empire has been the imagination of its founder and the tens of thousands of dreamers who followed him at the companies he founded, and the hundreds of millions who have visited Disney theme parks around the world. The Imagination! pavilion at Epcot celebrates the wondrous world that exists between our ears. Over the years this attraction was much beloved, much reviled, and much awaited. I guess it all has to do with the nature of your imagination.

MUST-SEE Journey into Imagination with Figment

Journey into Imagination with Figment invites guests to an open house at the Imagination Institute led by Dr. Nigel Channing, who promises to show us how the five senses can influence a person's mind's eye. "Today's theme," he tells us, is "how to capture your imagination."

Comic-actor Eric Idle (of Monty Python fame) returns as Channing, a role he originated at *Honey, I Shrunk the Audience* at Epcot. Channing's presentation, though, is interrupted by the surprise arrival of the freethinking Figment, a mischievous dragon who tries to show the ever-practical Dr. Channing and his guests that imagination works best not when it's controlled but rather when it's set free.

We're invited to explore sounds. "It's not about listening with your ears," says Figment. "It's listening with your imagination." In the dark a locomotive suddenly rumbles through the hallway. Says the shaken Dr. Channing: "I lost my train of thought."

In the sight laboratory Figment (as in "of imagination") has fun with a vision chart to prove that there is more to the imagination than meets the eye.

There are odiferous discoveries in the smell laboratory when Figment lets loose a skunk stink. "That's how you tell a skunk is not a rose."

And then we're invited into Figment's house, which is upside down to show how imagination can really come "home" when you look at things from a new perspective. Figment tells us, "There's more to sight than meets the eye."

All in all, the ride is a trifle of an entertainment for adults, although children will likely be entertained—but not quite as much as they were in the original version of the ride, which included some of the most unusual special effects at Epcot and was a clear favorite among youngsters. The ride introduced us to Dreamfinder and his pet purple dragon, Figment, on an expedition to collect colors, sounds, shapes, and stories with which to create new ideas.

Alas, every once in a long, long while, Disney suffers from a lack of imagination, and that seemed to be the case with the second version of the show, which dispensed with most of the "cuteness," instead creating a story based on the Imagination Institute that is featured in the fun-filled *Honey, I Shrunk the Audience* show. Dreamfinder was gone, and Figment was given only a tiny supporting role to Eric Idle.

The resulting dark ride was as flat as Spaceship Earth is round, little more than a very weak carnival fun-house show with upside-down rooms, a dark room filled with the sound of an approaching train, and lots of mirrors.

After going back to the drawing boards for a bit more, er, imagination, this attraction reopened in summer 2002 with the third version of the ride since the park opened—the only major double-reworking of an attraction anywhere at Walt Disney World.

MUST-SEE *Honey, I Shrunk the Audience* ≡FAST

This spectacular 3-D thriller takes off where the two original shape-altering Disney films (*Honey, I Shrunk the Kids* and *Honey, I Blew Up the Baby*) left off. In this case, it's the audience that shrinks instead of the kids. This is a theatrical performance that is simply not to be missed.

It begins outside the theater with a preshow sponsored by Kodak and based on its "true colors" advertising theme, an attractive and somewhat inspiring collection of photographs on the general idea of imagination and an extension of the imagination exhibit upstairs. Then we find ourselves as honored guests at the presentation of the "Inventor of the Year" award to Wayne Szalinski, played by actor Rick Moranis. Other members of the film cast also appear in the feature and are joined by funnyman Eric Idle. Finally, we are invited within to see a demonstration of some of Wayne's greatest new inventions, including the Dimensional Duplicator and the No Mess Holographic Pet System.

You'll go through the doors on the left side of the preshow auditorium into the theater and be asked to move all the way across a row to fill up all the seats. If you want to try to grab one of the best seats, hold back a bit until about twenty-five people have entered a row and then enter. As far as what happens next, we don't want to spoil the fun or play a cat-and-mouse game with you. (Oops—disregard that last hint.) The wild conclusion of the show comes when one of the machines goes berserk and ends up shrinking the entire audience down to toy size. "Stay in your seats, and we will blow you up as soon as possible," says Wayne.

The auditorium conspires with the 3-D images to complete the illusion with moving seats, spectacular lighting, special film effects, and unusual effects that will tickle your fancy and sprinkle you with laughter. The large theater seats 575 guests and will eat up a full waiting line inside the building; if the line stretches out onto the plaza, you can expect at least a forty-five-minute wait. Lines will ebb and flow at the theater, reached from an entrance to the left of the loading area for the Journey into Imagination with Figment ride. Go early or late to avoid lengthy waits, or make a reservation with a Fastpass ticket.

ImageWorks—The Kodak "What If" Labs
The upper floor of the Imagination! pavilion is given over to a clever Kodak exhibit where visitors can play with all sorts of high-tech video, audio, editing, and design devices. You can make sound and music by waving your arms and videotape yourself in super-slow motion, among other things.

■ THE LAND
Everyone has to eat, and The Land is a tasty collection of informative exhibits about food and our environment. The building, in part a giant greenhouse, also includes a popular food-court restaurant. The Land is one of the largest attractions at Walt Disney World. It covers some six acres and is as big as the entire Tomorrowland area in the Magic Kingdom. Stop and take a look at the huge mosaic at the entrance: Some 3,000 square feet in size, it is made of 150,000 separate pieces in 131 colors of marble, granite, slate, smalto (colored glass or enamel), Venetian glass, mirror, ceramic, pebbles, and gold.

In 2005 the pavilion became the home of the innovative Soarin' attraction, a transplant from Disney's California Adventure that takes guests on an amazing simulation of a hang-glider tour of the Golden State.

MUST-SEE Soarin' ≡FAST
You've got to ride this to believe it: your own hang glider for a virtual flight down the length of the Golden State. The amazing mechanism, a Disney first, lifts three rows of seats with eighty-seven passengers 40 feet into an 80-foot-high, dome-shaped movie screen. With your legs dangling beneath you, you move up and into the picture, banking with the hang glider as it soars from the Golden Gate Bridge in San Francisco to Mission Bay in San Diego and on to a special visit to a California icon that all started with a mouse.

The film swoops down so close to the ground and water you expect your feet to touch them, and then soars up into the clouds. Your field of vision is nearly completely surrounded; Disney even adds a whiff of orange blossoms and pine trees in the farms and forests.

There is no narration to the film, and none is needed. The scenes of the film, from start to finish, include:
■ banking through clouds and then down over the Golden Gate Bridge and out to sea

- winging down over rafters and fishermen in Redwood Creek
- flying over farmhands tending grapes in Napa Valley vineyards
- sailing out over the rugged coastline at Point Loma with fishing boats bobbing on the surf below
- swooping up the slopes of the mountains near Lake Tahoe, past oncoming skiers, and then skimming low over a tree-topped crest for a view of the lake itself
- banking a turn through Yosemite Valley past the falls and up toward Half Dome
- passing through fragrant orange groves near Camarillo
- flying into the rugged landscape of Anza Borrego State Park, the state's largest but relatively unknown park
- encountering six jets from the Air Force Thunderbirds
- passing closely across the aircraft carrier USS *Stennis* at San Diego and following close behind a Navy helicopter
- surfing along the foaming crest of ocean waves at Malibu
- cruising up the Harbor Freeway in rush-hour traffic and into downtown Los Angeles at nighttime
- visiting a party at Southern California's most famous theme park, a place called Disneyland

This attraction is one of the major draws at the park and includes a large outdoor waiting area as well as a hidden maze inside the building. If you see a crowd waiting outside, consider grabbing a Fastpass ticket and coming back later. You may also be able to shave quite a bit off your wait by entering a "singles" line, taking any available space on the hang glider.

This ride was created for Disney's California Adventure, the second park at Disneyland Resort in Anaheim. Based on the attraction's design in Anaheim, when you make your way to the front, the line splits to fill two identical theaters. Each holds three banks of gliders, marked a, b, and c, with three rows in each. If you have the chance, choose the center glider (b) and take a seat in the front row, marked row 1. You'll be rewarded with a spectacular view of nothing but the screen.

The funny safety briefing before you enter the theater stars Patrick Warburton, Elaine's annoying sometime-boyfriend "Puddy" from the *Seinfeld* sitcom. He plays "Patrick," the chief flight attendant.

To achieve the greatest clarity for the film, Imagineers used a 70 mm IMAX camera with a superwide-angle lens and shot at forty-eight frames per second, double the standard rate. All the scenes were shot from a helicopter.

The film is projected from above onto an upside-down IMAX screen. The seats are mounted on a simulator base with its movements linked to the scenes in the movie.

Star Tours, an older attraction at Disneyland and Disney–MGM Studios in Orlando, creates a similar illusion using larger seat movements. Through trial and error Disney engineers discovered that much smaller movements, coupled with visual screen cues, could create the same illusion. Where Star Tours seats move as much as 12 feet and pitch forty-five degrees, Soarin' seats move a scant 3 feet, with a six-degree pitch.

Water Me!

One section of the farm at Living with the Land includes a computer-controlled watering system that delivers individual amounts of moisture to plants as needed.

Soarin' was installed as an add-on to the building; the entrance to the ride replaced the former Food Rocks show.

⚡MUST-SEE⚡ Living with the Land ≡*FAST*

This is a boat ride through the past and future of agriculture. Disney Imagineers created a storm scene as an introduction to a tour that passes through a rain forest, desert, and plain—traditional sources of food—and then into some amazing experiments with hydroponic farms, cultivated shrimp and fish, and a desert made to bloom with crops with the assistance of high-tech irrigation.

The opening storm scene includes some very nice special effects with lightning and a rain forest, and a cast of animatronic creatures. Another significant change is that the opening segment of the ride is introduced by a woman, one of the few female voices in the park. Once the boats enter into the farming areas, the guide at the front of your boat will take over.

The fourteen-minute cruise visits:

- **The Tropics Greenhouse,** growing crops native to Southeast Asia, Africa, Latin America, and the southern United States. Rice, sugar cane, peanuts, cacao, bananas, and a 59-foot peach palm flourish under a 60-foot dome.
- **The Aquacell,** showcasing crops that swim: fish and other aquatic life including alligators, catfish, tilapia, sunshine bass, American eel, pacu, sturgeon, and the strange-looking paddlefish, which is cultivated for its caviar.
- **The Temperate Greenhouse,** featuring the concepts and technologies of sustainable agriculture, including intercropping of different plants to make the best use of soil and nutrients (coconut, cacao, and sweet potatoes in one example), integrated pest management, and specialized irrigation systems that reduce waste and increase crop production.
- **The Production Greenhouse,** where tons of tomatoes, peppers, lettuce, and other vegetables are grown for use in The Land's Garden Grill Restaurant and other Epcot restaurants. Land scientists utilize growing systems that are kinder to the environment and improve productivity.
- **The Creative House,** showing imaginative ways to grow crops without soil, hanging in the air, even on a space station.

Among the most educational of all the exhibits at Epcot, Living with the Land is also a good place for a quick break. Preschoolers may be bored, but anyone else is sure to find something to learn. Lines build by midday to as much as an hour in length; come early or late.

⚡MUST-SEE⚡ *Circle of Life*

The animated stars of *The Lion King* reappear as the "actors" in an environmental spectacular. Simba the lion, Timon the meerkat, and Pumbaa the warthog appear in colorful 70 mm glory, along with actors in a fable that begins when King Simba finds that Timon and Pumbaa are planning a new subdivision in the jungle, the "Hakuna Matata Lakeside Village." Simba warns his friends about the mistakes made by a creature who has from time to time forgotten how everything is connected in the Circle of Life. Those creatures, of course, are humans.

You'll learn about some of modern science's efforts to deal with thoughtful use of land in urban and rural settings around the world. The film includes scenes of polluted wildlife and an oil spill, an ironic contrast to the Exxon pavilion across the way. There is some very spectacular photography that builds off *The Lion King* film. For example, the famous thundering herds of animals of the cartoon move into a film of the real thing.

The auditorium for the *Circle of Life* is a bit strange for Disney World; once you leave the waiting area, you'll go down a series of narrow stairways into the seating area. It may be a difficult climb for some. Those who climb all the way down will have to put up with a sometimes overly loud soundtrack.

Other Attractions in The Land

Behind the Seeds Guided Greenhouse Tour. Serious gardeners and eaters will want to sign up to take this one-hour walking tour of The Land's greenhouses and labs, concentrating on soil-free gardening, fish farming, plant biotechnology, and pest management.

Sign up for the tour at the desk near the Green Thumb Emporium on the lower level; you can also call (407) 939–8687 to reserve a space in advance and obtain times and prices.

You'll learn all manner of secrets of hydroponics and aquaculture as well as seeing how Disney farmers created melons and squash with Mickey ears.

▌ THE LIVING SEAS

For years, this has been an ambitious but ultimately unsatisfying bust. There were one or two interesting exhibits here, but if you or your children are truly interested in learning about the watery two-thirds of our planet, you would be much better off making a visit to SeaWorld or a big-city aquarium.

There's still not all that much in the way of education, but Disney upped the entertainment ante a bit in 2006 with a high-tech, slow-speed ride: The Seas with Nemo & Friends.

Epcot Ecology

As a planned community, Epcot includes many interesting experiments in ecology. The huge Disney development uses a tremendous amount of water, which is a particular problem in the wet Florida environment. Some of the effluent of the wastewater treatment plant is sprayed on the 145-acre Walt Disney World Tree Farm to make use of nutrients in the water. Another project involves the growth of water hyacinths in a pond fed by the wastewater plant; the plants help purify the water by absorbing nutrients and filtering solids through their roots. Grown plants are harvested and composted for use as fertilizer.

Don't Read This

We don't want to spoil the illusion at The Living Seas, so, if you don't want to know an inside tip about the hydrolators, stop reading this sidebar right here. Okay? You've been warned. The hydrolators don't really dive down beneath the sea; the floor moves a few inches to simulate movement and bubbles move up the sides of the elevator. Then you walk out the door on the other side of the wall. It's the same principle used in the Haunted Mansion and in more dramatic fashion in other simulator rides.

▐MUST-SEE▐ The Seas with Nemo & Friends

The attraction uses technology that seems to have the stars of the film *Finding Nemo* swimming amid the live marine life of the 5.7-million-gallon aquarium in The Living Seas pavilion.

The undersea voyage begins aboard "clam-mobiles" in a colorful coral reef setting. Guests first meet Mr. Ray and his class on a field trip and learn that, not surprisingly, Nemo has wandered off. The journey to find Nemo continues as familiar characters, including Dory, Bruce, Marlin, Squirt, and Crush, help with the search. These deep-sea friends share virtual space with the pavilion's water world, one of the world's largest saltwater aquariums and home to more than sixty-five real species of marine life.

In the musical finale of the attraction, Nemo is happily reunited with his class and friends.

The inside and outside of The Living Seas has received many updates to connect it to the Nemo story. A grotto was installed outside with sculptures of some of the characters from the film, and one section of the aquarium within has been fashioned to reproduce the Great Barrier Reef of Australia, which many of the film's characters call home.

▐MUST-SEE▐ *Turtle Talk with Crush*

This most excellent little show was added in 2005. Disney Imagineers, working with Pixar animators, created a gnarly real-time computer graphics animation show starring the surfing turtle dude Crush, another of the stars of *Finding Nemo*.

Guests sit in rows of benches facing what looks like an aquarium screen; the littlest visitors can claim a piece of rug at the front. An underwater hydrophone descends into the "water" in the tank, and in swims Crush. "Whoa, check out all the human dudes in the human tank!" he says. With the hidden assistance of a computer and a pair of actors, Crush and his buddy Little Blue converse with the audience and answer questions.

Youngsters will love the show; adults will appreciate yet another glimpse at the future of animation and filmmaking.

Epcot DiveQuest/Epcot Seas Aqua Tour

Leave it to the folks at Disney to invent the ultimate dive site: guaranteed calm seas, no current, incredible visibility, vivid coral formations, more than sixty-five kinds of marine life, and an audience on the other side of a window at The Living Seas.

After suiting up in waist-deep water, groups of eight divers are guided by a Living Seas specialist for a twenty-minute dive, followed by a twenty-minute free-dive period. The entire three-hour program includes a presentation on marine-life research and conservation and a backstage overview of The Living Seas.

There are two versions of the tour: one for certified scuba divers, and another that uses a modern apparatus that encases swimmers in an air-filled helmet like an astronaut. In 2006 scuba sessions were priced at $140, and helmet sessions were a bit less. For information and reservations call (407) 939–8687.

EATS AND TREATS IN EPCOT'S FUTURE WORLD

■ INNOVENTIONS

Electric Umbrella. A large fast-food eatery inside Innoventions East offering burgers, chicken, and salads. An outdoor terrace is a good bet in temperate weather. The restaurant features an unusual electronic scoreboard for menus (which makes it easy to adjust offerings and prices). Main courses, priced from about $5.00 to $7.00, include a chicken sandwich with fajita seasoning, hot dogs, cheeseburgers, and a meatless burger with fries.

Fountain View Espresso and Bakery. Baked goods. Espresso, cappuccino, latte, cafe mocha, and other hot drinks priced at about $2.50. Also offered are coffees with Amaretto, Bailey's Irish Cream, Frangelico, or Sambucca for about $5.00, plus beer and wine. This is a good place—if you can get one of the relatively few seats—to sit and watch the fountain show. You can't see the fireworks from here, though.

Ice Station Cool. An unusual bit of marketing, this little igloo celebrates the global reach of Coca-Cola culture. A soda fountain offers free samples of soft drinks from around the world. On one visit the samples included Smart Watermelon from China, Kinley Lemon from Israel, Lilt Pineapple from the United Kingdom, Vegitabeta from Japan, and Krest Ginger Ale from Mozambique. You can also purchase Coke T-shirts in languages that include Japanese, Arabic, Russian, and Korean.

■ WONDERS OF LIFE

Pure and Simple. Within Wonders of Life, across from the AnaComical Players' stage. Waffles and fruit, salads, sandwiches, frozen yogurt, and sundaes. "Guilt-free goodies," $1.50 to $5.00. Well named for its healthful fare, presented in an attractive cafelike setting. Seating is at colorful blue metal tables and chairs, like something out of *The Jetsons.*

Special offerings priced from about $3.00 to $5.00 include a beta carotene salad (assorted veggies with a cantaloupe–balsamic vinaigrette dressing), venison chili soup, and a

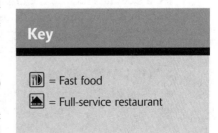

Key

= Fast food

= Full-service restaurant

Early Value Meals

Epcot sometimes offers discount early-bird meals at many of its restaurants for diners who arrive between 4:30 and 6:00 P.M. Check at Earth Station when you arrive at Epcot to see if this unadvertised special deal is in effect when you visit.

submarine with turkey pastrami, turkey ham, turkey breast, turkey salami, low-fat mozzarella, lettuce, and tomato on a multigrain roll. Sweets include nonfat yogurt sundaes, fruit cups, and fruit juice "smoothies."

■ THE LAND

Sunshine Season Food Fair. An attractive food court downstairs in The Land pavilion. One of the best things about eating at the Sunshine Season Food Fair in The Land is that everyone in your party can eat something different, shopping at the various stands and meeting at a table in the court. Just don't promise your kids a hot dog, a greasy burger, or fries when you arrive to eat; you'll have to get those elsewhere.

Stands include the Barbecue Store, offering beef and chicken sandwiches (about $5.00) or chicken and ribs (about $7.00); the Picnic Fare, selling cheese, fruit, and sausages; the Bakery, a fine place for bagels, rolls, muffins, cakes, and cookies; the Potato Store, selling baked potatoes with stuffing that includes cheese, bacon, and beef ($2.00 to $3.25); and the Cheese Shoppe, offering quiche, pasta, vegetable lasagna, and . . . cheese. Dessert counters include the Beverage House ($1.25 to $2.50) and the Ice Cream Stand ($1.50 to $2.75). Also, select a double-chocolate brownie, giant cookie, or apple pie. There is also a selection of beers, wine, piña coladas, and margaritas. All stands share the same kitchen, and there is some duplication; the same excellent brownie, for example, is available at several counters.

The Garden Grill. Upstairs in The Land pavilion. One of the most attractive and interesting full-service restaurants in Future World. The entire room revolves around a portion of the boat tour down below. It is now given over to character dining "experiences" starring Mickey, Minnie, and Chip 'n Dale.

The speed of rotation of the Garden Grill is adjusted to about one revolution per meal. The lunchtime speed is slightly quicker (about 448 feet per hour); dinnertime slows the turntable down to about 422 feet per hour. Either way, you're not likely to suffer from jet lag.

Parties holding reservations can bypass lines and enter directly into The Land pavilion within fifteen minutes of their reservation time.

Outside the entrance is a display of some of the fresh herbs and vegetables grown in the pavilion's greenhouses and served in the restaurant. You will see basil, chives, rosemary, parsley, thyme, and some beautiful peppers, beans, squashes, cucumbers, and eggplants.

■ THE LIVING SEAS

Coral Reef Restaurant. In the lower level of The Living Seas exhibit, to the right of the main entrance. Fish, shellfish, beef, chicken, and salads. Lunch, $6.00 to $15.00; dinner, $19.00 and up. Beer, mixed drinks, and a full wine list. Reservations are suggested; make them at the Earth Station. Open for lunch from 11:30 A.M. to 2:45 P.M., and for dinner from 4:30 P.M. to the closing hour for the park.

This place gives a new meaning to the idea of a seafood restaurant. You see food, the food sees you. We kept seeing diners nervously eyeing the passing sharks in the coral reef behind the huge windows alongside the tables; we suspect they worried they were going to be the seafood.

The best seats in the tank—er, restaurant—are eight tables along the glass wall. Other tables are as much as 20 feet from the fish. However, the restaurant is arranged in three terraces that give all guests a relatively good view of the aquarium wall. Anyhow, there is a fine selection of fish and shellfish; there are also some beef and chicken selections. Specialties include grilled fillet of tuna wrapped in plantains, the Coral Reef Clambake with half a lobster and shrimp, maple-glazed salmon, and steak and chicken offerings.

ATTRACTIONS AT WORLD SHOWCASE

The rest of the World's Fair at Epcot is the World Showcase, a collection of entertainment-education-tourism-trade exhibits from an unusual mix of countries. With the possible exception of the United Nations, nowhere else will you find Germany between Italy and China, or Mexico beside Norway.

While other parts of the vast Disney empire may be individually more impressive, there are few vistas more spectacular than the viewing area at the six o'clock position on World Showcase Lagoon. Displayed in a circle before you are the pavilions of the select nations of the world; all around is lush vegetation (sometimes adapted to the vagaries of central Florida weather), including tens of thousands of rose bushes and trees, Callery pears, Washingtonia fan palms, and camphor trees.

Most of the young staffers come from the country of the pavilion they work at, participating in the World Showcase Fellowship Program. During a one-year stay, the young people take part in a work-study curriculum.

As at any World's Fair, it is important to draw an important distinction here: Going to the Mexico pavilion is not the same as experiencing the ancient reality of Mexico. Seeing the spectacular movie at the Chinese exhibit does not mean you have been to Mongolia or Beijing, and taking the water ride at Norway does not qualify you to say that you have explored the Norwegian fjords. Instead, the pavilions—some better than others—do an excellent job of whetting the appetite for travel and educating us all on how different and alike we are. If you can get your kids excited about a visit to England or Canada or Italy, then a trip to Orlando may pay dividends all around; or, maybe it's your kids that have always wanted to go to Japan, and they needed to convince you.

■ MEXICO

The pavilion is set within a striking pre-Columbian-style pyramid, festooned with giant serpent heads and sculptures of Toltec warriors and patterned after the Aztec Temple of Quetzalcoatl at Teotihuacán. Quetzalcoatl, the god of life, is

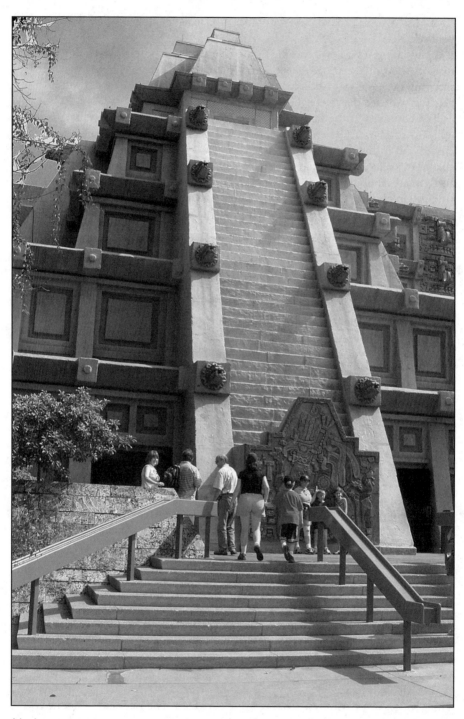

Mexico

represented by large serpent heads that can be seen along the entranceway.

The landscaping around the Cantina de San Angel depicts the arid desert regions of Mexico; the moist tropics of the Yucatan jungle are echoed with the lush greenery around the Mayan temple. Facing the Mayan temple, you see plants and flowers typical of the jungle; this section, with its several varieties of palm trees, is the most tropical area represented at Epcot. Heating systems hidden among the plants are used during the winter months to protect them from the cold and frost. One of the most notable plants in this area is the floss silk tree, located near the steps to the left of the temple. These showy trees present springtime blossoms and, in other seasons, an odd-shaped fruit hanging from its bare branches.

> ## Lemon Disney
>
> According to Disney insiders, Walt Disney loved lemony desserts, and many of the stands at The Land, and elsewhere at Walt Disney World, try to work as many lemon-flavored sweets onto the menu as they can.

Inside is a magical wonderland of a happy Mexican village. You'll enter into the colorful Plaza de Los Amigos, filled with carts selling handcrafted sombreros of varying sizes, toys, sandals, and other objects—sold at prices that are relative bargains within Walt Disney World. On a terrace near the "river," a mariachi band lets loose with its almost impossibly happy sound.

MUST-SEE *El Rio del Tiempo*

A charming, happy journey to Mexico—sort of a south-of-the-border version of the Magic Kingdom's It's a Small World—this six-minute boat ride is sure to appeal to children of all ages. There's a touch of Mexico's majestic past as a regional power, a greeting from a Mayan high priest, a humorous acknowledgment of the country's present day as a tourist mecca (enjoy the salespeople who scuttle from screen to screen to try to sell their wares), and a dazzling indoor fireworks salute as dozens of animated dolls dance around you. The indoor fireworks of *El Rio del Tiempo* ("The River of Time") are produced with cool fiber optics. The Mexican pavilion can become quite crowded at midday; I'd suggest a visit before 11:00 A.M. or after dinner.

■ NORWAY

The Land of the Midnight Sun has constructed one of the more interesting exhibits at Epcot. You'll enter on cobblestone streets of a simulated ancient village; take special note of the wood stave church modeled after the Gol Church of Hallingdal, built in A.D. 1250. Within is a display of Norse artifacts. There's also an interesting—and very expensive—set of stores offering clothing, crafts, and toys. Children will love the LEGOs table in the gift shop; LEGOs are made by a company in neighboring Denmark.

The pavilion incorporates four distinct Norwegian architectural styles. The Puffin's Roost and Kringla Bakeri are built in Setesdal style with grass roofs and thick log walls, and the Fjoring shop uses the gables of Bergen style. The castle represents the Oslo-style fourteenth-century Akershus, which still stands guard in the harbor of Oslo. The stucco-and-stone Informasjon building is built in Alesund style.

The roof of the pavilion is made of sod, a technique often used in traditional houses in mountainous regions of Norway as added insulation from the cold. At Epcot zoysia grass is used because it stays green year-round. Landscaping this pavilion was challenging because native Norwegian plants cannot survive the Florida heat. In their place, look-alike plants such as birch, maple, and sycamore are used to produce the same effect.

MUST-SEE Maelstrom ≡FAST

This is a dramatic and fun look at Norway from Viking times through modern day on a storm-tossed oil platform in the North Sea. You'll board Viking long-boats modeled after those used by Erik the Red 1,000 years ago and set sail into a world of fjords, forests, and the occasional troll. Some very young visitors may be momentarily scared by the "monsters"; all riders are likely to be thrilled by the indoor lightning storm in the North Sea.

You'll know you are in trouble near the end of the short four-minute ride when one of the trolls gets angry: "I cast a spell: back, back, over the falls." Sure enough, your boat will appear to travel over a cliff to land in the World Showcase Lagoon of Epcot before reversing direction for a gentle plunge down a waterfall. There's a movie at the end of the ride that I find much less thrilling than the ride; if you move quickly, you can walk right through the theater and out the door before the lights go down.

The Maelstrom ride can become quite crowded at midday; visit early or late. Shops feature trolls, beautiful (but pricey) knit sweaters from Scandinavia, trolls, leather items, trolls, candy, and trolls.

■ CHINA

One of the most successful of all of the Epcot pavilions at transporting the visitor to a foreign land, China's building is a small-scale but beautifully replicated version of Beijing's Temple of Heaven. On busy days look for dragon dancers and acrobats performing outside near the replica of the Zhao Yang Men ("Gate of the Golden Sun").

The Hall of Prayer for Good Harvests is a half-scale reproduction of the actual hall within the Temple of Heaven. There are twelve outer columns supporting the roof, representing both the months of the year and the twelve-year cycle of the Chinese calendar. Near the center of the room are four columns representing the four seasons; the columns support a square beam, which stands for Earth, and the assemblage is topped off by a round beam, representing heaven.

In Chinese culture age is respected, and gardeners want their plantings to appear old. Disney landscape architects selected trees with "corkscrew" trunks or "weeping" branches to help give the gardens a mature look. One of the trees, a weeping mulberry near the Nine Dragons Restaurant entrance, is one of the most impressive trees in Epcot. Other interesting trees native to China are the

The entrance to the China pavilion at Epcot's World Showcase

tallow tree, a plant with waxy fruit traditionally used to make candles and one of the few that changes colors in Florida's fall season.

MUST-SEE Reflections of China

The wonders of China are saluted with a magnificent Circle-Vision 360 film, *Reflections of China*. A crew of American and Chinese filmmakers worked together several years ago to capture new footage to update the pavilion's original film with footage shot in seven cities around the country.

Major additions include scenes of Hong Kong and Macau and updated images from modern Shanghai and Suchow, which Marco Polo called the Venice of the East (although the poet Li Bai, narrator of the film, suggests Venice might be better referred to as the Suchow of the West).

Simply breathtaking and not to be missed, the tour of China is guaranteed to open your eyes to the beauty and vastness of this still scarcely known nation. We've all seen pictures of the Great Wall, although never so spectacularly as presented here. Cameras enter into the fabulous Forbidden City of Beijing; you can look back over your shoulder at the gate through which you came. But then, there is more: the incredible Shilin Stone Forest, the Gobi Desert, the Grand Canal, tropical palms, and snowcapped mountains.

Circle-Vision films use nine cameras that capture a 360-degree view. For the original film, a crew had to carry the 600-pound camera 4,500 steps up the steep

How High's the Water?

You may not even notice as you cross it, but there is a small drawbridge between the Chinese pavilion and Germany near the Village Traders shop. Each day at about 5:00 P.M. the bridge lifts, and some of the floating props for the parade are taken through onto the lake for the nightly show.

slopes of Huangshan Mountain in Annui Province for what ended up as just a few seconds on the screen.

The theater has no seats. There are rails to lean upon—sitting on them is frowned upon—and small children and short adults may have a hard time seeing the screen without a lift.

Other Attractions in the China Pavilion

Land of Many Faces. An impressive exhibit that introduces many of China's ethnic minorities.

Yong Feng Shangdian Department Store. A shopping mall of merchandise from China, including silk clothing, embroidered items, and crafts. The huge collection includes some of the more interesting foreign items at Epcot, including silk robes, wooden toys, jewelry, and prints. You can also have your name written in Chinese characters on a scroll, T-shirt, or sweatshirt at a booth outside.

GERMANY

Wunderbar! This is a visit to a make-believe German village complete with a beer garden, teddy-bear toy shop, wine cellar, and a pastry shop of your dreams. The high wall at the back of the showcase is based on the Eltz Castle on the Mosel River, and Stahleck Castle on the Rhine. The statue in the center of the square is of Saint George and the dragon he slayed on a pilgrimage to the Middle East. Saint George is the patron saint of soldiers, and statues in his honor are common in Bavaria. Lining the front of the Germany pavilion is a row of sycamore trees, carefully pruned during the winter months. This style of pruning, or "pollarding," originates in Europe and is used to control the size of the trees in urban areas.

Attractions in the Germany Pavilion

Biergarten. Almost as loud and fun as a hall at the Oktoberfest in Munich— especially as the night goes on. The lively restaurant offers an all-you-can-eat banquet of red cabbage, sauerbraten, sausage, rotisserie chicken, and smoked pork loin. Desserts include apple strudel.

Der Bücherwurm. Here's a bookworm's delight, filled with books from and about Germany. The facade of the building is modeled after the Kaufhaus, a sixteenth-century merchants' hall in the Black Forest town of Freiburg.

Der Teddybär. You've been warned: This is a children-parent-grandparent trap full of fabulous toys, dolls, and various stuffed animals.

Die Weihnachts Ecke. Every day is Christmas in this shop full of ornaments, decorations, and gifts.

Glas und Porzellan. An outlet of Goebel, the glass and porcelain maker best known as the maker of Hummel figurines.

Süssigkeiten. We're uncertain whether to recommend you visit this shop on an empty or a full stomach. Let's put it this way: A full stomach will save you a lot of money. The cookies, candies, and pretzels are unlike anything you will find this side of Germany and are worth a trip from anywhere.

Volkskunst. A crafts market of clothing, carved dolls, cuckoo clocks, and more.

Weinkeller. The shop stocks several hundred varieties of German wines, as well as a selection of beer mugs, wine glasses, and other drinking items. Germans are serious about their beer; if you have any doubts, check out the mugs for sale at the Weinkeller. One of them is big enough to hold a couple of gallons of brew.

■ ITALY

Like China, the Italian pavilion is one of the more successful efforts in terms of giving the visitor a feeling of walking the streets of a foreign land. Take the time to study the various architectural styles. Out front is a 105-foot-tall *campanile*, or bell tower, a version of one of the landmarks of Saint Mark's Square in Venice, and the replica of the square itself is beautifully constructed. All that is missing are the pigeons, which explains why this version of Saint Mark's is so Disney-clean. The detailed replica of the angel on top of the *campanile* in the re-created Venice is covered with real gold leaf. The marble stones for the buildings, though, have no marble in them: They are actually fiberglass that has been painted and treated.

At the top of one of the columns at the entrance to Saint Mark's Square is a likeness of Saint Theodore, an important military leader in early Venetian history. Topping the other column is the winged Lion of Saint Mark's, the mythical guardian of the city of Venice. The stairway and portico alongside the Doge's Palace are drawn from Verona, while the town hall is reminiscent of the style of northern Italy.

While most of the buildings at Epcot are closed in a horseshoe shape, the Italy pavilion is open in the rear, drawing your eyes to the Italian cypress trees in the background. This architectural sleight of hand, along with the help of carefully planned landscaping, tricks the eye into believing the area is larger than it really is.

Landscaping around the garden area includes bougainvillea; citrus plants, including orange and lemon trees; and colorful blue, white, and pink hanging baskets. There is a planting of olive trees outside of Delizie Italiane, but no fruit is produced by these trees because of Florida's humidity. Near the gondolas at the edge of the World Showcase Lagoon, citrus and kumquat trees are planted to represent the Mediterranean region of Italy.

Outside the square look for the lively and irreverent performances of a visiting comedy troupe. Around the square is a collection of delicious and attractive stores:

Grumpy and Dopey Were Absent That Day

In the auditorium of the American Adventure, the twelve statues flanking the stage are said to represent the Spirits of America. On the right, from the back of the hall to the front, are Adventure, Self-Reliance, Knowledge, Pioneering, Heritage, and Freedom. On the left, from back to front, are Discovery, Compassion, Independence, Tomorrow, Innovation, and Individualism. The forty-four flags in the Hall of Flags represent the banners that have flown over the colonial, Revolutionary, and independent United States.

Delizie Italiane. An open-air market with sweet delicacies of all description.

La Cucina Italiana. Gourmet foods and wines, as well as fine cooking accessories.

Il Bel Cristallo. Fine crystalware, including colorful Venetian glass and porcelain figurines.

■ UNITED STATES

MUST-SEE **The American Adventure**

In our early visits to Epcot, the United States pavilion was one we chose to skip as the day got long. It's located at the very "back" of the park, and besides, we're Americans, so why should we be interested in something known as "The American Adventure"? Boy, were we ever wrong! The exhibit here is the ultimate in Disney animatronics, a rip-roaring, flag-waving show on a larger scale than almost anything else at Walt Disney World or anywhere else. The unlikely costars of the production are author Mark Twain and statesman and inventor Ben Franklin. Never mind that Twain wasn't born until forty-five years after Franklin died; such things don't matter when figures from history are brought back as robots.

The walls of the main hall are adorned with an interesting group of quotes from an unusual collection of Americans, including:

- **Wendell Willkie:** "Our way of living together in America is a strong but delicate fabric. It is made up of many threads. It has been woven over many centuries by the patience and sacrifice of countless liberty-loving men and women."
- **Walt Disney:** "Our greatest natural resource is the minds of our children."
- **Charles Lindbergh:** "I don't believe in taking foolish chances, but nothing can be accomplished without taking any chance at all."
- **Ayn Rand:** "Throughout the centuries there were men who took first steps down new roads armed with nothing but their own vision."
- **Herman Melville:** "Our blood is as the flood of the Amazon, made up of a thousand noble currents all pouring into one . . . we are not a nation so much as a world."

The twenty-nine-minute show starts with the Pilgrims landing at Plymouth Rock and moves on to the Boston Tea Party and Gen. George Washington's winter at Valley Forge. There's an eclectic collection of well-known and lesser-known figures of American history and culture. To Disney's credit, the pantheon of heroes here includes women, Native Americans, and African Americans. We meet characters such as Susan B. Anthony, Alexander Graham Bell, Frederick

Douglass, Chief Joseph, Martin Luther King Jr., Charles Lindbergh, and Teddy Roosevelt. On the cultural side are representations of Muhammad Ali, Lucille Ball, Marilyn Monroe, John Wayne, and Walt Disney himself. And don't overlook the imposing Georgian building itself and the paintings and statues in the hallways. Among special effects used in The American Adventure is multiplane cinematography, developed by Disney technicians to add the illusion of depth to classic animated films, including *Snow White and the Seven Dwarfs* and *Pinocchio.*

No Mistake

The clock on the facade of the United States building uses a IIII instead of IV for the four o'clock hour; this is an accurate reproduction of Georgian architecture of the time.

The buildings at the pavilion reflect American architecture from the late 1790s through 1830, including English Georgian, developed during the reign of King George III. Other examples are drawn from Williamsburg, Independence Hall, the Old State House in Boston, and Thomas Jefferson's Monticello home. By the way, the 110,000 "bricks" on the exterior of the main building are made from fiberglass formed and colored to appear the correct age. The landscaping is in the style of a historic formal garden in Philadelphia.

Lines at The American Adventure can build at midday but, except on the busiest days, are rarely larger than the seats in the large auditorium. The best seats are in the first few rows nearest the stage.

■ JAPAN

This typically understated but elegant Japanese setting features a reproduction of an eighth-century pagoda from the Horyuji Temple, the oldest completely preserved temple complex in Japan. Each of the five levels of the *Goju-no-to* (five-story pagoda) symbolizes one of the five basic elements: earth, water, fire, wind, and sky. Amateur gardeners will marvel at the detail in the rock gardens and ponds, and fish fanciers should check out the koi in the ponds. Rocks symbolize the long life of the earth; the water symbolizes the sea, a source of life.

Unlike many of the other World Showcase nations, about 90 percent of the plants used in the Japan pavilion are native to that country. In Chinese gardens ponds are still and reflective, while in Japan the water is running and active. Unlike Chinese gardens, Japan's are landscaped very meticulously, with every tree and shrub placed and maintained to achieve a specific look. Look for groupings of three, five, or seven plants in the garden; these are auspicious numbers in the Japanese culture. The red Gate of Honor (*Torii*) at the entrance to the Japanese pavilion is a sign of good luck. The gates were originally intended as perches for roosters to welcome the daily arrival of the sun goddess. The one at the pavilion is modeled after one in Hiroshima Bay.

Sipping Rice

Sake, pronounced *sah'-key,* is a colorless, sweet alcohol, sometimes called rice wine. It is made from rice fermented with yeast and is traditionally served warm.

Attractions in the Japan Pavilion

Bijutsu-Kan Gallery. A small museum of Japanese arts, culture, and craft. The exhibition is changed from time to time.

Mitsukoshi Department Store. A far distant branch of a large Japanese department store, offering a selection of clothing, dolls, toys, and trinkets. The food section includes some unusual items, such as fried sweet potatoes, shrimp-flavored chips, and tomato crackers. Gardeners may want to bring home a grow-it-yourself bonsai kit.

◼ MOROCCO

Step through the Bab Boujoulad gate to a beautifully detailed replica of the Koutoubia Minaret in Marrakesh. It's a world of fezzes, saris, and belly dancers. Bab Boujoulad is the main gate to the ancient city of Fez, known as the Medina. It was founded in the year 786 by the Idrissids. In the Medina section of the pavilion is a reproduction of the Chella Minaret in the capital city of Rabat. There is also a reproduction of the Nejjarine Fountain in Fez.

Sour orange trees, mint, and ornamental cabbages found here are typical of Morocco. Other landscaping includes an olive tree and a Senegal date palm to the right of the pavilion. The intricate tilework of the Morocco pavilion is among the most authentic re-creations of a foreign nation at Epcot; note that none of the tiles are perfect, because Muslims believe that only Allah is without flaw.

The folklore, dances, and music of Morocco are presented in the square outside the pavilion. Belly dancing and music from the regions of Tangiers, Fez, Casablanca, the Andaluz, and Marrakesh are presented at **Restaurant Marrakesh.** For more Moroccan culture, visit the **Gallery of Arts and History,** a museum of arts, crafts, and culture, with a changing display. Nearby is a branch of the

Moroccan tiling

Moroccan National Tourist Office, with information for visitors who would like to make a journey to the real thing.

Within the courtyard is a collection of fascinating shops, including **Casablanca Carpets,** for handmade Berber and Rabat rugs; **Tangier Traders,** for leather goods, woven belts, and fezzes; **Medina Arts,** for crafts; and **Jewels of the Sahara,** selling silver, gold, beads, and precious and semiprecious jewel items. There's a sign at the shops inviting shoppers to MAKE AN OFFER for items they want to purchase; give it a try by suggesting a price about half of the list price, and don't be surprised if the seller comes back with at least a small break from the original sticker.

■ FRANCE

Vive la France! France lives in a small-scale reproduction of a section of the streets of Paris, complete with an elegant theater, shops, and a bakery and sweetshop of your dreams. There's even a one-tenth-scale Eiffel Tower atop the pavilion. It's for appearance only, though—there is no top-level observation tower as there is in the real thing.

Take a few moments to look at the architectural styles, which include mansard roofs and ironwork harking from France's *Belle Epoque* ("Beautiful Age") in the late nineteenth century. The park on the right side of the pavilion is stocked with Lombardy poplars, looking somewhat like the famous setting of Seurat's painting *Sunday Afternoon on the Island of La Grande Jatte.*

If you look toward the shops, notice the *allee* (avenue or pathway) of trees ascending the incline. This *allee,* normally made up of linden trees in France, is created with Natchez crepe myrtle, which thrives in Florida's climate. To the right of this row of trees is Le Notre Garden, an embroidered parterre garden where 985 shrubs are shaped into a fleur-de-lis design.

Attractions in the France Pavilion

Impressions de France. Within the Palais du Cinéma is a lovely eighteen-minute film that hits all of the highlights of France—from Paris to Versailles to Mont Saint Michel to Cannes, and lots of lesser-known but equally beautiful settings, accompanied by lovely and familiar music, including "Gaité Parisienne" by Jacques Offenbach, "Trois Gymnopédies" by Eric Satie, "Carnival of the Animals" by Camille Saint-Saëns, "Claire de Lune" by Claude Debussy, "Daphnis et Chloé" by Maurice Ravel, and other familiar French works. The large screens extend 200 degrees around the theater, which has the added advantage of seats for all viewers. Lines build at mid-

Veiled Threat

Belly dancing first came to America in 1893 at the Chicago World's Fair when a Syrian dancer who called herself "Little Egypt" scandalized viewers with what later came to be known as the "hootchy-kootchy." Belly dancing is believed to have originated in Persia (now Iran) and is still popular throughout the Middle East and Morocco.

Eiffel Tiny

The one-tenth-scale replica of the Eiffel Tower was constructed using Gustave Eiffel's original blueprints.

day; visit early or late on crowded days. Stop and take a look at the postshow area, which is modeled after Les Halles, the former commercial marketplace of Paris.

Plume et Palette. One of the most high-toned of all shops in Epcot, with its entranceway modeled after one of the more famous decorative entranceways to the Paris Metro subway. The interior of the store and the showcases compete with the lovely gifts and artworks for sale here.

La Signature. Get a whiff of the perfumes and a peek at the clothing.

La Maison du Vin. This is a place for the gourmand. As its name suggests, it is a Gallic House of Wines.

Galerie des Halles. A bakery and candy store in a building that is modeled after the famous Parisian market.

■ UNITED KINGDOM

Merry Olde England (and the rest of the United Kingdom) is represented at Epcot by a selection of attractive shops and a first-class pub that sports a nice selection of British beers; it may be one of the few places in Florida where you can get a decent kidney pie.

Look for typical attention to detail in the construction of the buildings in the interesting streets of the United Kingdom. Never mind that the thatched roofs are made from plastic fibers (for fire protection) or the smoke stains applied by artists with paintbrushes; you probably didn't notice that until I pointed it out. The streetscape includes a thatched-roof cottage from the 1500s, a formal square with a Hyde Park–like bandstand, a London city square, and an exterior facade of the style of Hampton Court.

If you fancy you have a green thumb, or wish you did, be sure to check out the perfectly tended little English garden next to the Magic of Wales shop. The gardens include all sorts of roses from many parts of the former British Empire. (By the way, the secret garden also is an excellent place to watch the *Illumi-Nations* show on the lagoon.)

The perennial garden to the left side of the pavilion's promenade is filled with flowers that attract butterflies and features a chrysalis box that is home to developing butterflies. In the herb garden near the replica of Anne Hathaway's cottage, a variety of herbs grow year-round. This is called a "knot" garden because of the appearance of knots in the hedges. Farther around the corner is a hedge maze, with walls of Japanese yew, a plant often used to create shrub topiaries.

A glimpse of the United Kingdom

Attractions in the United Kingdom Pavilion

The Toy Soldier. Playthings for men and boys, women and girls of all ages. The shop's exterior is modeled after an ancient Scottish manor.

Lords and Ladies. More toys, of a slightly nobler fashion: chess sets, dartboards, beer mugs, stamps, coins, and more, inside a hall where the Knights of the Round Table would have felt at home.

Pringle of Scotland. Lay down your chips for beautiful knit sweaters and other articles of clothing.

The Queen's Table. Her highness may be the only one among us with the available cash to do some serious shopping here, but it's fun to poke (carefully) among the fabulous Royal Doulton china, figurines, and Toby mugs. The crests for four of the realm's most famous schools (Oxford, Cambridge, Eton, and Edinburgh) are displayed in the upstairs windows of the shop.

The Magic of Wales. A gift shop of small items and souvenirs from Wales; prices are the most reasonable among emporia here.

The Tea Caddy. Here you'll find considerably more kinds of leaves in bags and cans than you're likely to find at the corner grocery.

CANADA

The vast range of experiences of Canada is reflected in the landmarks of the pavilion. At the front is a native totem pole, out back is a scaled-down Canadian Rocky Mountain, and between is a scaled-down reproduction of the stone Château Laurier in Ottawa. The gardens of the Canada pavilion are the largest and most labor-intensive in Epcot's World Showcase and are based on the famed Butchart Gardens of Victoria, British Columbia, in western Canada. Seasonal displays of color are showcased there; throughout the year, 138 rose bushes bloom in this garden.

Attractions in the Canada Pavilion

O Canada! Another breathtaking Circle-Vision 360 movie that brings you up close and personal to bobcats, wolves, bears, and other creatures of the wild; to human glories such as the Cathédral de Notre Dame; to the ski slopes of the Rockies; and onto the ice of a hockey game in a scene so real you'll wish you had a goalie's mask on. Did we mention getting caught in the middle of the rodeo ring in the Calgary Stampede or the breathtaking camera ride down the toboggan slide at Québec City? The waiting area for the film is a cavelike mountain lodge from the Canadian Rockies. Be advised that you'll have to stand to watch this extraordinary eighteen-minute movie.

Northwest Mercantile. A modern-day version of a frontier trading post. You'll trade dollars (credit cards accepted, too) for sheepskins, lumberjack shirts, maple syrup, and Native American artifacts and crafts.

La Boutique des Provinces. Products from Canada's French-speaking regions, including Québec and parts of Ontario and the Atlantic provinces.

EATS AND TREATS IN EPCOT'S WORLD SHOWCASE

MEXICO

🍴 **Cantina de San Angel.** This cantina is located opposite the Aztec pyramid, beside the lagoon. Get a quick Mexican fix of tortillas, tostadas, and sweet churros (fried dough dipped in powdered sugar and cinnamon) at this attractive outdoor cafe. Small, round, wooden tables seat four under colorful umbrellas during the day and under high, soft-light lanterns at night. Meals are accompanied by Mexican music in a setting that includes native flowers on a tiled patio inside a stucco wall. The *platos Mexicanos* include corn or flour tortillas filled with chicken or beef, priced from about $4.00 to $6.00. Tacos, salads, and burritos, $3.50 to $6.00. Side dishes include refried beans or chips and salsa. Desserts, priced from about $2.00 to $3.00, include flan or churros. The cantina is an interesting place to view the nightly *Illumi-Nations* show over a cold beer or soft drink. Tables fill up early.

[🏠] [Y] **San Angel Inn.** This restaurant is inside a simulated Aztec pyramid in the center of the Mexican exhibit, our favorite location for a restaurant at Epcot. Diners sit on a terrace overlooking the passing boats on the River of Time (*El Rio del Tiempo*), under a make-believe starlit sky. It feels about as real as any Mexican place north of the border; in fact, the eatery is run by the same company that operates the well-known restaurant of the same name in Mexico City. Live percussion and a mariachi band add to the atmosphere. Look beyond the River of Time to view pyramids, a volcano, and a campfire.

The menu offers above-average Mexican fare, although a bit light on the spices. Specialties include *carne asada Tampiquena, huachinango a la Veracruzana,* tacos, burritos, and enchiladas. On visits we have made, lunchtime offerings have included the interesting and traditional *mole poblano* (chicken and spices with a chocolate-based sauce) and a combination platter (beef taco, enchilada, quesadilla, and avocado dip). At dinner we have been offered baked California lobster ($26) and camarones enchiladas (shrimp sautéed with pepper). Dos Equis and Tecate beers, margaritas, wine, and Mexican coffee with Kahlua, tequila, and cream are also available. Lunch or dinner children's offerings include soft tortilla with chicken or beef, fried chicken, or grilled beef taco. Traditional Mexican desserts include flan or *capirotada* (bread pudding). Lunch prices range from $5.00 to $15.00, and dinner is from $15.00. Children's menu. Reservations are suggested and necessary in the busy season.

■ NORWAY

[🍴] **Kringla Bakeri og Kafé.** This interesting cafe is located on the left side of the Norwegian pavilion, behind the replica of the church, and serves—what else would you expect?—fresh *kringles*. (All right, then: A *kringle* is a candied pretzel.) Also available are *vaflers*, which are waffles covered with powdered sugar and jam and other sweets. Sample the wonderful white-rice cream pudding or chocolate ball, like a 3-inch truffle. Pastries are $3.00 to $4.00. Open-faced sandwiches ($3.00 to $5.00) are very well presented for a medium-to-small serving. Offerings include tongue, beef, smoked salmon, mackerel, and ham. And, of course, there's a herring platter. Chairs and tables are available outside, between Norway's Ancient Church and the shops at the pavilion.

The Original Akershus

Oslo, the capital and major port of Norway, lies at the head of the Oslo Fjord. The earliest settlement was on the Akershus Peninsula, where a royal fortress was built about 1300. The building still stands, used for state banquets.

🏠 **Restaurant Akershus.** For many years this was a reasonable facsimile of a Norwegian eatery, with a *koldbord* buffet. Alas, it is now a Disney princesses character dining experience, with just a few hints of Norway. (For details see chapter 20.)

CHINA

🍴 **Lotus Blossom Cafe.** This is a quality fast-food restaurant located near the entrance to the China pavilion beside the Nine Dragons Restaurant. It offers covered outdoor dining in a cafe or patio setting. The dining area is tastefully decorated; the food is better than most fast-food operations. For the most variety for your money, try one of the combination platters. For a lighter meal, sample a bowl of soup for about $3.00. Stir-fry, egg rolls, sweet-and-sour chicken, soup, and more, $2.00 to $6.00. Chinese beer, tea, and soft drinks are available. Open for lunch and dinner.

🏠 **Nine Dragons Restaurant.** In a setting like an Asian palace, this quiet restaurant is located near the entrance of the China exhibit, on the left side as you enter. Look up as you walk into the waiting area to see an interesting golden dragon hanging from the ceiling. An ancient robe hangs on the back wall of the waiting area.

As fancy as it is, the selection of food, which is varied traditional Chinese cuisine in Mandarin, Cantonese, Kiangche, and Szechuan styles, is no better than many average Chinese restaurants and not as impressive as gourmet Asian eateries. Specialties include *kang bo* chicken and red bean ice cream. Chinese beer as well as specialty drinks and Chinese cordials also are available. Luncheon entrees range from $5.00 to $15.00; dinner entrees start at $15.00. A lunch sampler, offering unlimited portions of selected items, is priced at $14.75 for adults and $6.25 for children ages three to eleven. A dinner sampler for two is priced at $42.50. Reservations are required at busy times. Open daily from 11:00 A.M. through the closing time for the park.

OUTPOST

🍴 **Village Traders.** This is located in a dead area, long viewed as a holding place for a new pavilion, between Germany and China. A group of huts there offers vegetarian delights, including a "vegetable box" for $1.40 (you might call it a salad); the box with dips costs $2.00. A selection of fresh fruit is also available.

GERMANY

🏠 🍸 **Biergarten.** Located at the rear of the German exhibit off the Sommerfest courtyard, the Biergarten offers a loud and raucous atmosphere that gets louder as the evening wears on. Inside you'll feel like you are in a German beer hall at night. You'll dine at long tables, served by waiters and waitresses in alpine dress. The setting includes some small-town shops and a stage for the nightly musical shows.

Traditional German fare is served, including potatoes, pork, and bratwurst, served for lunch and dinner in all-you-can-eat banquet-style dining. The luncheon buffet, offered from 11:30 A.M. to 3:00 P.M., is priced at about $9.95 for adults and $4.75 for children age eleven and younger; offerings include sausages, rotisserie chicken, salads, red cabbage, and potatoes. At dinner the menu expands to include sauerbraten and smoked pork; prices increase to $15.75 for adults and $6.99 for children age eleven and younger.

Wash it all down with a huge thirty-three-ounce stein of beer (up to $7.50) or German wine and sit back and enjoy the floor show of oompah music and other lively tunes. All in all, a lot of noisy fun.

🏛 Y **Sommerfest.** Sommerfest offers German casual-food treats served at an attractive outdoor cafe located at the right rear of the German exhibit outside the Biergarten. You won't have any trouble finding this interesting and different establishment; follow the sharp odor of wurst and sauerkraut. Select a German beer to accompany one of the sandwich offerings. Bratwurst *und* strudel *und* Black Forest cake *und* beer, $2.00 to $4.00. Open for lunch, dinner, and snacks.

■ ITALY

🏛 **L'Originale Alfredo di Roma Ristorante.** This is not the original Alfredo's; the real thing is in Rome and credited with the creation of the creamy pasta fettuccine Alfredo. At Epcot you'll enter across a stone-paved square, beside the huge Neptune fountain and walled patio. The pink stucco exterior, stone benches, columns, and lanterns provide an appropriate atmosphere. A semiformal decor with interesting wallpaper and upholstered seating welcomes you to the cool and pleasantly lively interior. Check out the numerous photographs on the wall of the waiting area; you'll see many familiar personalities being served pasta.

The menu features freshly made pasta (including spaghetti, rigatoni, ziti, lasagna, and more) with various delectable sauces. Specialties include Cornish chicken legs in focaccia bread and oregano crust, *Ossobuco di Vitello,* and grilled salmon with Italian ratatouille in basil sauce. Other delights include *trenette al pesto Genovese* (imported linguine with Alfredo's pesto sauce), *scaloppine con funghi selvatici* (veal sautéed with demiglace, wine sauce, and wild mushrooms) and *ziti alla Mediterranean* (ziti with fresh mozzarella, Sicilian olives, and fresh tomatoes). House wines available by the glass or by the liter. There are strolling musicians at dinner. Lunch menu items range from about $5.00 to $20.00; dinner entrees start at $15.00. A children's lunch and dinner menu is offered. Reservations are required; stop by the Earth Station on the day you wish to dine.

■ UNITED STATES

🏛 **Liberty Inn.** The outdoor patio is a very pleasant, tree-shaded place offering umbrella tables and a bit of natural shade and colorful landscaping. The inside dining room is very spacious and has large window walls to maintain a bright, light atmosphere, even late in the day.

Minimalist Meals

The Japanese style of raw or lightly cooked foods in small, elegantly prepared portions is said to come from that nation's history of being overpopulated and short of both food and fuel.

There's nothing here to startle a youngster or, for that matter, to educate the palate of an adult, but the food is acceptable and typical of what many American families eat most of the time. The menu changes little between lunch and dinner. Offerings include a chicken breast sandwich served with french fries for about $5.00 for lunch or dinner. At dinner you can also choose a roasted half chicken with french fries and coleslaw for about $6.00. The evening offerings also include jambalaya, a southern stew that includes pork, shrimp, crawfish, chicken, sausage, vegetables, and rice. For the children there are fried chicken and hot dogs. Burgers, sandwiches, chili, and salads, $2.00 to $6.00. Open for lunch and dinner. Child's menu, $3.50 to $4.00.

JAPAN

Yakitori House. Yakitori is located in the rear left portion of the Japanese exhibit, behind the fountain, within the Japanese gardens in a replica of a teahouse in the 500-year-old Katsura Imperial Summer Palace in Kyoto. Dine indoors or outside; the rock-walled patio with fragrant landscaping is a pleasant getaway for lunch or dinner. By night, the patio is lit by lanterns.

The restaurant offers Japanese fast food, serving *yakitori* (skewered chicken basted with soy sauce and sesame), teriyaki chicken and beef, and *guydon* (a beef stew served over rice). The Shogun Combo offers a good selection, including beef teriyaki, seafood salad, and soups. Beef, chicken, seafood, and salads, $3.00 to $8.00. Open for lunch and dinner.

Japanese Shaved Ice. In hot weather the snack bar on World Showcase Lagoon just to the left of the Japanese pavilion sells *kaki-jori,* which is your basic snow cone done Japanese style with tasty fruit syrups. Flavors include cherry, strawberry, honeydew melon, tangerine, or mixed for $1.50.

Matsu No Ma Lounge. The lounge is located upstairs at the right side of the pavilion. Here you can sample sake (warm rice wine), Japanese beer, or exotic mixed drinks. One unusual specialty: sake martinis. Nonalcoholic drinks include Ichigo (strawberries, pineapple juice, lemon) and Mikan (Mandarin orange and pineapple juice with lemon). Appetizers include tempura, Kabuki beef or chicken, sashimi, and assorted Nigiri sushi. Exotic drinks, sushi, and more, ranging from about $2.00 to $8.00.

Teppanyaki Dining Room. This interesting restaurant, an entertaining and tasty break from the hubbub of Epcot, is on the second floor of the building on the right of the Japanese exhibit, above the Mitsukoshi Department Store. Groups of diners are assembled around a hot table, facing a chef equipped with a set of sharp knives; he carries salt and pepper shakers in holsters. Depending on the luck of the draw, your chef may be a multilingual comic, playing games with the chicken, shrimp, and beef as he slices and stir-fries the food. Teppanyaki fare is fresh and simple, featuring vegetables and meat over rice.

The dining experience is definitely not for someone who wants a leisurely and private time, but children—and adults who enjoy a floor show with their meal—are certain to have fun. Dinner entrees are the same as at lunch, but the prices are higher and the portions slightly larger. Other specialties include exotic alcoholic and nonalcoholic drinks. One summer favorite is the Sakura, made from strawberries, light rum, white curaçao, and lemon juice.

Lunch entrees range from about $10 to $20; dinner entrees are about $15 to $30. Children's menu available. Reservations are usually necessary; make them at the Earth Station on the day you want to eat.

Note that there are several teppanyaki-style Japanese restaurants nearby Walt Disney World; most offer better prices and smaller crowds.

Tempura Kiku. Tempura Kiku is located upstairs at the right side of the Japanese pavilion, next to the Matsu No Ma Lounge. Selections include batter-fried meat and vegetables, sushi, sashimi, shrimp, scallops, lobster, and fried beef and chicken strips. Exotic drinks from the lounge are available at the restaurant. Lunch entrees range from about $10 to $12; dinner entrees are about $15 to $23. Open from 11:00 A.M. to 3:00 P.M. for lunch and from 5:00 P.M. to park closing for dinner. Reservations are not accepted; there are only twenty-five seats.

■ MOROCCO

Restaurant Marrakesh. One of our favorite spots at Epcot, this place does a good job of making you feel as if you have traveled to an exotic place. When you arrive, wind your way through the Fez gate to the back of the Medina to find the Marrakesh amid the narrow streets and quaint shops.

Waiters in ankle-length *djellaba* robes, strolling musicians, and belly dancers provide an interesting and entertaining backdrop for a delightful meal. Even if you have to wait in the lobby briefly for your table, you'll be entertained by the music, native costumes, and decor. The dining area's raised dining rooms overlook the stage.

Among the traditional delicacies offered for lunch are *meshoui* (lamb roast in natural juices with rice, almonds, raisins, and saffron) and couscous (rolled semolina) steamed with garden vegetables, chicken, or lamb. Consider trying one of the sampler plates with small portions of various offerings for yourself or to share with someone. The dinner menu is similar but offers more variety and larger portions. Try the Tangier sampler for a selection of items, including specialties marinated in spices such as ginger, cumin, garlic with olives, paprika, and pickled lemon. It's all topped off with some delicious honey-sweetened pastries or crepes.

Lunch entrees range from about $10 to $15; dinner entrees are about $17 to $20. Children's lunch and dinner selections. Reservations are necessary in the busy season; stop by the Earth Station or sign in at the podium at the front of the Morocco exhibit. Best deal: lower-priced lunches.

🍴 **Tangierine Cafe.** Lentil salad, hummus, slow-roasted lamb, and *shawarma.* One of the best fast-food restaurants west of Casablanca.

🍴 **Moorish Cafe and Pastry Shop.** Baklava and other delectables.

🏠 FRANCE

🍴 **Boulangerie Pâtisserie.** This quaint bakery shop is across the narrow French street from the Bistro de Paris. It's a wonderful place to grab breakfast or a sweet snack any time of day. The bakery is managed by the Chefs de France, which is as tasty a recommendation as can be found at Epcot. Any of the tarts, apple turnovers, quiche Lorraine, and chocolate treats are good. Dark, flavorful coffee makes a good accompaniment for the sweet treats. Selections are priced from about $2.00 to $4.00.

🏠 Y **Bistro de Paris.** Upstairs over the Chefs de France, this bistro is entered through a rear door at the back of the building. A bistro is an intimate little cafe or pub, and that's what the designers of the Bistro de Paris had in mind in this lighter and (usually) quieter version of Chefs de France. The same master chefs designed the menu, which includes a variety of appetizers, soups, entrees, and desserts. Specialties include grilled beef tenderloin with mushrooms, glazed onions, and green peppercorn sauce; grilled swordfish with a tomato-béarnaise sauce; and sautéed veal tenderloin with apple and Calvados sauce.

Appetizers and entrees vary by season and are occasionally changed. In recent years offerings have included appetizers such as salad of duck liver pâté at $14.00, *gratin d'escargots de Bourgogne* (casserole of snails in herbal butter) at $7.50, cream of lobster soup at $4.50, or a mixed green salad with true Roquefort dressing and walnuts at $7.50.

Entrees have included a sautéed breast of duck with cherries and red wine sauce for $20; a rack of lamb with vegetables for two is $48. At least ten dessert items are available. On some visits I have been offered fruit and sherbet with raspberry sauce, and vanilla crème in a puff pastry shell topped with caramel sauce.

Dinner and lunch (in peak season only). Dinner entrees start at about $15 and rise from there. Children's menu. Reservations are available and necessary on busy days. Note that a window seat upstairs may be the best place in the park to view the nightly *IllumiNations* show.

🏠 Y **Au Petit Café.** This Parisian-style sidewalk cafe is located to the left of Chefs de France. You'll find it through the smell of fresh flowers coming from the many hanging baskets that adorn the posts that support the awning over the patio. The World Showcase is not quite the Champs-Elysées, but the little sidewalk cafe with its formal black-jacketed waiters gives a nice taste of the time-honored people-watching stations on the streets of Paris.

The menu includes traditional onion soup with cheese, coq au vin, and sautéed strip steak with Bordelaise sauce. Moderately priced offerings include such familiar items as quiche Lorraine and salads. Luncheon entrees range from $5.00 to $15.00; dinner plates begin at $15.00. Fruit sorbets, ice cream, pastry shells filled with light cream and chocolate sauce, and ice-cream soufflé with Grand Marnier sauce round out the menu. Children's offerings are about $4.00.

Open for lunch, dinner, and snacks. No reservations are accepted, and the waiting lines can become quite long on busy days.

Chefs de France. *C'est merveilleux!* Right here in Epcot, just across the way from umpteen hot dog and pizza stands, is a restaurant nearly as fine as any in France. The French chefs who are behind the restaurant are Paul Bocuse and Roger Vergé, operators of two of the country's finest restaurants, and Gaston LeNôtre, considered a national treasure for his pastries and desserts. The eatery is located on the ground floor of the large building at the left of the entrance to the France exhibit.

While retaining its Belle Epoque exterior styling, Chefs de France was quadrupled in size, incorporating the outdoor dining area formerly known as Au Petite Café. French windows swing open to let in the sounds of sidewalk musicians on warm days and a view of the World Showcase Lagoon for nightly spectaculars.

Enter this intriguing restaurant under the red awning off the stone-paved street of the France exhibit. The building is of classic French architecture with stone walls and a metal roof. Inside is an elegant French dining room complete with fresh tablecloths, paintings, and chandeliers. Table service is in elegant continental style with a bustling, active atmosphere. Pleasant and helpful personnel speak French (English, if you insist) and are ready and willing to help you make selections.

Lunch and dinner meals include ten or more salads and appetizers and about as many entrees. Menu items change from season to season. On recent visits we have seen fresh fillet of snapper and spinach baked in puff pastry, sautéed scallops and crab dumplings with lobster cream sauce, and sautéed tenderloin of beef with raisins and brandy sauce. As you might expect, desserts are worth drooling over, with plenty more than a dozen selections. We have dreamed about crème caramel (baked French custard with caramel sauce). All of this comes at only a slightly high price, compared to other Epcot table-service restaurants. Lunch ranges from $8.00 to $15.00; dinner begins at $15.00. Children's lunch and dinner menu. Reservations are suggested.

■ UNITED KINGDOM

Rose & Crown Pub and Dining Room. Located across the street from the main portion of the United Kingdom exhibit, the Rose & Crown is an interesting British dining experience. Ordinary pub food in England seems very exotic in Orlando. On previous visits we have been offered steak and kidney pie, lamb and barley soup, chicken and leeks, and fish and chips. The dinner menu expanded to include Cornish game hen, herb-roasted lamb, and Argyle prime rib with Yorkshire pudding. A selection of sweets, such as traditional sherry trifle, was also available. There is a decent selection of beers, stouts, and ales, including Bass from England, Tennent's from Scotland, and Guinness Stout and Harp ale from Ireland. They're sold by the pint and "yard" for those with powerful thirsts.

The decor is appropriately rough and dark, with elements of both city and country drinking establishments in the United Kingdom. Frosted and etched glass adds elegance to this beautiful setting.

The pub, which can become quite crowded, offers appetizer-size portions of the dinner menu. Lunch entrees range from $5.00 to $15.00; dinner begins at $15.00. Children's menu. Open for lunch, dinner, and snacks. Traditional afternoon tea served at 4:00 P.M. Reservations for the dining room are recommended and necessary on busy days; no reservations are accepted for the pub.

⊞ **Yorkshire County Fish Shop.** Classic fish and chips from a British institution. This counter offers some of the famous items from the Harry Ramsden's chain of fish-and-chips eateries. Ramsden opened his first humble hut in Guiseley near Leeds in 1928; today there are more than 170 outlets serving ten million customers per year. In British lingo, by the way, *chips* are what Americans call french fries; what we call *chips,* they think of as *crisps.*

■ CANADA

🏠 **Le Cellier.** Steaks, pasta, and seafood are served in a quiet corner of the park. Specialties include herb-crusted prime rib, salmon, and Prince Edward Island mussels. Ales and beers reflect Canada's brewing history, and dessert wines feature Canadian ice wine and late-harvest Rieslings. Lunch, served from noon to 4:00 P.M., has entrees priced from about $8.00 to $10.00; dinner is served from 4:00 to 9:00 P.M., with entrees from about $10.00 to $15.00.

EPCOT'S SPECIAL-EVENTS CALENDAR

Epcot includes an interesting range of special events, which in recent years has included Holidays Around the World at Christmastime, featuring a candlelight processional, the Christmas story presented at the America Gardens Stage, and a "living" Christmas tree. The events were free to all ticket holders, but Epcot also made available a specially priced ticket that offered entrance to the park, reserved seating at the processional, free preferred parking, and special discounts on Epcot merchandise.

Another favorite is Disney's Candlelight Processional, a retelling of the Christmas story. It is presented at least twice nightly at the America Gardens Theatre in World Showcase from just after Thanksgiving through December 30. Each program features a guest celebrity narrating the traditional story of Christmas, interwoven with music of the season by 450 choral voices, a fifty-piece orchestra, and a handbell choir. A limited number of seats are available to guests at Epcot, with lines forming several hours before showtime. Disney also sells Candlelight Processional packages that include dining at select Epcot restaurants and preferred seating at one of the shows. In recent years the packages began at about $40 for adults, not including admission to the park; a special package with an after–4:00 P.M. admission to Epcot sold for about $60.

Gardeners and nature lovers can soak up the grandeur of the gardens, topiaries, and flowers from late April through the end of May at the Epcot International Flower & Garden Festival. For information about this and other festivals at Epcot, call (407) 824–4321.

Many of the international pavilions have special celebrations on their national holidays. Chinese New Year is celebrated in February at China, Moroccan Throne Day is observed on March 3 in Morocco, and Italy holds a Carnivale Celebration at the opening of Lent.

CHAPTER NINE

DISNEY'S ANIMAL KINGDOM

DISNEY'S ANIMAL KINGDOM is a perfectly logical progression. After all, the entire worldwide Disney empire began with a mouse. Now there is a cast of more than a thousand animals at work at a wondrous kingdom that celebrates creatures real, extinct, and imaginary with rides and attractions, shows, dramatic landscapes, and close encounters with all sorts of exotic creatures. Mickey is still around, too.

From the moment you enter the park through a lush oasis, you are immersed in a meticulously re-created world: Africa and Asia brought to the swamps and meadows of Florida. Gardeners planted more than four million trees, plants, shrubs, ground covers, vines, epiphytes, and grasses from every continent but Antarctica.

And in 2006, the kingdom gained a high-speed encounter with a fantastic creature, the fabled yeti, at Expedition Everest. It's a roller coaster, but it's a *Disney* coaster . . . with all of the magic and joy from the minds of the Imagineers fully installed. The ride is wild but not untamed; most visitors should and will put it at the top of their personal must-see list even if they ordinarily avoid coasters.

Another new arrival is a dazzling live show starring Marlin and Nemo—an overprotective father and his curious son—called *Finding Nemo—The Musical*. The production, based on the hit movie, combines puppets, dancers, acrobats, and animated backdrops.

The employees of the park include more than 1,000 birds and mammals, plus iguanas, chameleons, and other reptiles. Disney recruiters traveled to Uganda, Zimbabwe, Ghana, Botswana, Cameroon, and South Africa to hire nearly one hundred college students, many seeking careers in the hospitality industry. You'll find Africans working at many of the gift shops and attractions in the park.

Disney's Animal Kingdom is 500 acres of sweeping vistas, including the wide-open plains of Africa populated by great herds of animals. By comparison, the Magic Kingdom is just 107 acres and Epcot just 260 acres. The park is located in the southwest corner of Walt Disney World at the end of the Osceola County

Parkway near All-Star Resorts. Although you wouldn't know it from the outside, it lies just north of U.S. Highway 192. Among the highlights:

- A safari across Africa, bringing us up close to real lions, elephants, zebras, giraffes, and dozens of other familiar and rare animals. There's a touch of an environmental message, too, with a harrowing chase after a group of elephant poachers.
- A stroll through Asia, where tigers rule the ruins of a maharajah's palace.
- A voyage millions of years back in time to rescue a dinosaur moments before a fiery meteor slams into Earth, dooming the entire species.
- A 3-D glimpse of the world from a bug's-eye view.
- A striking sculpture known as the *Tree of Life,* which sets the theme for the park with images of animals large and small.
- Disney's favorite creatures, Mickey Mouse and Minnie Mouse among them, strolling the park and making regular appearances in a beautiful garden.

The plant collection at Disney's Animal Kingdom includes 600 species of trees, 350 species of grasses, and 1,800 species of shrubs, vines, ferns, mosses, epiphytes, and perennials. All told, more than 100,000 trees and more than four million individual grasses and shrubs were planted or grown from seed. Architectural scale is reduced to allow trees to overshadow buildings; overall building height is limited to 30 feet, while the major trees of the park were at or above 40 feet at opening.

A PARK IS BORN

Disney's Animal Kingdom officially opened on Earth Day, April 22, 1998. Speaking at the dedication of Conservation Station in the park, Roy E. Disney, Walt's nephew and vice chairman of the company, said, "Just as this theme park has its roots in our films, it also presents a major departure. Once a movie is completed, it's done forever. On the other hand, Disney's Animal Kingdom—like the animal world itself—will evolve and grow. It's truly a living thing."

The dedication plaque for the park reads: WELCOME TO THE KINGDOM OF ANIMALS . . . REAL, ANCIENT, AND IMAGINED: A KINGDOM RULED BY LIONS, DINOSAURS, AND DRAGONS; A KINGDOM OF BALANCE, HARMONY, AND SURVIVAL; A KINGDOM WE ENTER TO SHARE IN THE WONDER, GAZE AT THE BEAUTY, THRILL AT THE DRAMA . . . AND LEARN.

MUST-SEES

The *Tree of Life*
(Discovery Island)

It's Tough to Be a Bug!
(Discovery Island)

Kilimanjaro Safaris
(Africa)

Pangani Forest Exploration Trail
(Africa)

Conservation Station
(Rafiki's Planet Watch)

Kali River Rapids
(Asia)

Maharajah Jungle Trek
(Asia)

Expedition Everest
(Asia)

Dinosaur
(DinoLand, U.S.A.)

Finding Nemo—The Musical
(DinoLand, U.S.A.)

Festival of the Lion King
(Camp Minnie-Mickey)

ANIMAL KINGDOM

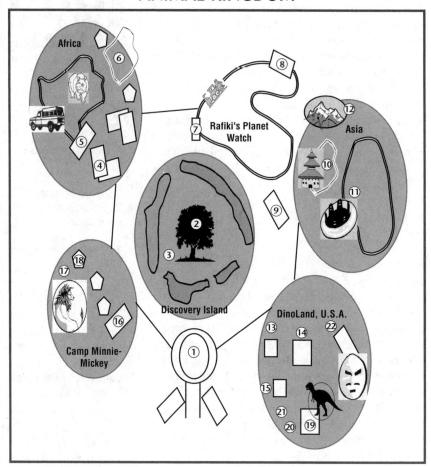

A hit with adults from the start, Disney's Animal Kingdom took a while to grab hold of the imagination of younger visitors since in the years since its opening, Disney has been focusing on rides, parades, and shows for children. However, Chester & Hester's Dino-Rama added a small midway of dinosaur-themed games and two rides—the TriceraTop Spin and the Primeval Whirl. There are also more Disney characters at the park, and some other amusements including talking remote-controlled trees and trash cans that prowl the waiting lines outside the park and within; look carefully, and you can spot the keeper dressed to blend in with the tourist crowd.

Animal Kingdom is the greenest of the theme parks in Orlando, and several years after the opening ceremonies, the growing foliage has filled out nicely. Although it is the newest Disney park in Orlando, Animal Kingdom harkens back to a comment by Walt Disney about Disneyland: "The trees will keep on growing, and the place will get more beautiful each year."

ANIMAL KINGDOM

<table>
<tr><td>① The Oasis</td><td>⑫ Expedition Everest</td></tr>
<tr><td>② The Tree of Life</td><td>⑬ The Boneyard</td></tr>
<tr><td>③ It's Tough to Be a Bug!</td><td>⑭ Fossil Preparation Lab</td></tr>
<tr><td>④ Harambe</td><td>⑮ Cretaceous Trail</td></tr>
<tr><td>⑤ Kilimanjaro Safaris</td><td>⑯ Pocahontas and Her Forest Friends</td></tr>
<tr><td>⑥ Pangani Forest Exploration Trail</td><td>⑰ Festival of the Lion King</td></tr>
<tr><td>⑦ Wildlife Express Train</td><td>⑱ Character greeting area</td></tr>
<tr><td>⑧ Conservation Station</td><td>⑲ Dinosaur</td></tr>
<tr><td>⑨ Flights of Wonder</td><td>⑳ TriceraTop Spin</td></tr>
<tr><td>⑩ Maharajah Jungle Trek</td><td>㉑ Primeval Whirl</td></tr>
<tr><td>⑪ Kali River Rapids</td><td>㉒ Finding Nemo—The Musical</td></tr>
</table>

ABOUT THE ANIMAL KINGDOM

Disney's Animal Kingdom is a more leisurely experience than the Magic Kingdom, Epcot, or Disney–MGM Studios. The beauty is in the details, and you'll miss a lot if you rush from attraction to attraction. There are seven main areas, each at the end of a spoke radiating out from the *Tree of Life* at the center of the park:

■ **The Oasis.** The entrance plaza leads into this very green and lush tropical garden. Most visitors will zoom right through; make time to explore the Oasis later in the day or on your way out.

■ **Discovery Island.** The island at the center of the park is home to the *Tree of Life* and *It's Tough to Be a Bug!*

■ **Africa.** You'll enter through the East African port of Harambe to some of the most spectacular parts of the park: the Kilimanjaro Safaris, the Pangani Forest Exploration Trail, and the Wildlife Express Train to Conservation Station at Rafiki's Planet Watch.

■ **Rafiki's Planet Watch.** The park's steam engine takes visitors for a journey to an inside peek at the care and preservation of wildlife at Conservation Station, and some hands-on participation at the Affection Section.

■ **Asia.** One of the most beautifully realized areas of the park, home to the very wet Kali River Rapids and the Maharajah Jungle Trek, a stroll through the jungles of Asia.

■ **DinoLand, U.S.A.** About as close as you could hope to get to the world of the dinosaurs. Explore the Cretaceous Trail and the Boneyard, and then load onto a Time Rover for a wild, high-tech trip back in time to the days when the dinosaur was king.

■ **Camp Minnie-Mickey.** An old-fashioned summer camp populated by Mickey and his pals, the Lion King and his troupe, and for those who prefer the real thing, some fascinating smaller animals.

The layout of the park is somewhat confusing because you cannot see landmarks; the *Tree of Life* is visible only when you are in the center of the park and cannot be seen from outlying lands. Study the map and pay attention to the signs. There's no Main Street or obvious gathering place, although the thriving port city of Harambe is likely to be a favored hangout for many visitors. Be sure to bring a hat and sunscreen; parts of the park are about as hot and exposed as, let's say, Africa.

The park is generally open from early in the morning until dusk; Disney has installed lighting on the savanna and may operate the park into the night on some of the busiest days of the year.

There remains quite a bit of undeveloped space available for expansion at the park. Disneyphiles note that the early renderings for the park included an area named Beastly Kingdom, the home of mythical creatures such as unicorns and dragons. And they point to the logo for Animal Kingdom, which includes a winged dragon in the middle of a march of real creatures. We can hope.

In 2006 **Mickey's Jammin' Jungle Parade** was presented daily, starting at the Tusker House Gate at Harambe Village, winding through the park, and exiting in Harambe. Among parade elements were soaring animated puppets including 8-foot-tall Party Animals and drum sculptures.

Finally, there is the question of the relative merits of Disney's Animal Kingdom versus its nearest major competitor for animal lovers: Busch Gardens Tampa Bay. Disney is way ahead on story and detail; Kilimanjaro has the real feel of Africa with nary a glimpse of a roller coaster, and native guides add a touch of realism. However, Busch Gardens has closer encounters with the animals, especially if you spring for the truck safari into the veldt, for about $35 extra. And it does have some awesome coasters. If you're limited to Orlando, Animal Kingdom will do you just fine; if you have the time, I'd recommend you also make a 60-mile expedition to Tampa.

THE OASIS

You'll enter the park though the cool green of this lush garden. Colorful and unusual animals inhabit a miniature landscape of streams, grottoes, waterfalls, and glades. It's a place of cool mists, fragrant flowers, and the sights and sounds of playful animals.

Most visitors are going to sprint through the Oasis to get into the park itself . . . and that's not a bad idea on a busy day. But do take the time to revisit the area, or at least make a more leisurely stroll when you leave at the end of the day. This is Disney's horticultural and animal Imagineering at its best, a lovingly created small world after all.

There are lovely and exotic plantings at almost every turn, and caves, waterfalls, and grottoes that offer welcome respite from the Florida sun. And tucked away are hidden animal delights, including tropical birds and small animals such as anteaters, tufted deer, muntjac, two-toed sloths, otters, macaws, and scarlet ibis. My favorites include the tree kangaroos. At the far end of the Oasis, a stone bridge crosses the Discovery River to bring visitors to Discovery Island.

Power Trip #1: Breakfast with the Animals

There are two good reasons to get to the park early and head for Harambe: First of all, the Kilimanjaro Safari is one of the biggest draws of the park, and lines build by midmorning. Second, many of the animals on the African savanna are morning creatures. (Lions, for example, sleep as much as eighteen hours a day and are particularly fond of siestas in the heat of the afternoon.) Dedicated animal lovers and photographers will want to arrive at the park as early as possible and head for Harambe. If you're lucky, you may be able to make two safari trips before most visitors park their cars.

For those who prefer thrills of a more mechanical nature, the wild Expedition Everest yeti-coaster is also a huge draw at Animal Kingdom. That doesn't mean you have to meet the yeti before breakfast; you can head for the Fastpass machine in Asia and grab a reservation for the thrill ride, and then build up your courage with a trip into the savanna.

If it's a warm morning, while you're in Asia you can also head for the Kali River Rapids for a wet tour through a tropical rain forest; if there's a chill in the air, you might want to wait for later in the day, although lines will build in the afternoon. Kali River Rapids also offers Fastpass reservations.

Walk through the thrilling Maharajah Jungle Trek while you're there. Move on to DinoLand, U.S.A., for Dinosaur and Camp Minnie-Mickey for the *Festival of the Lion King* show. Leave *It's Tough to Be a Bug!, the Tree of Life,* and the front of the park for last.

The live shows at the park fill quickly; one great strategy is to pick up a Fastpass for an attraction like the Kilimanjaro Safari or Expedition Everest and put it in your pocket while you head for a show. When the entertainment is over, you should be able to amble into an attraction without waiting in line.

Power Trip #2: A Contrarian's Tour

Okay, so we know that most visitors are likely to head first for the Kilimanjaro Safari or Expedition Everest, but you have other goals in mind. Take advantage of the major flow to the left side of the park in the morning by going in the other direction instead. Head first for DinoLand, U.S.A., for Dinosaur and then Camp Minnie-Mickey for the *Festival of the Lion King* show. Move counterclockwise against the flow toward Africa and the Kilimanjaro Safari. Catch lunch early, and then head out into the savanna during the noontime lull in search of snoozing cats and frolicking elephants or climb Mount Everest in search of the yeti. The cooling Kali River Rapids are definitely worth a visit; lines will build on warm afternoons.

The gardens are colored by hundreds of flowering trees from nearly every tropical and subtropical region on Earth, including jacarandas, tabebuias, calliandras, cassias, michellias, bauhinias, and tipuana. Disney landscapers promise plants and trees will be in bloom no matter what time of year you tour the park. The Animal Kingdom's population of plants is at least five times as large as the lush world of Epcot. All told, Animal Kingdom has more landscaping than the three other Walt Disney World parks combined.

On the African savanna the challenge includes keeping the huge area looking like a piece of Africa while dealing with the fact that many of the animals will insist on eating the landscaping. Elephants, for example, can completely devour large stands of their favorite grass. Handlers place precut leafy branches and 1,300 pounds of fresh grasses in various spots each day to attempt to lure some of the larger eaters away from the live vegetation.

Another challenge comes from Florida's occasional winter freezes. Water sprays help prevent frost, and heaters are used in some areas where the plants are lush and tropical.

DISCOVERY ISLAND

The crossroads of adventure at Disney's Animal Kingdom, this island of tropical greenery and equatorial architecture is the hub through which you'll pass to reach other lands.

The *Tree of Life* at Discovery Island

There are some 1,500 hand-painted wooden folk-art carvings scattered about, a fusion of pre-Columbian, Peruvian, African, and Polynesian forms. They were crafted on the island of Bali by native craft workers.

MUST-SEE THE *TREE OF LIFE*

Towering 145 feet above Discovery Island is the *Tree of Life*, 170 feet wide at its base and surrounded by shimmering pools and meadows filled with birds and small mammals noted for their playful behavior. The trunk of the tree is carved as an intricate swirling pattern of animal forms that symbolize the richness and diversity of animal life on Earth.

More than a dozen artists and Imagineers worked for seventeen months to create the 325 animal carvings, from majestic lions to playful dolphins, from humble armadillos to camels, baboons, and elephants. They had between six and ten hours to finish each sculpture before the plaster hardened.

Hungarian sculptor Zsolt Hormay assembled a team of artists from around the world. Native Americans carved the bear, bald eagle, bobcat, and mountain lion. Hormay himself sculpted the baboon, koala, and scorpion. The images were carved in a thin layer of cement attached to steel rods bent into the rough forms of the animals; some of the animals highest up in the tree are made of foam to reduce weight.

The tree itself has some 8,000 branches adorned with more than 103,000 artificial leaves that blow in the wind. The entire structure—built upon a framework designed with the assistance of an oil-rig builder—sways a bit in the wind. At its base are small pools and meadows that are home to animals that include otters, flamingos, capybaras, ducks, storks, cranes, cockatoos, lemurs, tamarins, tortoises, and red kangaroos.

⊞ MUST-SEE ⊞ *IT'S TOUGH TO BE A BUG!*

Like Spaceship Earth at Epcot, the central symbol of Disney's Animal Kingdom also houses an exciting attraction. Guests step inside the *Tree of Life* to experience a 3-D adventure about creatures of a much smaller scale than most of the others in the park: insects. Based on *A Bug's Life*, the animated film from Disney and Pixar (creator of *Toy Story*), the humorous film and special-effects theater provide a bug's-eye view of the world.

The queue for the 430-seat theater wends its way around the base of the *Tree of Life* before eventually ducking into a cool, dark room; listen carefully for the rustle, buzzes, and chirps of the stars of the show. While waiting, read some of the amusing movie posters promoting the greatest hits of insect cinema. Facetious titles include: *Web Side Story, Beauty and the Bee, My Fair Lady Bug, Antie, A Cockroach Line,* and my favorite, *Little House of Hoppers.*

When the doors open, pick out a place to sit on a log and admire the tangled-root and vine architecture all around. The orchestra of creatures tunes up below while a buzzing can be heard from the wasp-nest projection booth. Try to sit in the middle of the theater—midway in from both sides and halfway back from the screen—for the best 3-D effects.

The show is ready to begin. The announcer has a request: Please refrain from buzzing, chirping, stinging . . . or pollinating. With a pair of 3-D "bug glasses" in place, you're right in the midst of things as Flick, the ant master of ceremonies, welcomes visitors as honorary bugs and introduces us to some of the cast of millions: "Take it from an ant. It's tough to be a bug," says Flick. "That's why we've developed some amazing survival techniques."

Assisted by a pair of acorn weevils with a slingshot, Chili the Tarantula shows off his ability to throw poison quills. And yes, they're zooming out toward the audience. Next an acid-spraying soldier termite, "the Termite-ator," defends his mound by spraying intruders—that's us—in the seats below. The stinkbug soloist, Claire DeRoom, astonishes us with a malodorous performance. But the big artillery arrives with a villainous grasshopper, a bug on a mission to wipe out the audience of intruders. "You guys only see us as monsters!" he says. "Maybe

A Home for the Animals

Most of the animals in Animal Kingdom's Africa spend their days working the crowds on the Kilimanjaro Safaris and from along the Pangani Forest Exploration Trail, and then retire for the night to their hotel suites.

Most of the animals at the park were born in captivity at zoos and other preserves. Among the tasks undertaken by Disney animal managers was to give them more room to roam than most have ever known, while conditioning them to come to shelters each night for their own security and for daily care. Each area has its own sound signal used to summon animals to their "backstage" homes. The Thomson's gazelles have learned to come back to their shelter each night when they hear a "goose call." Giraffes respond to a coach's whistle, and zebras listen for a cowbell.

When the animals were first introduced to the African savanna and forest there were temporary fences erected. Subtle barriers including water, gratings, and hidden wires help reinforce the training.

it's time you 'honorary bugs' got a taste of your own medicine!" Suddenly we're under assault by a giant flyswatter, a blinding fog of "Bug Doom" spray, and a nasty hornet squadron.

I won't spoil the ending, but it does have a certain biting edge. The butterfly curtain closes, and the announcer reminds the audience to remain seated while all the lice, bedbugs, maggots, and cockroaches exit first.

AFRICA

The adventure into and across the wilds of Africa begins in Harambe, a well-aged, modern-day town on the edge of a wildlife reserve. Harambe (pronounced Há-rahm-bay) is based on the Arab-influenced Swahili culture and architecture of coastal Kenya, with white coral walls, thatched roofs, and a *hakuna matata* attitude toward life.

Disney Imagineers lavished a tremendous amount of detail on Harambe; be sure to read some of the signs and notes on the wall. The hand-plastered walls often expose their coral rock substructures. I was at first surprised to find that Disney had allowed the place to look so dusty on Grand Opening Day until I realized that the piles of wind-blown dirt inside the hallways of some of the buildings were actually created by designers and cemented into place.

At the end of Harambe's main street, an ancient gnarled baobab tree, a symbol of the African savanna, beckons visitors toward the Kilimanjaro Safaris. Check out the Ziwani Traders shop at Mombasa Marketplace to explore an interesting selection of hand-carved masks, sculptures, clothing, and assorted items from Kenya and other African nations. The decorative gourds on display are used by Masai tribes to hold milk until it is sour enough to meet their taste preferences.

Disney designers went back to Africa to obtain tribal craftsmen and traditional thatching grass to create the pole-supported thatched roofs of Harambe and the research outposts along Pangani Forest Exploration Trail. During construction, Disney imported thirteen Zulu craftsmen from Kwazulu-Natal in South Africa and fifteen trailer loads of thatch.

Trading their tribal garb for American blue jeans—and putting hard hats over familiar straw caps and bandannas—the builders did object to air-conditioning in their hotel rooms. They were eventually moved to houses where they could open the windows and let in the midsummer warmth of Florida.

The roofs were constructed with wild Berg thatch, which resists insects and decay and provides excellent insulation and waterproofing. The battens, which secure the thatch to hardwood rafters, are made of eucalyptus pods stripped bare, coated with mud, and kiln-dried to produce a mottled dark brown finish. The roofs are expected to withstand the effects of Florida's sun and rain for up to sixty years.

▪MUST-SEE▪ KILIMANJARO SAFARIS ≡FAST

The adventure begins in Harambe beneath a 40-foot-tall baobab tree, where the queue winds its way through a warehouse stocked with safari gear. The waiting area is huge—and well hidden from view. Be sure to check the posted wait time at the outside of the safari shed before staking your claim in line.

Disney has added a few touches that make the wait a bit less painful. Near the start of the covered portion of the line you'll circle around the base of Mzee Mbuyu baobab (Swahili for "Old Man Baobab"), one of the signature trees of the Harambe reserve. A bit later on, the queue passes through a few live-animal habitats, including that of a group of crowned cranes. Environmental messages play from video monitors overhead. The safari will help you learn about the importance of protecting animal life; the game warden quotes a Swahili saying: "What you see with your eyes you value with your heart."

Eventually you will be bouncing across the rugged terrain in an open-sided, thirty-two-passenger motor lorry; you can call it a safari truck. In the driver's seat is an experienced guide who will help identify the animals and keep in radio contact with a bush pilot flying ahead in a spotter plane. The trucks follow a twisting trail through a lush green forest, across small river crossings, and into the Serengeti grasslands rich with antelope, giraffes, zebras, baboons, rhinos, elephants, crocodiles, lions, hippos, and many more animals.

Crossing the Bongo Pool, where many animals come to drink, be on the lookout for black rhinos, among the most fascinating animals in Africa. They may be along the shores, wallowing in the water, or lurking just below its surface. If you're lucky, you may spot a glimpse of a rare okapi, a large mammal related to the giraffe but lacking the long neck. Rounding the bend, you'll come to a woodland of date and fan palms, the home of a colony of shiny black-and-white colobus monkeys.

A set of cascading waterfalls forms a pool that is home to African crocodiles, which can grow to as much as 20 feet in length, much larger than American alligators. A very rickety bridge crosses directly over their heads; do you think it's strong enough to support the weight of your safari lorry? Safely across, the safari emerges from heavy vegetation for a spectacular view of the vast savanna, where you'll see spotted giraffes, black-and-white-striped zebras, sable antelope, Thomson's gazelles, and speedy ostriches that are capable of outrunning the truck.

Kilimanjaro Safaris. © *Disney Enterprises, Inc.*

The landscape of the savanna includes strange vegetation such as maringa trees—known as sausage trees—with foot-long seed pods used by natives to make a lemonade-like drink. Termite mounds stand up to 20 feet tall. Out on the grasslands baboon families sightsee from rocks and trees as the trucks pass by. Around another bend a herd of elephants moves among the trees. The truck fords a small stream and moves into elephant company. If you're lucky, you may catch a glimpse of one or more lions; they are hard to spot, especially in midday when they're likely to be snoozing.

The driver communicates by radio with the spotter plane in search of "Big Red" and her elephant newborn, "Little Red," a favorite pair of pachyderms who were given their names because they seem to enjoy rolling in the rust-red dust. Keep your eyes open (and cameras ready) for a glimpse of white rhinos in nearby pools; you may spot kudu, scimitar-horned oryx, Zimbabwean Klipspringer, long-horned eland, and cheetahs out in the grasslands.

The beauty of the scene is soon disturbed by a message from one of the game wardens: It seems ivory poachers have wounded Big Red, and Little Red is missing. The bush pilot asks us to help out by forcing the poachers eastward along the gorge toward the waiting wardens. We hear the sound of the poachers' jeep ahead of us and even the sound of bullets. Off to our left we pass their hurriedly abandoned camp, fires still smoldering. And then comes the good news from the spotter plane: The poachers have been caught. As we come around a bend, we find a ranger training a rifle on a pair of poachers cornered inside their crashed vehicle. Beside it in the back of a small flatbed truck is a baby elephant still covered with rust-red dust; Little Red is safe and will be taken back to his mother.

Detouring around several waterfalls and across a 100-foot pool, we rejoin the main road and enter the most lush vegetation in all of the safari, a place of giant bamboo, palm, and other big-leaf trees. We are near the heart of gorilla country and the start of the Pangani Forest Exploration Trail.

About the Safari

The trucks sit high off the road and offer good views. There is a canvas awning that provides a bit of shade from the sun, but in heavy rain you can expect to get wet. Serious photographers will want to try to get one of the outside seats. No guarantee, but I saw more action on the driver's side of the vehicle.

The safaris run all day until dusk, and you are likely to see different animals each time you go for a trip. Most of the creatures are more active in the morning, often seeking cool shade for long siestas in the heat of the afternoon.

The Kilimanjaro Safaris are one of the major draws of Disney's Animal Kingdom, and they're likely to have long lines at certain times of the day. On busy days lines can reach to as much as two hours in midmorning and midafternoon, dropping to a reasonable fifteen minutes at lunch. It is almost always worthwhile to use the Fastpass system here. My suggestion is to arrive early and ride the safari before the crowds form and while the animals are most active, and then come back again in midafternoon for another safari. And don't stay away

Traffic on the road at Kilimanjaro Safaris

just because it may be raining a bit; some of the animals are much more active when it is cool or wet.

The animals all perform their roles well, but the unsung stars include Disney's landscaping crew. The trick was to find a way to simulate the wilds of Africa in an environment that includes moving safari trucks and free-ranging animals. Disney's planners laid out the plant bed lines using spray paint from a motorcycle moving at the same speed as the trucks because guests would experience the landscape at that speed.

The park's chief landscape designer took some horticultural tips from a wise old elephant while he was scouting Africa for savanna landscape materials; the animal grabbed some favorite snacking grass with its trunk and passed it over to the designer. The seeds from that grass were eventually planted at Animal Kingdom.

The rutted safari road is also part of the landscape design. The Imagineering team matched concrete with the surrounding soil, then rolled tires through it and tossed stones, dirt, and twigs into it to create a bumpy, remote African road in the wilds of Walt Disney World.

This is central Florida, of course, and not central Africa, so some creative compromises were necessary. The seven distinctive baobab trees were re-created in concrete, and the towering acacias are actually 30-foot-tall southern live oaks given a carefully maintained crew cut.

⛏ MUST-SEE ⛏ PANGANI FOREST EXPLORATION TRAIL

The end of the safari ride is also the beginning of the Pangani Forest Exploration Trail, where you can take a walk through the domain of two troops of lowland gorillas, observe hippos from an underwater viewing area, and get close to exotic birds in an aviary. Highlights include close-ups of African mammals, including hippos (with an over- and underwater viewport); you'll also be able to see families of lowland gorillas through windows in the gorilla observatory and from a swaying rope bridge that crosses through a small valley. And you can spy herds of antelope from a thatch-roofed observation station.

Many of the animals are too small or too shy to be seen from passing safari trucks; instead they are presented up close along the trail. One display shows cutaways into the burrows of naked mole rats—some of the most unusual creatures in the park. The creatures are actually not rats at all, but rather relatives of the common mole; they organize themselves like bees or ants, with a queen who is the center of society.

Giant African bullfrogs hop around a lily-pad pool outside a wildlife research center that features interactive displays and maps. Research areas include telescopes, video displays, and animal- and bird-spotting guides. At the exit from the research office you'll enter a canopy of trees filled with as many as thirty-five species of exotic tropical birds nesting among the palms and bushes. In pools below are many rare fish, including the colorful cichlid that is found only in Lake Tanganyika.

Moving across the aviary, you'll find another open-air shelter that has a dam on the far wall with a large panel of inch-thick glass holding back the millpond. The glass offers an above- and underwater view of a trio of giant hippopotamuses and a pair of coal-black African cormorants.

A bit farther along is a platform overlooking the savanna with a view of giraffes, tiny dik-diks, and other rare members of the antelope family grazing in knee-high grass.

The trail leads through a leafy canyon to the gorilla research camp. Experts answer questions and assist with research materials. Just beyond a large plate-glass window a family of gorillas—two females and a silverback adult male—make their home. Disney hopes for the patter of little gorilla feet in the years to come.

Beyond the research camp the path crosses a small canyon over a swaying suspension bridge to present another view of the gorilla family. On the other side of the bridge is another group of young male gorillas, part of a study of bachelor groups within the Gorilla Species Survival Plan (SSP), a program of the American Zoo and Aquarium Association. The end of the trail leads to Harambe station, where you can catch the **Wildlife Express Train** to Conservation Station at Rafiki's Planet Watch.

One of the most unusual plants here is a Brazilian flowering tree called Markhamia that normally grows as straight as a telephone pole in the rain forest. Grown from seed at the Animal Kingdom, the tree started out in a straight line until it reached a shade canopy above. Then it "turned on its blinker and

Chow Time

Food service for the 1,000 animal employees of Disney's Animal Kingdom is one of the more complex and demanding assignments in the park. Do you want to tell a 425-pound gorilla or a 3-ton rhino that supper is late?

A full-grown elephant chomps down something like 125 pounds of hay and pelleted chow each day. Anteaters don't eat just ants—they prefer a mix of ants and grubs.

Giraffes have their own smorgasbord hidden high up in the re-created baobab trees: hidden 16-foot-wide turntables deliver bamboo, willow, and acacia shoots throughout the day.

The park includes an eight-acre "browse farm" to feed the animals with a stand of acacia, hibiscus, mulberries, and shrubs to replace natural forage for giraffes, gorillas, baboons, elephants, and antelope.

made a sharp left-hand turn," said a landscape designer at the park. The plant grew toward the light, then made another sharp turn toward the sky, ultimately resembling a giant stair step.

RAFIKI'S PLANET WATCH

Here's your chance to get up close and personal with some of the employees of Disney's Animal Kingdom. Rafiki's Planet Watch includes an educational facility for humans and a hospital for animals as well as a lively petting zoo.

■ WILDLIFE EXPRESS TRAIN

The Wildlife Express departs from the East African Depot near Harambe. The colonial-style, narrow-gauge steam trains of the Eastern Star Railway offer a glimpse at some of the nighttime homes for the animals as well as some of the park's veterinary facilities.

"*Karibuni Harambe!*" announces the train conductor. ("Welcome to Harambe.") There's to be no drinking, no smoking, and "absolutely no cooking on board." And while we're at it: "*Kuwa macho wajangili!*" ("Keep a lookout for poachers!")

The puffing steam engines and open-air carriages hark back to British railroads in the mountains and jungles of far-off colonies. For nearly a century engines like these were shipped to South Africa, Rhodesia, and India to carry European explorers and the native populations to mines, agricultural areas, and animal lands. The passenger carriages are partially enclosed by waist-high, wood-louvered shutters; carpetbags, boxes, crates, and wicker luggage are stacked high on the roof. The classic depot is patterned after the stucco structures with open-air waiting areas built by the British in East Africa during the early 1900s.

The narrow-gauge (3.3-foot rail width) track was used in many areas where that design was easier to use along canyon walls and around horseshoe bends. Three engines and two sets of cars were built in 1997 by the model-railroad firm of Severn Lamb in Alchester, England, a few miles from William Shakespeare's cottage in Stratford-upon-Avon. The company makes trains for parks located around the world, including one in use at Disneyland Paris.

Each five-car train seats 250 passengers on side-facing benches for the 1.2-mile circle tour that runs down a shallow valley between Africa and Asia. The tour offers a behind-the-scenes look at the modern animal-care facilities, including night shelters for lions, elephants, warthogs, and antelope herds. On the return from Rafiki's Planet Watch, the train offers some peeks into the Asian area of Disney's Animal Kingdom.

▘▘▘▘▘ MUST-SEE ▘▘▘▘▘ CONSERVATION STATION

Conservation Station offers a backstage look at the veterinary headquarters and center for conservation programs at Disney's Animal Kingdom. Located in the north side of the park near the edge of Africa, Conservation Station is reached by a short journey aboard the Wildlife Express Train. From the depot it's a short walk through a jungle to a building dominated by a giant montage of animal faces, including those of the gorilla, wolf, elephant, lion, panda, turtle, baboon, and others.

Just inside the building, in the Hall of Animals, another mural presents hundreds of other animals looking directly at their visitors. "The animals are looking at you and to you—the human species," says curator Jackie Ogden. "Man represents both the greatest danger to the animals and their environment and the greatest hope." Here guests can meet animal experts and learn about the behind-the-scenes operations of the park and how they can help the animals they have met. Around the room are high-tech interactive computer displays and video observatories with a view into the park's veterinary operating room. Veterinarians may describe surgeries or procedures as they perform them; an attendant can relay questions and answers. The operating room includes blood analyzers, anesthetic equipment, and EKG machines; it even has a laparoscope connected to an overhead television monitor so guests can see into the bodies of patients during certain surgeries.

Animal-care experts are on hand to explain goings-on and to answer questions about many of the creatures. There are also regularly scheduled presentations allowing you to get up close and personal to live animals, including aardvarks, chinchillas, a miniature donkey, a golden eagle, goats, guinea pigs, rock hyrax, a great horned owl, porcupines, and rabbits.

To the right is a giant screen that projects a world map spotlighting eleven areas of the world where animals are most threatened by destruction of habitats and the encroachment of human civilization. Nearby is Animal Cam, four sets of computer touch screens that allow visitors to control cameras trained on

---

Train Buff Alert

The model for the engines at Disney's Animal Kingdom was discovered in the archives of the Indian Peninsula Railroad; they feature an unusual Aspinwall side-tank 2-4-2 design first built in 1898 at Horwich Locomotive Works in England. The stubby locomotives combine engines and tender in one car. Unlike the American-style engines at the Magic Kingdom, with their bells and low-moaning whistles, the whistles of the Wildlife Express sound like the scream of a wounded piccolo.

Although a handful of the nineteenth-century trains may still be operating in some isolated corners of the world, the Wildlife Express is believed to be the only train of its type now carrying passengers.

some of the animal habitats. A video and computer system called EcoWeb allows visitors to hear messages from well-known wildlife conservationists and to find out about ecological programs in their own backyards. Research activities directed from the facilities include radio transmitters that allow scientists to track the movement of herds, and endocrine studies that let scientists check on the health of animals without disturbing them.

Next comes a series of rooms with large picture windows that allow visitors to peek in on baby mammal nurseries; brooder rooms for birds, reptiles, and amphibians; and veterinary laboratories and operating rooms. On one of my visits, I observed a five-year-old female cheetah with a stomachache undergoing a barium series radiograph X-ray. Visitors watched the procedure through the glass, observing close-ups on a television screen. A team of eight keepers and veterinarians moved and positioned the animal, groggy from gaseous isofluorine anesthesia.

I don't usually make recommendations about visiting bathrooms, but you might want to take a side trip into the public facilities here. While you are tending to your business you can learn things such as the fact that an elephant pees as much as twenty gallons per day.

■ AFFECTION SECTION

This is your basic petting zoo, done very nicely in Disney style. Here you'll find pygmy goats, Nigerian dwarf goats, a miniature donkey, guinea pigs, and Tunis sheep, plus live demonstrations featuring unusual and exotic animals such as llamas, porcupines, aardvarks, and lesser anteaters. The animals have hideaways where they can escape over-handling from visitors.

Note the fanciful hand washer built into the snout of an elephant sculpture at the entrance.

ASIA

As you cross the Asia Bridge, you enter into the mythical Kingdom of Anandapur ("place of delight"), filled with the crumbling ruins of an ancient village, its temples, and even a maharajah's palace. In many small ways Anandapur is the most realistic and engaging area of the Animal Kingdom. We enter into a collage of Asian themes, including Nepalese, Indian, Thai, and Indonesian architecture, ruins, and animal carvings. A stand of trees grows from the ruins of a tiger shrine, and two massive monument towers—one Thai and one Nepalese—provide an idyllic setting for two rival families of gibbons who create a hooting racket all day.

The pathway from Harambe to Asia offers one of the best views of the *Tree of Life*. Overall, this is a place to go slow and enjoy the scenery, the animals, and the sense of place. Humankind and animals have lived in relative harmony for centuries here in the rain forest, but today the lush Asian lands are in danger: Fires are burning, trees are falling, and animals are losing their habitat. An environmental message about logging and development underlies much of this area.

:::::::: :::::::: MUST-SEE :::::::: **EXPEDITION EVEREST** ≡*FAST*

Okay, so a yeti is (we think) a fictional animal. This ride, though, is very much for real. Expedition Everest is a triumph of Imagineering, the latest and greatest peak in the Disney Mountain Range that began with the Matterhorn at Disneyland more than half a century ago. The spectacular thrill ride combines a high-tech roller coaster with the excitement of a close encounter of the hairy kind on a runaway railroad train.

The yeti, we're told, is an enormous creature that resides high in the Himalayan Mountains guarding the route to Mount Everest. At Disney's Animal Kingdom, mighty Everest stands just under 200 feet tall, beautifully crafted and designed.

Guests board an old mountain railway destined for the foot of Mount Everest. The train rolls through thick bamboo forests, past thundering waterfalls, along shimmering glacier fields, and it climbs higher and higher through the snowcapped peaks. But suddenly the track ends in a gnarled mass of twisted metal . . . and the train reverses direction to plunge backward through mountain caverns, fog, and icy canyons, heading for a face-to-muzzle showdown with the mysterious yeti—known to some as the abominable snowman.

Top speed for the train is a respectable 55 miles per hour, and the $100 million ride includes a 120-foot climb and an 80-foot first drop, which makes it among the gnarliest entertainments at Walt Disney World. (Space Mountain climbs only about 90 feet and goes no faster than about 28 miles per hour . . . in the dark.)

Disney's intent was to keep this ride within the bounds of a family attraction; the cars do not turn upside down. The steel tracks deliver an exhilarating, smooth ride that is well within the tolerance level of nearly all visitors, including my roller-coaster-averse wife, whom I cajoled into enjoying a trip into the Himalayas and back.

In a way, this ride harkens back to one of the earliest and most enduring attractions at the first Magic Kingdom, Disneyland in California. That ride involves a climb up a snowcapped mountain, and on the way down riders also meet the abominable snowman. But there has been a tremendous improvement in ride technology, animatronics, audio, and overall thrill factor between the 1959 opening of Matterhorn (even with a 1978 renovation) and the opening of Expedition Everest, the eighteenth peak in the Disney Mountain Range. (Other peaks include Space Mountain, Big Thunder Mountain, Splash Mountain, and other hills at the Disney parks around the world.)

At just under 200 feet tall, the mountain is more than 2 miles shorter than the real Mount Everest (which stands about 29,028 feet above sea level and 11,428 feet above its base camp), but there is a tremendous amount of detail in the Florida version of the mountain. The same is true of the "base camp" that surrounds Expedition Everest.

To create the sense of an enormous mountain range, Imagineers painted a mural of shadows across the face of the mountains. The range, with its glaciers and valleys, is a canvas of rockwork, carvings, and paintings that create a forced

Expedition Everest

perspective: Closer-in objects have a massive look, while appliqués trick the eye into perceiving far-off objects.

There's nearly a mile of track within and without the mountain. The railcars race forward, then backward and inside and outside the mountain. The ride vehicle is modeled after an antique steam engine built to haul tea; the cars carry thirty-four passengers, two abreast in seventeen rows. Riders must be at least 44 inches tall.

The trains depart from the mythical village of Serka Zong, which consists of several buildings, including a hotel, Internet cafe, and trekking supply store, all reflective of today's Nepalese architecture. In the Himalayan regions, villagers commonly preserve yak dung and dry it out on village walls. They later use the hardened material as fuel in their homes. Disney Imagineers re-created the look of these walls in the Serka Zong village area.

Disney Imagineers traveled to the Nepalese Himalayas to study the lands, architecture, colors, and culture to shape their design for the village. After a journey by jet, surrey, helicopter, and donkey, the group reached their destination, the thousand-year-old Ding Guo Shan monastery near Mustang.

Near the entrance is a canopy of prayer flags. Emblazoned with animal symbols, the banners are inspired by the Himalayan prayer flags that send thoughts and prayers to the wind. Throughout the village area, the yeti appears in architectural details, revealing its dual existence as earthly creature and mythological legend. Nepalese carvers created these special pieces based on their beliefs and local stories.

At the mandir, a traditional Himalayan shrine structure, wooden doors depict the creature in his very real realm, coming down from the mountain to snatch up a yak.

Just as the Chinese practice of arranging furniture based on feng shui is meant to create balance in the home, the earth-based red-black-white paint combinations of the Himalayas are ladled onto buildings for balance and protection. The yellow candle-drip effect over one village home signifies the residence of an old, well-established family, and firewood stacked on the roof indicates affluence.

The architectural style and cultural references of the village are a hybrid of Tibetan, Nepalese, and other design traditions found throughout the Himalayas. Each building was reproduced with great care and attention to detail so that structures appear to range in age from 50 to 300 years old. Imagineers sculpted concrete to re-create the look of the rammed-earth block (a technique where natives pound moistened earth with a mallet to create an adobe-like material) and stacked-stone buildings typically built to withstand rough Himalayan weather. Workers then sandblasted and physically distressed the structures with chain saws, hammers, blowtorches, and other tools to create uneven corners and sagging walls. Finally, artisans applied paints and stains to further the illusion of structural aging.

The three-story mandir, a pagoda-type building, was hand carved with 1,000 yeti images in Nepal, then shipped, aged, and reassembled at the Serka Zong site. A tall, brick-red block building with heavy wood doors and protective animal carvings represents a monastery similar to the one Imagineers visited in Nepal. A village entrance wall built of mani stones carved with auspicious symbols like the wheel of life, an endless knot, and other representations portends good luck. Carved totems representing the Tibetan phurba—a triple-sided ritual stake or dagger—are driven into the ground to contain threatening elements.

At least 8,000 props purchased mostly from Nepal add a lived-in look to the village and other areas of the Expedition Everest attraction. The authentic artifacts include a Mani Rimdu dance costume typically worn by a monk during a two-week festival, a 3-D yeti stamp from Bhutan, yeti dolls, a Nepalese Coke bottle, antique Chinese ceramics, and waterproof barrels designed for mountain treks.

More than 900 bamboo plants, 10 species of trees, and 110 species of shrubs were planted to re-create the lowlands surrounding Mount Everest. Some 1,800 tons of steel were used in the mountain structure, about six times the amount of steel that would have been used in a traditional office building of this size.

For thousands of years, diverse cultures along the Himalayan mountain range have believed in the yeti—some as a real, living being and others as a spiritual protector. Many believe that sightings of this mysterious, hairy creature mean the forest is pure, pristine, and undisturbed, and as the great forests disappear, so, too, does the yeti.

Disney's version of the yeti is based on a rare animal that lives not far from Everest, the golden monkey. With a strange, haunting face covered in hair everywhere but the smallest areas around the eyes and nose, blue skin, and unfathomable dark eyes, the golden monkey is the perfect model of a cold-climate primate.

⁞MUST-SEE⁞ KALI RIVER RAPIDS ≡*FAST*

Aboard twelve-passenger rubber rafts, adventurers zoom down the raging whitewater Chakranadi River through rapids and waterfalls and through dense jungles into a modern-day parable about the effects of thoughtless development. *Chakranadi* is a Thai word that means "river that runs in a circle."

Traveling into a huge bamboo tunnel, rafters are surrounded by a jasmine-tinged mist as they are lifted 40 feet to the river's headwaters. The tour begins with a close call with a geyser from the river bottom; if you're lucky, you'll watch the people sitting opposite you take a surprise shower.

At the top of a climb, a giant carved tiger face peers from behind a waterfall. Gliding on through a rain forest and temple ruins, the raft emerges from a thicket of bamboo, and the smell of jasmine is lost to the acrid smell of smoke from burning trees. The raft twists and spins through the river, swollen by uncontrolled runoff from rain, the unpleasant result of environmentally careless logging. Disaster narrowly avoided, more thrills await on a white-knuckle race through turbulent waters, some of the more energetic I've seen on a river-raft ride. The large rafts move comfortably; take advantage of the dry storage section

Kali River Rapids

in the center of the boat for backpacks. Depending on luck (and how heavily weighted down your raft is), you will end up somewhere between damp and drenched.

The setup to the ride has some lovely attention to details. The queue winds its way through a wooden temple; beyond the rails you can spot stone gods in the jungle. The counter at the entrance to the rapids holds a sign saying the owner is away, GONE TO TEMPLE. The shelves are stocked with native guidebooks, as well as Kodak film in Indian-language packaging. Speaking of queues: You can expect the water ride to be very popular on hot Florida afternoons. I'd suggest heading there early or late on crowded days.

▓▓▓▓ MUST-SEE ▓▓▓▓ MAHARAJAH JUNGLE TREK

At the end of the river ride lies a trail through an Asian wonder world, through temple ruins partially reclaimed by the jungle. Komodo monitor dragons, which grow up to 12 feet long, perch on rocks near a streambed. Across a wooden foot-bridge are families of bats, rare Asian birds, Malayan tapirs, and other exotic creatures. (Tapirs are strange creatures that look like a long-nosed pig dressed in a tony gray cardigan sweater. A distant relative of the rhinoceros and horse, tapirs are most active in the early morning and late afternoon.)

The ruins of a maharajah's palace are home to a group of Bengal tigers. Beyond them lie a herd of blackbuck antelope and Elds deer. The animals are visible from the top of a parapet, through a bamboo stand, and from a bridge amid the re-created ruins near an old herb garden. On one of the visits I made, I watched as one of the tigers spent much of the warm morning swimming back and forth in a moat. Gibbons let loose hoots as they swing from a Thai temple to a Nepalese monument tower.

Near the end of the trek is a walk-through aviary, home to species of ground-, mud-, and tree-dwelling birds. There's also a bat room, with visitors standing on the free side of an open wood grate with slats too wide for the creatures to pass through. (There's a go-round for those too squeamish to face the bats up close and personal.)

■ *FLIGHTS OF WONDER*

Birds swoop low over the audience gathered at Caravan Stage, a 1,250-seat amphitheater overlooking the Discovery River just across the bridge to Asia. *Flights of Wonder* demonstrates the skills of some of the world's most interesting birds, including falcons, macaws, vultures, hawks, and owls, in a twenty-five-minute show that is presented several times daily. The setting is the abandoned ancient aviary of the Rajahs of Anandapur, in a crumbling fortified town in Asia, a centuries-old way station on the fringe of the desert. The buildings are pockmarked to provide homes for some of the avian actors as they wait for their cues to perform. Others even fly from the top branches of the 145-foot-tall *Tree of Life* just on the other side of the Discovery River.

In essence, the story has devolved into a comedy act that may help answer the question, why did the fancy chicken cross the stage? We meet Bwana Joe, a jungle guide who's scared of animals, and a talented parrot who sings a few verses of "Camptown Ladies." Among the creatures are Harris hawks, a Barbary falcon, and Toco toucans that catch grapes at ten paces. A black-legged seriema, a large cranelike bird, body-slams a real-looking serpent. Tumbler pigeons do midair backward somersaults. Other stars include a green-winged macaw, king vulture, Eurasia eagle owl, and moulacan cockatoo. At some shows an augur buzzard flies out and lends a hand by scratching the head of the phoenix.

Although the show is carefully rehearsed, the birds are taught to show off their natural talent rather than perform tricks. Trainers demonstrate how birds respond to special audio or visual clues. Casting will vary from show to show. At one performance a troop of Indian runner ducks will dash across the stage on cue; another time the role might be taken by Abyssinian ground hornbills in flight.

DINOLAND, U.S.A.

A celebration of America's fascination with all things dinosaur, this section of the Animal Kingdom looks like a quirky roadside attraction of the 1950s, complete with an old Airstream trailer, a Quonset hut, pink (plastic) flamingos, and other bits of dino-Americana. You will enter into the area beneath the skeleton of a 50-foot-tall brachiosaurus.

DinoLand, U.S.A., features the Boneyard playground, a rambling open-air dig site filled with fossils where kids can slide, bounce, and slither through the bones of Tyrannosaurus rex, triceratops, and other long-gone giants.

▐MUST-SEE▐ DINOSAUR ≡FAST

Dinosaur is housed within what we're told is the "once-secret research project of the Dino Institute, built as a discovery center and ongoing research lab dedicated to uncovering the mysteries of the past." (Does this sound like Jurassic Park? More than a little, actually.) The attraction, which opened as Countdown to Extinction, was renamed in 2000 to support Disney's film of the same name.

Enter into the institute's rotunda, filled with murals, dioramas, and fossils telling the scientific theory of how the dinosaurs became extinct. A video starring Disney's favorite techno-geek Bill Nye explains that scientists now believe that an asteroid—6 miles across and traveling 60,000 miles per hour—slammed into Earth in a fiery crash sixty-five million years ago at the end of the Cretaceous era. The resulting "nuclear winter" blocked the sun and dropped temperatures for several years, devastating plant life. Much of the planet's animal life, deprived of food, followed into extinction.

As many as eighty guests at a time are ushered into a briefing room for a video conference with the director of the institute, Dr. Helen Marsh. "I hope you enjoyed the quaint exhibits in the old wing," she says. "Today that bare-bones approach is history. The Dino Institute has created the Time Rover—an amazing vehicle that can literally transport you to the age of the dinosaurs."

The idea is to take guests back to the start of the Cretaceous era for a thrilling but safe romp among the dinosaurs. And, we're promised, we'll be whisked back to the present day well before that asteroid crashes into the planet. As Dr. Marsh assures us, "The future is truly in the past." Of course, nothing could possibly go wrong, right? Meet paleontologist Grant Seeker (nudge, nudge: get the egghead joke?). He wants to use the Time Rover to retrieve a living, breathing iguanodon, and to do so, he needs to send us very close to the end of the Cretaceous period. You know, when the asteroid is due. Dr. Marsh is in charge, of course, and Seeker promises her the Time Rovers are properly programmed. But why is he winking at you?

Finally, we descend into the loading area for the twelve-passenger Time Rovers, three rows of four seats. Buckle yourself into a seat and put your cameras and personal belongings into the pocket in front of you; you're going to need your hands to hold on tight. And then we're off, into a cloud of fog and a blizzard of flashing lights . . . we're going back, back, back in time.

Suddenly we emerge into a sunless prehistoric forest, a place of strange insects and birds and the honking and shrieking of giant beasts. As our Time Rover climbs a small hill, the headlights reveal a styracosaurus. Nearby an alioramus indelicately dines on a giant lizard. As we move through the fantastic landscape, we can hear the voice of Seeker as he helps us search for the iguanodon of his dreams. He doesn't seem all that concerned about the sudden hail of meteorites that is falling from the sky, smashing into the vehicle and making it swerve off the road

Animal Kingdom's Top Ten

They're all stars, but here are ten of the most unusual and interesting creatures in the park:

▶ **1. Gerenuk.** An antelope with a pencil-thin neck, oversized ears, and delicate features, it stands on its spindly hind legs to feed on vegetation. Look for these otherworldly creatures on the savanna from Kilimanjaro Safaris or from the savanna overlook at Pangani Forest Exploration Trail.

▶ **2. Naked mole rat.** A homely, cold-blooded creature from Kenya and Ethiopia that lives in an underground colony centered around a queen, the only female in the colony capable of reproduction. Pink and virtually hairless, these members of the mole family seem to "moonwalk" along tunnels. A glass wall exposes the colony along the Pangani Forest Exploration Trail.

▶ **3. Marabou stork.** It's been called the "world's ugliest bird," and it's not hard to understand why: It sports a pickax bill, two unsightly pouches, and a naked cranium that has scablike spots. Standing as much as 5 feet tall, they were slaughtered in large numbers at the turn of the twentieth century for hatmakers who sought the downy feathers under the birds' tails. One of the largest groups in North America can be seen on the savanna.

▶ **4. Okapi.** One of the largest mammals discovered in the twentieth century, okapi are found only in the Ituri Forest of the Republic of Congo. Resembling a cross between a giraffe and zebra, it is a shy, solitary, and short-necked member of the giraffe family. They can be seen near the start of the Kilimanjaro Safaris tour and from the Pangani Forest pathway.

▶ **5. Sable antelope.** These large and aggressive antelope are from southern Africa and have scimitar-shaped horns that allow them to stand up to large predators, including lions. When at rest, they lie in a circular star pattern with their heads facing out and their young in the middle to protect them from predators. A herd of sable can be seen from the Kilimanjaro Safaris.

▶ **6. Carmine bee-eater.** One of the most beautiful African birds, it is about a foot long with an iridescent turquoise head and a flaming carmine red body. It performs amazing acrobatics in pursuit of bees, one of its favorite foods. One of the largest flocks in North America can be seen in the aviary on the Pangani Forest Exploration Trail.

▶ **7. Red kangaroo.** This marsupial's unusual reproductive system allows her to have one offspring at foot while another nurses and grows in her pouch and a third is in the embryonic stage; she can produce two kinds of milk at the same time for these different-aged joeys. Boomers (males) are reddish in color, while females are bluish gray. They can leap distances of up to 40 feet, reaching speeds of 30 miles per hour. A group can be seen in the *Tree of Life* area.

(continued)

▶ **8. Ring-tailed lemur.** About the size of a large house cat, gray with a long black-and-white striped tail, it spends its leisure time sunbathing. One of the few primates that gives birth to multiple young, its horrific screaming is mostly bluster. A colony can be seen in the *Tree of Life* area.

▶ **9. White rhinoceros.** Not really white—you go and tell him—but actually brownish gray, its name comes from a mistranslation of the Afrikaans word for "wide," which describes the animal's upper lip. This creature, as much as three tons in weight, has been poached for years for its horn, which is used for cere- monial dagger handles in northern Africa and in Chinese folk medicine. Though they don't swim, they like to take dips to cool off. They can be seen from the Kilimanjaro Safaris.

▶ **10. Black rhinoceros.** More rare than white rhinos, these animals from east- ern and southern Africa are also more aggressive. They use their hooked lip to grab the shrubs they eat. Fewer than 5,000 are left in the wild; like the white rhino, they have been poached for their horns. They can be seen on the sa- vanna from the Kilimanjaro Safaris.

According to Disney, most of the animals on display were born in zoologi- cal parks; others were rescued from endangered habitats or are orphans that have been saved by wildlife officials.

. . . and directly into the path of a fearsome carnotaurus. But wait! The big me- teor is on its way. Will Seeker manage to pull you back sixty-five million years to the Dino Institute before it hits Earth, or before you become a dino dinner? You will, of course, survive to spend another day at Disney. As you stumble out of the institute and back to the present day at the park, be sure to check out the secu- rity-camera images near the exit. Is that an iguanodon wandering the halls?

Everyone is going to enjoy the show, although some riders may find that the loud jumble of noises and flashes makes the story a bit difficult to follow. Others may find the ride itself a bit jarring. On a hot day it's worth a visit just for the air-conditioning.

The CTX Rovers are versions of the vehicles used at Disneyland's Indiana Jones Adventure, Temple of the Forbidden Eye ride. The Rovers use a Disney technology known as Enhanced Motion Vehicle, which controls the movement of the trans- port forward and backward, up and down, and side to side, as well as the sounds and some of the special effects of the ride. Each vehicle can stop, back up, slow down, or go faster based on computer decisions.

The dinosaur crew, in their order of appearance in Dinosaur, are Styracosaurus, Alioramus, Parasaurolophus, Raptor, Carnotaurus, Saltasaurus, Cearadactylus, Compsognather, and Iguanodon. According to Disney Imagineers, the show was cast as if it were a movie, with a hero and a villain. The hero is the iguanodon, a plant-eating dinosaur large enough to make an impres- sion anywhere he goes, but gentle looking with a wise, beaked face. Planners wanted to surprise visitors with a villain few had ever encountered in films, mu-

The entrance to Chester & Hester's Dino-Rama!

seums, or books: the carnotaurus. The name means "meat bull," and the creature matches its fearsome name with the blunt face of a bulldog, a gaping mouthful of savage teeth, and two huge horns. The creature in the show was based on a nearly complete skeleton of a carnotaurus that was uncovered in Argentina a few years ago. The audio-animatronic version, though, is larger and even more fearsome than the real thing—that's show biz.

Guests must be at least 46 inches tall to ride, and pregnant women and visitors who have medical conditions are advised against taking the ride.

■ CHESTER & HESTER'S DINO-RAMA!

The dinosaurs are in charge in this family ride area, which features a pair of carnival rides and half a dozen midway games. Chester and Hester's Dinosaur Treasures is a re-creation of a quirky roadside stand of the (believe it or not) pre-Disney era in America, selling all manner of dinosaur souvenirs. The fun fair includes carnival games like Ringosaurus, in which guests toss beanbags into dinosaur jaws.

TriceraTop Spin

This is a hub-and-spoke spinning ride; sixteen four-person vehicles move up, down, and around in a ride that transforms into a giant spinning toy top. The top rises to reveal—what else?—a dinosaur. Think of this ride as a Dino-Dumbo; it joins The Magic Carpets of Aladdin at the Magic Kingdom as a salute to the very popular Dumbo the Flying Elephant, also at the Magic Kingdom.

Primeval Whirl ≡FAST

Chester and Hester's homemade "time machine" is a wild "prehysterical" run that sends riders through curves, short drops, and the jaws of a dinosaur.

This is a Disneyfied wild mouse–like coaster featuring thirteen colorful four-seater cars on a pair of identical twisty and turny tracks of tight loops and short drops that take riders past flying asteroids and corny cartoon dinosaurs. A final descent drops into the gaping jaws of a giant dino fossil. The cars start out heading the same direction as the track, but then they are released to spin wildly. Riders must be at least 48 inches tall.

A spinning coaster sets off on Primeval Whirl in DinoLand, U.S.A.

■ THE BONEYARD

Not since the days of the dinosaurs has there been a playground like this: Bones, fossils, and reconstructed dinosaur skeletons are everywhere. Children of all ages can dig in the sand to uncover the pieces of the past (returning them later for other explorers to find). There's also a set of walkways, rope bridges, and slides that lead in every which way.

As you enter the area, you'll pass beneath the Oldengate Bridge, constructed from replica bones of a brachiosaurus, one of the largest creatures that ever walked the planet, standing some 52 feet tall and more than 80 feet long. The bones are based on casts of the actual fossil of a creature found in Colorado in 1900; the original is at the Field Museum in Chicago.

■ CRETACEOUS TRAIL

This walk through the past, where guests can wander through a garden of cycads, palms, ferns, and other surprising survivors from the age of the dinosaur, includes soft-shelled turtles and Chinese crocodiles. The cycad collection of more than 3,000 ancient fernlike plants is the third largest in North America. It includes direct descendants of four botanical epochs of plant evolution dating back hundreds of millions of years, such as ferns, mosses, conifers, broadleaf plants, and the first flowering plants. DinoLand, U.S.A., features twenty species of magnolia, a flowering plant that dates from the Cretaceous period.

MUST-SEE FINDING NEMO—THE MUSICAL

The undersea world that charmed audiences around the world in the hit film *Finding Nemo* comes to life in a new musical stage show, the first time that Disney has taken a nonmusical animated feature and transformed it into an original musical production. The show is presented several times daily in the enclosed Theater in the Wild.

The musical picks up the story of Marlin and Nemo, an overprotective clownfish father and his curious son, with the help of puppets, dancers, and acrobats. The show is presented against high-tech animated backdrops, with special lighting, sound, and other effects.

In the musical, Marlin and Nemo each travel on a separate journey that ultimately teaches them how to love and understand each other. The two have been separated, and Marlin will stop at nothing to get his son back, facing undersea challenges with his new friend, Dory. Meanwhile, Nemo, relocated to a fish tank in Sydney, makes new friends who teach him that he's stronger than he thinks. When news of his father's heroic journey reaches the tank, Nemo is inspired to do whatever is necessary to escape the tank and see his father again.

Marlin, Nemo, and Dory are represented by live performers operating larger-than-life puppets. Other characters appear in a diverse array of puppetry styles, including rod, bunraku, and shadow.

Finding Nemo—The Musical is the first major musical produced for Walt Disney World Resort by Disney Creative Entertainment, also responsible for *Disney's Aladdin* at the Disneyland Resort in California, *The Lion King* at Hong Kong Disneyland, *Twice Charmed* on the Disney Cruise Line, and *The Golden Mickeys* at Hong Kong Disneyland and on the Disney Cruise Line.

CAMP MINNIE-MICKEY

Since the Disney empire did start with a mouse (and then his girlfriend, and then various dogs, ducks, and other creatures), it was obvious from the start that some of the most famous animals of our time would have an area of their own. (And yes, Goofy is a dog.)

Just across the Discovery River southwest of Discovery Island, Camp Minnie-Mickey is a child's paradise of woodland trails and "meet-and-greet" pavilions, set in a northeastern forest of cedar and birch trees. Benches and other furniture were handcrafted by artisans from the Adirondacks. Each trail leading to a character meeting spot is themed to set up an exciting character encounter.

As guests cross a wood-hewn bridge from Discovery Island to Camp Minnie-Mickey, they stroll alongside a babbling brook to find lifelike images of Mickey,

Goofy, and Donald Duck at their favorite fishing hole. You'll also find Winnie the Pooh and Tigger camped out in a grove of maples and oaks.

▦ MUST-SEE ▦ *FESTIVAL OF THE LION KING*

Here's Disney's stagecraft at its best, a rollicking combination of Broadway, an indoor parade, and a circus. Oh yes, there are also stilt walkers, fire twirlers, singers, dancers, acrobats, and floats.

The theater is a 1,000-seat hexagonal timber structure. Guests are assigned to one of four triangular rooting sections: elephant, giraffe, warthog, and lion. Giant stages move in from four directions to bring us up close to Simba and other animal heroes of *The Lion King,* along with singers, dancers, and acrobatic performers costumed in African tribal garb or dressed to depict exotic African animals. The show opens with a rousing rendition of "I Just Can't Wait to Be King."

A 12-foot-tall figure of Simba rises from Pride Rock. To the left is Elephant Waterfall, where a playful pachyderm spouts water from his trunk. Across the way is a pair of swaying giraffe heads, and nearby is a jungle mesa topped by Pumbaa and Timon. The unbilled stars of the show, though, are a troupe of acrobats who perform a comic—but impressive—routine on a trampoline and trapeze at center stage. A pair of adagio dancers performs to "Can You Feel the Love Tonight?" and the girl returns later in a flying harness to soar above the crowd. Kids from the audience are brought forth for a production of "Wimboweh."

The twenty-eight-minute show is performed eight times daily. Lines can build at midday; one strategy to avoid crowds is to visit the show early, or aim for a show that takes place near starting time for one of the daily parades through the park.

▪ *POCAHONTAS AND HER FOREST FRIENDS*

Pocahontas takes to a rustic stage to help us discover the secret to saving America's forests and the creatures that live there. With the help of Grandmother Willow—a spirit in a tree trunk—as well as a live armadillo, red-tailed hawk, skunk, boa constrictor, and several rabbits, Pocahontas and the audience learn that only humans can save the animals and the forest from civilization. The twelve-minute show is presented through the day in a 350-seat outdoor theater. Trees offer shade to some of the seats.

EATS AND TREATS

There are several interesting fast-food restaurants in the park as well as one sit-down restaurant, the Rainforest Cafe, near the entrance. You'll also find snacks that include dinosaur legs (well, okay, they're large turkey legs) in DinoLand, U.S.A.; fresh-baked cookies in an Adirondack cabin at Camp Minnie-Mickey; and ice-cream bars that have the imprint of Simba's paw from stands throughout the park. And, unlike the Magic Kingdom, Disney's Animal Kingdom fully embraces alcohol. You can purchase beer in many of the restaurants, and there's

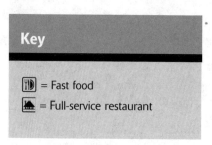

even a house brand of wine at a bar in Harambe.

The park can be quite hot in the Florida sunshine; be sure to drink lots of water to avoid dehydration. Bottled water is available from vendors, and there are free fountains in many locations.

▲ **Rainforest Cafe.** Somewhat hidden behind a 65-foot waterfall to the left of the entrance is a branch of the quirky Rainforest Cafe chain, the second outlet at Walt Disney World (the other is at Disney Village). There are entrances from inside and outside the park. (You'll need to have your hand stamped and hold on to your ticket to reenter the park; visitors coming just for the restaurant will have to pay for parking in the Animal Kingdom lot.)

The Rainforest Cafe is the only full-service restaurant at the park, and waits for seats in the 575-seat dining room can be as long as several hours. Advance reservations are not accepted, but arriving guests will be given a "passport" with an expected departure time for a dining "safari." Not coincidentally, a large gift shop lies between the check-in desk and the dining room, and your presence—and money—will be welcomed there while you wait. If your safari time is several hours in the offing, you could go back into the park.

There are other sights to see while you wait, though, including real parrots on perches below giant toadstools, giant cylindrical aquariums, and a bubbling water wall at the base of the juice bar. And you've got to love the stools at the bar—I wonder where the front halves of those animals went?

◼ DISCOVERY ISLAND

⊞ **Pizzafari.** One of the more Disneyesque places in the park, the inside of the restaurant is nevertheless worth a peek; the walls are covered with animal murals, and the ceiling is lined with colorful animal figurines. Small open-hearth-oven pizzas sell for about $6.00. Some have unusual toppings. Also available is a mesquite-grilled chicken Caesar salad.

⊞ **Flame Tree Barbecue.** Specializing in wood-roasted meats with tomato-based or mustard sauces, this eatery is open for lunch and dinner. There is indoor seating as well as an outdoor dining pavilion along the river. The menu includes smoked beef brisket, pork shoulder, and turkey for about $7.00, and barbecued rib platters for $8.50.

◼ DINOLAND, U.S.A.

⊞ **Restaurantosaurus.** This basic fast-food venue has a slightly altered McDonald's menu, minus the golden arches. You'll find Chicken McNuggets, Happy Meals, and french fries, plus hot dogs, sandwiches, and salads. Complete meals are priced at about $6.00. A daily character breakfast starring Mickey Mouse, Donald Duck, Goofy, and Pluto is also presented here.

■ AFRICA

▮D▮ **Tusker House Restaurant.** The restaurant sprawls out onto a weather-beaten outdoor patio. Open for breakfast, lunch, and dinner. Prices range from about $7.25 to $9.00 for chicken cooked on the rotisserie, roasted, grilled, or fried; plus prime rib, lasagna, and roasted vegetable sandwiches with tabbouleh.

▮D▮ **Kusafiri Coffee Shop & Bakery.** This attractive eatery features warm cinnamon rolls, coffee, espresso, cappuccino, and other delicacies. Kusafiri is designed like an East African bazaar, with Arabic archways and ceilings draped in exotic fabrics.

CHAPTER TEN

DISNEY–MGM STUDIOS

LET'S GO TO THE MOVIES: Disney–MGM Studios celebrates the magic of filmmaking and television. In recent years the park has begun to emerge from the shadows of the other, splashier parks at Walt Disney World. The first step was the installation of the Twilight Zone Tower of Terror, a wild journey that expands on a story from the revered television show. Then came the astounding *Fantasmic!* nighttime show and the Rock 'n' Roller Coaster Starring Aerosmith. For many visitors the final answer is still to be found at *Who Wants to Be a Millionaire—Play It!*, a live show that has outlasted the prime-time television hit. For the younger set, there's Playhouse Disney. And children of all ages will enjoy the audio thrills of *Sounds Dangerous*.

And several times a day the park explodes with high-octane thrills at *Lights, Motors, Action! Extreme Stunt Show*. The show features Hollywood-style stunts and special effects on cars, motorcycles, and Jet Skis in a 5,000-seat theater in the back-lot area.

A 122-foot-tall Sorcerer Mickey hat crowns the studios as its icon, representing the magic of show business and Disney wizardry. The 156-ton icon, at the end of Hollywood Boulevard directly in front of the Chinese Theater, salutes Mickey's famous role in the animated-classic *Fantasia*. (The hat, by the way, is a size 606⁷⁄₈. It would fit a 350-foot-tall mouse.)

The idea behind Disney–MGM Studios is to allow guests to step into some of the greatest—or at least the most popular—movies and television hits of the twentieth century. Not surprisingly, many of them are Disney hits, including *Beauty and the Beast*, *The Little Mermaid*, *Mulan*, *Toy Story*, and *Honey, I Shrunk the Kids*.

The overall theme of Disney–MGM Studios seems to be "Nothing is what it appears to be." This will be apparent from the moment you spot the park's distinctive Earfful Tower (a set of mouse ears atop a 130-foot-tall water tower) from outside the park, and the giant Sorceror's Hat that stands at the central plaza of the park. From there it's on to the movie-realistic New York street scenes and the inside magic of the studio production tours. You'll also be able to see the Twilight Zone Tower of Terror, a creepy derelict hotel. It's fun to think of the tower as a counterpoint to the squeaky-clean real hotels spread throughout Walt Disney World.

SPECTACLES AND PARADES

First of all, the *Fantasmic!* show is not to be missed. It is quite simply one of the best outdoor entertainments at any theme park anywhere. Also, be sure to find the time to stroll Hollywood Boulevard near the entranceway—I'd suggest coming back to this area at midday when the lines at attractions are at their longest. The boulevard is a continuous street theater. Pretty girls may be approached by "producers" handing out their business cards. Actresses on the prowl for producers will give men the eye; vain stars will expect you to swoon at their feet. Actors perform skits and gags from old silent films. The street actors stay in character all of the time they are "on"; for fun, try asking one of them for directions or some personal questions about their careers.

In 2006 the **Disney Stars and Motor Cars Parade** was performed daily, stepping off from the Star Tours gate and traveling down Hollywood Boulevard to exit near the front of the park at Crossroads. More than one hundred performers and crew take part in the parade—along with six guests from the park chosen as grand marshals. The cavalcade is made up of fifteen cars dating from 1929 to 1951; six of the vehicles are original, while the remainder are re-creations. The cars each salute famous Disney characters. Among the groups: *Toy Story,* featuring Buzz Lightyear and Woody, atop Andy's bed; Mary Poppins and Bert stroll down the street along with the dancing penguins alongside a colorful car decorated with old-fashioned carousel horses; and Luke Skywalker and Princess Leia fly through the parade aboard their space-travel machine in the *Star Wars* group. Recent additions include JoJo and Goliath, stars of the Disney Channel series *JoJo's Circus.*

MUST-SEES

Who Wants to Be a Millionaire—Play It!

Fantasmic!

Rock 'n' Roller Coaster Starring Aerosmith

Twilight Zone Tower of Terror

The Great Movie Ride

Sounds Dangerous

Indiana Jones Epic Stunt Spectacular

Star Tours

Voyage of the Little Mermaid

Playhouse Disney— Live On Stage!

Jim Henson's Muppet*Vision 3D

Lights, Motors, Action! Extreme Stunt Show

Disney–MGM Studios Backlot Tour

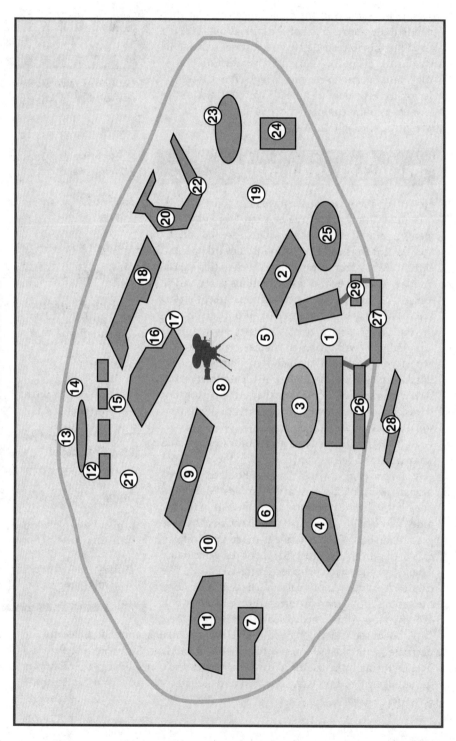

DISNEY–MGM STUDIOS

DISNEY–MGM STUDIOS

① Hollywood Boulevard
② *Beauty and the Beast—Live On Stage*
③ Echo Lake
④ *Indiana Jones Epic Stunt Spectacular*
⑤ Plaza
⑥ *Sounds Dangerous*
⑦ Star Tours
⑧ The Great Movie Ride
⑨ *Honey, I Shrunk the Kids* Movie Set Adventure
⑩ New York Street
⑪ *Jim Henson's Muppet*Vision 3D*
⑫ The Back Lot
⑬ Catastrophe Canyon
⑭ *Lights, Motors, Action! Extreme Stunt Show*
⑮ Soundstage 1
⑯ *Who Wants to Be a Millionaire—Play It!*
⑰ *Playhouse Disney—Live On Stage!*
⑱ Production Center
⑲ Sunset Boulevard
⑳ *Voyage of the Little Mermaid*
㉑ Disney–MGM Studios Backlot Tour
㉒ The Magic of Disney Animation
㉓ Rock 'n' Roller Coaster Starring Aerosmith
㉔ Twilight Zone Tower of Terror
㉕ *Fantasmic!*
㉖ First Aid
㉗ Entrance Plaza
㉘ Guest Relations
㉙ Lockers/strollers

In recent years Disney beefed up its shopping district on Sunset Boulevard to include a Planet Hollywood shop, joining the larger store at the chain's restaurant at the Disney Village Marketplace. The Sunset Boulevard area now includes the four biggest draws at MGM: *Fantasmic!*, Rock 'n' Roller Coaster, the Twilight Zone Tower of Terror, and the *Beauty and the Beast—Live On Stage* show. If you arrive late, or are visiting on a busy day, start your day with a glance at the Guest Information Board at Hollywood Junction at the top end of Hollywood Boulevard. A chalkboard here will tell you how long the waits are for many of the attractions at the park; the hosts are kept up-to-date by walkie-talkie reports from head counters. You may need to alter your Power Trip based on unusual conditions. One more note: The layout of the park makes it one of the hottest places in the Walt Disney World Resort. Be sure to wear a hat and use sunscreen any time of the year.

How does Disney–MGM Studios compare to the other movie-themed park in Orlando, Universal Studios Florida? In my opinion, anything within Walt Disney World offers a more polished and better planned experience than almost any other theme park. That said, Universal Studios Florida is larger and has several rides and attractions that are unlike anything else at Walt Disney World, including the Twister, Men in Black, Terminator 2, Earthquake, and *Shrek 4-D* attractions. (The other theme park across town, Universal's Islands of Adventure, includes the Jurassic Park River Adventure, plus phantasmagoric rides loosely based on cartoon characters such as the astounding *Amazing Adventures of Spider-Man* as well as some of the hairiest roller coasters for older kids of all ages.) If you have the time, I suggest you visit both Disney–MGM and Universal's two parks; if you are on a very tight schedule and must choose among them, I'd suggest Disney–MGM if you are with young children, Universal's Islands of Adventure for teens, and Universal Studios Florida for older parties.

CHRISTMASTIME AT DISNEY–MGM STUDIOS

MGM is also home each Christmastime to the Spectacle of Lights show on its Residential Street and Washington Square back lot. The display began as a private show that lit up the house of businessman Jennings Osborne; he—or at least his show—was eventually run out of Little Rock, Arkansas, because of electrical excess. The street is open for strolling each evening from just after Thanksgiving through early January. The back-lot tram tour is ended early each day to allow pedestrians to walk around.

The rest of the park is hardly neglected. Live plantings of poinsettias line the paths, a giant set of mouse ears adorns the landmark Earrful Tower near the road entrance to the park, and a spectacular Christmas tree occupies the plaza near Mickey's hat.

ATTRACTIONS AT DISNEY–MGM STUDIOS

MUST-SEE **WHO WANTS TO BE A MILLIONAIRE—PLAY IT!** ≡FAST
Together for the first time, two of Disney's biggest stars: Mickey . . . and Regis. Regis Philbin himself arrived at Disney–MGM Studios accompanied by Mickey Mouse and an armored car to hand the "keys to the hot seat" to hosts charged with re-creating the drama delivered in the television game show *Who Wants to Be a Millionaire?*

Premiering as a regular ABC series in January 2000, *Who Wants to Be a Millionaire?* soared in popularity to become the most-watched television series in the 1999–2000 season. A syndicated version of the show can be seen in major U.S. markets. The Disney-MGM version was still running in 2006, although its long-term schedule was uncertain.

Guests experience *Millionaire* in exacting detail, seated in a replica of the high-tech set, complete with the dramatically lit hot seat. The one difference: Guests play for points, not dollars, winning unique prizes along the way. Prizes range from collectible pins and hats to a grand prize of three nights for four persons on Disney Cruise Line.

The television show has waned in popularity, but the live show goes on at Disney–MGM Studios; the park adjusts the number of shows and the hours based on daily attendance. The live show takes place in a 600-seat studio located in Soundstages 2 and 3. The show eats up a lot of time—plan on at least an hour from getting in line to setup for the show and then about a thirty-minute performance.

Like the television show, the fastest finger determines the first contestant to sit in the coveted hot seat. All audience members play along, using individual keypads at their seats as their scores are tallied throughout the session. They also get involved when players use the "ask the audience" lifeline. Other guests could be called upon for help with the "phone a complete stranger" lifeline. The "phone

Power Trip #1: For Adults and Adventurous Kids

Arrive early. This tour allows for a quick fast-food lunch and a more leisurely dinner. Stop by the Production Information Window just inside the gates on the right side to see if there are any tickets for tapings of television shows. Before you start your day, draw up your list of personal must-sees. Order them into attractions that offer Fastpass reservations and those that do not. At Disney–MGM Studios you can obtain Fastpass reservations at *Who Wants to Be a Millionaire—Play It!*, *Jim Henson's Muppet*Vision 3D*, Rock 'n' Roller Coaster, Tower of Terror, Star Tours, *Indiana Jones Epic Stunt Spectacular*, *Voyage of the Little Mermaid*, and the *Lights, Motors, Action! Extreme Stunt Show*, which opened in 2005.

Lights, Motors, Action! changed the dynamic at the park, and its theater swallows up 5,000 people at a time, which allows for a relatively easy entrance and also reduces crowds elsewhere in the park while the show is under way.

If you're looking for thrills in the morning, I would go the length of Hollywood Boulevard and turn right and head down Sunset Boulevard toward the Twilight Zone Tower of Terror. Make a quick stop at the Fastpass dispenser for the Rock 'n' Roller Coaster, and then head for the still-short line at the Tower of Terror. If the lines are short and you are so inclined—if you can pardon that pun—check into the hotel again before the lines reach intolerable lengths later in the day.

Now head to the Rock 'n' Roller Coaster in Studio 15 to the left of the Tower of Terror. Once your stomach is back in its customary position, zoom out of Sunset Boulevard and back to Hollywood Boulevard; make a left at the first corner along Echo Lake. Note the Hollywood & Vine and '50s Prime Time Cafe as possible dinner stops; you may want to make a reservation as you go by.

Your next goal is to pick up a Fastpass for *Who Wants to Be a Millionaire—Play It!* If you can get in right away, go for the big bucks; if not, plan to come back in the afternoon with your pass in hand. Next, head for Star Tours. (Pass by the *Indiana Jones Epic Stunt Spectacular*—it'll wait for later.) After you're back from the moons of Endor, make a sharp left turn and visit *Jim Henson's Muppet*Vision 3D*, a treat for all ages. While you're in the area, check out Mama Melrose's Ristorante Italiano, another interesting food stop, or the Sci-Fi Dine-In Theater Restaurant, a must-see eatery; make reservations early for these dining options.

The next stop is The Great Movie Ride at the top of Hollywood Boulevard. (Along the way, you have passed by *Sounds Dangerous.*) Continue moving in a counterclockwise direction through the archway to the studio section of the park. It should be time for lunch now; the Soundstage Restaurant is in the studio area and is as good a fast-food stop as any other.

Go next to The Magic of Disney Animation tour; don't let youngsters talk

(continued)

you out of this visit—they'll enjoy the movie in the preshow, and you'll want to see the artists at work. Nearby is *Playhouse Disney—Live on Stage!*, a live production based on children's television shows including *Bear in the Big Blue House*, *Rolie Polie Olie*, *The Book of Pooh*, and *Stanley*.

At this point, you will have visited all of the attractions that have the longest lines. Backtrack or continue in a counterclockwise direction to see any shows you may have missed, such as the *Indiana Jones Epic Stunt Spectacular* (consult the daily schedule for show times), *Playhouse Disney—Live on Stage!* (for younger visitors), and the clever *Sounds Dangerous* for movie and Drew Carey fans. Finally, you'll want to end your day at one of the nighttime showings of *Fantasmic!* On a busy day you may need to secure a seat as much as an hour before show time.

Remember that crowds at many rides and restaurants will be shorter during the afternoon parade; check the schedule on the day you arrive.

Power Trip #2: For Young Children and the Adults Who Are with Them

This tour skips three rides that may be too wild for youngsters: Twilight Zone Tower of Terror, the Rock 'n' Roller Coaster, and Star Tours. Arrive early, and make restaurant reservations for lunch or dinner. Then head up Hollywood Boulevard and go straight to The Great Movie Ride. When you're through, enter into the studio section of the park and join the line for the *Voyage of the Little Mermaid* stage show.

You know your kids better than anyone else; some youngsters will love the *Lights, Motors, Action! Extreme Stunt Show*, while others may be frightened by the explosions and loud noises. Either way, the large theater takes in thousands of guests, making it easier to get into other attractions.

Head over to *Playhouse Disney—Live on Stage!* The next stop is the Disney–MGM Studios Backlot Tour. Now cross over the top of the park to visit the *Honey, I Shrunk the Kids* Movie Set Adventure and one of the outdoor stage shows.

It's time to go inside to take a load off your feet and your mind with some inspired silliness at *Jim Henson's Muppet*Vision 3D*, a treat for all ages. Go next to The Magic of Disney Animation tour.

Depending on the ages of your children, you may want to visit the *Indiana Jones Epic Stunt Spectacular* (consult the daily schedule for show times, and be aware that there are some loud noises and flashes in the show), *Playhouse Disney—Live on Stage!*, and *Sounds Dangerous*. And then end the night at *Fantasmic!*, a treat for all ages. Get there an hour early if the park is crowded.

a stranger" phones are spread around the theme park. One is in a corridor near the soundstages, a second is near the Fastpass machines for the show, and a third phone, just in case no one answers anywhere else, is in an office in the *Millionaire* production facilities.

Regis introduces the show in a video; local hosts use many of his mannerisms and shticks.

⬛ MUST-SEE ⬛ *FANTASMIC!*

The fabulous *Fantasmic!* nighttime music, light, water, and animation show, which has been thrilling visitors to Disneyland in California for years, made its way east to the Disney–MGM Studios and became an immediate hit. The show is presented twice nightly at a 6,500-seat amphitheater behind the Twilight Zone Tower of Terror off Sunset Boulevard; the stadium half-circles a 1.9-million-gallon lagoon. There's also room for another 3,000 standing guests, making it the largest amphitheater at Walt Disney World. On a pretty summer night, *Fantasmic!* will draw guests from all of the parks at Walt Disney World.

Under the baton of Mickey Mouse himself, the spectacular attraction features fifty performers and combines lasers, dazzling special effects, animation, and dancing waters synchronized to the melodies of beloved Disney classics. Three water-mist screens are used to project Disney animation.

The twenty-five-minute show takes guests inside the dreams of Mickey Mouse—a world where his magic creates dancing waters, shooting comets, animated fountains, swirling stars, balls of fire, and other amazing wonders. When Disney villains intrude on Mickey's fantasy and turn his dreams into nightmares, he uses the power of good to triumph over the evildoers.

The show opens subtly, with a faint musical note in a darkened theater. As the music swells, a brilliant light bursts in the night sky, illuminating the entire island and casting a spotlight on Mickey Mouse. Mickey's imagination gives him the power to make the waters dance as he conducts the musical score. Next an animated comet soars across the sky, sprinkling stars against a giant water-screen backdrop. Under Mickey's direction, the stars dance in unison to the "Sorceror's Apprentice"; as the stars burst forth in color, they transform into blooming floral images.

To the sounds of African drums and the chatter of wild animals, costumed animal characters emerge from behind the water screens to perform a version of "I Just Can't Wait to Be King" from *The Lion King*. A cascade of bubbles fills the water screens for a medley of hits, including "Under the Sea." Old friend Jiminy Cricket rises up the screen, trapped within a bubble; Jiminy escapes only to find Monstro the whale in pursuit. Love is in the air as we are visited by famous couples Pocahontas and John Smith, Cinderella and Prince Charming, Belle and Beast, Aladdin and Jasmine, Ariel and Eric, and Snow White and her Prince.

The merriment fades rapidly with rumbling thunder and crashing waves. The Evil Queen from *Snow White* brews a magical spell with the aid of lightning, flares, and smoke effects. Her plan to defeat Mickey brings together classic Disney villains Ursula, Cruella, Scar, Jafar, Maleficent, Hades, and others to harness the positive energy of Mickey and turn it to evil. Mickey is terrified when Maleficent unexpectedly transforms into a 40-foot-tall dragon whose breath ignites the waterway into a sea of flames that overtakes the island. But once again, it's Mickey to the rescue as the mouse rises high above the water, summoning forth a giant water curtain to surround the island. The fountains begin to dance again, smothering the fierce flames while Mickey defeats the dragon. When Mickey triumphs, Tinker Bell heralds the arrival of the good guys, and the *Steamboat Willie* riverboat full of all-time favorites comes steaming around the bend.

Fantasmic! is a major draw at the theme park every night, which means two things: Get to the amphitheater early to claim a seat (the gates open ninety minutes before showtime), and if you're not going to the show, take advantage of the fact that thousands of people will be out of circulation and not in line at major attractions such as the Twilight Zone Tower of Terror.

There are no bad seats, although the best view is about ten rows up from the water in the center of the amphitheater, roughly rows I through L. If it's a cool night and the wind is blowing from the stage, I'd recommend sitting a bit farther back—the wind can carry some cold mist into the seats. There's also no cover in the theater—the show will go on in light rain but is likely to be canceled in heavier weather.

▓▓▓▓▓ MUST-SEE ▓▓▓▓▓ ROCK 'N' ROLLER COASTER STARRING AEROSMITH
≡FAST

The Mouse meets hard-rockers Aerosmith for some bodacious partying at Walt Disney World's first serious roller coaster. The coaster is hidden within a building styled to look like the other working soundstages at Disney–MGM Studios. Stage 15, we find, is the headquarters of G-Force Records. We enter beneath a 40-foot-long Fender guitar into the record company's lobby, beautifully decorated with details that include carved guitar-head columns.

Here's the buzz: The mega–rock group Aerosmith is in the house, recording a new song. Even better, this must be the VIP tour, for we are ushered through the Artist's Entrance to the recording studio. Music blasts through the closed doors of Studios A and B, and then the door opens to Studio C. Alas, the recording session is over, but wait: There's the band listening to playback in the control room beyond. And they're happy to see us, too; what's a rock band without a following of frenetic fans? But then a producer rushes in to tell the boys they're already late for a major concert across town. Time to go . . . but not without the fans. It's time to order up the largest, fastest limousine in town.

We step out of the studio and into a wonderfully seedy Hollywood alley, the back door to the Lock 'n Roll parking garage and the Down Under Club. The concert is about to begin and there is no time to waste; we're ushered into our stretch limo, a twenty-four-passenger pink Caddy that shines with chrome. (There are six coaches, each with two rows of two seats.) Before you've got the time to ask yourself, "How'd a nice person like me end up in a place like this?" your vehicle is launched into a traffic tunnel and the chase is on. And I do mean "launched." The coaster accelerates from 0 to 57 miles per hour in 2.8 seconds. The takeoff is unusual because it is flat rather than up a hill; once the cars reach maximum speed, they will climb up to the top of the building under their own momentum.

From there it's a wild trip through Beverly Hills, downtown Los Angeles, over the traffic-jam intersection of I–10 and the 101, and through one of the Os of the HOLLYWOOD sign. The large signs and thirty sets are illuminated with black light. All of this is accompanied, of course, by a rock 'n' roll soundtrack performed by Aerosmith and blasted through 108 speakers in each train. (There are five different songs, so serious fans will have to ride at least that many times to hear all of the music.)

On one of my visits—before the coaster opened to the public—I was treated to an unusual viewing of the interior of the building with the

The entrance plaza at the Rock 'n' Roller Coaster Starring Aerosmith

lights on. The most amazing sight was the first climbing hill at the end of the launch tube—it heads almost straight up the rear wall. It's probably just as well that you won't have to see that stretch of track. At the top of the hill the coaster almost immediately goes into a double inversion. There's a third inversion a bit farther along in the ride.

Disney points out that the coaster was not adapted to fit within an already-built structure. Instead, the tracks were designed and installed at the park, and a building was put up around them. This is one reason, Imagineers say, the ride is as smooth as it is.

Riders must be at least 48 inches tall to ride. The coaster is located off Sunset Boulevard to the left of the Twilight Zone Tower of Terror.

⊟MUST-SEE⊟ TWILIGHT ZONE TOWER OF TERROR ≡FAST

You want terror? How about this thought: The tower is in control. The latest version of the Twilight Zone Tower of Terror multiplies the thrills inside the thirteen-story haunted hotel with technology that actually places the attraction in control of each ride experience.

Behold the mysterious Hollywood Tower Hotel, a relic of Tinseltown's golden age moved to Disney–MGM Studios, complete with a set of high-speed elevators guaranteed to fail on a regular basis. Imagineers have reworked the computer controls for this popular ride numerous times. The latest version randomizes the ride, with many lifts and drops, false starts, and unexpected drops.

The Twilight Zone Tower of Terror

You'll approach the hotel across its beautifully landscaped grounds; if the waiting line extends outside the building, you are in for a lengthy wait. Even before you enter the lobby of the abandoned hotel, there are signs of danger high up on the side of the 199-foot-tall building (the tallest structure anywhere at Walt Disney World): You'll see sparking electrical wires in a sign hanging above a gaping hole in the tower walls.

Legend says a full guest wing was once attached to that damaged wall. What happened to the wing? And more important, what happened to the people who were in the tower when it disappeared? Well, you'll be given a not-at-all-subtle hint of what lies ahead when you spot an out-of-control elevator cage plunging down the shaft, visible through open doors high on the outer wall.

Once inside, you'll be in the lobby, with the concierge's table and the front desk. Check out the rich details. For example, on the left side you'll see a dusty unfinished mah-jongg game and a pile of 1930s newspapers. Many of the furnishings of the lobby came from old hotels in Hollywood and Los Angeles, including the famed Jonathan Club, an L.A. landmark built in the 1920s.

Eventually you'll make it to the bellhop's podium, where you will be sent to one of the four libraries. (Warning: If you're prone to claustrophobia, you may feel uncomfortable in the library; then again, if the library scares you, the elevator will definitely terrify you.) The introduction begins in the darkened hotel library as a flash of lightning energizes a television in the corner. Our host, Rod Serling (long dead, but that doesn't matter in the Twilight Zone), tells the story of the dark and stormy night—Halloween of 1939, to be exact—when the guests disappeared from their elevator and stepped into a nightmare. We learn that when the lightning bolt struck, all the main elevators of the building were lost; only the creaky old service elevator still functions.

By the way, *The Twilight Zone* series never included a story about a haunted elevator at the Hollywood Hotel, but that didn't stop Disney Imagineers. Rod Serling's introduction to the ride was patched together from various unrelated segments of the show and augmented by a Serling imitator.

Next the library doors open to reveal the entrance to the hotel's basement, a creepy world of boilers, generators, and electrical boxes. It even smells like a basement. There's another waiting line down in the basement; the line splits into left and right queues that head to one or the other of the two elevator shafts in the building. The rides are the same, although the shaft to the right offers a brief view of the park from the top, while the left shaft overlooks the Disney road system.

The cars seat twenty-two passengers in three rows; new seat-belt systems for the ride may reduce capacity to twenty-one. If you want to sit in the front row of the car, you'll need to camp out on one of the spaces marked 1 or 2 in front of the elevator. To snag the center seat on the top row—a seat with an unobstructed view and a seat belt instead of safety bar to hold you in place—you'll want to ask for Seat 4 in Row 3. The elevator operator at the door may be willing to cooperate with you in making your choice.

The doors of the elevator will open on the first floor, where you will see a happy family and bellhop suddenly struck by lightning; the view changes to a star field. Your car will move forward into the lights and the shaft. When you arrive at the "fifth dimension," you will look out at what seems to be an elevator shaft. Wait a minute! Are you going up or sideways? And who are those people who seem to have hitched a ride in your elevator? They seem like ghostly doubles of you and those around you.

Finally, you are in the vertical elevator shaft in the most severely damaged part of the hotel; your cab rises up higher and higher. At each floor you can catch glimpses of the happy theme park outside. At the very top you will reach the damaged elevator motors; they are sparking and flashing ominously. The door opens for a view of the park. Guests watching from outside will be able to see the elevator cab hanging in space for a few seconds.

Every ride begins with a launch skyward. There's a brief moment of panic when the cables of the elevator seem to snap in a shower of electrical sparks. The vehicle then plunges, falling faster than the force of gravity. Then it lurches back upward, only to fall again and again.

The elevator cab is actually driven downward by high-power motors so that it travels faster than it would in free fall. Imagineers tell us that the two motors, on the roof, deliver horsepower equivalent to that of 275 Corvette engines. The rest of the way down, the cab travels in what the engineers call "controlled deceleration." That means putting on the brakes. And, by the way, the drop is advertised as a thirteen-story drop, but the top floor is the twelfth. Ah, but you got on the elevator in the basement.

The latest version uses computer-generated random sequences of rises and falls in the elevator shaft; not even the droll hotel "bellhops" know which specific sequence guests are queued to ride. It's the first Disney attraction in the world to offer random experiences. And the ride was also enhanced with ghostly apparitions, sustained weightless "air time," and cannon blasts of chilling air.

"We wanted the guest to feel completely out of control—not knowing what to expect next, and giving the die-hard fans a lot more to talk about," said Theron Skees, show producer for Walt Disney Imagineering.

Tower of Terror has been a favorite at Disney–MGM Studios since it opened in 1994. Changing the ride experience has always been part of the plan to keep the "terror" in the Tower. The computer controls allow Imagineers to add effects, change timing sequences, and completely alter the way the elevator moves.

Disney Imagineers tell us that designers had to keep the height of the hotel below 200 feet to avoid having to place an out-of-character flashing light on the roof to warn passing planes. The building itself is skewed slightly to emphasize the view of the damaged side of the hotel.

How good is the ride? Well, it definitely is worth a **MUST-SEE** in this Econoguide. But it is a very short experience once you are in the elevator, about two minutes with just ten seconds or so of drop. Personally, I love the ride, but I work real hard to avoid waiting in line for two hours for ten seconds of thrill. On busy days be sure to get to the park early and ride the Tower of Terror immediately, especially in the summer and during holiday periods. Or head for the Fastpass dispensers early.

In Anaheim a similar version of the Twilight Zone Tower of Terror opened at Disney's California Adventure in 2004.

MUST-SEE THE GREAT MOVIE RIDE

This is a celebration of some of the most famous movies of our time within a reproduction of the famous Mann's Chinese Theater in Hollywood. The interior of the Chinese Theater is a bittersweet reminder of how full of marvel the grand theaters of the early years of movies were and how ordinary our local multiplex mall theaters are. In the lobby you'll find what may be the world's most expensive slippers: Dorothy's ruby shoes from the 1939 MGM classic *The Wizard of Oz*. You'll also find a carousel horse from the 1964 *Mary Poppins* movie, and a portion of the set from the 1979 *Alien* film.

Your first stop is a waiting area in a theater that is continuously showing original trailers from some of the most beloved movies of all time, including *Singin' in the Rain; Fantasia; Footlight Parade* with Jimmy Cagney, Joan Blondell, and Ruby Keeler; and a stark preview of *Alien*. You'll go within all of those movies and more in the ride to come.

Your moving auditorium will be presided over by

Fly It Again, Sam

According to the Hollywood mythmakers, the Lockheed Electra 12A on display in the *Casablanca* set was used in the real movie. But film historians point out that the famed film was shot entirely within a Hollywood studio and the actors never came near a real airplane.

a host or hostess who will narrate the tour. After a few introductory scenes, though, your leader will be hijacked by a 1920s gangster or a Wild West desperado (depending on which set of seats you are in). Don't worry, though: The good guys always seem to prevail later on in the ride.

In addition to old Chicago and the West, the moving chairs visit "By a Waterfall" (with more than sixty animatronic dancers) from Busby Berkeley's *Footlight Parade*. From there the chairs move into the *Nostromo* spaceship, home of the Alien himself; an extended *Raiders of the Lost Ark* set including wriggling robotic snakes; the jungle world of *Tarzan;* Mickey Mouse's *Fantasia;* and finally a drive down the Yellow Brick Road of *The Wizard of Oz.* The last stop on the ride is a high-tech theater that surrounds you with the sound and images of a short film that strings together some of the best-known scenes of all time. Some visitors come back to see how many stars and films they can recognize as they fly by.

The Heart of Darkness

The spaceship that is invaded by the murderous alien of *Alien*—the most chilling scene of the Great Movie Ride—was named *Nostromo.* That name comes from a 1904 book by the Polish/English novelist Joseph Conrad, who spent much of his early life as a seaman on a succession of freighters.

The Great Movie Ride brings to Disney-MGM the same "moving theater" cars first introduced at the Energy pavilion at Epcot. The ride is worth a visit, although it could use a freshening; it has remained essentially frozen in time since Disney–MGM Studios opened. Insiders say that a reworking of the attraction, perhaps using some advanced virtual-reality technologies, may happen in years to come.

The sidewalk outside the ride includes hand- and footprints from celebrities minor and major. Look closely to find Pee-Wee Herman, dated 1984, before he became a persona non grata at Disney. Leonard Nimoy's handprint gives the V-shaped Vulcan "Live long and prosper" salute.

The lines for this attraction build at midday. If the lines extend outside the building, I'd suggest you come back at another time; there is still a lengthy queue within the theater. The ride itself takes about twenty minutes once you're seated. The ride was most recently touched up in early 2003.

▒MUST-SEE▒ *SOUNDS DANGEROUS*

How better to demonstrate the power of audio in storytelling than to take a whole audience of visitors and lock them up in the dark . . . with a high-tech stereo and 3-D sound system, that is. That's the idea behind *Sounds Dangerous,* starring comedian Drew Carey as a bumbling police detective.

Everything starts out like your basic television sitcom, with Drew in search of a smuggling ring. He's equipped with a hidden video camera and is in broadcast communication with headquarters. Ah, but something goes wrong, and the video camera shuts off . . . and we're all left in the dark. There's barely a peep of light in the auditorium. We can still hear Drew in our headphones, and we learn the entire story from his description and some truly amazing sound effects. Have you ever experienced a haircut and shave in the dark? There's a trip to the circus—watch out for those elephants.

Next, there is that jar full of killer bees; you don't suppose the glass will break, do you? Can you imagine the sound? Justice triumphs, and the smuggling ring is unmasked. It's all a clever lesson in how important a role sound plays in movies and television.

Outside the theater is an interactive playroom where you can experiment with some of the arts of movie sound, including a Foley stage for sound effects and computer stations where you can put your own voice or noises you select into a classic Disney cartoon.

▇▇▇▇ *MUST-SEE* INDIANA JONES EPIC STUNT SPECTACULAR ≡FAST

A cast of stunt performers, helped by a dozen or so volunteers from the audience, help Indy save Marion, the heroine of the film *Raiders of the Lost Ark,* from machine-gun-toting German soldiers, an airplane crash, and various other assaults. The set received a complete makeover in 2000, with new lighting, sound, and special effects. Many of the enhancements reflect technical advances that weren't available when the show first opened in 1989.

The stunt show starts with a real bang as a double for Indiana Jones rocks and rolls across the huge stage. It's a thirty-two-minute world of Nazis, Arab swordsmen, fiery explosions, and bad jokes. Inspired by the blockbuster film *Raiders of the Lost Ark,* the show re-creates scenes with seventeen stunt performers. The professionals are joined by about a dozen "extras" drawn from the audience. Wearing costumes appropriate for the Middle Eastern setting, they act as bystanders while Indiana saves Marion from the machine-gun fire of German soldiers and an out-of-control truck that explodes on impact.

The 2,000-seat covered outdoor theater—a good place to get out of the sun— fills up by showtime, even earlier on busier days. The best seats are in the center of the theater; they are filled first, and it is from this section that the "casting director" usually selects "extras" to participate. All must be over the age of eighteen; there's a ringer among them.

▇▇▇▇ *MUST-SEE* STAR TOURS ≡FAST

"Whenever your plans call for intergalactic travel," say the travel posters, "please consider flying Star Tours to the vacation moon of Endor." Loosely based on some of the original characters from *Star Wars,* Star Tours's atmosphere and excitement builds beautifully from the moment you walk beneath the huge space machine outside; it continues as you walk through the indoor waiting area that simulates a gritty space garage. The clumsy mechanics are our favorite flaky robots, R2D2 and C-3PO.

> **Another Big Adventure**
>
> The original voice of the robot pilot at Star Tours was none other than the exceedingly strange Paul Reubens, also known as Pee-Wee Herman. After Pee-Wee was, err, exposed as someone a bit out of the Disney mold, a new (less interesting) voice was dubbed in to replace his.

Most of the queue for Star Tours is inside the building; if the line reaches outside the building onto the plaza, you're facing a forty-five-minute wait. If the line extends outside and into the covered space "forest," you might want to plan your expedition to Endor for later in the day. Better yet: Grab a Fastpass.

When your time comes, you will enter a forty-passenger simulator cabin and meet your pilot, Captain Rex. The doors will close and your seat belts will tightly cinch before he informs you that this is his first trip. Too late—you're off. You'll make an uneasy takeoff and then blast (accidentally) into and through a frozen meteor, stumble into an active intergalactic battle zone, and finally make a wild landing at your goal, the vacation moon of Endor.

This is quite a wild ride, at about the same level of twisting, turning, and dipping as the Body Wars show at Wonders of Life in Epcot Center. It's a short ride, but a bit rough for the very young; pregnant women and those with health problems are advised to sit this one out.

After the ride, note the travel posters for other Star Tours destinations, including lovely Hoth and Tatooine. And watch this space: Disney insiders say a new Star Tours show, perhaps involving some new high-tech projection systems, is in the offing.

■ *WALT DISNEY: ONE MAN'S DREAM*

If you think you know everything there is to know about Walter Elias Disney, you're sure to be surprised at the rich display of memorabilia, films, and audiotapes gathered here. The walk-through exhibit and short film presented here were created as part of the celebration of the centenary of Disney's birth; we can only hope that it becomes a permanent part of Disney–MGM Studios.

Among the displays is a re-creation of Disney's original office in California. On the desk and walls are some of the original plans for Disneyland. You'll also see an audio-animatronic robot without its skin, models for the *Tree of Life* in Animal Kingdom, and the Twilight Zone Tower of Terror at Disney–MGM Studios. In cases are a 1964 silk organza embroidered dress worn by Julie Andrews in the "Jolly Holiday" musical number from the film *Mary Poppins,* and actor Guy Williams's costume from the *Zorro* television series of 1957–1959.

Some of the oldest images in the film show Walt in a Red Cross ambulance unit in France during World War I. When he was hired as an artist in Kansas City, some of his first cartoons were based on drawings he made while in France. Included in the film is a glimpse of his first successful character, Oswald the Lucky Rabbit; Disney lost control of the rights in a contract dispute. (The company recently purchased them back.)

Sounds Like . . .

The Foley stage is named after the acknowledged creator of the Hollywood sound-effects stage, Jack Foley. The same sort of devices were used in adding sounds to live radio dramas of the 1930s and 1940s. The work of the audio engineer is known as "sweetening" and includes the use of sound filters, the addition of echo, and the inclusion of sound effects.

Disney Imagineers decided that no one could tell Disney's story better than Walt Disney himself. Many of the sound recordings were of poor quality, recorded in Disney's backyard by his daughter for a series of magazine articles she was writing; engineers had to work around chirping birds, the squeaky noises of the hammock Walt was sitting in, and passing airplanes and cars. Twenty hours of recordings were distilled to about ten minutes of audio for the film. Imagineers also digitized and edited films and photos of Walt, some almost one hundred years old.

We see early incarnations of Mickey Mouse, and see Disney's important transition to the Silly Symphonies cartoons, a series of musicals without a central character. We learn how Disney put up the family fortune in 1935 to finance *Snow White*. With the profits of that film he built the studio that made the company a global success. In short order came classics *Pinocchio, Bambi,* and *Fantasia.*

Some of the images in the film show Disney's formative years on the farm in Marceline, Missouri; pictures on display at the exhibit include old images of Marceline that show how it influenced the design of Main Street, U.S.A., at Disneyland and the Magic Kingdom.

The attraction offers a wireless translation device for Spanish, Portuguese, Japanese, French, and German speakers.

▪MUST-SEE▪ *VOYAGE OF THE LITTLE MERMAID* ≡FAST

A salute to one of Disney's recent classics, this show is presented throughout the day at a theater that includes all sorts of bits and pieces of Disney magic, including snippets from *The Little Mermaid* and more than one hundred puppets, lasers, holographic projections, live performers, and audio-animatronic robots. The fifteen-minute show can draw huge lines on a crowded afternoon; during busy time it is presented as often as twenty-two times a day. If this film is a favorite of your youngsters, you would do best to head there early. Very young kids may become a bit startled by some of the special effects used in the show; prepare them ahead of time.

At the start of the show the curtain becomes running water, and laser beams overhead create the feeling we are descending beneath the waves. An opening sequence of black-light puppetry is especially enchanting.

▪MUST-SEE▪ *PLAYHOUSE DISNEY—LIVE ON STAGE!*

Jim Henson's *Bear in the Big Blue House* meets some new friends on stage at Soundstage 5, including stars from Disney Channel children's television shows *Rolie Polie Olie, The Book of Pooh,* and *Stanley.* Jamie, a human host, interacts with fifteen fun and furry puppets and characters in a show aimed at preschool and young audiences ages three to eight.

The 7-foot-tall Bear, who dances a mean cha-cha, wants to party with all of his friends, including Pip and Pop, a pair of rambunctious purple otters; Treelo, a green and blue lemur; and Tutter, a little blue mouse with a big heart. The problem is, you see, that Tutter is too shy to dance in front of strangers. And so,

Jamie tries to help, taking Tutter—and all of us in the audience—inside the world of Playhouse Disney, where we enter the magical robot world of Rolie Polie Olie, the bedroom of Stanley and Dennis the talking goldfish, and the Hundred-Acre Wood of Pooh, Tigger, Eeyore, and Piglet.

■ *BEAUTY AND THE BEAST—LIVE ON STAGE*

Off-off-Broadway, this twenty-minute live-action show at the outdoor Theater of the Stars uses elaborate props, extravagant costumes, colorful production numbers, and dramatic special effects to tell the fairy-tale love story of Belle and the Beast. Many elements from the film are also used in the stage show, including the recorded vocal talents of stage and screen stars such as Robby Benson (Beast), Angela Lansbury (Mrs. Potts, the teapot), Jerry Orbach (Lumière, the candelabra), David Ogden Stiers (Cogsworth, the clock), and young Bradley Pierce (Chip, the cup).

As the show opens, audiences are welcomed by "Be Our Guest," performed by a collection of dancing chefs, bubbling bottles, and a lovely sherbet parfait that becomes a beautiful showgirl. "The Mob Song" takes place in a dark forest pierced with streaks of lightning, wolves' eyes, and huge bats. Here Gaston leads the villagers on a rampage to "kill the beast." Belle proves that love conquers all as the Beast miraculously transforms—on stage—into a handsome prince! In the final scene Belle and her prince dance to "Beauty and the Beast," as recorded by Angela Lansbury, while surrounded by dazzling special effects, white doves, and serenading beaus and maidens.

Check the daily entertainment schedule for times.

■ *HONEY, I SHRUNK THE KIDS* MOVIE SET ADVENTURE

This most inventive playground is based on the hit movie about a mad inventor whose shrinking ray accidentally reduces his children and a few friends. Play areas include giant cereal loops, ants, spiders, a huge roll of film, and a leaky garden hose. The ground is carpeted in a spongy rubber. It's a great place for youngsters to burn off some energy, but be advised that it is quite easy to misplace a child in the playground. The best strategy is to station an adult by the single exit from the playground, rather than chasing through the various adventures.

▓MUST-SEE▓ *JIM HENSON'S MUPPET*VISION 3D* ≡FAST

We have to admit that we passed by this attraction the first few times we took our kids to the studios—Bert and Ernie and Kermit the Frog seemed a bit too silly, even for an eight-year-old. Were we ever wrong!

The fun begins once you enter the theater, which also happens to be Muppet World Headquarters. Pause just inside the entrance to read the office directory on the wall. Listings include the Institute of Heckling and Browbeating—Statler and Waldorf, Curmudgeons-in-Chief; the Sartorial Accumulation Division, run by Miss Piggy, of course; and the Academy of Amphibian Science, under the tutelage of Kermit the Frog. The security desk at the door advises that the guard will be back in five minutes, but the key is under the mat.

The preshow area for *Muppet*Vision* includes a wonderfully goofy collection of packing cases with equipment for the Muppet Labs (Tongue Inflators, Gorilla Detectors, and Anvil Repair Kits) and road-show suitcases for the Muppet band, Dr. Teeth and the Electric Mayhem, including paisley bell-bottoms, Nehru jackets, Beatles boots, and love beads. There's a big pink trunk that bears the label, MISS PIGGY SATIN EVENING GOWNS; below that are more satin evening gowns, and finally, the rest of the satin evening gowns. Another favorite: a cargo net filled with orange and green cubes labeled A-NET-FULL-OF-JELL-O in a tribute to original Mouseketeer Annette Funicello.

The real fun is within the beautiful 584-seat theater, which is decidedly more opulent than your neighborhood quintupleplex. There's a robotic all-penguin orchestra in the pit (they took the job just for the halibut) and a private box at the front for Waldorf and Statler. The film includes some marvelous 3-D special effects, as well as flashing lights, a bubble maker, smell-o-vision, and a surprise from the skies, as well as a live actor and a cannon.

Don't pass this extraordinary multimedia show by. If you don't have a kid with you, you can pretend you're with the ones in front of you in line. And when you leave, be sure to check out the statue outside: It's Miss Piggy as the Statue of Liberty. The same show now plays at Disney's California Adventure in Anaheim.

::::::: MUST-SEE ::::::: LIGHTS, MOTORS, ACTION! EXTREME STUNT SHOW ≡FAST

Motorized cinematic thrills, imported from Hollywood by way of Paris: A cast of about fifty and a fleet of more than forty customized and modified cars, motorcycles, and watercraft occupy a huge "set" fashioned after a Mediterranean

Lights, Motors, Action!

village. The theater is one of Walt Disney World's largest stages, allowing stunt drivers to demonstrate high-speed spins, two-wheeled driving, jumps, pyrotechnic explosions, high falls, and other gags much like those performed for movie and television cameras.

Not that it really matters, but the premise of the show involves the filming of a spy thriller, with production crew members, stunt managers, and a director and assistant director on the set. Youngsters will love the jumps and explosions; more sophisticated viewers may prefer the intricate auto ballet where the vehicles move in and among each other in a choreographed dance.

The most capable of the stunt cars has four forward and four reverse gears; the modified Opel Corsa had its engine removed and replaced—in mid-body—by a 1,300-cc motorcycle engine. For safety's sake there's just a one-gallon fuel cell within.

In addition to a special split-personality appearance by Herbie the Love Bug, one of the more interesting vehicles is one that performs some spectacular maneuvers moving in reverse. The car itself is reversed behind the dark glass; the driver is looking out the rear window with a steering wheel and pedals facing that direction. He wears a mask and uniform that makes it appear as if he is facing the other way.

Audiences enter through the garage as mechanics and technicians fine-tune the show vehicles; six large windows offer guests behind-the-scenes views. Among the unusual vehicles is one designed to drive backwards and another that splits in half. The various machines have different colors so viewers will know which is the hero's and which is under chase.

The set is surrounded by a high 5,000-seat stadium that brings guests close to the action. The grandstand is on the west side. If you visit before noon, you will be facing the rising and slightly cooler sun. At noon there is nowhere to hide, but by midafternoon you'll find a bit of protection.

The theater is part of a larger redevelopment of the back-lot area of Disney–MGM Studios that also includes new cityscapes, adding Chicago and San Francisco to the park's existing New York City skyline.

The show first debuted at Disney Studios Paris at Disneyland Paris.

⚫MUST-SEE⚫ DISNEY–MGM STUDIOS BACKLOT TOUR

Disney–MGM Studios was envisioned as a working movie lot, and the back-lot shuttle tour is a great way to see some of the real—and not-so-real—elements of moviemaking. As it has worked out, there have been only a relatively few major films produced in Orlando, and Disney's animation facilities have been shut down. Over the years films and TV shows made here have included episodes of *Star Search, Mickey Mouse Club, Live! With Regis & Kathie Lee, Talk Soup,* and professional wrestling shows. Bits and pieces of major films have been shot here, including *Honey, I Blew Up the Baby; Passenger 57; Oscar; Ernest Saves Christmas; Splash Too;* and the HBO Films series *From the Earth to the Moon.* Animators worked on parts of *The Little Mermaid, Beauty and the Beast, Pocahontas, Aladdin, Lilo and Stitch,* and *Brother Bear.*

The back-lot tour begins with a visit to the Water Effects Tank. This pool, home

Catastrophe Canyon on the Backlot Tour

of the *Miss Fortune* tugboat and other miniature or partial boat sets, demonstrates how technicians use fans, explosions, and a 400-gallon splash tank to recreate a raging storm and a battle at sea. Two volunteers from the audience get to play captains courageous. From there it's on to a walk through a portion of the prop warehouse. Signs indicate some of the more recognizable objects; pay attention to the tags on some of the items on the shelves for clues to the more obscure.

The large trams run continuously; lines are generally short in the morning and late in the day. Remember this: The left side of the cars (the first person into each row) is the wet side, no matter what the guide says at first. (Not very wet, by the way—more of a splash than a soaking.)

As you pull out of the tram station, you will first pass by the Car Pool, which includes some of the vehicles used in your favorite movies. The trams next pass through the Costuming shops. Artisans at the Scenic Shop can build just about anything and everything for the movies; you'll also glimpse the huge stock of lighting fixtures for filmmaking. The interior of a 747 plane was used for scenes in *Passenger 57;* it is part of an actual jetliner retired from Delta Airlines.

The back lot of the studios has a Residential Street that holds some vaguely familiar sights—you may recognize homes used in *Golden Girls, Empty Nest,* and many other movie and television settings. These are empty shells used for exterior shots; interior filming is done within sound-stages in California or elsewhere.

At the end of the street, you'll make a right turn past the Boneyard, home of some of the larger props from former movie productions. Look for the trolley from Toontown in *Who Framed Roger Rabbit?* and the UFO from *Flight of the Navigator,* among other props. Parked on a corner is a Gulfstream airplane owned by Walt Disney and used in 1964 during the scouting for land for Walt Disney World in Florida.

Finally it is on to a demonstration of large-scale special effects in the area known as Catastrophe Canyon, which simulates a working oil field in a narrow desert canyon. We won't spoil the fun except to point out that the "set" features a series of tanks storing 70,000 thousand gallons of water, hydraulic shaker tables, flames, explosions, and . . . your tram.

> ## Fill 'Er Up
>
> The oil field at Catastrophe Canyon bears the markings of Mohave Oil, a fictitious company that is also represented at the old-timey Oscar's Super Service Station on Hollywood Boulevard.

The tour includes a stop at the AFI Showcase, honoring American film heritage. Presented by the American Film Institute (AFI), the showcase includes rare movie artifacts and memorabilia, a video wall, and exhibits on the careers of AFI's twenty-five Life Achievement Award recipients. Among the many pieces of movie history that have been shown are Rosebud, the sled from *Citizen Kane;* Humphrey Bogart's suit from *The Maltese Falcon;* the cheesy little miniature saucer used in the 1955 sci-fi classic *The Day the Earth Stood Still;* and sketches from *Toy Story.* The showcase also has displays on film preservation and the various disciplines of filmmaking taught at the AFI Conservatory, including editing, directing, producing, cinematography, screenwriting, and production design. Funds raised from sale of items at the showcase go to AFI's preservation efforts, such as the restoration and distribution of the recently discovered 1912 film *Richard III,* the oldest surviving American feature film, found in the basement of a Portland, Oregon, home where it had lain untouched for some thirty years.

EATS AND TREATS

Disney–MGM Studios includes some of the more interesting eateries at Walt Disney World. Be sure to check when you arrive for Early Value Meals offered at some of the restaurants, and for special meal deals for youngsters.

🎬 **ABC Commissary.** This large fast-food cafeteria offers basic fare that includes burgers, large hot dogs, chicken breast sandwiches, and stir-fry chicken. Prices range from about $4.00 to $5.00. Children are offered hot dogs, chicken strips, and more for about $4.00.

🎬 **Backlot Express.** Between Star Tours and the *Indiana Jones Epic Stunt Spectacular,* this interesting setting for a burger and hot dog fast-foodery is set among the props of the Studio Shops. Offerings include charbroiled chicken with flour tortillas, burgers, hot dogs, chili, and chef's salad. Prices range from

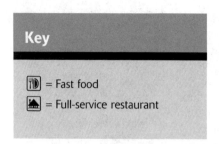

Key

[TD] = Fast food

[▲] = Full-service restaurant

$4.00 to $7.00. The condiment bar includes a healthy (and otherwise) selection of about two dozen toppings.

[TD] **Dinosaur Gertie's Ice Cream of Extinction.** Across from the *Indiana Jones Epic Stunt Spectacular,* here you can get cold treats from within the belly of a dino, or so it appears. Some of the same items can be purchased from wagons around the park. The eatery's name is a tribute to Gertie the Dinosaur, one of the first animated cartoon stars; Gertie was a big hit in 1914 in vaudeville shows. Open seasonally.

[▲] **'50s Prime Time Cafe.** The cafe is located along Echo Lake, near the *Indiana Jones Epic Stunt Spectacular.* Step right into a kitchen of the 1950s; Mom will greet you at the door, and your waitress will stand by to make sure you clean your plate. Luncheon appetizer offerings include Mom's Chili over angel-hair pasta for about $4.00, Dad's Bachelor Chili for about $2.50, and fried zucchini for about $3.00. Entrees include Magnificent Meatloaf, chicken potpie, Granny's Pot Roast, and the All-American Burger, for about $8.00 to $15.00. Dinner offerings include Auntie's Roasted Lamb and a charbroiled T-bone steak. Prices range from about $13 to $23. Book reservations early.

[▲] **The Hollywood Brown Derby.** At the end of Hollywood Boulevard and near the entrance to the studios is one of the nicer restaurants within any of the Disney theme parks. The Brown Derby was the "in" restaurant and nightspot of Hollywood in the 1930s. Owner Bob Cobb reportedly told his friends that food was all that mattered. In fact, he said his menu would be so good that people would eat out of a hat, so he built his restaurant in the shape of a derby.

This replica of the Hollywood landmark features an Art Deco interior and drawings of movie stars on the walls. Lunch includes the famous Cobb salad introduced at the original Brown Derby, as well as corned beef and cabbage and pasta with seafood. Prices range from about $9.00 to $18.00. Dinner entrees include peppercorn-crusted tuna with balsamic syrup, sautéed grouper, rack of lamb, and tomato-garlic penne. Prices range from about $15 to $24.

[TD] **Hollywood & Vine.** Casual dining at a lunch and dinner buffet that features fresh-roasted meats and poultry, seafood, pasta and vegetable selections, and a dessert bar.

[▲] **Mama Melrose's Ristorante Italiano.** In the streets of New York near the *Muppet*Vision* theater and Star Tours attractions, this very attractive eatery is filled with the enticing smells from the wood-fired pizza oven. *Tutta La Pasta Che Puoi Mangiare* (all the pasta you care to eat) costs about $10.50; grilled tenderloin of beef is priced at about $14.00. Other offerings include fresh fish, vegetable lasagna, and chicken marsala. Your basic (small) pizza sells for about $9.50 and is available in basic, Italian combo, four-cheese, chicken, and pesto varieties, among others. There are also vegetarian, ham, Mexican, and other varieties. The child's menu includes spaghetti, pizza, hot dogs, and chicken strips, for about $4.00 to $6.00. There are 292 seats available, but things can become quite hectic between 1:00 and 3:00 P.M. Reservations are accepted.

📺 Min and Bill's Dockside Diner. This diner is on Echo Lake; it operates seasonally. Belly up to the hatchway in the SS *Down the Hatch,* moored at a dock on the studio pond. Snack offerings include nachos with cheese, fruit cup, Danish, soft yogurt, and ice-cream sodas. Prices range from about $2.00 to $3.00.

🎭 Playhouse Disney's Play 'n Dine at Hollywood & Vine. Sing, dance, and dine with characters from *JoJo's Circus, The Little Einsteins,* and other shows for breakfast and lunch.

🎭 Sci-Fi Dine-In Theater Restaurant. Behind Monster Sound and across from Star Tours, the Sci-Fi is a must-see eatery, among the most unusual settings of any restaurant anywhere. Each group of diners is shown to their table—inside a little convertible—by a parking attendant. Each four-seat car with a 1955 license plate faces a large drive-in movie screen showing coming attractions for weird and wonderful science-fiction movies of the 1950s and 1960s. Reservations are essential.

On one visit, the films included *Cat Women of the Moon, Devil Girl from Mars* (a creature without mercy), *The Horror of Party Beach* (teenagers, beach, rock 'n' roll, bikers, and atomic monsters), Peter Graves in *It,* and the original trailers for *Attack of the 50 Foot Woman.* (The girl in one of the horror films says to the guy she is with, "I expected to be frightened on my wedding night, but not like this.") The reel of trailers also includes a few newsreels; it runs about forty-five minutes before repeating itself, which is enough time to order, eat, and leave.

All in all, the Sci-Fi Restaurant is a hoot. The food is appropriate for a drive-in theater—very ordinary, but that's not really the reason you came. Samples from the menu include Journey to the Center of the Pasta, Attack of the Killer Club Sandwich, Return of the Killer Club Sandwich, Revenge of the Killer Club Sandwich, and Beach Party Panic (fillet of fish, of course). Prices range from about $8.00 to $12.00. At dinner look for some of the same dishes, plus Red Planet (linguine and tomato sauce) and Saucer Sightings (a rib-eye steak), with entrees priced from about $10 to $17.

📺 Starring Rolls Cafe. Fresh from a makeover in 2005, this small eatery, almost hidden to the right of the Brown Derby, offers an expanded menu of sandwiches, salads, pastries, and handcrafted chocolates.

📺 Studio Catering Company. Off the streets of New York and next to the *Honey, I Shrunk the Kids* playground, this outdoor fast-food restaurant is sheltered under a corrugated tin roof. Just outside is an ice-cream and sundae bar.

📺 Sunset Market Ranch. As you rush to or from the Twilight Zone Tower of Terror, don't overlook the attractive outdoor eatery on Sunset Boulevard. Included in this area are Rosie's Red Hot Dogs, Catalina Eddie's frozen yogurt stand, and Echo Park and Anaheim Produce fruit and vegetable stands. The market is a tribute to the famed Los Angeles Farmer's Market.

📺 Toy Story Pizza Planet. This pizza parlor near Star Tours has a collection of the latest in video games—or is it the other way around?

Fishy Statue

Note the statue near the Studio Catering Company. It's the actual mermaid fountain from the 1984 film *Splash.*

CHAPTER ELEVEN

DISNEY WATER PARKS

ON HOT NEW YORK CITY SUMMER DAYS when I was a kid, we sometimes managed to unscrew the covers from fire hydrants and turned them on: instant water park! Over the years water parks have grown much more ambitious. All over America you'll find 100-foot towers of fiberglass and steel lubricated with rushing water. Beneath them you will find swimming pools that have massive wave machines. But once again, leave it to Disney to take what has become the ordinary water park and make it extraordinary. It's all in the setting.

Disney's watering holes—Blizzard Beach and Typhoon Lagoon—are state-of-the-watery-art. They are a great way to cool off and have a ton of fun on a hot summer (or summerlike) day—a season that in Florida can extend from March and sometimes February through December. Note that one or the other park may be closed during the quiet periods in January and February for refurbishment.

If you've got an all-parks admission ticket, it's not a bad idea to plan on splitting your day into thirds: Start at one of the theme parks in the morning, break away to a water park in the heat and crowds of the afternoon, and then return to one of the theme parks in the evening for more rides and the nightly fireworks or parade. If you're on an a la carte plan, jump at the chance to unwind at a water park on the hottest day of your trip. And don't overlook Wet 'n Wild, nearby to its owner, Universal Studios Florida.

The water parks have fast-food eateries, but you can also bring your own lunch in a cooler; no bottles or alcohol are allowed.

BLIZZARD BEACH

You are, of course, perfectly willing to suspend disbelief—that's why you're at Walt Disney World in the first place. So you'll have no problem getting this concept: After a freak storm dumped a ton of snow on Orlando, Blizzard Beach was quickly constructed as Florida's first ski resort. Unfortunately, temperatures quickly returned to normal, so what we have here is a ski resort for swimmers. The sixty-six-acre Blizzard Beach is built around 90-foot Mount Gushmore, served by a chairlift to the top of the ski jump. This is no bunny hill; nearly every one of the seventeen slides are a few notches above the level of Typhoon Lagoon over on the other side of Walt Disney World. It also has the only ski lift I know of where there's a beach umbrella over the chairs. One of Disney's top Imagineers involved in the design of the park said that Blizzard Beach grew out of a daydream about a winter resort inside of a snow globe. Other concepts included a beached cruise ship. The final result includes some lovely puns, beginning with the official mascot, a creature named Ice Gator.

A few of the water slides include:

- **Downhill Double Dipper.** The world's first side-by-side racing slide.
- **Summit Plummet.** This is the big one, the ski jump starting 120 feet up. (It actually begins at a platform 30 feet above the top of Mount Gushmore!) As far as we know, it is the highest free-fall water slide in the world. From below it looks as if skiers—er, sliders—are heading off a ski jump at the top of the mountain. Sliders may reach a top speed of 60 miles per hour down the 500-foot slide at an angle of sixty degrees; the slide passes through a ski chalet on the way down. For those in training for the water-slide Olympics, there's a timing clock at the bottom to report your results. Disney claims Summit Plummet is the fastest water slide in the nation.
- **Slush Gusher.** If you make it to the top of Mount Gushmore but lack the courage to take the dive, you can take a slightly easier way to the bottom: Slush Gusher, a double-humped slide about half the length of the plummet but still a spectacular plunge delivering speeds of as much as 50 miles per hour.
- **Runoff Rapids.** This is another way off the top, inner-tube ride that suddenly drops into a dark section within a pipe.
- **Snow Stormers.** "Snowmaking" jets spray water over the course as you bounce your way to the bottom on Snow Stormers, a twisting and turning inner-tube slide that looks like a slalom ski course. (By the way, if you want to avoid a long line for the chairlift, you can climb the stairs to the top; when you get to the 138th step, you'll be ready for a cooling plunge.)
- **Teamboat Springs.** A record-setting six-person, 1,200-foot raft ride down through waterfalls.
- **Toboggan Racers.** An eight-lane competitive water slide; unlike the other slides, this one puts riders head-first on a mat.

Whoa!

It's you against gravity as you plunge down the flumes at Typhoon Lagoon and Blizzard Beach. You can somewhat control your speed, though, by the way you lie down. Fastest: Lie on your back with your hands over your head. Arch your back so that only your shoulders and heels touch the track. Fast: Lie on your back with your hands crossed on your chest and your ankles crossed. Slow: Sit up. Slowest: Walk back down the stairs.

Blizzard Beach

- **Melt Away Bay.** A 1.2-acre wave pool at the base of Mount Gushmore.
- **Cross Country Creek.** The creek circles the park, pushing visitors on inner tubes on a 0.5-mile circuit. It also passes through an ice cave where the "icicles" melt onto the paddlers below.
- **Ski Patrol Training Center.** Activities for the younger hotshots include the T-bar at the Ski Patrol Training Center, where you can hang on to an overhead trolley for a trip over—or into—a pool.
- **Thin Ice Training Course.** This presents a pathway across treacherous icebergs in the pool.
- **Krinkle Tin Slide.** An enclosed pipe that deposits sliders into a deep pool.
- **Tike's Peak.** For the youngsters, miniature versions of Mount Gushmore's slides and a snow castle fountain.

Blizzard Beach is a hot draw and may attract crowds beyond your tolerance during busy times of the year; a contrarian approach calls for taking advantage of Typhoon Lagoon instead. Disney planners will close admission to the park once the lot is full. Only guests at Disney resorts arriving by bus will be admitted, so come early during peak times.

Disney installed a set of automated ticket machines at the entrance to the park to expedite the ticketing process. Guests can purchase single-day waterpark tickets at the machines using a credit or debit card or their on-property hotel ID cards.

TYPHOON LAGOON

According to Disney legend, this was once a beautiful tropical resort until a rogue typhoon roared through. What was left standing was knocked down by an earthquake. Oh, and then there was a volcanic eruption. (Sounds like a lovely place to vacation.) Despite all this the villagers refused to give up, and they rebuilt their paradise in and among the ruins.

The fabulous water slides are built into realistic miniature mountains. The huge wave pool has a sandy beach, and the river-rafting ride passes through jungle canopies, a rain forest, and caves. There is hardly any sign of the artificial nature of the park—the water that cascades down the mountain emerges from rivers and creeks without a pipe in sight.

Mount Mayday is one of the tallest peaks in Florida, even if it is a Disney-created simulation. It rises some 90 feet into the air and is topped by the wreckage of the shrimp boat *Miss Tilly*. The smokestack on the boat erupts in a plume of water every once in a while, adding to the cascades all around.

A recent addition is **Crush 'n' Gusher,** a white-knuckle "water coaster." Riders are whisked along a

Electricity Overhead

Thunderstorms can come up quickly and powerfully in Florida, especially in the late afternoons of hot days. Lifeguards will clear the pools and slides of Typhoon Lagoon or Blizzard Beach if a storm is near, and they may even close the park if necessary.

Slip, Sliding Away

According to local myth, more than a few bikini tops have flown away on the old Kowabunga. Always trying to please, Disney has built a little viewing stand at the bottom.

I spent part of an afternoon there—strictly for research purposes—but the only lost articles I observed were sunglasses. By the way, I'd strongly recommend wearing an eyeglasses strap or carrying your glasses in your folded hands when you ride one of the slides. You should also use plenty of sunscreen.

series of flumes and spillways that weave through what appears to be a rusted-out tropical fruit–processing plant. There are three fruity spillways to choose from—Banana Blaster, Coconut Crusher, and Pineapple Plunger—running as much as 420 feet from start to end.

The namesake central pool is **Typhoon Lagoon,** which is almost three acres in size. Every ninety seconds you can catch some of the world's largest human-made waves, walls of water as high as 6 feet tall. You'll hear a thunderlike rumble as the wave is generated and a scream from the bathers as the water is released. Two sheltered pools, Whitecap Cove and Blustery Bay, serve the less adventurous, with shallows for young children.

Hang on to your bathing suit as you drop 51 feet, at speeds of up to 30 miles per hour, down the three 214-foot-long **Humunga Kowabunga** water slides, enclosed in dark tunnels. Do we actually pay good money and wait in line for the privilege of falling this far, this fast? The moment of truth will come when you reach the top; try not to stop and consider the folly of it all. There's nothing to do but to lie on your back, cross your ankles, and fold your arms over your chest. Once you've survived, come back another time and try the slide with your eyes open.

Or try the nearby **Storm Slides.** The three body slides, Rudder Buster, Jib Jammer, and Stern Burner, crash through caves, geysers, and waterfalls. Each of the slides is somewhat different—on a busy day you'll have to take the slide assigned by the lifeguard at the top of the stairs. If you have a choice, our favorite is the center slide (Jib Jammer), which passes through an unexpected dark tunnel midway down the hill. The top speed on the slides is about 20 miles per hour, which seems mighty fast.

Up before Down

As enjoyable as Typhoon Lagoon is, be aware that there is quite a bit of climbing involved in using the slides. There is a bit less climbing if you use the ski lift at Blizzard Beach, but you can expect long lines at busy times there.

Mayday Falls and **Keelhaul Falls** let you loose on a large inner tube through waterfalls, fountains, caves, and more. Mayday is the taller and longer of the slides, about 460 feet in length. Keelhaul is shorter, about 400 feet, but features sharper twists and turns.

Entire families can go for a relatively tame whitewater adventure at **Gang Plank Falls.** Your circular boat will work its way down the mountain in and among waterfalls and obstacles. Don't say the wrong thing to the person who loads your raft at the top of the slide—with the flick of a wrist, he or she can send your raft under the waterfall at the loading zone. The rafts can hold up to five or six persons, and you may end up with strangers if lines are long. For the youngest swimmers, **Ketchakiddie Creek** features water slides, boats, squirting animals, and other toys for children only.

Finally, you can take a tour on the lazily flowing **Castaway Creek** that circles the park for almost half a mile; it takes about thirty minutes to circle completely around. If the traffic gets too thick or if the float is too lazy, you can get out and walk in the 3-foot-deep creek or even leave and cross the park to your starting place.

Perhaps the most unusual attraction at the park is the **Shark Reef,** where guests get to strap on a snorkel and float through an artificial coral reef in and among small nurse and bonnethead sharks, as well as thousands of other colorful little fishies. We're assured that these are peaceful creatures. In fact, naturalists worry more about visitors damaging the fish with their suntan lotions and other pollutants; you'll be asked to take a shower first. It's an absolutely captivating experience and highly recommended.

Lockers and sometimes-crowded changing rooms and showers are available along the right side of the lagoon as you face Mount Mayday. You can also rent towels. During the summer the park is open into the evening; in spring and fall it often closes as early as 5:00 P.M. Typhoon Lagoon typically closes for maintenance in January or February.

We have found that dragging a towel and shirt around the park is more of a nuisance than it is worth—you can't bring the towel up the waiting line for slides, and the exits are usually not in the same place as the entrances. If it's warm enough to go swimming, you might want to do without a towel. Although you are allowed to wear water shoes and glasses, you should take care to hold on to both in the water and on slides.

Snack bars in the park include Lowtide Lou's, Leaning Palms, Typhoon Tilly's, and Let's Go Slurpin'. Prices range from $3.00 to $5.00 for fried chicken, burgers, and fried-fish dishes; you can also get soft drinks, beer, and ice cream. There's also a gift shop, Singapore Sal's Saleable Salvage, where you can buy bathing suits, T-shirts, and souvenirs. They also have sunscreen; you can save a few dollars or more by shopping at a drugstore outside the park.

Note that during the off-season in the early months of the year, Typhoon Lagoon is closed on Saturday.

Surfing Lessons

Here's your chance to hang ten: On selected mornings the surf boys and gals at Typhoon Lagoon offer surfing lessons. Surf's up for two and a half hours before the park opens. The waves in Typhoon Lagoon's surf pool are set to range from 3 to 6 feet high, which is better than you'll find at many surfing beaches.

Beginners can take the "Learn to Surf" lesson, but if you're already a gnarly surfboard dude, there's also the "Private 100 Waves Surf Event," with higher and stronger waves. Prices begin at about $135; call (407) 939–7529 for reservations.

CHAPTER TWELVE

DOWNTOWN DISNEY: DISNEY WEST SIDE, PLEASURE ISLAND, MARKETPLACE, CIRQUE DU SOLEIL

A CITY OF ENTERTAINMENT the size of Walt Disney World deserves its own downtown. We need a place to unwind at the end of a long day of business, do some shopping, and catch a meal at a place that doesn't use paper napkins and plastic forks. Of course, the business of Walt Disney World is Disney entertainment, and so Disney has created its own very quirky metropolis of restaurants, nightclubs, shops, and theaters. For information about Downtown Disney, call (407) 939-2648.

Set in a crescent curve along one shore of Buena Vista Lagoon, the 120-acre Downtown Disney is made up of:

■ **Downtown Disney West Side.** The hottest area of downtown, home to a collection of "celebrity" restaurants, the indoor virtual theme park DisneyQuest, and one of the world capitals of weird, Cirque du Soleil.

■ **Downtown Disney Pleasure Island.** The original downtown district for adults, it includes a collection of unusual clubs and restaurants.

■ **Downtown Disney Marketplace.** Here you'll find all things Disney as well as a mega-LEGO store and an outpost of the Rainforest Cafe.

Parking is free at Downtown Disney, but sometimes you may feel as if you have parked in East Overshoe, Iowa; there are more than 7,000 spaces in several lots. Valet parking is available for $5.00 after 5:30 P.M. If you are staying somewhere at Walt Disney World, consider using bus transportation from your hotel to Downtown Disney.

DOWNTOWN DISNEY WEST SIDE

⬛ MUST-SEE ⬛ DISNEYQUEST

Disney's most far-out park exists within the purple walls of DisneyQuest, a place that stands at the cutting edge of virtual entertainment. Disney's theme-park-in-a-box has its own version of the corporate icon: "Hurricane Mickey," a swirling version of Walt Disney's classic cartoon mouse.

In 2006 general admission was $35, and tickets for children (ages three to nine) were $29. The pass provides all-day use of the facility, including all the video games and pinball you can play. Everyone must have a ticket to enter, and guests age twelve and younger must be accompanied by an adult. Annual passes, priced at $89 for general admission and $71 for children, are also available. Some multiday tickets for Walt Disney World also include admission to DisneyQuest as an option.

The 100,000-square-foot building was a five-story flagship for Disney's hopes for a chain of similar attractions in dozens of domestic and international locations. Alas, the second DisneyQuest, in Chicago, closed in 2001. Disney estimates people will make visits of two to three hours. The attraction is usually open from 10:30 A.M. until midnight; there is a capacity limit, and long lines can be expected from time to time, especially on rainy days. Call ahead for more information and special hours during holiday periods.

You enter DisneyQuest through the "Cybrolator," an elevator-like conveyance. Your bumbling guide is *Aladdin*'s madcap Genie of the Lamp. When the doors open, you find yourself standing at the Ventureport, a crossroads of adventure leading to four entertainment environments.

Though you will probably be eager to begin your quest, take a moment to soak in one of the most amazing interiors at Walt Disney World. The crossroads puts you in the middle of a gigantic armillary sphere, an ancient astronomical instrument composed of rings representing the positions of important circles of the celestial sphere. It's a stunning piece of work easily missed.

Many of the DisneyQuest attractions are designed to be changed or updated regularly. In recent years, among the features has been **Pirates of the Caribbean: Battle for Buccaneer Gold,** a high-tech challenge inspired by one of the most popular attractions at the Magic Kingdom. A crew of four boards a ship-themed motion platform and then

MUST-SEES

DisneyQuest

Cirque du Soleil:
La Nouba

House of Blues

Wolfgang Puck Cafe

Bongos Cuban Cafe

Planet Hollywood

The Adventurers Club

BET SoundStage Club

The Comedy Warehouse

Rainforest Cafe

works together as captain and cannoneers on an action-packed, five-minute journey. The 3-D adventure culminates in a final showdown with Jolly Roger and his ghost ship.

At **Radio Disney SongMaker,** you can enter a private sound booth to produce your own greatest hit, combining lyrics and music styles to create a one-of-a-kind song. SongMaker offers a choice of a few dozen musical styles, including hip-hop, swing, country, dance, and even opera or yodeling. Song titles range from the serious ("I Love You Mom") to the downright silly ("My Dog Gets More Dates than I Do") and serve as the inspiration for the lyric lines guests string together to form the song. More than a thousand vocal performances by professional studio singers and top musicians are available. You can download the song to a CD (for an extra charge) to show your family and friends your debut as a musical producer.

The Explore Zone gateway is through the tiger's head from Aladdin's Cave of Wonders.

A crowd favorite is the **Virtual Jungle Cruise,** in which visitors are able to navigate a primeval world, where dangers include hungry dinosaurs and a cataclysmic comet. Guests strap their feet into toeholds on a real raft and paddle their way in a virtual reality re-creation of the wildest white-water expedition ever.

You can fly through the streets of Agrabah on a hunt to release the Genie in **Aladdin's Magic Carpet Ride,** an entertainment that was previewed in a prototype version at Epcot several years ago. Sitting on motorcycle-like simulators and wearing virtual-reality headgear, players become Abu the monkey on a tour on Aladdin's flying carpet in search of the Genie of the Lamp. Participants compete against the clock and each other.

At Score Zone you can go sword-to-sword with supervillains as you fly through a 3-D comic book world in **Ride the Comix!** As many as six visitors at a time put on head-mounted virtual-reality helmets and brandish laser swords against Disney villains.

Rescue Earth colonists under attack in **Invasion! An Extra-TERRORestrial Alien Encounter** while piloting a planetary walker. This is an extension of the Alien Encounter attraction at the Magic Kingdom. You travel in X-S 5000 Rescue Units, developed to defend human colonists from a succession

DisneyQuest

of nasties. Among the creatures are Alien Warbeasts and riders, slow but numerous Alien Grunts, and bloodthirsty Alien Heavy Weapons Commanders.

You can become the joystick on a human-size motion base—a Hover-Disc Motion Base—and hip-check your friends in **Mighty Ducks Pinball Slam.** A hydraulic system lifts the discs slightly off the floor, and players maneuver their ball on the screen by moving their bodies. It's fun to play and to watch.

The Create Zone is an Imagineering studio where you can design the roller coaster of your dreams . . . and then buckle up and ride your creation on **Cyber Space Mountain,** a 360-degree pitch-and-roll simulator. You'll begin at a computer console where you can select ride elements—lifts, drops, rolls, loops, and just about any diabolical twist of fate you'd like to try with some 10,000 feet of virtual track to play with. Ride elements include figure eights, spirals, barrel rolls, loops, banked S-curves, camelbacks, and straightaways. Then you're off on a ninety-second ride inside a simulator that can roll like a barrel, climb, and drop—in some ways it is more radical than the real thing.

You can learn some of the secrets of Disney animation at the **Animation Academy,** an eighteen-seat video training classroom. The entry to the Replay Zone is through a retro art collection from the moon-crazy '50s; on the other side are three levels of classic rides and games with a futuristic twist. Climb into a bubble-top bumper car and shoot it out with oversized playground balls in **Buzz Lightyear's AstroBlaster.** There are two passengers in each car—one driver and one gunner. If you hit a target on another vehicle, they'll spin out.

There's a section of carnival games with rewards, including Dumbo's Water Race and Mickey's Lunar Rally. There's even a Game Graveyard where the golden oldies of video gaming live on.

DisneyQuest includes a pair of unusual fast-food eateries as well: FoodQuest, offering salads, sandwiches, pizza, and fun food, and Wonderland Cafe, with indulgent desserts, including offerings from the Cheesecake Factory. For information call (407) 828–4600 or consult www.disneyquest.com.

⊞⊞⊞ MUST-SEE ⊞⊞⊞ CIRQUE DU SOLEIL: *LA NOUBA*

Wonderfully weirder than most anything else at Walt Disney World, Cirque du Soleil's *La Nouba* brings together an international cast of sixty performers twice daily, five days a week, in a 70,000-square-foot, 1,671-seat theater that resembles a concrete circus tent with a 160-foot-tall mast.

The Montreal-based circus has no elephants and dancing tigers, and its aerialists and clowns march to a decidedly different beat from what you'll find under any other big top. Created in 1984 by one-time street performer Guy Laliberté, Cirque du Soleil is a striking mix of the circus arts and street entertainment. The circus has permanent show facilities in Las Vegas at the Treasure Island, MGM Grand, Mirage, New York–New York, and Bellagio casinos. Other shows tour in Europe, Asia, and North America.

The name of the show comes from an Algerian French phrase, *faire la Nouba,* which roughly translates as "party hearty." The strangeness begins with a nightmare opening scene with a startling moment when a bicyclist pedals by upside down, suspended from a wire. And the weirdness goes on from there, including

Cirque du Soleil's *La Nouba* at Downtown Disney West Side. *Photo courtesy of Cirque du Soleil*

the introduction of a raft of creatures who rise up from beneath the floor.

There's a bit of a story involving *La femme de ménage* (The Cleaning Lady), who seems to discover this strange world going on behind the scenes, and there's a wonderfully bizarre strong man who prances about making comically menacing poses.

Among acts that steal the show are four Chinese girls and their diabolos, a form of large yo-yo. Holding two sticks linked by a string, they slide, juggle, and toss a musical wooden spool while performing flips in the air. And then there is *Equilibre sur chaises* (Balancing on Chairs); the solo star stacks furniture he has found in the imaginary attic of *La Nouba* in order to light a chandelier, which mysteriously rises just beyond his reach every time he tries to get to the last candle. The artist defies gravity and the laws of physics as he balances precariously on a stack of six chairs, two books, and a baby carriage atop a table elevated 16 feet in the air. When he finally manages to reach the chandelier, now 34 feet in the air, he throws in a handstand before lighting the last candle.

The *Grands Volants* (Flying Trapeze) sets up four pendulum-like swings on two different levels to carry a team of perfectly synchronized aerialists 53 feet above the stage. Timing is key when all four trapezes are swinging in tandem and the aerialists switch places—barely inches away from colliding.

A group of bicyclists in modern dress climbs and descends stairs, performing some heart-stopping maneuvers at the edges of the stage and open pits. One of the bikers hops his bike over the body of a draftee from the audience. My favorite act came near the end when a whole troupe of acrobats performs on the power track and trampoline that rise from beneath the stage. They become human spider-men, launching themselves and climbing the walls of a building that rises from the stage. And then somewhere in the amorphous story, the cleaning lady kisses a frog and finds her prince.

All in all, this is a spectacular way to spend ninety minutes. It's not cheap, though: In 2006 tickets for *La Nouba* were priced from $61 to $95 plus tax ($49 to $76 plus tax for children ages three to nine). The show schedule varies from season to season. In the busy summertime, advance purchase is essential.

Sight lines in the U-shaped theater are very good; the best seats are in the center about midway up from the stage. Tickets in the 100 series are on the lower level, and those in the 200 series are in the balcony. No photography or videotaping is permitted. The music and sound effects are rather loud, which may be a problem for some guests and children. The show is under contract to Walt Disney World through the year 2010; the show may change slightly over that time as some of the acts rotate in and out.

■ AMC PLEASURE ISLAND 24

This was already the most successful multiscreen theater complex in Florida when it had a mere ten screens; the place expanded to two dozen screens a few years ago, making it the largest cineplex in the state. Eighteen of the theaters feature "stadium seating"—two with balconies and three-story-tall screens. For show times call (407) 298–4488 or consult www.amctheatres.com.

■ VIRGIN MEGASTORE

A state-of-the-art music, video, and book mecca, the circular, three-level store features 300 CD listening stations and an elevated exterior stage for live performances.

■ DOWNTOWN SHOPS

Also on the West Side is a collection of eclectic shops, including:

■ **Guitar Gallery.** Selling one-of-a-kind and celebrity model acoustic and electric guitars.

■ **Hoypoloi.** An unusual gallery of art glass, ceramics, sculpture, and other decorative items.

■ **Magnetron Magnetz.** All things magnetic, and not just refrigerator stickups, although you can buy those, too. Every few minutes the store's "magnetic generator" comes to life, energizing the whole place and all that is within it in wondrous ways.

■ **Sosa Family Cigars**. Stogies from a renowned Cuban family in a store modeled after the living room of founding father Don Juan Sosa Acosta.

■ **Starabilias.** Nostalgic and collectible old stuff, run by the founder of a similar store at the Forum Shops at Caesars Palace in Las Vegas.

■ DISNEY WEST SIDE RESTAURANTS

▪MUST-SEE▪ ▲ **House of Blues.** (407) 934–2583; www.hob.com. The sign out front of the huge 500-seat restaurant and 2,000-seat music hall, television production, and radio broadcasting facility reads: IN BLUES WE TRUST. The place is modeled after an old-time Mississippi juke joint, with rusted metal and fall-down wood trim. It gets even funkier inside, with a collection of folk-art paintings and sculptures.

Live blues, R&B, jazz, and country music are presented nightly, plus a rollicking Sunday Gospel Brunch. The restaurant features eclectic cuisine with a Delta heritage. Signature dishes, priced from about $9.00 to $22.00, include jambalaya, the Elwood (chicken breast Cajun style), the Jake Burger, and étouffée. There is, of course, a gift shop that sells souvenirs and, more important, books about blues and folk art and well-known and obscure blues recordings.

There's even a blues time for youngsters ages four to fifteen. *Gumbo Yo Yo*, a live, interactive stage show, is presented Saturday mornings, focused on teaching the House of Blues mission of "Unity in Diversity" through comedy, music, and storytelling. Tickets are available at the door, or by calling ahead; parents and children of other ages are free. A portion of ticket-sales proceeds goes to the International House of Blues Foundation to support various educational outreach programs.

▪MUST-SEE▪ ▲ **Wolfgang Puck Cafe.** (407) 938–9653; www.wolfgangpuck.com. The famed chef's first Florida restaurant features his innovative California cuisine in a casual setting adorned with colorful mosaic tiles. Specialties include wood-fired pizzas with toppings such as spicy chicken and smoked salmon.

There are 550 seats inside in three dining rooms, plus a walk-up Wolfgang Puck Express restaurant. Inside is a sushi and raw bar, a casual-dining restaurant downstairs with some seats allowing a view of the kitchen, and a more upscale, reservations-only restaurant upstairs with a view of Buena Vista Lagoon.

The decorating bill for the place was said to reach $8 million. Be sure to check out the bar counter, which includes a spread of $30,000 worth of semiprecious stones, and the tile work out front.

▪MUST-SEE▪ ▲ Ⓨ **Bongos Cuban Cafe.** (407) 828–0999. A Cuban cafe/nightclub created by Latin superstar Gloria Estefan and her husband, Emilio, brings the sizzle of Miami's South Beach to Disney. A giant concrete pineapple outside and elaborate mosaic murals inside speak of the hot, hot, hot heyday of Cuba in the 1940s and early 1950s; there's even a Ricky Ricardo look-alike working as a greeter.

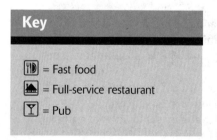

Key

🍴 = Fast food

▲ = Full-service restaurant

Ⓨ = Pub

The 471-seat restaurant includes a menu created by Quintin and Carmen Lario, founders with the Estefans of Larios on the Beach, a very popular eatery on Miami's South Beach. The Cuban style of cooking, *comidas criolla* or Creole, combines tropical and European elements. Staples include white sweet potatoes, squash, corn, rice, beans, and simmered sauces known as *soffritos*.

MUST-SEE 🎬 **Planet Hollywood.** (407) 827–7827; www.planethollywood.com/restaurants/orlando.shtm. This three-story, 400-seat restaurant, on its own plot of land between West Side and Pleasure Island, is one of the busiest eateries on the planet. The club, which has several major film stars among its owners, including Sylvester Stallone, Arnold Schwarzenegger, Bruce Willis, and Demi Moore, is a cinema equivalent to the Hard Rock Cafe chain. (Not at all coincidentally, there is a Hard Rock restaurant at Universal Studios Florida across town.)

The restaurant is decorated with movie and TV scripts, artifacts, and costumes; the sounds of music and film clips echo throughout. Surprisingly, the food is above average, including huge Caesar salads, Cajun chicken breast, hot wings, burgers, and pizza. Entrees start at about $10. Restaurant open daily from 11:00 A.M. to 1:00 A.M.

DOWNTOWN DISNEY PLEASURE ISLAND

Merriweather Adam Pleasure, also known as MAD Pleasure or the Grand Funmeister, disappeared in 1941 on a circumnavigation expedition of the Antarctic. By 1955 his beloved home island was in disrepair; the coup de grace was administered by a rogue hurricane. The six-acre island languished in ruins until it was rediscovered by Disney archaeologists, who painstakingly rebuilt the town. If you believe that story, perhaps you'd like to join the Pleasure Island Histerical Society, whose plaques dot the landmarks of Pleasure Island, which is located next to Disney Village. Even if you don't, a visit to Pleasure Island is a worthy nighttime entertainment.

The outdoor stages and gathering places of Pleasure Island are used regularly for street parties for New Year's Eve, Mardi Gras, and just about anything else you could want to celebrate and on just about any night of the year.

Pleasure Island shops and clubs open at 7:00 P.M. Admission is $20.95; visitors younger than age eighteen must be accompanied by an adult twenty-one or older. Pleasure Island is included in Park-Hopper tickets at Walt Disney World, and annual passes are available at roughly the price of three one-day admissions.

MUST-SEE 🍸 **THE ADVENTURERS CLUB**
Kungaloosh! Welcome to the decidedly unusual private club of Mr. Pleasure and his friends. Don't worry, though, you'll be welcomed as a guest . . . and offered a free membership and a secret password. We're sworn to secrecy ourselves, but it begins with a K and ends with a loosh. You'll enter five strange rooms filled with strange actors and you, their guests. Stick around and see what happens.

The Adventurers Club is one of the most entertaining "performance spaces" you'll find at Walt Disney World. According to the cover story, this is the place where Mr. Pleasure stored the strange items he brought back from his journeys; it's enough fun just to cruise among them. You'll likely meet the curator, the maid, and other oddball friends of Pleasure who will share their stories, and you'll be invited to enter into the library for an oddball show, including the Balderdash Cup Competition, the Curator's New Discovery, the Second Annual Radiothon Talent Show, the Maid's Sing-a-long, and the Bon Voyage Party. Get in early and grab a seat in the main parlor on the lower level. There's no pressure to buy drinks; you can just sit and watch the strange goings-on.

MUST-SEE ▣ BET SOUNDSTAGE CLUB

This upscale waterfront club features jazz, rhythm and blues, soul, and hip-hop in live performances, as well as programming from BET SoundStage Network. BET operates Black Entertainment Television, a cable programming service.

MUST-SEE ▣ THE COMEDY WAREHOUSE

This place is a hoot, offering an evening of improvisational humor, with somewhere between a PG and R rating—by Disney standards it can get downright risqué. (I'll leave it to the comics to express themselves, but on one of my visits the skit—directed by instructions called out by the audience—progressed to a love scene on the beach in which Ariel the mermaid lost her strategically placed seashells and was revealed to be a man.) There were even a few gentle jibes at Disney, including a fake movie poster on the wall advertising a film dubbed as *Dumbo, First Blood.*

There are several shows each night; the club is small and seats are often filled well before showtime. If you want to sit through two sessions, you'll have to exit and get back in line for a later show. From time to time television crews tape comedy specials here. When a "name" comedian is appearing, there may be an extra charge for admission.

When you are offered a seat in the amphitheater-like club, think twice about whether you really want to sit by a telephone. You don't suppose it may ring during the show, do you?

As at all of the clubs here, you will be approached by a waiter or waitress, but you do not have to purchase anything if you don't want to. Drink prices include small beers for about $3.00, up to a sixty-ounce pitcher for about $9.00. Special drinks include Laughter Punch, made with Midori, rum, and pineapple juice. Sodas, popcorn, pretzels, and banana splits are also available.

■ MANNEQUINS DANCE PALACE

This contemporary club has a rotating dance floor and a high-tech (recorded) sound, light, and dance show starring the Pleasure Island Explosion Dancers, on stage several times each night. There are also a bunch of strange mannequins scattered about, bubble machines, and more. You must be at least twenty-one to enter.

■ MOTION

Bodies are always in motion at this two-story temple of groove that stands at the border between Downtown Disney Pleasure Island and Downtown Disney Marketplace. A disc jockey spins the hottest chart hits nightly, backed by a huge video screen, pulsing speakers, and swirling lights.

🏠 RAGLAN ROAD IRISH PUB AND RESTAURANT

A little piece of the old sod, featuring authentic Irish food, drink, and live entertainment. The eatery includes four antique bars, each more than 130 years old and imported from Ireland. These grand fixtures were crafted from rich woods, such as mahogany and walnut, and feature marble adornments, leaded glass, and ornate detailing. To complete the authenticity, and in keeping with tradition, a wide selection of cold, creamy and fresh Irish beers, and fine Irish whiskies are served.

The menu offers bistro-style Irish fare made with fresh ingredients, including dishes such as Raglan Rack (rack of lamb on a delicate Irish stew consommé), Kevin's Kudos (oven-roasted loin of bacon with an Irish mist glaze, served with braised cabbage and creamed potato), and Salmon of Knowledge (fresh grilled salmon with a hickory-scented maple sauce). The large space seats 600.

Raglan Road is a thoroughfare in south Dublin, and a work of the same name by Irish poet Patrick Kavanagh was made into a song that was covered by artists including U2, Sinead O'Connor, and Van Morrison. The Irish-owned company behind the restaurant is also responsible for the Nine Fine Irishmen restaurant at the New York–New York Hotel & Casino in Las Vegas.

■ ROCK 'N' ROLL BEACH CLUB

Live bands perform the classics of rock; a DJ spins stacks of vinyl—well, stacks of CDs, anyway—during breaks. Be sure to check out the second floor, where you'll find a selection of pool and air-hockey tables and video and pinball machines, as well as a shark hanging from the ceiling with a bikini top in its teeth. Menu items include pizza by the slice.

■ 8TRAX

If you can remember what an 8-track tape player was, you'll understand the basic concept of this celebration of the '70s (starring The Doors, Iron Butterfly, Janis Joplin, bell-bottoms, beanbag chairs, and lava lamps). The dance floor includes your basic disco mirror ball and a fog machine.

DOWNTOWN DISNEY MARKETPLACE

When the going gets tough, the tough go shopping. The Marketplace is one of Disney's most interesting collections of shops, including a large LEGO outlet and the mother of all Disney Stores. There's also another outlet of the unusual Rainforest Cafe chain.

You can drive to the Village and park in the huge parking lot (it adjoins and mixes with the spaces for Pleasure Island), or you can take a water taxi from the Port Orleans Resort, Dixie Landings Resort, or the Disney Vacation Club. The stores are open from 9:30 A.M. to 10:00 P.M.

Of course, there are lots of shops selling T-shirts, sweatshirts, and hats with pictures of Mickey or Minnie, but perhaps the single largest collection is at the warehouse-size **World of Disney,** with twelve rooms of toys and souvenirs, clothing (including Disney lingerie!), and more.

A recent addition to the World of Disney is the Bibbidi Bobbidi Boutique, part of the store's Princess Room. Here youngsters can be made up pretty as a princess. The boutique, "owned' by the Fairy Godmother and "operated" by Fairy Godmothers-in-Training, offers a menu of fancy updos, glitter makeup, and dazzling nails designed to pamper princesses ages three and up. Walk-ins are accepted, but reservations are strongly encouraged (call 407–939–7895); the last appointment of the day is at 5:30 P.M.

Nearby young adventurers can pretend to sail the high seas and hoist the Jolly Roger in the Adventure Room. Young heroes and heroines can fill treasure chests and skulls with pirate plunder, create their own seafaring hat, and interact with Rusty Blade and his talking parrot pal, Pollyanna.

Another favorite is the **LEGO Imagination Center,** a retail shrine to the little plastic bricks. It features an outdoor play area and huge LEGO models, including a sea serpent rising out of Buena Vista Lagoon and a UFO model complete with an alien family. The store features every LEGO product available in the United States, including blocks, games, puzzles, bedsheets, and clothing.

It's Christmas all the time at **Disney's Days of Christmas,** where you can purchase American and European ornaments and Disney holiday merchandise. (By the way, during the Christmas holiday period there's ice-skating on a small rink at Downtown Disney Marketplace, the only outdoor rink in Florida. Skate rentals are available.)

You'll be able to indulge that chocolate addiction with a visit to **Ghirardelli Soda Fountain & Chocolate Shop,** where you'll find chocolate in all forms, as well as sundaes, shakes, malts, and more. The shop is designed like a turn-of-the-twentieth-century San Francisco shop.

Designated Drinkers

Note that the drinking age in Florida is twenty-one, and visitors to Pleasure Island who are not obviously over that age will be required to show proof of their birthdate. Once "carded," you'll receive a wristband you can wear for the rest of the evening. There is, however, no requirement that you buy any drinks in any of the clubs—just say "no," and you'll be left alone to watch the shows.

■ DOWNTOWN DISNEY MARKETPLACE RESTAURANTS

The major restaurants in the Downtown Disney Marketplace–Pleasure Island area are located outside the turnstiles between Pleasure Island and Disney Village and can be visited without purchasing a ticket.

🍴 **Cap'n Jack's Restaurant.** A little bit of Cape Cod in a pretty setting on the village lake. Specialties include lobster tails, crab claws, clams, chowder, and frozen margaritas. Prices range from $5.00 to $15.00. The children's menu features pasta, $4.00. Open for lunch and dinner from 11:30 A.M. to 10:00 P.M.

🍴 **Earl of Sandwich.** A 220-seat casual restaurant with freshly prepared hot sandwiches, salads, and desserts.

🏠 **Fulton's Crab House.** (407) 934–2628. By the shores of Disney's inland sea is a seafood restaurant on a re-created paddle wheeler. The crab house promises to change its menu daily to reflect the latest and greatest seafood available in season. (They'll even post the air-freight bills on the wall!) Entrees, from about $15 to $35, include Nantucket bay scallops, mustard-crusted trout, and Fulton's cioppino. Appetizers begin with a well-stocked oyster bar and also include such delicacies as alderwood-smoked salmon with potato crostini lemon-chive cream. Open for a popular character breakfast with seatings at 8:00 and 10:00 A.M., lunch daily from 11:30 A.M. to 4:00 P.M., and dinner 5:00 P.M. to midnight. Dinner entrees about $20.

McDonald's Ronald's Fun House. A one-of-a-kind outpost of the fast-food chain, featuring fanciful rooms and decor based on Ronald McDonald and some of his McDonaldland friends. Among the settings: Ronald's Dining Room, with a formal 20-foot serpentine dining area; Birdie's Music Room, featuring a giant french fry organ; and Grimace's Game Room, with video monitors. Oh, and it sells burgers and fries, too.

Portobello Yacht Club. (407) 934–8888. This first-class Northern Italian eatery's offerings range from thin-crust pizza cooked in a wood-fired oven ($7.00 to $8.00) to steak, chicken, and fish dishes. Lunch salads, priced from about $5.00 to $8.00, may include *insalata Caesar di pollo* (Caesar salad with chicken). A sample of entrees, priced from about $13 to $25, includes *Spiedini di Gamberi,* charcoal-grilled garlic shrimp on a rosemary skewer; center-cut pork chop with herb crust; veal rib eye breaded and sautéed with a balsamic vinaigrette topping; and *Spaghettini alla Portobello,* a house specialty including Alaskan crab, scallops, clams, shrimp, and mussels with tomatoes, garlic, olive oil, wine, and herbs. A children's menu is also available.

Open daily 11:30 A.M. to midnight; call for reservations.

MUST-SEE **Rainforest Cafe.** (407) 827–8500; www.rainforestcafe.com. Wild and wacky, with trees, birds, crocodiles, and rainfall . . . real and animatronic. This is not your basic roadside cafe, unless your neighborhood eatery sports an animatronic gator at the door, an active (simulated) volcano, and a menu that emphasizes nonendangered fish, beef from countries that pledge not to deforest their lands for grazing, and some imaginative vegetarian offerings as well. Every once in a while the room lights go dim, and a (dry) thunderstorm breaks out inside the restaurant. Be sure to check out the wishing pond to the right of the entrance. The spectacular parrots on perches are real; the huge alligator below is not.

Specialties include the Amazon Natural herbal burger constructed of nuts, grains, and beans; Rumble in the Jungle, roasted turkey tossed with Caesar salad and stuffed into a pita bread; Jamaica Me Crazy!, grilled pork chops dusted with Jamaican and Cajun seasonings; and Rasta Pasta, with bow-tie pasta, grilled chicken, walnut pesto, broccoli, red peppers, spinach, and fresh herbs in a garlic cream sauce.

Lines for the 550-seat restaurant can become oppressive at prime lunch and dinner hours; your best bet is to come earlier or later than the crowds. Of course, you can also while away the time in the impressive gift shop. Open for lunch and dinner from 10:30 A.M. to 11:00 P.M. Another Rainforest Cafe is located at the entrance plaza to Disney's Animal Kingdom.

Wolfgang Puck Express. Lunch and dinner service for California-style pizzas.

CHAPTER THIRTEEN

EDUCATIONAL OPPORTUNITIES AND TOURS AT WALT DISNEY WORLD

LET'S BE HONEST ABOUT IT: A trip to Walt Disney World is first and foremost a journey in search of fun. But that doesn't mean you can't justify your visit as an educational experience. Feeling bad about taking your kids out of school to plunge down the Tower of Terror, spin on the Teacups, or zoom the Test Track? How about giving them a little homework, Mickey-style?

SHOULD YOU TAKE YOUR KIDS OUT OF SCHOOL?

In the best of all worlds, probably not. There are enough interruptions in the normal school year as it is. However, if work and school vacation times do not coincide, or if you are taking our advice seriously and trying to avoid crowds, there are ways to work with your schools.

Meet with your children's teachers to determine if there are particular times when an absence of a few days (wrapped around or including a weekend or minor holiday) will not make a big impact on schoolwork. Consult your school calendar in search of local holidays or "workshop" half days. See if you can coordinate special assignments for your children. If there is an upcoming unit on Mexico, for example, perhaps they could be assigned to produce a report with research performed at Epcot Center's Mexico pavilion.

BEHIND-THE-SCENES TOURS

One of the secrets of Walt Disney World is the range of fascinating tours of its parks and facilities available to visitors. Some of the tours are offered directly to the public, while others are part of hotel packages (the Deluxe Plan and the

Grand Plan among them), and others are offered to visiting school and corporate groups. For information call (407) 939–8687. Ticket prices range from about $20 to $200; some tours also require purchase of an admission ticket to the parks. Tours change by the season. Call for information. In 2006 a typical set of tours included:

■ **Keys to the Kingdom.** A four-and-a-half- to five-hour tour of the history, heritage, and philosophies of the Magic Kingdom, and a quick peek backstage, including the underground Utilidor system. Offered daily. About $60, plus admission ticket to the park.

■ **Backstage Magic.** The ultimate in insider peeks, this seven-hour expedition includes the Utilidor tunnel system beneath the Magic Kingdom and backstage technology at Epcot and Disney–MGM Studios. Includes lunch. Offered Monday to Friday. About $199 per person; theme-park admission is not required.

■ **Disney's Family Magic Tour.** A two-and-a-half-hour organized scavenger hunt inside the Magic Kingdom for kids of all ages. Tickets $27, plus admission to the park.

■ **Mickey's Magical Milestones Tour.** A two-hour narrated tour that explores the history of the world's most famous cartoon mouse, as seen at the Magic Kingdom. Each ticket $25, plus park admission.

■ **The Magic Behind Our Steam Trains.** A three-hour visit to the Disney roundhouse as engineers prepare the Magic Kingdom's steam-engine trains for their daily travels. No cameras permitted. Offered Monday, Thursday, and Saturday. About $40, plus admission ticket to the park.

■ **Gardens of the World.** A three-hour study of selected gardens in Epcot's World Showcase, conducted by a Disney horticulturist; includes tips to bring home to your own garden. Offered Tuesday and Thursday. About $59, plus admission ticket to the park.

■ **Hidden Treasures of World Showcase.** Three-hour walking tours of Epcot's World Showcase to point out the subtle details of the architecture. Offered Tuesday and Thursday. About $59, plus admission ticket to the park.

■ **Undiscovered Future World.** Inside the shows and technologies of Future World at Epcot on a four-and-a-half-hour tour. Offered Monday, Tuesday, Friday, and Saturday. About $59, plus admission ticket to the park.

■ **Dolphins in Depth.** Up close and personal with some of the residents of the Living Seas at Epcot in a three-hour knee-deep wading adventure. Offered weekdays. About $150; admission ticket to the park not required. Minors must be accompanied by an adult age eighteen or older.

■ **Backstage Safari Tour.** Three hours behind the scenes at Disney's Animal Kingdom, with visits to animal care and feeding facilities and meetings with keepers. Offered Monday, Wednesday, Thursday, and Friday. About $65, plus admission ticket to the park.

■ **Wild by Design.** A three-hour Animal Kingdom tour focusing on the architecture and art of the park. Offered Tuesday, Thursday, and Friday. About $58, plus admission ticket to the park.

- **Around the World at Epcot.** A two-hour experience tooling around the World Showcase on a Segway Human Transporter. All tickets $80, plus admission ticket to the park.
- **Epcot DiveQuest.** A three-hour plunge into the pool at Epcot's The Living Seas, for certified open-water scuba divers. Offered daily. About $140. Gear provided; no theme-park admission ticket is required.
- **Epcot Seas Aqua Tour.** A two-and-a-half-hour in-the-water experience for non-scuba-certified visitors at Epcot's The Living Seas. Offered daily. Wet suits provided. About $100; no theme-park admission ticket is required.
- **Behind the Seeds.** A one-hour inside peek at the growing areas within Epcot's The Land. Offered daily. Adults $12, children $10, plus admission ticket to the park.
- **VIP Tour.** For a mere $750, plus admission to the parks, you can hire a private guide who will design an itinerary, escort you to the best seats in the house for shows, and otherwise give you the VIP treatment. The tour is priced at $125 per hour, with a six-hour minimum. You can arrange for the tour through Disney Special Activities at (407) 560–4033.

CHAPTER FOURTEEN

INSIDE THE WORLD OF DISNEY

THE INSIDE STORY OF HIDDEN MICKEYS

Hidden Mickeys began as an inside joke among Walt Disney Imagineers, the artists and engineers who design Disney parks and attractions. As word spread of these subtle tributes to Walt's famous mouse, serious fans of all things Mickey began to include the search as part of the entertainment at the park.

Imagineers include Hidden Mickeys when designing, building, or putting the finishing touches on a new attraction or hotel, hiding silhouettes, profiles, and other images of Mickey Mouse in murals, queue areas, and even golf course sand traps. There is no official count of how many Hidden Mickeys exist throughout the Walt Disney World Resort, and over the years some have come and gone. Here are some of the less-obvious places to look.

■ MAGIC KINGDOM

■ **Haunted Mansion:** In addition to the 999 or so ghosts in the old house, there is at least one mouse: a Hidden Mickey formed by an arrangement of dishes on the table in the banquet scene.

■ **Splash Mountain:** A Hidden Mickey enjoys a lazy day on the river in the final scene before the watery splash; a pink cloud floating high above the *Zip-A-Dee Lady* paddle wheeler bears a striking resemblance to a profile of Mickey lying on his back.

■ EPCOT

■ **Norway:** While you're waiting in line for the Maelstrom, check out the mural overhead. A burly Viking sports a pair of Mickey Mouse ears.

■ **Spaceship Earth:** Mickey has his own constellation just beyond the attraction's loading area.

■ DISNEY–MGM STUDIOS

- **Aerial view:** Disney–MGM Studios offers one of the largest Hidden Mickeys: The Hollywood Plaza area and surrounding buildings in front of the Chinese Theater actually form a giant Mickey Mouse face when viewed from the air.
- **Rock 'n' Roller Coaster Starring Aerosmith:** A pair of Hidden Mickeys are worked into the tile floor in the attraction's rotunda.

■ DISNEY'S ANIMAL KINGDOM

- **Pizzafari Restaurant:** Mickey can be "spotted" on a wall mural, cleverly hidden among leopard spots.
- **The Boneyard:** In the woolly mammoth dig site, Mickey has been formed with a fan and two hard hats.
- **Rafiki's Planet Watch:** There are more than twenty-five Hidden Mickeys among the murals, tree trunks, and paintings of animals.

■ RESORTS

- **Disney's Magnolia Golf Course:** Mickey is remembered by golfers around the world for his contribution to the sixth hole, where a Hidden Mickey forms a giant sand trap that looms ominously close to the green.
- **Disney's Eagle Pines and Osprey Ridge Golf Courses:** Mickey's head is used as a putting green at the courses' clubhouse area.
- **Disney's Grand Floridian Resort & Spa:** A Hidden Mickey is found on the weather vane atop the convention center.
- **Downtown Disney Marketplace:** Interactive fountains at the entrance of the shopping, dining, and entertainment district form Mickey's familiar silhouette.

ROBOT CAST MEMBERS: AUDIO-ANIMATRONICS

Some 1,600 employees at Walt Disney World are at their jobs twenty-four hours a day without a lunch break, pay no taxes, and are constitutionally unable to file a complaint. Then again, we are talking about wicked witches, evil grasshoppers, nasty dinosaurs, and unpleasant ghosts. To be fair, some are nicer folk: singing bears, wisecracking birds, and some of the more notable presidents of the United States. These dedicated workers, of course, are members of the mechanical corps of audio-animatronics robots. The Disney-developed technology electronically combines and synchronizes voices, music, sound effects, character movements, and other show elements.

The system was first developed more than fifty years ago as Walt Disney planned Disneyland. The challenge to animate the theme-park figures fell to WED Enterprises (now known as Walt Disney Imagineering), the Disney creative design, development, and engineering subsidiary. Among the staff were many of the famed Disney animators. The earliest experiments utilized simple mechanical devices such as cams and levers to animate miniature models of human figures such as Dancing Man, a 9-inch-tall tap-dancing vaudevillian programmed to mimic the dance steps of entertainer Buddy Ebsen.

Cams were tedious to cut, and the movement they could induce was limited to the diameter of the cams. Disney Imagineers combined the cam-and-lever design with hydraulic and pneumatic controls to achieve more versatility in the moving animals of two early Disneyland attractions, Nature's Wonderland and Jungle Cruise. But the actions remained simple. With help from studio sound experts and electricians, Imagineers abandoned cams and levers and devised a system to control the actions with solenoids activated by magnetic recording tape. This form of audio-animatronics technology was introduced in the summer of 1963 with the opening of the Enchanted Tiki Room at Disneyland.

Programming lifelike movements in animal characters proved easier than in human figures. To record the sequence of signals that would animate the human figures, Wathel Rogers, considered the father of audio-animatronics technology, was rigged up with a harnesslike device. As he moved, the various actions were recorded as a series of electrical signals. The programming was painstaking. For instance, a figure of Abraham Lincoln created for the 1964 New York World's Fair incorporated fifty-seven moves, including twenty-two different head movements, all of which had to be acted out in correct sequence by the wired-up animator.

In 1969 Imagineers turned to the rapidly developing technology of computers. A variety of movements are first recorded onto a computer disk; animators can later edit the movements and sequence them. The finished show is controlled by a digital-animation playback system that simultaneously relays data and cues to speakers, lights, special effects, and audio-animatronics figures. As technology progressed into the 1980s, so did the control system. Today a control system animates the audio-animatronics figures for both Epcot and the Magic Kingdom from a single remote location.

Sophisticated computers have enabled audio-animatronics animators to achieve greater subtleties

Suspended Animation

A recurring rumor about dear old Walt Disney is that he chose to be cryogenically frozen when he died of lung cancer in 1966, in hopes of a defrost in another day and age. Actually, according to the company, he went to the other extreme and was cremated before burial at the famous Forest Lawn Memorial Park in California.

Mouse Duds

Mickey Mouse's closet includes more than 175 different outfits, ranging from a scuba suit to a tuxedo. Minnie Mouse's wardrobe contains some 200 outfits, including everything from a cheerleader ensemble to evening gowns.

in body language and expression, including a pioneering walking movement by Ben Franklin during a scene of The American Adventure at Epcot. Franklin's head tilts and nods, his body twists, individual fingers of his hand move, his torso moves forward and to the side, and his mouth pinches right and left. In all, there are some forty separate movements in that scene alone.

The state of the art at the park is the audio-animatronics A-100 technology, which incorporates compliance technology that enables movements and gestures to be even more fluid and realistic. However, programming remains as painstaking as ever. It generally takes about eight hours to animate one second of movement.

The first audio-animatronics A-100 figure was the Wicked Witch, who debuted in The Great Movie Ride at Disney–MGM Studios in 1989. Other A-100 figures include the carnotaurs in the Dinosaur attraction at Disney's Animal Kingdom.

Among the most complex A-100 figures is Hopper, a 9-foot, four-armed grasshopper with sixty-eight functions who appears in *It's Tough to Be a Bug!*, also at Disney's Animal Kingdom.

DISNEY CRUISE LINE

Ahoy, Mickey! *Disney Magic* and *Disney Wonder* are just like any other cruise ship . . . except for those six letters on the bow and all that they mean for guests. The *Disney Wonder* makes three- and four-day cruises to the Bahamas, featuring a visit to Nassau and Castaway Cay, Disney's private Bahamian island. *Disney Magic* sails alternating weeklong cruises to the eastern and western Caribbean, including a stop at Castaway Cay. The eastern trip visits St. Maarten and St. Thomas, and the western trip goes to Key West, Grand Cayman Island, and Cozumel. Both vessels are based at Port Canaveral on Florida's east coast, about an hour away from Orlando.

As part of the celebration of the fiftieth anniversary of Disneyland, *Disney Magic* was sent through the Panama Canal to sail from a Los Angeles–area port for the summer of 2005, making three- and four-day trips to Mexico and Catalina Island. In 2007 *Disney Magic* will cross the Atlantic for a summer of sailing in the Mediterranean, sailing ten- and eleven-day cruises from Barcelona, Spain.

Disney had great success with its West Coast itineraries, and the European sailings are likely to be in great demand as well. The company has had plans for a third ship sitting on the shelf for several years as it waits the optimum financial moment.

Disney built its ships with adults as well as kids in mind. Youngsters have their own deck, Disney's Oceaneer Adventure, which is open late into the night. Features include Disney's Oceaneer Club, a play area for younger kids, and Disney's Oceaneer Lab, which offers electronic games played on giant video walls and interactive computer activities. Teens have their own private hangout on each of the ships. On *Disney Magic* the hangout is The Stack, a club up high

The Disney Cruise Line fleet. *Copyright © 1999 The Walt Disney Company*

in the hollow forward funnel (one of the two smokestacks is just for show). The equivalent on *Disney Wonder* is Aloft. Each is a cross between a college dormitory and a trendy coffee shop, loaded with comfy couches and overstuffed chairs. Adults can dance the night away at Beat Street or Route 66, adult nightclub districts with dance, jazz, and improv comedy clubs.

Guests rotate to one of three themed restaurants each evening. French continental cuisine is offered at Lumières on *Disney Magic* and Triton's on *Disney Wonder*. The flavors and spirit of the Bahamas is featured at Parrot Cay. And then there is Animator's Palette, where the room magically transforms from a black-and-white artist's sketch to full-color animation over the course of dinner. There's also Palo, an adults-only restaurant, and a kids-only pizza parlor. After dinner families can enjoy one of three Broadway-style shows at the Walt Disney Theatre or catch a movie at the Buena Vista Theatre. And there's Studio Sea, a nightclub for the entire family.

The ships, built in Trieste, Italy, feature a "classic exterior design reminiscent of the majestic transatlantic ocean liners of the past." They have in many ways delivered on the promise, with some of the most elegant shipboard spaces I have seen, and a vessel with stunning lines that will please even the most finicky cruise connoisseur. I don't recall the *Queen Mary* offering Disney character breakfasts and shows, though.

You can book passage on one of the ships through a travel agent or through Disney Cruise Line's Web site, www.disneycruise.com. (For full details on the Disney cruise line, you can consult another title in this book series, *Econoguide Cruises*.)

DISNEYLAND PARIS

The French have an apt phrase: *Le plus ça change, le plus c'est la même chose.* It means: "The more that changes, the more things are the same." The French hate American culture, right? Tell that to *La Belle au Bois Dormant* (Sleeping Beauty), *Blanche-Neige et les Sept Nains* (Snow White and the Seven Dwarfs), and, of course, to Mickey Mouse (no translation needed). Most of all, tell that to the millions of visitors who head 20 miles east of the City of Lights to Marne la Vallée, home of the City of Mickey. The resort opened in 1992. For information consult www.disneylandparis.com.

Should you go all the way from North America to visit Disneyland Paris? Well, on the one hand, this is one of the most advanced theme parks in the world, decades younger than the Magic Kingdom in Orlando and the even older Disneyland in Anaheim. But it is also very similar, albeit with a French accent. For us the beauty of Disneyland Paris is this: It's a wonderful way to convince the kids to go to France to visit the Cathedral of Nôtre Dame, the Louvre, the Champs-Elysées, Versailles, the Pompidou . . . and Mickey and Minnie.

On several of my trips I chose to make Disneyland Paris my base, venturing west to Paris and Versailles five days in a week and spending two days in the park. Hotels at the park, although not cheap, are still less expensive than many hotels in downtown Paris. The RER train service to Paris (about forty-five minutes by rail) is easily accessible, or you can rent a car and use the highways.

Although Disneyland Paris is very much an outpost of American culture, as defined by Walt Disney and refined during a half century by the moviemaking and theme-park empire he created, there is nevertheless a definite French and European gloss to the park. But worry not: Though the rides and attractions are narrated in French, you'll find English and other translations readily available. Nearly every park employee speaks multiple languages, and English is very common.

■ MAGIC KINGDOM

The Magic Kingdom is laid out very much like its cousins in California and Florida. One exception: The American Tomorrowland is called Discoveryland in France. Among the highlights of the park:

■ **Phantom Manor.** This highest-tech version of this Disney classic (known as the Haunted Mansion in Florida and California) has 999 ghoulish French ghosts. The story, if you need one, involves a bride who was jilted at the altar. Forever in her wedding dress, she haunts the house and all who visit.

■ **Pirates of the Caribbean.** Yo, ho, ho . . . this is one of Disney's very best. A slightly Frenchified version of the classic watery adventure, it's a cruise into the middle of a pirate raid on a Caribbean island town. Among the highlights are a moonlit battle scene as your boat passes beneath the guns of two warring ships; cannonballs land all around in the cool water. Pay attention, too, to the jail scene where a group of pirates tries to entice a mangy dog to bring them the key. The

Main Street, U.S.A., in Disneyland Paris. *Courtesy Disneyland Paris.* © *Disney*

ride includes a wondrous collection of animatronic humans and animals, including robotic chickens and pigs.

- *Indiana Jones et le Temple du Peril* (**Indiana Jones and the Temple of Doom**). A truly wild roller coaster that careens through the long-buried ruins of the Temple of Peril, right-side up, upside down, and straight at the waters below. In 2000 Disney turned up the thrills a few notches by reworking the track, mounting the cars backward, and sending guests on a ride that lets them concentrate on where they've been instead of where they're heading. The mine cars back their way through a spiraling inverted 360-degree loop.
- *Le Château de la Belle au Bois Dormant* (**Sleeping Beauty's Castle**). The centerpiece of the park is this very European castle. Located upstairs is *La Galerie de la Belle au Bois Dormant* (Sleeping Beauty's Gallery), which displays the story of Sleeping Beauty through hand-painted storybooks, stained-glass windows, and finely woven tapestries. Beneath the castle is *La Tanière du Dragon* (The Dragon's Lair), where a huge animatronic dragon sleeps restlessly.
- **Dumbo the Flying Elephant.** A worldwide favorite for youngsters, who wait in line (along with their cranky parents) for the chance to ride on Dumbo in a circular pathway above Fantasyland.
- **It's a Small World.** Every little girl's wildest dream: a world of beautiful dancing dolls from all over the world. There is nothing to get your heart beating here, but even the most cynical—including little boys and adults—will probably find something to smile about in this upbeat boat ride.

- **Star Tours.** The Starspeeder 3000 departs regularly on a short and eventful voyage to outer space in this simulator ride based on the *Star Wars* films of George Lucas.
- *Le Visionarium.* A Cinematronic 360-degree theater presents a beautifully produced film about French science-fiction author Jules Verne in a spectacular time-travel adventure that soars through Europe. A version of that film was imported to the Magic Kingdom at Walt Disney World in Orlando as *The Timekeeper;* that show closed in 2006.
- **Space Mountain: *De la Terre à la Lune* (From the Earth to the Moon).** A triumph of imagineering, this is a roller-coaster trip to the moon. This version of the classic ride goes way beyond the originals at Disneyland and Walt Disney World, beginning with the takeoff: Every thirty-six seconds the *Cannon Columbiad* launches a twenty-four-passenger rocket train through its barrel. Space travelers shoot to the top in a heart-stopping 1.8 seconds, floating through a moment of zero gravity at the top before descending in the dark through the trip from Earth to the Moon with upside-down spirals and twists and turns.

WALT DISNEY STUDIOS

The second park in Paris, opened in spring 2002, celebrates the art and science of television and moviemaking. The two major attractions at the park are France-ified versions of major draws at Disney–MGM Studios in Orlando: the Studio Tram Tour (which goes into a simulation of a movie back lot), and the Rock 'n' Roller Coaster Starring Aerosmith. Other presentations include the Art of Disney Animation, The Stunt Show Spectacular, and Flying Carpets over Agrabah.

CinéMagique ,is a new attraction created exclusively for the Walt Disney Studios Park; guests take a trip through the silver screen and experience some of the best moments from one hundred years of European and American cinema.

Armageddon Special Effects takes its name from the science-fiction blockbuster of the same name, re-creating some of cinema's most spectacular moments and unveiling special-effects secrets.

TOKYO DISNEY RESORT

Hai, Mickey-san. If ever proof was required of the global impact of American popular culture, it came with the opening of Tokyo Disneyland in 1983. The park, 6 miles outside of Tokyo, is owned by a Japanese company under license to Disney. In 2001 Tokyo DisneySea Park opened alongside. Outside of the theme parks is Ikspiari, a themed entertainment district.

TOKYO DISNEYLAND

This Japanese version of the Magic Kingdom includes familiar Disney attractions as well as new shows such as Pinocchio's Daring Journey, The Eternal Seas, and Meet the World. Instead of Main Street, U.S.A., you'll find **World Bazaar** as the gateway to **Adventureland, Fantasyland, Tomorrowland,** and **Westernland.**

Adventureland attractions include the Jungle Cruise, Enchanted Tiki Room, and Pirates of the Caribbean. In Westernland you'll find the Mark Twain Riverboat, Tom Sawyer Island, The Golden Horseshoe Revue, and Country Bear Jamboree. At Toontown the cartoon characters are in charge.

Fantasyland includes the Pinocchio ride, plus It's a Small World, Haunted Mansion, Snow White's Adventure, and the Mickey Mouse Revue. There are also venerable favorites Dumbo the Flying Elephant and Cinderella's Golden Carrousel.

Tomorrowland includes yet another Space Mountain, as well as Meet the World, an attraction based on Japanese history and the country's influence on the rest of the world.

■ TOKYO DISNEYSEA

Tokyo DisneySea overlooks Tokyo Bay, adjacent to Tokyo Disneyland. Surrounded by water (and aided by construction tricks that seem to extend the horizon of a small moat), the entrance to the park is anchored by a globe-shaped fountain known as the AquaSphere, alive with the flow of water. Representing our Earth, the "water planet," the AquaSphere is covered by cascades of water that flow down and around the globe, mysteriously clinging to its surface. The seven lands at the park include:

■ **Mediterranean Harbor,** a Disney version of a southern European seaport that includes Venetian gondolas, the DisneySea Transit Steamer Line that links to Lost River Delta, and the *Renaissance,* a re-creation of a galleon used during the Golden Age of Exploration.

■ **Mysterious Island,** which celebrates Jules Verne. Guests venture to the ocean floor to explore the lost city of Atlantis in *20,000 Leagues Under the Sea* and take a thrilling journey far below an active volcano in *Journey to the Center of the Earth.*

■ **Mermaid Lagoon,** a place for younger visitors to explore the "under the sea" world of Ariel and all her friends from the classic Disney animated film *The Little Mermaid* with seven kiddie attractions.

■ **Arabian Coast,** home to Aladdin and his playful Genie pal from *1001 Arabian Nights.* Attractions include Sindbad's Seven Voyages and the Magic Lamp Theater.

■ **Lost River Delta,** a place where Indiana Jones would feel right at home. Visitors can search for the fountain of youth in the wild ride Indiana Jones Adventure: Temple of the Crystal Skull on a perilous journey through the secret corridors of a foreboding Central American pyramid.

■ **Port Discovery,** which allows us to travel across the horizons of time to a futuristic marina that celebrates the thrills, adventure, and excitement of new frontiers in the sea and sky. Attractions include StormRider, Aquatopia, and the DisneySea Electric Railway.

■ **American Waterfront,** which nostalgically showcases the harbors of New York and Cape Cod at the beginning of the twentieth century. Located on the park's main waterfront in Mediterranean Harbor, the Tokyo DisneySea Hotel Mira-

Costa offers breathtaking views of the park and Tokyo Bay. The park is next to Tokyo Disneyland and connected by monorail. For information consult www .tokyodisneyresort.co.jp.

HONG KONG DISNEYLAND

Ni Hao, Mickey Mouse. Hong Kong joined the world of Disney in September 2005. The park is located on 310 acres of Lantau Island, about thirty minutes by rail from central Hong Kong. For information consult www.hongkongdisney land.com and look for the button that gives an English translation.

The park includes four lands and two themed hotels:

- **Main Street, U.S.A.** City Hall, Hong Kong Disneyland Railroad, Main Street Vehicles
- **Tomorrowland.** Space Mountain, Buzz Lightyear Astro Blasters, Orbitron
- **Fantasyland.** Sleeping Beauty Castle, The Many Adventures of Winnie the Pooh, *Mickey's PhilharMagic,* Fantasy Gardens, Dumbo the Flying Elephant, Mad Hatter Tea Cups, Cinderella Carousel, Snow White Grotto
- **Adventureland.** Jungle River Cruise, Tarzan's Treehouse, *Festival of the Lion King,* Rafts to Tarzan's Treehouse, Liki Tikis
- **Hong Kong Disneyland Hotel.**
- **Disney's Hollywood Hotel.**

PART III

UNIVERSAL ORLANDO

CHAPTER FIFTEEN

A BURGEONING UNIVERSE

ORLANDO IS NO LONGER A SMALL WORLD AFTER ALL. It's more of a Universal place. The kingdom of the Mouse now has some serious—and fun—competition across town at the growing Universal Studios empire. Universal Orlando now offers two theme parks, a water park, a sprawling nighttime dining and entertainment complex, and several impressive hotel resorts. The bottom line: You could spend at least two days of an Orlando visit here, with more to come. The following are all part of Universal Studios:

- **Universal Studios Florida.** Celebrates the worlds of moviemaking and television.
- **Universal Studios Islands of Adventure.** One of the most advanced theme and thrill parks in the world, with a collection of high-tech simulators, roller coasters, and strangeness unmatched at Walt Disney World.
- **Universal Studios CityWalk.** A lively rock, blues, and culinary magnet by night.
- **Resorts.** The first three of five large resort hotels are open: the elegant 750-room Portofino Bay Hotel, the 650-room Hard Rock Hotel, and the 1,000-room Royal Pacific Resort. Two additional hotels planned for years to come will bring the total number of rooms on the park property to about 5,000.
- **Wet 'n Wild.** The Wet 'n Wild water park nearby on International Drive is one of the best aqueous entertainment places anywhere.

And if that's not enough, Universal Studios has been noodling around with plans for 2,000 more acres of land on the other side of Interstate 4 that may one day hold a few more theme parks, another group of resort hotels, and other attractions.

In 2004 French company Vivendi Universal and General Electric Company completed a merger of Universal's Hollywood studio, its theme-park empire, and other U.S. entertainment assets with GE's television network NBC and cable television holdings, which include CNBC, MSNBC, Telemundo, the USA Network, and the Sci-Fi Channel.

The deal created a new company called NBC Universal, which will compete with entertainment giants Walt Disney, Viacom, and News Corp, owner of Fox

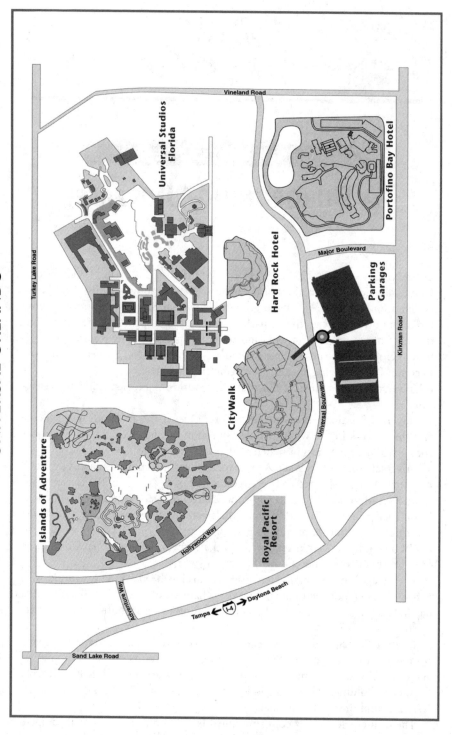

UNIVERSAL ORLANDO

Universal Studios Islands of Adventure by night. *Copyright © 1999 Universal Studios Orlando*

and DirecTV. NBC Universal is 80 percent owned by GE; as part of the deal, Vivendi was granted the option to sell its 20 percent stake at market prices beginning in 2006.

Universal is the country's third-largest motion-picture studio, behind Sony and Disney's Buena Vista. Some analysts say the new company may sell off its theme park operations to concentrate on television and film holdings.

THE UNIVERSAL STORY

It was almost a century ago that movie legend Carl Laemmle began to allow visitors—at 25 cents a head—to come to his studios to watch silent movies being made. The tours at Universal Film Manufacturing Company in Hollywood were stopped when sound was added to film; in 1964 the renamed Universal Studios reopened its doors to visitors. Universal's Hollywood lot became the third most popular tourist attraction in the nation. On the tour visitors board trams that take them in and around the historic back lot and soundstages of Universal City and along the way into some very special attractions based on some of the movie company's greatest hits. In 1990 Universal moved east to Florida with the opening of Universal Studios in Orlando. Here are a few things to know about the sprawling resort, now home to two theme parks:

Universal Orlando Tickets

Prices were in effect in early 2007 and are subject to change. One-day tickets are valid at either Universal Studios Florida or Universal Studios Islands of Adventure. Multiday tickets allow moving back and forth between the parks on any day the tickets are in use. Prices do not include tax. Universal Orlando offers a variety of discounts such as AAA, AARP, HIA, and the Orlando MagiCard, and offers a discount for online purchases at www.universalstudios.com. From time to time Universal offers a second- or third-day free extension to one-day or two-day passes.

	ADULT	CHILD (ages 3 to 9)
ONE-DAY	$63.00	$52.00
Admission to Universal Studios or Islands of Adventure on a single day.		
ONE-DAY/TWO-PARK	$77.00	$67.00
TWO-DAY/TWO-PARK	$109.95	$109.95
Admission to Universal Studios and Islands of Adventure for two days; unused days do not expire. Includes park-to-park entrance on same day. Also includes free CityWalk Party Pass.		
SEVEN-DAY/TWO-PARK	$85.00	$85.00
EXPRESS PLUS PASSES	$99.95	$99.95
Bypass the regular lines at many attractions at the Universal Studios Florida or Islands of Adventure theme parks. Prices vary from $15 to $40 for a one-day, one-park upgrade, or $25 to $50 for a two-day, two-park upgrade, depending on the time of year; the highest prices apply when you might need the pass the most.		
TWO-PARK PREMIER ANNUAL PASS	$179.95	$179.95
Entrance to both parks every day of the year. Includes discounts on food and merchandise and lodging at on-site hotels.		
TWO-PARK POWER ANNUAL PASS	$119.95	$119.95
Free parking and discounts on food and merchandise and lodging at on-site hotels. Not valid during peak summer periods, Christmas, and spring break periods.		

ORLANDO FLEXTICKETS

Prices were in effect in 2006 and are subject to change. Prices do not include tax. Visit any of the parks within the same day. Parking fee required only once each day at first park visited.

	ADULT	CHILD
Four-Park Orlando FlexTicket	$189.95	$155.95
Unlimited admission to Universal Studios Florida, Universal Studios Islands of Adventure, SeaWorld Orlando, and Wet 'n Wild Orlando. Valid fourteen consecutive days.		
Five-Park Orlando FlexTicket	$234.95	$199.95
Unlimited admission to Universal Studios Florida, Universal Studios Islands of Adventure, SeaWorld Orlando, Wet 'n Wild Orlando, and Busch Gardens Tampa Bay. Valid fourteen consecutive days.		

Parking	$10.00
Preferred Parking	$14.00
Valet parking	$16.00

For information call (407) 363–8000, or consult www.universalorlando.com.

■ Universal Studios Florida is more than twenty years newer than most of Walt Disney World, and Universal Studios Islands of Adventure is as state of the art as theme parks come. Both parks include some of the most spectacular and modern rides and attractions in the world, well beyond Pirates of the Caribbean.

■ The facility is a working studio, producing television shows, music videos, commercials, and the occasional movie.

■ Universal Studios CityWalk offers some very sophisticated places to eat and to party, and best of all, it sits at the entrance to both theme parks. You can break away from the rides for lunch or dinner, or end your day there. This is a worthy competitor to Downtown Disney at Walt Disney World.

A ferry leaves CityWalk for one of the hotels.

The best times of year to come to Universal Orlando are the same as for other area attractions. Arrive between September and November, between Thanksgiving and Christmas, or in mid-January, and you may be able to walk around like you own the place. Show up during Christmas break, Easter vacation, or midsummer, and you'll meet what seems like the entire population of Manhattan, Boston, or Cleveland in front of you in line. Universal Orlando is open 365 days a year.

Hours of operation of the parks are adjusted based on projections for attendance and are subject to change. Check before you make plans for late evenings. Some of the shows are opened on a staggered basis. When you first walk in the door at a quiet time of year, you may find that some of the shows don't offer performances before 11:00 A.M. or noon; head for the rides first.

UNIVERSAL EXPRESS PLUS

Few things are less exciting to theme-park visitors than to find ninety-minute waiting lines at attractions. Lines will never completely go away, but Universal Studios joined Walt Disney World in offering guests a way to make an appoint-

How to Get to Universal Orlando

Universal Orlando is located near the intersection of I–4 and the Florida Turnpike in Orlando. The main entrance is about a half mile north of I–4 at exit 75B–Kirkman Road (Highway 435). Another entrance is located on Turkey Lake Road.

From Orlando International Airport: Take 528 west (the Beeline Expressway) toward Tampa and Walt Disney World. Watch for signs to I–4 east (to Orlando); take the Universal Studios exit 75B.

From Walt Disney World: Take I–4 east (to Orlando) to the Universal Studios exit 75B. Or take Universal Boulevard (formerly Republic Drive) into the park.

ment for a bug hunt with the Men in Black or to zoom with mythical monsters at Dueling Dragons. At Universal Studios, though, special access comes at a cost, although it does not require visitors to obtain a scheduled admission pass.

The new scheme, instituted by Universal in 2006, is called Express Plus, and it costs between $10 and $50 above the price for an admission ticket, depending on the time of year and the number of days.

VERY, VERY IMPORTANT PERSONS

Universal Studios offers two types of VIP tours for people who hate to wait in line. (Like, who doesn't?) The basic VIP tour is a five-hour guided walking tour of either one of the Universal parks with as many as twelve guests; two-park tours take about seven hours to complete. Visitors are given priority entrance to at least eight attractions. Even your car gets special treatment: The package includes free valet parking.

At Universal Studios Florida the tour usually includes Revenge of the Mummy, Jaws, Twister, Back to the Future: The Ride, E.T. Adventure, and Men in Black: Alien Attack. At Universal's Islands of Adventure, the tour usually visits Incredible Hulk Coaster, Dudley Do-Right's Ripsaw Falls, Jurassic Park River Adventure, The Amazing Adventures of Spider-Man, The Cat in the Hat, Dueling Dragons, The Eighth Voyage of Sindbad, and Dr. Doom's Fearfall.

Prices vary depending on time of year, with higher rates on busiest days. Universal offers nonexclusive tours that gather together strangers for the day, and exclusive tours in which you can invite as many as a dozen friends and family or go all by yourself for the day.

In 2006, available VIP tours included:

- **One-day/one-park nonexclusive Tour.** $100 to $120 per person.
- **One-day/two-park nonexclusive Tour.** $125 to $150 per person.
- **One-day/one-park exclusive tour.** $1,400 to $1,600 for a group of as many as twelve persons.
- **One-day/two-park exclusive tour.** $1,700 to $2,000 for a group of as many as twelve persons.

The tours do not include lunch. As expensive as the tours are, they may make sense if you are forced to visit the park on a day when all the major rides have ninety-minute waits. About a dozen tour guides are available. One downside is that you'll miss some of the clever entertainment presented in the waiting lines; then again, you'll miss the waiting lines. For information and reservations for a VIP tour, call Universal Studios VIP Tours at (407) 363–8295.

UNIVERSAL TIME- AND MONEY-SAVING TIPS

One way to save time, and perhaps a bit of money, is to purchase your tickets ahead of time from Universal's Web site, www.universalorlando.com. The site sometimes offers special ticket deals not available at the gates. You can arrange to pick up tickets at the park or pay to have them shipped to you.

You cannot bring a cooler past the turnstiles, but there's no rule against stuffing a sandwich and a plastic bottle of soda or juice in a backpack. It's a long hike (and moving sidewalk) from the parks to the garage, but you could save quite a bit of money by packing a lunch and keeping it in a cooler in your car.

Unless the parks are very, very crowded (in which case you might want to rethink your schedule), Preferred and VIP parking offer only slightly better parking options than a space in the regular section of the garage. One important tip: Write down the name of the level and the spot where you are parked and keep it in your wallet. Don't expect to rely on your tired memory ten hours later—the garage is huge, and if you're anything like me, you'll have little chance of remembering whether you left your nondescript white rental car in King Kong or Jurassic Park and whether you went up or down an escalator to the moving sidewalk.

CHAPTER SIXTEEN

UNIVERSAL STUDIOS FLORIDA

RIDE THE MOVIES, and then surf the TV shows. While you're at it, immerse yourself in one of the most thematically consistent theme parks in the world. Universal Studios Florida is a place where fans of Hollywood's greatest hits can extend the experience of the big screen into thrilling and clever state-of-the-art rides and shows. This is the home of *The Mummy, Jaws, The Terminator, E.T.,* and *Beetlejuice*. Kids of all ages can meet Woody Woodpecker, Barney, Fievel, Curious George, Jimmy Neutron, and Shrek. Fans of the classics can pay tribute to Lucille Ball, Hollywood makeup magicians, stunt artists, and even animal-star actors.

And then there is the supremely weird world of *Men in Black,* the ultimate bug hunt. The huge techno-thriller ride merges a high-tech ride mechanism with some of the liveliest animatronics in Orlando. There's also Woody Woodpecker Kidzone, home of *Animal Planet Live!,* E.T. Adventure, *A Day in the Park with Barney,* Fievel's Playland, Woody Woodpecker's Nuthouse Coaster, and the wet and wild Curious George Goes to Town.

The wraps have come off Revenge of the Mummy—The Ride, a high-tech indoor roller coaster that salutes the successful *Mummy* films with what its creators call a psychological thrill ride. And then an even creepier offering arrived: *Fear Factor Live,* which invites guests to stick their head in a box of scorpions, eat chocolate-covered bugs, or dangle from a rope . . . and pay for the privilege.

Nickelodeon Studios, which used to tape some of its shows at the park, pulled out in 2005, taking with it the famed Green Slime Geyser. A number of the channel's cartoon characters are still featured in Orlando, though.

Bigger, flashier, louder . . . and circular: In 2006, the park introduced *Universal 360,* a new show that projects the sights and sounds of some of Hollywood's greatest hits onto three-story-high spheres floating in the lagoon, plus one of the largest laser displays in Florida, accompanied by music and fireworks.

Images will come from within the four spheres and from locations all around the lagoon. The screens will be locked into place for the nightly show, but they can be moved for special events, possibly to add a bit of special panache to Halloween Horror Nights or holiday celebrations. The show is expected to be presented through the summer season.

ATTRACTIONS AT UNIVERSAL STUDIOS FLORIDA

■ WORLD EXPO

▌MUST-SEE▐ Revenge of the Mummy—The Ride

If an encounter with the Mummy is not scary enough for you, how about meeting up with the creepy guy while zooming forward and backward and on your side . . . in near-complete darkness. There's a bit of weightlessness, some 3.5-G weigh-downs, and, oh yes, a flaming ceiling, too.

You'll enter into the Museum of Antiquities, which is actually the set of yet another *Mummy* movie. Strolling among the cameras, klieg lights, and costumes, you'll see some snippets of a behind-the-scenes documentary being made about the new movie.

Wonder of wonders: It seems that strange things have been happening on the set. Some members of the crew think the place may even be . . . cursed. It seems possible that this movie set may actually be a real archaeological dig, and perhaps there's been a bit of extracurricular grave robbing.

Be that as it may, you're given the extraordinary opportunity to take a little train ride into the Mummy's catacombs. The vehicles are industrial carts used by the archaeologists to bring supplies into the dig, and discoveries out. The train starts out slowly, like a dark ride.

It won't take much of a ride before you realize that things really are a bit askew: Parked off to the side is another train, this one filled with tourists just like you, wearing theme park T-shirts, holding cameras . . . and quite mummified. This is not a good thing.

One of the mummies manages to croak out a

MUST-SEES

Revenge of the Mummy—The Ride
(World Expo)

Men in Black: Alien Attack
(World Expo)

Back to the Future: The Ride
(World Expo)

Fear Factor Live
(World Expo)

E.T. Adventure
(Woody Woodpecker's Kidzone)

Animal Planet Live!
(Woody Woodpecker's Kidzone)

Earthquake—The Big One
(San Francisco/Amity)

Jaws
(San Francisco/Amity)

Twister
(New York)

Shrek 4-D
(Production Central)

Jimmy Neutron's Nicktoon Blast
(Production Central)

Terminator 2 3-D
(Production Central)

UNIVERSAL STUDIOS FLORIDA

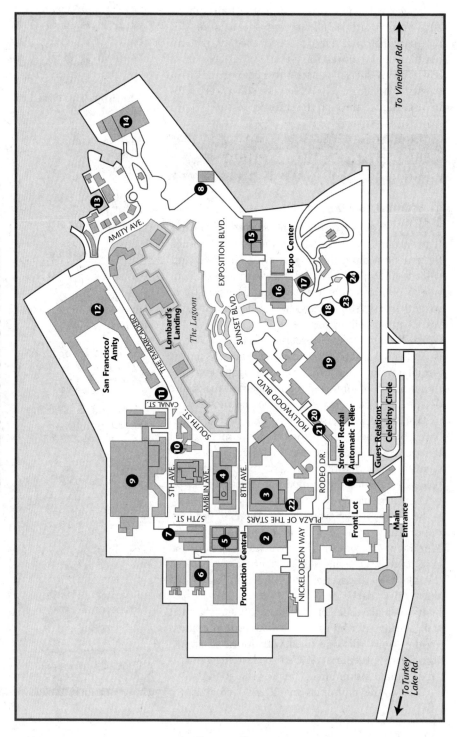

UNIVERSAL STUDIOS FLORIDA

① Production Central Information
② Jimmy Neutron's Nicktoon Blast
③ *Shrek 4-D*
④ Future attraction
⑤ The Boneyard
⑥ Production Studios
⑦ *Twister*
⑧ Men in Black: Alien Attack
⑨ Revenge of the Mummy—The Ride
⑩ Performance stage
⑪ *Beetlejuice's Graveyard Review*
⑫ Earthquake—The Big One
⑬ Jaws

⑭ *Fear Factor Live*
⑮ Back to the Future: The Ride
⑯ *Animal Planet Live!*
⑰ *A Day in the Park with Barney*
⑱ Fievel's Playland
⑲ E.T. Adventure
⑳ *Universal Horror Make-Up Show*
㉑ *Terminator 2 3-D*
㉒ Lucy: A Tribute
㉓ Woody Woodpecker's Nuthouse Coaster
㉔ Curious George Goes to Town

warning, but then the chief mummy appears with the ultimate threat: He'll be happy to take our souls. The train moves on to a dark room, and suddenly animatronic warriors burst out of the walls toward the train. Huge flames erupt from an altar, and the ceiling fills with fire. As the train rolls forward toward a descending stone door, it suddenly drops below.

That may sound like a successful escape, but actually the train has arrived at what is obviously a dead end. After that sinks in for a moment, the train is suddenly launched backward and uphill into a roller-coaster ride through the interior of the tomb. The track never goes completely upside down, but there are turns banked as much as eighty degrees and a few very sharp drops in total darkness.

Along the way you'll see computer-generated special effects and creatures projected onto fog and mist and hear a soundtrack intense enough to wake the dead.

The Revenge of the Mummy is a very successful merger of a scary dark ride, cinematic special effects, and a state-of-the-art roller coaster using linear induction motors, which allow smooth and rapid launches of the train in either direction and varying speeds. The ride builds on and improves on other fabulous rides, such as Indiana Jones at Disneyland, its cousin Dinosaur at Disney's Animal Kingdom, Journey to Atlantis at SeaWorld Orlando, and one of the archetypes for indoor thrill rides, Space Mountain at Disneyland and Walt Disney World. The ride, ten years in research and development, debuted simultaneously at both Universal Studios Hollywood and Universal Orlando.

"This is in many ways the next sequel of *The Mummy*," says director Stephen Sommers, who consulted with Universal on the ride.

The ride's launch system uses the same technology employed in futuristic magnetic levitation trains, thrusting riders forward, backward, and forward again. Utilizing engineering techniques gleaned from the Mars robotic range vehicle, the attraction includes a skeleton warrior who literally leaps into the riders' vehicle to defend his netherworld tomb.

Universal's ride producers traveled to Egypt and the British Museum in

Power Trip #1: An Express Tour (for a Price)

If you're willing to pay for the privilege, you can skip the lines at most of the attractions at either of Universal's theme parks. In 2006 an Express Plus Pass sold for a premium of $10 to $40 for a one-park/one-day upgrade to a regular admission ticket, or $20 to $50 for a two-park/two-day upgrade, depending on the time of year. The highest prices apply when you might need the pass the most. Guests at one of the three hotels on Universal Studios's property can obtain a pass as part of their accommodations package.

Power Trip #2: First Things First

Lines at some of the more popular attractions can build to as much as ninety minutes on busy days. This Power Trip puts you on a fast track for the major magnets in the morning, with a more leisurely pace for the rest of the day. For thrill seekers, Revenge of the Mummy—The Ride will grab hold of most visitors; head there first or last to avoid the crowds. Tied for second place for the same crowd are the intergalactic bugs at Men in Black, the rock-'em sock-'em *Terminator 2 3-D* show, and *Fear Factor Live*.

Younger visitors are going to want to visit Jimmy Neutron's Nicktoon Blast and *Shrek 4-D*.

Head for your first target as soon as you arrive and work your way down your list until the lines get too long; grab an early lunch and venture out again when the rest of the crowd comes in for a break. The same theory usually works at dinner.

London to make the ride's shadowy interior environment more realistic. Details range from glistening golden amulets to dusty canopic jars containing the grisly remains of the haunted long-deceased royalty portrayed in the ride.

You may be be able to skip around long lines at any time of the day by volunteering for the single-rider line. The singles line, though, avoids the interesting features of the waiting queue—but saves a lot of time.

The seats in the cars are rather tight and may be a bit uncomfortable for tall or large people. More of the action occurs on the left side of the ride, so snaring a seat on that side should be a priority. Seats at the back of the cars have a slightly rougher ride than those at the front and middle.

MUST-SEE Men in Black: Alien Attack

You are aware, of course, that the twin observation towers of the New York World's Fair of 1964–1965 and the Saint Louis Arch aren't really mere American architectural landmarks. They are, of course, actually landing beacons for alien spacecraft. If you didn't know that, then maybe you also wouldn't realize that the entrance to a pavilion called "The Universe and You" isn't really an ordinary theme-park attraction, either. You see, what we've got here is the cleverly hidden global headquarters of the Men in Black (MIB) organization. And you, you're about to become the newest recruit in the MIB army.

You'll enter an elevator in what just might seem like an ordinary office building, and then come out into the fantastic coffee-break room where you can chat with some of the friendly (but very sassy) alien workforce; from there it's on to the immigration center. The ride begins with a training lecture by MIB director Zed (voiced by actor Rip Torn, who played the role in the movie) warning new trainees that aliens are living among us.

Our job is to round them up and keep track of them. In fact, a shuttle is ready to take off immediately to deport some rather nasty alien criminals to

The headquarters of the Men in Black

Planet LV-428. After a lecture on the finer points of alien spotting and the proper use of alien zappers, visitors are turned loose on their very own training mission. Ah, but something goes wrong: The space shuttle bound for Planet LV-428 has crashed, and armed aliens are running around New York City, something that—despite appearances to the contrary—is not an ordinary occurrence in the Big Apple.

Your six-passenger training vehicle (with two rows of three seats) heads out into the streets, and suddenly the bugs are everywhere: in the windows, hanging from the lampposts, and peeking out of mailboxes. There are two similar but not identical tracks, with a pair of vehicles competing against each other and the aliens. It's zap or be zapped in a wild, cosmic turkey shoot—if the alien wins a duel, your vehicle will spin out of control.

The end of the adventure lies within the slimy belly of the largest animatronic creature ever built, a warehouse-size 30-foot-tall alien bug with 8-foot teeth and 20-foot claws. You'll receive an individual score, a group score, and the score of the vehicle you competed against. There are about thirty different endings for your experience, and fellow recruit Will Smith will give you an appropriate send-off.

Men in Black is a ride-through interactive video-game experience, a wackily weird entertainment that combines the state-of-the-art ride mechanism of The Amazing Adventures of Spider-Man, some of the dizzy fun of The Cat in the Hat, and an improvement over the intergalactic target-shooting at the Magic Kingdom's Buzz Lightyear's Space Ranger Spin. The ride, located between Back to the Future and *Fear Factor Live,* is reputed to be the largest dark ride ever built, with more than an acre and a half under roof. The building is the largest at the park.

Outside the building there are free lockers to hold your stuff while you take on the aliens. Lines can build at this attraction; consider joining the fast-moving singles line to fill in open spaces on bug-zapping vehicles.

A few pointers from professional bug-zappers:

■ Any seat is as good as the next, although some of the zappers are in better shape than others. If you get one that doesn't seem to be working properly, be sure to complain to one of the ride operators at the end of the ride. You'll be doing the next rider a favor, and you just might earn a free pass to the front of the line for another try.

■ The worst possible score is "Nice try" (100,000 points); the highest score is an almost impossible 999,999.

■ The basic trick is this: Keep your finger on the trigger at all times and never let go. You'll never run out of ammunition and you just might hit something.

■ There's no rule against shooting the same alien over and over, and for some of them the points you earn will double and triple.

■ When you shoot at the aliens hiding behind the windows, your field of fire will expand to a cone, giving you a better chance of hitting them.

■ When you finally see the Big Bug, push and hold the little red button hidden under the zapper's holster for a 100,000-point bonus.

And just for fun, keep an eye out for famed director and producer Steven Spielberg. He's sitting on a park bench just short of the scanner, reading a newspaper (with an article about *Jurassic Park 3* on the front page). Watch carefully, and the newspaper will lower to reveal an alien holding up Spielberg's head.

▓ *MUST-SEE* ▓ Back to the Future: The Ride

Dive into the world of the record-breaking movie trilogy *Back to the Future* in Universal's incredible simulator adventure. This is about as wild a ride as anything you'll find in Florida, with the possible exception of the real Space Shuttle.

It seems that weird Doc Brown is back home and conducting new time-travel experiments. He has created another vehicle—an eight-passenger Time Vehicle that is faster and more energy efficient than anything before . . . or since. That's the good news. The bad news is that Biff Tannen has broken into the Institute of Future Technology and threatens to end the universe as we know it! It's up to you to jump into your own modified DeLorean and chase down Biff.

Surrounded by images and sound and buffeted by the motion of your flight simulator, you will soar into Hill Valley in the year 2015, blast back to the Ice Age

Don't Say You Weren't Warned

Back to the Future is described as a "dynamically aggressive ride." Visitors suffering from maladies including dizziness, seizures, back or neck problems, claustrophobia, motion sickness, and heart disorders, as well as pregnant women, are advised to sit this one out. The ride also won't work for persons of a certain size or shape who cannot fit into the seats and safety harness. We suspect you know who you are.

If you are prone to dizziness or upset stomach on wild rides like Back to the Future or the Jimmy Neutron's Nicktoon Blast, you might want to take one or two Dramamine motion-sickness tablets at the start of the day (before you take any rides). They work like a charm. Check with your family doctor first, especially if you are taking any other medications or if you have any allergies or unusual conditions. And be aware that the pills may make you a bit sleepy; you may want to assign a designated driver for the end of the day.

for a chilling high-speed encounter with canyons of sheer ice, and explode into the Volcanic Era for a once-in-a-lifetime encounter with a Tyrannosaurus rex and then through a volcano and over the edge of a molten lava fall.

This is a state-of-the-art attraction that combines an amazing 70 mm film with a set of simulator ride vehicles (bearing Florida license plates OUTTATIME). The 80-foot-diameter domed Omnimax screens occupy all of your peripheral vision, making the screen seem to vanish and take you into the scene.

The director of the Back to the Future ride-film was renowned movie special-effects designer Douglas Trumbull, who created special effects for hits including *2001: A Space Odyssey* and *Close Encounters of the Third Kind*. The four-minute movie portion of the ride took two years to make and cost as much as a feature film. Elaborate hand-painted miniatures were created for the filming. The preshow and the movie in the ride itself were made specially for the simulator. Doc Brown (Christopher Lloyd) and Biff Tannen (Thomas Wilson) took part in the movie, but Marty McFly (Michael J. Fox) is nowhere to be seen.

The Institute of Future Technology in the waiting area features actual props from *Back to the Future* and other movies in the series, including a set of hoverboards (futuristic skateboards without wheels) and the all-important flux capacitors for time travel. Check out the bulletin board in the waiting area, which has the names of some of the visiting scientists who have offices in the building. They include guys by the names of Thomas Edison, Albert Einstein, and Francis Bacon.

Coming Attraction

If you have really sharp eyes and a good sense of balance, keep an eye out during your wild Back to the Future ride for the movie poster on the wall in Hill Valley; it advertises *Jaws 19*.

Meeting Spot

If you need to meet someone after the Back to the Future ride, pick a specific spot such as the Jules Verne Train, because there are two exits from the building. Ask for advice from one of the attendants on the proper place to wait.

There are actually two identical rides in the building, each with its own set of twelve eight-seater DeLoreans and movie dome. Each area has cars on three levels with three cars at the top, five in the middle, and four at the bottom. Universal insiders say the very best experience can be had by sitting in the front row of the center car on the second tier; dispatchers call it Car 6. This particular vehicle is in the absolute center of the movie dome, and you cannot easily see any other cars that might distract from the illusion. At about the midway point of the waiting line visitors are divided among three ramps, one to each level. If you can manage to go through portal number two to the middle level, you will have a one in five chance of grabbing a choice seat in magic Car 6. If you are concerned about getting motion sickness, you may want to try to get onto the lower level of the ride. (Speaking for myself, I prefer a Dramamine in the morning and Car 6.)

When you enter the holding room for the simulator, try to maneuver near the door to get a seat in the front of the car. (Some visitors find the small waiting room a bit confining; you can ask the attendant to leave the door open if you feel it necessary. Trust me: A much more intense experience is coming.) As you wait to board the simulator, pay attention to the little movie about time-travel safety; we enjoyed watching crash dummies "Fender" and "Bender" at work. Also note the glass case, which includes some juicy little details for fans of the film. In the famous Car 6, you'll find a notepad discussing the results of various flights in which Doc Brown reports he discussed the theory of electricity with Benjamin Franklin and philosophy with Mark Twain. On one of the flights, Brown reports he attended a presidential inauguration, noting that "she is quite a woman." When you feel the floor rumble beneath your feet, you'll know the car is returning to its base.

The DeLorean vehicles rise about 8 feet out of their garages at the start of the movie. Once in the air, four actuators drive the car—three for vertical and one for fore-and-aft movement. Although it may feel as if your car is soaring and dropping hundreds of feet, the entire range of movement for the vehicle is about 2 feet. To give the feeling of traveling through space, the cars are surrounded with a fog made from liquid nitrogen.

At one time, this was the busiest attraction in the park, and waits could extend to ninety minutes or more. The ride still draws crowds on the busiest of days, but if you come on a slow day or show up early or late in the day, you can go back to the future without spending too much of today in line.

Remember that the crowd you see out on the plaza is only about half the backup—there are internal walkways and hallways as well.

Each ride takes nearly five minutes, with about ninety-six persons entering each of the two simulator theaters at a time. By the end of a quiet day, there may be no line at all. But it still takes five minutes or so to walk into the gate, up the stairs, into a waiting room for one of the simulators, and into your seat. Before or after you join the line, check out the large prop to the left of the building. The Jules Verne Train was used in the closing scene of *Back to the Future III,* when Doc Brown returns from 1885 in this steam engine adapted to become a time machine.

MUST-SEE *Fear Factor Live*

Are you ready to pay $50 for the privilege of eating worms, sticking your head in a tub of scorpions, or diving off a helicopter into a 3-foot-wide tub of grape Jell-O? Me neither.

Participants in the *Fear Factor Live* show at Universal Studios are spared from some of the most frightening or disgusting stunts from the successful television reality show, but there should be more than enough *ee-yoos* and *aahs* to satisfy the viewers in the audience. The show, which replaces the *Wild, Wild, Wild West Stunt Show,* is the first major crossover resulting from the purchase of Universal Studios by GE, which also owns NBC, where the television show was a major hit.

In each show park guests compete against each other in a progression of extreme stunts. The stunts were developed with help from *Fear Factor*'s creators and are designed to test the physical and emotional limits of each contestant. Members of the audience can pitch in by blasting contestants with water and air and controlling obstacles on stage. In addition, audience members can spin the "Wheel of Fear" and confront their own phobias.

Participants take part in a series of progressively extreme stunts, guided by a host who reinforces the complexity and risks associated with the stunts performed in the attraction. Just like the television show, the host begins the show with a disclaimer: "The stunts you are about to see were designed and supervised by trained professionals. They are extremely dangerous and should never be attempted by anyone, anywhere, anytime." Except right here in a Universal Studios theme park, I guess.

Outside of the theater is a casting-call booth where guests are invited to audition to take part in the show. Each selected contestant is videotaped to later air during their performance.

Employing the same technology utilized in live television broadcasts, the videotaped highlights are transmitted electronically to an elaborate *Fear Factor Live* editing booth located within the attraction. The footage is edited and readied for closed-circuit broadcast during each contestant's performance.

Each performance involves as many as eighteen volunteers, and each show is different because of the varying mix of participants. The heart of the show involves three extreme stunts; at the completion of each, two participants exit via the "Walk of Shame," until one winner remains.

Stunts include:

■ **The Endurance Hang.** Six contestants stand, harnessed atop horizontal trusses 30 feet in the air. A small platform protrudes at their feet, and a thin trapezelike bar suspended by two cables hangs before them. At the proper moment the platform falls from beneath them and the six contestants attempt to hang on as long as possible. (Just to make it interesting, while they are hanging there, two children from the audience have the chance to try to distract the contestants by blasting them with "air cannons" that send out pulses of offensive odors.)

▪ **The Eel Tank Relay.** Hanging from an overhead bolt, four contestants dangle in shackles inches above the ground. In this multitasked stunt, the contestants must free themselves from the shackles and sprint across a giant spinning turntable until they reach the tank of slithering eels. A collection of signature yellow *Fear Factor* flags lie beneath the eels. The first two contestants to successfully plunge into the tank of eels, grab and secure the flags to a designated pole suspended above the rotating turntable, and ingest an unusual mixture of blended ingredients—a secret *Fear Factor Live* smoothie—move to the final challenge.

▪ **Shock 'n' Awe.** In a setting reminiscent of Frankenstein's laboratory, the two final contestants are lowered onto tables and outfitted with electrical wire contraptions. With their arms extended in front of them, the contestants are directed to rotate spinning wheels located on either side of the tables. The faster the wheels spin, the more electricity they generate. The first contestant to release the spinning wheel is eliminated; the loser is launched backwards via an elaborate reverse bungee pull that ignites a pyrotechnical explosion. Huge electrical sparks splash across the stage . . . and into the audience.

Just to keep things moving, while the contestants on stage are preparing for their big stunts, members of the audience (mostly kids) get to take part in smaller excitements. Some may include:

▪ **You Are What You Eat!** Entomophagy (the art of eating insects) is practiced worldwide, delivering a delicious high-protein dinner. All of the delicacies served in *Fear Factor Live* are FDA approved. Two opposing teams of young volunteers compete for the honor of devouring the most chocolate-covered insects.

▪ **The Desert Hat Challenge.** The lucky volunteer sits on stage with a large Plexiglas box carefully placed over his or her head. The goal: Stay calm inside the box after it is filled with a load of emperor scorpions. (The emperor scorpion is the largest of all known scorpions, with some giants reaching up to 8 inches in length and weighing more than two ounces. Emperor scorpions are not deadly, though their sting could be painful.)

Fear Factor Live is produced similar to a live broadcast, with eight fixed cameras strategically positioned throughout the attraction and accompanied by several roving cameras. Technicians capture action as it occurs and feed it back to an editing suite, where the footage is cut and broadcast onto a pair of 10-foot-tall screens.

Each thirty-minute show accommodates as many as 1,500 guests. A similar show was also opened at Universal Studios Hollywood.

■ WOODY WOODPECKER'S KIDZONE

▪▪MUST-SEE▪▪ E.T. Adventure

One of the best-loved movies of all time is given life in this imaginative ride, which begins where the film *E.T.* left off. You will share a bicycle with our favorite extraterrestrial in a voyage across the moon to save E.T.'s home, a planet dying for lack of his healing touch. In celebration of the twentieth anniversary of the making of the film, the ride was given a reworking that nearly doubled its passenger capacity and added some new features.

As marvelous as the ride itself is, don't overlook the incredible fantasy world of the waiting area. Video monitors display a documentary about the making of the film with cast members Drew Barrymore, Henry Thomas, and Dee Wallace Stone, along with insight from director Steven Spielberg on how he brought his vision to life. Guests in line also see a video presentation by Search for Extraterrestrial Intelligence (SETI) scientist Frank Drake, who offers commentary on the film from a scientific perspective and demonstrates a sampling of radio frequencies picked up by radio telescopes searching for extraterrestrial life.

In the preshow room an introduction by Spielberg tells the story of E.T.'s quest to save his home after receiving an urgent message from his teacher, Botanicus. Your own adventure starts when you register at the door and are cast as an actor in the coming adventure; be sure to hold on to the special card you are given until it is collected as you climb onto your bicycle.

The entrance line wends its way through a mysterious redwood forest populated with all sorts of human and otherworldly creatures. All around you government agents search for E.T. Finally, you are at your bicycle—enlarged to include twelve seats. As your bicycle takes off, you are pursued by police cars with searchlights. You'll seem to climb higher and higher through a fiber-optic star field, until the city beneath you looks like a toy set. Director Steven Spielberg created a phantasmagoric cast of new characters for the adventure, including Botanicus, Tickli Moot Moot, Orbidon, Magdol, Big Zoms, Tympani Tremblies, Water Imps, Horn-Flowers, Gurgles, Squirtals, and Churtles. Will you arrive home at the Green Planet in time? Well, yes. The celebration begins as E.T.'s friend Tickli Moot Moot laughs again, Orbidon sparkles, and Magdol sings. Baby E.T.s will dance and play all around you, and E.T. will thank you . . . personally.

The huge miniature city beneath your bicycle includes 3,340 tiny buildings, 250 ultracompact cars, and 1,000 streetlights. The stars twinkle from some 4,400 points of light. The music for the ride was written by Academy Award–winning composer John Williams, also responsible for the movie score.

▪MUST-SEE▪ *Animal Planet Live!*

Animal stars, including many refugees from animal shelters, take center stage at *Animal Planet Live!* The show brings the Animal Planet television network's favorite shows together with behind-the-scenes movie magic. *Animal Planet Live!* features video clips from such popular Animal Planet television shows as *Emergency Vets, The Planet's Funniest Animals, The Jeff Corwin Experience, Wild on the Set,* and the network's lively animal sports programs.

Many of the animal stars featured in *Animal Planet Live!* have extensive credits in film and television production. In recent years the stars of the show included:

▪ Meesha, the talented gray Himalayan who costarred with Robert De Niro and Ben Stiller as Jinx, the toilet-using cat, in *Meet the Parents.*

- Sniffles, a rescued raccoon, who shared the spotlight with Jim Carrey in *Ace Ventura: Pet Detective.*
- Spooner, a four-year-old Australian shepherd, who was discovered at an animal shelter before landing his breakout role in the Baha Men's video "Who Let the Dogs Out?"

The open-air stadium, the former home of the Animal Actors Stage, can accommodate 1,500 people for its twenty-five-minute show; it is a good place to take an afternoon break when lines at attractions are longest and the sun is at its hottest.

Woody Woodpecker's Nuthouse Coaster

Equal rights for kids: Why should adults have all the thrills? In 1999 the Woodster arrived with his own kid-size roller coaster, installing a brilliant red 800-foot-long track through a cartoon factory, and there are lots of small surprises for young riders. This ride is not The Hulk or Dueling Dragons—the monster rides next door at Universal Studios Islands of Adventure—but then kids aren't allowed on those coasters anyway. Think of Nuthouse Coaster as a thrill ride with training wheels.

The coaster reaches a top speed of 22 miles per hour and climbs to a maximum height of 28 feet; the sixteen-car train takes ninety seconds from start to finish. Riders must be at least three years old and able to sit up; kids under 48 inches tall must be accompanied by an adult.

Woody Woodpecker's Nuthouse Coaster. *Copyright © 1999 Universal Studios Orlando*

Curious George Goes to Town

Curious George Goes to Town

Everyone's favorite mischievous monkey now has a home at Universal Studios Florida. (For the record, he pushed aside the creepy Psycho House movie false front that had stood on a hill nearby. We suppose that's a good thing.)

It's a wet and wonderful world. It seems that George has let loose a bit of havoc by freeing the animals from their cages, leaving the doors open for kids to climb through. Following George's footsteps into the town's plaza there's a dream of a playground, centered around a room packed with 12,500 foam balls to throw, shoot, and dump on each other. Outside, a pair of balconies face each other across the plaza with water cannons. Up above, two 500-gallon buckets fill up every few minutes and then dump their load on watchers below. Restrooms are nearby for changing clothes.

Fievel's Playland

Now here's serious entertainment for the very youngest visitors to Universal Studios, and a good place to burn off some energy. The playground, based loosely on the *American Tail* animated movies, is located between the E.T. Adventure and *Animal Planet Live!* The surroundings are padded with a soft absorbent surface to protect kids who might fall. It includes a carnival air pillow for jumping and a 30-foot climbing net.

The kids-only water slide has a measuring post at about 40 inches that says: IF YOU AIN'T THIS TALL, BRING AN ADULT. Another sign warns that the slide will give you wet breeches, and this is quite true. The slide itself, on a small raft, is short and not nearly as wild as bigger rides at water parks. The line for the slide can

Studio Lingo

As you stroll the back lot, look for the three types of movie sets. A "facade" is a false front that has nothing behind it. A "shell" has a front, back, and side, but no useable interior space. A "practical set" is a shell that can be used for movies or other purposes.

become quite long, and parents who do not accompany their kids will probably want to park themselves at the bottom of the slide to retrieve them.

It might be possible to let your kids run loose at the playground while an adult waits in line at E.T.; I'd suggest you keep them out of line for the water slide, though, since it would be impossible to retrieve them quickly if they were way up in the queue.

A Day in the Park with Barney

This interactive musical show and hands-on educational playground stars the ubiquitous purple dinosaur; his best friend, Baby Bop; and her big brother, BJ. Actors at the 350-seat theater-in-the-round teach lessons about life through song, dance, and play.

Special effects take guests through the seasons of the year with wind, falling leaves, light rain, and even snow; clouds and stars appear magically on a projection screen. Songs include some of Barney's favorites, such as "Mr. Knickerbocker," "If You're Happy and You Know It," and his chart-topping hit, "I Love You." Adults are excused unless accompanied by an insistent youngster.

Visitors enter the attraction through a landscaped park to a central courtyard where a statue of the dino-star is surrounded by playful streams of water. Gently winding paths meander through the park, inviting guests to try out the interactive Humming Stone, a kaleidoscope, or the sand sculpture wheel.

The centerpiece is the Barney Theater, of course. In the preshow area, visitors are met by a new character, Mr. Peekaboo, a bumbling but good-hearted fellow who introduces himself to the crowd with a lighthearted but forgetful song. When children remind him of who they came to see, he urges them to use their imaginations . . . encouraged by a colorful waterfall wall that beckons them into the theater.

After the show children of all ages are invited into Barney's backyard, which features interactive delights that include a water-harp that plays music as visitors run their fingers through its streams of water, and a wood-pipe xylophone. Brightly colored rocks emit musical tones when stepped on, and rainbow lights sparkle everywhere.

■ SAN FRANCISCO/AMITY
▮▮▮ *MUST-SEE* ▮▮▮ Earthquake—The Big One

Why in the world would any sane human being want to travel all the way to Orlando, fork over a not-small number of hard-earned bucks, and then wait in a long line for the privilege of walking right into a devastating earthquake? Well, it has to be because this ride is devastatingly fun. This spectacular attraction is based on the 1974 motion picture *Earthquake*, which was the first movie in history to win an Academy Award for special effects. (Before the ride begins, be sure to check out the photos along the walls of the preshow area. Universal researchers uncovered a treasure trove of photos from the family of a survivor of the 1906 San Francisco earthquake.)

Six visitors—usually three women, a man, and two kids—are picked as extras and "grips" for a demonstration of movie special effects. The kids get to fulfill an ultimate fantasy: dropping (foam) boulders on a bunch of adults. The male extra is in for a surprise dive.

Before the action you'll see a short film about some of the special effects used in the original movie. Most interesting is probably the miniature city constructed for one of the most spectacular scenes in the movie. It took six months to build, at a cost of about $2.5 million, and about six minutes to destroy; the actual sequence in the movie takes even less time than that.

I'd suggest you move all the way across the rows in the demonstration area so you can move quickly to the train for your choice of seats. When the demonstration is over, you will enter into a re-creation of a subway station in Oakland and board a subway train heading to Embarcadero Station in San Francisco.

The front of the 200-seat train is to your left; the best car for the ride is the second car from the front. The first row of each car has a somewhat blocked view; try to grab a seat in the middle. The right side of the train (the far side of the row as you get in) has the best view of the flood; the left side of the train (where the last person in the row gets on board) is closest to the explosions and the train crash.

The train pulls out of the station and under the bay to Embarcadero Station. Suddenly, something goes very wrong. The train begins to shake violently, lights flicker, and the ceiling starts to collapse. The street above your head caves in, and a huge propane tanker truck crashes through the ceiling and toward you. But that's only the beginning: Another train bears down on you at high speed, aiming for a head-on crash. Finally, a huge tidal wave races your way. Cut!

Heavy Effects

The special effects of Earthquake—The Big One are among the most spectacular ever created for an amusement park. To begin with, the rocking and rolling of the simulated earthquake would actually register a whopping 8.3 on the Richter scale. The mega-tremor releases 65,000 gallons of (recycled) water every six minutes. The falling roadway slab weighs 45,000 pounds. By the way, the tracks themselves remain stable; all of the rocking and rolling is done by lifters within the train itself.

▌▌▌▌ MUST-SEE ▌▌▌▌ Jaws

Just when you thought it was safe to go back to Florida, Universal Studios went and opened Jaws, a spectacular ride based on the movie classic that kept millions out of the ocean thirty years ago . . . and still does. The ride was given a sprucing-up and some of the effects turbocharged a bit in 2006; the flames, splashes, and the teeth are bigger and better than ever.

It's always the Fourth of July when you visit the picturesque seaside resort of Amity. You can walk the boardwalk and try your hand at carnival games or grab a sticky snack. And, of course, you are certainly going to want to hop aboard the Amity Harbor tour boat for a peaceful cruise.

Out of Business

On the streets of San Francisco, note the impressive facade of Ferries & Cliff, one of the biggest department stores in the city at the turn of the twentieth century. It collapsed in the great earthquake of 1906 and was never rebuilt, except at Universal Studios.

The five-minute jaunt starts out well enough. The vicious shark that had previously terrorized Amity hangs lifeless from a hook in the village. What could possibly go wrong? Well, okay, we imagine you have guessed what lies ahead. Your boat will motor gently around the corner and past a pretty little lighthouse to find a wrecked tour boat just like the one you're in. A few moments later the harbor explodes with terror as an awesome 32-foot-long, three-ton killer great white shark arrives to invite all of you to lunch. His lunch, that is. It starts with a quick glimpse of a dorsal fin that zips past and then under your boat. Then he comes back!

Your boat captain will attempt to save the day, firing rifle grenades in a desperate attempt to stop the attacker. Somehow he will steer the boat into the safety of a deserted boathouse. Hah! Suddenly there's a crash on the side of the boathouse, and the wall all but comes down with the force of Jaws breaking through.

Now it's a race for survival as the boat is chased by the frenzied creature. The captain wildly fires his gun, hitting a chemical tank along shore, and the lagoon fills with burning fuel as he attempts to break for safety on a barge that carries the main power supply cable to Amity Island. Once again the shark attacks, but

Jaws attacks a passing boat.

this time he grabs hold of the main power cable: instant fish fry! At last you're safe . . . right?

Some young visitors may find the explosions and the hot steam that envelops you at the end of the ride frightening; the fright level of the Jaws ride has been ratcheted up a bit in recent years. The left side of the boat is definitely the place to be for the more adventurous traveler; that's the side closest to the explosions, fire, Jaws, and . . . water.

The fifth row of the boat lines up directly with the shark in some of the most spectacular scenes. When the ride first opened, Universal set decorators included a pair of mouse ears in the shark's mouth, but the top brass decided it was too scary for youngsters . . . and Disney.

> ## Expensive Stains
>
> The New York streets are made of concrete; a mold was applied to make the roads appear to be constructed of cobblestones. All of the cracks in the road, bubble gum on the sidewalks, and rust stains on the stone (Styrofoam, actually) walls were applied by artists.

The Jaws ride employs space-age underwater technology never before used in an amusement attraction. The 32-foot shark is made of steel and fiberglass, with a latex skin; its teeth are made of urethane. When it attacks, it moves through the water at realistic shark speeds of 20 feet per second, with thrusts equal to the power of a 727 jet engine. The seven-acre lagoon holds five million gallons of water, and there are eight boats. Much of the New England memorabilia scattered about was found in Gloucester, Massachusetts, and surrounding fishing towns.

Other Attractions in San Francisco/Amity

Amity Games. Down by the waterfront, there's a movie-set version of a boardwalk, complete with games of chance that in recent years have included Short Shot basketball, Milk Can Menagerie, Shark-Banger (a version of the familiar whack-a-mole game), Wave Roll, Goblet Lob, Quarter Pitch, Hoop Toss, and Dolphin Dash.

■ NEW YORK
MUST-SEE Twister

Here's your chance to step into a room with a murderous tornado. That's the story line of this spectacular attraction, based on the wildly successful movie of the same name and basically the same story.

Guests entering into the waiting line find themselves in an outdoor field littered with re-creations of some of the film's props and artifacts. The setting is Wakita, Oklahoma, population 585. You'll see old farm equipment, an Esmoo Dairy truck with its signature cow symbol, and a collection of storm-tracking vehicles. Monitors overhead show footage of actual tornadoes.

Eventually you'll make your way into the preshow area, where actor Bill Paxton deadpans his way through an introduction to the art and special effects used in the film. The 300-mile-an-hour twister in the film, Paxton says, is classified as an "F5, a once-in-a-lifetime monster tornado." Some call a twister of that magnitude the "finger of God," he tells us. Actress Helen Hunt livens up the place

A New York street set

later with more details about filming in and around the real town of Wakita, in "tornado alley." Some of the scenes in the film, we learn, were enhanced with the winds produced by a commercial jet engine. The room is decorated with actual props from the film.

We enter into what is left of Aunt Meg's home, destroyed by a twister in the film, and from there into one last area where we look out on the Galaxy Drive-In, a scene from the movie. The marquee at the theater promises a night of horror. Drink in the details. You'll hear the sound of crickets. Look for the shadow of a worker inside Erik's Garage. If you watch very carefully, you'll see a snippet of the famous shower scene from *Psycho* on the screen.

But it's showers of another sort that grab our attention. Rain begins to pelt the drive-in; we're somewhat protected by the tin roof over the shelter where we stand. The storm begins to intensify. A window in the projection booth shatters. A storm-chaser truck, with the film's "Dorothy" experiment on its flatbed, blows in from the left and knocks over a fire hydrant. A bolt of lightning splits a tree, and the wind and rain are suddenly very intense. The flimsy tin roof over our heads doesn't provide much shelter anymore.

Finally, the event that has drawn us volunteers: A five-story tornado grows before our eyes. We feel the wind, see the finger of God, and hear its freight-train rumble. Was that an Esmoo cow flying over our heads? Then a truck slides across the parking lot to strike the gas pumps outside of Erik's Garage. A line of flame moves toward the leaking gas. Boom!—and it's over . . . and we lucky survivors get to walk out into the gift shop, a place where you can buy souvenirs that declare to the world that you have been to a place where cows fly.

Twister replaced the *Ghostbusters* attraction that had a long run there; the building was almost completely rebuilt within its exterior shell. Twister was originally scheduled to open in 1998 but was delayed out of respect for several Florida communities ravaged by real tornadoes in February of that year.

A trip through the Twister attraction will take about twenty minutes, plus the length of the waiting line. The tornado scene itself takes only about two and a half minutes. If the outdoor queue is full when you arrive, expect about an hour's wait; if the line extends out the door and onto the street, you'd probably be better off coming back later.

Beetlejuice's Graveyard Revue

The ultimate in graveyard rock, this tuneful singing and dancing show is presented in a shaded outdoor amphitheater and stars everybody's favorite creep, Beetlejuice, and a monstrous cast of characters that has over the years included Wolfman, Dracula, Frankenstein, the Phantom of the Opera, and the Bride of Frankenstein. The background music is tape-recorded, but the singing and dancing are live and very entertaining, although the very young and older adults may find it a bit loud.

Over the years it's been fun to listen to some of the inside jokes: At one show, Beetlejuice took a gander at the creepy old horror set and commented, "Hey, it looks like Tim Burton's summer home." He introduced Frankenstein as "a man

The home of *Beetlejuice's Graveyard Revue*

of many parts—all of them used." And the Bride: "this month's cover girl from *Popular Mechanics.*"

Beetlejuice's Graveyard Revue is even better at night: The crowd is usually a bit more rowdy, and the lighting effects look especially impressive against the dark sky. Check the schedule for the hours of performance.

Beetlejuice is a character on loan from Warner Brothers, while the rest of the awful actors are from Universal classics.

Other Attractions in New York

Arcade. As if you needed any more excitement, there is a state-of-the-art video arcade in the New York section that offers a good selection of current games.

◼ PRODUCTION CENTRAL

▦ MUST-SEE ▦ *Shrek 4-D*

Shrek 4-D, presented in fabulous 4-D OgreVision, is the latest installment in the fractured fable of Shrek, the swamp-dwelling 700-pound ogre with poor hygiene.

The fifteen-minute film includes new animation and special OgreVision effects, including multidimensional images, surround sound, a bit of touch, and a smidgen of smell.

Shrek 4-D picks up the tale from where the Academy Award–winning Best Animated Feature left off. Shrek is on his honeymoon with the beautiful Princess Fiona and their persistent companion, Donkey, bridging the story between the original film and the DreamWorks Pictures sequel, *Shrek II.*

When you enter the attraction, you'll be ushered into a forbidding preshow chamber based on the dark and dank recesses of Lord Farquaad's dreaded dungeons. On multiple screens, they'll be greeted by the vertically challenged Farquaad himself, who, in his first posthumous appearance, informs guests of his ghostly scheme to haunt Shrek, Fiona, and their donkey companion.

After you settle into your specially designed seats in the main auditorium, you'll put on OgreVision glasses that will transport you into the story. About those seats: They include tactile transducers, pneumatic air propulsion, and water spray nodules, and they are capable of both vertical and horizontal motion. In other words: This is not your basic lounge chair.

Once again there is trouble in the faraway kingdom of Duloc. En route to their honeymoon at enchanted Fairytale Falls, the three travelers are interrupted by the ghost of Lord Farquaad, intent on taking his fearsome revenge. The adventurers and the audience are transported into the center of an adventure including an aerial dogfight between fire-breathing dragons and a steep plunge down a 300-foot waterfall.

The film brings back the talents of Mike Myers (Shrek), Eddie Murphy (his chatterbox companion, Donkey), Cameron Diaz (Princess Fiona), and John Lithgow (the vengeful Lord Farquaad).

Production Schedule

To find out if there are tickets available for studio audiences for shows in production, or for information about films in production at the studios, call the Guest Services office at (407) 224–6355.

Shrek 4-D

If you're stuck in the waiting line, you can entertain yourself a bit by perusing the clever posters and signs. On the Duloc Community Bulletin Board you'll learn that there's a big sale at Sir Crazy Ernie's Ye Old Discount Sporting Goods Outlet, which predates Nike's slogan with its own motto: "Joust Do It!"

Some of the pillars carry copies of *The Medieval Times,* with banner headlines: "Lord Farquaad Returns from Grave!" (A smaller headline expands: "Still very very short.")

And then there are posters for features at the Duloc Googoplex: *Thelonius 2: Judgment Proof* and *Claws* are coming.

Finally, just outside the entrance to the dungeon you'll find advertisements for Dulocland, the local theme park, which sounds ever so slightly like somewhere in the Disney empire. Our favorites include Lord Farquaad's Enchanted Tick Room, located at the entrance to Parasiteland, and The Flyin' Talking Donkey. ("You'll hurl in your Tea Cups when you ride Donkbo.")

Within the doors of the dungeon, the preshow is conducted by a wisecracking host; the patter is mostly funny, although some young children may need a bit of reassurance. (If you're standing beneath the overhead Iron Maiden torture device, you may be warned you're in a designated "splash zone.")

Our guide greeted us: "Welcome, prisoners, to Duloc, the happiest totalitarian dictatorship on Earth." We received various instructions, along with warnings of floggings for misbehavior; the good news, we were told, was that after ten floggings we would receive a complimentary frozen yogurt.

The film itself is a state-of-the-art 3-D presentation that includes a few special sensory tricks and some funny puns and sly references to modern-day films. One of the fight sequences devolves into a gravity-defying kung fu sequence straight out of *The Matrix;* in a graveyard sequence, Donkey tells us, "I feel dead people."

There's also a *Star Wars* canyon chase aboard Dragon. And at the end Donkey gives proper credit: "Behind every successful donkey there's a fire-breathing dragon."

The attraction opened in 2003 simultaneously at Universal Orlando, Universal Studios Hollywood, and Universal Japan, marking the first time an Oscar-winning animated film has been developed as a film-based theme-park attraction. In Orlando the show occupies the former home of Alfred Hitchcock: The Art of Making Movies, with an hourly capacity of as many as 2,400 guests.

▌MUST-SEE▐ Jimmy Neutron's Nicktoon Blast

Got some spare time? How about assisting Jimmy Neutron, boy genius, in his quest to prevent the evil Ooblar from the planet Yokian from enslaving Earth? Go ahead—it'll be a blast.

It seems that Ooblar has stolen Jimmy Neutron's newest rocket creation, the *Mark IV.* You'll blast off on a rocket trip—along with everyone else in the specially designed theater—to follow Jimmy, his best friend, Carl, and Jimmy's faithful robotic dog, Goddard, on a wild chase that just so happens to also involve many of Nickelodeon's most popular 'toons, including SpongeBob SquarePants, the Fairly Odd Parents, Hey Arnold!, the Rugrats . . . and someone who looks a lot like Elvis. The adventure begins with a romp through a cartoon version of Universal Studios.

Jimmy Neutron's newest invention is a device that allows him to snoop on what's happening in the real world. He will discover that evil, egg-shaped aliens called Yokians are using mind control to threaten the future of Earth. You are given the chance to help him save the planet, hopping aboard a Rocket Pod to roar, spin, crash, and careen into the action.

Jimmy Neutron, star of the Academy Award–nominated film and box-office hit *Jimmy Neutron: Boy Genius,* was the first computer-generated animated character developed by Nickelodeon for simultaneous use on television, film, and the Internet. The film follows Jimmy, his dog, Goddard, and his eclectic friends and family as they experience life in Retroville. Jimmy, a typical kid who happens to be a genius, creates gadgets to improve his everyday life. But his inventions go awry more often than not, and hilarious trouble often follows.

The attraction blends a new Jimmy Neutron adventure with sophisticated computer graphics, state-of-the-art ride technology, and programmable motion-based vehicles that move in sync with the film. The vehicles were originally developed for The Funtastic World of Hanna-Barbera, the previous occupant of the building in the Production Central section of the park, not far from the main entrance.

Visitors leave the theater into a Neutron-theme play area and a gift shop. Kids (and the adults they bring with them) can enter the play area through the shop without having to wait for a seat in the theater.

SoundStage 54

Here's a high-priced parking lot for some of the vehicles and large props of current and older Universal movies. In recent years you could gawk at vehicles from films including *The Mummy Returns, Jurassic Park III, The Fast and The Furious, Blue Crush,* and *The Bourne Identity.*

■ HOLLYWOOD

MUST-SEE *Terminator 2 3-D*

He's back . . . and with a vengeance. This is a tour de force of film, live action, and computerized special effects that puts the audience in the middle of an epic battle between and among the fearsome "cinebotic" robots, stunt performers, and the reunited stars of *Terminator 2*: Arnold Schwarzenegger, Linda Hamilton, Robert Patrick, and Edward Furlong, along with director James Cameron and special-effects wizards from the series. In this newest Terminator adventure—which begins in the present day and jumps to the Los Angeles of 2029 covered in the film—Cyberdyne Systems, the dreaded creators of Skynet and its fearsome Terminator cyborgs, has moved its corporate headquarters to Universal Studios Orlando's Hollywood Boulevard.

Guests twist and turn in their seats as menacing Cyberdyne Systems "T-70" cinebotic warriors train their sights on random targets, firing across the theater. The audience will leap back in three-dimensional shock when the T-1000 Terminator "cop" from the *Terminator 2* movie morphs to life before their very eyes, then cheer with relief as Schwarzenegger's T-800 cyborg literally charges off the screen to save the day astride a 1,500-pound Harley Davidson "hog" that actually lands on the stage and then dives back into the screen and into the scene. And not to spoil the fun, but you'll want to hold on to your seats for the jaw-dropping finale. You'll understand what we mean when your feet are back on solid ground.

The show begins with a super entertaining preshow sales pitch by a Cyberdyne associate. "Imagine a world where butterflies run on batteries," she asks, expecting you to do so with happy anticipation, "where human error is a thing of the past. Our goal is complete control of global communication." Just after the associate unveils Skynet, a computer-controlled defense system, something goes wrong with the promotional video: It seems that hackers have broken into the system to warn us against Cyberdyne.

Terminator creator James Cameron, who directed this third installment of the saga, regards *Terminator 2 3-D* as a true sequel to his earlier blockbusters. "It's definitely the next film," he said. "The only difference is this film is only twelve minutes long, and you can't see it in just any theater."

Because the audience is in the present day, the story uses T-70 cinebots, a design of robots not seen in the movies, which take place several decades in the future. The six T-70s each stand 8 feet tall; they rise from their hiding places along the walls of the theater with the aid of a hydraulic system.

The attraction marked the first time interlocking three-dimensional images were projected onto multiple screens, surrounding guests in 180 degrees of action. For its climactic third act, the film opens up from one 50-foot center screen to simultaneous projection on three screens, arranged at 60-degree angles for a sense of enveloping the audience. Spanning 165 feet, *Terminator 2 3-D* was the world's largest 3-D installation when it opened, and the first to use the triple-screen setup and six 70 mm Iwerks projectors. According to its producers, the twelve-minute film was, frame for frame, the most expensive film ever produced.

Live-action portions of the film took place in a two-week shoot at Kaiser Eagle Mountain, an abandoned steel mine in Desert Center, California, rebuilt in spectacular fashion to resemble Los Angeles after a nuclear war. More than a hundred cars, trucks, and buses were hauled in from wrecking yards and strewn about the 1-million-square-foot location set. The background consisted not of mock-ups, but of actual buildings that were blown up during filming, lending a scale authenticity that surpassed many big-budget Hollywood action flicks. Additional scenes were shot on a Los Angeles soundstage, where an elaborate 24-foot "miniature" of Skynet, the pyramid-shaped headquarters of Cyberdyne Systems, was constructed. Through the magic of cinema trickery it will appear to be 800 feet tall on screen.

The show has a seating capacity of 700 and can accommodate about 2,400 guests per hour. Much of the waiting area for the show is within the Cyberdyne building; if lines extend out onto the street, you may want to come back later in the day. The best seats for the 3-D effects are from the middle to the back of the theater; the best seats to see the live action, including the arrival of the Harley on stage and the frozen breakup finale, are in the third or fourth row, in the center.

Lucy: A Tribute

On the left side of Rodeo Drive, keep your ears open for the world's largest in-door collection of Lucy screams. If you are a fan of Lucille Ball and everyone around her, you'll be enthralled with this collection of photos, scripts, and memorabilia and a continuous showing of episodes from her television show. Among my personal favorites is Lucy as part of a barbershop quartet.

There is a diorama showing how the original television show was filmed in front of a live audience. The original TV show was unusual in that the creators worked with three or four permanent sets that stood side by side in the studio, avoiding the flimsy-looking sets typical of television shows at the time. The permanent setting also allowed for more advanced lighting, allowing cameras to move quickly from one area to another. All of the sets were painted in carefully chosen shades of gray to control the contrast of the finished black-and-white film.

We don't know very many other places in the world where you can see a collection of Desi Arnaz's conga drums or view some of the original scripts from *I Love Lucy*. There's a Lucy trivia quiz, including questions like, "What was the biggest laugh in Lucy history?" Here's a hint: The answer involves Lucy, Ricky, a bunch of raw eggs, and a wild and romantic dance.

Desi Arnaz was born as Desiderio Alberto Arnazey Acha III in Santiago, Cuba, in 1917. The son of a Cuban senator, he lived in great luxury until the revolution of 1933, when his family fled the country. Arnaz worked at various jobs, including cleaning birdcages. Eventually he got a job in a band and soon became one of the leading band leaders in New York. Signed to the lead in the New York musical *Too Many Girls,* he played a Latin football player. When he went to Hollywood to play his role in the movie version of the show, he met the studio ingenue Lucille Ball, and in late 1940 they began a bicoastal marriage.

After World War II, looking for a way to work together in Los Angeles, Lucy and Desi hired the writers of Lucy's radio show *My Favorite Husband* and produced a pilot for *I Love Lucy.* Their new company, Desilu Productions, became the largest television and film production company in Hollywood. Arnaz died in 1986; Lucy passed on in 1989.

Universal Horror Make-Up Show

This show used to be called the "gory, gruesome, and grotesque" makeup show, and that pretty much sums it up, although they did leave out "gross." Most everyone loves a good monster or horror movie. Here's your chance to learn some of the secrets behind the special effects. For example, where else would you find the recipe for gore: shrimp sauce, oatmeal, and red dye.

Among the devices demonstrated in the twenty-five-minute show is the teleportation scene from *The Fly,* somewhat humorously reenacted on stage. A film clip explains how Meryl Streep is turned around in her body in *Death Becomes Her,* a special effect that involved blue-screen technology. Streep was videotaped walking backward wearing a blue bag over her head, and then her face was electronically superimposed onto the bag for the effect.

Among recent additions were elements of *Van Helsing,* which joined Universal's long string of horror films.

Some children may find the show to be much too gory, gruesome, and grotesque: Parents be warned. One extra from the audience—almost always a woman seated down front—gets her arm sliced open and suffers other simulated indignities. There are 355 seats in the theater, and visitors are often turned away at midday; go early or late on busy days. The show may not be offered during the quietest times of the year.

Universal Horror Make-Up Show

SPECIAL EVENTS

Most any day in the summer and during holiday periods the rest of the year you can expect a high school or college marching band to high-step around the park at midmorning. And Universal Studios also regularly throws itself a party for special events; call (407) 363–8000 for calendar updates. Some of the special events include:

- **New Year's Eve Celebration.** A blazing fireworks show and other seasonal entertainment welcome the new year.
- **Mardi Gras at Universal Studios Orlando.** Presented each year from mid-February through the end of March or early April, and featuring fifteen or so full-size floats from the streets of New Orleans, Universal Studio's version of Mardi Gras includes more than 200 costumed street performers, including stilt-walkers, fire-eaters, unicyclists, and ten marching bands. In addition, more than 150 elaborately costumed characters will ride on the floats; many of them are guests selected from the audience. The parade takes place nightly at closing time; admission is included in the day's ticket. In addition, major musical groups perform onstage each Saturday during the Mardi Gras celebration, and the park's restaurants will add New Orleans favorites, including crawfish, jambalaya, and étouffée. You can also buy a potent Hurricane, a rum-based drink concocted by New Orleans institution Pat O'Brien's, a restaurant that has another location at Universal CityWalk.
- **Fourth of July.** A special fireworks show, with music from movie favorites.

EATS AND TREATS

There are some interesting choices for food at Universal Studios, including a variety of foreign and ethnic foods. There are many more choices, too, with the opening of Universal CityWalk. You can leave Universal Studios Florida (get your hand stamped for reentry) and go out to lunch or dinner at CityWalk, choosing from a nice variety of unusual to haute cuisine.

In 2006 the park introduced the **Universal Meal Deal,** an all-you-can-eat day pass. For about $19 for one park or $23 for two parks on one day, you can make multiple visits to selected fast-fooderies; each time you can select an entree, side dish, and dessert. Drinks cost extra, and there is supposed to be no sharing. . . .

At Universal Studios Florida, participating restaurants in 2006 were Mel's Drive-In, Louie's Italian Restaurant, and the International Food and Film Festival. (See chapter 17 for a listing of participating eateries at Islands of Adventure.)

There is a little-used exit from the park in Production Central near Jimmy Neutron's Nicktoon Blast (and the former site of Nickelodeon Studios) that leads to Hard Rock Cafe and NBA City, as well as offers a shortcut that connects to Universal Studios Islands of Adventure and Universal CityWalk.

■ HOLLYWOOD FRONT LOT

Beverly Hills Boulangerie. Just inside the entrance gates, at the corner of Plaza of the Stars and Rodeo Drive, the Boulangerie offers a selection of sandwiches, coffee, and drinks.

Sweets include cherry turnovers, cheese Danishes, overstuffed muffins, macadamia nut and chocolate-chip cookies, croissants, hazelnut éclairs, and slices of Key lime pie, for about $2.00 to $3.00.

Cafe La Bamba. This attractive eatery lost its Mexican flavor in favor of more ordinary fare such as barbecue baby-back ribs, rotisserie chicken, and barbecue pork, for about $7.00 to $10.00. The cafe is decorated like an old villa, with fancy pillars and art (albeit with a cafeteria line within). During Universal's celebration of Mardi Gras, the restaurant takes on a New Orleans menu. A quiet bar near the entrance offers a variety of alcoholic beverages and soft drinks.

Mel's Drive-In. Here you can get burgers, hot dogs, salads, chips, and drinks in a 1950s diner, modeled after the eatery from *American Graffiti*. You can't miss Mel's: Just look for the garish pink and blue building with its large neon sign on the corner of Eighth and Hollywood Boulevard. Unless you are a child of the '50s, you may not immediately appreciate the true beauty of the pink and white 1956 Ford Crown Victoria parked next to an absolutely cherry 1957 black Chevrolet out front.

Inside, a sock-hop theme prevails, with period music and booths that have individual jukebox selectors. Check out the old 45 rpm records pasted to the wall and the pedal pushers worn by the attendants. Notice I didn't say "waitresses."

Forget the personal, at-table service you knew in the '50s, because you have to stand in line to retrieve your fast food here. You'll also have a lot of company in line at this popular place.

Schwab's Pharmacy. This classic old-time drug-store fountain is just waiting to be discovered. It's on Hollywood Boulevard next to the Brown Derby Hat Shop and hard to miss. Look for the giant blue neon sign, and walk into the bright white drug-store fountain area.

Schwab's Pharmacy

Triple A

Most of the gift shops and several of the sit-down restaurants within Universal Studios will give a 10 percent discount to AAA members; bring your card.

This is a typical 1950s drugstore, with a few booths and seating around a curved counter. Soda jerks in blue jeans, white shirts, and classic paper hats take your order and prepare the treats while you watch. The walls are decorated with vintage photos from the original Schwab's in Hollywood and some of its famous patrons.

If you remember the '50s with its custom, hand-made ice-cream treats (or even if you don't), you'll have a hard time selecting from the familiar Schwab's offerings. Main courses include hot dogs and turkey or chicken-salad sandwiches for about $6.00 or $7.00. Ice-cream cones and milk shakes sell for about $2.50 to $3.50. Schwab's is also a good place to pick up an emergency supply of aspirin, Tylenol, Rolaids, or cough drops—some of which you may need after the treats. They also sell Dramamine, useful to some for thrill-ride relief.

WORLD EXPO

International Food and Film Festival. In the rear of Expo Center, next to Back to the Future, this food court offers American, Chinese, German, Italian, and Greek fast food. The advantage of this eatery is evident to families: Everyone in the party should be able to indulge their own tastes in one place. Gyros, brats, burgers, pizza, and more, $2.00 to $8.00.

WOODY WOODPECKER'S KIDZONE

Kid Zone Pizza Company. Pizza, chicken fingers, and snacks.

SAN FRANCISCO/AMITY

Lombard's Seafood Grille. Housed in an elegant 1800s warehouse, this is, by most visitors' accounts, the most attractive restaurant in the park, with a nice view of the lagoon. Lunch entrees range from about $8.00 to $15.00 for adults and $3.50 to $5.00 for children. Dinner entrees start at about $15.00 and reach to about $25.00 for adults and $5.00 to $8.00 for children.

Specialties include steak, pasta, and seafood. Fish choices include swordfish, grouper, tuna, mahimahi, salmon, and lobster, priced at market rates from about $15 to $25. You can begin your meal with New England clam chowder or lobster bisque. Other entrees include pan-seared bison rib eye for $24 and buffalo burgers for $10.

Entrees for lunch include fish and chips, grilled chicken, crab cakes, New York strip steak, or chicken and chive fettuccine. The signature sandwiches include the Lomberger (a hamburger on a sourdough bun with Swiss, cheddar, or Boursin cheese), fried grouper on sourdough with a dill rémoulade sauce, and a veggie burger on a seven-grain bun.

Midway Grill. This is the place to get carnival fare: grilled Italian sausage with peppers and onions for about $6.00, Philly cheese steak for about $6.50, plus Nathan's hot dogs and chicken fingers.

Lombard's Seafood Grille

TD **Captain Quint's Seafood and Chowder House Restaurant.** You'd almost have to know this little eatery was here or find it by accident as it's tucked into the back of Pier 27. Draft and imported bottled beer complement the limited but rather nice selection of barbecue pork sandwiches, clam chowder, and hot dogs. Prices range from about $8.00 to $15.00.

TD **Richters Burger Company.** Named Richter, as in Richter scale, this eatery offers The Big One (a $6.00 burger with fries), The San Andreas (chicken breast on bun with fries), and The Trembler (a hot dog platter with fries). Entrees range from about $5.00 to $8.00. Located directly opposite the entrance to Earthquake, Richters's back tables have a view of the lagoon.

TD **San Francisco Pastry Company.** At the front of Pier 27, on the Embarcadero across from Earthquake—The Big One, the European cafe opens off of brick-paved streets, and the patio overlooks the lagoon. Offerings include San Francisco–style pastries and sweets, croissant sandwiches, espresso and cappuccino, and the best selection of beers at any casual restaurant in the park. Prices range from $4.00 to $8.00.

■ PRODUCTION CENTRAL

TD **Classic Monsters Cafe.** (Seasonal.) This cafe offers a gustatory celebration of some of Universal's greatest monster hits. You'll order your food from a cafeteria line and take it back to one of four monstrous dining areas stocked with artifacts and memorabilia from great movies: Egypt (including items from *The Mummy*), a Gothic haunted house (*Phantom of the Opera* and *Frankenstein*), outer space (films such as *This Island Earth*, one of the worst sci-fi movies ever made, so bad it's a classic), and a sea-creature lair (*Creature from the Black Lagoon*). Items on display include original scripts, props, posters, and costumes. The background music includes great hits from monster films and even some parodies such as *The Rocky Horror Picture Show*.

Appetizers include chef, Caesar, and chicken and shrimp Caesar salads priced from about $3.00 to $9.00. Pastas include four-cheese ravioli, penne pasta, linguine primavera, and wood-fired oven pizza from about $7.00.

■ NEW YORK

Finnegan's Bar & Grill. Finnegan's occupies a prominent position on Fifth Avenue across the street from the former home of Kongfrontation. In movie-set style, the corner Regal Cafe is just another entrance to Finnegan's. This is a typical New York City community bar, complete with brick-paved sidewalk and awning-covered entrance. The neon signs in the windows add to the festive saloon atmosphere. The pressed-tin ceilings are high and accented with hanging lights and slow-moving fans.

Traditional Irish fare is served, including stews and meat pies. Lighter items include a Blarney baguette filled with your choice of roast beef, corned beef, ham, or turkey with wedge fries for about $9.00, and a Shamrock steak sandwich, also for about $9.00. It's Saint Patrick's Day every day here, including Irish stew with lamb, potatoes, and fresh vegetables for $7.95. And there is London Times fish and chips (fish fillets in ale batter with fries and malt vinegar), wrapped in a paper cone that is a replica of the front page of the *London Times,* for about $10.50. And, of course, there is corned beef and cabbage (about $11) every day. Other offerings include shepherd's pie and bangers and mash (hot dogs and mashed potatoes), each for about $10.

Louie's Italian Restaurant. Located right on Universal's Fifth Avenue at Canal Street, Louie's offers a wide selection of Italian specialties, from antipasto to pizza, soups to salads, plus pasta and ices. You can also buy beer. The portions are large and the food fresh. Pizza is available by the slice for about $3.50 or by the pie from about $16.00 to $18.00.

CHAPTER SEVENTEEN

UNIVERSAL STUDIOS ISLANDS OF ADVENTURE

UNIVERSAL'S ISLANDS OF ADVENTURE is the most technologically advanced, wild and woolly theme park in Orlando. It's got something for everyone, with thrill rides, spectacular simulations, entertainment, worlds of wonder for children of all ages, and delights for the eye at most every turn. This is also Florida's most beautiful theme park by night, a world of fire and water, fog and light.

On 110 acres, roughly the same size as the Magic Kingdom at Walt Disney World, are the world's first duel racing roller coasters; the first combined 3-D film, live action, and moving motion base simulator; and a high-speed coaster that has a zero-G heartline inversion.

The crown jewel of Islands of Adventure is **The Amazing Adventures of Spider-Man,** an attraction that is unlike anything else anywhere on the theme-park planet. If comparisons must be drawn, think of Back to the Future and *Terminator 2 3-D*—on wheels. Then there are the awesome roller coasters. The glowing-green **Incredible Hulk Coaster** dominates the skyline as you drive by on Interstate 4 and overhangs Marvel Super Hero Island to your left as you enter the park. A couple of times a minute the area rumbles with the launch of a train 150 feet up the takeoff tunnel and then echoes with the screams of the riders as they immediately enter into an inverted zero-G roll. Not to be overlooked is the mind-boggling spaghetti bowl of red and blue tracks in the back right corner of the park; the two **Dueling Dragons** coasters run side by side, above, below, and straight at each other.

It certainly gets hot in Florida, but you'll have plenty of opportunities to take a shower with your clothes on at entertaining water rides **Dudley Do-Right's Ripsaw Falls** and **Popeye & Bluto's Bilge-Rat Barges.** You can visit places heretofore only viewed in the mind's eye, at state-of-the-art simulations

MUST-SEES

The Amazing Adventures of Spider-Man
(Marvel Super Hero Island)

Incredible Hulk Coaster
(Marvel Super Hero Island)

Doctor Doom's Fearfall
(Marvel Super Hero Island)

Dudley Do-Right's Ripsaw Falls
(Toon Lagoon)

Popeye & Bluto's Bilge-Rat Barges
(Toon Lagoon)

Jurassic Park River Adventure
(Jurassic Park)

Pteranodon Flyers
(Jurassic Park)

Dueling Dragons
(The Lost Continent)

Poseidon's Fury
(The Lost Continent)

The Eighth Voyage of Sindbad
(The Lost Continent)

The High In The Sky Seuss Trolley Train Ride!
Seuss Landing

The Cat in the Hat
(Seuss Landing)

Caro-Seuss-el
(Seuss Landing)

One Fish, Two Fish, Red Fish, Blue Fish
(Seuss Landing)

such as the **Jurassic Park River Adventure, Triceratops Discovery Trail,** and **Poseidon's Fury.** And then there is **Seuss Landing,** where the wonderfully weird world of Dr. Seuss comes to life for children of all ages.

At the park's opening ceremonies in 1999, Steven Spielberg, creative consultant to Universal Studios, gave an interesting insight to the design process: "Making a theme park is like making movies and plays, and then building an entire city to contain them." The adventure begins at the Port of Entry and continues through five "islands" connected by walkways, bridges, and a water taxi. Clockwise from the Port of Entry, you'll find Marvel Super Hero Island, Toon Lagoon, Jurassic Park, The Lost Continent, and Seuss Landing.

PORT OF ENTRY

You'll present your passport (admission ticket, actually) at a dramatic plaza in the shadow of a towering lighthouse modeled after the famous Pharos light at ancient Alexandria. If you have a moment, check out the notice about currency exchange rates at the USIOA Guest Services booth. In addition to cash, credit cards, traveler's checks, and currency from a number of major nations of today, you can also learn that USIOA values one Spanish doubloon as four pigs and one donkey, and one Alsatian franc at one goose.

Give yourself a few moments to enjoy the attention to detail around you at eye level and up above. My favorite sign in the Port of Entry: SOOTHS SAYED WHILE YOU WAIT.

Notable shops in the Port of Entry include Universal's Islands of Adventure Trading Company (the major souvenir shop of the park), Silk Road Clothiers (travel gear, leather bags, and jewelry), Island Market and Export (gourmet foods from around the world), and Ocean Trader Market (carvings from Africa, mehndi skin colorings from India, and more exotica). At the end of the shopping district lies the entryway to the park itself, a pass through a set of gates held back by impressively large chains.

Power Trip #1: An Express Tour (for a Price)

If you're willing to pay for the privilege, you can skip the lines at most of the attractions at either of Universal's theme parks. In 2006 an Express Plus Pass sold for a premium of $10 to $40 for a one-park/one-day upgrade to a regular admission ticket, or $20 to $50 for a two-park/two-day upgrade, depending on the time of year. The highest prices apply when you might need the pass the most. Guests at one of the three hotels on Universal Studios's property can obtain a pass as part of their accommodations package.

Power Trip #2: Go Early, Stay Late

Face it: Islands of Adventure is one bustling place. The biggest draws are the major thrill rides, The Amazing Adventures of Spider-Man, Dueling Dragons, and the Incredible Hulk Coaster. On a Florida sizzler (which can happen almost any time of the year, but especially from May through September), Jurassic Park River Adventure, Dudley Do-Right's Ripsaw Falls, and Popeye & Bluto's Bilge-Rat Barges are likely to draw long, hot lines of guests in search of a cooling drench. And if you're intent on riding the simple but charming Pteranodon Flyers, don't wait too late in the day either. You'll need a kid as an escort, though.

Follow the basic Econoguide strategy: Arrive early, head deep into the park to your number one goal, and try to stay one step ahead of the crowds, who will likely work their way from front to back. Eat lunch and dinner early and head for major attractions while other park visitors wait in line for food.

Remember that Jurassic Park, Dudley Do-Right, and Bilge-Rat Barges are not billed as water rides for nothing. (So, too, for One Fish, Two Fish, Red Fish, Blue Fish for the kiddies.) Consider whether you want to start the day with a wet bottom, especially on a cool day.

MARVEL SUPER HERO ISLAND

Imagine an entire island populated by superheroes the likes of Spider-Man, The Hulk, and the Fantastic Four. For most of us this place is eerily familiar, a step into the fantasy comic-book pages of yesterday and today. Just like in the cartoons, the storefronts are generic. You'll find a store named "Store," an arcade "Arcade," and a frozen-ice stand advertised as "Frozen Ice." You'll also find a trio of awesome thrill rides guaranteed to make you marvel.

UNIVERSAL STUDIOS ISLANDS OF ADVENTURE

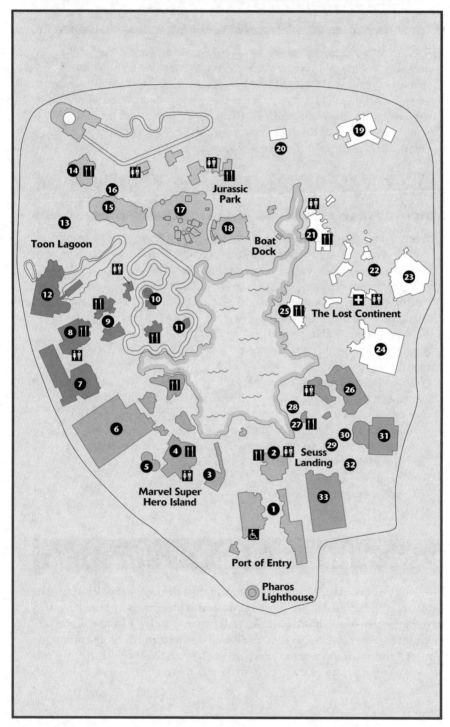

UNIVERSAL STUDIOS ISLANDS OF ADVENTURE

① Port of Entry shops
② Confisco Grille
③ Incredible Hulk Coaster
④ Cafe 4
⑤ Doctor Doom's Fearfall
⑥ The Amazing Adventures of Spider-Man
⑦ Special events
⑧ Comic Strip Cafe
⑨ Comic Strip Lane
⑩ Popeye & Bluto's Bilge-Rat Barges
⑪ Me Ship *The Olive*
⑫ Dudley Do-Right's Ripsaw Falls
⑬ Storm Force Accelatron
⑭ Jurassic Park River Adventure
⑮ Thunder Falls Terrace/Camp Jurassic
⑯ Pteranodon Flyers
⑰ Triceratops Encounter

⑱ Jurassic Park Discovery Center
⑲ Dueling Dragons
⑳ Flying Unicorn
㉑ Enchanted Oak Tavern (and Alchemy Bar)
㉒ Mystics of the Seven Veils
㉓ *The Eighth Voyage of Sindbad*
㉔ Poseidon's Fury
㉕ Mythos Restaurant
㉖ The High In The Sky Seuss Trolley Train Ride!
㉗ Green Eggs and Ham Cafe
㉘ If I Ran the Zoo
㉙ Caro-Seuss-el
㉚ Moose Juice Goose Juice
㉛ Circus McGurkus Cafe Stoo-pendous
㉜ One Fish, Two Fish, Red Fish, Blue Fish
㉝ The Cat in the Hat

MUST-SEE THE AMAZING ADVENTURES OF SPIDER-MAN

You've got to see this, though you still won't believe it. Quite simply, this is the state of the art in theme-park rides: a 3-D video, virtual-reality motion base simulator on wheels. There's nothing like it anywhere else in the universe.

There's an outdoor queue in the delivery docks of that well-known New York newspaper, the *Daily Bugle*, home of mild-mannered photographer Peter Parker. (Background information for the comically impaired: The bite of a radioactive spider changed shy high-school student Peter Parker into a superhero with the speed, agility, and strength of a spider. He earns his keep as a cameraman, acting as a one-man vigilante army whenever he can spare the time.) Eventually, we make our way into the lobby of the *Bugle*. Spend some time to soak in the attention to detail in the waiting area. It begins with a collection of headlines of recent events you may have missed while you were away on vacation; for example, "Terror Coast to Coast: Magnetic Mutant Seizes Missile Base." There are also some *Bugle* editorials by the unknowing Spider-Man detractor J. Jonah Jameson, who asks: "Is Spider-Man Through?"

Past the hallway we enter Peter Parker's office and darkroom. Look closely at the name on the door; it seems that the previous occupant of the small room was named "Broom Closet." Signs on the wall give the *Bugle*'s operating procedure: "Remember! First get the pictures. Then get the stories. And after that . . . safety first."

Next we enter the newsroom. Lights flash on old-style telephones, an incongruous mix with modern computer screens. Note the color scheme: Most everything in the background is in pale green, like the muted backgrounds of a comic book. The foreground is decorated in bright posterlike colors.

There is news in the air. Headlines trumpet: "Emergency Declared! Statue of

Short Story

Alas, the smallest visitors to Universal's Islands of Adventure will be unable to ride the fastest and wildest attractions. Don't fight the rules; they are there for the child's protection. Here are the minimum heights:

▶ **Pteranodon Flyers:** 36 inches

▶ **The Amazing Adventures of Spider-Man:** 40 inches

▶ **Jurassic Park River Adventure:** 42 inches

▶ **Dudley Do-Right's Ripsaw Falls:** 44 inches

▶ **Popeye & Bluto's Bilge-Rat Barges:** 48 inches

▶ **Doctor Doom's Fearfall:** 52 inches

▶ **Dueling Dragons and the Incredible Hulk Coaster:** 54 inches

▶ **The High In The Sky Seuss Trolley Train Ride!:** 34 inches

Note that even if a child meets one of the lower height requirements, he or she must be accompanied by an adult on restricted rides if he or she is under 48 inches in height.

Liberty Stolen!" Who could possibly have done such a dastardly deed other than Doctor Octopus, Electro, Hydro-Man, Hobgoblin, and Scream, aka The Sinister Syndicate?

Drafted as a civilian posse, we're given the chance to join with Spider-Man to retrieve the missing national treasure. Our vehicles are "Scoops," more formally known as "Surveillance Communications Patrols." A funny cartoon tells of the dos and don'ts about loading into the car. Watch carefully and see if you can spot the funny jab at the Test Track at Disney's Epcot; it comes during the cartoon's recommendation that you be sure to use the Scoop's lap bars.

Each car holds a dozen volunteers in three rows of four. Two Scoops are loaded at the same time. The rows are numbered from the rear of each vehicle (and assigned a name for a section of the *Daily Bugle*'s circulation area in New York City). Row 1 is Queens, the back row of the second vehicle in line. Row 2, Bronx, is the middle row. Row 3, Brooklyn, is the front row. In the first vehicle in line, Row 4, Coney Island, is the back of the bus. Row 5, Staten Island, is in the middle. Row 6, Manhattan, is the front row. All of the seats in the Scoop vehicle give a good view of the action. The front row offers the most dramatic views— without someone else's head between you and the action—but the middle and last rows offer the most motion.

Now we're off on a 20-block tour of New York City, a huge acre-and-a-half set where we are thrust into the middle of a battle between good and evil. Seen through our 3-D glasses, Spider-Man greets us, and then things go seriously wrong. Flaming pumpkins and spewing water pipes hurled by the forces of evil seem to fly toward riders and smash into the vehicle. It all comes to a chilling conclusion when Doc Ock takes aim at us with his Doomsday Anti-Gravity Gun. One blast sends us 400 feet in the air, and then into a 400-foot free fall. If you're wondering whether you should take out new flight insurance, remember that it's all simulated—a technology known as "sensory drop." That doesn't mean it doesn't feel very real.

Here's an insider tip: At one point on the ride, you'll pass a movie theater; there's a phone number listed for tickets and information. I'll save you the effort of trying to write it down: Call (407) 224–1783.

Here's what you'll hear: "Thank you for calling. Due to the recent unpleasantness caused by Doc Ock and his gang of villains, we will be closed until further notice or at least until Spider-Man can make our city safe again."

According to Universal Studios, the challenge in creating Spider-Man was to get guests directly involved in the action as they viewed 3-D films and moved at high speed past props and special effects. The technology employs a "moving point of convergence" and uses twenty-five large-format movie projectors and dozens of smaller projectors.

I went for a behind-the-scenes peek at the control room for the high-tech ride. There I saw with my own eyes what my mind had refused to believe. The actual rise and fall of the vehicles—including the "400-foot drop" that is at the heart of the ride—is only about 3 or 4 feet. Knowing the secret, I went back and rode the Scoop once more—and I still felt the bottom of my stomach rising to meet my throat as we "fell" forty stories.

MUST-SEE INCREDIBLE HULK COASTER

It seems that Dr. Bruce Banner is playing around with the rules of physics once again, conducting special gamma-ray accelerator tests. We lucky visitors are offered the chance to participate in the experiment. How can we say no? In a ride of about two minutes and fifteen seconds, the thirty-two passengers, seated four abreast, experience seven rollovers and plunge into a pair of deep subterranean tunnels.

Not that you're going to be able to read this book—or remember much of what I wrote here—while you're riding on The Hulk, but here's a summary of your ride. Your trip begins when your car is catapulted in three seconds up a 150-foot launch tunnel with the same force as a U.S. Air Force F-16 fighter attack jet on takeoff. After you exit from the tube at 40 miles per hour, there's an immediate twist onto your back in a weightless heartline roll more than 110 feet above the ground. The cars then dive at 60 miles per hour in a steep plunge toward the water, and then straight back up 109 feet. Still with me? Okay, now you go into a sharp twist into an upside-down roll to the right, then a tight turn and upside-down roll to the left . . . followed by yet another plunge to the water. Back up you go, into a narrow oblong loop, upside down at the top, of course.

You complete the front side of the ride with a drop to—and below—the surface of the lagoon and beneath a bridge full of gawkers crossing from the Port of Entry to Marvel Super Hero Island. Coming up from the tunnel, you make a slow, twisting climb to the left, which ends in a sideways loop. From there you're into an upside-down loop and into a semi-hidden area of the park behind the Hulk building. Out back where there are few witnesses, you flip over and then plunge upside down to Earth and immediately back up into one inverted loop and then another, and then onto your side in a small, tight loop that goes upside down at the top. If you have your eyes open, you may be able to see the end of the ride, but between here and there are a few more high-G twists and turns to burn off speed. Whew! Now you can say you've experienced The Incredible Hulk. Was it good for you, too?

Incredible Hulk Coaster

The queue for The Hulk begins outside and wends its way into the Gamma Radiation Testing Zone, your basic sci-fi cartoon laboratory with flashing lights, green overhead pipes, and video monitors that tell the story of the experiment through the words of Dr. Bruce Banner. (In case you're not an expert on all things Marvel, scientist Bruce Banner's basic constitution was altered when he was caught in the rays of a gamma bomb explosion; he's a nice enough guy as long as you don't get him angry or agitated. When he is, he transforms into the rampaging Incredible Hulk, glowing a lovely shade of green.)

Just short of the loading area, the line splits. Keep to the left for a seat in the front car, or keep to the right to enter the faster-moving line for the rest of the train. At night the metal coaster track glows an eerie green, an especially dramatic sight for guests walking across the bridge to the island; the tracks loop over and then under the walkway.

If you've got anything loose—a camera, a purse, false teeth, spare change—look for the lockers just outside the boarding area and use the space. You'd be amazed what will fall into the net below the first loop.

▋MUST-SEE▋ DOCTOR DOOM'S FEARFALL

Looming above the island are a pair of 200-foot towers of steel. Victor Von Doom, absolute dictator of the otherwise insignificant nation of Latvaria, has

much bigger goals: total world domination. The creation is Doctor Doom's infernal device to drain fear from all visitors.

You enter through the portals of the Latvarian Embassy, guarded by a squad of Doctor Doom's army in their armored finery. Doom's enemies, of course, are the Fantastic Four, although to tell you the truth, these guys did absolutely nothing to prevent the bad doctor from sending me shooting up a tower into the sky. (Before you get in line, check out the imprints in concrete from bodies that have fallen from the top of the tower. Not! Well, imprints are there, but it's a bit of showmanship by the designers of the ride.)

We lucky visitors are strapped into four-passenger

Doctor Doom's Fearfall

seats on the outside of the tower, feet dangling free below. With a sudden burst of energy, the seats zoom 150 feet up the tower; there's a brief pause of weightlessness at the top, and then a powered descent back down the track to the bottom. This ride gives many of us about as much of the feel of weightlessness as we're going to experience until we win a ride on the Space Shuttle. (As we flew up the tower, the press credentials on a lanyard around my neck floated off and hung in space at the top. I had just enough time to reach out and grab it.) The chairs give you two or three bounces on the way down. When your feet and the rest of you are more or less back on terra firma, you'll exit the ride into a video arcade.

■ STORM FORCE ACCELATRON

A dizzying spin for younger visitors, located to the right of the entrance to the Incredible Hulk Coaster, the Accelatron features the powers of the X-Men superheroine, Storm, in a battle to defeat Magneto. As you enter a geodesic dome topped by a 20-foot lightning rod, you learn that Storm, majestic mistress of weather, has requested the aid of her mentor, Professor Xavier, and all the visitors who stop by. Guests board the circular Power Orb, specially designed by Professor Xavier to convert human energy into electrical forces through the power of "cyclospin." Recruits can hold onto the Power Orb's rudder, spinning the Accelatron faster and faster, generating enough power to defeat Magneto. Translation: a high-intensity spinning-teacup carnival thrill ride.

TOON LAGOON

This is a place where the funnies come to life, from the snowcapped peaks of Ripsaw Falls to Popeye's ship, *The Olive*, to Wimpy's burger stand. Comic Strip Lane salutes cartoon heroes old and new. In addition to Cathy and Shoe and the Marvel superheroes, you'll also find cutouts of classic toon characters such as Pogo, Snuffy Smith, Little Orphan Annie, Betty Boop, Beetle Bailey, Hagar the Horrible, Krazy Kat, and Dennis the Menace.

Hanging from the storefronts and trees are cartoon blurbs. A few samples: DON'T HAVE THE MUSHROOM PIZZA BEFORE YOU RIDE RIPSAW FALLS. My favorite, hung outside of Blondie's: I HAVE A FEELING PEOPLE CAN READ MY THOUGHTS. Also outside of Blondie's is a fun photo opportunity: Pose a family member or friend pulling on Marmaduke's leash; turn your camera sideways, and you can expect a picture right out of the comic books.

▪▪▪▪▪▪ _MUST-SEE_ ▪▪▪▪▪▪ DUDLEY DO-RIGHT'S RIPSAW FALLS

Dudley Do-Right must save Nell from evil Snidely Whiplash in this wild flume ride. It's a familiar setting for Dudley, the dim-bulb Canadian Mountie who was part of the beloved *Rocky and Bullwinkle Show*. Our assignment is to help Dudley on a wild and wet rescue attempt through a lagoon and log flume that ends with a drop through the roof of a ramshackle dynamite shack (the sign for which says DANGER ZONE. HIGHLY KAMBOOMABLE.) and a dive 15 feet below the surface of the water.

Dudley Do-Right's Ripsaw Falls

Toon Lagoon

You'll work your way up through queues that wind outside the building and then within. There is, of course, water, water, everywhere. The plunging logs splash onto the queue below, and water cannons fire spurts here and there. When you finally enter the building, you'll learn the story of Ripsaw Falls, told with tongue decidedly planted in cheek. Movie posters advertise such slightly skewed hits as *Saw Wars, Paws,* and *Three Men and a Grizzly.* You'll meet the Beaver and the Bear, performing a stand-up comedy routine (actually a hang-up comedy routine from their mounted position on the wall). Listen carefully to the very bad jokes, including a few gentle jabs at the Mouse across town. I guess it is a small world after all. (My favorite sign at the loading platform: PLEASE REMOVE HATS AND ANTLERS.)

There are three rows of seats in the loglike car. You can load as many as six per log if you're very friendly with another person in your party, one behind the other in the same seat. The first lift takes you out on a floating pathway with a great view of Toon Lagoon and other parts of Islands of Adventure. When you emerge from a mine section, you find our heroine, Nell, fit to be tied. Then Dudley loses his train of thought; we all regain it quickly when we seem to meet an oncoming locomotive. (Get it?)

After several false drops, you come to the big one. In case you miss the point, a sign warns: SCENIC OVERLOOK AHEAD! The plunge down the falls is dramatic . . . and wet. The front row of the log gets soaked, the middle gets wet, and the third seat gets seriously damp. But a good time is had by all. "And so," you are told, "our hero proves a Mountie always gets his man, but not always his girl."

The busiest time of the day for this ride is the middle of a hot day; lines are shorter in the morning when it is cooler, and at the end of the day, presumably because most people don't want to ride home with wet pants.

MUST-SEE POPEYE & BLUTO'S BILGE-RAT BARGES

The villainous Bluto is the proprietor of this establishment, and so you can count on things going awry. Popeye tells us that "Bluto has taken me girlfrien' Olive down the White Waters of Sweet Haven. I need shipmates to join me rescue. Don't ferget to bring yer spinach." You might want to bring a rain parka, too.

We start out on a path for Popeye's pleasant boat ride, but we come to a detour in the waiting line erected by Bluto. Suddenly we are in the line for Bluto's boat, which seems like a much less friendly cruise line. The long and complex queue eventually wends its way into Bluto's office. Among the awards and plaques for evildoing is a framed greenback labeled FIRST DOLLAR STOLEN.

The twelve-passenger circular rafts move along at a zippy 16 feet per second. There are lots of spins and tight turns, but only a short drop. That doesn't mean you won't get wet, though. If the splashes from the rapids and the unexpected geysers don't get you, one of the kids up on the deck of Me Ship *The Olive* just may have you in the sights of his water cannon.

This is, after all, just another raft ride, not all that different from another Orlando attraction, Kali River Rapids at Disney's Animal Kingdom. Where the Bilge-Rat Barges shines, though, is in the theming. There are funny little surprises at every turn, including Bluto's Boatwash, and various other opportunities for some extra wet surprises. You will get wet, especially in the seat of your pants. You're in most danger when your side of the raft is moving backward into a wave. There is a covered storage area in the center of the raft, but you'd do better using a locker for valuables or leaving them with someone on shore.

Popeye & Bluto's Bilge-Rat Barges

◾ ME SHIP *THE OLIVE*

This fun spot for kids has some great slides and hidey-holes. There are also water squirters to aim at the Bilge-Rat Barges passing by below. There are bells to ring and telescopes, and all sorts of toys. Actually, this place is worth a visit by kids of all ages just for the view of the lagoon and the rest of the park from the upper level.

JURASSIC PARK

The dinosaurs are back, and here's your chance to meet them face to face. The robotic creatures (you didn't really expect scaly flesh and blood, did you?) take over the Jurassic Park River Adventure. Elsewhere you will meet dinos up close and personal at the Triceratops Discovery Trail, check in on the DNA recombination process at the Jurassic Park Discovery Center, and hitch a ride on the back of a pteranodon for a prehistoric bird's-eye view of the park.

The entry to this part of Islands of Adventure wends its way through tropical jungle that is enclosed by electric fences and alarms. Beyond the mists of the ancient forests, you can hear distant roars. (Be sure to make a return visit to this area if you're in the park at night.)

▦ MUST-SEE JURASSIC PARK RIVER ADVENTURE

Hop aboard a small boat for a pleasant little journey back in time, the ever-flowing river. We are, of course, in the ultimate theme park, the world of the dinosaur brought back to life by scientists who have extracted dino DNA from an ancient insect trapped in amber.

The boats carry twenty-five persons, in five rows of five seats, into a beautifully landscaped, ferny re-creation of Earth as it existed millions of years ago. "The river flows through a newborn world, where giants walked the earth," says our guide. "Welcome to . . . Jurassic Park."

First stop on our voyage is Ultrasaur Lagoon, home of a species of gentle vegetarian giants who pose no threat to us. From there we float into Stegosaur Springs, where the natives seem just a bit more threatening—but we're harmless tourists, right? Next is Hadrosaur Cove, and here the inhabitants are suddenly not very hospitable at all. In fact, one of them roars up out of the water so close to our boat that it diverts us into the wrong channel: We're pushed through the Jurassic Park Animal Control Gate Number 13 into the Raptor Containment Area. And that's not good at all.

Alarms and flashing lights are everywhere. We see the remains of a crashed tour boat just like ours (reminiscent of the destroyed boat at Jaws in Universal Studios Florida). Close by, a pair of small spitters fights over the remnants of a Jurassic Park uniform. As we pass farther along, we come beneath a crane holding a crate marked RAPTOR TRANSPORT UNIT. Something inside is moving around and making nasty noises. Will it drop on our heads? And then we are into the warehouse building. We are pushed way back against our seats as the boat makes

The Jurassic Park Discovery Center glows by night. *Copyright © 1999 Universal Studios Escape.*

a very steep climb in near darkness. At the top we seem to pause for just a moment—and then we plunge back to the surface of the lake, in an 84-foot dive down one of the longest, fastest, and steepest water descents anywhere.

This is, of course, a water ride at heart, and you will get wet. The first row gets soaked, with a bit less water as you move toward the back of the boat. You can use one of the lockers outside the waiting queue for valuables; in recent years use of the lockers has been free for one hour, with a charge of $1.00 for each additional thirty minutes. (When the park is very busy, the waiting time may well extend more than an hour, putting you into the red.)

The long queue splits left and right to a pair of loading stations. As long as you have to wait in line, you might as well learn something about the various species of dinosaurs in the park; there's an informative video on overhead screens. (By the way, gardeners will be thrilled by the plantings around the ride and along the river pathway.) The ride is a near duplicate of the original Jurassic Park attraction at Universal Studios Hollywood.

▆ JURASSIC PARK DISCOVERY CENTER

At this interactive educational experience, you can observe as a raptor is hatched from an egg, examine dinosaur skeletons, and learn how biochemists at Jurassic Park brought these prehistoric creatures back to life.

One of the stations demonstrates DNA sequencing in a process that is supposed to mix a bit of your personal characteristics with those of a compatible

Halloween Horror Nights

Hundreds of monsters, maniacs, and mutants crawl out from the back lot from mid-October through Halloween. This is an amazing effort, not for the squeamish or very young. Scattered about the park are a half dozen dark mazes populated by all manner of creepy creatures that are scarified with the aid of sound effects, fog machines, and laser projectors. The park attracts huge crowds for the Halloween Horror Nights; a separate admission ticket is required. The event had been held at Universal Studios Florida for many years before moving over to Islands of Adventure.

dinosaur. You begin by choosing between ancient creatures that were herbivores or carnivores, armored or camouflaged, large or small, and members of herding groups or solo folk. Then you lean into a "brain scanner" that takes a video image of your face, and give a simulated snippet of your DNA to a sampler that scans your hand. The final step is an instruction to the computer to genetically recombine your DNA with your receptor dinosaur. The result: a new dinosaur with a bit of your face and personal characteristics. For some reason the dino I created was not carrying a reporter's notebook.

At another station a lab technician assists you in using a "pre-emergent nursery scanner" to examine the life growing within huge eggs. There's also a neutrino scanner that examines fossils in a wall of rock.

At Beasaurs you can use a periscope-like device to get some idea of how the world looked through the eyes of a dinosaur—an unusual effect when you consider that for many of the beasts, their eyes were on opposite sides of their head.

The Discovery Center is an ambitious attempt at edutainment but falls a bit flat; I expect Universal will step up the investment here in years to come.

MUST-SEE PTERANODON FLYERS

Here's a chance to get a prehistoric bird's-eye view of the island, soaring in a chair beneath the 10-foot wings of one of these flying dinosaurs. This very simple, charming ride immediately proved to be much too popular for its own good. Universal planners thought of the ride as a diversion for the kids, and it surely is attractive to youngsters. But its simple charm and the view of the park it offers made it appealing to adults as well. The result: There can be lengthy lines for the very short ride. There are only three of the two-seater birds on the track at any one time. Lines can stretch to an hour or more, and, alas, the ride is way too short to justify that. The rule: Adults need to be accompanied by a child except during the first half hour that the park is open.

The two-seat metal birds are pulled by a chain lift about 40 feet into the air and then descend under the quiet power of gravity along a winding track that circles above Camp Jurassic. The chairs move along at a brisk but unthreatening speed, swinging out from side to side a bit as they move around turns.

Some youngsters may be uncomfortable riding alone, but they must be willing and able to occupy their own seat. There is both a lap bar and a seat belt to hold riders in place, and there are no loops and dives on the track.

■ TRICERATOPS ENCOUNTER

At this dino-petting zoo humans can pet a "living" dinosaur for the first time ever. Trainers at the feed and control stations teach guests about the biology of the 24-foot-long, 10-foot-tall triceratops. Here's your chance to get up close and personal with a real, live dinosaur. You'll meet Chris, who is making a visit to the veterinarian for a case of the sniffles. Well, okay, she's not real, but she moves around, interacts with her concerned doc, and sniffles and sneezes. (You have been warned.)

Guests are escorted through in groups of about thirty, stepping onto a scale near the entrance for a group weigh-in. Our small contingent totaled about 6,315 pounds, or about the weight of a small triceratops, we were told. The walk-through to the encounter begins at the Jurassic Park Game Warden Station. There you'll be able to look at—and touch—all sorts of buttons and switches on the control system for the park. Yes, you really can play with the switch that turns on or off the electric-fence systems, the surveillance cameras, and all the other safety systems that are there to protect us from the beasts outside the compound. I'm sorry to have to tell you this, but: The switches aren't really connected to anything. And the dinosaurs aren't real. (You knew that already, right?)

The next stop is a lab area (including lockers of Dilphosaurus Acid Protection Suits). You'll find huge bales of "Dino Chow" as well as samples of stomach contents and dino dung. Then we're in the examining room with Chris. Attendants there will check her temperature, listen to her vital signs, and collect a sinus sample and a urine sample, which is something you don't see every day. There are a few other bathroom jokes here, as well, which you can experience for yourself without my help. Chris, powered by high-tech hydraulics and robotics, moves and responds to trainers and visitors. A lucky visitor will get to pet the gentle giant.

Note that Triceratops Encounter may not be open during quiet times of the year.

■ CAMP JURASSIC

Sitting in the shadow of Jurassic Park River Adventure, this children's play area includes a fantastic collection of climbing nets and slides. Some of the areas are nicely shaded.

At the base of the climbing area is the Amber Mine, stocked with glowing gems (some including insects trapped in the amber, which according to the story of *Jurassic Park* was the source of the dinosaur DNA for the resurrection of the beasts). Outside the mine, be sure to step on the large dino footprints on the walkway. (If you don't step on them on purpose, you're almost certain to do so by accident.) Each print triggers a mighty or mini roar from the maker of the mark, along with an accompanying rumble in the ground below your feet.

Best of all, there is only one exit from Camp Jurassic, so you can let the kids run free and park yourself at the gate to catch them if they start to wander off toward the dinosaurs and other lures. Note that the climbing nets look a lot flimsier than they are. There are steel cables hidden within the webbing of many of the supports.

THE LOST CONTINENT

A crumbling statue of Poseidon, the Greek god of the sea, presides over a land lost long ago in the mists of time. Exotic traders peer from behind mountains of rich fabrics and precious metals, inviting guests to join them in the search for even greater treasures.

MUST-SEE DUELING DRAGONS

"A stroll through this forest can be a dangerous proposition," says Merlin. "Living within it are two fierce dragons. One breathes fire; the other breathes ice. In order to escape, you must prove your bravery by mounting the back of one of the creatures and riding it to freedom." That's the good news. The bad news is that we're talking about a roller coaster here—one of the most terrifying yet conceived.

Dueling Dragons features two intertwined tracks that whiz guests over, under, and around each other through the trees of a medieval forest and then out over Dragon Lake. From the top of the 125-foot common lift, the Fire Dragon drops to the left and the Ice Dragon heads off to the right, with each track following its own layout. But they don't stay apart forever—three times the coasters zoom straight at each other, turning away or diving above or below each other at the last moment. At times the two tracks and their passengers—their feet dangling below (or above) them—are separated by a mere 12 inches.

The seats in the dragons are four abreast with eight rows, for a total of thirty-two volunteers; the cars are suspended from the overhead track except when they are upside down and the track is under your head. The tracks invert five times during the ride of about two minutes and twenty-five seconds. As each train is loaded, a computer calculates its weight and decides which of the two

Dueling Dragons. *Copyright © 1999 Universal Studios Orlando*

coasters should leave first and at what speed, so that the near-collisions occur right on schedule.

Here's something you don't see in a press release every day: Universal says the queue for the Dueling Dragons, at 3,180 feet, is the longest and most elaborate waiting line in the world. Trust me, it just goes on and on and on. The good news is that because there are two separate coasters, the line moves twice as fast, gobbling up about 3,264 riders per hour. The bad news is that nevertheless, this is one very long line. If you arrive at the coaster and find the line reaching to the outside of the queue, you're in for a wait that might reach two hours.

Just when you think you're heading for the loading station, the queue takes off in another direction into a whole new yard full of lines. Finally you enter into the building in a medieval churchlike setting, a place of shattered glass and crumbled stones that once was a fair castle, where Merlin will tell you the story of the dueling dragons. Slow down a bit to read the inscription in the open book in the next room. It's Merlin's entreaty to the gods to release us all from the thrall of the dragons: "Serpent of fire, obey my command. Abandon your hold upon this land." "Dragon ice, abominable scourge, from this blighted land diverge."

The next waiting area (yes, there's still more) is a creepy cavern marked with the scrawls of ancient graffiti artists. DON'T BE A BONEHEAD, one says, just above a collection of skulls. Another reads, ENTER IN PEACE, EXIT IN PIECES. Finally, it is time to "choose thy fate." The waiting line diverges into the final queues. Head left to Fire, right to Ice.

The two loading stations are next to each other, and there is one final queue for those visitors who insist on sitting in the front of the car. The cars leave the station about the same time, climbing the hill in tandem and taking off on their near-collision course together. The Fire track is a few seconds faster to the finish. Coaster experts say that the Ice side offers better twists and turns; sit toward the front for the best views of the next close encounter. Fire is a bit wilder; ride at the back for the best whips. Trust me: Anything that is not locked up will fall out. Use the lockers outside the queue to store your possessions.

Here's a tip for photographers: On the sidewalk directly in front of the coaster is an interconnecting red and blue circle surrounding a bronze plate. If you stand on the plate and wait, you'll be treated to a view of all three of the near-collisions between the two coasters.

MUST-SEE POSEIDON'S FURY

The Global Discovery Group has discovered the long-lost Temple of Poseidon, and you're invited for a visit. Unfortunately, the leader of the expedition, Professor Baxter, has disappeared. You're left in the hands of a rather shaky tour guide.

This walk-through show has some of the most technologically advanced special effects at the park, mated with a somewhat confusing story line; in 2002 the show's story was given its second complete rewrite. It's something about a battle between Poseidon and the evil Darkenon for control of the seas. We learn that "he who holds the Trident gold has Poseidon's power." The rest of the story was completely underwater for me.

Poseidon's Fury

You'll enter the building through the moldy, crumbling ruins of an ancient city. Once you're inside, the hallway is very dark, damp, and cool, barely lit by flickering lamps. When your eyes finally adjust to the light, check out the interesting details on the walls and ceilings, including the shell sconces on the walls.

You move on to the next room, a creepy stone temple with an elaborate puzzle-door, which, you learn, is the portal to Atlantis. It's like a giant bank-vault door; when the pieces finally align, a vortex to Atlantis is revealed. As befits a visit beneath the sea, this is one wet and wild vortex. Pay close attention when the door opens: A splash turns into a roaring tube of water that flows up and around you as you move into the world of Atlantis. This is definitely a frizz-the-hair, fog-the-glasses kind of place, but you won't get wet.

Then you are welcomed to the spectacular Temple of Poseidon, with a view through windows into the undersea world. Poseidon himself and his army of followers fill a dramatic water screen across the room. (The images are dramatic, an even better, indoor version of Disney's *Fantasmic!*) The ensuing battle between the gods fills the room with fire, and water, and fog—and with victory, a sudden return to the other side of the vortex.

MUST-SEE THE EIGHTH VOYAGE OF SINDBAD

Apparently, seven voyages were not enough for this great hero of the past, and so he sets out once again on a great search for riches. Here's the story line in three sentences: "We're as rich as kings," says Kebab. "Yes, but only if we can make it back alive," replies Sindbad. And, look: "The princess is imprisoned in a circle of fire!" So, you see, the goal is to escape the clutches of evil, with the riches—and the princess—intact.

Sindbad and his friend Kebab ("Shush, Kebab," says Sindbad at one point in the story) are entreated by the captive princess to snatch away the enchanted jewel "The Sultan's Heart." But when they do so, the lovely princess transforms into the evil sorceress Miseria, who proceeds to torment Sindbad, Kebab, and the real princess. ("That's so typical," says Kebab. "Give your girlfriend a big rock and she changes on you.")

The show involves explosions, fireworks, and other pyrotechnics. There are also a few wet surprises. One splash zone is in the middle section of the center of the theater near the mast; another is down low on the right side.

When Miseria and her henchmen battle against Sindbad and his buddy, you'll see them throwing axes, hammers, knives—and a kitchen sink. The finale features Miseria's flaming plunge from the upper level of the set into the pond below. (Watch carefully and see if you can spot a stuntman in a flame-resistant suit substituting for Miseria at the last moment.)

There are 1,700 seats in the canopied theater, which should allow for enough space for last-minute arrivals except on the busiest of days. While you're in the area, be sure to pause to contemplate the statue outside the entrance to the theater. There's a hidden camera and speakers within, along with an array of water hoses. The controller—with his or her hands on the spray buttons—talks with the guests. It's fun to watch or participate.

■ FLYING UNICORN

At the end of a meandering path under the trees between Jurassic Park and the Lost Continent are traces of long-lost mythical creatures, fairies, and gnomes. According to legend, an ancient wizard gathered scraps of knights' armor, wood from magic castles, and iron from witches' cauldrons to build a cart resembling the noble steed he rode as a young man. As he was constructing the vehicle, he came across a miraculous find: a unicorn's horn, which he placed on the head of the cart.

The fountain at *The Eighth Voyage of Sindbad*

Flying Unicorn

When he did so, it came alive, soaring over the treetops. Translation: This is a relatively tame roller coaster for younger visitors that tops out at about 20 miles per hour. One nice feature is that some of the cars can accommodate visitors in wheelchairs.

■ MYSTICS OF THE SEVEN VEILS

One of the stranger offerings at a theme park, a team of rent-a-psychics operates under a tent near Sindbad's show. You can buy readings from five minutes to half an hour, for about $10 to $50. Or you can send the money to me, and I'll send you the tea leaves from my last cup of Lipton's.

SEUSS LANDING

On ten whimsical acres where Dr. Seuss's famous characters come to life, this is the most fun part of the park, a draw for kids of all ages. There's hardly a straight line to be found on the island, and Universal's horticulturists have even managed to find and grow some strangely misshapen trees to match the strange foliage of the books of Dr. Seuss. (Some of the palms were transplanted from southern Florida, where they had been bent by the fury of Hurricane Andrew.)

Near the entrance to the land near the Port of Entry is a dedication to Theodore Geisel, better known under his pen name. "We dedicate this land to Dr. Seuss. May his genius forever be on the loose." At the other end of the land, beneath an arch at the entrance to The Lost Continent is a Seussian quote: "Think left and think right. Think low and think high. Oh, the things you can think up, if only you try!"

⚏ MUST-SEE ⚏ THE HIGH IN THE SKY SEUSS TROLLEY TRAIN RIDE!

Gliding above the world of Seuss Landing, this whimsical trolley-train gives visitors a great view of the park and a few special surprises.

The suspended trains pass through scenes from some of Dr. Seuss's most popular books. At the "Inking and Stamping" room, guests will be greeted by Sneetches looking for places to imprint the famous Sneetch Stars. In the "Star

Wash" room, guests are immersed in a flurry of bubbles while their Stars are cleaned, sprayed, and sparkled.

As the trains move outdoors, you'll get a bird's-eye view of One Fish, Two Fish, Red Fish, Blue Fish; The Cat in the Hat; and the rest of Seuss Landing—including a trip *through* the Circus McGurkus Cafe Stoo-pendous restaurant.

Riders must be at least 34 inches tall; guests under 48 inches in height must be accompanied by an adult.

This ride has had one of the longest incubation periods of any attraction at a theme park, anywhere. The track and much of the infrastructure for the ride were put in place in 1999 with the opening of the park; its original name was planned to be Sylvester McMonkey McBean and His Very Unusual Driving Machines. For the next seven years the ride was closed to the public, but the trolleys were dispatched to move through Seuss Landing from time to time.

⫶ MUST-SEE ⫶ THE CAT IN THE HAT

This ride through the pages of Dr. Seuss's best-known book is one of the best dark rides anywhere. (The ride is the most Disney-like attraction at Universal's Islands of Adventure, the highest possible compliment for a ride aimed at youngsters.)

Up to 1,800 guests per hour travel on six-passenger couches through eighteen scenes from the book. At the heart of the ride is a 24-foot revolving, mind-bending tunnel. The couches twist and turn and spin on their bases. The adventure features more than thirty robotic characters, including the Cat himself and the mischievous Thing 1 and Thing 2. Those Things tear the house apart in wonderful ways, and then race to make everything right once Mom comes back home. "Should we tell her about it?" we're asked. "Well, what would you do if mother asked you?" We're not sure.

⫶ MUST-SEE ⫶ CARO-SEUSS-EL

It's claimed that this is the most elaborate and interactive carousel ever built—who are we to argue with Dog-a-lopes and Cowfish? Seven different Seuss characters, a total of fifty-four mounts, circle around; the creatures will respond to their riders in wonderfully weird ways. Characters include Cowfish from *McElligot's Pool*; Elephant-birds from *Horton Hatches the Egg*; AquaMop Tops and Twin Camels from *One Fish, Two Fish, Red Fish, Blue Fish*; Dog-a-lopes and Mulligatawnies from *If I Ran the Zoo*; and Birthday Katroo from *Happy Birthday to You*. If you fear the ride will make you or your child ill, you can ask the attendant to disable the car's spin.

The Cat in the Hat comes to life at Seuss Landing.

One Fish, Two Fish, Red Fish, Blue Fish. *Copyright © 1999 Universal Studios Orlando. All rights reserved.*

ONE FISH, TWO FISH, RED FISH, BLUE FISH

Young visitors (and lucky adults in their company) steer one of twelve two-passenger Seussian fish up and down 15 feet in the air as they travel through water spouts and streams. Topping off the ride is an 18-foot-tall sculpture of the "Star Belly Fish" of the story.

You know which fish you are. If the song says that one fish should go down and red fish should head for the sky, pay attention unless you'd like a free bath from the water cannon on the next turn.

IF I RAN THE ZOO

This interactive playground tells the story of Gerald McGrew and his quest to create a totally different zoo of strange and unusual animals. The three areas include Hedges, Water, and the New Zoo. At McElligot's Pool you can drop a coin in the creature's mouth if you'd like to see what happens. Let me give you a hint: The humor here is not dry. (By the way, Universal promises to give all of the coins to charity.)

EATS AND TREATS

By theme-park standards, Universal has done a great job of creating interesting food fare at Islands of Adventure, from green eggs and ham to Dagwood sandwiches and from burgers to exotic Asian noodle dishes. Fast-food meals will likely cost about $10 with a drink; the upscale Mythos and the quirky Confisco Grille offer restaurant service for about $12 to $20 for entrees alone.

In 2006 the park introduced the **Universal Meal Deal,** an all-you-can-eat day pass. For about $19 for one park, or $23 for two parks on one day, you can make multiple visits to selected fast-fooderies. Each time you can select an entree, side dish, and dessert. Drinks cost extra, and there is supposed to be no sharing. . . .

At Islands of Adventure, participating restaurants in 2006 were Circus McGurkus Cafe Stoo-pendous, Comic Strip Cafe, and Captain America Diner. (See chapter 16 for a listing of participating eateries at Universal Studios Florida.)

■ PORT OF ENTRY

🏠 **Confisco Grille and Backwater Bar.** Run by a band of thieves, this unusual and inventive restaurant is on the right side of the Port of Entry as you near the lagoon. The "thieves," of course, are the waitstaff, but the manager may warn you that if you find something missing from your table to let him know; he'll see about getting it back for you.

The unusual lobby features some odd mechanisms and stairways to nowhere. Inside there's Kraft paper on the tabletops and the smell of a wood fire in the air. On recent visits specialties, priced from about $10 to $20, included Thai chicken salad, pad Thai, fajitas (beef, chicken, or shrimp), a portobello mushroom burger, Shrimp Alla Confisco, and a grilled sirloin steak. Side orders include Confisco fries for about $4.00, served in a cone with dipping sauces such as Buffalo style (hot sauce and blue cheese) and Southern style (peach chipotle barbecue sauce).

There's also a character breakfast at Confisco Grille with a most unusual duo: Spider-Man and The Cat in the Hat. In 2006 the meal was offered Thursday through Sunday from park opening to 10:30 A.M. and was priced at $15.95 for adults and $9.95 for children. For reservations call (407) 224–4012.

🍴 **Croissant Moon Bakery.** This pleasant bakery has only a handful of inside tables. Specialties include soups and salads for about $3.00 each; unusual sandwiches, priced at about $7.00, include peppered roast beef with smoked Gouda cheese and smoked turkey with Brie. And there is a sumptuous spread of cakes, cheesecakes, and cookies, priced about $2.00 to $3.00.

■ MARVEL SUPER HERO ISLAND

🍴 **Cafe 4.** A salute to the Fantastic Four (scientist Reed Richards; his wife, Sue; her kid brother John Storm; and Ben Grimm), this cafe is near the entrance to Spider-Man. Offerings include pizza by the slice (about $3.50) or the pie (up to $17.45), with topping choices including cheese, pepperoni, and barbecue chicken with Boursin cheese. Other specialties, priced from about $5.00 to $8.00, include an Italian hoagie, sausage sub, minestrone soup, and Caesar salad.

Blondie's: Home of the Dagwood

 **Captain America Diner.** Good old American fare, including chicken sandwiches, burgers, and Freedom Fighter french fries, with diner-style entrees from about $5.00 to $7.00.

■ TOON LAGOON

 **Blondie's: Home of the Dagwood.** We're talking real sandwiches here, huge stacks of stuff between slices of bread. Of course, the featured sandwich includes the Dagwood (ham, salami, turkey, bologna, and Swiss and American cheeses). The Dagwood and other handfuls are priced at about $7.00. You'll also find vegetable soup and salads.

 **Comic Strip Cafe.** Offering just what you'd expect comic-book heroes to order, this cafe has counters serving fish and chips, Chinese, Mexican, and pizza and pasta offerings.

 **Wimpy's.** You already know what kind of food this guy likes. Just head for the counter marked "bovine perfection." Wimpy promises, by the way, that he "personally supervises the culinary construction of each hamburger." Alas, the burgers cost more than a nickel, and you'll have to pay for them today, or on Tuesday (if your visit is on a Tuesday). A basic burger with fries is about $5.00. If you insist, you can also order a chicken sandwich or chili dog for about $7.00. And attention, Popeye: There's even a spinach salad for $3.00.

 **Cathy's Ice Cream.** The weight-conscious comic-strip heroine's favorite food is offered to all.

■ JURASSIC PARK

 **Pizza Predattoria.** Small personal pies, including pepperoni and barbecue chicken with pineapple, are priced at about $7.00. Other entrees include meatball sandwiches and a Caesar salad in a pizza crust. There's also a combination platter of pizza, salad, and soda for about $9.95.

 **The Burger Digs.** A basic fast-food joint offering burgers, cheeseburgers, and grilled chicken for about $6.00 to $9.00.

 **The Watering Hole.** You've got to like a bar in Jurassic Park that advertises itself as the "home of the original lounge lizard." The walk-up outdoor stand offers coffee and a full range of drinks, including rum runners, piña coladas, and margaritas, priced at about $3.00 plain or $5.00 with a shot of alcohol. There's also a nice selection of imported beers and microbrews.

A Musical Escape

Among the delights of the park is a suite of original music composed and performed as a background theme. A different soundtrack is heard in each of the five islands, as well as in the Port of Entry. Musicians from around the world came together in the resonant chambers of a desanctified monastery and professional studios in Seattle to make a recording that was one of the most ambitious musical events ever.

Port of Entry features music performed by a Javanese gamalan, a traditional orchestra, which traces its roots from A.D. 230. It consists mainly of percussive instruments, including gongs, drums, bells, and wooden-keyed xylophones, as well as violins, flutes, and zithers. The music changes as the visitor walks through an exotic bazaar, culminating in a grand, lush signature theme as guests pass under a grand arch and, like explorers discovering a new world, view the one-hundred-acre vista of the Islands of Adventure for the first time.

A Celtic band recorded additional music for the Port of Entry and for The Lost Continent. The band included some of the most ancient instruments in Western culture, including the bagpipe, double oboe, flute, and harp. Also featured in the recording are a pennywhistle, a handheld Celtic drum known as a "bohdran," a concertina, and an Irish alto flute.

Also contributing to music for The Lost Continent was a Greco-Etruscan band, featuring instruments from the Middle East, India, and Greece. Among instruments were a Greek lyre called a "kithara," a wind instrument played with a double reed known as a "shawm," a stringed instrument from Western Asia named a "cembalo" with strings struck by a pair of small hammers, a stringed instrument from India called a "vina," a sitar and its larger cousin the "surbahar," a long-necked Indian lute known as a "tambura," a pakawaj talking drum, and a bowed stringed instrument carved from a single block of wood called a "sarangi."

At Seuss Landing musicians brought the fantastic sounds of cartoons to life. The result was a score that involved some newly created but wacky instruments, including a harp that used rubber bands instead of strings. For Toon Lagoon, where two-dimensional cartoons populate the landscape, they worked with familiar melodies such as "The Sailor's Hornpipe" (better known to us as Popeye's theme) and music from the beloved cartoons of Jay Ward, creator of Rocky and Bullwinkle.

■ THE LOST CONTINENT

🏠 **Mythos Restaurant.** The showpiece of the Islands of Adventure, Mythos lies on the shore of the Inland Sea within a volcanic rock formation. Stop and take a look at the intricate details on the Mythos building, with carvings and hidden figures, in some ways a rocky version of the striking *Tree of Life* at Disney's Animal Kingdom. The interior is like a limestone cavern.

Appetizers, priced from about $5.00 to $10.00, include tempura shrimp with wasabi and soy, and grilled asparagus with citrus butter. Salads include poached artichoke. Entrees, priced from about $10 to $20, include linguine with Thai spices, including mint and cilantro; grilled yellowfin tuna Niçoise with kalamata vinaigrette; and grilled chicken sandwich with Vidalia onions, fontina cheese, and green-olive mayonnaise.

Enchanted Oak Tavern (and Alchemy Bar). Designed to commemorate the oak tree trunk in which legend says Merlin was frozen by the Lady of the Lake, this eatery on The Lost Continent features oak-fired barbecue dishes and Dragon Scale Ale. The great sorcerer himself may make guest appearances if you're lucky. Entrees, priced from about $7.00 to $15.00, include chicken and ribs, barbecue spare ribs, and hickory-smoked chicken.

■ SEUSS LANDING

Green Eggs and Ham Cafe. What else do you expect on the menu than this famed dish from Dr. Seuss? There's more, of course, but don't you want to try something green? (In case you were wondering, the eggs are colored with parsley puree.) Entrees at the outdoor walk-up window are priced about $6.00, including green eggs and hamwich, hamburgers, and cheeseburgers.

Circus McGurkus Cafe Stoo-pendous. This is a fun place to eat with animated mobiles of Seuss circus creatures overhead. Above the seats is a section of track from High In The Sky Seuss Trolley Train Ride!; suspended trains pass by from time to time. Booths are named after Seuss characters, including "Rolf from the Ocean of Olf" and "The Drum-Tummied Snumm."

Entrees include basic kid stuff like deep-fried chicken, lasagna, pepperoni pizza, meatballs and spaghetti, and the like. Entrees are about $7.00. There's also the old standby of alphabet soup for a relative bargain of about $3.00.

Moose Juice Goose Juice. This drink stand offers moose juice (also known as Turbo Tangerine) or goose juice (sour green apple). Both are available fresh or frozen for $2.00 to $3.00. If you can't decide between them, order a mix of both.

Green Eggs and Ham Cafe

CHAPTER EIGHTEEN

UNIVERSAL CITYWALK ORLANDO

IN ORLANDO, EVEN ADULTS DESERVE a place all their own. (Kids can come along, too, most of the time.) Universal CityWalk, a thirty-acre day-and-night entertainment center, serves as the front door to Universal Studios Florida and Universal Studios Islands of Adventure. Visitors are deposited there when they exit one of the two gigantic parking garages. The two-tiered promenade wraps around a four-acre lagoon.

Admission to CityWalk is free, and visitors can come and go between Universal Studios Florida and Universal's Islands of Adventure; your options for lunch or dinner are greatly improved by the addition. Some of the venues have a cover charge of about $3.00 to $5.00 in the evening when there is entertainment and may have a higher entrance fee for some special events. You will, though, have to park your car in Universal's lot and pay an $8.00 fee for the privilege, something that is not popular with some visitors.

In 2006 Universal offered two nighttime deals: a CityWalk Party Pass for $9.95 for all clubs, except for special events, or $13.95 for club access and a ticket to a movie at the Universal Cineplex. Both prices did not include tax.

The Meal & Movie Deal, for $19.95, included a special-menu meal at one of the CityWalk restaurants and a movie ticket; tax and gratuity was included. Participating restaurants included Bob Marley's, Hard Rock Cafe, Jimmy Buffett's Margaritaville, NASCAR Cafe, NBA City, Pastamoré, Pat O'Brien's, and Latin Quarter. For information call (407) 224–2489.

At certain times of the year, Universal allows free entry to the clubs with a current ticket stub from one of the theme parks.

On the moving sidewalk from the parking structure into CityWalk, to your right is the Hard Rock Hotel. A bit farther in the distance to your right is the elegant Portofino Hotel. At the end of the walkway you will find yourself in

CityWalk. Head right to Universal Studios Florida and left to Universal's Islands of Adventure.

The first CityWalk was opened at Universal Studios Hollywood and was an immediate success. At Walt Disney World, Pleasure Island and Downtown Disney West Side were clearly influenced by that success in California.

For many visitors the best thing about CityWalk is its proximity to the two theme parks at Universal Orlando. For the first time in Orlando, it is possible to exit a theme park and walk to a sophisticated dining and adult entertainment district for lunch or dinner and then return to the park.

For dinner reservations in CityWalk, call (407) 224–3663; you'll also find a reservations cart near the Universal Cineplex.

A CITYWALK WALKABOUT

■ BOB MARLEY—A TRIBUTE TO FREEDOM

At Bob Marley's the room is hot, the music is hot, the dancing is hot, and some of the food is hot: The jerk chicken with black bean sauce will clear out your sinuses nicely.

The restaurant is a one-of-a-kind celebration of music and culture based around the music and philosophy of Jamaican reggae legend and cultural icon Bob Marley. The restaurant and club are patterned after Marley's actual home and garden in Kingston, Jamaica. In a touch of realism, it is not air-conditioned. It includes an inner courtyard that is open to the sky, and there's a stage for performances.

The menu features light Jamaican fare, including meat patties, roti, Red Stripe beer, and grapefruit-flavored Ting soda. Typical menu items include sweet and spicy mango chicken wings, jerk-marinated chicken breast served on cocoa bread, Jamaican beef or vegetable patties in a flaky crust, and Jamaican-style oxtail in brown sauce. Entrees range from about $8.00 to $10.00.

Open for dinner weekdays from 4:00 P.M. to 2:00 A.M., and lunch and dinner on Saturday and Sunday from 11:00 A.M. to 1:30 A.M. There is a cover charge of $5.00 after 8:00 P.M. For information call (407) 224–2262 or consult www.bob marley.com.

■ CITYJAZZ

CityJazz is very elegant, a wood-trimmed cathedral to jazz that is endowed with impeccable acoustics. The Down Beat Jazz Hall of Fame honors the musicians hallowed in the pages of *Down Beat* magazine since 1952, and the stars of today are featured at a live-performance stage. Nearby is an outdoor stage facing Central Plaza for small performances. A much larger stage offers seats facing the water; it is used for major concerts.

Open for drinks from 8:00 P.M. to 1:00 A.M. Sunday through Thursday and 7:00 P.M. to 2:00 A.M. on Friday and Saturday. The Down Beat Jazz Hall of Fame Museum is open from 3:00 to 6:00 P.M. There is a cover charge of $5.00 after

8:30 P.M., with higher charges for special performances. For information call (407) 224–2189.

■ BONKERZ COMEDY CLUB

Laugh until you go bonkers at shows Thursday, Friday, and Saturday nights at 8:00 P.M. Doors open at 6:30 P.M. Admission is $7.00 per person, or included with a CityWalk Party Pass. All guests must be eighteen or older. For information and reservations call (407) 629–2665.

■ THE BUBBA GUMP SHRIMP CO. RESTAURANT & MARKET

The Oscar-winning movie *Forrest Gump* has inspired this chain of seafood restaurants, which features—of course—lots of shrimp, as well as other seafood specialties, steak, sandwiches, and other casual fare. For information consult www.bubbagump.com.

■ EMERIL'S ORLANDO

Bam! From the bayous of Louisiana, this sophisticated and "kicky" culinary hot spot features chef Emeril Lagasse's Creole-based cuisine. The focal point is a bustling open kitchen where diners can watch their meals being prepared. A squad of waiters descends on tables to deliver meals to every diner at the same moment—they call it "gang service."

Located in a separate building near the waterfront, this is a very upscale eatery—not a cheap date. A meal for two with wine can easily hit $200. And speaking of wine, the house collection holds something like 12,000 bottles. Lagasse himself makes occasional appearances.

Appetizers include New Orleans barbecue shrimp and spinach and bacon crusted oyster gratinée, priced from about $8.00 to $12.00. Entrees, priced from about $18 to $38, include hickory smoked-lemongrass roasted duck, andouille-crusted Texas redfish, grilled Black Angus sirloin strip steak, and roasted Atlantic salmon. Wood-fired pizzas included wild and exotic mushroom truffle, goat cheese and rock shrimp, sweet barbecue salmon, and Southwestern-style seafood with cilantro–black bean sauce. There's also a six-course "degustation," or sampler, served to the entire table.

Open daily for lunch from 11:30 A.M. to 2:00 P.M. and dinner from 5:30 to 10:00 P.M., and until 11:00 P.M. on Friday and Saturday. For information call (407) 224–2424 or consult www.emerils.com/restaurants/orlando_emerils/.

■ THE GROOVE

The Groove is a high-tech, high-end dance club with all of the requisite toys: fog machines, strobes, spotlights, and video screens. Oh, and the music was so loud that I could barely take notes. The walls are decorated with all things dance, from funk to disco to the Folies Bergère and even a bit of exotic dancing. One of the prized posters advertises an appearance by Josephine Baker at the Folies Bergère in Paris.

The Blue Room is like a set from the *The Jetsons,* serving martini drinks such as the Hippie Chick and the Mood Ring. The Green Room is a spooky place lit

Hard Rock Live at Universal CityWalk. *Copyright © 1999 Universal Studios Escape. All rights reserved.*

by electric candles, featuring scotch and aperitifs such as Nectar of the Gods. The Red Room (reminiscent of an old, old bordello, or so I am told) offers fruit drinks including the Scarlet Letter and the Red Velvet. The club includes live performances by Universal/MCA acts.

Open nightly from 9:00 P.M. to 2:00 A.M., and until 3:00 A.M. Thursday through Saturday. Guests must be twenty-one or older to enter. Cover charge is $5.25. For information call (407) 224–2227.

■ HARD ROCK CAFE ORLANDO

The world's largest Hard Rock Cafe includes a 650-seat restaurant. There is, of course, a gift shop. The spectacular eatery replaced the earlier version at Universal Studios Florida.

Hard Rock Cafe features classic American cuisine in a high-energy atmosphere, surrounded by rare and unique pieces of memorabilia from the past five decades of rock 'n' roll. Signature dishes, priced from about $8.00 to $13.00, include Pig Sandwich, meat loaf, grilled fajitas, veggie burgers, portobello mushroom sandwich, and the Outrageous Hot Fudge Brownie.

Open from 11:00 A.M. to 2:00 A.M. or later. For information call (407) 351–7625 or consult www.hardrock.com.

■ HARD ROCK LIVE

The first live-concert venue in the chain is modestly fashioned after the Roman Forum in a modern "retro" style. Capable of accommodating 2,800 people—with 1,800 in seats—Hard Rock Live hosts concerts by cutting-edge and rock-classic artists.

More than 140,000 square feet in size, complete with imposing columns, majestic archways, and a grand entrance, the hall includes the latest in sound and light technology. The arena includes opulent luxury boxes as well as general seating.

The Hard Rock Live House Band, which includes members who have backed up some of rock's greatest names, performs Monday through Thursday. Cover charge is $9.00.

Ticket prices for headliner acts vary by performer. For information call (407) 351–7625 or consult www.hardrock.com/live2/live.asp.

■ JIMMY BUFFETT'S MARGARITAVILLE CAFE

Perched like a parrot on the edge of the CityWalk lagoon, this quirky restaurant celebrates the island music and lifestyle of cult hero–musician Buffett. There are, of course, margaritas on tap; in fact, they may flow out of a bubbling volcano. The cafe is appropriately located overlooking the water near the bridge to Islands of Adventure.

Food is "high-end" bar food, including seafood, "cheeseburgers in paradise," and other fare related to Buffett's songs. The Volcano Bar erupts with margaritas, and there are also themed areas, including the Shark Bar and the 12-Volt Bar. If you don't catch the references, just ask the nearest Parrothead, who may sing you the appropriate line from the master.

Typical entrees range from about $13 to $17 and include Calypso mahimahi, Jimmy's Jammin' Jambalaya, crab cakes, and coconut tempura-fried shrimp.

Open for lunch and dinner from 11:00 A.M. to 2:00 A.M. There is a cover charge of $7.00 on Thursday, Friday, and Saturday. For information call (407) 224–2155 or consult www.margaritaville.com/orlando.

■ LATIN QUARTER

Hot, hot, hot: This is the place to come for a salsa beat and a delicious spread of Hispanic food from twenty-one nations from Mexico to South America. Add in a dance floor and the infectious music, and you'll see why this place is one of the liveliest in CityWalk. A dance troupe, including some outrageous costumes, performs salsa, merengue, tango, and other hot, hot, hot routines.

The extensive menu includes appetizers priced from about $5.00 to $8.00, including *ceviche de vieiras y camarones* (snapper and shrimp marinated in a spicy lemon and lime juice with jalapeños, tomato, and cilantro), *nachos casi machos* (plantain-chip nachos with Monterey Jack cheese and jalapeños), and *tamal en majo de maiz con mujo* (cornmeal stuffed with seasoned pork wrapped in a corn husk and served on a black bean puree).

Entrees, priced from about $14 to $25, include *churrasco a la parilla* (grilled skirt steak with chimichurri sauce over garbanzo beans sautéed with ham and chorizo sausage), *costillas de Cornero al morno* (spiced rack of lamb), and *atun a la cana de Azucar* (sugarcane tuna loin on a bed of roasted garlic boniato).

Open from 11:00 A.M. to 1:30 A.M. for lunch and dinner. There is a cover charge of $7.00 on Thursday, Friday, and Saturday. For information call (888) 745–2846.

NASCAR Cafe

■ RED COCONUTS CLUB

CityWalk's newest "ultra lounge," which replaced the Motown Cafe, is on the upper level of CityWalk and offers signature martinis, VIP bottle service, and a gourmet appetizer menu. There's live music or a DJ daily, transitioning from Sinatra to jazz to modern grooves.

Visitors must be at least twenty-one, and a $7.00 cover charge or CityWalk Party Pass is required.

■ NASCAR CAFE

This is fast food of a different sort, with diners immersed within rows of gleaming Nextel Cup cars, a surround-sound video wall, electronic and multimedia games, and various memorabilia and artifacts from the world of NASCAR racing. The atmosphere continues on to the menu and the pit-crew waitstaff. Car parts are everywhere, of course. An entire race car hangs over the bar on the ground floor, surprisingly close to the ground-floor video arcade, where you'll find driving games (including a Virtual Reality Race Simulator, priced at about $5.00 per ride).

The menu includes basic American food, some of the items named in honor of racing heroes. Offerings are priced from about $8.00 to $10.00 for burgers (including a Daytona chili burger and a vegetarian Gardenburger) and from about $11.00 to $20.00 for entrees such as the Bill France Pork Chop, the DW Dude Filet (Darrell Waltrip's steak of choice), the Crew Chief Roasted Chicken, and a chicken pastry potpie. Appetizers, priced from about $6.00, include Talladega Tenders, Winston Cup Wings, Supercharged Chili, and popcorn shrimp.

Open daily from 10:00 A.M. to 10:00 P.M. No cover charge. For information call (407) 224–7223 or consult www.nascarcafeorlando.com.

■ NBA CITY

A high-energy cafe next door to the Hard Rock Cafe and near the entrance to Universal Studios Islands of Adventure, this is the first in what is intended to be a new chain of theme restaurants, a partnership between the National Basketball Association and Hard Rock Cafe. Outside is the tallest basketball player in Orlando since Shaquille O'Neal left town, a gigantic hoopster in bronze. Down below are handprints from NBA stars, including Hakeem

Olajuwon, Charles Barkley, and WNBA star Sheryl Swoopes. You won't be the first to place your small mitt in theirs.

The restaurant includes the CityWalk Cage, a dining area featuring contemporary American cuisine with entrees such as steak, chops, and pizza priced from about $9.00 to $20.00; the NBA City Playground, with games and attractions; and the NBA City Club, where guests can watch live and classic games.

Typical entrees include grilled Caribbean jerk mahimahi, maple-glazed pork chops, pastrami Reuben, burgers, and steaks. Pasta specialties include chicken bleu cheese, shrimp a la vodka, and grilled salmon and bow ties.

Open from 11:00 A.M. to 2:00 A.M. No cover charge. For information call (407) 363–5919 or consult www.nbacity.com.

NBA City

■ PASTAMORÉ

This lively outdoor street cafe has a few indoor seats. Specialties center around panini, priced about $10, including *panini al verdura,* with beefsteak tomatoes, grilled eggplant, fresh basil, olive oil, and balsamic vinegar; *panini capicola,* with Italian meats and fontina cheese; and *panini di polle é pesto,* with grilled marinated chicken, fontina cheese, and pesto mayonnaise. Entrees, priced from about $10 to $20, include cherrystone clams steamed with Italian sausage, garlic Boursin steak, chicken parmigiana, risotto with grilled chicken or shrimp, and fettuccine carbonara. You can also order a family-style sampler with antipasto, pasta fagioli, salad, a choice of entrees, and dessert for $21.95 per adult and $6.95 for children. There's also antipasto and salad selections, along with a selection of Italian and domestic beers and wines. Desserts include ultrarich Italian gelato ice cream; flavors include cappuccino, pistachio, and chocolate with hazelnuts.

The cafe is open from 8:00 A.M. to midnight, and the small restaurant operates from 5:00 P.M. to midnight. For information call (407) 224–2244.

■ PAT O'BRIEN'S

This is a replica of the famous watering hole in New Orleans, with a Main Bar and a Dueling Pianos bar. Famed for its old-world character and flaming fountain patio, Pat O'Brien's is also the birthplace of the world-famous Hurricane drink. The restaurant's wine collection features more than 4,000 bottles, with many of them on display around the dining room. An extensive cigar humidor is located within the "chimney" of the eatery.

Founded in 1933 as Club Tipperary, one of the leading speakeasies of its time, Pat O'Brien's moved to its New Orleans location in 1942. The CityWalk outpost is a close replica of the original, built of weathered redbrick, wrought iron, and dark wood fixtures. Overhead in the entranceway are seven muskets representing the seven countries that have at one time or another occupied New Orleans.

Pat O'Brien's does a great job of transporting the feel of New Orleans to Orlando. Upstairs over the open courtyard are a few handsome smaller rooms. Among them is the Briars Suite, named in honor of Napoleon Bonaparte's favorite retreat on the Isle of Saint Helena, where Napoleon came to visit and all but refused to leave.

I sampled a fiery jambalaya, a lot different from the weak imitations you may find at your neighborhood diner. Entrees, priced from about $8.00 to $10.00, include a N'awlins po'boy with fried shrimp, Bourbon Street chicken, and a muffuletta sandwich. It's the drinks that are the stars, though. Among favorites are the Fuzzie Leprechaun (vodka, peach schnapps, Blue Curaçao, and pineapple and orange juice), the Hurricane (rum or vodka and fruit juices), and the Skylab (rum, vodka, apricot brandy, and Blue Curaçao).

Open for lunch and dinner from 11:00 A.M. to 1:00 A.M. There is a cover charge of $5.00 to enter the Dueling Pianos bar, which is open from 6:00 P.M. to 2:00 A.M. nightly (from 8:00 P.M. on Sunday and Monday) and restricted to guests twenty-one and older. For information call (407) 224–2106 or consult www.patobriens.com/orlando.html.

■ UNIVERSAL CINEPLEX

This twenty-screen, 5,200-seat Cineplex Odeon theater complex employs state-of-the art projection and sound systems. The seating is laid out in a stadium design, assuring unobstructed views. One of the theaters, especially large and lavish, is used for movie premieres. For information and showtimes call (407) 354–5998.

■ CITYWALK SHOPS

- **Cartooniversal.** Character apparel and souvenirs.
- **Cigarz at CityWalk.** Cigars, of course, and fine tobacco, as well as cordials, single-malt Scotch, and coffees.
- **Dapy.** Wind-up, flashing, beeping, and clicking toys and gifts. Dapy, which originated in Paris, is related to Spencer Gifts and Universal itself.
- **Endangered Species.** A clothing and gift shop that has an environmentally aware message.
- **Fossil.** An upscale version of the trendy watch, sunglasses, and accessory marketplace.
- **Fresh Produce.** Apparel in fruit and vegetable colors.
- **The Island Clothing Store.** Tommy Bahama, Lilly Pulitzer, and other beach and resort wear.
- **Quiet Flight.** Beachwear and ware.
- **The Universal Studios Store.** Did you expect a Disney store?

PART IV

SEAWORLD ORLANDO

CHAPTER NINETEEN

SEAWORLD ORLANDO, DISCOVERY COVE BY SEAWORLD

FOUR-FIFTHS OF EARTH'S SURFACE IS WATER, and more than five million visitors a year swim upstream to visit SeaWorld Orlando, the world's most popular marine-life park. SeaWorld's appeal has always been its focus on nature and its amazing collection of marine creatures, but in recent years it has had to deal with two powerful competitors: the animal attraction of Disney's Animal Kingdom and the human appeal of thrill rides at Universal Orlando and Walt Disney World. In the new millennium SeaWorld has begun to expand its base with attractions that celebrate thrills as well as animals.

The big fish—or mammal, actually—around here is **Shamu,** and in 2006 SeaWorld opened a spectacular new show called **Believe** that puts on display some astounding animal behavior backed by impressive staging and music.

The king of the untamed animals at the park is **Kraken,** the longest, tallest, steepest, and perhaps the most stomach-churning roller coaster in Florida. Kraken flies alongside another thrill ride, **Journey to Atlantis,** an unusual mix between a coaster and a water ride. In 2006 even the kiddies got their own thrill ride, a "family-friendly" roller coaster named **Shamu Express.**

Across the road from SeaWorld is its unusual cousin, **Discovery Cove.** Think of it as a marine attraction where the animals outnumber the human visitors and where the food and service are more like first-class resort than a fast-food drive-through. Visitors pay handsomely for the luxury. And though SeaWorld has disclosed very little in the way of details, plans are under way for the opening of a marine-themed water park.

Blue Horizons, presented at the Whale and Dolphin Stadium, is another very enjoyable live animal show. When the sun sets in summer and peak seasons, don't miss *Mistify,* a light show presented on a 60-foot-high mist screen accompanied by water fountains, flames, and fireworks.

MUST-SEES

Believe

The Waterfront

Kraken

Journey to Atlantis

Wild Arctic

Key West at SeaWorld

Shamu's Happy Harbor

Shamu Express

Blue Horizons

Manatees: The Last Generation?

Clyde and Seamore Take Pirate Island

Pets Ahoy!

Terrors of the Deep

Located ten minutes south of downtown Orlando and fifteen minutes from Orlando International Airport at the intersection of Interstate 4 and the Beeline Expressway, SeaWorld is open every day at 9:00 A.M., with extended hours during the summer and holidays. Call (800) 327–2424 or (407) 351–3600 for more information, or consult www.seaworld.com. Discovery Cove is adjacent to SeaWorld. For information and reservations call (877) 434–7268 or consult www.discoverycove.com.

SEAWORLD ORLANDO

SeaWorld has a pleasantly different feel from many other attractions in central Florida, including Walt Disney World and Universal Orlando. The emphasis is on all things natural: marine animals, birds, and lots of greenery. Most of the scheduled shows take place in outdoor theaters that seat as many as 5,000 visitors. With the rare exception of the busiest days, you won't see waiting lines; simply walk into the theater about fifteen or twenty minutes before the event and pick a seat. If the theater is full, you'll be invited to return for a later show. (Saturday and Sunday are generally the busiest days of the week at the park, with Monday through Thursday the quietest.) Average attendance at SeaWorld is about 15,000 per day, with summer and holiday peaks of almost twice that level.

SeaWorld estimates it should take about eight hours to tour the entire park. I recommend that you see the shows first and then spend the remaining time visiting areas not regulated by the clock. If you really want to see it all, plan on arriving at opening time (usually 9:00 A.M.) and staying through dusk.

Try to arrive for any presentation at least fifteen minutes ahead of showtime. This gives you the best chance at the seat you want and allows you to view the preshow activities offered at some of the theaters. Most shows are just short of thirty minutes long. Presentations usually start right on time, but you should be able to slip in a couple of minutes late without disturbing the show.

GUIDED TOURS AND VIP ACCESS

SeaWorld offers a variety of tours and special programs, including the following. (Park admission is not included. Call to confirm prices and availability.)

- **Adventure Express.** Includes front-of-line access to Kraken, Journey to

Power Trip #1: Thrills and Chills

If you want to make the most of a thrill-filled day at SeaWorld, head for the coasters early in the day. Here's one scenario: When the gates open, start your day with an eye-opener on the Kraken roller coaster. When you're back to earth, head next door to Journey to Atlantis, another top draw for thrill-seekers. (If the morning is chilly, though, you might want to wait until later in the day before enjoying Atlantis's somewhat wet thrill.) Then make a beeline to Wild Arctic for a simulated but still chilly helicopter adventure.

Now, pick up the schedule of shows and work your way through the park for the rest of the day. Sometime in the late afternoon, the lines at the coasters and the simulator will probably be short enough for a return visit. End your day at the Shamu Rocks America finale at Shamu Stadium.

Power Trip #2: Seeing the Shows

Many visitors to SeaWorld come for the traditional animal shows and to stroll through the attractive grounds; they get sufficient thrills from their up-close visit with Shamu. Begin your tour by studying the park map and show schedule you'll receive at the entrance gate. Take note that some of SeaWorld's shows and events are presented only a few times each day. Decide which of these you most want to see, and then work the schedule. Don't miss the best of the best: **Believe** and *Blue Horizons*. Children of all ages are also sure to enjoy *Clyde and Seamore Take Pirate Island.*

The schedule is designed to allow you to walk from show to show easily. Your best bet is to see the scheduled shows in the order they occur from your arrival time; after you've done that, spend the rest of your day viewing exhibits and visiting any rides that appeal to you, like Kraken, Journey to Atlantis, and Wild Arctic. This may sound inefficient, but the SeaWorld property isn't all that large; you can crisscross a few times if you need to.

Atlantis, and Wild Arctic; reserved seating at selected shows; a box lunch; and a behind-the-scenes visit to meet and touch a penguin. On one of my visits, I was escorted into the housing for Magellanic penguins, native to the Falklands and Chile; they are not on display to the public. The six-hour guided tour requires reservations; call (800) 406–2244. Adults $89, children $79, plus park admission.
- **Dolphin Nursery Close-up Tour.** A sixty-minute guided tour to the dolphin nursery with an animal-care specialist. All tickets $40, plus park admission.
- **Marine Mammal Keeper Experience.** Guests will show up for "work" at 6:30 A.M. and spend the day alongside trainers and rehabilitation staff. Limited to three guests per day, ages thirteen and older, the package includes lunch, a T-shirt, and a seven-day pass to SeaWorld. The cost in 2006 was $399 plus tax.

SEAWORLD

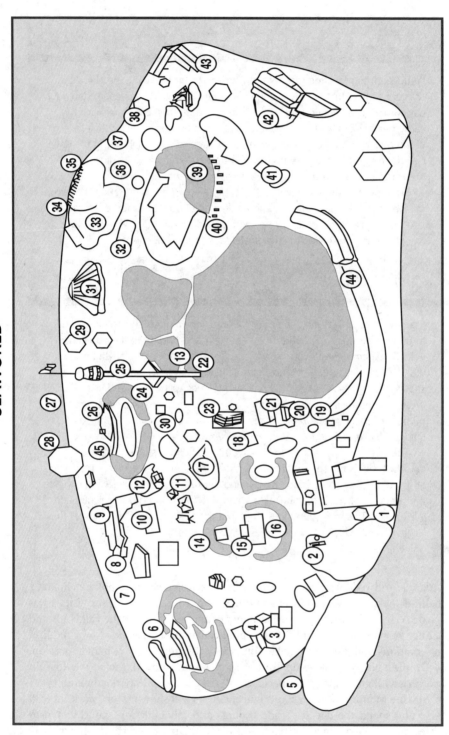

SEAWORLD

① Ticket Plaza	㉕ Sky Tower
② Treasure Isle–Ice Cream	㉖ Pacific Point Preserve
③ Key West at SeaWorld	㉗ Kraken
④ Dolphin Stadium	㉘ Journey to Atlantis
⑤ Stingray Lagoon	㉙ Terrors of the Deep
⑥ Manatees: The Last Generation?	㉚ Special events
⑦ Special exhibits	㉛ Nautilus Theatre: *Odyssea*
⑧ Jewels of the Sea Aquarium	㉜ Paddleboats
⑨ Penguin Encounter	㉝ Clydesdale Hamlet
⑩ Mama Stella's Italian Kitchen	㉞ Hospitality Deli
⑪ Dockside Cafe	㉟ Anheuser-Busch Hospitality Center
⑫ Pets Ahoy Gifts	㊱ Midway Games Area
⑬ Seafire Inn	㊲ Play area
⑭ Tide Pool and Caribbean Tide Pool	㊳ Radio Control Boats & Trucks
⑮ Tropical Reef	㊴ Shamu Stadium: Believe
⑯ Flamingo Exhibit	㊵ Shamu: Close Up!
⑰ SeaWorld Theater: *Pets Ahoy!*	㊶ Mango Joe's Cafe
⑱ Tropical Rain Forest	㊷ Wild Arctic
⑲ Pelican Exhibit	㊸ Shamu's Happy Harbor/Shamu
⑳ Spoonbill Exhibit	Express
㉑ Makahiki Luau	㊹ Atlantis Stadium
㉒ The Waterfront	㊺ Sea Lion and Otter Stadium: *Clyde*
㉓ Waterfront shops and restaurants	*and Seamore Take Pirate Island*
㉔ Pearl Dive	

■ **Behind-the-Scenes Tours.** One-hour walking tours focusing on particular topics. Predators Tour explores the world of sharks and includes a backstage visit at Shamu Stadium. The Polar Expedition Tour goes inside Wild Arctic. Saving a Species Tour visits the rescue and rehabilitation facilities at the park. A separate admission ticket is required. Adults $16, children $12.

■ **Sharks Deep Dive.** Participants don SeaWorld wet suits and either snorkel or scuba dive within a shark cage, traversing a 125-foot-long underwater habitat teeming with an array of more than fifty sharks, including sand tigers, sandbars, Atlantic and Pacific black tips, and nurse; sawfish; plus thousands of schooling fish. Guests use new equipment that permits underwater time without the need for scuba certification. In 2006 the cost was $150 per person, which includes a "Sharks Deep Dive" T-shirt and a shark information booklet and poster. You'll also need an admission ticket to the park. The experience is limited to a small number of guests for the two-hour program.

■ **Beluga Interaction Program.** A group of guests will meet with an educator to learn about the mystery of beluga whales and then change into wet suits to get up close with the creatures to touch and feed them and assist trainers in communicating with the whales. Participants must be at least thirteen years of age. A separate admission ticket is required. For prices and information call (800) 327–2424.

■ **Camp SeaWorld and SeaWorld/Busch Gardens Tampa Bay Adventure Camps.** SeaWorld's education department offers more than 200 summer-camp classes, including sleepover programs inside the shark tunnels and adventures for kids as well as the whole family. For information call (866) 468–6226 or (407) 363–2380.

ATTRACTIONS AT SEAWORLD

⊞ MUST-SEE ⊞ THE WATERFRONT

The heart of SeaWorld is The Waterfront, a five-acre zone filled with shows, theme restaurants, and shops and boutiques. Included within are three maritime neighborhoods: High Street, Harbor Square, and Tower Island.

Strolling entertainers include the Harbormaster, a salty old sea captain who regales travelers with fish tales and plays music with bottles or brandy glasses. The Longshoremen entertain visitors with street comedy and stunts. Sailors and fishermen walk about with colorful tropical birds.

Each night during the summer and holiday periods, a dazzling display of light, water, and fire ends the day at SeaWorld with Mistify. The show is visible from anywhere around the central lake, but front row is at The Waterfront.

The Waterfront at SeaWorld. *Photo courtesy of SeaWorld*

High Street

Artisans from around the world showcase their wares on elegant High Street. Nestled among the shops is The Seafire Inn. Chefs prepare stir-fry dishes on a 4-foot Mongolian wok. By night, The Seafire Inn is the home of the Makahiki Luau.

Harbor Square

Harbor Square is at the center of The Waterfront and hosts daily performances by the "Seaport Symphony," a band of chefs who make music with pots and pans, along with more traditional instruments.

Harbor Square also is home to The Waterfront's largest restaurant, Voyagers Wood-Fired Pizza. Food preparation turns performance art as chefs "Dominic and Luigi" create pizzas the old-fashioned, high-flying way.

Mermaid dreams

Tower Island

Jutting out into the lake is Tower Island, a place to see and be seen. At the base of SeaWorld's famous 400-foot-tall Sky Tower landmark, a re-creation of an ancient fortress has been turned into the SandBar, a pub overlooking the picturesque harbor. Guests can dine on upscale appetizers such as sushi and enjoy signature martinis and frozen drinks while listening to live musicians.

⬛ MUST-SEE KRAKEN

Rising up out of the sea, or at least up out of SeaWorld, is a monster of a roller coaster, Kraken. With the sudden explosion of roller coasters in Orlando, including the fabulous Dueling Dragons and The Hulk at Universal Studios Islands of Adventure, and the raucous Rock 'n' Roller Coaster at Disney–MGM Studios, SeaWorld waited an extra season to introduce the highest, fastest, and longest coaster in town, located alongside the Journey to Atlantis ride.

Kraken is a floorless and topless coaster. Before you get too excited, let me explain what that means; we're not talking about the dress code. Coaster seats are

SeaWorld Tickets

Prices, which do not include 6 percent tax, were in effect in early 2007 and are subject to change. Discounts are offered for tickets purchased over the Internet through www .seaworld.com; visitors can print their own numbered ticket before heading to the park. From time to time the park offers discounts to Internet ticket buyers. The park also regularly offers a second-day-free deal that allows visitors to return to the park.

	ADULT	CHILD (ages 3 to 9)
ONE-DAY SEAWORLD TICKET	$64.95	$53.95
FOUR-PARK ORLANDO FLEXTICKET	$189.95	$155.95
Unlimited admission to Universal Studios Florida, Universal Studios Islands of Adventure, SeaWorld Orlando, Wet 'n Wild. Valid fourteen days.		
FIVE-PARK ORLANDO FLEXTICKET	$234.95	$199.95
Unlimited admission to Universal Studios Florida, Universal Studios Islands of Adventure, SeaWorld Orlando, Wet 'n Wild, and Busch Gardens Tampa Bay. Valid fourteen days.		
SEAWORLD ORLANDO/ BUSCH GARDENS TAMPA BAY VALUE TICKET One day at each park	$99.95	$89.95
SILVER PASSPORT SEAWORLD ANNUAL PASS	$94.95	$84.95
SILVER PASSPORT SEAWORLD, BUSCH GARDENS ANNUAL PASS	$144.95	$134.95
SILVER PASSPORT SEAWORLD, BUSCH GARDENS TAMPA BAY, ADVENTURE ISLAND ANNUAL PASS	$189.95	$179.95
GOLD PASSPORT SEAWORLD ORLANDO TWO-YEAR PASS	$144.95	$134.95
GOLD PASSPORT SEAWORLD ORLANDO, BUSCH GARDENS TAMPA BAY TWO-YEAR PASS	$219.95	$209.95
GOLD PASSPORT SEAWORLD ORLANDO, BUSCH GARDENS TAMPA BAY, ADVENTURE ISLAND TWO-YEAR PASS	$279.95	$269.95
PLATINUM PASSPORT SEAWORLD ORLANDO, BUSCH GARDENS TAMPA BAY, ADVENTURE ISLAND TWO-YEAR PASS	$309.95	$299.95

Parking $10.00

mounted on a pedestal a few feet above the wheels and track. There is no "car," no roof or sides, and riders' feet will dangle off the bottom of their chairs.

Think of being strapped into your favorite chair and taking off up a 149-foot-high hill and then careening off into space at speeds of up to 65 miles per hour. Oh yes, and your chair turns upside down seven times, with elements including a cobra roll, a zero-gravity roll, several vertical loops, and some flat spins. The first drop is an impressive 144 feet, heading into a 101-foot diving loop. All this with a view of nothing but sky or ground.

Greek and Norse myths say Kraken was a massive underwater beast held prisoner by Poseidon. At SeaWorld, the sea serpent has been set free—and boy, is he ever angry. The waiting line features some displays of baby eels—Kraken's offspring, we are told.

A good portion of the 4,177-foot-long track runs over water. The track plunges underground three times; one stretch dives below the lagoon. Riders stay pretty dry, but onlookers are rewarded with a major splash as the coaster goes by.

The track runs fairly close to the ground for most of its path, rising and falling like the undulating back of a serpent. One very nice touch: At the top of the lift hill, there's a false drop just for effect, and then an extended flat stretch where you can contemplate the plunge that's ahead.

The ride takes about three minutes and thirty-nine seconds. There are usually three trains on the track (eight cars of four passengers each), accommodating about 1,500 riders per hour. The Swiss-designed ride is unique in Orlando, although it is similar to a ride named the Medusa at Six Flags Great Adventure in New Jersey.

MUST-SEE JOURNEY TO ATLANTIS

This unusual attraction is part water ride, part roller coaster, and totally wild. SeaWorld's first thrill ride delivers two of the steepest, wettest, fastest drops anywhere. Here's the concept: Journey to Atlantis plunges riders into the middle of a fierce battle between good and evil for the lost city of Atlantis.

According to historical lore, the city of Atlantis sank beneath the waves eons ago. Now it has risen again in the Greek fishing village of Thera. The Atlantis set spans an area larger than six football fields and towers taller than a ten-story building.

You'll enter into an eight-passenger fishing boat, two per row. The front and back seats offer the best ride; you may get slightly less wet in the middle row. The boats enter into an underwater setting with coral, an area filled with what SeaWorld calls "aqualusions." The attractive siren Allura, representing evil, and Hermes, the force of good, play happily together for a few moments before the siren morphs into a wicked creature. (Hermes, the golden sea horse that transforms into a glittering guide, looks like a horse, but he is actually a fish. Hermes's live counterparts, yellow Indo-Pacific and lined Caribbean sea horses, reside in aquariums in the gift shop.)

Riders are pulled into Atlantis and the dark and mysterious depths of the siren's lair. (The piercing scream of the angry siren is actually made up of a combination of eight animal voices, including a lion, bear, and rattlesnake.) Suddenly the boats nosedive 60 feet at a sixty-degree angle, reaching a speed of up to 50 miles per hour through a tidal wave of water. (Just to add insult to injury, there is a bank of coin-operated water hoses at the bottom of the first 60-foot water drop for spectators to use on riders.)

Journey to Atlantis

You'll fall through a dark vortex with fog and light. A second drop of just 9 feet may get you wetter than the big fall. Allura calls: "Leaving so soon? I think not!" Then each fishing boat is drawn back up into the building, this time connected to the rails of a roller coaster. The coaster drop is also about 60 feet, with sharp S-curves and other elements. And there's one more big splash at the base of the coaster's drop. The last, most spectacular drop is unlike any other. Cars nosedive at highway speeds into a series of careening S-curves before emerging into the daylight.

The attraction adds some spectacular "aqualusion" effects to give us a view of an ancient city beneath the water. Statues seem to come to life and then magically transform into rivers of shimmering water. Entire sets appear and then disappear, metamorphosing into Olympian vistas. Advanced technology uses hologram and LCD images. Nearly 24,000 fiber-optic lights illuminate the travels of Hermes, the attraction's hero, who guides guests beyond the dark depths of the siren's dangers to relative safety. The attraction is located at the back of the park near Kraken and between the manatee display and Penguin Encounter; guests driving on International Drive can see the superstructure along the right side of the road. The ride is usually much more crowded on hot summer days, when the idea of a cool bath and high speed is relatively attractive. Avoid Atlantis just after one of the major shows lets out.

The entire trip takes about seven and a half minutes. You do not want to bring any cameras or other items not meant to get wet. There are unlocked storage cubbies for riders at the loading area; rental lockers with keys are also available before you get in line. Note there is a 42-inch height minimum.

Be sure to check out the Jewels of the Sea Aquarium Gallery inside the gift shop at the base of the building that supports the ride; it includes eight aquariums, including an unusual glass tank set into the floor. Beneath your feet are stingrays and various fish; over your head are bonnethead sharks.

⦙MUST-SEE⦙ WILD ARCTIC

The Wild Arctic coexists in balmy central Florida, a combination of a state-of-the-art simulator ride and an impressive re-creation of some of the wonders of the frozen north. The adventure begins with a thrilling "flight" over the frozen north in the jet helicopter *White Thunder* to the remote Base Station Wild Arctic, surrounded by the beauty of the arctic and kicking up snow at takeoff in a race to outrun an approaching storm.

As the chopper flies out of the hangar, the arctic landscape unfolds. The journey is relaxing—at first—as the sweeping vista is filled with frozen mountains, glacier peaks, and clouds. The craft's diving and banking levels out over the sea, and passengers are treated to a spectacular view of narwhals, walruses, and other marine life.

Unsettled briefly by buffeting winds and blinding fog banks, the jet helicopter swoops toward the pack ice for a closer view of polar bears. The radio crackles a warning: The blizzard is bearing down. Following the frigid Franklin Strait, the helicopter skims low over the arctic sea. At Larsen Sound a huge glacier fills the horizon. Gently touching down on the ancient frozen floe, visitors absorb the beauty—until a deep rumbling starts, and the copter starts to tumble into a deep crevasse. The copter smacks into the sea just as the rotors reach full thrust. We make a spectacular escape through the close walls of an ice cavern and eventually to the base station.

There are three helicopter simulators in the Wild Arctic building, each seating fifty-nine people. The attraction accommodates up to 1,800 guests per hour when all three simulators are in operation. Wheelchair access is provided. High-definition video laser-disc projectors provide the visual stimulation, backed up by 1,200-watt, six-channel laser-disc sound systems. Each cabin moves six ways—yaw, pitch, roll, heave, surge, and sway. Sometimes the cabin moves as much as 9 feet, and in some directions it moves at speeds up to 24 inches per second.

Stepping from the simulator, guests enter a chilly passageway into a frozen wonderland of Base Station Wild Arctic with ice walls, where they will come close to some of the real animals that live at the North Pole. Forget you're in Florida and buy into the story: The base station was built by modern scientists around the decrepit hull of a 150-year-old British exploration ship frozen in the ice for all these years, a unique vantage point for viewing arctic sea life, including polar bears, beluga whales, and walruses. The viewing position allows views of the animals above and below the water as they forage for food, dive, swim, and interact with base-station workers.

Realistic Fantasy

The structure that houses Journey to Atlantis is modeled after a Greek palace, Knossos. Hieroglyphics on the walls of the attraction are duplicates of ones taken from murals and pictorial works in historical Etruscan books. In filming for the attraction, Santa Barbara, California, stood in for Greece.

Ask the Experts

Do you have a question about aquatic animals? SeaWorld experts promise to reply to questions submitted to them by e-mail at shamu@seaworld.org or by phone at (800) 237–4268.

High-tech equipment sits in and around the ship's remains, with measuring devices next to old anchors and video receivers perched on old shipping crates. The base station makes extensive use of computers and touch-screen monitors to allow guests to communicate with reports from field researchers, and guests can use computers to communicate with research base "scientists." You'll be able to gauge your ability to hold your breath against polar bears (two minutes), beluga whales (twenty minutes), walruses (twenty-five minutes), and the local champion, harbor seals (twenty-seven minutes).

The arctic is a place of mystery to most people, assumed to be a frozen desert. Instead, it is a vast, ever-changing ocean, teeming with life and closely linked to the rest of the planet. Among the stars of Wild Arctic are Klondike and Snow, a pair of polar bears. Abandoned by their mother at birth, the bears were hand raised by experts at the Denver Zoo. Weighing about 1.3 pounds at birth, the male, Klondike, will weigh about 1,800 pounds by adulthood and the female, Snow, about 900 pounds. Lack of space at the zoo demanded the bears be relocated, and in late 1995 the pair were brought to Orlando.

They live in a special enclosure that includes a chilly (fifty degrees) pool that contains 900,000 gallons of manufactured seawater and is stocked with fish. (The cubs had never seen live food and had to learn how to fish for themselves.) The bears' hunting instincts are further satisfied with morsels hidden in nooks and crevices of the habitat.

Polar bears are among the most beautiful and dangerous of animals and are found only in the arctic. The animals are born white; their coats turn yellow in the summer sun and turn white again after a spring molt. The hair itself is hollow to trap warm air, oil coats their fur, and a thick layer of fat provides insulation from the cold. When awake, polar bears spend much of their time stalking or feeding on seals, walruses, and sometimes even beluga whales.

Beluga whales, sometimes known as "sea canaries," are born gray and turn white as they age, making a natural camouflage from predators as they move among the icebergs and ice floes. They weigh from 1,500 to 3,300 pounds and measure from 10 to 15 feet long. Like other toothed whales, belugas "echolocate," sending out sonarlike sounds to find breathing holes in the ice and to locate prey such as squid, octopi, shrimp, and a wide variety of other bottom-dwelling fish. Walruses have one pair of flippers in front and a second in back. A thick layer of fat, or blubber, helps regulate heat loss.

Children may explore polar bear dens (without the bears) or pop their heads through openings in a simulated ice floe, just as they saw the harbor seals doing before them.

⚟ MUST-SEE ⚟ KEY WEST AT SEAWORLD

This showcase for the island beauty and funky tropical charm of the southernmost city in the United States has a mix of New England and Bahamian architecture, framed by stands of palm trees, hibiscus, and bougainvillea. Visitors stroll along river rock and pathways and boardwalks; restaurants feature Caribbean cuisine. Street performers and vendors and perhaps a tightrope walker brighten the landscape. The five-acre site is on the park's east side, alongside Manatees: The Last Generation? Naturalistic animal habitats allow up-close encounters and interaction with bottlenose dolphins, sleek stingrays, and one of the world's few saltwater-adapted reptiles, the sea turtle.

Key West at SeaWorld

The largest section at Key West is Dolphin Cove, home to more than two dozen inquisitive bottlenose dolphins, the species most often seen in the coastal waters of the Gulf of Mexico and off Key West. A wave maker moves chilled seawater through the deep 600,000-gallon pool, creating tides that ebb and flow. There is also an area where guests can touch and feed the animals. And an underwater window allows glimpses of the dolphins below the surface.

At Turtle Point, you can come up close to threatened and endangered species of sea turtles, including the green, loggerhead, and hawksbill. The hunting of sea turtles was a major industry in Key West until federal laws protecting the animals were enacted in the 1970s.

Stingray Lagoon, a longtime local favorite at SeaWorld, features a wide variety of graceful rays, including cownose, Southern, roughtailed, Atlantic, and yellow stingrays, as well as guitar fish. Visitors are encouraged to touch and feed the 200 or so rays. These fascinating creatures swim close to the edge of the pool, where you can easily rub their rubbery skin and feel their fins; their poison sacs have been removed, and these stingrays are used to humans. A new nursery cove exhibits newborn rays. Nearby is Sunset Square, with Key West–theme shops, restaurants, and entertainment.

MUST-SEE SHAMU'S HAPPY HARBOR

If you asked active, adventurous kids to design the ultimate outdoor playground, they might come up with something just like this. Shamu's Happy Harbor is, quite simply, one of the most spectacular playgrounds we have ever seen. In the learned opinions of the kids we asked, it stands head and monkey bars over Fievel's Playground at Universal Studios; *Honey, I Shrunk the Kids* Movie Set

Adventure at Disney–MGM Studios; and Tom Sawyer Island at the Magic Kingdom. We cannot imagine higher praise.

And *higher* is the word that comes to mind first. The central feature of the three-acre playground is a pair of gigantic nets that each extend about 40 feet in the air. The netting—actually double netting to prevent accidents—winds back and forth and makes turns like flights of stairs. Way up at the top is a tire swing, safely allowing youngsters to fly out as if into space.

The base of the net lets out into a long slide. Down below is Pete's Water Maze, a pirate ship with water cannon, a large sand play area, and other activities. On very hot days you might want to dress your children in bathing suits and let them cool off on the small wet slides there. Parents can park at the bottom of the net and keep an eye on their kids as they climb; a snack bar serves the area. Most of the area is under a roof, blocking the sun and some rain.

If all of this is too rambunctious for your young ones, they can explore Boogie Bump Bay, a special area for small ones that includes bubble bikes, a mini-ball crawl, an air bounce, a fence maze, and many other activities appropriate to their size.

MUST-SEE SHAMU EXPRESS

Okay, it's not Kraken—unless you're viewing it through six-year-old eyes. Shamu Express, which opened in 2006 at Shamu's Happy Harbor, is a "family-friendly" roller coaster that packs just enough thrill: more than 850 feet of track and a top speed of 26 miles per hour.

Also added to the area is a jellyfish-themed tower ride called **Jazzy Jellies,** which lifts and spins families. And **Swishy Fishies** is a teacup spin ride around a giant waterspout.

MUST-SEE MANATEES: THE LAST GENERATION?

SeaWorld is doing its part to answer the question the name of this attraction poses with a "no." This fascinating attraction winds through a riverlike setting filled with the gentle manatee giants, as well as turtles, fish (including tarpon, gar, and snook), and birds. A seamless, 126-foot-long acrylic panel permits underwater views. Nearby is a nursing pool built for manatee mothers and their babies, and there's also the Manatee Theater, which presents a special film using Bi-Vision technology with stunning underwater footage to make it seem as if you are completely surrounded by manatees.

The manatee is an air-breathing marine mammal; when it submerges, special muscles pinch the nostrils tightly closed to keep the water out. If you look carefully, you will also see sparse hair on the manatee's skin. Manatee calves nurse from their mothers. Some people believe that the myth of the mermaid arose from manatee sightings by sailors; they had to have been out to sea a long time to make such a mistake. Interestingly, though, the word *manatee* is believed to be derived from a Carib word meaning "a woman's breast."

In the wild an adult manatee dines exclusively on plants; each day a full-grown specimen may eat as much as one hundred pounds of sea grass, water hyacinths, and other types of plants. At the park the favorite food for the manatees is romaine lettuce, one of SeaWorld's bigger expenses. If you're in the viewing area at one of several feeding times, watch as the manatees use their flippers almost as hands to grab the lettuce.

All of the manatees on display have been rescued from their only natural enemy—man. Most have been injured by propellers on boats, fishing nets, or plastic items thrown in the water by boaters. Adult manatees are released back into the wild once they are able to survive there. Orphans will probably spend the rest of their lives in the park.

Also on exhibit are some of the vehicles and equipment used by SeaWorld's Beached Animal Rescue Station. Since 1973 the park's marine animal experts have rescued more than a hundred manatees found seriously injured, ill, or orphaned in the wild. The crews are also called upon to help at dolphin and pygmy sperm whale strandings.

One of the slogans in the manatee area is "Extinction is forever. Endangered means we still have time."

> ## Gator Gar
>
> The fish that you see in the manatee ponds that look at first glance like alligators are something known as alligator gar (*Lepisosteus spatula*). From the side they look ordinary, but from the top and bottom they certainly could fool all but the bravest.

■ PACIFIC POINT PRESERVE

This re-created coastal setting for California sea lions and harbor and fur seals is a great way to get up close and personal with some of SeaWorld's most amusing aquatic creatures. Able to swim at birth, a harbor seal pup stays close to its mother for short nursing periods. The female's fat-rich milk helps the pup to more than double its weight by the time it is four to eight weeks old. Then the pup is weaned, goes its own way, and fends for itself.

You'll be able to purchase a package of smelt to feed the seals. Washing stations are nearby to help remove the smell of smelt from your hands. Note that if you want to see and feed them, seals and sea lions are not morning creatures; they are most active in the midday sun.

■ ANHEUSER-BUSCH HOSPITALITY CENTER

SeaWorld is owned by Anheuser-Busch, which also owns Florida attractions Busch Gardens Tampa Bay and Adventure Island, and other parks around the United States. The Hospitality Center offers a bit of the corporate message along with free samples of the company's beers.

Set amid tropical lagoons and lush foliage, the center displays antique brewery equipment, including a century-old Studebaker wagon used for hauling more than six tons of Budweiser beer behind a team of Clydesdale horses. At the Clydesdale Hitch Barn, guests can watch stable hands suit up the majestic horses in their harnesses and formal attire before their twice-daily parades through the park.

Clydesdales are descended from the great war horses of Europe, brought to North America around 1842 to pull delivery vehicles. Anheuser-Busch introduced a team of Clydesdales and a bright red brewery wagon to celebrate the end of Prohibition in 1933.

A full-grown Clydesdale stands about 18 hands tall at the shoulders (about 72 inches tall) and weighs between 2,000 and 2,300 pounds. Ten or more of the giant Clydesdale workhorses are on display at any given time, either in the outside paddock or in indoor stalls near the Hospitality Center. These huge horses, the symbol of Anheuser-Busch, are sometimes dressed in elaborate harnesses and hitched to their famous wagon to march in procession through the park. The driver of an eight-horse hitch pulling a beer wagon like the ones at SeaWorld must wrestle more than forty pounds of reins to control the horses. A Clydesdale horseshoe measures 20 inches end to end and weighs about five pounds.

After viewing the Clydesdales, adults can sample Anheuser-Busch products, including Michelob and Budweiser beers. A separate counter offers soft drinks and snacks at the going SeaWorld prices. An outside terrace offers a quiet, shady spot for sampling and resting and also provides a good view of the associated gardens and waterfalls and the Clydesdale paddocks close by.

SHOWS AT SEAWORLD

⋮ MUST-SEE ⋮ BELIEVE

A truly astrounding achievement, Believe is a killer-whale ballet presented on a spectacular aquatic stage at Shamu Stadium. The show, introduced simultaneously at all three SeaWorld parks (Orlando, San Diego and San Antonio), showcases the Shamu family of killer whales in a show in which the animals—weighing between 6,000 and 10,000 pounds—move to the beat of a specially composed musical score. SeaWorld trainers developed sixty whale behaviors that are used in the show.

The set is dominated by a 30-foot-high tail fluke flanked by four huge LED video screens that operate independently and also move together to create a single, 80-foot-wide panoramic screen. These screens provide guests at Shamu Stadium with views of the whales from above- and below-water cameras, including, for the first time, a camera suspended directly over the main show pool.

The audio system for Believe is the most sophisticated ever constructed for a SeaWorld show, involving nearly one hundred speakers throughout the stadium. The musical score was recorded by the Prague National Symphony Orchestra.

The 5,200-seat Shamu Stadium, a short walk down the hill from the Atlantis Stadium on the same side of the lagoon, was built around a five-million-gallon saltwater pool that is home to the killer whales, the stars of the show.

The majestic, mysterious killer whale mostly lives in a world unto itself, traveling in pods from frigid waters off the coast of Iceland to warmer climates near the tip of South Africa. On islands off the coast of Argentina, researchers have observed them hunting in great packs and called them the "wolves of the sea." Whales are aquatic mammals and not fish, though they are good swimmers. Killer whales can remain submerged up to twelve minutes before surfacing.

Killer whales have shown an unusual capacity for sharing special relationships with humans. In the show, many of the whales' actions are prompted by trainers' hand signals. For example, when the trainer holds up an open hand toward the audience, the whales face the audience and open their mouths. Also listen carefully for the faint sound of high-pitched training whistles during the show.

The best seats in the stadium—if you don't mind getting wet—are in the first six rows. Here you will be able to see under the water through the glass wall of the tank, as well as the show up above. If you prefer to stay dry, sit toward the front of the second bank of seats, in the middle of the stadium. You'll have a good view of the video screen and of the platform where the whales frequently beach themselves during the show.

Don't say we didn't warn you: The lower fifteen rows are marked as the "splash zone." That may at first seem like a bit of overkill—it does not seem possible that a whale can send water up that high over the glass. And in fact, for the first three-quarters of the show only those brave souls in the very closest seats are likely to be splashed by one of the animals as it passes by. But don't congratulate yourself too soon. The conclusion of the show is one wet finale. Wet as in water that washes over the top of the glass in a spectacular wave and soaks the people in those front fifteen rows. Water. Wave. Soaks. Fifty-five-degree saltwater. Actually, it's two waves. Get the picture?

One problem with the stadium shows at SeaWorld is that when one of the presentations lets out, a large number of people are deposited onto walkways leading toward the restaurants. If you are planning to eat after a show, head directly to a restaurant or consider sending someone ahead to place an order.

■ SHAMU: CLOSE UP!

SeaWorld's 1.7-million-gallon killer-whale research facility allows visitors to get closer than ever to Shamu and his friends. It also allows scientists opportunities to study the development of killer whales. The habitat is located alongside the Shamu Stadium and includes shallows that encourage the whales to engage in some of their favorite activities: back scratching and tummy rubbing. Special devices include a huge scale, capable of measuring weights up to 40,000 pounds.

MUST-SEE *BLUE HORIZONS* (WHALE AND DOLPHIN STADIUM)

Dolphins leap from the water, humans plunge from above on bungees, and Broadway meets the seafront at *Blue Horizons*, a show that opened in mid-2005.

A young girl's vivid imagination sets the stage for an extravaganza of graceful dolphins, ominous false killer whales, and a rainbow of exotic birds, including blue and gold macaws, Andean condors, and sun conures. The action comes from below the water, where specially trained dolphins leap as high as 25 feet

Dolphins visit guests at Key West.

A Dolphin's Life

Bottlenose dolphins inhabit temperate and tropical waters throughout the world and are the most common dolphin species in the United States, from Cape Cod to the Gulf of Mexico. They live in groups known as "pods" or "herds," varying in size from two to fifteen animals. The members of the pod rank themselves and establish dominance by smacking their tails against the water, butting heads, and other actions.

above the surface, sometimes carrying divers. From above, aerialists, dressed in costumes symbolizing sea and sky, plunge off the elaborate set into the water or launch skyward.

The twenty-minute show is set to an original musical score played by the Seattle Symphony Orchestra, and it is performed on a 100-foot-wide, 40-foot-tall stage and in front of an extension of the see-through wall enclosing the pool at the Whale and Dolphin Stadium. The set was designed by Stanley Meyer, who worked on the Broadway musical *Beauty and the Beast.*

The park's dolphins had to learn a number of new behaviors and accept cues from unseen handlers. The birds in the show will fly over the audience, circle, and then soar off to a landing place on the set, in an explosion of color in the sky and water.

Pseudorca crassidens, or false killer whales, have a beautiful, solid-black color and smooth features; these fast swimmers are up to 25 feet long.

The first four rows, especially toward the center of the arena, are the wet seats. The views from anywhere are good, but the best seats are mid-stadium within the first ten rows. The stairs to the seats in the stadium are quite steep and might pose a difficulty for some people; the easiest seats are at the bottom, where you may get a bit wet, or at the top, where you are the farthest away.

MUST-SEE CLYDE AND SEAMORE TAKE PIRATE ISLAND (SEA LION AND OTTER STADIUM)

This is a dramatic tale of treasure, treachery, and the quest for fish, beginning somewhere in the Caribbean as a pirate ship sails by an island inhabited by two marooned buccaneers. But when an otter purloins the treasure map and seeks the assistance of the stranded pirates, who will end up with the gold?

Some of the funniest bits at SeaWorld are to be found here, at the 3,000-seat Sea Lion and Otter Stadium. The humans in this show are more than actors: They are skilled animal handlers who are chosen for their animal knowledge as well as their acting ability. The stars are the sea lions, a tiny otter, and the only trained walrus we've ever seen.

Depending on the time of day and season, much of the stadium may be facing the sun; come early to find a shaded area. The first four rows are marked as "splash zones"; we're talking about little spurts, nothing like the tsunamis at Shamu Stadium. Early arrivals also get to watch the talented mime make fun of late arrivals, one of the most popular mini-shows at SeaWorld.

■ PELICAN EXHIBIT

On the left side of the walkway toward the Atlantis Stadium is a small but spectacular collection of pelicans. Among the birds you will see there are American white pelicans, denizens of marshy lakes and the Pacific and Texas coasts; they winter chiefly in coastal lagoons from Florida and southern California south to Panama. Unlike Florida brown pelicans, white pelicans do not dive for their food. Instead they fish in groups, capturing their prey cooperatively by forming a crescent, beating their wings, and driving the fish into shallow water, where they use their large pouched bills to catch and then swallow their meal.

■ *ODYSSEA* (NAUTILUS THEATRE)

Under the sea, with a bit of a Las Vegas circus, *Odyssea* is a thirty-minute spectacle combining acrobatic feats, lively music, and dazzling special effects. Scenes include an antarctic landscape with high-flying, playful "penguin" characters who bounce, tumble, and flip on trampolines; aerial performers who fly through the air in intricate formations, appearing to glide through a glittering green kelp forest; a contortionist, balanced inside a giant seashell, who twists, bends, and undulates into seemingly impossible shapes; and giant, accordion-like "tube worm" characters who perform a colorful, rhythmic dance.

The air-conditioned theater has 2,400 seats, enough for last-minute arrivals on all but the most crowded day.

▓ *MUST-SEE* *PETS AHOY!* (SEAWORLD THEATER)

An all-star cast of more than 130 features potbellied pigs, cats, dogs, birds, the occasional rat, and a few not-so-well-trained humans in a skit with a vague sea adventure theme. This is one of the best animal shows I've seen; if there was an Academy Award for furry and feathered creatures, these would be my nominees.

In some shows an aspiring young actor or actress even gets into the act, costarring with a sloppy-kissing Great Dane. Finally, guests receive training tips for their own pets. Before you make excuses for the limited repertoire of your own pets at home, consider that nearly all the performers come from animal shelters.

Bad PR

Sharks have gotten a great deal of bad PR. Two times more people die of bee stings each year than succumb to shark attacks.

CONTINUOUS-VIEWING EXHIBITS

A number of SeaWorld exhibits are open all day without scheduled events. You can enter them for a quick walk-through or a leisurely study. The premier facilities of this type at SeaWorld include Key West at SeaWorld, Terrors of the Deep, Penguin Encounter, and Tropical Reef. You'll see a number of other interesting places as you walk through SeaWorld, including a tropical rain forest and Pacific Point Preserve.

MUST-SEE TERRORS OF THE DEEP

You will find yourself immersed in the secret hiding places of menacing eels, venomous fish, hungry barracuda, and . . . sharks. The unique collection of creatures in this exhibit can be potentially dangerous, it is true, but the message of this exhibit is clear: "Respect them, don't kill them." For example, sharks have a bad reputation for attacking humans, but there are few documented instances of wanton attack. As with most injurious encounters between humans and sea creatures, these attacks usually are the result of mistaken identity: The human was mistaken for food.

A short video at the entrance offers some excellent background; don't rush through. The shark movie and aquarium portion of the show are timed to give you about twenty-five minutes to view the tunnel area and the other displays. If you rush through these sections, you'll have to stand in line waiting your turn for the shark theater. The show takes about forty minutes, including the film and walk-through.

The first aquarium displays more than 500 eels in a 10-foot-deep tank. Grouper, snapper, lookdowns, and jacks—predatory fish that are native to the same ecosystems inhabited by eels—are housed nearby. A high-tech system simulates the currents and wave action of the reef, and a single light source is placed to simulate the sun.

Hungry Sharks?

Sharks eat only about once a week. Check with the park for the current feeding schedule; if you can make it, you will understand what the term "feeding frenzy" really means. This is not an experience for the squeamish.

The best part of this exhibit is the acrylic tunnel that runs through the bottom of the aquarium; you can walk through the tank to view the "terrors." The clear viewing tunnels can support the weight of 372 elephants, which is more than strong enough to keep you and the 450 tons of water above you apart. One of the scenes from the film *Jaws 3-D* was shot inside the shark tunnel. SeaWorld's education department occasionally schedules sleepovers within the tunnels for school groups.

Among the creatures you'll see are moray eels (some more than 6 feet long), spotted morays, and purple-mouthed eels. After the first tunnel you'll come to a display of venomous lionfish and scorpion fish. The graceful lionfish will captivate you with their movement and the colors of the fins that hide their dangerous spines. Scorpion fish show how they camouflage themselves in the sand and wait for an unsuspecting meal to swim overhead.

A separate tank showcases clown fishes, with beautiful but highly poisonous spines. Also on display are nasty surgeon fish. When they are agitated, they will sweep their tails and threaten antagonists with their spines; a swipe from one of the razor-sharp extensions can seriously slash another fish or injure a fisherman attempting to remove them from nets or hooks.

There's also a collection of barracuda, creatures that ordinarily feast on fish, squid, and shrimp, attacking with a single swift strike at speeds of as much as 28 miles per hour. Viewed from the side the barracuda is hard to miss, but from the front the slender fish is nearly invisible. Barracuda attacks on humans are rare and accidental. Murky water makes it hard to see, and barracuda are apt to confuse shiny objects such as jewelry for fish. Swimmers in tropical waters are advised not to be between the fish and the sunny surface of the water.

The final stop on the journey comes when you descend 15 feet below the surface to the territory of the shark through a 6-inch-thick clear acrylic tube. You'll travel through the 125-foot-long shark-filled habitat on a PeopleMover, as dozens of nurse, brown, bull, and sand tiger sharks swim overhead and in front. Among the shark skeletons on display is a set of jaw bones from a 17-foot male great white caught in western Australia. If you are claustrophobic and choose to avoid the tunnel, simply exit to your left through the unmarked door beside the tunnel entrance. You can wait for the rest of your party at the end of the line.

■ PENGUIN ENCOUNTER

The largest, most technically advanced exhibit of its kind, this is home to hundreds of penguins (from the antarctic) and alcids (from the arctic). The science center goes beyond entertainment to educate guests about the need to protect and preserve polar life.

In a setting so realistic that you can expect to see snowflakes inside, this exhibit moves you past living arctic and antarctic displays on a 120-foot PeopleMover. Glass windows give an unobstructed and unobtrusive view above and below the water, where stately king penguins, gentle gentoos, and bounding rockhoppers live. (By the way, the largest penguins at SeaWorld Orlando are the king penguins; at SeaWorld of California there's a colony of emperor penguins, which are the largest in the world.) At the alcid exhibit you'll come face-to-snout with more than a hundred puffins, buffleheads, smews, and murres from the arctic. While these are not related to penguins, they are considered their ecological counterparts.

SeaWorld animal experts match temperature and daylight as closely as possible to the animals' native territory so their seasons change as they would if they

Penguin and Eggs

If you see groups of penguins huddled along the back wall of the exhibit, chances are they are hatching eggs. SeaWorld has a very successful penguin breeding program.

Penguin Encounter

were living in the wild. After the ride past the live exhibits, you enter a hall with many fascinating, lighted displays. Press on the kid-size handprints within each display to hear a recorded message.

Be sure to stop at the SeaWorld Learning Center just past the moving walkway. A globe depicts antarctic explorers. You will see Scott's expedition of 1910 to 1913, and his somewhat friendly adversary Amundsen's from 1910 to 1912. Also featured is Drake's route around South America from 1578 to 1579, and Cook's expedition from 1712 to 1715, which was the first known circumnavigation of the antarctic—marked on the map as TERRA INCOGNITA.

Hot House

When it's snowing in the penguin exhibit, these fascinating animals are swimming in fifty-five-degree water. That's cold to us, but compared to the thirty-two-degree refrigerated air of their enclosure, it is like a penguin day at the beach.

■ TROPICAL REEF AND CARIBBEAN TIDE POOL

More than 1,000 tropical fish live in this 160,000-gallon exhibit, the largest South Pacific coral reef display in the United States. The Caribbean Tide Pool gives you close-up views of tropical fish and invertebrates such as starfish, sea urchins, crabs, and anemones. Smaller aquariums exhibit clown fish, sea horses, and octopi.

■ SKY TOWER

This 400-foot needle tower can be seen from miles around SeaWorld, marking the park location and helping you find your way in. Once inside the park, you can ride a sit-down, circular elevator to the top for a panoramic view of SeaWorld and much of central Florida. Take your SeaWorld map on this five-and-a-half-minute ride; it will help you orient yourself to the layout of the park as well as other attractions in the area, such as Walt Disney World, which you can see from your rotating perch.

Admission is not included in the daily park pass; in 2006 tickets were $3.00. The elevator may not operate during heavy winds or other bad weather.

OTHER ATTRACTIONS AT SEAWORLD

Flamingo Boats. A fleet of flamingo-shaped paddleboats head out into a small part of the lagoon; they're a pleasant break from the hustle and bustle of the park. Two-seater boats rent for about $6.00 per hour.

EATS AND TREATS

In general, SeaWorld food offerings are a bit simpler than you will find at Epcot or Universal. Menus are more limited, but the food generally is of high quality, and the portions are large. By the way, watch out for marauding seagulls. They are quite capable of swooping down and grabbing some of your food if you are eating at one of the outdoor restaurants.

Two recent additions at SeaWorld are places where the tableside entertainment has a certain fishy appeal: Sharks Underwater Grill and Dine with Shamu.

 Sharks Underwater Grill. SeaWorld squeezed a dining room into the Terrors of the Deep building, offering views from your table through ceiling-to-floor windows into a 660,000-gallon tank that is home to some fifty sharks of various species, including sand tiger, sandbar, nurse, blacknose, and Atlantic black tip. If you're lucky, you may witness participants in the **Shark Deep Dive,** which allows a few guests each day to descend into the tank within a shark cage. The Floribbean-style menu has an emphasis on seafood, delivering a meal well beyond typical theme-park fare. Typical offerings include Caribbean seafood pasta with spiced shrimp, scallops, and fish; oak-grilled filet mignon with jerk seasoning; and a seafood sampler. Advance reservations can be made by calling (407) 351–3600; priority seating can be arranged by calling (800) 327–2420 or visiting the information counter at the front gate.

 Dine with Shamu. This is a seafood buffet backstage at Shamu Stadium. Park trainers give lectures during meals, which will be scheduled at various times during the day. Tickets for adults are about $37, children

Key

 = Fast food

 = Full-service restaurant

(ages three to nine) about $19. Park admission is not included. For reservations call (800) 327–2420, or visit the information counter at the front gate.

📷 **Shamu & Crew Character Breakfast.** Meet some of the park's most famous residents—or at least people wearing their costumes (don't tell the kids)—at The Seafire Inn at 9:10 A.M. daily in season. Adults $14.95, children $9.95. Reservations are required.

📷 **Makahiki Luau.** The nightly shindig as the sun sets at the Waterfront's Seafire Inn is a bountiful celebration filled with ancient customs, rhythmic music and dance, authentic costumes, and the cuisine of the Pacific Islands. The entertainment begins with the arrival of a tribe in a ceremonial boat. Dancers perform the native dances of Tahiti, Fiji, Marquesa, and Hawaii.

The meal, served family style, includes mahimahi in piña colada sauce, Hawaiian chicken, sweet-and-sour pork, tropical salad and fruit, fried rice, stir-fried vegetables, seasonal desserts, and beverages.

In 2006 tickets were $45.95 plus tax for adults and $29.95 for children ages three to nine. Park admission is not required and is separate from the price of the luau. For reservations call (800) 327–2420 or consult www.seaworld.com.

There's also a special version of the luau presented during the holiday season: the **Makahiki Christmas Luau.**

🍴 **Smoky Creek Grill.** Picnic tables with umbrellas are available dockside overlooking the Atlantis Lagoon, with a back-door view of the ski show from the lagoon-side seats. Offerings include hickory-smoked chicken or ribs, coleslaw, and roll. Entrees are $5.00 to $7.00.

🍴 **Mama Stella's Italian Kitchen.** Near the Penguin area, this pleasant restaurant with indoor seating offers spaghetti for about $5.00 and pizza for about $4.00. You can also purchase a garden salad and garlic bread.

🍴 **Mango Joe's Cafe.** Here you can get chicken or beef fajitas, fried fish, and club sandwiches, priced from about $6.00 to $12.00. Children's meals include chicken or steak fingers served with french fries for about $4.00. (About those "fingers": They are grilled pieces of meat, not fried. We'd vote them among the best snacks at the park.) The chicken fajitas at Mango Joe's are quite good.

🍴 **Dockside Cafe.** An outdoor cafe near the Sea Lion and Otter Stadium, Dockside serves hamburgers and sandwiches ($5.00 to $6.00) and interesting salads and desserts ($2.00).

DISCOVERY COVE

Theme parks are crowded, impersonal, and expensive. Not so at Discovery Cove, which opened in 2000 across the road from SeaWorld Orlando. At Discovery Cove you're greeted by a concierge, escorted to your personal chaise in the shade of a thatched roof, offered a reservation for your lunch or dinner, and, most importantly, given an appointment to swim with the dolphins and get up close and personal with a pool full of bat rays and 10,000 tropical fish.

Discovery Cove Tickets

Discovery Cove tickets include a full day's use of the park; a supervised swim with the dolphins; use of a mask, snorkel, swim vest, towels, and lockers; plus lunch or dinner. Tickets also include a seven-day pass to SeaWorld Orlando or Busch Gardens Tampa Bay, valid in the week before or after your visit to Discovery Cove. Tickets can also be expanded, for a fee, to include all three parks. Prices, which do not include 6 percent tax, were in effect in early 2007 and are subject to change. Visitors younger than six are not permitted in the dolphin pool.

In recent years ticket prices have been slightly higher in the peak season from mid-March through the end of October. We list here the price ranges as they were in effect for 2007.

In 2006 Discovery Cove introduced the **Evening Experience**, an all-inclusive package limited to just 150 guests per night, from 3:00 to 9:00 P.M. The package includes a shallow-water dolphin encounter, snorkeling in the coral reef, hand-feeding birds in the aviary, and dinner and cocktails at Laguna Grill. The package was offered on selected dates between the end of May and September 1.

	ALL GUESTS
ALL-INCLUSIVE GENERAL ADMISSION DAY*	$259–$279
NON-DOLPHIN SWIM DAY*	$159–$179
EVENING EXPERIENCE*	$259
TRAINER FOR A DAY	$429–$449

*Discovery Cove tickets include a seven-day pass to either SeaWorld Orlando or Busch Gardens Tampa Bay. To extend the ticket to include both SeaWorld Orlando and Busch Gardens and fourteen days of use, add $30 to ticket price.

The experience is uncrowded, personal, relaxing . . . and very expensive. Admission to the park is limited to about 1,000 visitors per day by reservation, with an entrance fee in 2006 of $249 to $279 per person.

How can they justify that price? Consider that the ticket includes admission, as well as a full meal, towels, umbrellas, lockers, snorkels, vests, lounges, and hammocks. Then add in a scheduled swim with the dolphins (which used to sell for $159 at SeaWorld all by itself) and a one-week pass to SeaWorld across the street (worth about $80) or Busch Gardens Tampa Bay, and you may be able to find a way to justify buying a set of admission tickets to Discovery Cove. That said, it's still $996 to $1,116 plus tax for a family of four, a world record for theme-park prices. It makes sense if you want to take a swim with the dolphins, and if you make use of the SeaWorld pass for at least a second day of your stay.

The heart of the thirty-acre park is Dolphin Lagoon, home to about thirty of the friendly marine mammals. Guests receive an appointment for the lagoon; children below the age of six are not permitted. Groups of three guests receive personal instruction from a trainer in shallow water and then enter the lagoon to swim and play with the dolphins.

Guests visit dolphins at Discovery Cove.

At Coral Reef swimmers and snorkelers can opt to play hide-and-seek with rainbows of 10,000 tropical fish in a million-gallon pool. Brightly colored angelfish and delicate butterfly fish compete for attention with silvery jacks, black-and-white spadefish, and more than seventy-five other species. Swimmers also come within inches of barracuda and sharks—safely isolated from the pool behind clear panels in the water. At another point the hull of a shipwreck has acrylic panels that hold off barracudas on the other side.

Ray Lagoon is a quiet, protected area where guests can snorkel, wade, and play with hundreds of southern and cownose stingrays, gentle animals that can grow up to 4 feet in diameter.

The quarter-mile-long Tropical River meanders its way throughout most of Discovery Cove, passing by beaches, walkways, and rocky lagoons. There is a dense tropical forest, an Amazon-like river, a tropical fishing village, and an underwater cave. The river ranges in depth from about 3 to 8 feet; all visitors must wear one of the park's swim vests, which provides just enough buoyancy to let you float along.

Swimmers pass under a waterfall on the Tropical River to enter an immense Aviary that is home to some 300 colorful birds from around the world. Many are trained to eat from the hands of guests.

The aviary holds softbills such as starlings and thrushes, roseate spoonbills, multicolored Turacos, nectar-eating lorries, and tawney frogmouths. Among the smaller residents are finches, honeycreepers, and hummingbirds; a large-bird sanctuary holds some creatures as large as 4 feet tall, such as toucans and red-legged seriema.

The saltwater in the reef and dolphin pool are maintained at seventy-eight degrees; the freshwater river is a constant eighty-five degrees. The park makes its own saltwater; it is not chlorinated, but instead treated with ozone and other chemicals not threatening to wildlife.

Visitors check in for the day at a reception area like a grand hotel. A concierge schedules time with the dolphins and hands out a pass with a charge account for any purchases made at the park. The buildings at the park are designed with a tropical theme, many with real thatched roofs. All visitors are given a pass for a meal, which will feature stir-fries and grilled fish. If you insist on spending more money, you can also purchase snacks or a second meal, beer or wine, photos, gifts, and souvenirs.

Discovery Cove also offers a Trainer for a Day program. For a fee of $419 to $449 per person, a group of up to twelve guests can spend the day working with the trainers and animals at the park and also receive lunch, use of the park, and a seven-day pass to SeaWorld Orlando.

Snorkeling in the Coral Reef at Discovery Cove. *Photo courtesy of SeaWorld*

PART V

DINNER SHOWS AND CHARACTER MEALS

CHAPTER TWENTY

DINNER SHOWS AND CHARACTER MEALS

IF YOU'RE ON VACATION, why should the entertainment stop when you sit down to eat? That's the thinking behind one of the fastest-growing industries in Orlando and the surrounding area—the dinner show. You can watch the North and South battle the Civil War real friendly like, and you can pull apart a chicken with your bare hands while knights on horseback joust for your entertainment. And that's just the beginning: There are more than a dozen major dinner shows inside and outside Walt Disney World. Nearly every one of them has something unique to offer.

Prices for adults generally range from about $25 to $45 and usually include all courses and drinks; be aware that almost every show offers discounts from the listed price. You may be able to buy cut-rate tickets to dinner shows from ticket booths in hotels or on tourist roads; shop around a bit for the best deal.

One word of warning: Most of the shows try to pad their nightly take with all sorts of gimmicks. They'll try to sell you photos taken in the lobby, photos taken at your table, souvenir booklets, flags, and other items. If you're not in the market for extra trinkets, just say no.

Call for hours of performance for any show; in the busiest seasons some theaters will have two shows in a night.

WITHIN WALT DISNEY WORLD

The dinner shows at Walt Disney World resorts generally require advance reservations and purchase of tickets. Call (407) 934-7639 for reservations; most times of the year you'll need to do this weeks or even months before arrival. Guests at hotels within the park get a head start for reservations, too. Prices and times are subject to change.

■ HOOP-DEE-DOO MUSICAL REVUE

This Western singing and dancing show at Pioneer Hall in Disney's Fort Wilderness Resort features all-you-can-eat chicken, ribs, corn, and strawberry shortcake. This is a hugely popular, raucous, thigh-slappin', hee-haw of a show; if that's the sort of entertainment you like, this is a fine example. Entertainment includes piano and banjo music, terrible jokes and gags, and an audience-participation washboard finale. In between is a bit of improvisational humor as cast members make up songs about some of the guests in the audience.

Veterans observe that although this is an all-you-can-eat adventure, the courses (including fried chicken and barbecue ribs) come and go pretty quickly, and there is a show to watch, too. Disney also trimmed a half hour off the starting time of the late show by shortening the overall performance and turnaround times a bit.

If you're not already at Fort Wilderness as a guest and plan to use Disney transportation, you'll need to leave about an hour before your showtime to make connections to the resort and walk to the Pioneer Hall, which is located near the beach on Bay Lake. There is also a parking lot at Fort Wilderness.

The large hall has two levels; the best seats are at the front of the balcony or a few rows back from the stage on the main level. Seats are assigned at the time of the reservation. Seatings are at 5:00 and 7:15 P.M., with a 9:30 P.M. show in high season. Adults about $50; children (three to eleven) $25. For reservations and information call (407) 939–3463, or (407) 824–2803 on the day of the show. Reservations are necessary most days; a walk-up waiting list is also begun at Pioneer Hall about forty-five minutes before showtime.

■ DISNEY'S SPIRIT OF ALOHA DINNER SHOW

This all-you-can-eat feast at Disney's Polynesian Resort features tropical appetizers, Lanai roasted chicken, Polynesian wild rice, South Seas vegetables, dessert, wine, beer, and other drinks. It's all accompanied by singers, hula dancers, fire twirlers, and other entertainment. The show, and the food, was upgraded a bit in late 2003; it used to be called the Polynesian Luau.

There's a partial roof over the dining room, with the stage open to the sky; mosquito repellent is worth adding to your preshow preparations in bug season. The show is much more dramatic when it is dark; the early show in summer is presented while it is still light. (By the way, it is possible to see portions of the show from the courtyard of the Polynesian Resort without paying for a seat and meal.)

Guests at park resorts can reserve seats when they reserve their rooms; others can make reservations within thirty days of the day of the show. Seatings Tuesday to Saturday are at 5:15 and 8:00 P.M. Adults about $50; children (ages three to eleven) $25. For reservations call (407) 939–3463.

NEARBY WALT DISNEY WORLD

■ ARABIAN NIGHTS DINNER ATTRACTION

Arabian Nights features beautiful horses, handsome caballeros, pretty young women, and a theatrical presentation in one of Orlando's largest and oldest dinner theaters. This is first and foremost a horse show: More than fifty of them, including Arabians, Lippizans, Andalusians, Belgians, and Percherons, perform in the 1,200-seat Palace of Horses. Favorite stunts include "Airs above the Ground" maneuvers, a chariot race, and a most unusual square dance on horseback.

The story tells of Princess Scheherazade on the eve of her wedding; the palace genie summons the greatest horse performers and riders to participate in the celebration. Somewhere along the way there's an act that salutes the Big Apple, set to "New York, New York" with horses clad in tuxes (and tails). And the finale is performed to "Proud to Be an American."

The dinner features prime rib, salad, and wedding cake; vegetarian meals are also available. The meal is accompanied by beer, wine, and soft drinks. The serving staff is extremely solicitous, and the audience is much less rowdy than at some of the other dinner shows in town.

Arabian Nights is one of the only family-owned attractions in the area; it is the creation of Mark and Galen Miller, who previously owned an Arabian show farm near Gainesville, Florida. Mark Miller is also one of the founders of the Black Stallion Literacy Project, together with Tim Farley, son of Walter Farley, author of the famed children's book *The Black Stallion*.

Nightly performance times vary from season to season and within the week; call for information.

In 2006 admission was about $46 to $57 for adults and about $20 to $31 for children (ages three to eleven). Special discounts are regularly offered on the show's Web site and through tourist guides in the Orlando area. Located at 6225 West Irlo Bronson Highway (U.S. Highway 192), east of the intersection with Interstate 4 in Kissimmee. For information call (800) 553–6116 or (407) 239–9223, or consult www.arabian-nights.com.

■ CAPONE'S DINNER & SHOW

Set in 1931 gangland Chicago, this musical comedy review with guns has an unlimited Italian buffet that offers items such as lasagna, baked ziti, sausage and peppers, baked chicken, and pasta salad, plus beer, wine, sangria, and rum runners. Special discounts are regularly offered at the show's Web site and through tourist guides in the Orlando area. Adults and seniors about $46; children (age twelve and younger) about $28. Located at 4740 West Irlo Bronson Highway (US 192); (800) 220–8428 or (407) 397–2378; www.alcapones.com.

■ DOLLY PARTON'S DIXIE STAMPEDE

A hootin' and hollerin' show featuring thirty-two horses, pigs, chickens, ostrich racing, and a herd of buffalo moved into a new arena near Walt Disney World in 2003.

Country singer Dolly Parton has built an empire of theme parks and dinner shows in the South; her Orlando theater is a $28 million investment that includes a 1,200-seat arena along I–4 between the Disney parks and SeaWorld.

The show is mostly built around horses. Breeds include quarter horses, the gentle and heavily muscled horse of the American cowboy. You'll also see Appaloosas, originally bred by the Nez Perce tribe. Belgian draft horses, 2,200-pound behemoths whose large size and wide hooves make them perfect for hauling loads, pull Conestoga wagons along the arena floor.

Performances include Roman Riding, a special type of trick riding featuring a team of two horses moving side by side with one rider standing astride both. Another feature is barrel racing, a fast-paced race that requires tight turns at breakneck speed. The ninety-minute show concludes with a patriotic tribute written by Parton that adds thirty trained doves to the menagerie.

The meal, served without silverware unless you insist, delivers a whole rotisserie chicken, hickory-smoked barbecue pork, vegetable soup, and an apple turnover.

We are fans of Dolly Parton's musical offerings, many of which have the ring of real country and Southern culture. That said, the Dixie Stampede show does not seem authentic. The supposed story line is about the "friendly and fun rivalry between the North and South," presenting the U.S. Civil War as a dispute about "different ideas of patriotism." Servers outfitted in Confederate or Union uniforms deliver dinner and make appearances on the "stage," a dust-free dirt arena. You'll see horse-drawn magic tricks, "snowfall" on a nineteenth-century New York scene, and jousting with swords. There's a silly chicken chase and competition among selected audience members playing "horsey" with broomsticks. The music is less than memorable, and surprisingly, doesn't feature Parton except in a forgettable finale.

The original Parton show opened in 1988 outside the entrance to Parton's theme park, Dollywood, in Pigeon Forge, Tennessee. Other shows are presented in Branson, Missouri, and Myrtle Beach, South Carolina.

A Roman Rider at Dolly Parton's Dixie Stampede.
Photo courtesy of Dolly Parton's Dixie Stampede

Medieval Life

A little piece of ancient Spain, Medieval Life includes a truly amazing collection of tools, personal items, and some of the darker elements of the Medieval times, including dungeons and torture chambers. This place is for real—an exhibit unlike most anything else in central Florida or elsewhere in the United States.

Your visit will start at the architect's house, the home of one of the most respected members of the community. The craftsmen exhibits include authentically dressed tradesmen and artisans, including potters, blacksmiths, millers, carpenters, and glassblowers.

Then—parents of young children be warned—it's into the dungeon, where you'll see replicas and real instruments of torture that include the garrote, iron torture masks known as "branks," and the interrogation chair, a large wooden chair covered with sharp iron spikes used to "convince" a person charged with a crime to offer a confession. And be prepared to explain—or steer your kids around—a few real chastity belts.

Admission is free to ticket holders for the Medieval Times show, and the exhibit is open two hours before showtime daily. If you want to make a separate visit to the branks and belts, tickets in 2006 were $3.50 for all visitors. Medieval Life is located at 4510 West Irlo Bronson Highway, off Highway 441 in Kissimmee; (800) 229–8300 or (407) 396–1518; www.medievaltimes.com.

In Orlando the Dixie Stampede offers daily shows at 6:30 P.M., with a second show at 8:30 P.M. during busy times of the year. Horses are on display outside the arena each day from 10:00 A.M. to showtime.

A special Christmas program proved very popular, with as many as five performances per day from early November through mid-January.

The show is located at 8251 Vineland Avenue, off exit 68 of I–4 between Walt Disney World and SeaWorld. Admission for adults in 2006 was $47.19. Price includes the Carriage Room show, the ninety-minute main show, and a four-course Southern-style meal. For information and reservations call (866) 443–4943 or (407) 238–4455, or consult www.dixiestampede.com.

■ MEDIEVAL TIMES DINNER & TOURNAMENT

Come to dinner as the guests of the royal family in the eleventh century. The feast includes spectacular pageantry, dramatic horsemanship, swordplay, falconry, sorcery, and a jousting contest. The meal—which is served without silverware—includes a hearty vegetable soup, roasted chicken, spare ribs, potato, and dessert, plus beer, sangria, and soft drinks.

Medieval Times is one of the old-timers among dinner theaters, dating back more than twenty years in Florida, nearly forty years in Spain, and about 1,000 years in history. Twenty-five years ago, Jose De Montaner converted his farm in Majorca, Spain, into a barbecue dinner show and then a medieval-theme show for tourists. There are now Medieval Times dinner attractions in California (near Disneyland), New Jersey, Illinois, Texas, South Carolina, Maryland, and Toronto, Canada.

The entertainment takes place in the 1,100-seat Great Ceremonial Hall. Seats are not reserved, so arrive early for the best seats (down low at midcourt). The show begins with some impressive demonstrations of horse training and riding skills, including the Carousel, a display of intricate horse maneuvers.

According to the company, about 500,000 visitors a year come to the show. The attraction underwent a multimillion-dollar face-lift that was completed in 2006, improving the exterior of the building with new features and landscaping.

The tournament begins with knights on horseback with lances galloping at full speed toward 3-inch hoops suspended from posts; the next challenge is a javelin toss on horseback. The final confrontation pits knights against each other in jousting tournaments and hand-to-hand fighting.

The latest version of the show adds a princess and a "confrontation between a turncoat warrior and a surprise defender of the crown." A new equine star is a coal-black Friesian stallion, in stark contrast to the white Andalusian stallions ridden by most of the other actors.

Alongside the theater is the Medieval Life exhibit, an extraordinary collection of strange artifacts brought over from Europe.

Adults about $50 plus tax, children (age twelve and younger) about $34. Tickets include admission to Medieval Life. 4510 West Irlo Bronson Highway (US 192), near Highway 441 in Kissimmee; (800) 229–8300 or (407) 396–1518; www.medievaltimes.com.

■ MURDERWATCH MYSTERY DINNER THEATRE

A lively evening of food, song, and murder is presented in the attractive restaurant, with above-average dinner buffet fare at Baskerville's within the Grosvenor Resort at Walt Disney World Village. The restaurant has a replica of Sherlock Holmes's 221B Baker Street office on display.

We enjoyed a campy, funny show involving an engagement party for the daughter of a mafia don. Before we could begin the salad course, an FBI agent (who also played the piano) checked out our table for bombs, listening devices, and leftovers. Other characters, including detective Shirley Holmes, worked the tables during the show. Before the night was over, the dopey chanteuse was murdered, the marriage was off, and a good time was had by all.

Tickets in 2006, including dinner, were $39.95 for adults and $9.95 for children (ages nine and younger). Presented Saturday evening with one or two shows per night. Grosvenor Resort, 1850 Hotel Plaza Boulevard; (800) 624–4109 or (407) 827–6534; www.murderwatch.com.

INTERNATIONAL DRIVE/UNIVERSAL STUDIOS AREA

■ MAKAHIKI LUAU AT SEAWORLD

Eat, drink, and be entertained by the Hawaiian Rhythms troupe. (Located at The Seafire Inn at SeaWorld; you do not need a ticket to the park, and the luau price does not include admission.) The meal features items such as mahimahi in piña colada sauce, Hawaiian chicken, and sweet-and-sour pork. Adults $45.95, children (ages three to nine) $29.95. Dinner served from 6:30 to 8:45 P.M. nightly. 7007 SeaWorld Drive; (800) 327–2420 or (407) 363–2559.

■ PIRATE'S DINNER ADVENTURE

Ahoy, mateys! Just off International Drive near Wet 'n Wild and Universal Studios Orlando, the impressive set includes a full-scale pirate ship afloat in a 300,000-gallon indoor lagoon. Pirates swing from ropes over your head, and battles rage all around. The story, if it's important to you, involves the lovely Princess Anita and her court, held hostage by the dastardly Sebastian the Black. The meal includes roast chicken and prime rib. Presented nightly. After the show, guests can attend the Pirate's Buccaneer Bash to mingle with cast members and attempt to learn the latest dance steps. Adults $51.95 plus tax, children (ages three to eleven) $31.95. 6400 Carrier Drive; (800) 866–2469 or (407) 248–0590; www.orlandopirates.com.

■ SLEUTHS MYSTERY DINNER SHOW

Step into the scene of the crime. Mix with the characters, search for clues, and help track down the culprit. Among recent titles in the troupe's repertoire are *Kim and Scott Tie the Knot, Lord Mansfield's Foxhunt Banquet,* and *The Show Must Go On.* You'll also eat dinner along the way. One to four shows per night. Adults $47.95 plus tax, children (ages three to eleven) $23.95. Discount coupons are found in many magazines and flyers aimed at tourists. 7508 Republic Drive, off International Drive behind Wet 'n Wild; (800) 393–1985 or (407) 363–1985; www.sleuths.com.

DISNEY CHARACTER MEALS

For reservations for character meals at Walt Disney World properties, call (407) 939–7741 or (407) 939–3463. The mix changes regularly. Be sure to call to check on current offerings.

■ **Baskerville's Character Breakfast Buffet.** Baskerville's at Grosvenor Resort. Breakfast with a changing cast of characters. Call (407) 828–4444 for reservations and current schedule.

■ **Beach Club Buffet.** Cape May Cafe at Disney's Beach Club Resort. Admiral Goofy and friends; 7:30 to 11:00 A.M. daily. Adults $18.99, children (ages three to eleven) $10.99.

■ **Chef Mickey's Fun Time Buffet.** Disney's Contemporary Resort. Starring

Mickey and his gang. Breakfast from 7:00 to 11:30 A.M. Adults $18.99, children (ages three to eleven) $10.99. Dinner from 5:00 to 9:30 P.M. Adults $27.99, children (ages three to eleven) $12.99.

■ **Cinderella's Gala Feast.** Disney's Grand Floridian Beach Resort. Dinner buffet features Cinderella and friends and performances on *Big Bertha,* a century-old band organ. Served from 4:30 to 8:20 P.M. Adults $28.99, children (ages three to nine) $13.99.

■ **Cinderella's Royal Table.** Once Upon a Time Breakfast in King Stefan's Banquet Hall in Cinderella Castle. Cinderella and friends. Daily from 8:00 to 10:20 A.M. Includes breakfast and photo. Adults $31.99, children (ages three to eleven) $21.99. Fairytale Lunch in Cinderella Castle. Daily from 3:00 to 9:00 P.M. Includes lunch and photo. Adults $33.99, children (ages three to eleven) $22.99. Magic Kingdom admission ticket and reservations required.

■ **Crystal Palace in the Magic Kingdom.** Winnie the Pooh and friends for breakfast on Main Street from 8:00 to 10:30 A.M. Adults $18.99, children (ages three to eleven) $10.99. Lunch from 11:30 A.M. to 2:45 P.M. Adults $20.99, children, $11.99. Dinner 4:00 P.M. to closing. Adults $27.99, children $12.99. Magic Kingdom admission ticket required.

■ **Donald's Breakfastosaurus.** Restaurantosaurus in DinoLand, U.S.A. Breakfast buffet with Donald Duck and friends from park opening until 10:30 A.M. Adults $18.99, children (ages three to eleven) $10.99. Animal Kingdom theme-park admission required.

■ **Garden Grill.** Chip 'n Dale's Harvest Feast. Lunch with Mickey and friends at The Land pavilion of Epcot Center. Lunch from 11:00 A.M. to 3:00 P.M. Adults $20.99, children $11.99. Epcot admission ticket required.

■ **Garden Grove Character Breakfast.** Walt Disney World Swan. Goofy, Pluto, and friends. Saturday and Sunday 8:00 to 10:30 A.M. Buffet: adults about $16.95, children (ages three to eleven) about $8.50. Menu items also offered.

■ **Gulliver's Grill Character Dinner.** Walt Disney World Swan from 6:00 to 10:00 P.M. Goofy and Pluto on Saturday, Sunday, Tuesday, Wednesday, and Thursday. Rafiki and Timon on Monday and Friday. Adults about $24.95, children (ages three to eleven) about $10.95.

■ **Liberty Tree Tavern Character Dinner.** Goofy's Liberate Your Appetite Character Dinner. Dinner from 4:00 P.M. to park closing with Goofy, Minnie, Pluto, and friends. Adults $27.99, children (ages three to eleven) $12.99, plus theme-park admission to the Magic Kingdom.

■ **Mickey's Backyard BBQ.** Disney's Fort Wilderness Resort & Campground. Mickey and friends for dinner at 6:30 P.M. Thursday and Saturday from March through December, with several additional performances at busy times. Adults about $40, children (ages three to eleven) about $25. Gratuity included.

■ **'Ohana Best Friends Breakfast.** Disney's Polynesian Resort. Starring Lilo and Stitch. 7:00 to 11:00 A.M. daily. Adults $18.99, children (ages three to nine) $10.99.

■ **Playhouse Disney's Play 'N Dine.** Fans of JoJo and Goliath from *JoJo's Circus* and June and Leo from *The Little Einsteins* will join other Playhouse Disney TV stars during breakfast and lunch at Hollywood & Vine restaurant at Disney–

MGM Studios. A buffet breakfast is served daily from 8:00 to 11:20 A.M., and lunch from 11:40 A.M. to 2:25 P.M. Adults $22.99, children (ages three to nine) $13.99.

■ **Princess Storybook Dining at Restaurant Akershus.** Norway pavilion at Epcot. Dine with the princesses: Belle, Jasmine, Snow White, Sleeping Beauty, Mary Poppins, Pocahontas, Cinderella, Ariel, Alice, and Mulan. Breakfast from 8:30 to 10:10 A.M. Adults $22.99, children (ages three to eleven) $12.99. Lunch from 11:40 A.M. to 2:50 P.M. Adults $24.99, children (ages three to eleven) $13.99. Dinner from 4:20 to 8:40 P.M. Adults $28.99, children (ages three to eleven) $13.99. Epcot theme-park admission required.

■ **Sunday Disney Character Breakfast.** Watercress Café at the Buena Vista Palace Resort, Hotel Plaza. Minnie, Pluto, and Goofy on Sunday from 8:00 to 10:30 A.M. Order from menu or buffet. Adults about $15.95, children about $9.95.

■ **Supercalifragilistic Breakfast at 1900 Park Fare.** Disney's Grand Floridian Resort & Spa. Mary Poppins and friends, daily from 8:00 to 11:10 A.M. Adults $18.99, children (ages three to eleven) $10.99.

■ **Wonderland Tea Party.** A tea party at Disney's Grand Floridian Resort starring Alice and the Mad Hatter. Lunch is served weekdays from 1:30 to 2:30 P.M. Children (ages four to ten) $28.17.

PART VI

SPORTS AND RECREATION

CHAPTER TWENTY-ONE

DISNEY'S WIDE WORLD OF SPORTS AND RECREATION WITHIN WALT DISNEY WORLD

DEPENDING UPON YOUR POINT OF VIEW, Walt Disney World is either four theme parks surrounded by ninety-nine holes of golf or a country club so huge it holds within it four theme parks. Or the place is so big that it can park a baseball stadium, professional tennis complex, and track fieldhouse in one corner and an Indy-class auto racetrack in another without running out of popcorn and liniment. If there were no Magic Kingdom, Epcot, Disney–MGM Studios, or Animal Kingdom, the Walt Disney World resort would deserve recognition just for its sports complexes.

DISNEY'S WIDE WORLD OF SPORTS

Lace up your sneakers, Mickey: Disney's Wide World of Sports offers world-class athletic facilities for man, woman, and mouse. It's a field of dreams for more than thirty sports. The 220 acres of facilities include a handsome baseball stadium; a softball quadraplex; a fieldhouse that has six professional-quality basketball courts; ten tennis courts, including a stadium court; four soccer fields; and much more.

The site, which draws its name from the famous ABC sports television show—now part of the Disney corporate family—is home to more than 170 amateur and professional sports events each year, including the NFL Tampa Bay Buccaneers training camp, the Major League Baseball Atlanta Braves spring training camp and exhibition games, the Pop Warner Super Bowl, AAU National Championship events, the Sports Experience interactive play area, and the All-Star Cafe sports-themed restaurant.

In 2006 visitors could purchase a day pass to the facilities for $10.28 plus tax for adults and $7.71 for children (ages three to nine) and observe training and many amateur tournament activities anywhere on the property. Parking is free. Special events, such as spring-training baseball games, have an additional charge. Tickets for all events are available through Ticketmaster outlets or by visiting the box office at the entrance to the complex. For updated schedules call the Disney's Wide World of Sports Information Line at (407) 363–6600 or consult www.disney worldsports.com or http://dwws.disney.go.com/wideworldofsports/index. The sports complex is within Walt Disney World, near U.S. Highway 192; it can also be reached on an internal bus via a transfer at the Blizzard Beach station.

Among the facilities at Disney's Wide World of Sports are the following:

■ **Baseball Stadium.** A field with major-league dimensions, 9,500 permanent seats, and a grass lawn beyond the outfield for casual seating. The Atlanta Braves work out and play their home spring-training games in February and March of each year. The handsome stadium is reminiscent of sturdy 1950s-style architecture. It includes a number of nice touches, such as extra-wide seats and a pair of concession stands that face the field so fans won't miss a pitch if they're off on an emergency safari for hot dogs. Serious baseball fans and just about anyone else will appreciate how close you can get to the game. Seats are mostly exposed to the rain or sun, except for rows P through U of the lower deck. Alas, the retro manually operated scoreboard was replaced by an electronic board in 2003; for technical reasons, the jumbo TV screen in centerfield was removed.

Tickets are usually available for all games; the biggest draws include the New York Mets, Boston Red Sox, New York Yankees, and Cleveland Indians. The largest crowd at the park gathered in 2001 when 11,335 came to see Mark McGwire and the Saint Louis Cardinals. The schedule of teams changes from year to year.

The spring-training home season includes about sixteen games from late February through the end of March; there are also intrasquad games and practice sessions. For information call (407) 939–1500. Tickets range from about $13 to $21 and are available at the stadium or through Ticketmaster at (407) 839–3900.

For the first two weeks of spring training there is no charge to enter the stadium to watch workouts and intrasquad practices.

■ **Tampa Bay Buccaneers Training.** In recent years the NFL team has conducted preseason training at Wide World of Sports from late July to late August. Admission is free to watch workouts and scrimmages; there are no formal games. Check with Disney before making plans for 2006 and beyond.

■ **The Milk Fieldhouse.** Six hardwood basketball courts with main-floor seating for 5,000 spectators.

In 2006, the NBA Pre-Draft Camp was held for the first time at the Milk Fieldhouse. The camp brings together top prospects to work out and be evaluated by league coaches, general managers, scouts, and front-office executives. Some of the practice games were broadcast nationally.

■ **Softball/Baseball Quadraplex.** Six softball diamonds with bleachers; three Major League–size fields with 500 seats each.

- **Track and Field Complex.** A 400-meter polyurethane track, long jump and triple jump runway, and other facilities.
- **Tennis Complex.** Ten clay courts, nine of them lighted. One thousand permanent seats at center-court stadium, with additional temporary seating available.
- **Beach Volleyball.** Five sand courts. All the facilities are open to organized tournaments only.
- **Official All-Star Cafe.** Just outside the main entrance to the baseball stadium, a spectacular outpost of the themed dining restaurant also features stages for special events and sports radio and television shows. Nearby is a huge Foot Locker Super Store, stocked with the latest in athletic gear.

WALT DISNEY WORLD GOLF COURSES

Disney is one version of golfing heaven. Ever on the search for a cute phrase, Disney has taken to calling it "The Magic Linkdom." It's a way for Mom and Dad and even junior to come to Walt Disney World without having to spend all their time in the company of a bunch of cartoon mice. For general information consult www.disneyworldgolf.com.

There are three price ranges for tee times at Disney golf courses. One rate is for guests staying at one of the Walt Disney World resort hotels, a second tier of rates is for guests who purchase a Disney Annual Golf Membership, and a third set of prices applies to day guests not staying at Walt Disney World. There are also discounted twilight rates available at certain times of the year.

There are five championship-level eighteen-hole golf courses within the World, plus the nine-hole Oak Trail practice course. Two of the courses are good enough to be stops on the PGA Tour. The Funai Classic at Walt Disney World Resort is played in October on the Palm and Magnolia courses.

Instruction is available through the Walt Disney World Golf Studio at the Magnolia driving range. The fee is $50 for a half-hour lesson for adults, or $30 for juniors (seventeen and younger). Call (407) 824–2270 for reservations. Junior golfers can also participate in a five-day-long summer golf camp.

Magnolia

At the Shades of Green (formerly the Disney Inn). Named for the more than 1,500 magnolias on the course, this course plays to 6,642 yards from the middle tees and is the setting for the final round of the Walt Disney World Golf Classic. There's water on ten of the eighteen holes. In 1993 the Magnolia received a complete face-lift by course architect Joe Lee. The Garden Gallery offers breakfast, lunch, and dinner.

Courses, Rated

According to the pros at the courses, here are the difficulty levels from most difficult to easiest:

1. Osprey Ridge
2. Palm
3. Magnolia
4. Eagle Pines
5. Lake Buena Vista

Golf Fees

Prices were in effect in early 2007 and are subject to change. Carts included. Rates do not include tax. Resort guests can reserve tee times as much as ninety days in advance; day guests can reserve up to thirty days in advance. All reservations must be guaranteed with a credit card. For reservations call (407) 939–4653. You may also be able to reserve a starting time on the same day you want to play by calling the pro shop at each course directly. Complimentary transportation is provided to guests at Walt Disney World resort hotels coming to play at one of the courses; contact the valet desk or bell services for assistance. Replay rates are 50 percent of full rate on the same day, on a space-available basis, and may not be reserved in advance.

Times for twilight rates vary during the year; price allows play for as many holes as possible before nightfall. In recent years the courses offered a Summer Price Slice Special from mid-May to late September, with reduced prices in the hot hours after 10:00 A.M. There are also reduced-price "twilight special" tee times after 2:00 or 3:00 P.M. daily. Replay rates are 50 percent of the full rate on the same day and cannot be reserved in advance. Higher rates are generally in effect from September to late April.

Note that only soft-spike (nonmetal) golf shoes or tennis shoes are permitted on the course, and proper golf attire, including shirts with a collar and Bermuda-length shorts or slacks, are required.

	DAY VISITOR	RESORT GUEST	TWILIGHT RATE	SUMMER RATES
EAGLE PINES	$129	$119	$65	$60–$119
OSPREY RIDGE	$145	$135	$75	$50–$109
MAGNOLIA	$135	$125	$70	$45–$99
PALM	$119	$109	$60	$45–$94
LAKE BUENA VISTA	$99	$89	$55	$45–$89

OAK TRAIL (nine-hole walking course)

Adult	$38; $19 for replay
Junior (seventeen and younger)	$20; $10 for replay

(Reduced rates for midday tee-offs, on space-available basis, and cannot be reserved in advance. Pull carts are available for $5.00.)

RENTALS

Men's deluxe clubs	$55
Men's premium clubs	$55
Women's deluxe clubs	$55
Oak Trail clubs	$15
Range balls	$7.00 per bucket
Shoes	$10

LESSONS

Adult forty-five-minute private lesson	$50
Junior forty-five-minute video lesson	$50

The Disney Golf Studio offers lessons and videotape analysis. Pro shop: (407) 824–2288. Course information: par 72. Yardage: 5,232–7,190. Course/slope ratings: 69.4–74.9/125–136.

Palm

Considered the second most difficult course at Walt Disney World, it is included among *Golf Digest*'s top twenty-five resort courses. It plays to a relatively short 6,461 yards from the middle tees, but water and sand seem to be almost everywhere. The eighteenth hole has been rated as the fourth toughest on the PGA Tour. Also located at Shades of Green, it shares the Garden Gallery and pro shop with the Magnolia course. Course information: par 72. Yardage: 5,311–6,957. Course/slope ratings: 69.5–73.9/126–138.

Lake Buena Vista

A wide open and heavily wooded course that reaches to 6,655 yards, extending from the Disney Village Clubhouse. Located at Disney's Village Resort near the Hotel Plaza. The Lake Buena Vista Restaurant in the clubhouse serves breakfast, lunch, and dinner. The Lake Buena Vista Golf Studio offers lessons and analysis. Pro shop: (407) 824–3741. Course information: par 72. Yardage: 5,194–6,819. Course/slope ratings: 68.6–73.0/123–133.

Osprey Ridge

By most accounts the most difficult course at Walt Disney World, it was designed by acclaimed golf-course architect Tom Fazio. The course includes a circulating eighteenth-hole routing with holes that play in every direction. The course extends a total of 6,705 yards from the middle tees, including some remote tropical settings. Some of the tees, greens, and viewing areas are as much as 25 feet above grade; much of the earth was moved from the excavation at nearby Eagle Pines.

The namesake "ridge" plays an important role in the course: You'll climb the ridge for the tee for hole 3, the green for hole 12 is built into its side, and the green for hole 16 is atop it. Located at the Bonnet Creek Golf Club, it includes the Sand Trap Bar & Grill, a lunch spot with a view of the greens. The Bonnet Creek Golf Studio offers lessons and analysis. Pro shop: (407) 824–2675. Course information: par 72. Yardage: 5,402–7,101. Course/slope ratings: 69.5–74.4/ 123–131.

Eagle Pines

Eight of designer Pete Dye's courses are included in *Golf* magazine's top fifty. Unlike the high mounds and ridges of Osprey Ridge, this newer course offers a low profile, although many balls will end up in the surrounding pines. Eagle Pines plays 6,224 yards from the middle tees and is considered a bit more forgiving than the other courses. Dye included a lip on the edge of fairways along water hazards to reduce the number of wet balls. The course shares the Bonnet Creek Golf Studio, pro shop, and Sand Trap restaurant with Osprey Ridge.

More Golf, You Say?

In addition to the Walt Disney World courses, there are dozens of municipal, public, and semiprivate golf courses in and around the Disney area in Orange County. Here is a selection:

▶ **Crystal Brook Golf Course.** Kissimmee; (407) 847–8721. Public, nine holes.

▶ **Cypress Creek Country Club.** Orlando; (407) 351–2187. Semiprivate, eighteen holes.

▶ **Dubsdread Golf Course.** Orlando; (407) 246–2551. Municipal, eighteen holes.

▶ **Eaglewood.** Orlando; (407) 351–5121. Public, eighteen holes.

▶ **Eastwood Golf & Country Club.** Orlando; (407) 281–4653. Semiprivate, eighteen holes.

▶ **Falcon's Fire Golf Course.** Kissimmee; (407) 239–5445; www.falconsfire .com. Public, eighteen holes.

▶ **Grand Cypress Resort.** Orlando; (407) 239–4700. Resort, forty-five holes.

▶ **Hunter's Creek Golf Club.** Orlando; (407) 240–4653. Public, eighteen holes.

▶ **International Golf Club.** Orlando; (407) 239–6909. Resort, eighteen holes.

▶ **Kissimmee Golf Club.** Kissimmee; (407) 847–2816; www.kissgolfclub.com. Public, eighteen holes.

▶ **Lake Orlando Golf Club.** Orlando; (407) 298–1230. Public, eighteen holes.

▶ **Marriott's Orlando World Center.** Orlando; (407) 239–4200. Resort, eighteen holes.

▶ **Meadow Woods Golf Club.** Orlando; (407) 850–5600. Semiprivate, eighteen holes.

▶ **MetroWest Country Club.** Orlando; (407) 299–1099; www.metrowest orlando.com. Semiprivate, eighteen holes.

▶ **Osceola Golf Club.** Kissimmee; (407) 348–4915. Public, eighteen holes.

▶ **The Pines.** Orlando; (407) 647-4067. Public, eighteen holes.

▶ **Ventura Country Club.** Orlando; (407) 277–2640. Semiprivate, eighteen holes.

▶ **Wedgefield Golf & Country Club.** Orlando; (407) 568–2116. Semiprivate, eighteen holes.

▶ **Winter Park Municipal.** Winter Park; (407) 623–3339. Municipal, nine holes.

▶ **Winter Pines Golf Club.** Winter Park; (407) 671–3172. Public, eighteen holes.

▶ **Zellwood Station Country Club.** Zellwood; (407) 886–3303. Semiprivate, eighteen holes.

Course information: par 72. Yardage: 4,838–6,772. Course/slope ratings: 66.6–72.5/119–135.

Oak Trail Executive Course

At the Shades of Green, this nine-hole, 2,913-yard, par 36 course has small rolling greens and elevated tees. It's no pushover, though, and has some of the most difficult greens at Walt Disney World. No golf carts are allowed. Course information: par 36. Yardage: 2,552–2,913. Course/slope ratings: 64.6–68.2/107–123.

■ MINIATURE GOLF

Winter Summerland Miniature Golf

In true Disney fashion, this pair of miniature golf courses is unlike any you will find in your neighborhood shopping mall. It seems late one Christmas Eve, Santa was flying back to the North Pole and glanced down to see an unbelievable sight: snow in Florida at Blizzard Beach. It was, Santa decided, the perfect place for a vacation getaway for his hardworking elves, a Winter Summerland.

The only thing the area lacked was a golf course. The elves took care of that, dividing the area into two camps, one that enjoyed the warm Florida sun and another that preferred the snow and cold of the North Pole. And so they built two courses: a "sand" course and a "snow" course. On the summer course Santa slumbers beneath a large mound of sand, and inner tubes litter the "beach." Parked nearby is a small aluminum "Elfstream" camper. The winter course includes Squirty the Snowman, who stands in the way and sprays golfers with water if they get too close. Whichever course you choose, you'll end up in an old log campground lodge for the final hole; you'll need to putt your ball between two model trains that circle below a decorated Christmas tree. When you put the ball in the cup, you'll travel through cyberspace for a special greeting direct from Santa.

The course is located off the parking lot of Blizzard Beach, to the right of the ticket plaza. Both courses are open from 10:00 A.M. to 11:00 P.M. daily; greens fees for either course are $10.75 plus tax for adults and $8.50 plus tax for children. A second round of golf is offered for a 50 percent reduction. For information call (407) 560–3000.

Fantasia Gardens Miniature Golf

The original small golf course at Walt Disney World offers two eighteen-hole courses near the Swan, Dolphin, and BoardWalk Resorts. Hippos dance, fountains leap, and broomsticks march at the course, with a theme taken from Disney's classic animated film *Fantasia*. The course includes hazards based on the film. At "Toccata & Fugue" good shots are rewarded with musical tones. "The Nutcracker Suite" features quirky obstacles, including dancing mushrooms. "The Pastoral Symphony" presents a 40-foot-tall Mount Olympus with waterfalls. At "The Dance of the Hours," good timing and accuracy are needed to pass *Fantasia*'s famous alligator and hippo *pas de deux*. Then there is "The Sorcerer's Apprentice," starring Mickey Mouse, his troop of out-of-control broomsticks, and dazzling water effects.

Alongside is Fantasia Fairways, a par 3 or 4 putting course with exaggerated contours, water hazards, and sand traps, with holes ranging from 40 to 75 feet. Both courses are open from 10:00 A.M. to 11:00 P.M. daily; greens fees for either course are $10.75 plus tax for adults and $8.50 plus tax for children. A second round on the same day is available at 50 percent discount. For information call (407) 560–8760.

THE WALT DISNEY WORLD SPEEDWAY

The Walt Disney World Speedway, a $6 million, 1.1-mile course to the left of the access road to the parking lot for the Magic Kingdom, is home to the Richard Petty Driving Experience. The program moves motor-sports fans out of the grandstands and into the driver's or passenger's seat of an authentic stock car capable of speeds of up to 145 miles per hour. Program offerings include the eight-lap Rookie Experience, and the Experience of a Lifetime, a series of three ten-lap sprints. For those who'd rather leave the driving to a pro, Richard Petty Driving Experience also offers the Ride-Along Experience, including three laps as a passenger in a stock car with a professional driver, traveling at a top speed of 145 miles per hour.

Instructors put participants through the paces in all sessions, beginning with classroom instruction on safety and fundamentals. It continues with on-track technique for handling, passing, and drafting with the stock cars. Programs are run with a lead car ahead of the students. The instructor is in the lead car, with two students following single file about six to eight car lengths apart. The lead instructor car is in radio contact with a flagger, pit road instructor, and coordinator.

Driving experiences are available for those at least eighteen years of age with a valid driver's license and the ability to drive a vehicle equipped with a standard transmission. Fans at least sixteen years of age can participate in the Ride-Along Experience. Riders under eighteen years of age must be accompanied by their parent or legal guardian.

Prices in 2006 began at $105.44 with tax for the Ride-Along Experience. The Rookie Experience of eight laps was priced at $403.64 including tax, and the more expansive King's Experience (one eight-lap and one ten-lap drive) cost $767.69 with tax. The ultimate Experience of a Lifetime (three ten-lap sprints) was priced at $1,330.19 with tax.

Racing is conducted daily except Tuesday and Thursday. For information on the program, call (800) 237–3889 or (407) 939–0130, or consult www.1800 bepetty.com.

The speedway also offers a most unusual souvenir for racing fans. After tearing around the 1-mile course in an authentic stock car, guests can purchase the same Goodyear Racing Eagles that are used on the 630-horsepower machines. The tires are used for approximately 100 laps around the speedway before they are changed. Once the tires are removed from the cars, they are stacked in the showroom store, where guests can purchase them for $5.00 each.

The tires have been taken home for use as wall hangings, coffee-table bases, and swings; some fans haul them to races to get the autographs. The original cost of a set of Goodyear Racing Eagles with rims ranges from about $500 to $1,200.

The raceway hosted the Disney World Indy 200 in 1996, drawing tens of thousands of fans and creating a major slow-speed traffic jam. That event is no longer on the Indy Racing League schedule.

ON THE WATER

■ WALT DISNEY WORLD MARINAS

Walt Disney World offers the country's largest fleet of pleasure boats, more than many navies of the world. There are three major areas: the Seven Seas Lagoon, which sits between the Magic Kingdom and the Ticket and Transportation Center and is surrounded by the monorail; Bay Lake, the largest body of water, which includes Discovery Island; and the Buena Vista Lagoon, a thirty-five-acre body of water that fronts on Pleasure Island and Disney Village.

Marinas are located at the Contemporary Resort, Fort Wilderness, Polynesian Resort, Grand Floridian, Caribbean Beach, Yacht Club, and Beach Club. You'll also find a rental counter at Disney Village, where a variety of boats are available for rental to day visitors as well as guests at Disney resorts. In the summer waiting lines for boats can become lengthy at midday.

Guests at some of the Disney resorts can purchase a pass that includes unlimited use of boats during their stay; if you're planning to make use of Disney's navy more than twice during a weeklong stay, the pass will save you money.

Among the marinas' many offerings:

■ **Parasailing.** The sky is the limit for parasailing adventures high above Bay Lake. Single and tandem fliers get a bird's-eye view of the Magic Kingdom at altitudes nearing 450 feet for seven to ten minutes. Instead of the usual water approach, the special boats permit takeoff and landing from the back of the craft. Prices start at $90 for one and $140 for tandem flyers. For reservations call (407) 939–0754.

■ **Pedal boats.** One-person pedal boats, rented for about $6.50 per half hour, are available at most marinas. Canoes or kayaks for canal paddling can be rented at the Fort Wilderness Bike Barn (407–824–2742) for about $6.50 per half hour.

■ **Sailboats.** Wind-powered vessels, from little two-seater Sunfish and speedy Hobie Cat catamarans to heavier six-seater Capris, are available at Contemporary, Polynesian, Grand Floridian, Fort Wilderness, Yacht Club, and Beach Club marinas. Prices range from about $20 to $30 per hour.

■ **Slow boats.** SunTracker pontoon boats putter about, very slowly, from Disney Village and other resort marinas. Rentals cost $42 per half hour.

■ **Tubing.** Rates start at $125 per hour for up to five guests. For information call (407) 939–0754.

■ **Wakeboarding.** Rates start at $140 per hour for up to four guests. For information call (407) 939–0754.

Water, Water Elsewhere

Not to drink, but to swim in, boat and water-ski on, and parasail over. In addition to the offerings within Walt Disney World, there are numerous places for aquatic recreation in the Orlando area:

▶ **Turkey Lake Park** offers sand beaches, a swimming pool, and nature trails. For general information call (407) 299–5594.

▶ You can rent a houseboat for cruising on the Saint Johns River through **Hontoon Landing Marina**. For information call (800) 248–2474 or consult www.hontoon.com.

▶ Experienced divers can explore the Atlantic or Gulf Coasts or inland springs with equipment from **The Dive Station**. For information call (407) 843–3483 or consult www.divestation.com.

■ **Water Mouse.** Small and low powered, they're still zippy enough to be a lot of fun. They rent by the half hour for about $23; children younger than age twelve are not allowed to drive. Available at Contemporary, Polynesian, Grand Floridian, Fort Wilderness, and Disney Village.

■ **Waterskiing.** The sports center at the marina at the Contemporary Resort offers a variety of water sports, including waterskiing, kneeboarding, and wakeboarding, on Bay Lake near the Magic Kingdom with guidance from a professional instructor. Rates start at $140 per hour for up to five guests. For information call (407) 939–0754.

General information on many water activities is available by calling (407) 824–2222. You can also call the Fort Wilderness Marina at (407) 824–2757.

■ GUIDED PONTOON CRUISES

Nightly guided pontoon cruises, timed to coincide with nighttime shows at Epcot and on Bay Lake, are offered at several resorts.

Each night a pontoon boat, with a capacity of up to fifteen persons, departs any of the lakeside resorts for a circle of Bay Lake; the charge (with a driver) is $120 for a party of up to ten persons. A moonlight pontoon cruise on Bay Lake, including champagne and snacks, costs $175 for up to seven persons and $230 for up to twelve guests.

Each evening a pontoon boat departs Disney's Yacht Club at 8:40 P.M. for a visit to Crescent Lake and the World Showcase, with a great view of the nightly *IllumiNations* show at Epcot. The cost is $160. A similar cruise, at the same price, leaves the BoardWalk resort. For information call (407) 939–7529.

■ FISHING WITHIN WALT DISNEY WORLD

Though not quite a Florida wilderness experience, the fishing is still pretty good on Bay Lake, Lake Buena Vista, Crescent Lagoon, and other waterways within

Walt Disney World. Trophy-size largemouth bass in the fourteen-pound range lurk in lakes and canals almost within casting distance of Cinderella Castle.

During construction of the Magic Kingdom in the late 1960s, more than 70,000 bass fingerlings were released into Bay Lake and Seven Seas Lagoon. Organized fishing tours didn't start until 1977, leaving the bass to grow and breed undisturbed for years. The result is some spectacular fishing that has even caught the attention of professional bass anglers. Three professional bass-fishing events—FINS, Bass & Race, and Bass & Golf—have been held on Bay Lake and Seven Seas Lagoon and televised on ESPN. The heaviest largemouth bass caught and recorded at the Vacation Kingdom was fourteen pounds, six ounces.

Two-hour guided catch-and-release tours on Bay Lake and Seven Seas Lagoon are offered daily on an advance-reservation basis, using pontoon boats. Boats are fully stocked with rods, reels, cold drinks, and a camera to prove you're not telling "fish stories." Prices range from about $200 to $230 for as many as five people for two hours; four-hour trips for as many as five guests cost $395, with a charge of $90 for each additional hour. No fishing license is required. Disney also offers a two-hour guided experience designed just for children ages five to twelve. Cost is $30 per child.

Tours start at Disney's Polynesian, Contemporary, Grand Floridian, Wilderness Lodge, and Fort Wilderness Resort docks on Bay Lake and Seven Seas Lagoon; at Disney's Yacht Club and Beach Club Resorts and Disney's BoardWalk on Crescent Lake; and at Downtown Disney Marketplace and Disney's Port Orleans Resort. For information and reservations for a fishing tour as much as two weeks in advance, call (407) 939–7529 and choose option 4.

Guests at Fort Wilderness or Disney Village can fish from the shore or on any of the canals. Equipment is available for rent at the Bike Barn (rods and reels) or at the Fort Wilderness trading posts (cane poles and lures). There is also the Fishin' Hole on Ol' Man Island at Disney's Dixie Landings Resort hotel. The hole is stocked with bass, bluegill, and even catfish; bamboo poles and bait are provided. After all that, though, you'll have to return the fish to the pond after you catch them; this fishin' hole is just for sport. The cost is about $4.00 per hour, with a family rate of about $13.25 for up to six people. For information call (407) 934–5409.

■ POOL AND BEACH SWIMMING

Guests at Disney resorts are surrounded by water, with swimming encouraged almost everywhere. There are more than 5 miles of white-sand beach along the shores of Bay Lake and Seven Seas Lagoon. Both bodies were engineered by Disney; sand was mined from beneath the lake muck during construction.

Beaches can be found at Contemporary, Grand Floridian, Caribbean Beach, Fort Wilderness, Polynesian, Yacht Club, and Beach Club Resorts. At certain times of the year, swimming may be restricted because of environmental or health concerns because of algae and natural bacteria growth; check with the resort for information.

All of the hotels within Walt Disney World offer swimming pools, some more exotic than others. For example, water slides can be found at the Polynesian and

Caribbean Beach Resorts. Use of these pools is restricted to guests at Disney resorts. Day guests looking for cooling water are encouraged to visit Typhoon Lagoon or Blizzard Beach.

◼ SNORKELING

Get up close and personal with leopard and nurse sharks, rays, rainbows of tropical fish, and an upside-down sunken ship without venturing into the ocean at Shark Reef at Disney's Typhoon Lagoon water park. Entrance and use of snorkel gear is free with admission to Typhoon Lagoon.

◼ SWIMMING WITH THE FISHES

Certified divers and adventurous swimmers can slip into dive gear for an encounter with creatures of the deep without having to visit the ocean at the Epcot DiveQuest/Epcot Seas Aqua Tour within the six-million-gallon aquarium at Epcot's Living Seas pavilion. The tank is home to thousands of creatures, from angelfish to 300-pound sea turtles. The DiveQuest program welcomes certified divers on expert-led tours. There are also sessions that use modern equipment that encases swimmers in an air-filled helmet that does not require scuba certitifcation. Rates, which include equipment, are about $140 for a two-and-a-half-hour experience for scuba and a bit less for the helmet equipment. For information call (407) 824–4321 or (407) 939–8687.

◼ SURFING

Never mind that Walt Disney World is 50 miles inland; you can still learn to hang ten. Surfing lessons are conducted at Typhoon Lagoon's 2.75-million-gallon wave pool before it is opened to the public on selected mornings. The pool produces waves from 3 to 6 feet high every ninety seconds—and no sharks are allowed.

You can take a Learn to Surf lesson for beginners. If you're already a gnarly surfboard dude, there's also the Private 100 Waves Surf Event, with higher and stronger waves for experienced surfers. Prices begin at about $135. Call (407) 939–7529 for reservations.

OUT AND ABOUT

◼ TENNIS COURTS WITHIN THE PARK

Most tennis courts are open to Disney guests at no cost. Some high-maintenance clay courts require a fee. For information on tennis clinics and instruction, call Disney's recreation information line at (407) 939–7529. Instruction, including Peter Burwash International courses, is presented at the Grand Floridian and Disney's Contemporary Resort. A private adult lesson costs $75 per hour; two adults can share a one-hour lesson for $40 each. A group clinic costs $15, and a game against the club pro is $75.

■ **Disney's Contemporary Resort.** (407) 824–3578. The Racquet Club has six lighted clay courts, open to all resort guests from 7:00 A.M. to 6:00 P.M. Rates are $8.00 per hour, or $50.00 per family for the duration of the stay. Racquets and ball machines are available for rent.

■ **Disney's Grand Floridian Beach Resort.** (407) 824–3000. Two groomed clay courts are available to resort guests by reservation from 8:00 A.M. to 9:00 P.M. at no charge. Racquets and ball machines are available for rent.

■ **Disney's Yacht Club & Beach Club Resort.** (407) 934–7000. Two hard courts are available to all resort guests from 7:00 A.M. to 10:00 P.M. for no charge; no reservations are taken.

■ **Disney's Fort Wilderness Homes/Campgrounds.** (407) 824–2742. Two hard courts are available to resort and day guests from 8:00 A.M. to 5:00 P.M. for no charge; no reservations are taken. Racquets available for rent.

■ **Disney's Old Key West Resort.** (407) 939–7529. Two hard courts.

■ **Disney's BoardWalk Resort.** (407) 939–7529. Two hard courts.

■ HORSEBACK RIDING

Trail rides depart from the Trail Blaze Corral at Fort Wilderness campground several times a day. The horses are very gentle, and experience is not required for the forty-five-minute guided tour. Only one rider per horse is permitted, and there is a weight limitation of 250 pounds. Riders must be at least nine years old. The rides cost about $42.

Call (407) 824–2832 between 8:00 A.M. and 3:30 P.M. for information and reservations. Get there by driving to the Fort Wilderness parking lot and taking the Disney bus from there to the park. Or you can hop a short boat ride from the Magic Kingdom across Bay Lake.

Nearby is the Fort Wilderness Petting Zoo, a small, pleasant shaded area that has goats, sheep, horses, and other animals. Admission to the zoo is free. There is a fee of about $3.00 for the pony ride—one of the best deals in Walt Disney World. An adult leads the very docile steed around the track.

■ HAYRIDES

A hay wagon leaves Pioneer Hall at Fort Wilderness every night at 7:00 and 9:30 P.M. for a forty-five-minute tour. Tickets are $8.00 for adults and $5.00 for children. Sign up at the booth outside Pioneer Hall.

■ BIKING WITHIN WALT DISNEY WORLD

More than 8 miles of bicycle paths can be found at Fort Wilderness and at the Disney Village Resort; other places to bike include some of the spread-out resorts such as Caribbean Beach. In an unusual departure for Disney entertainment, use of the paths is free—that is, if you bring your own bike. You can pick up maps wherever bicycles are rented.

Bikes can be rented at the Bike Barn at Fort Wilderness, the Villa Center at Disney Village, or the marina at Caribbean Beach. Rates are about $8.00 per hour or $22.00 per day; tandems (bicycles built for two) can be rented at the Bike Barn. Surrey bikes rent for $18 to $23 per half hour. Call (407) 939–7529 for information. Places where you can bike ride include the following:

■ **Port Orleans and Dixie Landings.** A 2.5-mile tour around the Carriage Path and along the riverfront. Dixie Landings: single or tandem bikes at Dixie Levee near the marina. Port Orleans: single or tandem bikes at Port Orleans Landing near the marina.

■ **Fort Wilderness Resort and Campground.** More than 8 miles of roads and trails in and among forests, beaches, trails, waterways, and boardwalks. Single and tandem bikes are available at the Bike Barn.

■ **Disney's Village Resort and Disney Vacation Club.** Easy riding along the golf course, waterways, and residential streets of the resort. You'll have to share the road with cars, buses, golf carts, and joggers. At this location bicycles are available for rental only to guests at a resort within the park. Village Resort: single bikes at the Reception Center. Vacation Club: single and tandem bikes at Hank's Rent 'n Return.

■ **Disney's Caribbean Beach Resort.** A leisurely, flat circuit around Barefoot Bay Lake, including bridges to Parrot Cay Island and other interesting destinations. Rent single bicycles at the Barefoot Boat Yard.

■ JOGGING

Lace 'em up for a run on one of Walt Disney World Resort's scenic jogging trails. A sylvan 2.2-mile trail offers guests a view of Disney's Fort Wilderness Resort and Campground. The 1.4-mile promenade around the lake at Disney's Caribbean Beach Resort is ideal for jogging. Small jogging trails are offered at Disney's Contemporary Resort, Disney's Polynesian Resort, and Disney's Grand Floridian Resort and Spa. You can also take a leisurely three-quarter-mile stroll on the promenade that surrounds Crescent Lake and connects the Epcot resorts.

■ WALT DISNEY WORLD MARATHON

Only in Walt Disney World can thousands of runners visit four continents in a few hours, passing through a magical castle, down Hollywood Boulevard, and past the Eiffel Tower. The fourteenth annual Walt Disney World Marathon was held January 7, 2007, with a half-marathon the day before. Each year nearly 25,000 people take part in the two events. Registration information is available at www.disneyworldsports.com.

The race wends its way through all four Walt Disney World theme parks, past famous landmarks such as Spaceship Earth at Epcot and the Mickey's Sorcerer's Hat at Disney–MGM Studios and right through Cinderella Castle at the Magic Kingdom. A new theme and entertainment treat greets the athletes each year. Runners can expect to be greeted by more than a few unusual sights along the way, including Mickey Mouse in jogging shoes.

Disney invites even first-time marathoners to compete, allowing a generous seven-hour time limit (the winners usually finish in about two and a half hours). All athletes who complete the race receive a special Mickey Mouse–shaped gold medal, and athletes who complete the half marathon in less than three and a half hours receive a Donald Duck version. There's also a hotly contested wheelchair marathon.

Registration for each year's marathon and half marathon begin in January. For the 2007 marathon, fees were $100 for the marathon and $90 for the half marathon. Registration can be done online at www.runningnetwork.com or www.disneyworldsports.com. A paper application can be requested by calling (407) 939–7810. Special marathon lodging packages are available by calling (407) 939–7810.

■ DISNEY HEALTH CLUBS

■ **Disney's BoardWalk Inn & Villas.** Muscles and Bustles Health Club. Nautilus, circuit training, steam rooms, massage. Open daily from 6:00 A.M. to 9:00 P.M.

■ **Disney's Contemporary Resort.** Olympiad Fitness Center. Nautilus, circuit training, cardiovascular, sauna, massage, tanning booths. Open daily from 6:30 A.M. to 8:00 P.M.

■ **Disney's Grand Floridian Beach Resort.** Spa & Health Club. Whirlpools, saunas, steam rooms, couples treatment room, personal training, massage therapies, and body treatments, including facials, water therapy and soaks, manicures, pedicures, and leg treatments. Open daily from 6:00 A.M. to 9:00 P.M. For reservations call (407) 843–3000. A day pass sells for $15; a length-of-stay pass is $30 for an individual or $45 for a family of as many as five members.

■ **Disney's Yacht & Beach Club Resorts.** Ship Shape Health Club. Nautilus, cardiovascular equipment, weight training, sauna, spa, steam room, massages. Open daily from 6:00 A.M. to 9:00 P.M. A day pass sells for $15; a length-of-stay pass is $25 for an individual or $45 for a family of as many as five members.

■ **Disney's Old Key West Resort.** Exercise Room. Nautilus, free weights, massages. Open from 6:30 A.M. to midnight.

■ **The Villas at the Disney Institute.** Spa & Fitness Center. Cybex, cardiovascular equipment, private treatment rooms, steam room, sauna, whirlpool. Open daily from 6:00 A.M. to 8:00 P.M. Call (407) 827–4429 for reservations. A day pass sells for $15; a length-of-stay pass is $35 for an individual or $50 for a family.

CHAPTER TWENTY-TWO

OUTSIDE WALT DISNEY WORLD: PARTICIPANT AND SPECTATOR SPORTS

WALT DISNEY WORLD is not the only game in town: There's also professional baseball, basketball, football, and, if you can believe it, ice hockey.

MAJOR LEAGUE BASEBALL SPRING TRAINING

Spring training is a dream fulfilled for the serious baseball fan and an enjoyable sojourn for the casual observer. You are so close to the superstars of baseball, the young hopefuls trying for a one-in-a-million spot on a major league roster, as well as some of the greats of yesteryear soaking up the spring sunshine as coaches. Listen to the enthusiastic chatter of the ball players: talk of "taters" (home runs), "hacks" (swings), and "beep" (batting practice).

There are two parts to Florida's Grapefruit League: the training and the not-quite-prime-time practice games. Pitchers and catchers usually arrive in Florida in mid-February to work themselves into shape with exercise and steadily lengthening throwing sessions. Their teammates usually arrive a week or two later. In general, the teams can be found at their practice fields each morning until early afternoon; check with the spring-training sites before heading out. At most parks there is no admission charge for the workouts, and you may be able to wander in and among the superstars. Most teams invite many of their upper-level minor-league players as well as promising rookies to their camps; you'll see uniform numbers as high as ninety-nine. And once the big-leaguers depart, many leave behind their minor-league farm teams, who play a full summer season in the Florida League.

Practice games begin about March 1, and most early games take place in the afternoon. Toward the end of the season, in early April, some games may be scheduled under the lights. Teams tend to play nearby neighbors to cut down on travel time; some of the games are "split squad," meaning that half of the large preseason roster may be playing elsewhere at the same time. Ticket prices range from about $5.00 to $20.00. You can usually obtain tickets as late as the day of the game, except for the more popular matchups, such as Yankees versus Mets or Mets or Yankees versus Red Sox.

If you're a golfer, you might want to check out a course near one or another of the training camps; many players and coaches share that sport and can be found on the links in the afternoon.

As we know, of course, Disney wants it all, and so it came as little surprise to learn that Walt Disney World has snared a major-league team of its own—at least as a spring-training tenant. The Atlanta Braves make their Florida base at Disney's Wide World of Sports. (See chapter 21 for more details.)

Outside the theme park, other nearby training camps are for the Houston Astros, Kansas City Royals, Florida Marlins, and Detroit Tigers.

■ SPRING TRAINING CAMPS WITHIN AN HOUR OF WALT DISNEY WORLD

Tickets for many spring-training events can be purchased through the Tickets .com Web site, www.tickets.com; through Ticketmaster, www.ticketmaster.com; or through the individual Web sites of the major-league teams, which can be accessed through www.mlb.com. You can also consult the online schedules and news posted by Spring Training Yearbook at www.springtrainingmagazine.com.

- **Atlanta Braves.** The Braves train at Disney's Wide World of Sports within Walt Disney World. For information call (407) 939–4263. Tickets: $13 to $21.
- **Cleveland Indians.** Chain O' Lakes Stadium, Winter Haven. About 32 miles south of Walt Disney World. Call (863) 293–3900 for information or (866) 488–7423 for tickets. Tickets: $7.00 to $21.00.
- **Detroit Tigers.** Joker Marchant Stadium, 2301 Lakeland Hills Boulevard, Lakeland. About 36 miles southwest of Walt Disney World. (863) 688–8075. Tickets: $9.00 to $16.00.
- **Houston Astros.** Osceola County Stadium, 1000 Bill Beck Boulevard, Kissimmee. Located off U.S. Highway 192, 1.5 miles west of Florida Turnpike exit 244. (321) 697–3200. Tickets: $15 to $18. The Osceola County Stadium and Sports Complex is also the summer home of the Osceola Astros of the Florida State League at the Class-A professional level; their season is in the summer. The complex includes a 5,120-seat stadium, four other practice fields, and a clubhouse and training facilities.

■ OTHER GRAPEFRUIT LEAGUE TEAMS IN FLORIDA

- **Baltimore Orioles.** Fort Lauderdale Stadium, 5301 NW Twelfth Avenue, Fort Lauderdale. About 200 miles south of Walt Disney World. (800) 236–8908 or (954) 776–1921. Tickets: $8.00 to $18.00.
- **Boston Red Sox.** City of Palms Park, 2201 Edison Avenue, Fort Myers. About 145 miles southwest of Walt Disney World. (877) 733–7699 or (239) 334–4700. Tickets: $10 to $44.
- **Cincinnati Reds.** Ed Smith Stadium, Twelfth and Tuttle, Sarasota. About 116 miles southwest of Walt Disney World. (941) 954–4464. Tickets: $7.00 to $14.00.

The atmosphere at baseball spring training is much more casual than during the Major League season.

■ **Florida Marlins.** Roger Dean Stadium, Jupiter. About 150 miles southeast of Walt Disney World. (561) 775–1818. Tickets: $5.00 to $23.00.

■ **L.A. Dodgers.** Holman Stadium, Dodgertown, 4101 Twenty-sixth Street, Vero Beach. About 104 miles southeast of Walt Disney World. (722) 569–6858. Tickets: $8.00 to $18.00.

■ **Minnesota Twins.** Lee County Sports Complex, 14100 Six Mile Cypress Parkway, Fort Myers. About 150 miles south of Walt Disney World. (800) 338–9467 or (239) 768–4279. Tickets: $16 to $20.

■ **New York Mets.** Thomas J. White Stadium, 525 NW Peacock Boulevard, Port Saint Lucie. About 125 miles southeast of Walt Disney World. (772) 871–2115. Tickets: $6.00 to $25.00.

■ **New York Yankees.** Legends Field, 1 Steinbrenner Drive, Tampa. About 75 miles southwest of Walt Disney World. A modern 10,000-seat home; tickets sell quickly. Call (813) 875–7753 or (813) 879–2244 for ticket information. Tickets: $13 to $19.

■ **Philadelphia Phillies.** Bright House Networks Field, Clearwater. The Philadelphia Phillies moved into an impressive new stadium in Clearwater for the 2004 spring-training season. It is also home to the Class-A Clearwater Threshers, a Philadelphia farm team. Clearwater is about 90 miles southwest of Walt Disney World. (727) 442–8496. Tickets: $8.00 to $25.00.

■ **Pittsburgh Pirates.** McKechnie Field, 1750 Ninth Street West, Bradenton. About 105 miles southwest of Walt Disney World. (941) 748–4610. Tickets: $6.00 to $11.00.

■ **Saint Louis Cardinals.** Roger Dean Stadium, 4751 Main Street, Jupiter. About 150 miles southeast of Walt Disney World, near Palm Beach. (561) 775–1818. Tickets: $5.00 to $22.00.

■ **Tampa Bay Devil Rays.** Tropicana Field, 1 Tropicana Drive, Saint Petersburg. About 92 miles southwest of Walt Disney World. (888) 326–7297 or (727) 825–3250. Tickets: about $7.00 to $19.00.

■ **Toronto Blue Jays.** Knology Park, 311 Douglas Avenue, Dunedin. About 90 miles southwest of Walt Disney World, near Clearwater. (727) 733–0429. Tickets: $13 to $18.

■ **Washington Nationals.** Space Coast Stadium, Viera. About 70 miles southeast of Walt Disney World, near Melbourne. (321) 633–4487. Tickets: $5.00 to $18.00.

NBA BASKETBALL

The **Orlando Magic** of the National Basketball Association play at the T. D. Waterhouse Centre (the former Orlando Arena) from October to April of each year.

The arena, at 600 West Amelia Street, opened in 1989. There are 15,291 seats for basketball beneath a spectacular video screen used for replays and special encouragements to the fans. Tickets have been easier to obtain in recent years as the team's fortunes have waned; seats cost from $10 to $110, with some premium or VIP seats priced higher. For ticket information call (407) 916–2255 or (800) 462–2849, or consult www.nba.com/magic.

ARENA FOOTBALL LEAGUE

The Orlando Predators play a fourteen-game schedule at the T. D. Waterhouse Centre (the former Orlando Arena) from January to May. The league features eight-man "Ironman" football on a 50-yard indoor field; with the exception of the quarterback and an offensive specialist, players must play both offense and defense. Tickets are priced from about $6.00 to $100.00. For more information call (407) 447–7337 or consult www.orlandopredators.com.

THE CITRUS BOWL

The Capital One Bowl college football game is held at the 70,000-seat stadium in early January of each year, pitting the champions of the Big Ten Conference against the Southeastern Conference (SEC). For information call (407) 849–2500 or consult www.fcsports.com.

HORSEBACK RIDING

■ **Grand Cypress Equestrian Center.** $45 trail rides and $85 to $150 (for experienced riders only) for trail rides; private lessons $55 per half hour, $100 per hour. Located at 1 North Jacaranda, off Highway 535, Orlando. (800) 835–7377 or (407) 239–4700; www.grandcypress.com/equestrian_center.

RODEO

■ **Kissimmee Rodeo.** Every Friday from 8:00 to 10:00 P.M., except during December. Adults $18.00, children $9.00. Located at the Kissimmee Sports Arena, 958 South Hoagland Boulevard. (407) 933–0020; www.ksarodeo.com.
■ **Silver Spurs Rodeo.** Kissimmee. The largest rodeo east of the Mississippi, with bull and bronco riding, steer wrestling, and more, is held for one weekend in

mid-February and early October only. The Silver Spurs began in March 1944 during World War II as a fund-raising event to sell war bonds. In 2003 the rodeo moved into a new indoor facility at Osceola Heritage Park. Call (321) 697–3495 for tickets, priced from about $10 to $25, and (407) 847–4052 for information; www.silverspursrodeo.com.

GREYHOUND RACING

■ **Melbourne Greyhound Park.** Put your money on the dogs. Matinee and evening race schedule varies seasonally; call for information. Live races conducted year-round, augmented by the Club 52 poker hall. The track is located in Melbourne. (321) 259–9800; www.melbournegreyhoundpark.com.

■ **Sanford-Orlando Kennel Club.** Racing year-round, nightly at 7:30 P.M. except Sunday, and matinees Monday, Wednesday, and Saturday at 12:30 P.M. General admission $1.00, clubhouse $2.00. The track is located at 301 Dog Track Road, Longwood. (407) 831–1600; www.floridagreyhoundracing.com.

ROLLER SKATING

Skate Reflections. Roller skate to the latest music on 17,000 square feet of solid maple floor. Located at 1111 Dyer Boulevard, Kissimmee. (407) 846–8469; www.skatereflections.com.

Hunting and Fishing Licenses

Fishing (fresh and saltwater) and hunting licenses for persons age sixteen and older may be obtained from the Osceola County Tax Collector's office. For information consult www .osceolataxcollector.com/ hunting-fishing.html. More information is available from the Florida Game and Fresh Water Commission at (407) 846–5300 or the Florida Marine Patrol (saltwater fishing) at (800) 342–5367. Some tour services also serve as agencies for appropriate licenses.

FISHING

■ **Backcountry Charter Service.** Inshore saltwater trips on the Indian River near the Kennedy Space Center and on the Saint Johns River. (800) 932–7335; www.floridabackcountry.com.

■ **Bass Anglers Guide Service.** (407) 656–1052; www .fishing-boating.com/bassanglers.

■ **Bass Challenger Guide Service.** (407) 273–8045; www.basschallenger.com.

BUNGEE JUMPING

The Orlando area seems to feature more bungee-jumping establishments than you could shake a tourist at; it's a very changeable industry, with cranes or towers moving from one open lot to another. If this is the sort of thing you're looking for, cruise Irlo Bronson Highway or International Drive and look up.

BOATING AND CRUISES

- **Airboat Rentals U-Drive.** Adults, $40 per airboat up to four adults; electric boats $25 for up to six adults. Airboats, electric boats, and canoes available for rental and use in a cypress swamp. Located on Shingle Creek at 4266 West U.S. Highway 192, Kissimmee, a half mile east of Medieval Times. (407) 847–3672; www.airboatrentals.com.
- **Boggy Creek Airboats.** Guided tours in Florida wilderness; night alligator hunts available in summer. Boats zip along at speeds of up to 45 miles per hour between walls of tall grass. Adults $18.95, children (ages three to twelve) $14.95. Located at Southport Road in Kissimmee. (407) 344–9550; www.bcairboats .com.
- **Rivership *Romance*.** Cruises on the Saint Johns River. The 110-foot-long steel-hull ship was built in 1942; it spent its first fifty years plying the cold water of the Great Lakes carrying coal and iron ore, and later troops patrolling the locks at Sault Ste. Marie during World War II. In later years it served as a working vessel on the lakes and was involved in search-and-rescue missions, including the sinking of the *Edmund Fitzgerald,* made famous in a song by Gordon Lightfoot. In 1995 the ship was gingerly moved 2,700 miles from Chicago on inland waterways, across the Gulf, and into the canals and rivers of Florida, where she was completely re-furbished.

Dinner cruises Friday and Saturday nights ($46 to $54); no children younger than age sixteen. Three-hour lunch cruise Wednesday and Saturday: adults $38; four-hour lunch cruise Monday, Tuesday, Thursday, and Friday: adults $48.50. Located at 433 North Palmetto Avenue, Sanford. (800) 423–7401 or (407) 321–5091; www.rivershipromance.com.

Boating Away

The Kissimmee Waterway, a 50-mile-long series of lakes, connects Lake Tohopekaliga with Lake Okeechobee and, through that body of water, with both the Atlantic Ocean and the Gulf of Mexico. There are boat ramps at Granada (2605 Ridgeway Drive) and Partin Triangle Park on Lake Tohopeka-liga, and at Sexton on Fish Lake (2590 Irlo Bronson Highway [US 192]), all in Kissimmee.

SIGHTSEEING BY AIR

- **Orange Blossom Balloons.** One-hour sunrise champagne hot-air-balloon flights over central Florida and the theme parks. Adults $175, children (ages ten to fifteen) $95 with adult. Departs from the Days Inn Maingate West, near Disney. (407) 239–7677; www.orangeblossomballoons.com.
- **SkyScapes Balloon Tours.** $425 per couple. Private flights for couples and families, $185 per adult and $125 per child. 5755 Cove Drive, Orlando. (407) 856–4606; www.skyscapesballoontours.com.

CHAPTER TWENTY-THREE

ORLANDO AND KISSIMMEE ATTRACTIONS AND SHOPPING

ORLANDO-KISSIMMEE ATTRACTIONS

■ GATORLAND

Gatorland is about as real a place and as un-Disney a theme park as you are likely to find in central Florida, and it is one of our favorite places in the world. It is, quite simply, a shrine to the alligator, and when they say they have the world's largest collection of the fascinatingly creepy creatures, they're not exaggerating: There are thousands of them at every turn in this fifty-acre park, which draws some 400,000 visitors each year.

Gatorland is one of the older attractions in central Florida, dating from 1949. Over the years the park has grown from a handful of alligators with a few huts and pens into the Alligator Capital of the World and an active breeding station. You'll stroll along a boardwalk through a cypress swamp to see gators, herons, and dozens of other wild creatures. Other creatures on display include snakes, deer, goats, talking birds, and even a Florida bear. Semi-brave visitors can even "pet" an alligator—a baby with its mouth taped shut. The park is also a mecca for bird-watchers, with thousands of native birds nesting in the area, making use of the alligators as protectors of their nests from natural predators such as raccoons and opossums. There is a walk-in aviary, home to a flock of Australian lories that may come to perch on your hand.

The Jungle Crocs of the World display features Nile, Cuban, American, and Australian saltwater crocodiles in a swamplike setting. Visitors meander through the swamp on a raised walkway. Each of the species of crocodiles has a slightly different stalking behavior, according to Gatorland experts. Cuban crocs tend to attack on land, while their saltwater cousins usually hide under the surface of the water and explode out to snap at any tempting target. You can take a slow tour

A trainer gets up close and personal at Gatorland.

of this exhibit, as well as to the ten-acre breeding marsh, on a small-scale railway.

Florida "Crackers" (the term comes from the sound made by bullwhips cracking over the heads of cattle) were the first alligator wrestlers—of necessity. They would often have to fight gators that had grabbed calves for a snack. At Gatorland you'll see an exhibition of stunt wrestling in the 800-seat Wrestlin' Stadium. Another highlight is the Gator Jumparoo, where giant alligators nearly 15 feet long and 1,000 pounds jump out of the water to be hand-fed. There's also a small water park for kids, Lilly's Pad.

There are more than a thousand alligators at the park; Gatorland keepers manage about fifty to seventy-five hatchlings per year. Younger animals are tagged or chipped with an electronic marker to allow keepers to identify and track them. Some senior citizens, more than forty years old, are monitored based on their descriptions.

The biggest alligator at the park, about 14.5 feet long, lives in the main lake; there's also a huge crocodile named Alf, about the same size and believed to be the biggest American crocodile in captivity. Gatorland also has a saltwater crocodile named Morton, who was nearly 12 feet long at less than ten years old. Morton is from a species known to grow to more than 20 feet long and live more than fifty years, so he has an excellent head start and a good chance at becoming a record animal. Another notable large alligator is Chester, brought to the park from a checkered career around Chestnut Park in Tampa. He was accused of having a taste for neighborhood dogs.

Gatorland offers a line of alligator boots, belts, wallets, and meat. Yes, meat: Pearl's Smoke House offers smoked alligator ribs, deep-fried gator nuggets, and gator chowder. The nuggets, of course, taste just like chicken. The meat is not harvested from animals at the park.

The animals in the park are active year-round, but insiders say May is the best time to visit; birds in the park are most active, and alligators are on the prowl in breeding season. The park is open daily from 9:00 A.M. to 6:00 P.M. Visitors should allow several hours; to catch the full cycle of shows, I'd suggest arriving early or at lunchtime. Tickets in 2006 were $19.95 for adults and $12.95 for children ages three to twelve. Located at 14501 South Orange Blossom Trail (Highway 441) in Orlando, about a twenty-minute drive from Walt Disney World. (800) 393–5297 or (407) 855–5496; www.gatorland.com.

■ GREEN MEADOWS FARM

The ultimate petting farm for children of all ages, Green Meadows Farm includes a two-hour guided tour with introductions to more than 300 animals, including pigs, cows, goats, sheep, donkeys, chickens, turkeys, ducks, and geese. Everyone gets to milk a cow, and children can go for pony rides, a tractor-pulled hayride, and a ten-minute train ride.

This is a lovely place for animal lovers of all ages to while away a warm afternoon; the farm setting could not be more different than a theme park but has real oohs and aahs at every turn. On one of our visits the tour came to a complete halt in front of a pen occupied by three-day-old Vietnamese potbellied pigs. My children fell in love with some of the exotic chickens, including a variety named *mille fleurs* ("thousand flowers") because of the intricate pattern on their back.

The farm is one of six similar operations around the country, the brainchild of Bob and Coni Keyes of Waterford, Wisconsin. It started in Wisconsin when that farm began to allow visitors to come and pick vegetables and raspberries. It expanded from that to allow urban youngsters to get up close to farm animals. There are similar farms in Illinois, California, New Jersey, and New York.

The farm is located in the town of Kissimmee. Take U.S. Highway 192 east toward Kissimmee; turn right at Poinciana Boulevard and go 5 miles to the farm. Admission: $19; children age two and younger are admitted for free; seniors, $16. Open every day but Thanksgiving and Christmas from 9:30 A.M. to 5:30 P.M. For information call (407) 846–0770 or consult www.greenmeadowsfarm.com.

■ THE HOLY LAND EXPERIENCE

A "living Biblical museum" spread over fifteen acres near Universal Studios Florida. The place re-creates in elaborate and authentic detail the city of Jerusalem and shows its religious importance between the years 1450 B.C. and A.D. 66. A cast of characters re-creates stories and events included in the Bible. Guests enter the Holy Land Experience through the Jerusalem City Gate and into a re-creation of a first-century street market with Middle Eastern music, village craftsmen, and themed gift shops.

The Wilderness Tabernacle is home to a twenty-minute multimedia presentation that examines Israel's ancient priesthood. The Qumran Dead Sea Caves represents the caves where the Dead Sea Scrolls were hidden by the Essenes, an ancient Jewish religious sect, during the first century; they were discovered in 1947. Other areas at the park include the Via Dolorosa (the "way of suffering"), the street that Jesus walked on his way to Calvary to die on the cross. At the end of the path is a tranquil garden with a replica of the tomb of Jesus near Jerusalem. Throughout the day dramatists or musicians depict the death, burial, and resurrection of Jesus.

The Temple of the Great King is a half-scale representation of Herod's Temple, which stood upon hallowed Mount Moriah in first-century Jerusalem. Within is a theater presenting *The Seed of Promise*, shot on location in Jerusalem. Also, just off the Byzantine Cardo (the main Byzantine Road) is a building housing the world's largest indoor model of first-century Jerusalem. The 45-foot-long by 25-foot-wide model is believed to be a historically authentic reproduction of the city as it stood in the year A.D. 66.

In 2002 the Scriptorium: Center for Biblical Antiquities opened. The museum, built in the fourth-century Byzantine architectural style, houses a collection of biblical artifacts, ancient cuneiform, scrolls, and manuscripts.

The attraction is located at Conroy and Vineland Roads, off exit 78 of Interstate 4. Operating hours vary; call for times. Admission: adults $29.99, children (ages six to twelve) $19.99. For information call (866) 872–4659 or (407) 367–2065, or consult www.theholylandexperience.com.

■ ORLANDO SCIENCE CENTER

Orlando's science museum is a hands-on exploration of our environment and the universe. You'll be greeted by live animals in an 8,000-gallon cypress swamp. You can become a Cosmic Tourist in an exploration of space, or travel through the human body as a piece of food in BodyZone.

The Darden Adventure Theater features daily performances by the Einstein Players, and the Dr. Phillips CineDome and planetarium offers a selection of IMAX films and special presentations. At the Crosby Observatory visitors can view the night sky using Florida's largest public refractor telescope.

Admission is $14.95 for adults and $9.95 for children ages three to eleven, including exhibits plus one film or planetarium show. Senior tickets $13.95. After 4:00 P.M. admission is reduced by $5.00 for all tickets. Parking is $3.50.

Located at 777 East Princeton Street, the center is open Tuesday through Thursday from 9:00 A.M. to 5:00 P.M., Friday and Saturday from 9:00 A.M. to 9:00 P.M., and Sunday from noon to 5:00 P.M. Closed Monday. For information call (888) 672–4386 or (407) 514–2000, or consult www.osc.org.

■ RIPLEY'S BELIEVE IT OR NOT!

This is one strange place—something that will be immediately obvious when you look at the building. Think of it as the leaning museum of Orlando, and

The Babies of Ripley's

The Orlando Ripley's made it into the *Wall Street Journal* in late 1995 with a "believe it or not" of its own: Eight of the twenty staffers at the museum became parents in a single year, each after touching an African fertility totem in the office lobby. A ninth pregnancy was a delivery woman for an air express company.

you'll get the idea. Among the oddities here are a replica of the *Mona Lisa* made from slices of toast, a 1907 Rolls-Royce constructed from more than a million matchsticks, and extraordinary humans, including the world's tallest man and Liu Ch'ung, the man with two pupils in each eye. The Orlando branch of the chain of museums also includes a portion of the Berlin Wall, a reproduction of Van Gogh's self-portrait created from 3,000 postcards, and a Disasters Gallery.

This is a must-see for visitors who have a taste for the bizarre; it's even stranger than a theme park that celebrates a talking mouse. Allow about ninety minutes for a self-guided tour. Located at 8201 International Drive, 1 block south of Sand Lake Road, the attraction is open daily from 9:00 A.M. to 1:00 A.M. Admission: adults $16.95, seniors $14.95, and children (ages four to twelve) $11.95. For information call (407) 363–4418 or consult www.ripleysorlando.com.

■ SKULL KINGDOM

A haunted family attraction, this shrine to scarification stands at the top of International Drive, across from Wet 'n Wild. Enter, if you dare, through the Giant Skull Entrance. The theming never lets up, from the ticket booth within a giant winged dragon to a spiderweb chandelier in the entry chamber, where groups of visitors are divided into small groups to walk through the sprawling building.

The concept is "fun and fright," which is accomplished with some high-tech apparatus, including hydraulics, smoke machines, robotics, and theatrical lighting. Live actors pop out of the walls and respond to the actions of visitors—without touching them. One of the final sections of the adventure presents a fully animated alien that will knock your knees extraterrestrially.

The Skull Kingdom is open weekdays from 6:00 to 11:00 P.M. and weekends from noon to 11:00 P.M. In July and August the attraction is open daily from noon to 11:00 P.M. Day admission, $8.99; after 5:00 P.M., $14.04. The recommended minimum age is eight. For information call (407) 354–1564 or consult www.skullkingdom.com.

There's also a Magic Show and Dinner offered regularly; it includes pizza, soda, and beer. Adults $19.75, children seven and younger $15.97. Combination tickets including admission to Skull Kingdom were priced in 2006 at $28.25 for adults and $24.45 for children.

■ *TITANIC*–SHIP OF DREAMS

The *Titanic* lives again in this high-tech re-creation of some of the more interesting details of the great ship, at The Mercado on International Drive. The attraction features actors in period costume who share the stories of those aboard and also includes more than 200 artifacts from private collections, many on public display for the first time.

Among them are a deck chair recovered from the Atlantic following the sinking, first-class china and dinnerware, personal letters on *Titanic* stationery that survived the sinking, and a life jacket. The controversial letter of deceased *Titanic* survivor Nellie Walcroft, purchased at auction in England, is included in the display. The letter sheds new light on the disaster and stirs up fresh controversy. Walcroft tells of the alleged shooting of some steerage passengers who attempted to find a place on one of the doomed *Titanic*'s lifeboats.

Also on display is memorabilia from the movie *Titanic,* including a costume worn by Leonardo DiCaprio, plus items from older classics, including *A Night to Remember* and *The Search for Titanic,* hosted by Orson Welles.

The attraction is located at The Mercado, 8445 South International Drive, and is open from 9:00 A.M. to 9:00 P.M. In 2006 tickets were $19.95 for adults and $12.95 for children (ages six to eleven). For information call (407) 345–9337 or consult www.titanicshipofdreams.com.

▓ WET 'N WILD

It's all in the name in this large water park, owned by nearby Universal Studios Florida. According to industry sources, Orlando's Wet 'n Wild is the busiest water park in the country, drawing about 1.3 million visitors in recent years, a bit more than Walt Disney World's Blizzard Beach and Typhoon Lagoon.

The park, which opened in 1977, claims the mantle as the world's first water park. Today, with the assistance of a bit of heated water, it is one of the nation's only water parks to be open year-round.

Although it doesn't have the Disney "theme" magic, Wet 'n Wild does have some of the wildest—and most unusual—water rides anywhere around. Attractions at the park include **Bomb Bay,** where volunteers climb into a snug compartment shaped like a large bomb with fins and are slowly maneuvered onto a ledge hanging out over a six-story water slide. When the spring-loaded bomb bay doors open, the rider plunges into a near free fall at speeds close to 30 miles per hour through an angled chute.

The **Lazy River** tube ride meanders through a re-created bit of Florida's past, with old boat docks, rustic billboards, and not a mouse in sight.

Blue Niagara features 300 feet of intertwined looping slides that twist from six stories above the park to a splash landing. **The Surge** dispatches a four-passenger bouncing tube down a 600-foot path that includes high banked turns.

Der Stuka, claimed to be one of the highest, fastest water slides in the world, sends riders in a free fall down a 250-foot slide, and then allows them to coast to a stop along a 115-foot-long water runway. At the **Black Hole** a two-person raft is propelled by a thousand-gallon-a-minute blast of water for a thirty-second runaway journey through 500 feet of twisting, turning darkness.

Bubba Tub sends groups of five people splashing down a triple-dip slide. **The Flyer** is a watery toboggan run with 80-foot-long toboggans. And at **Hydra Fighter** riders sit in back-to-back swings equipped with water cannons. By regulating water pressure, they'll be able to control how high and fast the swing goes. Serious players can send their gondola swinging ninety degrees or more from perpendicular. About once an hour the area's lifeguards take to the ride to show amateurs how it's really done.

A recent addition was **Disco H₂O,** a four-passenger tube that drops down an enclosed flume toward a watery disco club complete with lights, mirror balls, and groovy music. **The Storm** drops guests from a chute into a giant open bowl—kind of like a bathroom commode—where they spin in descending circles to a splash landing. **The Blast** is a new design for a two-person tube ride that features many twists and turns, explosive pipe bursts, and drenching waterspouts that lead up to a final waterfall plunge.

Our favorite here is **Knee Ski.** You'll snap on a life vest and a helmet and then plant your knees in a surfboard. Hold on to the handle for dear life as you are launched out onto the lake and towed by an overhead cable around a half-mile course. We've yet to see someone make it completely around on the first try, but after a few exciting tries, most visitors master the Knee Ski. My hotshot teenage daughter couldn't get enough of this unusual ride, but I was perfectly happy to make it around once before retiring to a beach umbrella.

You can also ride a wakeboard, pulled around a portion of the pond on the **WakeZone** cableway. At **Wild One** you and a friend ride on a pair of bouncy tubes pulled around the pond by a Jet Ski; there's an additional charge.

All three of the pond rides—Knee Ski, WakeZone, and Wild One—are open from May through September from noon to dusk.

There's also the **Surf Lagoon** wave pool and the **Kids' Park,** with smaller versions of the park's most popular rides.

Located at 6200 International Drive, just off I–4, the park is open year-round, depending on weather conditions. For most of the year, the park is open until 5:00 P.M.; from June until Labor Day, it is open until 7:00, 9:00, or 11:00 P.M. During summer nights there's a concert stage on the deck of the Surf Lagoon Wave Pool for nightly music and entertainment, and the park is open late.

Admission before tax: adults $34.95 and children (ages three to nine) $28.95. Tube rental was $4.00; you can also rent a towel or a locker. Other tickets offered include a weekday annual pass and an every-day annual pass priced at about the cost of two days of tickets. Admission is also included as part of the Orlando FlexTicket passes; see chapter 15 for prices. For information call (800) 992–9453 or (407) 351–1800, or consult www.wetnwild.com/orlando.

SMALLER AREA ATTRACTIONS

■ **Congo River Golf & Exploration Company.** Three locations: 5901 International Drive, Orlando; (407) 248–9181. 6312 International Drive, next to Wet 'n Wild, Orlando; (407) 352–0042. 4777 West US 192, 3 miles east of I–4, Kissimmee; (407) 396–6900; www.congoriver.com. A miniature golf course and more, with exploration games, an arcade, and go-karts (International Drive) or paddleboats (Kissimmee). At the Kissimmee location the two courses are the

Stanley and the more difficult Livingstone. Golf fees: $10.45 for eighteen holes, $14.50 for thirty-six holes; children, $8.45 for eighteen holes, $12.50 for thirty-six holes. Opens at 10:00 A.M.

- **Haunted House at Old Town.** 5770 West Irlo Bronson Highway, Kissimmee; (407) 397–2231; www.old-town.com. Two floors of spooks and special effects. Adults $10.00, children (ages ten and younger) $6.75. Open noon to 11:00 P.M. daily.
- **International Trolley & Train Museum/Trainland.** 8990 International Drive, Orlando (behind Pointe*Orlando); (407) 363–9002. Toy trains from the 1920s to the present, one of the largest indoor model-train layouts in the country, and a gift shop for collectors. Adults about $8.00, seniors and children (ages three to twelve) $6.00.
- **Katie's Wekiva River Landing.** 190 Katie's Cove, Sanford; (407) 628–1482. The Wekiva River is located in east-central Florida within Orange, Seminole, and Lake Counties. The watershed encompasses about 130 square miles. Fossils of long-extinct mammals, including saber-toothed cats, mastodons, and giant sloths, have been found along its length. Native Americans, including the Timucuans and the Seminoles, lived along the riverbanks for some 7,500 years. Downstream canoe runs, with equipment rental and shuttle service. Open 8:00 A.M. to sunset. Call for rates. Runs range from 6 to 19 miles.
- **Kissimmee Go-Karts.** 4708 West Irlo Bronson Highway, Kissimmee; (407) 396–4800. Indy-style and double-seater go-karts on a nearly mile-long track that goes over and under bridges. $3.75 per lap; multi-lap tickets also available. Children must be at least eleven years old.
- **Monument of States.** Lakefront Park, downtown Kissimmee. Erected in 1943, the Monument of States is a 50-foot-tall solid concrete structure. More than 1,500 stones represent every state in the nation and twenty-one foreign countries. Minerals and ores include gold and silver, plus chrome, cobalt, copper, iron, lead, platinum, and zinc. Stones include agate, alabaster, alva, coquina, coral, diamond-bearing rocks, feldspar, flint, Florida keystone, granite, limestone, marble, meteors, mica, petrified wood, petrified teeth and bones, quartz, sandstone, schist, slate, stalactites, stalagmites, and travatia.
- **Pirate's Cove Adventure Golf.** www.piratescove.net. Two locations: 8501 International Drive, Orlando; (407) 352–7378. 12545 Highway 535, Crossroads Shopping Center, Lake Buena Vista; (407) 827–1242. A clever pirate-theme golf course, with two eighteen-hole challenges at each location. Both courses $13.49 for adults, $12.49 for children.
- **Pirate's Island Adventure Golf.** 2845 Florida Plaza Boulevard, Kissimmee; (407) 396–7484; www.piratesislandgolf.com. Two eighteen-hole courses set in a tropical paradise. Adults $7.95, children $6.95. All-day play, $9.95.
- **Race Rock.** 8986 International Drive, Orlando; (407) 248–9876; www.racerock .com. A restaurant packed with racing cars and memorabilia, including stock, funny, and Indy cars, plus monster trucks, hydroplanes, and dragsters. Open Sunday through Thursday from 11:30 A.M. to 10:30 P.M. and Friday and Saturday to 11:00 P.M.

- **Reptile World Serpentarium.** 5705 East Irlo Bronson Highway, St. Cloud; (407) 892–6905. Cobras and dozens of other poisonous snakes. Open Tuesday through Sunday from 9:00 A.M. to 5:30 P.M. Adults $5.75, students $4.75, and children (ages three to five) $3.75.
- **River Adventure Golf.** 4535 West Irlo Bronson Highway, Kissimmee; (407) 396–4666. Water-theme courses. All tickets $7.95; children younger than age four free.
- **SAK Comedy Lab.** 380 West Amelia Street, downtown Orlando; (407) 648–0001; www.sak.com. A small, informal storefront theater that features improvisational and scripted comedy shows. The young cast works without a net, and unlike the Comedy Warehouse at Pleasure Island, there are no Disney minders anywhere on the SAK Comedy Lab property. Among alumni is Wayne Brady. Two shows on Friday and Saturday at 8:00 and 10:00 P.M. General admission is $13. Call for specials.
- **WonderWorks.** Pointe*Orlando, International Drive, Orlando; (407) 351–8800; www.wonderworksonline.com. It's hard to miss this place, even in the midst of the wall-to-wall, grab-your-eye tourist district: It's the place that looks exactly like it has fallen from the sky and landed upside down on International Drive.

  WonderWorks is a place where science has gone crazy—a sort of hands-on science museum for children of all ages. Here's the cover story: Since the end of World War II, the super-secret WonderWorks laboratory has been located on a remote, uncharted island off Florida—within the Bermuda Triangle—and has served as a haven for investigators of the unexplainable. But in 1997 something went awry in a top-secret experiment to harness the power of a tornado: The energy vortex lifted the research lab from its foundations and dropped it, upside down, in Orlando.

  Inside the building you'll find hands-on demonstrations of the forces of nature, including a hurricane chamber, the Earthquake Experience, and an anti-gravity room. In the Physical Challenge Lab, you can try out the Shocker Chair, test your coordination on a virtual balance beam, play virtual basketball, and arm wrestle a computer. In the UFO Lab you can split your image and distort your body, make music with a theramin or computer drums, and morph your voice. Guests can also attend the Outta Control Dinner Show, a ninety-minute magic show and pizza dinner.

  The attraction is open daily from 9:00 A.M. to midnight. Plan to stay for at least two hours in the building; Mom and Dad may want to shop next door. Adults $19.95, children (ages four to twelve) $14.95. Admission for dinner magic show: adults $21.95, or $37.95 combination with WonderWorks admission; children $14.95, or $21.95 with WonderWorks admission. A package that includes admission to the attraction, the dinner show, and one laser tag game sells for $1.00 more.
- **A World of Orchids.** 2501 Old Lake Wilson Road, Kissimmee; (407) 396–1887; www.aworldoforchids.com. Here you'll see botanical gardens and an arboretum containing an ever-changing display of more than 2,000 varieties of orchids, which bloom throughout the year. The world's largest permanent indoor display

of rare and exquisite flowering orchids was created by Kerry and Chris Richards, internationally recognized orchid growers and owners of a Miami orchid nursery. Open daily except Monday from 9:30 A.M. to 4:30 P.M. Admission is free.

OTHER ATTRACTIONS OUTSIDE ORLANDO

▉ BOK TOWER GARDENS

Florida's historic bell tower, centerpiece of a magnificent garden, is at Florida's highest point—all of 295 feet. Bok Tower Gardens was dedicated in 1929 to the American people by Dutch immigrant Edward Bok, Pulitzer Prize–winning editor of the *Ladies' Home Journal.* Some of the fifty-seven bronze bells weigh as much as twelve tons. The 128 acres of gardens include thousands of azaleas, camellias, magnolias, and other flowering plants. The gardens are home to a colony of wood ducks and more than one hundred other species of birds. A forty-five-minute carillon recital is presented daily at 3:00 P.M. Located in Lake Wales, about 55 miles south of Orlando, off U.S. Highway 27 to Alternate 27, the gardens are open daily 8:00 A.M. to 6:00 P.M. Adults $10.00, children (ages five to twelve) $3.00. For information call (863) 676–1408 or consult www.boktower.org.

▉ CYPRESS GARDENS ADVENTURE PARK

Florida's first theme park, established in 1936, Cypress Gardens became semi–world famous as the home of the famous water-ski team Dixie Belles in hoopskirts, and thousands of varieties of plants, birds, and other creatures. The park closed in early 2003 after several years of declining attendance, but it was rescued in late 2004 under new ownership with fresh investments in shows, thrill rides, and other entertainment.

The new owner of Cypress Gardens, who also operates Wild Adventures in Valdosta, Georgia, was assisted by massive subsidies and involvement by Florida state and local government.

The lush, green park off US 27 is near Winter Haven, Florida, about forty-five minutes from Orlando. The famed botanical gardens include more than 8,000 varieties of plants from ninety countries.

The original founder of Cypress Gardens was Dick Pope Sr., who closed his first Florida real-estate deal at the age of twelve. When the local market went bust in 1927, he went into the public relations business, promoting some of the first outboard motors with races across the state. In the heart of the Depression, Pope convinced federal agencies to beautify and rebuild the canals and lakes around Winter Haven. Pope dreamed of a tropical paradise in the middle of a muck-filled marsh.

The lush gardens opened in 1936. Boat rides were added two years later. The Dixie Belles arrived in 1940 when park employees dressed warmly for an unseasonable cold snap. If you find a Dixie Belle in a huge hoopskirt and other heavy accoutrements sitting out in the broiling Florida sun year-round, don't fret: She has a parasol as well as a hidden air-conditioning vent in the bench below.

Cypress Gardens's first water-ski show took place in 1943 when a group of local skiers gathered on Lake Eloise to entertain military troops on leave. Since then skiers have recorded more than fifty world records, including the first four-tier human pyramid. In the 1950s and 1960s, Elvis Presley and Esther Williams made films here.

Today, two areas, Adventure Grove and Paradise Pier, showcase rides for all ages at Cypress Gardens. Set along a boardwalk in the style reminiscent of vintage amusement parks, the offerings include children's favorites, fun-for-the-whole-family attractions, and heart-pounding thrill rides.

Transportation through the park is made easy with the Citrus Line Railroad and Cypress Cove Ferry Line.

The water-ski capital of the world lives on as skiers take to the water and sky in an explosive show that will leave guests laughing as well as gasping in wonder at gravity-defying feats. The Royal Palm Theater presents *Cypress Gardens on Ice*. And, of course, the Dixie Belles are back to grace the gardens.

Visitors can discover the enchantment of the Living Garden and end the day with a spectacular laser-and-fireworks show over Lake Eloise. Guests will be able to enjoy a variety of seasonal events, such as a Halloween "spooktacular" and the magical Christmas Wonderland.

The Star Haven Amphitheater hosts free concerts as part of the admission to the park, with shows ranging from country, bluegrass, rock, pop, oldies, gospel, contemporary Christian, R&B, and more. (Guests are encouraged to bring in lawn chairs to set up in festival-style seating. A block of covered reserved seating is also available at an additional charge.)

You can take a peaceful walk through the park's historic botanical gardens, stroll along Topiary Trail, or allow yourself to be surrounded with the spectacular beauty of hundreds of colorful butterflies fluttering through the lush foliage at **Wings of Wonder.**

Jubilee Junction is a bustling village featuring old-fashioned food and shopping including crafts.

Triple Hurricane is the park's signature wooden coaster, styled in the out-and-back design reminiscent of early boardwalk "woodies." **Swamp Thing!** is a suspended coaster that soars and swoops over Paradise Pier. **Okeechobee Rampage** is a modern steel coaster with left-right swerves, sudden speed bursts, and camelbacks.

Fiesta Express is a small wild-mouse coaster, aimed at younger and more cautious visitors. **Galaxy Spin** is another smaller coaster with spaceship cars that twist and turn along the track, spinning all the while!

Thunderbolt lifts passengers in a slow and agonizing ascent up its formidable tower, pauses for a precarious moment, and then plunges 120 feet to the ground in a high-speed free fall.

Delta Kite Flyers is reminiscent of the park's historic water-ski show; strapped-in guests lie on their stomachs and take off into the wild blue yonder with the sensation of free flight.

Inverter is a head-over-heels, over-the-top excitement swing ride. **Pharaoh's Fury** is an Egyptian barge that catapaults back and forth at speeds as high as 80 miles per hour. **Yo-Yo** looks like its name: a circular swing 25 feet above the ground.

At **Disk'O,** passengers are strapped to a circular deck on a motorcycle-style seat, looking out; the deck rotates while swinging from side to side. **Mega Bounce** is a cousin of the old Tilt-A-Whirl ride—cars navigate up and down at the end of long arms as they spin around the center tower.

Family-oriented rides include the **Paradise Sky Wheel,** which lifts guests 100 feet into the air above Paradise Pier, with great views of the entire park. The **Boardwalk Carousel** is a classic double-deck merry-go-round with a menagerie of brightly painted animals.

The **Citrus Line Railroad** carries visitors along a track that enters both Paradise Pier and Adventure Grove; the conductor gives a narration of the history of Cypress Gardens.

Held over from the original park, the **Sunshine Sky Adventure** rises sixteen stories in the air, slowly revolving; views extend as far as 17 miles on a clear day.

Visitors can board either the *Gardenia* or *Bougainvillea* for a relaxing ride along the shoreline of Cypress Gardens on the **Cypress Cove Ferry Line** between the north and south ends of the park.

Children of all ages can slip down the **Fun Slide;** they climb to the top of the 90-foot summit and then zoom down the slippery slope. Other kiddie rides include the **Rio Grande Train, Super Trucks, Dizzy Dragons,** and **Junior Rampmasters.**

The signature show at the park is *Top Fun Ski Academy,* a spoof of the movie *Top Gun* that features gravity-defying jumps and feats of daring. *The Living Garden* comes to life with performers, animated fountains, and lighting.

Other shows include *Wild West Shenani-Guns, Pirates of Cypress Cove,* and the evening fireworks-and-laser show, *Night Magic.*

Also included in admission is Splash Island Water Park, located alongside Cypress Gardens. Features include **Catchawave Bay,** a 20,000-gallon wave pool. **Rain Fortress** is one of the largest interactive wet-play areas in North America.

Major water slides include **Double Dip Zip,** a two-slided tube complex rising four stories into the air. The six-story **Tri-Phoon** features two lightning-fast speed slides and one dizzying body slide.

Finally, in 2005, the parent company of Cypress Gardens purchased the famed Starliner roller coaster, which had entertained guests since 1963 at Panama Beach in Florida. The coaster is expected to be installed at Cypress Gardens for the 2007 season.

Admission in 2006 was $39.95 for adults and $34.95 for children (ages three to nine) and seniors (ages fifty-five and older). Parking $9.00. For information call (863) 324–2111 or consult www.cypressgardens.com.

■ FANTASY OF FLIGHT

This celebration of the wonders of flight was built around the personal collection and dream of founder Kermit Weeks. The sprawling 300-acre facility includes indoor and outdoor displays of antique and unusual aircraft dating from near the dawn of flight and featuring World War I and II fighting craft. There are also several multimedia exhibitions, including a chilling re-creation of a World War I battlefield and a walk through a B-17 Flying Fortress. A state-of-the-art flight simulation known as Fightertown puts visitors at the controls of a World War II fighter on a Pacific mission; the eight planes are mounted on a full-motion simulator base that responds to your movements of the stick and rudder. As you fly your mission, you'll be in radio contact with a controller and the other fliers in your air group.

Visitors can also venture above the central Florida countryside in a hot-air balloon for an extra charge, and there are also opportunities to fly in a vintage biplane. During busy times a pilot will present the Aircraft of the Day from the vintage collection, meeting with guests and discussing the plane before he or she takes it to the skies for a demonstration.

Weeks, born into a wealthy oil family, put together his first home-built aircraft at the age of seventeen. A few years later he was flying in aerobatic competitions. He twice won the U.S. National Aerobatics Championship.

Fantasy of Flight, located in Polk City, off exit 44 of I–4, about 20 miles southwest of Walt Disney World, is open daily except Thanksgiving and Christmas Day from 9:00 A.M. to 5:00 P.M. Adults $24.95, children (ages five to twelve) $13.95, and seniors (age sixty and older) $22.95. Tickets include admission to exhibits and Fightertown Flight Simulators. For information call (863) 984–3500 or consult www.fantasyofflight.com.

■ KENNEDY SPACE CENTER VISITOR CENTER

The home base of the Space Shuttle is the fifth most popular attraction in Florida, drawing nearly three million visitors each year; it's also one of the best tourist bargains anywhere. The space center is about 55 miles from Orlando, and there's enough to occupy you for a full morning or afternoon. Here's your chance to wander through the *Explorer,* a full-scale replica of the Space Shuttle, accurate down to the switches in the cockpit. The Gallery of Space Flight includes a fabulous collection of spacecraft, moon rocks, and other items. The 140,000-acre space center itself is an interesting wildlife area with some fifteen endangered species making their homes there. Watch for alligators in the canals along the roadways; the cape is also home to numerous wild pigs.

The entry to the center is themed after the International Space Station, complete with huge replicas of the station's solar panels. Robot Scouts is a walk-through exhibit that introduces NASA's most far-reaching space explorers, the robotic planetary probes. Highlights include the Viking Mars lander, Cassini Saturn probe, Lunar Prospector, and Hubble Space Telescope.

A live stage show, *Mad Mission to Mars 2025,* includes the comic antics of Professor Pruvitt and his wacky colleagues, Kelvin, WD-4D, and Dr. Gimbal. They magically transform guests into "astronaut trainees" and virtually transport them to the Red Planet. The film *Quest for Life,* presented at the Visitor Complex, explores the mysterious spark of life that made our planet unique in the solar system. The film blends recent findings on the planet Mars with theories from leading scientists, and it reveals how the process that led to life on

Earth may have been replicated on as many as two billion other planets that are believed to have the needed ingredients.

At the International Space Station Center, workers are assembling elements of the $30 billion orbiting research facility that will be jointly operated with the Russians. Visitors view a video about the program, narrated by one of the astronauts who will help assemble the craft in space.

The LC39 Observation Gantry gives an eagle's-eye view of the Space Shuttle as it is prepared for flight. It stands just a half mile from one launchpad and a mile from the other, and it also allows a peek into the massive Vehicle Assembly Building, where the pieces of each spacecraft are brought together before flight.

The Kennedy Space Center tour offers views of Space Shuttle Launch Pads A and B, the Vehicle Assembly Building, and an authentic 365-foot-long *Saturn V* moon rocket—one of only three in existence—housed in the new *Apollo/Saturn V* center. The Firing Room Theater re-creates the atmosphere of the original firing room as it existed during the *Apollo* era. The Lunar Surface Theater restages the fateful moments of *Apollo 11*, when astronauts Neil Armstrong and Buzz Aldrin placed the first human footprints on the moon.

Spectacular IMAX movies are shown on the huge screen of the IMAX Theater. One of the most popular is the thirty-seven-minute *The Dream Is Alive*, which shows astronauts living and working in space. Also check out the Astronauts Memorial, which honors the twenty-four American astronauts who gave their lives in the line of duty (including the crews of the *Columbia*, *Challenger*, and *Apollo 1* spacecraft, as well as others killed in training accidents). The 42-foot-high Space Mirror is set by a quiet lagoon near the entrance.

With luck, you may see one of the Space Shuttles—mated to its external tank and rockets—moving down the 3.5-mile road from the Vehicle Assembly Building to the launchpad on board a transporter. The entire assemblage weighs about twelve million pounds. Shuttles typically spend several weeks on the pad as they are prepared for launch. Most orbiters return for a landing on a special runway at the space center, making a double sonic boom as they cross over central Florida. It is especially interesting to visit the center while a Shuttle is in orbit; the air crackles with radio traffic to and from the orbiter, and special displays track the progress of the current mission.

Visitors can spend as much time as they want at each attraction; buses are available to transport guests from location to location on a frequent schedule. The center tends to be less busy on weekends than weekdays and is open every day of the year except for Christmas Day, from 9:00 A.M. to dusk. The visitor center may be off-limits on launch days, and bus tour routes may be altered or canceled when rockets are being prepared or launched. Heightened security concerns require inspection of all bags; large bags and luggage are not permitted.

Attractions at the space center include the Astronaut Hall of Fame. For visitors who really want to get a bit of the feeling of being an astronaut, there is ATX—The Astronaut Training Experience; participants get to try out a multi-axis trainer and a one-sixth-gravity chair as well as a private tour of the center. Tickets for ATX sell for about $225 for adults.

A massive *Saturn V* moon rocket. *Courtesy Kennedy Space Center Visitor Center*

In 2006 a Maximum Access badge for a tour of the space center, the Astronaut Hall of Fame, and unlimited IMAX films cost $38 for adults and $28 for children (ages three to eleven). A Standard Access badge, which includes just the tour and the IMAX films, sold for $31 for adults and $21 for children.

Tickets for the Astronaut Hall of Fame, outside of the the space center on State Road 405 in Titusville, are also available separately, at $17 for adults and $13 for children (ages three to eleven).

The NASA Up Close Tour combines an admission badge with a guided tour that gives guests a closer drive-by of launchpads, the Vehicle Assembly Building, and the Shuttle landing strip. In 2006 tickets were $22 for adults and $16 for children (ages three to eleven), plus the cost of a Maximum or Standard Access badge.

"Lunch with an Astronaut" is offered daily at 12:30 P.M. Prices, not including purchase of a Standard Access or Maximum Access badge, were $22.99 for adults and $15.99 for children ages three to eleven. Tickets may be purchased online at www.kennedyspacecenter.com or by calling (321) 449–4400. Tickets may also be purchased in the Visitor Complex on the day of the event, if not previously sold out.

The Cape Canaveral: Then and Now Tour ventures to the location of some of the original *Mercury, Gemini,* and *Apollo* launchpads. In 2006 tickets were $22 for adults and $16 for children (ages three to eleven), plus the cost of a Maximum or Standard Access badge.

The center is located off Highway 405, NASA Parkway, 7 miles east of U.S. Highway 1. From Orlando take Highway 528 (the Beeline) to Highway 407, about one hour total driving time. From Atlantic Coast Florida take exit 78 off

Interstate 95. Follow signs for Kennedy Space Center. For information call (800) 572–4636 or (321) 449–4444 in Florida, or consult www.kennedyspacecenter.com.

Space Shuttle Launch Viewing

From outside the space center, the best places to watch a launch are along US 1 in the city of Titusville and along Highway A1A in the towns of Cocoa Beach and Cape Canaveral on the Atlantic Ocean. If you'd prefer to view the launch from the space center, free launch-viewing passes that permit vehicles to enter the space center and park at a site 6 miles from the pad are available by sending a letter three months in advance of a launch date to NASA Visitor Services, Mail Code: PA-Pass, Kennedy Space Center, FL 32899.

The visitor center at the Kennedy Space Center also sells about 1,500 tickets to board buses to a viewing site 6 miles from the launchpad. You can purchase tickets online through the www.kennedyspacecenter.com Web site. In 2006 tickets, which include admission to the Visitor Complex, were priced at $38 for adults and $28 for children. In addition, if there is an afternoon launch, you may be able to park at the visitor center and watch the blastoff from there. Tickets are generally available six weeks before a scheduled launch.

Current information on launches is available by calling NASA at (321) 449–4444, or consult www.kennedyspacecenter.com or NASA's Web site at www.spaceflight.nasa.gov.

■ LION COUNTRY SAFARI

The nation's first drive-through zoo when it opened in 1967, the park includes more than 1,000 wild animals from all over the world, including giraffe, eland, bison, elephant, rhino, zebra, ostrich, and antelope, wandering free over hundreds of acres. There's also a petting zoo and an amusement area that includes paddleboats, a boat ride, and an old-time carousel.

In 2006 the park finally had to erect a fence between visitors and lions, the first such barrier; cars still drive through most of the park, but the lions are kept separate on a large island. The fence was installed because some visitors would ignore warnings and open windows or doors near the large cats. Other areas, home to animals including antelope and buffalo, remain open and unfenced.

You'll use your own vehicle to drive through the preserve; the car cannot have broken windows. Convertibles and other inappropriate vehicles must be exchanged for available rental cars. In 2006 rental rates were a reasonable $10 to $18 for ninety minutes.

The park is located on Lion Country Safari Road, Loxahatchee, 18 miles west of West Palm Beach off exit 99 of the Florida Turnpike. Loxahatchee is about 175 miles from Orlando. For information call (561) 793–1084 or consult www.lioncountrysafari.com. Open daily from 9:30 A.M. to 5:30 P.M. Adults $20.95, children (ages three to nine) $16.95, seniors (sixty-five and older) $18.95. Parking $3.50.

■ SILVER SPRINGS

Silver Springs has been drawing visitors to its natural beauties since the early 1800s. In the 1860s steamboats explored the area, and in 1878 Silver Springs became famous for the invention of glass-bottom boats for display of underwater wonders. Six of the original *Tarzan* movies were filmed at Silver Springs in the 1930s and 1940s; *The Yearling*, starring Gregory Peck and Jane Wyman, was filmed there in 1946. And more than one hundred episodes of the *Sea Hunt* television series, starring Lloyd Bridges, were filmed at Silver Springs from 1958 to 1961.

Divers have mapped and explored what is said to be the largest spring system in the world, the source of up to two billion gallons of water daily. Discoveries at the site have included fossilized mastodon teeth dating back 10,000 years, a giant ground sloth claw, and a mammoth tooth from the Pleistocene period. In addition, several species of troglobitic life, including crayfish, have been found.

Attractions at Silver Springs include the following:

■ **Panther Prowl.** Features rare Florida panthers and their close relative, the eastern cougar, in an outdoor habitat of trees, caves, and ponds.

■ **World of Bears.** This may be the only place in Florida where guests can see majestic grizzly and Kodiak bears, plus three other ursine species. Recent arrivals include a pair of Asiatic black bears and two Sun bears from Southeast Asia.

■ **Big Gator Lagoon.** A half-acre cypress swamp habitat with more than two dozen of Florida's largest alligators adds to the extensive collection at the park. Another exhibit showcases a white American alligator, one of only seventeen known specimens in the world.

■ **Glass-bottom-boat tours.** Visitors can cruise in glass-bottom boats on a tour that explores seven natural formations, including Mammoth Spring, the world's largest artesian limestone spring. Creatures in the nearly pure spring include alligators, turtles, garfish, and largemouth bass. Along the riverbanks are great blue heron, cormorants, ibis, egrets, raccoons, and river otters.

■ **Jeep Safari.** Takes passengers on a four-wheel-drive vehicle into a jungle that is home to free-roaming wildlife, including African waterbucks, two-toed sloths, Brazilian tapirs, and four species of deer. The highlight of the safari is a trip through a 3-foot-deep pit teeming with alligators.

■ **Lost River Voyage.** Explores an untouched cypress jungle, a glimpse of wild Florida as it was thousands of years ago. At Cypress Point you may be lucky enough to see Sonek, one of several Florida beasts claimed to be the world's largest American alligator.

■ **Festival of Lights.** From about Thanksgiving to New Year's Eve, Silver Springs celebrates with a Festival of Lights, a central Florida version of a winter wonderland.

Silver Springs is open daily from 10:00 A.M. to 5:00 P.M., with extended hours in the summer and on holidays. Admission in 2006: general $32.99; children ages three to ten, $23.99; and seniors $29.99. For information call (352) 236–2121 or consult www.silversprings.com.

A combination ticket with Wild Waters was priced in 2006 at $3.00 above Silver Springs admission prices.

The Silver Springs and Wild Waters Super Pass entitles the pass holder to a full year of concerts, special events, and rides at Silver Springs, plus daily admission to

A glass-bottom boat explores Silver Springs. *Photo courtesy of Orlando/Orange County Convention & Visitors Bureau*

the Wild Waters water park next door. In 2006 the annual pass was priced at $62.99 for adults and children and $48.99 for seniors (ages fifty-five and older).

The **Wild Waters** water park offers nine flumes, including the Twin Twister, a pair of 60-foot flumes for two-person inner tubes; the Tornado water ride; and the 450,000-gallon Wave Pool. The Lazy Bones River sends guests on a slow tour of an 800-foot jungle waterway, and the Cool Kids Cove children's play area is a version of an 1800s riverboat with water cannons, net cage bridges, water slides, and more.

The water park is open spring through early fall. Call for operating schedules. Prices in 2006 were $23.99 plus tax for general admission and $20.99 for visitors under 48 inches tall. Parking $6.00. For information call (352) 236–2121 or consult www.wildwaterspark.com.

■ WEEKI WACHEE SPRING

Mermaids abound at this old water park on the Gulf Coast. Presentations include an underwater show based on the original Hans Christian Andersen story *The Little Mermaid,* as well as a Wilderness River Cruise, a Birds of Prey Show, and a petting zoo. Adults $21.95, children (ages three to ten) $15.95. Parking $3.00. North of Tampa on U.S. Highway 19 at the intersection with Highway 50. For information call (352) 596–2062 or consult www.weekiwachee.com.

Next to Weeki Wachee Spring is the Buccaneer Bay water park, open from mid-March to early September.

■ VALIANT AIR COMMAND WARBIRD AIR MUSEUM

Here you'll see historic displays of aircraft and aviation memorabilia from World War I, World War II, Korea, and Vietnam. Adults $12.00, seniors $10.00, children (ages three to twelve) $5.00. Open daily from 10:00 A.M. to 6:00 P.M. 6600 Tico Road, Titusville (near the Kennedy Space Center); (407) 268–1941; www.vacwar birds.org.

SHOPPING

To heck with mice, sharks, and whales—for some folks, the ultimate Orlando recreational activity is shopping. And the millions of visitors to the entertainment attractions of Orlando have become a tremendous lure to retailers. Bring an empty suitcase with you and leave time for some of the shopping adventures listed here.

■ **Altamonte Mall.** 451 Altamonte Road, Altamonte Springs (north of Orlando, east of I–4 on Highway 436); (407) 830–4422; www.altamontemall.com. Macy's, JCPenney, Gap, Cache, The Limited, Sears, and more than 175 specialty shops. Open Monday through Saturday from 10:00 A.M. to 9:00 P.M. and Sunday from 11:00 A.M. to 6:00 P.M.

■ **Belz Factory Outlet World/Festival Bay.** Located at the north end of International Drive, past Kirkman Road; (407) 352–9611; www.belz.com/factory. A huge collection of factory-outlet shops, with more than 170 companies represented in two enclosed malls and four shopping centers, all within walking distance of each other. Manufacturers include L'eggs/Hanes/Bali, Pacific Sunwear, Timberland, Rack Room Shoes, Royal Doulton, Bass, Stride-Rite, Mikasa, Van Heusen, Oshkosh B'Gosh, Guess Jeans, London Fog, Danskin, Pfaltzgraff, and Samsonite. Open Monday through Saturday from 10:00 A.M. to 9:00 P.M. and Sunday from 10:00 A.M. to 6:00 P.M.

■ **The Florida Mall.** Intersection of Sand Lake Road (Highway 482) and South Orange Blossom Trail (Highway 441); (407) 851–6255; www.shopsimon.com. Macy's, Dillard's, JCPenney, Saks Fifth Avenue, Sears, and 200 specialty shops. A new wing opened in 2002, adding Nordstom, Lord & Taylor, and other high-end retailers. With the new construction, the mall, already the largest in central Florida, grew to 2 million square feet. Open Monday through Saturday from 10:00 A.M. to 9:00 P.M. and Sunday from noon to 6:00 P.M.

■ **The Mall at Millenia.** Orlando gained another major mall in late 2002, at I–4 and Conroy Road. The upscale mall features Bloomingdale's, Macy's, and Neiman Marcus, along with high-end boutiques from Tiffany, Gucci, and Lacoste. The mall is located about a mile from the Florida Turnpike and Universal Studios Orlando and about fifteen minutes from Walt Disney World. For information call (407) 363–3555 or consult www.mallatmillenia.com.

■ **Mercado.** 8445 International Drive; (407) 345–9337. A small but interesting collection of shops and eateries, Mercado includes more than sixty specialty shops, including Designer Gear, Magic Max, and the *Titanic* Gift Shop. Restaurants include P'zazz, Bergamo's, and La China. There's also Cricketers Arms, an English pub. In the International Food Court, you'll also find Balti House (serving fast Indian food), The Butcher Shop, Mahi Mahi Bistro, Tropical Café, The Sandwich Gallery, and The Latin Grille. At night the grounds and shops are alight with twinkling lights, and free entertainment is presented in the courtyard. Shops are open from 10:00 A.M. to 9:00 P.M. daily; restaurants and bars close later.

■ **192 Flea Market.** 4301 West Vine Street (US 192), Kissimmee; (407) 396–4555. A full-time, free-admission market with as many as 400 dealer booths under one roof. Disney souvenirs, jewelry, crafts, clothing, and more. Open daily from 9:00 A.M. to 6:00 P.M.

■ **Orlando Premium Outlets.** 8200 Vineland Avenue, Orlando; (407) 238–7787; www.premiumoutlets.com. An upscale outdoor mall featuring Banana Republic, Calvin Klein, Dooney & Bourke, Kenneth Cole, Timberland, and Versace.

■ **Pointe*Orlando Entertainment Center.** International Drive at Universal Boulevard; (407) 248–2838; www.pointeorlandofl.com. This sprawling retail and entertainment center features more than sixty shops, a twenty-one-screen movie multiplex, and several restaurants. It's located across International Drive from the Orange County Convention Center. An eye-catching roadside attraction is WonderWorks, designed to look like a three-story, upside-down mansion that landed atop a brick warehouse. A redevelopment project in 2006 added a central courtyard with more stores and eateries, including B. B. King's Blues Club, Tommy Bahama Cafe and Emporium, and Brighton Collectibles.

Restaurants include Adobe Gila's, Hooters, Johnny Rockets, and the Capital Grille. You'll also find the Muvico Pointe 21 Theaters, plus shops such as AIX Armani Exchange, Bimini Shoes, Chico's, Express, Foot Locker, and Victoria's Secret.

You'll have to pay to park in the parking garage, although the ticket can be validated for free parking with purchase of a movie ticket or food and beverage at one of the participating restaurants.

Pointe*Orlando shops are open Monday through Saturday from 10:00 A.M. to 10:00 P.M. and Sunday from 11:00 A.M. to 9:00 P.M. Many restaurants and bars stay open later.

PART VIII

TAMPA

CHAPTER TWENTY-FOUR

BUSCH GARDENS TAMPA BAY AND NEARBY ATTRACTIONS

BUSCH GARDENS IS A WELCOME GETAWAY from the concrete of Walt Disney World and environs, drawing three million visitors a year to its 355 acres, home to more than 2,800 animals.

Busch Gardens Tampa Bay opened as a hospitality center for the Anheuser-Busch brewery in Tampa in 1959, showcasing a collection of exotic birds and some of the Busch family's collection of African animals. In 1971, when the era of Florida as theme park began, the company began a massive expansion of Busch Gardens. The brewery that was the original reason for Busch Gardens Tampa Bay closed at the end of 1995; part of that land at the heart of the park was used for the massive wooden roller coaster, **Gwazi.**

Today the park is like stepping onto the African veldt—albeit a veldt with a sky ride above and a passel of outrageous roller coasters on the horizon. In 2005 Busch pushed the thrill level up a few notches with the opening of **SheiKra,** billed as the nation's first dive coaster.

Visitors can enter into the veldt on **Rhino Rally,** an off-road safari among elephants, white rhinos, antelopes, alligators, cape buffalos, warthogs, and other exotic African species. The Gwazi coaster joins other recent expansions, including **The Edge of Africa** up-close animal safari and the spectacular **Montu** coaster in the Egypt area of the park. Another recent addition was the flashy *KaTonga* musical show at the Moroccan Palace Theater, and **Cheetah Chase,** a wild-mouse minicoaster.

The map of Florida looks so huge to many visitors that the thought of a drive from Orlando to Tampa seems like an all-day drive; it's not. Measured from the intersection of Interstate 4 and U.S. Highway 192, Tampa Bay is an easy 70 miles; at 65 miles per hour to the gates of SeaWorld, about seventy-five minutes. Although it is only about 70 miles away, Tampa Bay is on the other coast of Florida and sometimes has a different weather pattern than Orlando. One March day we left Orlando in heavy rain and arrived to find the sun blazing in Tampa.

The busiest times of the year are similar to those of the Orlando attractions: June to Labor Day and spring and Easter breaks. Other times of the year bring large crowds of foreign visitors, including planeloads from South America and Brazil. Lines, though, rarely are anywhere as long as those you'll find at Walt Disney World or Universal Studios Florida during peak summer and holiday periods.

Busch Entertainment Corporation operates parks including Busch Gardens in Tampa and Williamsburg, Virginia; SeaWorld in Orlando, San Antonio, and San Diego; Adventure Island in Tampa; and the Sesame Place theme park in Langhorne, Pennsylvania.

Operating hours are 9:30 A.M. until 6:00 P.M. Extended hours into the evening are offered in summer and over selected holiday periods. To get there from Orlando, take I–4 west about 60 miles to Tampa. Exit at Interstate 75 north and find the Fowler Avenue off-ramp (exit 54). From there, follow signs to the park.

BUSCH GARDENS ATTRACTIONS

■ MOROCCO

This re-creation of the exotic city of Marrakesh features unusual architecture and demonstrations of Moroccan crafts, snake charmers, the Mystic Sheiks of Morocco marching band, and the Sounds of Steel, a five-man steel-drum band. Serious shoppers may enjoy a visit to the brass store just past the ticket booths; an artisan/importer from Morocco offers an impressive display. And, if you like to pay to carry someone else's corporate slogan or ad campaign, check out the Rabat Label store, where you can buy just about any article of clothing or sporting equipment with one or another Anheuser-Busch logo on it.

KaTonga (Moroccan Palace Theater)

KaTonga takes guests on a journey to the heart of Africa in a forty-minute musical celebration of animal folklore. The show follows a day in the lives of aspiring storytellers, called griots, as they strive to become masters of their craft. To accomplish this rite of passage, the performers evoke traditional African stories.

MUST-SEES

Akbar's Adventure Tours
(Egypt)

Montu
(Egypt)

Myombe Reserve: The Great Ape Domain
(Nairobi)

Rhino Rally
(Serengeti Plain)

The Edge of Africa
(Serengeti Plain)

Serengeti Safari
(Serengeti Plain)

R. L. Stine's Haunted Lighthouse
(Timbuktu)

Kumba
(Congo)

Congo River Rapids
(Congo)

SheiKra
(Stanleyville)

Gwazi
(Stanleyville)

Stanley Falls Log Flume
(Stanleyville)

Tanganyika Tidal Wave
(Stanleyville)

BUSCH GARDENS

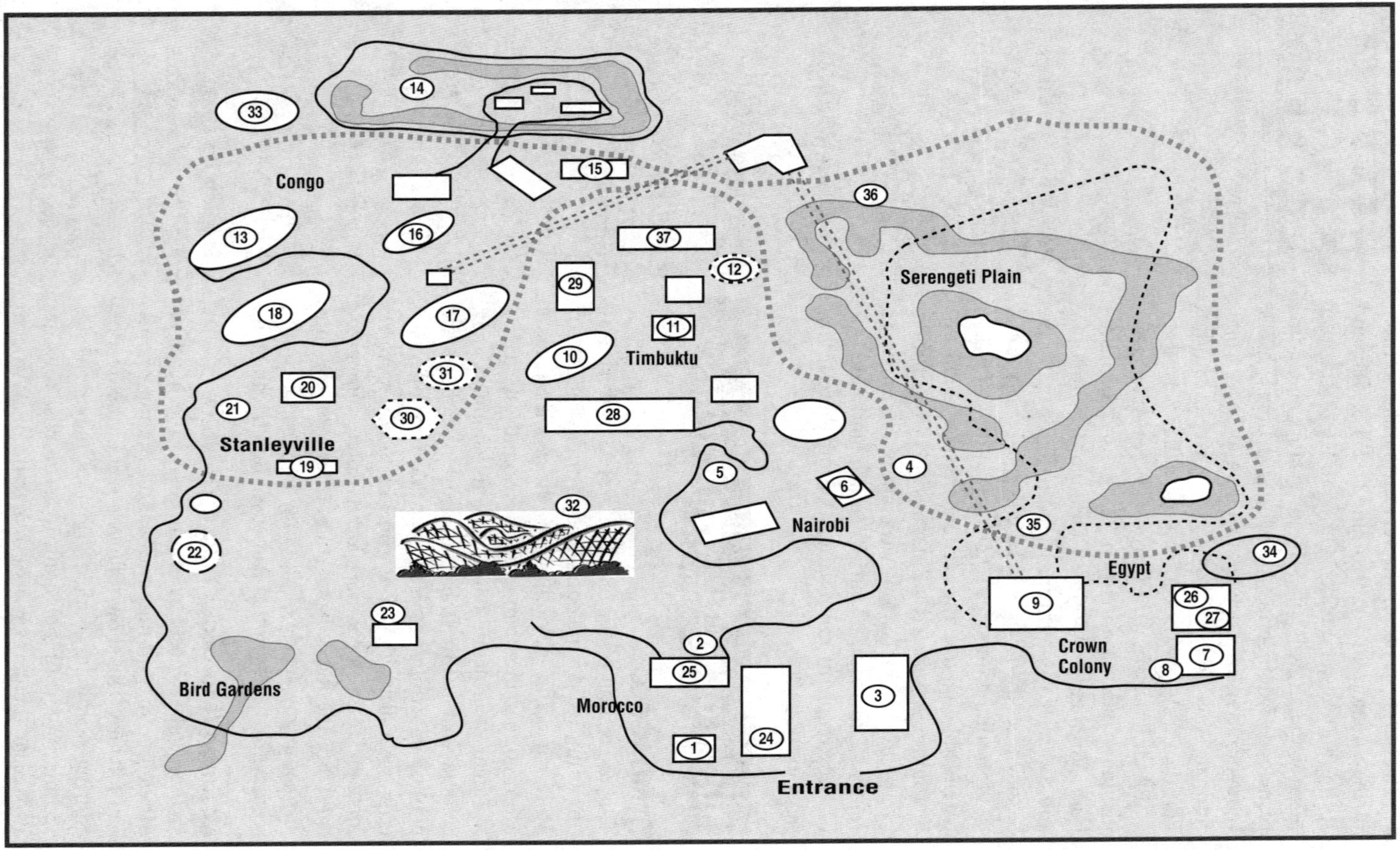

Congo
Stanleyville
Timbuktu
Serengeti Plain
Nairobi
Egypt
Crown Colony
Morocco
Bird Gardens
Entrance
1
2
3
4
5
6
7
8
9
10
11
12
13
14
15
16
17
18
19
20
21
22
23
24
25
26
27
28
29
30
31
32
33
34
35
36
37

BUSCH GARDENS

① Marrakesh Theater
② Sultan's Tent
③ Moroccan Palace Theater
④ Aldabra Tortoise Habitat
⑤ Myombe Reserve: The Great Ape
   Domain
⑥ Train station
⑦ Akbar's Adventure Tours
⑧ Clydesdale Hamlet
⑨ Skyride and Monorail Station
⑩ The Scorpion
⑪ Carousel Caravan
⑫ The Phoenix
⑬ The Python
⑭ Congo River Rapids
⑮ Congo Station Transveldt Railroad
⑯ Claw Island
⑰ Stanley Falls Log Flume
⑱ Tanganyika Tidal Wave

⑲ Stanleyville Station Transveldt Railroad
⑳ Stanleyville Theater
㉑ Zambezi Theater
㉒ Land of the Dragons
㉓ Hospitality House
㉔ Boujad Bakery
㉕ Zagora Cafe
㉖ Crown Colony House
㉗ Anheuser-Busch Hospitality Center
㉘ The Kasbah
㉙ The Oasis
㉚ SheiKra
㉛ Bazaar Cafe
㉜ Gwazi
㉝ Kumba
㉞ Montu
㉟ The Edge of Africa
㊱ Rhino Rally
㊲ *R. L. Stine's Haunted Lighthouse*

The show, which replaced the long-running *World Rhythms on Ice* show, makes use of the Broadway-caliber theatrical facilities of the Moroccan Palace. The show is presented by a cast of eighteen, including the griots, puppeteers, dancers, and acrobats.

The stories reveal life in the jungle through the life-changing experiences of four African animals. Whirly, a young monkey, learns that confidence requires risk to succeed. Kipopo, the caterpillar, looks inward to find her true self before morphing into a beautiful butterfly. An overbearing bullfrog, Rok Rok, is taught the treasure found in respecting and listening to others. And Kilinda, an African crowned crane, brings together animals and people in a survival story of epic proportions.

KaTonga's creators include some of Broadway's most renowned and experienced talent, among them famed puppet designer Michael Curry. Best known for his award-winning work on Broadway's *The Lion King*, Curry's signature giant puppets were featured in New York City's Times Square Millennium celebration and Broadway shows including *Kiss of the Spider Woman* and *Crazy For You*. Choreographer Abdel Salaam, founder and artistic director of New York's Forces of Nature Dance Theater Company at Cathedral of St. John the Divine, brought traditional African and pop dance to the production.

◼ EGYPT

MUST-SEE Akbar's Adventure Tours

Hold on to your hats—and your wallets—when you embark upon the wacky journey led by comedian Martin Short, starring as Akbar, a shady Egyptian tour

Power Trip for Summer and Holiday Periods

Begin your Busch Gardens tour by studying the schedule of entertainment you receive at the front gate. Depending on the time of year, some major shows, such as *KaTonga* at the **Moroccan Palace Theater**, are presented many times a day, while other entertainment may be scheduled only once or twice a day. Adjust your Power Trip to include any shows on your must-see list.

SheiKra is one of the top draws; head there early in the day, at lunchtime, or late in the day. The **Rhino Rally** off-road safari is attractive to many others; its thrills are much more sedate. To see more wild animals, head there in the cool morning. Back to thrill rides, the other big draws are the **Gwazi** double-track roller coaster, followed closely by **Montu** in Egypt and **Kumba** in the Congo. You can count on lengthy lines at all three of these attractions in the heart of the day. Go early or around dinnertime to make the most of your time.

R. L. Stine's Haunted Lighthouse, in Timbuktu, draws mostly younger crowds deep into the park; the 3-D film will accommodate about 2,000 people per hour, so waits should not be too terrifying.

While you're in Kumba's neighborhood, check out **Congo River Rapids**. On the occasional chilly day, you might want to store a dry sweatshirt in a locker before you ride. Now try the relatively biteless (but still intimidating) **Python** roller-twister-coaster.

When you're through, the majestic tigers on **Claw Island** will probably seem tame, but they're certainly worth a visit. Of the two other water rides, **Stanley Falls** may be more fun, but the **Tanganyika Tidal Wave** is more dramatic. What the heck: Ride 'em both.

Animal lovers will want to arrive early at **The Edge of Africa** to experience a close-up encounter with hippos, lions, giraffes, and more. For a different type of thrill, consider signing up early in the day for one of the **Serengeti Safari** truck tours into the animal preserve.

If you are not in the mood for an immediate upside-down rattle and roll, you can instead start the day by bearing right from the entrance toward Crown Colony to visit the wacky **Akbar's Adventure Tours** simulator adventure (open in high season only). Once you return to Florida, backtrack to the **Skyride** to view the Serengeti Plain from above.

When you've accomplished all your goals, take a leisurely circuit of the park on the **Transveldt Railroad.**

guide hanging on to a shoestring travel business. His newest product is a simulated journey across Egypt, which he desperately hopes will save his business from repossession by Stanford "Don't call me Stan" Wharton (played by comedian Eugene Levy). Equipped with his brother Omar's home movies, Akbar embarks on his greatest venture ever. (Note that the tour is not open on off-season days; if your heart is set on a visit to Egypt—even in the hands of Akbar—call ahead to confirm the operating schedule.)

Visitors waiting to board the simulator will see posters depicting some of the awesome attractions of the tour—and they won't be able to avoid noticing the very humble means by which Akbar proposes to take them there. Before boarding, you'll meet Akbar himself, the "world's greatest tour guide."

In a preshow film Akbar takes us into his workshop, where his possessions are being removed by Stanford Wharton. After a bit of friendly persuasion by his "baby" brothers Corky and Chip, Stanford reluctantly agrees to give Akbar one more chance at success with his homemade simulator. And then you'll be face-to-face with the simulator: Homemade may be too kind a description. Perhaps "nouveau dump" would be a bit more accurate. But Akbar promises that no misfortune could possibly befall anyone on the maiden voyage. You believe him, right?

The journey begins on camelback, jostling through a bustling marketplace as merchants and pedestrians dive for safety. Weaving and banking just above the desert surface, the simulator, now a biplane, struggles up into the sky to reveal a perilously close encounter with the ancient pyramids. From there it is on to the Sphinx, and this time it's not a near collision: Let's just say that the big cat receives a long-overdue face-lift.

Once the simulator regains control, it's on to the excavation of the forbidden tomb, riding on an out-of-control mine train. The train somehow gets on the wrong track and ends up in a spooky, skull-filled chamber. The monstrous guardian of the chamber expresses its displeasure with Akbar's intrusion by sending the visitors hurtling through a vortex and out of control.... Did you expect anything less?

Akbar's Adventure is located just outside the gates to Egypt, the former home of the Questor simulator. There are two simulator cabins, each seating fifty-nine guests. The total length of the show is about six minutes, which gives an hourly capacity of about 1,416 passengers. All kidding aside, the simulators themselves are very high-tech, with each cabin hydraulically powered to move in six directions—pitch, roll, yaw, heave, surge, and sway. The audiovisual system is based on an eight-channel laser video-disc surround system.

MUST-SEE Montu

The world's largest inverted steel roller coaster, named after a hawklike sun god worshiped by ancient Egyptians at Thebes, soars across nearly 4,000 feet of track and includes three first-of-a-kind elements:

- The Immelmann, an inverse loop named after a German stunt pilot.
- The world's largest vertical loop on an inverted coaster, at 104 feet.
- Two vertical loops slanted at forty-five-degree angles, known as a "batwing." Coaster experts say these are the wildest stretches.

The approach to the loading area for the ride is through a portal in a spectacular 55-foot-tall wall decorated with hand-carved hieroglyphs. As the trains leave the loading station, they drop toward a pond that is home to several live crocodiles. Other elements include a camelback maneuver that delivers three seconds of weightlessness, sweeping arcs crossing over and under the tracks of the Transveldt Railway, and a corkscrew finale.

Peaking at speeds in excess of 60 miles per hour, Montu reaches a maximum G-force of 3.85 at certain points during the three-minute trip. Riders must be at least 52 inches tall.

There are three trains made up of eight cars, each of which holds four passengers across for a total of thirty-two riders per train. The cars hang from the top and swing out from side to side; the foot platforms drop out when the train departs, leaving feet dangling below the car. At one point the swooping cars dive as close as 18 inches above the ground. The tracks dive into three Egyptian-theme tunnels below ground.

Visitors to Egypt can also tour a six-room replica of King Tutankhamen's tomb as it looked when it was first discovered by archaeologist Howard Carter in the early 1920s. Young visitors will be able to dig

Montu mid-roll. *Photo courtesy of Busch Gardens Tampa Bay*

through a sandpit with buried artifacts of the ancient culture. The area also includes shopping bazaars for the older visitors. Items for sale at the **Golden Scarab** and **Treasures of the Nile** shops include handblown glass and cartouche painting on scrolls.

Transveldt Railroad

The train offers some of the best close-up views of the animals on the Serengeti Plain between the Nairobi and Congo stations. Other portions of the track offer a tourist's-eye view of the back sides of the Python and Scorpion roller coasters. The train is a three-quarter-scale replica of an African steam engine and cars, and the engine is an unusual combination of energy sources, using propane gas to boil water for steam that powers an electric generator for the wheels.

Busch Gardens Tampa Bay Tickets

Prices were in effect in early 2007 and are subject to change. Prices do not include 7 percent tax. Note that Busch Gardens offers single-day, multiday, and multipark tickets at a discount on its Web site, www.buschgardens.com.

	ADULT	CHILD (ages 3 to 9)
SINGLE-DAY TICKET	$61.95	$51.95
PARKING $9.00		
BUSCH GARDENS/ADVENTURE ISLAND TWO-PARK UNLIMITED (One day at each park)	$99.00	$85.00
BUSCH GARDENS TAMPA BAY/ SEAWORLD FLORIDA VALUE TICKET (One day each at Busch Gardens Tampa Bay and SeaWorld Florida in Orlando)	$85.00	$85.00
FIVE-PARK ORLANDO FLEXTICKET (Unlimited admission to Universal Studios Florida, Universal Studios Islands of Adventure, SeaWorld Florida, Wet 'n Wild, and Busch Gardens Tampa Bay. Valid fourteen consecutive days.)	$234.95	$199.95
BUSCH GARDENS TAMPA BAY SILVER PASSPORT (Valid for twelve months. Includes parking.)	$94.95	$84.95
BUSCH GARDENS TAMPA BAY GOLD PASSPORT (Valid for twenty-four months. Includes parking.)	$144.95	$134.95
BUSCH GARDENS/ADVENTURE ISLAND SILVER PASSPORT (Valid for twelve months. Includes parking.)	$144.95	$134.95
BUSCH GARDENS/ADVENTURE ISLAND GOLD PASSPORT (Valid for twenty-four months. Includes parking.)	$219.95	$209.95
BUSCH GARDENS/SEAWORLD ORLANDO SILVER PASSPORT (Valid for twelve months at both parks. Includes parking.)	$144.95	$134.95
BUSCH GARDENS/SEAWORLD ORLANDO GOLD PASSPORT (Valid for twenty-four months at both parks. Includes parking.)	$219.95	$209.95
BUSCH GARDENS/ADVENTURE ISLAND/ SEAWORLD ORLANDO SILVER PASSPORT (Valid for twelve months at all three parks. Includes parking.)	$189.95	$179.95
BUSCH GARDENS/ADVENTURE ISLAND/ SEAWORLD ORLANDO GOLD PASSPORT (Valid for twenty-four months at all three parks. Includes parking.)	$279.95	$269.95
BUSCH GARDENS/ADVENTURE ISLAND/ SEAWORLD ORLANDO PLATINUM PASSPORT (Valid for twenty-four months at all three parks. Includes parking.)	$309.95	$299.95
ADVENTURE ISLAND TICKETS (Valid for one day)	$34.95	$32.95

The Transveldt Railroad

■ NAIROBI

▐MUST-SEE▐ Myombe Reserve: The Great Ape Domain

This animal habitat features six lowland gorillas and eight common chimpanzees in a tropical-forest setting. Gorillas include Lash, a twenty-plus-year-old, 330-pound silverback male who was hand raised by surrogates at the Cincinnati Zoo after his mother died. Also resident is a social group of five gorillas on a long-term breeding loan from Emory University in Atlanta.

Visitors enter the three-acre habitat through dense foliage to a clearing that has a glass wall where they can observe the chimps; passing through a bamboo thicket, guests come upon the gorillas at the base of a mountain between waterfalls in a simulated tropical rain forest. (On cool days boulders near the viewing areas are heated to draw the animals near.) There are chimp nests scattered in the trees; some are as much as 70 feet off the ground.

At each turn in the reserve, you will see educational displays that tell you about the lives of the gorillas and how humans are threatening their natural environment. Some things you'll learn: A young female uses blades of grass and stems to extract termites, a chimp delicacy; chimps, who eat mostly fruit, use plants for medicinal purposes to kill parasites, fungi, and viruses; and before chimps were observed using tools, it was assumed that humans were the only ones to do so.

Aldabra Tortoise Habitat

Opposite the train station you'll find a collection of gigantic tortoises, including the Aldabra tortoise, often found on Aldabra Island in the Indian Ocean. Brought back from near extinction, Aldabras often weigh as much as 600 pounds when mature and are seen here in large groups wallowing in mud or shallow lagoons. In the same area you may also see an African spurred tortoise, Africa's largest land tortoise. They span the continent along the southern fringe of the Sahara Desert to the Red Sea.

■ SERENGETI PLAIN

The largest open area of the park, this eighty-acre natural setting features more than 800 animals in free-roaming herds of camels, elephants, zebras, giraffes, chimpanzees, rhinos, Cape buffalos, gazelles, greater kudus, and hippos. The Transveldt Railroad circles the plain, while the Skyride passes overhead. Rhino Rally ventures into the plain.

Several years ago, the northern part of the plain was converted into a twenty-six-acre **White Rhinoceros Habitat,** showcasing the park's endangered white rhinoceros. Park guests can get an up close view of the white rhinos via the Serengeti Express Train, which traverses the habitat. The Skyride and Rhino Rally also will provide views of these endangered animals. Sable antelope, greater kudu, Defassa waterbuck, sitatunga, wildebeests, ostriches, and African crowned cranes also share this terrain.

▦ MUST-SEE Rhino Rally

There are real safaris in Africa, and theme-park safaris in Florida. And there are water rides and roller coasters just about anywhere you could toss a guidebook. But only at Busch Gardens Tampa Bay will you find Rhino Rally, a safari/water ride/coaster that is the most unusual ride at Busch Gardens and pretty much unmatched anywhere else. The Rhino Rally cuts through sixteen of the sixty-five acres of the Serengeti Plain on an eight- to ten-minute expedition.

From the international Rally Plaza, seventeen guests at a time board a special version of a Land Rover for a journey into the midst of white rhinoceroses, elephants, Cape buffalos, Nile crocodiles, zebras, antelopes, warthogs, flamingos, wildebeests, gazelles, and other species. So far, what we've got here is a version of the Kilimanjaro Safari at Disney's Animal Kingdom, but it goes way on from there.

After a tour through the preserve—you'll see different animals at different times of the day and weather conditions—the truck begins to cross a pontoon bridge across a raging white-water river. Suddenly the bridge breaks loose, send-

Serious Shoppers Only

Busch Gardens offers a plan for visitors who want a quick shopping spree at one of the shops just inside its gates. Buy your ticket, go forth and shop, and be back at the Guest Relations booth within thirty minutes, and you will be given a refund of your ticket. (You'll have to pay for parking, though.) We're told that some visitors make a mad dash from the gate to the Smokehouse restaurant for take-out ribs or chicken.

ing the truck down the river, through a canyon, and under a waterfall. The one-of-a-kind ride uses a roller coaster–like track hidden beneath the water, transporting the truck back to the plaza. In some ways the ride is derived from SeaWorld Orlando's Journey to Atlantis, another unique entertainment that combines a roller coaster with a flume ride. Rhino Rally can take about 1,600 guests per hour.

MUST-SEE The Edge of Africa

In the largest animal expansion in the park's history, guests to The Edge of Africa venture forth on a safari in search of hippopotamuses, giraffes, lions, baboons, meerkats, crocodiles, hyenas, and more. Among rock outcroppings and giant termite mounds, expeditioners will also discover species such as vultures and meerkats in areas offering distant views of the Serengeti Plain. The area makes use of moats and other hidden barriers to preserve the appearance of the wild. Roaming safari guides and naturalists offer guests educational facts about the various animals and regions.

The trek into the fifteen-acre compound begins with an exploration of the remains of an old fishing village, a riverine habitat where hippos, baboons, and various species of fish coexist. A glass window allows up close observations of hippos from above and below the surface of a pool. Hippos, born underwater, ordinarily stay beneath the surface for three to five minutes but can remain submerged for as long as thirty minutes. As the excursion continues, you'll come to a Masai village where members of the nomadic African tribe have vacated one of their many temporary homes. The reason for the hasty exit becomes apparent when you discover the lions and hyenas that have taken over the village.

Look for the visitor information center posting the day's animal sightings and diets. As you move into the area, watch for sleeping lions in one of the abandoned safari vehicles parked in the compound; lions spend as much as eighteen hours a day relaxing. In the wild they would spend their waking time hunting, but at Busch Gardens they receive catered meals of about seven pounds of raw meat several times per week. (The much smaller hyena, along with the lion, one of the most feared hunters in the jungle, eats as much as one hundred pounds of food—including animal bones—per week.)

MUST-SEE Serengeti Safari

I enjoy roller coasters well enough, but for me the real thrill at Busch Gardens Tampa Bay is a very special tour available to only a handful of visitors each day: the Serengeti Safari. Several times a day, as many as twenty visitors clamber on board an open flatbed truck for a one-hour visit behind the fences of the sixty-acre Serengeti Plain, with close-up views of giraffes, zebras, and hippopotamuses, among other animals. A park guide accompanies visitors on the truck.

It's a fabulous opportunity for camera buffs and animal lovers of all ages. On one trip a herd of giraffes ambled over to our truck to snack on apples, with a few friendly nips at hats and jackets; into the middle of the giraffes came a group of nearsighted ostriches

A giraffe visits guests on the Serengeti Safari.

that pecked at anything within reach. A good time was had by all, including the animals; several of the giraffes loped along behind the truck to bid us good-bye.

Only four to six truck tours are conducted each day; in 2006 the charge was $33.99 plus tax and the cost of park admission. There is a twenty-guest limit per truck, and no children under age five are allowed. Depending on the time of year, the thirty-minute safaris go out three to five times per day. You can book a trip at the Edge of Africa gift shop near the entrance when you arrive; you can also prebook a place on the 11:15 A.M. safari by calling (813) 984–4073.

Other Attractions in the Serengeti Plain
Petting Zoo. Great for the kids, at this unusually attractive petting zoo you can get as close as you can to some of the animals.

Nairobi Station Animal Nursery. The nursery is home to Busch Gardens's newest and littlest arrivals, including tiny birds, alligators, and snakes, set in a replica of an African hospital of yesteryear. The clinic includes operating rooms; X-ray, laboratory, and recovery areas; and brooder rooms for birds.

Elephant Wash. This is just what it sounds like: Ponderous pachyderms stand still for showers several times a day. Nearby is a small enclosure where guests can climb onto a seat on the back of an elephant for a short ride.

■ CROWN COLONY

The Skyride

This open cable-car ride from the Crown Colony to the Congo and back passes above the Serengeti Plain and then deep into deepest, darkest amusement-park land, with good views of the Scorpion and the Congo River Rapids. This is a lovely way to see the park on a nice day; when it is not, the ride can be a bit chilly, and it is shut down in high winds and inclement weather.

Clydesdale Hamlet

Some of Anheuser-Busch's famous corporate symbols can be visited in their stables here. The largest adults can be as tall as 6 feet at the shoulder and weigh about a ton.

■ TIMBUKTU

The Timbuktu area of Busch Gardens re-creates an ancient desert-trading region and combines thrill rides with a large games area. The area was redecorated in 2003 with new signs, banners, and colorful fabric awnings to create a festive Arabian atmosphere.

A portion of the Sultan's Arcade, located in the heart of Timbuktu, was converted into The Oasis, where guests can enjoy a variety of snacks and beverages.

The Scorpion

The Scorpion is by most accounts in the middle between Python and Kumba on the wildness meter. It goes up to the top of its tower, then down and to the left at 55 miles per hour before entering a full 360-degree loop into a series of corkscrew descents that put you on your side. Parental guidance: The exit to the ride is in a different area from the entrance. You must be at least 42 inches tall to ride.

▓ *MUST-SEE* R. L. Stine's Haunted Lighthouse

R. L. Stine's Haunted Lighthouse is a spooky, twenty-two-minute adventure film that combines 3-D visual technology with special theatrical effects for an exciting "4-D" experience. Based on an original story by the popular *Goosebumps* author, the film stars veteran actors Christopher Lloyd, Lea Thompson, and "Weird Al" Yankovic and was directed by Joe Dante, who also made *Gremlins*.

The story tells of two children vacationing with their family at a beach who meet a salty sailor who spins a tale of a haunted lighthouse. The adventure begins when a mysterious young boy leads the disbelieving children to the lighthouse.

The high-tech presentation uses four digital projectors; guests wear special glasses to allow 3-D visual effects to pop off the screen. Surround-sound speakers are built into the seats, which also include tactile and sensory effects in the seat backs and frames.

The creators of the film researched more than sixty lighthouses in North America in the quest for a filming location. In the end the qualities of multiple lighthouses were combined, and a lighthouse set was built on a soundstage in Culver City, California. Beach scenes were filmed at Point Dume State Preserve's Zuma Beach in California.

The film combines computer-generated imagery, animation, and live action. The soundtrack is an original score performed by the Seattle Symphony Orchestra with the accompaniment of a jazz ensemble and twenty-member chorus.

The theater—converted from the former home of the Dolphins of the Deep show—is located across from The Kasbah. It seats 750 guests with room for 750 more in line in the lobby. The same show also premiered at Busch Gardens Williamsburg, SeaWorld San Diego, and SeaWorld San Antonio.

Other Attractions in Timbuktu

Cheetah Chase. It's hard to keep a good mouse down, which explains the arrival of this somewhat wild and jouncy little coaster in Timbuktu in 2004. The ride was moved from Busch Gardens Williamsburg, where it was formerly called Wild Maus; it replaced the Crazy Camel at the same location near the exit of the Haunted Lighthouse 4-D Theater.

The 1,213-foot-long track allows individual cars to reach a top speed of about 28 miles per hour, but the ride feels much faster because of the tight turns. And the open structure makes it feel as if you are soaring off into the clouds, even though the maximum height above ground is just 45 feet.

Carousel Caravan. A most unusual merry-go-round, featuring desert camels and Arabian horses.

The Phoenix. A dry boat ride that gives new meaning to the term rock 'n' roll. The platform moves forward and then backward with increasing power until riders make a complete pass up and over the top a few times. This is a bigger and wilder version of the amusement-park pirate-ship ride.

Sandstorm. An aerial whip.

■ CONGO

⁞ MUST-SEE ⁞ Kumba

Kumba means "roar" in a Congo dialect. It might have been a better idea to call the ride "Aiyeeeee!" or some other such scream. Kumba is one of the largest and fastest steel roller coasters in the country, reaching speeds in excess of 60 miles per hour and putting as much as 3.75 Gs on the bodies of its lucky riders.

The coaster includes several unusual elements, including a diving loop, which plunges riders into a loop from a height of 110 feet; a camelback, a maneuver that creates three seconds of weightlessness while spiraling 360 degrees; a 108-foot vertical loop, the world's largest; a cobra roll that turns passengers upside down as they twist around a spectator bridge; and more ordinary super-coaster thrills, including an oblique loop, a vertical spiral, and a double corkscrew-shaped twist. But the ride itself is even wilder than its description—longer and with more twists and turns than three or four ordinary coasters put together. Riders are securely locked into place with an overhead harness and are seated four across. The outside seats give the best view—that is, if you are able or willing to turn your head while moving.

Upside down on Kumba

Before I scare you off, consider the fact that Kumba's roar is much worse than its bite. You are moving so fast that you hardly realize that you are on your head or your side or your back. And if it makes you feel any better, know that my then-nine-year-old daughter led the family onto the ride one morning; she rode it once with me and her big brother, a second time with her brother, and a third time by herself when we all insisted on a rest.

The ride is very nicely integrated into the bushes and trees of the park, with many of the dips and turns hidden in the landscaping. You can walk beneath much of the track, too, which offers a great view for spectators and bragging rights to successful riders. You must be at least 52 inches tall to ride and in good physical condition. Did I mention that I started that day with two Dramamine tablets?

The Python

Only at a park like Busch Gardens would a roller coaster like the Python have to settle for second-class status behind Montu and Kumba. The Python includes wicked twists and turns and a 360-degree double spiral, and cars reach speeds of more than 50 miles per hour. All that said, the Python is a very short ride; you'll be back at the loading station before your heart has returned from your throat.

If you're a little uncertain about your roller-coaster credentials, you may want to try your stomach at Python, then move on to Scorpion, go on to Kumba, and finally to Montu. Riders must be at least 48 inches tall.

MUST-SEE Congo River Rapids

Riders sit in a twelve-passenger circular air raft and are let loose on a churning white-water trip in an artificial river with rapids, logs, and other boats in the way. We'd tell you to sit at the back of the boat to avoid getting soaked, but the darned thing keeps turning around.

The ride won't get your heart pounding quite as fast as one of the flume trips, but it's still a lot of fun and cooling on a hot day. Riders have to be at least 38 inches tall, or at least two years old and in the company of an adult. On the bridge that overlooks the rapids beneath the Kumba track there are coin-operated water cannons that can be aimed at rafts below. Put a quarter into the Congo Water Blasters and add a little extra water to the raft riders passing by.

Other rides in this area include Ubanga-Banga Bumper Cars, the Monstrous Mamba octopus ride, and more kiddie rides.

Claw Island

In a valley below a pedestrian bridge is a hideaway where you can get as close as you may ever want to a rare white Bengal tiger.

A Congo River Rapids raft approaches a geyser. © *Busch Entertainment Group*

■ STANLEYVILLE

MUST-SEE SheiKra

Dive! Dive! Not a submarine, but a spectacular new diving roller coaster named after a species of African hawk that swoops almost straight down to grab its prey.

In the case of SheiKra, which opened in the spring of 2005, there is no "almost" involved. After a ride up a forty-five-degree lift hill to a height of 200 feet, the coaster plunges toward the ground at a ninety-degree angle. In case you've forgotten your geometry, that means the cars dive straight down, reaching a speed of 70 miles per hour.

SheiKra is the first of its kind in the United States, and only the third of its design in the world—the other two (which are not quite as extreme) are in Europe and Taiwan, and the Swiss manufacturer has given Busch Gardens an exclusive on the design for the next few years.

SheiKra is the first dive coaster to incorporate an Immelmann loop, a water splash, and a second ninety-degree, 138-foot drop through an underground tunnel. The ride also includes a 360-degree climbing carousel. SheiKra's 3,188 feet of steel track offers a total ride time of just over three minutes. Riders will experience a maximum of 4 Gs.

There are three cars per train, with riders strapped into place (with overhead "horse collar" harnesses) eight across, for a total of twenty-four riders per train.

The Stanleyville area was rebuilt to accommodate the new ride. The Stanleyville Smokehouse was taken down and replaced by the new 500-seat Zambia Smokehouse built into the coaster structure; guests at the restaurant have a close-up view of the ride. The former orangutan habitat at the ride location will be relocated elsewhere in the park.

The loading station for Gwazi. *Photo courtesy of Busch Gardens Tampa Bay*

MUST-SEE Gwazi

In African legend, or at least African theme-park legend, Gwazi is a fierce creature possessed of a lion's body and a tiger's head. At Busch Gardens Tampa Bay, the lion and tiger each other for 1.5 miles, heading right at each other on six "flyby" maneuvers in which they come within just feet of each other at crossing speeds of near 100 miles per hour. We're talking about a roller coaster, of course, and this is a truly amazing ride.

The double-track wooden coaster has two different sets of rails. Gwazi Tiger has a section of slalom track, more like a bobsled than a wooden coaster. Gwazi Lion's highlight is a nearly continuous series of spirals. As the two trains crest at the top of the 90-foot lift hills, both drops are on a "stingline," allowing riders to see the opposite train charging straight at them. At the last possible moment, the trains veer to the side. In the fourth of six flybys, each train arcs at a fifty-one-degree angle; the fifth flyby delivers an extended weightless stretch on a parabola of track.

Top speed for the coaster is a zippy 50 miles per hour; when the two trains head at each other, engineers consider them moving at a "crossing" or "closing" speed of 100 miles per hour. Though the wooden coaster follows an old concept, constructed out of more than 1.25 million board feet of lumber and more than two million bolted connections, modern technology is also applied. Computer sensors attached to both tracks monitor Gwazi's trains, regulating their spacing along nearly 7,000 feet of track. The computer also manages the braking systems, a far cry from the days when an operator had to physically pull a huge hand brake to slow down a train at the station.

Where's Timmy?

A few years back the park added a habitat for a white rhino by the name of Timmy. His home can be seen only by guests sailing by high in the air on the Tanganyika Tidal Wave.

MUST-SEE Stanley Falls Log Flume
You'll fall over the edge of a 43-foot plastic cliff in a hollowed-out log. Lines build at midday; visit early or late in the day to avoid long waits.

MUST-SEE Tanganyika Tidal Wave
Boats depart regularly for a pleasant little cruise through lush, tropical foliage. Sounds relaxing—that is, until your twenty-passenger boat plunges over the edge to fall 55 feet into a splash pool. The result is a huge wave—really huge—that wets the passengers but can really soak observers standing in the wrong place on the walkway below. For an excellent view of the tidal wave, climb the bridge and stand within the glass-walled tunnel. If you are riding, the back of the boat gets wet the least. You must be at least 42 inches tall to ride.

■ LAND OF THE DRAGONS
Busch Gardens's children's play area is built around a shaded three-story tree house and is home to Dumphrey, a friendly imaginary beast. Kids are invited to explore the winding stairways and mysterious towers of the tree house. The area also includes a children's theater, slides, a rope climb, a ball crawl, and a gentle waterfall. The rides area includes a mini-size Ferris wheel, a flume ride, and a dragon carousel.

■ BIRD GARDENS
This is the oldest area of the park, built in the shadow of the original brewery in 1959. The lush foliage includes nearly 2,000 exotic birds and birds of prey, representing 218 species and including one of the largest managed flocks of Caribbean flamingos.

Some of the park's most famous species are seen here. Eagles on display near the old brewery site include golden and American bald eagles. The koala habitat also includes Dama wallabies and rose-breasted cockatoos.

The park's Chilean flamingos ordinarily live in large colonies on brackish lagoons in South America. Their bent bills are fringed at the edges, and they filter out mud and retain shrimp and algae when held upside down in the water.

Other Attractions in Bird Gardens

Koala Display. A series of educational exhibits leads up to the home of the park's koalas, among the most unusual animals at Busch Gardens. You'll glide past the glass cages on a moving sidewalk; at the end you can also climb up some stairs to a stationary viewing area. Koalas are marsupials, unusual mammals with a pouch that covers the mammary glands on the abdomen. In the Americas the only current species of marsupial is the opossum.

Lory Landing. Bird-watching soars to new heights at Busch Gardens's aviary, featuring more than seventy-five colorful and unusual tropical birds from around the world. The environment is designed as if it were a deserted island with waterfalls, floral landscapes, vine-covered trellises, and ponds. It is the home to lorikeets, hornbills, parrots, avocets, touracos, and other brilliantly colored species. In a large free-flight area, visitors become human perches as lorikeets land on arms, shoulders, and heads to feed on nectar (sold for a nominal fee).

Closer to the aviary's entrance, separate enclosures offer views of several types of endangered parrots, including thick-bills, red-tailed black cockatoos, hyacinth macaws, and hawk-headed parrots. Amateur bird-watchers will find feathered facts and artifacts such as eggs tucked into surrounding trees, as well as species identification signs and notes describing threats to the species' native habitats.

Busch Gardens Bird Show. Several performances each day of a show that includes macaws, cockatoos, and birds of prey in flight.

Lizard Habitat. A showcase for Asian water monitors, crocodile monitors, rhinoceros iguanas, and green iguanas from regions that include Indonesia, South America, and the Caribbean.

Hospitality House. The patio nearby fronts on a small pond, patrolled by a flock of geese; it's one of our favorite places for a break from the sun and crowds. Free samples of Anheuser-Busch beer are offered, along with a simple sandwich-and-pizza menu. A musical variety show including ragtime jazz piano is presented on a small stage.

SPECIAL PROGRAMS

For a lucky few, there are some very special ways to go behind the scenes at Busch Gardens. Most sell out early in the day. All tour prices are in addition to park admission. For additional information on any of these tours, contact the Guided Tour Reservations Center at (813) 984–4043.

- **Adventure Thrill Tour.** Four- to five-hour tours that include priority show seating; front-of-the-line access to most major rides, including all roller coasters and water rides; and lunch. Adults $74.99, children (ages three to nine) $54.99. Park admission is required but not included in the price.

- **Animal Adventure Tour.** A two-hour behind-the-scenes walking and off-road truck tour hosted by the animal care staff. All guests $119.99 (includes park admission).

- **Guided Adventure Tour.** Four- to five-hour tours that include the Serengeti Safari, animal interactions, priority show admission, front-of-the-line access to most rides, and lunch. Adults $94.99, children (ages three to nine) $84.99. Park admission is required but not included in the price.

- **Elite Adventure Tour.** Four- to five-hour tours that include the Serengeti Safari, animal interactions, VIP show seating, guided walks through animal habitats, breakfast and lunch, parking, and camera. All guests $199.99. Park admission is required but not included in the price.

- **Serengeti Safari Tour.** A thirty-minute trip in an open truck out on the Serengeti Plain, including the opportunity to feed giraffes. Tours go out five times daily; the trucks carry as many as twenty guests per tour. Minimum age is five. In 2006 all tickets were $33.99.

- **Saving a Species Tour.** A forty-five-minute truck tour that includes visits to the giraffes and rhinos. In 2006 all tickets were $44.99.

- **Sunset on the Serengeti.** The evening begins at the Crown Colony's Brew Master's Club for a sampling of premium lagers. Then the tour continues into the Serengeti Plain to hand-feed giraffes and encounter other African wildlife . . . and drink a bit more beer. The one-hour tour, for guests age twenty-one and older, was priced at $39.99 per person.

- **Ultimate Adventure.** An exclusive all-day VIP tour with priority entrance to rides and shows and other special features. Tickets in 2006 were $249.99 (includes park admission).

In addition to the tours, Busch Gardens offers a variety of educational programs; check with the park for a schedule. Among the offerings is Zoo Camp, five different weeklong summer-camp programs for children from kindergarten through ninth grade. For information call (877) 248–2267.

EATS AND TREATS

▌MOROCCO

🕮 **Boujad Bakery.** This is an exotic place to grab a bit of breakfast or a sweet at any time of the day. Check out the gigantic blueberry and other types of muffins; also sold are impressive turnovers and pastries for $2.00 to $3.00 each.

🕮 **Zagora Cafe.** This exotic outdoor bazaar setting is the place to get unexotic burgers, onion rings, and turkey sandwich platters, priced at about $7.00.

The Crown Colony House restaurant

CONGO

📶 **Vivi Storehouse.** Near the Python coaster, this restaurant is open in the peak season only from 11:45 A.M. to 4:00 P.M. Offerings include sandwich platters for about $6.00, as well as chicken fajitas.

CROWN COLONY

🏠 **Crown Colony House.** This lovely 240-seat restaurant has spectacular views of the Serengeti Plain from its glass-walled Veldt Room. (There are only about a dozen tables next to the windows in the Veldt Room, and they go fast. No reservations are accepted.) Another interesting location is the Library, stocked with antique books and a collection of photographs from colonial days in Africa. A piano player entertains during meals.

Featured is Crown Colony's Famous Family Style Chicken Dinner—platters of batter-dipped chicken, coleslaw, soft yeast rolls, dressing, mashed potatoes and gravy, garden vegetables, and cranberry relish. The fare is about $10 per person.

The least-crowded times to visit are before noon, and from 4:00 to 5:30 P.M.; each day a throng heads for the restaurant about 12:15 P.M., when the midday ice show lets out.

TIMBUKTU

📶 **The Kasbah.** Timbuktu's signature restaurant, Das Festhaus, was renovated and renamed in 2003, taking on an Arabian desert theme with palm trees, colorful fabrics and tassels, and multicolored lanterns hanging from the ceiling. The Kasbah features continuous entertainment throughout the day. The former menu of German and Italian dishes was expanded to more relevant offerings.

STANLEYVILLE

📶 **Zambia Smokehouse.** The old Stanleyville Smokehouse was torn down to make room for SheiKra in 2005, which probably deeply upset fans of the place's slow-smoked chicken, beef brisket, and pork ribs,

Key

📶 = Fast food

🏠 = Full-service restaurant

served with french fries and coleslaw. But not to worry: A new smokehouse was integrated into the SheiKra coaster. Prices range from about $5.00 to $9.00. Grab a bunch of napkins and prepare for a tasty mess.

🍴 **Bazaar Cafe.** Features barbecue beef sandwich platters and salads.

◼ BIRD GARDENS

🍴 **Hospitality House.** Offerings include pepperoni and Chef's Combo pizzas, at $3.00 to $4.00 per slice. Tampa sandwiches—salami, turkey, cheese, and salad on a roll—sell for about $5.50. Free samples of Anheuser-Busch beers for adults.

ADVENTURE ISLAND

Although the tidal wave and rafting expeditions at Busch Gardens are guaranteed to dampen your hairdo, if you want to get really wet, you may want to head around the corner to Adventure Island. The twenty-two-acre water park, also owned by Busch Entertainment, offers giant speed slides, body flumes, diving platforms, inner-tube slides, a wave pool, water games, a white-sand beach, and volleyball courts.

Among the many water rides at the park are:

◼ **Wahoo Run.** This tunnel raft ride sends five riders down six stories and more than 600 feet of unforeseen drenching twists, drops, back-to-back curves, and turns. The thrill slide has a unique design that careens riders through alternat-

Wahoo Run at Adventure Island. *Photo courtesy of Busch Gardens Tampa Bay*

ing daylight and darkness and four waterfall curtains. The rafts are propelled by more than 10,000 gallons of flowing water per minute in a 9-foot-diameter tube.

- **Aruba Tuba.** A "tubular" slide that twists in and around and below Calypso Coaster; the ride can be enjoyed by solo riders or two at a time.
- **Calypso Coaster.** A spiraling snakelike ride down an open flume in an inner tube or raft for two.
- **Rambling Bayou.** A slow float along a winding river around bends, under bridges, and through a human-made rain forest.
- **Caribbean Corkscrew.** Takes riders from a four-story tower down a fully enclosed, twisting translucent tube.
- **Water Moccasin.** A triple-tube water slide that cascades riders downward and through a spiral before dumping them in a pool.
- **Tampa Typhoon.** A free-fall body slide that drops from a height of 76 feet before it levels out in a slick trough.
- **Gulf Scream.** A speed slide in which riders can go as fast as 25 miles per hour down a 210-foot slide.
- **Everglides.** Takes riders down a steep 72-foot double slide on water sleds that hydroplane up to 100 feet over a splash pool; a lift system carries the sleds back to the top of the slide platform.
- **Runaway Rapids.** A 34-foot-high artificial mountain that features five separate curving and twisting water flumes as long as 300 feet.
- **Paradise Lagoon.** A 9,000-square-foot swimming pool fed by waterfalls. Built into the surrounding cliffs are 20-foot-high diving platforms, a cable drop, a cannonball slide, and tube slides. Stretching overhead across the pool is a hand-over-hand rope walk.
- **Endless Surf.** A half-acre pool that mechanically produces 3- to 5-foot waves for body and rubber-raft surfing.
- **Splash Attack.** A huge water playground that offers squirt guns, waterfalls, slides, and a huge bucket that dumps water.

The addition of heating for the outdoor pools permits the park to be open from Valentine's Day through October; at the beginning and end of the season the park is open on weekends only.

YBOR CITY

In 1885 Cuban cigar factory owner Don Vicente Martinez Ybor (pronounced EE-bore) fled the political and labor unrest of Cuba to establish his cigar empire in Tampa. The factories prospered and attracted Cuban, Spanish, Italian, German, and Jewish immigrants in what became known as "Mr. Ybor's City." At its peak the district had 200 cigar factories with 12,000 *tabaqueros* (cigar makers) producing about 700 million cigars a year.

In the early part of the twentieth century, the Depression and Prohibition took their toll on the city, and the cigar district declined. But in the last decade, Ybor City has come back. Today it is a lively Latin Quarter with wrought-iron balconies, brick streets, boutiques, coffeehouses, restaurants, and nightclubs.

Visitors can stop by **Gonzalez y Martinez Cigar Factory** at Seventh Avenue and Twenty-first Street to watch *tabaqueros* hand-rolling cigars. You can also see cigars being made at the **Ybor City State Museum.** The museum complex covers half a city block and includes an ornamental garden and three restored cigar workers' houses called *casitas,* meaning "little houses."

Florida's oldest eating place, the **Columbia Restaurant** first opened on Seventh Avenue in 1905. Patrons used to gather in the small cafe to drink steaming cups of Cuban coffee and discuss the news of the day. Today the Columbia continues to be run by the fourth and fifth generations of its founder, Casimiro Hernandez Sr.

The Columbia, named after the anthem, "Columbia, Gem of the Ocean," is the largest Spanish restaurant in the nation, occupying an entire city block and offering eleven dining rooms with seating for up to 1,660. Diners are entertained by flamenco dancing most nights. For reservations and information call (813) 248–4961; www.columbiarestaurant.com.

A recent development in Ybor City is **Centro Ybor,** an entertainment complex anchored by the historic Centro Espanol social club. The $45 million, two-level development includes a twenty-screen Muvico Movie Theater, Improv Comedy Club, GameWorks interactive arcade, a museum and visitor center, shops, and restaurants.

The **TECO Line Streetcar System** began rolling through Ybor City in late 2002, returning trolley cars to the area after a long absence. Electric streetcars ran throughout Tampa and Ybor City and were a common way for cigar rollers to

Flamenco dancers at the Columbia Restaurant in Ybor City

The TECO Line Streetcar in downtown Tampa

get to work in the factories before the cars came rolling to a stop in 1946.

The new streetcars, replicas of the originals, transport passengers from downtown Tampa through the Channel District and into Ybor City, with ten stops along its 2.4-mile route.. The Ybor Station on Seventh Avenue will eventually house a streetcar museum and a restored original 1923 Birney Safety Car.

The streetcars take approximately twenty-two minutes to make all the stops along the route. The streetcars run seven days a week, with extended hours on the weekend, and a one-way fare costs $2.00.

Tampa Bay is also a magnet for sports fans. Perhaps the best-known local team is the **Tampa Bay Buccaneers,** winners of the NFL Super Bowl in 2003. The team plays at Raymond James Stadium. The $168.5-million stadium features "Buccaneer Cove," a 20,000-square-foot replica of an early 1800s seaport village, complete with a 103-foot-long, cannon-blasting pirate ship.

The National Hockey League's **Tampa Bay Lightning** play at the St. Pete Times Forum, which, despite its name, is actually in downtown Tampa. On the other hand, major league baseball's **Tampa Bay Devil Rays** play at Tropicana Field in St. Petersburg.

The **New York Yankees** have been holding their spring-training games in Tampa since 1988. Legends Field, which evokes the original Yankee Stadium in the Bronx, was built in 1996 for the Yankees.

The Tampa Bay Devil Rays hold their spring training at Florida Power Park's Al Lang Stadium in St. Petersburg. In addition, the **Toronto Blue Jays** and the **Philadelphia Phillies** spring train in nearby Dunedin and Clearwater, respectively.

For more information on attractions and accommodations in Tampa, call the Tampa Bay Convention and Visitors Bureau at (813) 223–1111 or consult www.visittampabay.com.

In St. Petersburg is the surprising **Salvador Dali Museum,** which claims the most comprehensive collection of the renowned Spanish artist's work. Much of the collection was gathered by A. Reynolds Morse and Eleanor Morse over a forty-five-year period and displayed in their Cleveland home. After a search that drew national attention, a marine warehouse in downtown St. Petersburg was rehabilitated, and the museum opened to the public in 1982.

The museum includes ninety-five oil paintings, with oils spanning from 1917 through 1970, including the Impressionist and Cubist styles of his early period, abstract work from his transition to Surrealism, and the famous surrealist canvases for which he is best known.

The museum, located at 1000 Third Street South in St. Petersburg, is open daily. Admission is $15 for adults, $10 for students age ten and older. Admission on Thursday is $5.00 from 5:00 until 8:00 P.M.

For information call (727) 823–3767 or consult www.salvadordalimuseum.org.

THE FLORIDA AQUARIUM

Florida was here long before the Mouse, and one of the most spectacular collections of creatures that have an aquatic link can be found at the Florida Aquarium, along downtown Tampa's waterfront. Alligator hatchlings, roseate spoonbills, river otters, mangrove forests, coral reefs, and thousands of fish are among the exhibits awaiting visitors.

The Florida water story begins at the **Florida Wetlands Gallery,** which features nearly fifty juvenile American alligators, river otters, and great horned owls. The **Florida Bays and Beaches Gallery** has a display that includes bonnethead sharks, Southern stingrays, flounder, and bighead sea robins.

The **No Bone Zone** is designed for younger visitors, with low tanks and plenty of hands-on opportunities. This unique 1,200-square-foot exhibit focuses on invertebrates, animals without backbones. The main feature is the **S.C.U.M.** touch tank—a 600-gallon tank where visitors can touch **S**ea stars, **C**rabs, **U**rchins, **M**ollusks, and other invertebrates from the world's oceans.

The heart of the Florida Aquarium is its **Coral Reefs Gallery,** an unusual glimpse into a habitat ordinarily only explored by divers. The design simulates a 60-foot dive from shallow-water reefs to deeper, darker waters. At the top of a walking tour, visitors discover a variety of corals populated by grouper, moray eel, and parrot fish. From there is a descent through the reef face into an underwater coral cave with viewing windows.

There is also an underwater theater, which faces a stunning 43-foot-wide, panoramic window. There you'll see coral colonies silhouetted by beams of sunlight from the surface, with brightly colored fishes and wandering sharks. Several times a day divers descend into the tank, sometimes conducting question-and-answer sessions by radio with viewers on the other side of the window.

Another key exhibit actually takes place outside the aquarium, aboard a 64-foot catamaran. *The Bay Spirit* takes as many as forty-nine passengers out into Tampa Bay on an EcoTour expedition to visit bottlenose dolphins, manatees, and birds that make their home in the deepwater port.

Tickets to the aquarium in 2006 were $17.95 for adults, $12.95 for children (ages three to twelve), and $14.95 for seniors. Combination tickets, which include aquarium admission, EcoTour, and a behind-the-scenes tour, were $37.95 for adults, $27.95 for children, and $34.95 for seniors. For information call (813) 273–4000 or consult www.flaquarium.org.

THE MUSEUM OF SCIENCE AND INDUSTRY (MOSI)

MUST-SEE

The amazing, expanding Museum of Science and Industry in Tampa has tripled in size to become the largest science center in the Southeast. Permanent exhibits include **The Amazing You,** where you can tour the human body in all its complexity, from DNA to cells to organs to individuals; the *Challenger* **Learning Center,** a living memorial to the crew of the shuttle orbiter *Challenger,* with a replica of a space vehicle and mission control; the **BioWorks Butterfly Garden;** and a flight simulator. The **IMAX Dome Theater** presents a changing series of big-screen films.

A permanent exhibit showcases a pair of 75-foot-long diplodocus skeletons guarding the lobby. The skeletons were from remains found in Wyoming. The dinosaurs were believed to weigh about twenty tons when they flourished in the western United States during the Jurassic period. *Diplodocus carnegii* were named in honor of industrialist Andrew Carnegie, who funded the expedition that recovered the first specimens in 1901. (*Diplodocus* means "double beam," referring to the chevron-shaped vertebrae in the creature's tail.)

Another high-flying attraction is the museum's high-wire bicycle, a carefully counterbalanced bike that allows riders to pedal across a 98-foot-long cable suspended 30 feet above the floor.

A major addition to MOSI's Our Place in the Universe exhibition is the Flight Avionics simulator; the motion simulator can hold up to fifteen people at a time for a five-minute "flight." The scenery and story of the adventure are changed periodically. There is a $3.50 additional charge for each visit.

The Saunders Planetarium, one of the most popular attractions at the museum, moved to MOSI's newest facility in 2005. The expanded area also houses three other exhibit areas: Activate!, Investigate!, and Kids Create! Located just past the building entry, Activate! explores motion and physical activity. Investigate! introduces more focused, thinking-based experiments that both challenge and build skills of observation, logic, analysis, and imagination. The experiment stations in Investigate! invite guests to spend time together solving puzzles and exploring scientific concepts. Kids Create! is an activity-rich workshop where guests can apply knowledge, skill, and creativity to the process of "making."

The Busy Box is an activity space specifically designed for children five and under. The Saunders Planetarium and Verizon Challenger Learning Center will be moved to the new facility. Future plans include an outdoor science park.

MOSI is located at 4801 East Fowler Avenue, 1 mile north of Busch Gardens Tampa Bay. For information call (800) 995–6674 or (813) 987–6000, or consult www.mosi.org. For information about IMAX films, call (877) 987–4629.

Admission prices to the museum in 2006, including one IMAX film, were $23.95 for adults, $19.95 for children (ages two to thirteen), and $21.95 for seniors (age sixty and older).

INDEX